# A Human Voyage

## Exploring Biological Anthropology

Anne Keenleyside

TRENT UNIVERSITY

Richard Lazenby

UNIVERSITY OF NORTHERN BRITISH COLUMBIA

NELSON / EDUCATION

**NELSON** / **E D U C A T I O N**

**A Human Voyage:**
**Exploring Biological Anthropology**

by Anne Keenleyside and Richard Lazenby

**Vice President,**
**Editorial Director:**
Evelyn Veitch

**Editor-in-Chief,**
**Higher Education:**
Anne Williams

**Acquisitions Editor:**
Maya Castle

**Senior Marketing Manager:**
Amanda Henry

**Developmental Editor:**
My Editor Inc.

**Photo Researcher and**
**Permissions Coordinator:**
Jessie Coffey

**Senior Content Production Manager:**
Natalia Denesiuk Harris

**Production Service:**
MPS Limited, A Macmillan
Company

**Copy Editor:**
Matthew Kudelka

**Proofreader:**
Dianne Fowlie

**Indexer:**
David Luljak

**Senior Production Coordinator:**
Ferial Suleman

**Design Director:**
Ken Phipps

**Managing Designer:**
Franca Amore

**Interior Design:**
Peter Papayanakis

**Cover Design:**
Johanna Liburd

**Cover Images:**
Steve McAlister/Getty Images
(human skull); DNY59/iStockphoto
(compass)

**Compositor:**
MPS Limited, A Macmillan
Company

**Printer:**
RR Donnelley

**Library and Archives Canada**
**Cataloguing in Publication Data**

Keenleyside, Anne, 1962–

A human voyage : exploring
biological anthropology / Anne
Keenleyside, Richard Lazenby.

Includes bibliographical references
and index.
ISBN 978-0-17-647345-7

1. Physical anthropology—
Textbooks. I. Lazenby, Richard A.,
1952–  II. Title.

GN60.K37 2010   599.9
C2010-904362-6

ISBN-13: 978-0-17-647345-7
ISBN-10: 0-17-647345-9

This book is dedicated to our mentors, colleagues, and friends Shelley Saunders (AK and RL) and Mark Skinner (RL), who started us on this voyage.

*Anne Keenleyside and Richard Lazenby*

# Brief Contents

# Table of Contents

# Preface

*"The important thing is not to stop questioning. Curiosity has its own reason for existing."*
—Albert Einstein (1879–1955)

## WHY THIS BOOK NOW?

There seems to be no shortage of textbooks in the field of biological (also called physical) anthropology; many have been released in new editions. As university teachers, we have "field-tested" several of these over the past 20 years or more. So you might reasonably ask: Why yet another? The simple answer is that the time has arrived for this particular book; indeed, it is possibly well overdue. In recent years a number of texts have appeared as "Canadian Editions," which is to say, the (usually) American version has included Canadian content written by a Canadian biological anthropologist whose name then appears in the list of authors. This additional content cites research by, or profiles of, scholars working in Canadian universities and colleges, or studies conducted on Canadian populations. In fact, the book you hold in your hands was originally conceived as a "Canadianized" edition of a popular American textbook. When the editors at Nelson proposed the somewhat brash idea of tackling the much larger project of writing an entirely new text—the first such book written by Canadian biological anthropologists for Canadian postsecondary students—we welcomed the opportunity (perhaps with more than a little naïveté). And thus *A Human Voyage* was launched!

The growth of the field in Canada is such that it is clearly time for such a text. The professional association for the discipline, known as CAPA/ACAP (a rather long acronym for the much lengthier title Canadian Association for Physical Anthropology/l'Association Canadienne d'Anthropologie Physique) has grown considerably since its inception in the early 1970s (see Chapter 1) and now boasts well over 160 members (c. 2009) representing several generations of teachers and their students. As well, university and college courses in the field (and in related subjects such as human ecology, human adaptability, medical anthropology, and forensic anthropology) have seen enrollment increase steadily over the past several decades; also growing is the number of graduate programs leading to advanced degrees (M.A. or Ph.D.). This growth is reflected in a broad range of nationally and internationally recognized academic scholarship, carried out not just in Canada but around the world, which covers virtually all facets of the discipline from the latest developments in evolutionary theory to interpretations of the fossil record, insights into nonhuman primate ecology and behaviour, modern population biology, and applied biocultural anthropology.

As teachers, one lesson we have taken from our own students over the years is that their conceptual and theoretical learning is greatly enhanced when practical examples and references resonate geographically, socially, and culturally. As we suspect many of our colleagues across Canada have done in the past, we often bring in materials reflecting Canadian scholarship to supplement those provided by the text, even in the recently evolved Canadian editions of existing (non-Canadian) texts. The intent of *A Human Voyage* is to put that knowledge and experience "between the covers." This book, then, is unabashedly Canadian in its focus and content, but not to the point of being parochial. An important point we make throughout *A Human Voyage* is that human biocultural diversity crosses national boundaries: research done in Canada has significance around the world. At the same time we acknowledge that these boundaries and the political and economic entities that create and maintain them can have profound impacts on human biology—the history of colonization and the health of Aboriginal populations in Canada and elsewhere stands as one of many such examples, as does the unique geographic distribution of rare traits such as Tay-Sachs disease (see Chapter 13), which has followed population migration over the ages.

# CONNECTING THE DOTS ...

Textbooks in biological anthropology typically adhere to a particular structure, beginning with an overview of the discipline's history, a bit of evolutionary theory, and some dabbling (at times outright wading) into the genetic mechanisms underlying population variation. This is then followed by a number of chapters discussing the evolutionary history and biobehavioural diversity of our closest living relatives, the nonhuman primates. This overview sets the stage for introducing the story of our own evolving lineage of the past several million years, beginning in Africa and tracing the global expansion of human migration. Eventually we end up in the here and now, and conclude with several chapters discussing modern population biology, its historical antecedents and geographic patterning. This is a logical, tried-and-true model, and in writing this text we have chosen to follow a similar structure. The benefit in doing so is that it provides a text that will have a familiar feel for the instructor, which in turn will make for an easy transition when adapting its content for the student.

In keeping with this model, *A Human Voyage* is presented as 16 chapters divided into four sections: **Deep Currents** introduces the history of biological anthropology as a field of study and its development in Canada, as well as the theoretical foundation and structure of human variation; **Tropical Currents** traces the evolution of our nearest primate relatives and the fascinating adaptations and behaviours expressed by those species still among us; **Ancient Currents** delves into the 7-million-year-old story of how our particular ancestors came to be human, amidst all the speculation and controversy; and **Modern Currents** focuses on the complex variations that exist among living human populations, how they came about, and their importance for humanity as we look forward into the 21st century and beyond.

## A Few Comments for the Student

This is *your* book—it was written for students with little or no background in the field and in such a way as to make the story of human evolution not only accessible but also enjoyable. However, in reading *A Human Voyage* you will see that the path into our past is not always clearly defined, and you may well wonder how we know anything at all! Do not be deterred—this is simply science at work. The possibility that we could have several plausible explanations for how we came to be as we are today is a cornerstone of modern science (a classic example being the adoption of upright walking discussed in Chapter 8). However, it is also true that while a number of credible scenarios *may* be proposed based on available evidence, there was in fact *only one* pathway taken by those many generations of your ancestors and their descendants—step-by-step-by-step. The journey along that pathway culminated in the diverse, complex global species—modern *Homo sapiens*—of which you are a member. It is quite possible, if not actually probable, that none of our current interpretations is an entirely accurate account of that voyage, though the weight of evidence may favour one over other reasonable explanations. This is why we have titled this book *A Human Voyage* rather than *The Human Voyage*, which would presume that somehow we possessed a complete and precise understanding of the past. This is a claim no one can justifiably make.

Our hope is that this text and the course you are taking will encourage a critical perspective and sense of wonder in each of you. Many of the exercises suggested at the end of each chapter are intended to assist you in this regard—to have you challenge what you have just read in the previous pages. These exercises and understanding the Core Questions posed at the outset and answered at the conclusion of each chapter are your best bet to getting the gist of its content, and perhaps doing very well in the course you are taking. In that regard *A Human Voyage* is as much about the art of questioning as it is about our current understanding of our species—its diversity, its history, and its (possible) future. As the authors of *A Human Voyage*, we will gauge its success by the degree to which it leaves you, the student, feeling somewhat dissatisfied with the descriptions, interpretations, and arguments provided, considerably more aware that there is a very robust—though still imperfect—body of evidence detailing humankind's evolutionary story, and much less complacent and accepting of the current state of our species and its impact on this planet.

## SUPPLEMENTS

### Instructor's Manual/Test Bank

The combined Instructor's Manual/Test Bank by Alexis Dophin, University of Western Ontario, offers lesson plans with student and instructor activities for each chapter, as well as a bank of multiple-choice, short-answer, and essay type questions to consider for tests and exams. ISBN 978-0-17-647438-6.

### *A Human Voyage* Website

**(http://www.humanvoyage.nelson.com)**

Available free to students, this Web-based supplement provides:
- True/false, multiple-choice, and essay-type questions
- Crossword puzzles
- Flashcards
- EarthWatch Journal
- Research Online

### PowerPoint Lecture Slides

This chapter-by-chapter presentation slideshow by Andrea Waters-Rist, University of Calgary, provides an overview of chapter content with selected text images. Available as a download on the text's website.

### Image Bank

A bank of images from the text is available to enhance your own classroom presentations. Available as a download on the text's website.

## ACKNOWLEDGMENTS

This labour of love would not have been possible without the help and support of numerous friends and colleagues. At Nelson, we wish to thank sales representative Erin Carlson for planting the idea in our head to do this project, and acquisitions editor Scott Couling for recognizing the need for this text at this time. Special thanks go to our senior development editor Katherine Goodes at My Editor Inc., for her patience and persistence in keeping us on schedule and on budget! Thanks also go to Nelson's permissions coordinator Jessie Coffey, senior content production manager Natalia Denesiuk Harris, acquisitions editor Anne-Marie Taylor, copy editor Matthew Kudelka, and project manager Gunjan Chandola (MPS Limited, New Delhi).

We also acknowledge the support of our colleagues across Canada and beyond who shared many of their stories, insights, and images to make this a better book. We are especially grateful to the following colleagues who contributed written material and photographs for the book: David Begun (University of Toronto), Julie Cormack (Mount Royal University), Alan Cross (Simon Fraser University), Jerry Cybulski (Canadian Museum of Civilization), Michelle Drapeau (Université de Montréal), Linda Fedigan (University of Calgary), Tracey Galloway (University of Toronto), Todd Garlie (US Army Research, Development and Engineering Command [RDECOM], Natick, Massachusetts), Carol MacLeod (Langara College), Tina Moffat (McMaster University), Mary Pavelka (University of Calgary), Mark Skinner

(Simon Fraser University), Matt Skinner (Max Planck Institute for Evolutionary Anthropology), and Matt Tocheri (National Museum of Natural History, Smithsonian Institution).

We also thank Henry Schwarcz (McMaster University) and Jane Evans (NERC Isotope Geosciences Laboratory, UK) for their helpful comments, and the following individuals for contributing many of the wonderful photographs in the book: Ann Broadberry (UBC School of Nursing), Ian Colquhoun (University of Western Ontario), Tosha Dupras (University of Central Florida), Lisa Gould (University of Victoria), Kayla Hartwell (Wildlife Care Center of Belize, Belmopan, Belize), Bonnie Kahlon (McMaster University), Mary Pavelka (University of Calgary), Tracy Prowse (McMaster University), Pascale Sicotte (University of Calgary), Travis Steffens (Researcher/Photographer, Ankarafantsika, Madagascar), and Andrzej Weber (University of Alberta). Thank you to Leah Andrews (Adam Scott Collegiate, Peterborough) for doing some of the background research for the book, and to our students for their encouragement. Special thanks go to those who participated in the reviewing process and whose comments helped bring this text to fruition:

David Begun, *University of Toronto*

Paul Erickson, *St. Mary's University*

Jaime Ginter, *Trent University*

Gray Graffam, *University of Waterloo*

Tina Moffat, *McMaster University*

Eugène Morin, *Trent University*

Anna Lucy Robinson, *Lambton College*

Kymberley Snarr, *Laurentian University*

Peter Stephenson, *University of Victoria*

Finally, we are eternally grateful for the support given and the sacrifices made by family and friends, who never let us forget that biological anthropologists are human, too!

## ABOUT THE AUTHORS

### Anne Keenleyside

Anne Keenleyside is an Associate Professor of Anthropology at Trent University in Peterborough, where she has been based since 2002. She received her Ph.D. in anthropology from McMaster University and also holds a Bachelor of Education degree from the Ontario Institute for Studies in Education. Her primary research interests are the health and diet of past populations. She has conducted fieldwork in the Canadian Arctic, Siberia, Russia, Romania, Bulgaria, and Tunisia, and is best known for her research on ancient Greek colonial populations on the Black Sea, and for her analysis of the skeletal remains of members of the last expedition of Sir John Franklin (1845–1848) to the Canadian Arctic. She has been nominated for several teaching awards, and received a merit award for teaching at Trent in 2004. Among the courses she offers are introductory biological anthropology, forensic anthropology, paleopathology, and human adaptability. When not preparing lectures or writing papers, she can be found strolling the aisles of Home Depot pondering her next home renovation project.

### Richard Lazenby

Richard Lazenby is an Associate Professor and a founding member of the Anthropology Program at the University of Northern British Columbia, Prince George, B.C. Richard arrived at UNBC in 1994 after receiving his Ph.D. at McMaster University (1992) and a brief sojourn as a Post-Doctoral Fellow at the University of Guelph. His overarching research interest is to understand how life history (growth, aging, diet, activity) shapes skeletal morphology at both the microscopic and macroscopic levels. Most recently he has been working with colleagues at the University of Calgary and at the Max Planck Institute for Evolutionary Anthropology in Leipzig, Germany, exploring the application of 3D microcomputed tomographic imaging to investigate patterns of asymmetry related to hand use in humans, nonhuman primates, and fossil hominins. When not in the classroom or lab or tromping through the bush on behalf of the British Columbia Coroner's Service or the RCMP, he can be found wandering along forest service roads or trails with his "best friend," Belle.

# SPECIAL FEATURES OF THE BOOK

## Chapter Openers

The opening of each chapter begins with an overview that summarizes the content that will be covered in that chapter. A list of core concepts introduces students to key ideas that will be introduced and discussed. A series of core questions posed at the beginning of each chapter highlights the major topics that will be covered. These are answered at the end of each chapter, allowing students to gauge how well they have engaged with the chapter's content.

## Maps, Photographs, and Illustrations

Colourful visuals, many of which are unique to this text, are used to illustrate key concepts and information and to help students master the material.

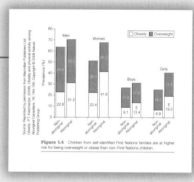

## Pedagogical Boxes

Each chapter includes one or more "Ped Boxes," which delve more deeply into the subject matter and history of biological anthropology. These boxes take three forms:

**Retrospection** Boxes emphasize key ideas or seminal developments in the field's literature and provide insight into how the discipline has taken shape over the years.

**Focus On** Boxes provide in-depth analysis of particular topics covered in the chapter. They are located adjacent to the relevant content.

**Profile** Boxes—written by some of our colleagues—illustrate the exceptional scholarship typifying biological anthropology in Canada. We could have included many more of these, but somehow our editors felt that a 1,000-page text might not be appropriate!

## Key Terms and Glossary

Each chapter contains a running glossary to help solidify key terms and concepts. A cumulative glossary is provided on the textbook's website. Definitions of **Key Terms** are given in context, immediately adjacent to where ideas and language are first introduced. Marginal notations providing **Web links** to Internet sites also provide key ancillary information.

**taxon**
a formal designation of biological classification (pl. taxa)—e.g., we are all members of the taxon *Homo sapiens*

## Chapter Summaries

Reviews at the end of each chapter and answers to the core questions posed at the beginning of each chapter are designed to help students reinforce their understanding of the material.

## CRITICAL THINKING QUESTIONS

1. Now that you have an understanding of the scope of the discipline of biological anthropology, identify two or three aspects of your *own* biology that you would like to know more about. Why do these interest you? How would you study them? In what ways would an awareness of your own biology impact the lives of those around you (family, friends, people you don't know).
2. In North America, much of the early research in biological anthropology was conducted on skeletal remains recovered from archaeological sites, representing the remains of Aboriginal peoples' ancestors. This work is still carried out today, though within a community-based research or consultative framework in which local First Nations bands are active participants and contributors to the research program. What do you think are the benefits of such an approach? What limitations to research, if any, might follow from it?

## GROUP DISCUSSION QUESTIONS

1. Discuss the relevance of biological anthropology as an applied field in the 21st century. What challenges facing humanity might the discipline help address in terms of finding "solutions"? How might it do so? (Possible examples: population growth, re-emerging diseases, environmental toxicity, global warming.)
2. Discuss why some fields within biological anthropology have gained so much attention in popular culture, while others have not. (Possible examples: forensic anthropology or primatology versus human biology or medical anthropology.)

## Group Discussion and Critical Thinking Questions

Provocative questions at the end of each chapter are designed to critically engage students with the chapter content. These include questions emphasizing individual learning as well as group/seminar-style discussion.

## RESOURCES AND READINGS

- L. Sawchuk and S. Pfeiffer, eds. (2001), "Out of the Past: The History of Human Osteology at the University of Toronto." **https://tspace.library.utoronto.ca/citd/Osteology/pfeiffer.html**
- The Canadian Association for Physical Anthropology / L'Association Canadienne d'Anthropologie Physique (CAPA/ACAP), **http://www.capa-acap.info**, is a good place to begin to learn about the discipline and its members in Canada. It includes links to history, training, field schools, annual meetings, and more. Similarly, the American Association of Physical Anthropologists (AAPA) maintains a comprehensive website, **http://physanth.org**, as does the Human Biology Association, **http://www.humbio.org/joomla**.

## Suggested Readings

These resources, many of them by well-known Canadian biological anthropologists, allow students to explore in greater detail particular topics covered within each chapter.

## Bibliography

In-text citations throughout the book provide the sources from which the materials are drawn. All sources cited are listed at the back of the book in a comprehensive bibliography.

# A Human Voyage

**Exploring Biological Anthropology**

# Chapter 1

# Introduction to Biological Anthropology

## OVERVIEW

As practised in North America, biological anthropology is one of four major fields of anthropology and encompasses a multitude of subspecialties. Though the history of biological anthropology goes back to the late 18th century, only in the past 60 years has the discipline emerged as a modern field of scientific inquiry—one that emphasizes process, adaptation, and variation. Today, biological anthropology embraces a biocultural perspective, especially in the study of modern human diversity. Through basic research, the discipline has made it clear that humans are uniquely evolved organisms in a complex system of ecological, physical, and cultural environments, past and present. An applied research focus addresses contemporary social questions, including those arising from forensic science, medical anthropology, and nutritional anthropology.

## CORE CONCEPTS

- biocultural perspective
- multidisciplinary and interdisciplinary research
- basic and applied research

## CORE QUESTIONS

- What is so compelling about human variation as a field of study?

- How does a biocultural perspective benefit a discipline such as biological anthropology?

- Why are fields as distinct as primatology and forensic anthropology considered subspecialties within biological anthropology?

- How does one best understand the history of biological anthropology as it has developed in North America?

*Civilization is a movement and not a condition,*
*a voyage and not a harbour.*

Arnold J. Toynbee (1889–1975)

# PROLOGUE: IN THE BEGINNING ...

*A young male hominin[1] stands quietly at the edge of a marsh, some 1.6 million years in the past, at a place we now know as East Africa. He is watching a small herd of impala that have gathered on the far side. It is the end of the dry season and water is everywhere, deep and swift in channels braiding through the wetland, which was much more easily crossed before the rains came. The hominin walks on two legs, as did his ancestors, though much more at ease than did they. This form of locomotion is an uncommon sight on the sun-drenched African savannah, but it allows for efficient travel over long distances, carrying pear-shaped chopping tools roughly fashioned from flint, or long, sharpened sticks. His upright posture affords him a view of the open plain not available to the four-footed predators—the forebears of leopard and lion—with whom he must compete for his dinner and be wary of lest he become theirs. He is more than one-and-a-half metres tall and not yet an adult—still, much taller than his ancestors. His frame is lean, his legs long—features that suit his species well, for they must follow herds of wildebeest and antelope across open country where shade is scarce. As he stands at the marsh edge, gentle breezes wash over his long torso and limbs. Even though warm, they whisk away beads of sweat from his skin, cooling his body. The grasses weave to and fro, brushing against his hairless, darkly pigmented legs. He sees that there is no easy crossing at this point; the impala should be safe for now. But it has been several days since his family made their last kill, and scavenging has been poor; the hominin suffers the impatience of youth and chooses to pursue the prey on his own. In doing so he learns a harsh lesson—biology and cultural adeptness cannot in every instance protect one from rash choices. The water in the bog is deeper than he imagined, the bottom softer. He struggles to move forward, then to turn back, but is caught in the mire. Soon he cannot move at all, and the more he struggles to loosen his feet, the more deeply his long legs sink into the mud. He falls helplessly forward into the water, among the rushes and grasses; his arms find nothing solid beneath him to keep his head above the murky surface ...*

Though lost to his family and the community of early humans, our young hominin was only temporarily lost to history. His misfortune became amazingly good fortune for a small band of his large-brained descendants, baking under the hot African sun. The year was 1984. With finely crafted tools of steel and synthetic fibre, they painstakingly excavated his almost complete fossilized skeleton from the dry sediments of his once watery grave. The bones and associated evidence preserved in the deposits that captured him, carefully recovered, analyzed, and interpreted, would reveal his history, which was, in fact, part of your own ...

So ...

Welcome to the story of yourself, of your parents and grandparents, of your children, and of your children's children. Welcome to the story of human generations, of relatives you have never met and will never meet. It is a remarkable story, deep in dust, in bone and blood and stone. It is a story distinguished by some degree of certainty but also by much ambiguity, a story filled with mystery and imbued with wonder. It is a story written and rewritten and waiting to be written yet again, perhaps by you. Welcome to your evolution!

## BIOLOGICAL ANTHROPOLOGY: A DIVERSITY OF INTERESTS AND AN INTEREST IN DIVERSITY

**biological anthropology**
the study of the biological origins, evolution, and contemporary diversity of humans and their primate relatives

**Biological anthropology** is the scientific study of humankind as one variety of animal among many, as living beings whose intention on conception is to be born, become sexually mature, find a mate (or two, or three ...), reproduce, grow old, and die. Along the way, we must find ways to nurture our bodies as well as our minds. To these ends, we eat food, eliminate waste, heal wounds, and avoid or survive disease. We satisfy curiosity, play joyfully, and encounter anger, love, jealousy, and grief. Many of these experiences are shared

---

1. "Hominin" is a term we use to refer to members of our ancestral lineage. This fictionalized account portrays the last moments of the "Nariokotome Boy," also known by his Kenya National Museum designation WT 15000, an almost complete skeleton of *Homo ergaster* discovered in 1984–85.

**Figure 1.1** Biology ties together all living things. Both the common chimpanzee and the common lab mouse have figured prominently in developing a better understanding of ourselves, even though one is a much closer relative.

with other organisms, closely related and otherwise (Figure 1.1). Some are arguably unique to the domain of human experience; each, however, conjures up questions of keen interest to biological anthropologists (see, for example, Meredith Small [1995] for an interesting take on love and sex, or Wrangham and Peterson [1996] on male violence as an evolved characteristic). The human expression of life events is the product of our particular evolutionary history, and to fully appreciate what we are all about from birth to death, generation to generation, we need to appreciate how these features appeared and were shaped over several million years of ancestral births, reproductions, and deaths.

Not all of us, of course, succeed in life's undertakings; failure in whole or in part is common. Many conceptions do not reach full gestation, let alone maturity; or they do so but become children whose growth is compromised by circumstances such as poverty, ill health, and ecological, social, or political instability. Some of us do not find mates or reproduce, while our siblings have several mates (not necessarily in succession) and scads of children. Some have lives filled more with grief than with love. This is the fullness and richness of the human condition, and it underscores what is most real about the living world—the **variation** within it. Joseph Weiner (1979, 5), a noted environmental physiologist and biological anthropologist, once observed that "it is not so much the fact of variation, but the significance of variation which demarcates the new bio-anthropology." The significance of that variation, for those humans now living and for their ancestors' ancestors, is what biological anthropology as a field of inquiry aims to discover, explore, and understand.

**variation**
observable differences within a class of objects, the source of which may be genetic or environmental or both in interaction

## ANTHROPOLOGY'S SCOPE: WHO WE ARE, WHAT WE ARE, WHY WE ARE

There is a good chance that you have already determined what your "major" will be during your undergraduate career. It may even be anthropology! But there are a number of other possibilities: biology, chemistry, psychology, mathematics, political science, geography, economics, First Nations studies, history, gender studies, or sociology … the list goes on. (We know this because we have had such students in our own classes.) The fact that a course in biological anthropology attracts students from diverse backgrounds illustrates two important points. First, there is something inherently compelling about the story of "us," of humankind. In this age of an "electronically shrinking planet" (a concept that the Canadian literary critic and communications theorist Marshall McLuhan [1911–1980] popularized as the "global village"), it is understandable that we wonder about where we came from, our similarities and differences, and our relationships. "Difference" surrounds us, especially in countries such as Canada, where Aboriginal peoples (the original migrants) have been living for many thousands of years and where in recent centuries immigration has done so much to shape our society (Figure 1.2). It is no

**CHAPTER 1** Introduction to Biological Anthropology

**multidisciplinary**

an investigative approach that brings the expertise of a number of disciplines to bear on a particular question within an existing field of study

**interdisciplinary**

an investigative approach bringing diverse fields together to create a new arena of study

**anthropology**

the global and comparative study of humankind, past and present

**holistic**

the integrated study of all aspects of human life, biological, cultural, historical, psychological, etc., in order to develop a comprehensive view of the whole of the human condition

**Figure 1.2**   Canada's population is a rich mosaic of peoples and cultures from around the globe.

Toronto Star/GetStock.com

surprise, then, that reflections of our origins and diversity confront us every day. The subject matter of biological anthropology is often the focus of cover stories in literary fiction, Hollywood movies, in popular magazines, and on educational television. The subspecialty of forensic anthropology alone has become extremely prevalent in popular culture. The second point, equally important, is that anthropology is becoming increasingly **multidisciplinary** *and* **interdisciplinary** and is drawing from and contributing to many other fields that study humankind and our primate relatives past and present (see Box 1.1.)

In North America, biological anthropology is one of several subfields in the larger domain of **anthropology** (from the Greek *anthropos,* meaning "human" + *logy,* meaning "to speak of") (Figure 1.3). Anthropology is a broad discipline that crosses the social, life, and physical sciences; it is dedicated to the historical, **holistic,** and comparative

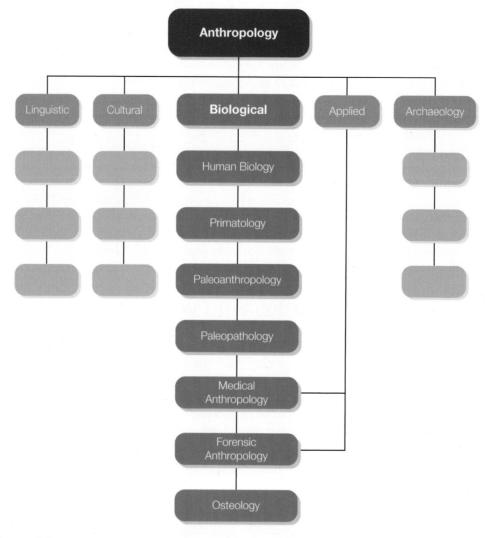

**Figure 1.3**   The diverse interests of anthropology are reflected in the breadth of its major subfields, the specializations within them, and the application of anthropological knowledge.

# BOX 1.1 FOCUS ON... Collaboration

Collaboration, or the sharing of ideas, information, and research effort across fields, characterizes many disciplines. This reflects two interdependent phenomena. The first is that the questions we pose often do not have clearly defined boundaries: they are "fuzzy" questions that touch on a number of subject areas, each of which can bring something to the table in search of a fuller comprehension. The second is that our particular subject of study—humankind—is not reducible to the bits and pieces that researchers of an earlier generation studied as distinct entities. We have since learned that the whole is vastly greater—and a lot more interesting—than the sum of its parts! A multidisciplinary approach describes the situation where researchers from different fields of study combine their efforts to address a particular question or research theme using the methods and bodies of theory from within their own discipline. Interdisciplinarity, on the other hand, develops when new insights emerge from the integration of concepts from other fields into a novel perspective or understanding, often creating new fields of inquiry (e.g., feminist studies).

Let us look at a couple of examples to illustrate what we mean.

In the opening section to this chapter we presented a vignette covering a moment in the life—and death—of what eventually became an extremely important fossil discovery, the so-called Nariokotome Boy from West Turkana, East Africa, dated to ca. 1.6 million years (see Chapter 10). This fictionalized account described not only what this individual looked like, but aspects of his environment (plants, animals, climate, geography) and behaviour (diet, mobility, culture). In the true spirit of *multidisciplinary* research, this diverse information was compiled from the work of specialists from numerous fields—paleoanthropology, paleontology, geology, paleoecology,

chemistry, and physics, to name a few—all working together on one great story: the discovery of who this individual was, and where, when, and how he lived (Walker and Leakey 1993).

Our second example illustrates *interdisciplinary* research. One of the great challenges facing public health today—in Canada and around the world—is the **pandemic** described by the World Health Organization (WHO) as "globesity." A significant proportion of humanity now tip the scales in the categories of overweight and obese (OW-OB). As a debilitating condition, OW-OB shows no respect for age, gender, class, or nationality; it crosses all boundaries. The costs to the health care system and to the economy more generally run into billions of dollars. Also, when viewed at the community level, we often find inequities in the **prevalence** of OW-OB. Recently, one of us (Lazenby) took part in a study to document childhood OW-OB in Prince George, British Columbia. An important finding was that, though the prevalence of OW-OB was high in the sample as a whole, children of First Nations ancestry were more at risk for being OW-OB than non–First Nations children—a pattern well established for Canada as a whole (Figure 1.4).

This difference was not rooted in ancestral biology (and we did not expect it to be), but in history and political economy. We could fully understand the pattern of OW-OB among Prince George schoolchildren only by integrating information describing the social and economic determinants of health—education, income, housing, family structure, access to health care. These in turn had to be contextualized within a colonial and post-colonial historical framework. What emerged from this interdisciplinary analysis was a broader, more nuanced understanding of the variation in human biological outcomes produced by nonbiological forces.

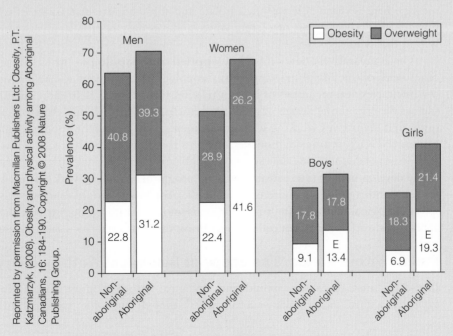

**Figure 1.4** Children from self-identified First Nations families are at higher risk for being overweight or obese than non–First Nations children.

**pandemic**

a disease affecting populations across a large area, typically used in reference to a global occurrence

**prevalence**

the proportion of a population exhibiting a particular feature at any one point in time.

**cultural anthropology**

the study of the structure and function of human societies, usually from a cross-cultural perspective

**ethnography**

the comparative study of cultures

**archaeology**

the systematic study of past human lifeways through an analysis of human interactions with and modifications of the environment, including the origin and development of technology

**anthropological linguistics**

the study of the origin, evolution, and use (social context) of languages

**thermoregulation**

the adjustment of body temperature within a normal physiological range under varying environmental conditions

**biocultural**

a research perspective that recognizes the interrelationship of biology and the many facets of culture, including technology and social behaviour

**applied anthropology**

a subfield emphasizing project-based, problem-oriented, practical applications of anthropological knowledge

study of human diversity. What do we mean by this? Simply that among all the various fields that study "humans" (including psychology, sociology, political science, economics, and history), anthropology is concerned not with a particular aspect of what makes us what we are, but with *all* aspects. Moreover, anthropology aims to discover the threads that weave together all the characteristics that make each of us not only unique as an individual, but also a part of a larger collective enterprise—that of humanity. Historically, the subfields of anthropology complementing biological anthropology are cultural anthropology, archaeology, and anthropological linguistics. **Cultural anthropology** focuses on comprehending the meaning and origins of social and cultural complexity through **ethnography**, while **archaeology** investigates the material record of human history (written and otherwise) extending some two and a half million years into the past. **Anthropological linguistics** examines the origin, evolution, and structure of language(s), the relationships among them, and the social use of language in managing human affairs.

An important consideration is that, while each of these subfields is very much its own distinct discipline, with particular bodies of theory and method, all are part of anthropology.[2] Archaeologists, for example, also study social and cultural complexity, its origins and development, and thus use many of the models of cultural anthropology; anthropological linguists have produced language maps charting the prehistoric migrations of human populations, which closely approximate similar maps produced through genetic analyses (Cavalli-Sforza 1997). Cultural anthropology, archaeology, and linguistics often contribute to the field of biological anthropology as it searches for a fuller understanding of humans as biological organisms. A good example of this integrative approach is Kurki and colleagues' (2008) comparative study of body-size proportionality in small-bodied foragers from past and present South African and Andaman Island populations.

Kurki and her coworkers examined the correspondence of body size and shape to climate, **thermoregulation**, and energetic efficiency using subsistence adaptation, archaeological history, and linguistic affinity to define samples and to explain the observed patterns of variation. Such studies exemplify what we refer to as a **biocultural** perspective, which recognizes that throughout human history, culture has in many ways influenced biological variation by acting as a mediator between individuals and their environment. Similarly, cultural differences may be significantly affected by biological differences within and between human populations (as we explore in Part IV of this book, *Modern Currents*). An essential message here is that while we often isolate and study a particular aspect of what we are as humans, that aspect is part of a larger whole and can only be fully appreciated by situating it within that whole.

The comparatively new subfield of **applied anthropology**—which has roots in all the other fields of the discipline—applies anthropological knowledge to challenges arising from the intricacies and inequities of human relationships, as well as to more practical questions such as the ergonomic design of clothing, vehicles, and furnishings. Applied anthropologists often find themselves working with government agencies and/or nongovernmental organizations (NGOs) seeking solutions to problems that may be local (e.g., forensic anthropologists assist police forces at crime scenes) or global (e.g., nutritional anthropologists contribute to the development of international food aid programs). Applied work is a full-time vocation for some anthropologists; more often, though, people who would otherwise consider themselves biological, cultural, linguistic, or archaeological anthropologists don the cloak of the applied anthropologist when called on to bring their expertise to a specific issue at hand.

## Fields Within Fields: The Scope of Biological Anthropology

In the past in Canada, you would find biological anthropologists working in universities, typically within anthropology departments, though in some instances in archaeology

---

2. Specialization is typical of almost all fields of study, including the other branches of anthropology, reflecting the rapid growth and diversification of "science" from the late 19th through the 20th centuries.

departments (e.g., at Simon Fraser University and the University of Calgary). Today, biological anthropologists can be found outside the traditional venue of anthropology departments. For example, a number of our colleagues now teach and carry out research within anatomy and cell biology departments associated with medical schools, and others have pursued independent careers as consultants. Some work for nongovernmental agencies such as PATHCanada, as well as in museums—for example, the Canadian Museum of Civilization in Gatineau, Quebec. These changes reflect how the discipline has broadened its areas of inquiry and application, now that innovative theory and analytical methods have expanded the scope of the field. To take one example, it might surprise you to learn that by studying genetically distinct strains of mice, biological anthropologists have developed a better appreciation of how genes regulate growth and development to create novel **cranial morphology** (Hallgrímsson et al. 2007; Figure 1.5); this in turn has helped us better understand problems such as cleft palate in humans. You might think it a stretch to jump from mice to people, but it is not as great a leap as it would seem, given that the genetic program regulating many aspects of development has been highly conserved[3] over tens of millions of years of evolution and is shared widely among mammals (see Chapter 4).

**cranial morphology**
the relative size and shape configuration of the various bones of the skull

In much the same way that anthropology comprises several major subfields, biological anthropology includes a number of specializations, all bound by a common interest in understanding more about who we are, where we came from, how we live, and how we behave. There is considerable communication and cross-fertilization of information and ideas among

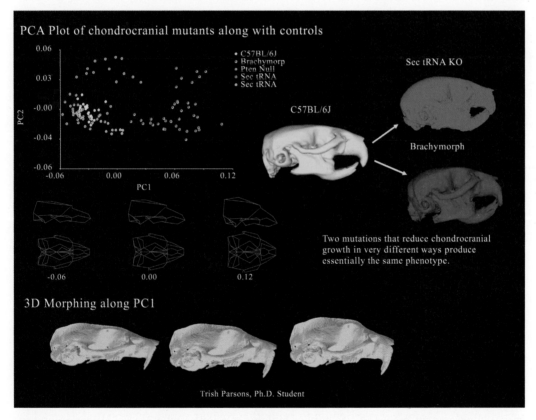

**Figure 1.5** Benedikt Hallgrímsson and his colleagues at the University of Calgary use 3D microcomputed tomographic imaging of different mouse strains to understand the regulation of facial growth and development. This work is relevant to mammalian evolutionary history as well as to understanding defects of human development, such as cleft palate.

Courtesy of Benedikt Hallgrimsson

3. To speak of something as "conserved" in the context of evolutionary biology is to suggest that there has been very little genetic change over millions of years. Interestingly, however, the regulation of that highly conserved genetic program may well have changed over time, leading to new evolutionary outcomes (see Chapter 4).

**Figure 1.6** In 1999 the rare discovery of partial remains of a mummified individual in northwestern B.C. provided unique insight into the lives of First Nations people.

Courtesy of Al Mackie

http://web.uvic.ca/~chpc/index.htm

these specializations, and now and then some very intense disagreements as to "how things work" as well! This is something we hope you will come to appreciate as you progress through your course and this text.

Biological anthropologists approach human diversity and variation from two basic directions: that of the living, and that of the dead. Regarding the latter, their studies focus on the hard tissues—bones and teeth—which survive decomposition for considerable lengths of time. However, in extraordinary circumstances, such as might be encountered with forensic work or in archaeology (e.g., mummification), we are fortunate to be able to study the soft tissue remains of deceased individuals.

For example, in 1999 the partial remains of a young man, no older than many of you, were discovered emerging from melting glacial ice in northwestern B.C., near the Yukon border (Figure 1.6). Named Kwäday Dän Ts'ínchi (Long Ago Person Found) by the Champagne and Aishihik First Nations in whose traditional territory the discovery occurred, this individual was found associated with a number of artefacts, including clothing and hunting implements. The biological and cultural remains offered a unique window into the life of one of our First Nations ancestors (Beattie et al. 2000). Only with the exceptional cooperation and goodwill of all involved—the scientific community and the Champagne and Aishihik First Nations elders, band leaders, and community members—have we come to know an individual who lived 550 years ago. This project exemplifies the success of **community-based research** within a biocultural framework (Schell et al. 2007).

Discoveries such as Kwäday Dän Ts'ínchi are as rare as they are significant. More often, biological anthropologists studying the past glean information from the varied surfaces, internal structures, and chemical composition of bones and teeth. And it is not simply a matter of those who work with the dead talking with "like-minded" colleagues: an exciting synergy results when our knowledge of lives once lived merges with knowledge of lives being lived now. For example, our understanding of the disease experience among First Nations peoples today has been illuminated by the study of the physical signs of ill health seen in skeletal remains of past populations (Waldram, Herring, and Young 2006). We know, for example, that the increased prevalence of dental disease among indigenous peoples is a product of the transition to "Western" diets with their excess of refined carbohydrates, as pre-contact populations show little evidence of tooth decay.

**community-based research**

an approach in which investigators work directly with a community to develop, organize, and implement a research program

## Skeletal Biology

An undergraduate curriculum in biological anthropology typically includes a course in human **osteology**. The study of bones and teeth has long been a mainstay of the discipline. There are many reasons why. The skeleton is the last biological tissue to decompose and is often preserved for hundreds or even thousands of years (and once fossilized, millions of years). It is the only permanent record of the human biology of peoples who are no longer among us. And it is rich in information, whether one is studying an individual skeleton or a collection of skeletons sampled from past populations (Katzenberg and Saunders 2008). Besides indicating fundamental features such as age and sex, bones and teeth bear a history of population affinity, environmental adaptation, growth and development, health and disease, diet, and activity (either as general aspects such as sexual division of labour, or regarding specific activities such as occupation), as well as signals of cultural practices, including migration, mobility, and marriage patterns. Developments in the analysis of bone chemistry, including **isotopes** of carbon, nitrogen, and oxygen, have expanded our horizons by pinpointing

**osteology**

the descriptive and comparative study of bones and teeth

http://www.paleopathology.org

http://www.eskeletons.org

specific population relationships, cultural practices, human–disease interactions, and diet. One interesting example is the application of isotope data to establish the time frame for the cultural practice of infant weaning (Katzenberg, Herring, and Saunders 1996). Our bodies incorporate various chemical isotopes from the foods we eat into our tissues, making it possible to identify the makeup of an individual's diet over the course of his or her lifetime from preserved remains (such as bones, teeth, and hair). Using this approach, Tosha Dupras and Matt Tocheri (2007) compared isotopes of carbon ($\delta^{13}$C) and nitrogen ($\delta^{15}$N) from juvenile and adult skeletons excavated from the Roman period (100–450 CE) site of Kellis, Egypt (Figure 1.7) and were able to show that weaning occurred by three years of age in that population.

**Figure 1.7** Skeletal biologist Tosha Dupras excavating at the site of Kellis, Egypt.

Courtesy of Tosha Dupras

**isotope**
a measurable form of a chemical element varying in the number of subatomic particles (protons and neutrons)—e.g., $^{12}$C and $^{14}$C are different isotopes of carbon, with the latter having two extra protons

As a branch of osteology, **paleopathology** focuses on characterizing patterns of disease and trauma in archaeological human remains. Many illnesses and injuries leave telltale marks on or within bones and teeth, and paleopathologists study these marks in order to understand how human populations in the past suffered from, and coped with, life's many challenges. Some skeletal changes clearly show a specific cause (e.g., syphilis or a broken bone). Many paleopathological studies, however, report on the presence of generalized, non-specific disease stress or overall patterns of wounds reflecting the kinds of weapons used in ancient times. In these cases skeletal changes may suggest disease processes, chronic exposure to infectious agents (e.g., bacteria or parasites), environmental challenges such as food shortages resulting in malnutrition, or activities associated with occupation or interpersonal violence. For example, Keenleyside and Panayotova (2006) relate cranial lesions in 3rd to 5th c. BCE Greek colonists on the Black Sea to diet and infectious or parasitic diseases (Figure 1.8). In a different vein, Faccia and Williams (2007) have shown that the pattern of vertebral lesions known as "Schmorl's nodes" seen in modern people experiencing chronic back pain can be informative regarding the degree to which humans in the past may have suffered from this debilitating condition. Clearly, we have as much to learn about the past from the present as we have about the present from the past.

**paleopathology**
literally, the study of ancient disease and trauma

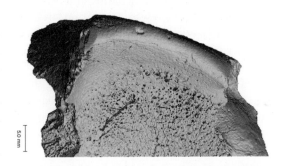

5.0 mm

**Figure 1.8** A porous lesion within the orbit of the eye, known as cribra orbitalia, is an example of a nonspecific marker of metabolic disease or parasitic infection, seen here in a young adult male from the Kalfata necropolis from the ancient Greek colonial site of Apollonia Pontica.

Courtesy of Richard Lazenby

http://www.paleoanthro.org

## Paleoanthropology

Few specializations within biological anthropology receive as much media attention as **paleoanthropology**, the study of human evolution as represented in the fossil remains of our **hominin** ancestors and those of our primate relatives (Figure 1.9). This attention is not owing to the spectacular nature of such discoveries, because most cannot be described that way. Rather, interest in paleoanthropology is due more to the fact that fragments of bone and tooth eked out of parched desert terrain, or excavated from deep in caves, may have huge implications for understanding—possibly even rewriting—human evolutionary history. In 2007, Matt Tocheri

**paleoanthropology**
the study of human evolution through fossils and the circumstances in which they are found

**hominin**
a term inclusive of modern humans and their bipedal ancestors

**Figure 1.9** Paleoanthropologist Matthew Skinner examines the fossilized facial skeleton of a prehistoric monkey recovered from the site of Asbole, Afar, Ethiopia.

Courtesy of Matthew Skinner

and his colleagues found themselves under an intense media spotlight when their 3D analysis of wrist bones from the controversial *Homo floresiensis* skeleton from Indonesia indicated that this discovery, dating between ca. 95 to 17 thousand years ago (Morwood et al., 2009), was anatomically quite primitive, more similar to our million-plus-year-old relatives in Africa (Tocheri et al. 2007; and see Chapter 10). Such stories hold a deep fascination for many of us, inside and outside the field of paleoanthropology.

The study of the fossil record of human evolution can be laborious, with fieldwork often carried out in inhospitable landscapes and in areas of the world having long histories of political instability (such as the Horn of Africa, where a number of momentous discoveries—including that of the famous "Lucy" partial skeleton[4]—have been made). And once found, the analysis—cleaning, reconstruction, description, and comparison—may require months or years of additional painstaking effort, though typically in the more welcoming and benign surroundings of a museum or university laboratory. However, the rewards of this research can be as immense as the task itself. In the past 50 years, our view of human evolutionary history has been transformed several times, from one of a rather simplistic more-or-less linear evolutionary "tree" perhaps only 2 million years in the making, to one viewed today as a complex (and complicated) "bush" occupied by numerous ancestors and descendants and extending into the past as much as 6.5 million years.

Interpretation of this rich record has brought forth keen and at times raucous debate during which very different and even opposing views have been advanced. These disputes may revolve around whether a particular fossil find should be considered a hominin at all. If it is generally agreed to be one, debate may then centre on which **taxon** it belongs to. Indeed, questions have been raised as to how many hominin taxa should be recognized at all, and of these, which gave rise to later forms. That such disagreements occur should not lead you to conclude that paleoanthropology is in acrimonious disarray. Quite the contrary, these debates are healthy and reflect serious attempts to make sense of natural biological variation from fragmentary "windows" widely dispersed in space and time. In spite of these limitations, there is a broad consensus regarding how we define ourselves and view the major developments that characterize the evolution of humankind (see Part III Ancient Currents).

## Human Biology

**Human biology** is the branch of biological anthropology that aims to understand modern population diversity, its historical antecedents, and its relationship to the lived environment. In other words, it aims to discover *what* and *who* we are in the context of *where* and *when* we are. A human biologist may just as easily be found in a North American urban neighbourhood studying the relationship between socioeconomic status and childhood obesity (Moffat et al. 2005) as in a rural village in the Himalayas studying breastfeeding and wage labour (Moffat, Galloway, and Latham 2002), or investigating the factors underlying infant death in Aboriginal communities in Manitoba early in the 20th century (Moffat and Herring

**taxon**
a formal designation of biological classification (pl. taxa)—e.g., we are all members of the taxon *Homo sapiens*

http://hmb.utoronto.ca

**human biology**
a branch of biological anthropology that examines modern population diversity

---

4. "Lucy," discovered in 1974 in the Afar region of Ethiopia, has the more formal scientific name of *Australopithecus afarensis* (see Chapter 9).

1999) (Figure 1.10). The underlying theme in each of these studies is the relationships among biology, culture, and environment, with the understanding that "environment" is defined quite broadly to include not just a person's physical surroundings but also the social and political circumstances within which they grow, live, work, raise families, and die.

Historically, human biologists have documented population variation in growth and development through measures such as body size, shape, and proportion—a method known as **anthropometry**. Comparative studies of height, weight, and muscle and fat mass can be very informative about population health and nutrition. Similarly, understanding how different human populations adapt morphologically and physiologically to environmental extremes (e.g., Arctic cold, desert heat, tropical humidity, and high altitude **hypoxia**) has been a keen subject of study for human biologists interested in human **adaptability**. High-altitude populations in the Andes, Tibet, and Ethiopia, for example, are known to have evolved different metabolic pathways (e.g., red blood cell concentration) in coping with the stress of low oxygen availability above 4,000 metres (Beall 2006).

**Figure 1.10** As a human biologist, Tina Moffat—shown here with her research assistant, Lakhpa Lama (middle) and a village elder in 1998—studies how modern populations adapt to diverse physical and social environments.

Courtesy of Tina Moffat

**anthropometry**
the measurement of body form

**hypoxia**
low oxygen availability, characteristically associated with high altitude

**adaptability**
the tendency for an organism to achieve increased functional capacity through a modification of body form and/or physiological pathway when faced with an environmental stressor

Many human biologists are interested in the impact of "modernization," during which significant transformations occur in the political economy of local populations. An excellent example of this approach is the long-term study of changes in Inuit growth, development, and health during the transition from traditional to modern ("Western") lifeways in the latter half of the 20th century, including the shift from subsistence hunting to wage labour, from "country" to processed foods, and from levels of relatively high activity to increasingly more sedentary lifestyles (Shephard and Rode 1996). This transition has been linked to changes in fertility patterns, increases in morbidity and mortality (illness and death), near-epidemic levels of adolescent suicide, and rising challenges from accumulating environmental toxins, such as PCBs and dioxins (Van Oostdam et al. 2005). Similar approaches have been used to study pastoral peoples in varying habitats, such as Africa, the Andes, and Siberia (e.g., Leonard and Crawford 2003).

In the past two decades the field of **molecular anthropology** has emerged as a driving force in understanding the genetic basis for modern population variation. This subfield studies the structure of **DNA** and identifies the actions of specific genes. The Human Genome Project (Collins, Morgan, and Patrinos 2003) has now mapped the entire human **genome** (though the precise function of most of our genes remains a mystery). Interestingly, scientists have recently completed a similar project to map the Neandertal genome (see Chapter 11). Developments in molecular genetics have expanded our understanding of how species variation may be produced through the process of development, leading to a new shift in evolutionary theory known as evolutionary developmental biology (see Chapter 4).

**molecular anthropology**
the study of population diversity at the level of the gene and its products (both structural and regulatory proteins)

**DNA**
deoxyribonucleic acid, the fundamental genetic material of life

**genome**
the total complement of an organism's DNA

## Primatology

One of the more memorable lines ever delivered in a classic Hollywood film was uttered by Robert Armstrong in the role of film director Carl Denham during the closing scene of the original 1933 epic *King Kong* (© 1933 RKO Pictures): "It wasn't planes that did the job.

http://primatology.net

T'was Beauty that killed the Beast." Beauty in this instance was Canadian actress Fay Wray, and the "Beast" was a larger-than-life gorilla, discovered on remote "Skull Island" as the object of worship and reverence by the local population. We suspect that Edgar Wallace and Merian C. Cooper, who wrote and produced the film, would have benefited from a course or two in **primatology**, the scientific study of the biology and behaviour of nonhuman primates (prosimians, monkeys, and apes). While it is true that human societies have developed symbolic relationships with our nearest relatives throughout recorded history, it is also true that the *anthropological* study of primates is younger than the original version of *King Kong*.

Primatologists[5] study nonhuman primates for two fundamental reasons. First, primates are inherently interesting—as much as any other creature, from bacteria to blue whales. They live fascinating lives beyond the realm of human experience, about which we are naturally curious. In this sense, we study primates to understand primates. At the same time, we study primates to understand ourselves. We are closely related, and to some nonhuman primates, *very* closely related. In this respect, primates are models—they serve as windows into our evolutionary past as well as into our present, into how our ancestors may have lived many millions of years ago and how we behave today (Strum and Fedigan 2000). The fundamental point here is that the individual reading this sentence at this moment (that would be you) is a primate, but one very particular kind of primate. And as you will find out in this course, you can learn much about yourself by knowing more about your nearest relatives.

Public awareness of primates and their relationship to ourselves owes less to cinematic blockbusters than it does to the work of specific individuals working in the field, famously studying the larger-bodied and seemingly more socially complex great apes, such as the chimpanzee (Jane Goodall), the gorilla (Dian Fossey, whose life and tragic death also captured Hollywood's gaze), and the orangutan (Biruté Galdikas). Of course, we now appreciate that behavioural complexity is a characteristic feature of nonhuman primates generally, and not just apes. Why, for example, should Madagascar prosimians choose to be active at dawn and dusk rather than during the day (Colquhoun 2006; Figure 1.11)? How do social behaviours such as infanticide interact with ecological factors such as food distribution to determine group size in New and Old World monkeys (Chapman and Pavelka 2005)? Why should human children and chimpanzees share a fondness for beginning a painting with the colour yellow and drawing in diagonal lines (Zeller 2007)? Should it surprise us that humans are not the only primate with an archaeological record of stone tool use (Mercader et al. 2007)? As even these few questions suggest, nonhuman primates present us with diverse opportunities to better know ourselves. These and many other interesting questions are pursued further in Part II Tropical Currents.

**Figure 1.11** Primatologist Ian Colquhoun studies social behaviour in black lemurs of Madagascar.

Courtesy of Sylvie Colquhoun

In the domain of primatology, conservation is an area of increasing importance (see Chapter 15). Nonhuman primates have evolved highly complex relationships with their habitats, often serving as **keystone species**, and thus are highly susceptible to dramatic changes imposed by human activity (e.g., deforestation, poaching). As a consequence, they have come to occupy a prominent and unenviable status on the list of endangered and threatened species (see the International Union for the Conservation of Nature's *Red Book*). Vietnam, for example, is home to 25 primate species and subspecies, only two of which (the rhesus and the long-tailed macaque) are ranked as "Least Concern." Primatologists alone cannot resolve such dire situations, but they can provide the knowledge that will better enable responsible governments and agencies to seek solutions.

---

5. Humans are one among many different kinds of primates, and for comparison it is often convenient to make the distinction between humans and nonhuman primates. A "primatologist" may come from different disciplines, such as anatomy and psychology, as well as anthropology.

## Applied Biological Anthropology

As noted earlier, an "applied" discipline is one in which the methods and models developed within an academic field are brought to bear ("applied") on present-day problems or needs of human societies. Biological anthropologists undertake applied projects in a number of areas, including forensic science, health and wellness, and ergonomics.

Forensic anthropologists are often called on to assist local police forces, coroner services, or medical examiners[6] to identify human remains that—as a result of natural causes or human intention—cannot be identified through more common methods (Figure 1.12). Many of these "case files" are suspicious deaths and subject to criminal investigation; others may represent the outcome of accident or misfortune. In each case, the forensic examination aims to provide biological information pertinent to identity (age, sex, body size, ancestry) and to the circumstances of death (e.g., evidence of trauma, elapsed time since death). It is not uncommon that the remains submitted for examination turn out to be nonhuman (e.g., mammals such as bear or deer), or bones from unmarked archaeological burials. In the past two decades, a number of forensic anthropologists have worked on large multidisciplinary teams under the auspices of prominent organizations such as the United Nations or Physicians for Human Rights to investigate mass graves resulting from armed conflict (Figure 1.13). These can be particularly difficult exercises. Often, many bodies are involved, there is evidence of brutal violence, and partly decomposed soft tissue is present; all of this is compounded by the trying nature of political realities (local, national, and international) and by the presence of family members seeking answers (Skinner and Sterenberg 2005).

In the area of population health, biological anthropologists are contributing to the subspecialty of **medical anthropology**. Health forms one of the major intersections of biology and culture, influencing not only the experience of disease but also perceptions of wellness (Parker and Harper 2006). Within this domain, community-based approaches are shown to provide benefits beyond an understanding of this intersection. Under this model, local communities work in partnership with researchers to design, implement, and publicize

http://www.forensicanthro.com

**medical anthropology**
a branch of applied anthropology examining the interplay of culture, biology, health/wellness, disease/illness, and the art of medicine, both traditional and Western

**Figure 1.12** Richard Lazenby and forensic odontologist Dr. David Hodges recover remains from a cremated homicide victim in northern B.C.

Courtesy of Richard Lazenby

6. Different provinces in Canada have different administrative structures providing public oversight to death investigation. British Columbia, for example, has a Coroners Service, and Alberta a Medical Examiners Office.

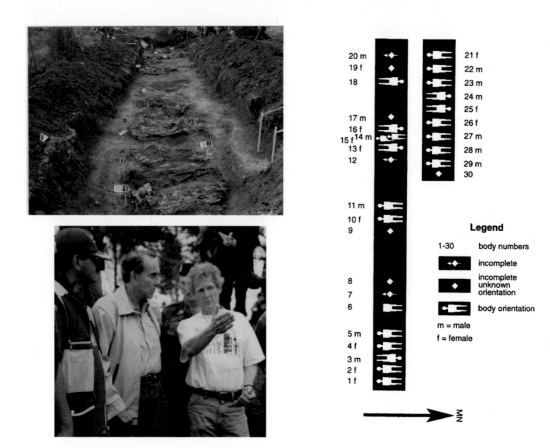

**Figure 1.13** Forensic anthropologists often assist in the excavation of human remains to gather evidence for crimes against humanity and to provide closure to survivors. Here, Dr. Mark Skinner (gesturing in lower image) discusses excavation strategy for a mass grave in the former Yugoslavia.

Courtesy of Mark Skinner

research. Sylvia Abonyi, a Canada Research Chair in Aboriginal Health in the Department of Community Health and Epidemiology, University of Saskatchewan, has been working with Aboriginal communities in northern Saskatchewan to document local understanding and experience with HIV/AIDS and Hepatitis C (Research Project Steering Committee 2006). Tracey Galloway has been studying growth and nutrition in rural Canadian schoolchildren (Galloway 2007), thus contributing to public health programming for elementary schools. Ethnopharmacologist Charles Leduc and his colleagues (2006) have documented a number of local plants traditionally used by the Eeyou Istchee Cree of northern Quebec, which may provide more culturally resonant pharmacologic benefit in treating Type II diabetes (the prevalence of which has dramatically increased among Eeyou Istchee adults in the past decade).

## A SCIENCE OLD AND NEW

http://www.medanthro.net

Earlier in this chapter we quoted Joseph Weiner on the significance of variation, which he saw as central to defining a "new" biological anthropology. Change occurs in all fields of study as new ideas and ways of thinking emerge, new discoveries are made, and revolutionary technologies are developed. Think of the incredible transformation of communication studies over the past two decades—the term "URL," now defined in the *Oxford English Dictionary,* did not exist prior to 1992! Biological anthropology has also witnessed significant changes in perspective (albeit less dramatic) (see Box 1.2) and is marked by an investigatory shift from varieties "*of* mankind" toward variation "*within* humankind."

The roots of the "old physical anthropology"[7] can be traced to Johann Friedrich Blumenbach (1752–1840), a comparative anatomist trained at Göttingen, Germany, whose M.D. thesis *De generis humani varietate nativa* provided an account of the origin of the five "races" of "man."[8] Blumenbach's classification was based on a comparative study of records of encounters with distant peoples by European traders and explorers and on a collection of skulls brought back from these journeys (Figure 1.14). In keeping with the prevailing view of his time (see Chapter 2), Blumenbach adhered to a **monogenist** view of human origins, according to which differences among varieties arose from local environmental circumstances rather than from independent "creations."

While Blumenbach's classification may have been "racial" and consistent with the use of the term in 18th-century natural history, it was not "racist" as we understand that term today. Blumenbach believed that varieties of "man" graded from one into another over geographic distance and that the differences in cultural and technological "accomplishment" among varieties could be ascribed to disparities in "opportunity" rather than innate character (Bhopal 2007; see Chapter 13). We should emphasize two points regarding Blumenbach's interest in skulls. First, it was common in the 18th and 19th centuries for comparative anatomy to focus on the head, especially cranial size and shape. The practice of **craniometry** was a clear reflection of

**monogenist**
from monogeny, meaning "single origin"; the view, consistent with biblical accounts, that humans were created once, with subsequent dispersal and modification; the contrasting view, according to which varieties ("races") of humankind were created separately, is known as polygeny, or "many origins"; these meanings are also applicable to the genetic concepts of monogenic and polygenic as defined in Chapter 3

**craniometry**
literally, the metrical assessment of the size and shape of the human skull

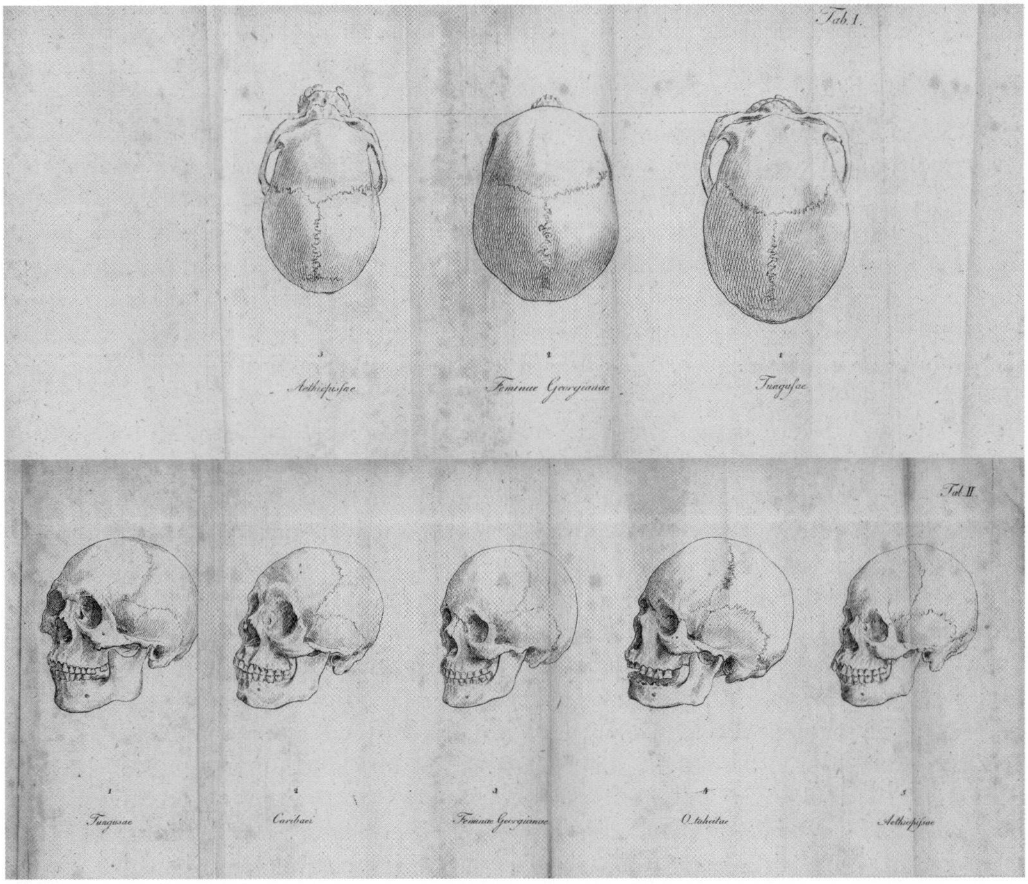

**Figure 1.14** Blumenbach noted distinctive differences in cranial size and shape among his "five varieties of man."

Blumenbach, J.F. "De Genesis Human Varietate native", Plates I & II. [*K.32.43/2]. Image courtesy of the Edinburgh University Library.

7. "Physical anthropology" was the name given to the field we now refer to as biological anthropology, at the beginning of the 20th century. That label reflected the discipline's emphasis at the time on observable and measurable physical features of human populations.

8. Blumenbach had originally agreed with Linnaeus's classification of humankind as four varieties (see Chapter 2). Later, though, in the 3rd edition of his book (1795), he added a fifth, the Malay.

the significance attached to the brain—the mind in particular—which was seen as the locus of intellect and reason. Second, while Blumenbach did not rank his varieties from first to last, many who followed him did (see Gould 1996) and for much of the 19th and early 20th centuries the discipline of physical anthropology was vexed with questions of race and notions of in-born qualitative differences.

Before the Second World War, research in biological anthropology was very much typological and descriptive, concerned less with variation within populations than with documenting physical distinctions between them. Most practitioners were not anthropologists at all, having been trained mainly in anatomy or psychology. Nonetheless, in fields such as osteology, primatology, and paleoanthropology, important discoveries were made. For example, in 1925 Raymond Dart (1893–1988), a South African professor of anatomy, reported on the original discovery of *Australopithecus africanus*, a putative early human ancestor (see Chapter 9). Similarly, in the 1930s the Canadian anatomist Davidson Black (1884–1934; Figure 1.15), at the time working at the Peking University Medical College, brought to light remains of another hominin fossil form, which he named *Sinanthropus pekinensis* (now known as *Homo erectus*). These paleoanthropological discoveries added fuel to the debate regarding where humankind originated: Africa, Asia, or Europe? The enigmatic (and as it turned out fraudulent) Piltdown Man, "discovered" in England in 1911, was a preferred progenitor for our species in many eyes, a view having more to do with class and race than with scientific rigour.[9] In 1931 the English zoologist and anatomist Sir Solly Zuckerman (1904–1993) published *The Social Life of Monkeys and Apes* based primarily on captive studies of baboons. This was one of the earliest works outside of psychology to explore behaviour in nonhuman primates.

In North America, anthropologists and anatomists were hard at work establishing the discipline through descriptive and comparative studies of human and nonhuman primate skeletons. This research was carried out for the most part on excavated remains from Native American archaeological sites or on anatomical preparations of anatomy school cadavers and unclaimed bodies.[10] Early in the 20th century, Aleš Hrdlička (1869–1943) became the first curator of physical anthropology at the Smithsonian Institution's National Museum of Natural History. His comparative study of crania from Alaska, Siberia, and Asia led him to propose that Aboriginal peoples colonized the Americas by migrating across the Bering Strait some 15,000 years ago.

A prominent voice in the field's development was Franz Boas (1858–1942). Initially trained in physics and geography, Boas later studied physical anthropology in Berlin in the 1880s. He also undertook ethnographic studies of Aboriginal peoples of the Pacific Northwest (primarily B.C.). Boas is largely responsible for establishing the discipline of anthropology as an independent academic field of study in North America. His contributions to the early development of biological anthropology are numerous. Notably, he undertook the first **longitudinal** study of child growth in North America, a project ultimately including more than 90,000 schoolchildren recruited from several cities, from Oakland, California, to Toronto, Canada (Jantz and Spencer 1997). However, one of Boas's most significant contributions was his research on stature and head size in adult immigrants from Southern and Eastern Europe and their American-born children. Under contract to the U.S. Immigration Commission, Boas and his assistants measured more than 18,000 subjects and found that the children were both taller and had larger heads than their parents. This study demonstrated that biological "potential" is not a fixed entity, but is influenced by the environment in which growth occurs. While not without controversy (Gravlee, Russell, and Leonard 2003; Sparks and Jantz

**Figure 1.15** Davidson Black, one of the early discoverers of the fossil hominin known as *Homo erectus*, in China.

Courtesy of the Becker Medical Library, Washington University School of Medicine

**longitudinal**

the repeated measurement of the same individuals over a given time interval—e.g., every year for five years. While costly and time consuming, longitudinal studies provide the most robust assessment of growth variation

---

9. The Piltdown forgery was a concoction of fragments of modern human cranium with a modified orangutan jaw. While the actual perpetrator(s) have never been conclusively identified, it is generally held that the purpose of the fraud was to reinforce and justify prevailing views that the progenitors of humankind could be linked directly with the dominant European (particularly British) ruling classes (Spencer 1990).

10. Two major sources of such osteological remains are the Hamann-Todd Collection at the Cleveland Museum of Natural History (with more than 3,000 individuals) and the Smithsonian Institution's Terry Collection (with 1,700-plus skeletons). In Canada, the J.C.B. Grant Collection at the University of Toronto is a more modest (202 known individuals) but nonetheless significant resource for comparative osteological research.

2003), Boas's research on immigrants and their children remains a seminal work in the study of human adaptability. It was also one of the first scientific rebuttals of the growing spectre of the American **eugenics** movement.

In Canada, biological anthropology as a formally organized academic discipline is much younger than its American counterpart. Indeed, for the most part it developed following the post-Washburn transition of the field from the "old" to the "new" (see Box 1.2), though some important research did take place in the pre–Second World War era. One example is the University of Toronto anatomist J.C.B. Grant's 1929 study, *Anthropometry of the Cree and Saulteaux Indians in Northeastern Manitoba,* published by the Archaeological Survey of Canada.

The establishment of the field in academia is largely a product of the development of the Canadian university system in the early and mid-1960s, during which new institutions were built and staffed and those already existing were expanded to add new departments and increase faculty numbers. The roots of modern Canadian biological anthropology can be traced to the (then) National Museum of Man in Ottawa,[11] where Larry Oschinsky was Curator of Physical Anthropology between 1958 and 1963 (Ossenberg 2001), and to the University of Toronto, where, following his appointment in 1958, James Anderson taught anatomy and human osteology in the Department of Anthropology (Jerkic 2001). Research at this time was heavily weighted toward the comparative skeletal biology and osteology of

**eugenics**

literally "true breeding," a social philosophy proposing that humankind might be improved through direct intervention in reproduction, including the restriction or elimination of particular groups deemed unworthy

**typology**

a static perspective of the world ascribed to the 4th-century BCE Greek philosopher Plato, in which "ideals" or "types" were perceived to be real, and variation as observed in the world was considered a deviation from ideal reality

---

| BOX 1.2 | **RETROSPECTION: Sherwood L. Washburn (1951) and the New Physical Anthropology** |
| --- | --- |

*"In the past, physical anthropology has been considered primarily as a technique. Training consisted in learning to take carefully defined measurements and in computing indices and statistics. The methods of observation, measurement, and comparison were essentially the same, whether the object of the study was the description of evolution, races, growth, criminals, constitutional types, or army personnel. Measurements were adjusted for various purposes, but measurement of the outside of the body, classification, and correlation remained the anthropologist's primary tools [...] If a new physical anthropology is to differ effectively from the old, it must be more than the adoption of a little genetic terminology. It must change its ways of doing things to conform with the implications of modern evolutionary theory [...] The new physical anthropology has much to offer to anyone interested in the structure or evolution of man, but this is only the beginning. To build it, we must collaborate with social scientists, geneticists, anatomists, and paleontologists. We need new ideas, new methods, new workers. There is nothing we do today which will not be done better tomorrow."*

Sherwood Washburn (1911–2000) was one of the more influential figures in modern biological anthropology. His work in primate anatomy and behaviour—continued and developed by many of his students, whose interests ranged widely—transformed the discipline from one mired in Platonic **typology**

to one that embraced a population-based perspective in which variation among members of a group was key to understanding biological adaptation and evolution. According to Washburn, this approach required a consideration of process (how things happen), function (how things work), comparison (how things differ within and among living and extinct forms), and evolution (where and when things appear). He was among the first in our discipline to champion the use of experimental approaches; he introduced the notion (borrowed from paleontology) of **mosaic evolution**; and he argued that it was necessary to incorporate ideas, methods, and results from other disciplines in order to produce a more comprehensive understanding of primate and human origins, evolution, and adaptation. Washburn was critical of perspectives that ignored biological realities ("race") or that embraced them at the expense of anthropological realities ("sociobiology").

Washburn's 1951 article was published at a time of significant change in the biological sciences, known as the "New Synthesis" (see Chapter 2), which merged the then distinct fields of population (laboratory) genetics and naturalistic (field) biology. This was a transformational shift in those disciplines, which up until then had studied evolution more or less independently. It was Washburn's paper that brought that revolution into the arena of human and primate anatomy and biology. In time, it led to a renaming of the field from "physical" to "biological" anthropology, to reflect the change from (physical) description to (biological) process.

Source: "The New Physical Anthropology," *Transactions of the New York Academy of Sciences,* ser. II, 13 (1951): 258–304.

---

11. The name was changed to the Canadian Museum of Civilization following a national competition in 1986.

**mosaic evolution**

the concept that functional complexes in organisms have independent evolutionary histories and have changed at different times and rates in the fossil record

**Table 1.1** Biological anthropologists holding Canada Research Chair (CRC) appointments as of 2010

| Name | Department / institution | Area of specialization |
| --- | --- | --- |
| Shelley Saunders* | Anthropology, McMaster University | Human disease and population origins |
| Christine White | Anthropology, University of Western Ontario | Bioarchaeology and isotopic anthropology |
| Robert Hoppa | Anthropology, University of Manitoba | Skeletal biology |
| Linda Fedigan | Anthropology. University of Calgary | Primatology and bioanthropology |
| Sylvia Abonyi | Community Health and Epidemiology, University of Saskatchewan | Aboriginal health |
| Mark Collard | Archaeology, Simon Fraser University | Human evolutionary studies |
| Julio Mercader | Archaeology University of Calgary | Tropical forest archaeology |
| Megan Brickley | Anthropology, McMaster University | Bioarchaeology of human disease |
| Dan Sellen | University of Toronto | Human ecology and public nutrition |

*Dr. Shelley Saunders was the first recipient of a CRC in biological anthropology; Dr. Saunders passed away in 2008.

**ossuary**

a repository for collections of human skeletal remains. In pre-contact Canada, these typically were large secondary burial pits containing the commingled remains of dozens of individuals who had earlier been interred in separate primary graves

Aboriginal archaeological populations, with Oschinsky focusing on Arctic-adapted peoples and Anderson emphasizing southern Ontario groups as represented by **ossuary** samples. At the same time, both these pioneers also took part in major studies of childhood growth in Canada and the United States. It would be reasonable to state that most biological anthropologists in the postsecondary education and museum systems in Canada (and many abroad) can trace their academic pedigree to the doctoral program at the University of Toronto, beginning in the late 1950s and early 1960s (Jerkic 2001). This would include many of the founding members of the Canadian Association for Physical Anthropology / L'Association Canadienne D'Anthropologie Physique (CAPA/ACAP) – whose first scientific meetings were held in Banff, Alberta, in 1973 – as well as the authors of this text.

Though the early years emphasized research on the skeletal biology of past populations, the specializations of human biology and primatology were also becoming established toward the end of the 1960s and early 1970s. Prominent human biologists included Frank Auger at the Université du Montréal, Jamshed Mavalwala and Emöke Szathmáry at the University of Toronto, and Joseph So and Hermann Helmuth at Trent University. Similarly, primatology was developing a strong presence, with (among others) Frances Burton (Toronto), Anne Zeller (Waterloo), and in western Canada, James Paterson (Calgary), and Linda Fedigan (Alberta, now at Calgary). Growth of the discipline in Canada has been quite exceptional over the past four decades; many institutions have a number of biological anthropologists on staff, often in different academic departments. By now, several generations of professors and students have gone on to become professors mentoring students of their own (we highlight a number of these mentorships throughout this text). Moreover, all of the various specializations have strong, internationally recognized participation, and exceptional graduate training opportunities exist in each. Indeed, no fewer than nine scholars contributing to the field of biological anthropology have been appointed to the prestigious Canada Research Chairs program (Table 1.1).

# SUMMARY

Biological anthropology is one of several major subfields of anthropology, which is the study of humankind in all its aspects. Biological anthropologists, in turn, may belong to a particular sub-specialization within their field—for example, skeletal biology, paleoanthropology, primatology, or human biology. Regardless, a central theme is the study of patterns of variation within and between human (and nonhuman primate) populations, their evolutionary and developmental origins, and what this might mean for understanding ourselves as a particular kind of animal. Biological anthropologists today employ a biocultural perspective, recognizing that biology and culture are intertwined both symbolically and functionally. It was not always so, however; the roots of the discipline (as with anthropology generally) were descriptive and comparative. This static perspective was challenged in the latter half of the 20th century, with a shift from an "old" to the "new" biological anthropology, with the latter emphasizing diversity and adaptation.

# CORE REVIEW

### What is so compelling about human variation as a field of study?

Humans are in many ways a paradox—we are animals, but not like other animals; as individuals we are different from other individuals, but also the same. We feel we have control over much of our lives, but at times we feel powerless in the face of diseases such as cancer or as members of lower socioeconomic classes. At the same time, we are also the only species capable of articulating these questions: What am I? Where did I come from? Why am I different from (or the same as) my neighbour? The compelling part of all this is that, while humans are biologically unique as individuals, collectively in many ways we are not. As the most socially, culturally, and technologically complex creatures to have ever walked the planet, we desire to acknowledge our biology; yet in many ways we often feel a need to suppress it. Our nature compels us to know ourselves, but at the same time we remain somewhat aloof as to what that knowledge might tell us. Biological anthropology attempts to provide the history and context to this paradox, to make us comfortable with being a particular kind of animal.

### How does a biocultural perspective benefit a discipline such as biological anthropology?

More than any other organism, humans adapt to their physical surroundings through culture (which includes belief systems, political economy, and technology). Culture in this way forms an interface between human biology and the environment. So, in order to fully understand the biology of humankind, one needs to examine its relationship with culture as a force that promotes and at the same time limits biological expression. A biocultural perspective is one that offers this broader view of what human biology is, but also of what it means in a particular nonbiological context—that of culture.

### Why are fields as distinct as primatology and forensic anthropology considered subspecialties within biological anthropology?

Though their work is very different in emphasis and scope, a primatologist studying how primates use deception to manipulate other primates, or how they vary in reproductive strategies, or how they use tools to process food, provides as significant a contribution to understanding humankind as a forensic anthropologist devising new methods to determine sex, age at death, or body size in skeletal remains, or helping gather evidence for use in war crimes trials. Fundamentally, all of the various subspecializations within biological anthropology are concerned with the "human condition," its origins and diversity in time and space.

### How does one best understand the history of biological anthropology as it has developed in North America?

Biological anthropology grew out of a 19th-century tradition of description and comparison, with an interest in documenting differences between human populations.

Measurement of skeletal remains, primarily skulls, laid a foundation for later work recording differences according to sex and age. An emphasis on understanding variation, its evolutionary origin, and population diversity did not really take hold until the latter half of the 20th century, during which the discipline diversified into several major subspecializations, including paleoanthropology, human biology, and primatology. Skeletal biology remains a significant area of inquiry, though it now applies a biocultural model—one that recognizes that all aspects of human biology, including bones and teeth, are influenced by our social and behavioural environments as much as by our physical surroundings.

# CRITICAL THINKING QUESTIONS

1. Now that you have an understanding of the scope of the discipline of biological anthropology, identify two or three aspects of your *own* biology that you would like to know more about. Why do these interest you? How would you study them? In what ways would an awareness of your own biology impact the lives of those around you (family, friends, people you don't know).

2. In North America, much of the early research in biological anthropology was conducted on skeletal remains recovered from archaeological sites, representing the remains of Aboriginal peoples' ancestors. This work is still carried out today, though within a community-based research or consultative framework in which local First Nations bands are active participants and contributors to the research program. What do you think are the benefits of such an approach? What limitations to research, if any, might follow from it?

# GROUP DISCUSSION QUESTIONS

1. Discuss the relevance of biological anthropology as an applied field in the 21st century. What challenges facing humanity might the discipline help address in terms of finding "solutions"? How might it do so? (Possible examples: population growth, re-emerging diseases, environmental toxicity, global warming.)

2. Discuss why some fields within biological anthropology have gained so much attention in popular culture, while others have not. (Possible examples: forensic anthropology or primatology versus human biology or medical anthropology.)

# RESOURCES AND READINGS

- L. Sawchuk and S. Pfeiffer, eds. (2001), "Out of the Past: The History of Human Osteology at the University of Toronto." **https://tspace.library.utoronto.ca/citd/Osteology/pfeiffer.html**

- The Canadian Association for Physical Anthropology / L'Association Canadienne d'Anthropologie Physique (CAPA/ACAP), **http://www.capa-acap.info**, is a good place to begin to learn about the discipline and its members in Canada. It includes links to history, training, field schools, annual meetings, and more. Similarly, the American Association of Physical Anthropologists (AAPA) maintains a comprehensive website, **http://physanth.org**, as does the Human Biology Association, **http://www.humbio.org/joomla**.

# 2 Science and the Development of Evolutionary Theory

## OVERVIEW

The scientific method, in which hypotheses formulated from existing theory are tested by observation and experiment, has become a powerful tool for the study of nature. The development of modern science through the application of reason inspired a new interpretation of the world. It was once thought that our world was static, hierarchical, and recently created. By applying the scientific method we learned that in fact, it is geologically ancient as well as characterized by biological variation, geographic diversity, and species succession through time. This advance in knowledge culminated in Darwin's theory of evolution and its mechanism of natural selection. Though modified and extended since its appearance in 1859, evolution remains the only comprehensive framework for understanding contemporary population variation within and between species as well as the origins of that variation.

## CORE CONCEPTS

■ world view, scientific method, contingency, theory and paradigm, hypothesis, essentialism, Great Chain of Being, scientific revolution, uniformitarianism, diversity, evolution, adaptation, natural selection

## CORE QUESTIONS

■ What is Western science? How does science differ from other world views?

■ How did early Greek philosophy hamper the development of evolutionary thought?

■ What scientific advances of the 14th to 18th centuries led to the development of Darwinian evolutionary theory?

■ What essential insights did Darwin bring to his theory of evolution by natural selection?

A new scientific truth does not triumph
by convincing its opponents
and making them see the light, but rather
because its opponents eventually die,
and a new generation grows up
that is familiar with it.

Max Planck (1858–1947)

# PROLOGUE: WORLD VIEWS AND THE ELEPHANT'S CHILD

*"I keep six honest serving-men*
*(They taught me all I knew);*
*Their names are What and Why and When*
*And How and Where and Who."*

Rudyard Kipling (1902)

**adaptation**

a state of existence or a process by which an organism is or becomes better suited to its circumstances of life

**niche**

the conditions of environment in which an organism lives, including climate, space, predator–prey relationships, mate availability, etc.

**morphology**

study of the size, shape, and configuration of an organism and its various parts

**analogous**

a similarity in structure or function resulting from independent adaptation to comparable circumstances in life, rather than evolutionary descent

**pheromone**

a chemical signal capable of causing a specific response in members of the same or closely related species

**epistemology**

the study or theory of knowledge, including its production, validation, and application

**secular**

separate and apart from religious tradition or edict, worldly

**methodology**

the study of the methods applied to research generally or within a particular discipline

**Darwinism**

evolution resulting from natural selection acting on random variation in populations, through which more fit individuals are favoured in "the struggle for existence"; as conceived by Charles Darwin

These lines introduce Kipling's "The Elephant's Child," one of his *Just So Stories*. The story of the Elephant's Child recounts how all living elephants came to have "long noses." In other *Just So Stories,* we learn how the camel acquired its hump, the leopard its spots, and the rhinoceros its skin (and even why people in Africa are darkly pigmented!). Two ideas are common to these accounts: change and **adaptation**. In Kipling's stories, the long-nosed elephant, the spotted leopard, and the humped camel are more suited to their particular ecological **niches** than their pre-existing bulbous-nosed, unspotted, and humpless forebears. Each has become—in a manner *just so*—somehow more fit to its circumstances of life.

To contrive a "Just So" story to explain all that exists in nature is one way for us to appreciate the "what and why and when" of things. But it is not an especially satisfying one, if only because it provides very simplistic (albeit humorous) explanations for what are extremely complex and variable **morphologies**. The Elephant's Child's curious encounter with a conniving crocodile (Figure 2.1) does not really help us understand how an elephant's trunk develops during gestation as a fusion of the embryonic nose and upper lip, or why the African elephant has two lobes at the tip of its trunk (**analogous** to "fingers") and the Asian elephant only one, or how a bull elephant uses its trunk to detect **pheromones** produced by a sexually receptive female. Each of these developmental, anatomical, and physiological adaptations requires more thoughtful consideration of its separate yet interdependent "what and why and when."

All human cultures have world views that they apply to make sense of the physical, biological, and historical domains of nature, their relationships and interdependencies, and in particular how people, as creatures both similar to and different from other animals, fit into that magnificent complexity. Some world views develop as magico-religious **epistemologies**. Two-well known examples are the Judaeo-Christian Old Testament Book of Genesis (1st millennium BCE) and the Five Classics of K'ung Fu-tzu (Confucius; 551–479 BCE). Others develop from more **secular**, material traditions. The most widely accepted of these latter world views arose during the European Enlightenment of the 17th to 19th centuries, an era in the development of Western civilization characterized by the application of reason and the scientific method in pursuit of more intellectually satisfying answers to "what, why, and when." Originating in the late 15th and early 16th centuries with discoveries by Nicolaus Copernicus, Leonardo da Vinci, Johannes Kepler, and Isaac Newton, among many others (and deeply rooted in Grecian, Arabic, and Asian philosophies and sciences—see Box 2.1), the "Scientific Revolution" transformed not just *what* we understood of the world, but *how* we understood it.

In this chapter we introduce science as a way of knowing and explore its **methodology**. In particular, we examine the development of **Darwinism** which is to this day the unifying conceptual framework for contemporary biology,

**Figure 2.1** Sketch of Elephant's Child and crocodile from Kipling's *Just So Stories.*

From *Just So Stories for Little Children* by Rudyard Kipling. Originally published/produced in Macmillan & Co.: London, 1902 © The British Library Board. (12809.t.64, opposite 72). Reprinted with permission.

including biological anthropology. Because all evolution, both organic and intellectual, derives from predecessors, this chapter also presents an overview of the people, events, and circumstances that were central to the development of evolutionary thought and theory from its pre-Enlightenment origins to the publication of Darwin's *The Origin of Species* in 1859.

# WHAT IS SCIENCE?

In reading this chapter, you should realize that "science" is not something foreign, something "out there" done only by supposedly highly intelligent people (i.e., scientists). In fact, science is a way of knowing. Every one of us applies it to almost every decision we make, usually without realizing that we are "doing science." We could be comparing brands of dish soap at the market, playing Ultimate Frisbee, or scheduling our time. Consider the following statement: "Students who do not read the text will have the same grade, on average, as those who do read it." This proposition can be examined as a scientific problem. Information could be collected from a number of students describing the degree to which they are either "readers" or "non-readers," and their resulting course grades compared using an appropriate statistical test. Science begins with a problem or a question, the solution to which requires gathering suitable observations or evidence from appropriate subjects, followed by a careful analysis and interpretation of results (which may or may not support our expectations). Thus, we might wonder whether there is a relationship between the cost of dish soap and its cleaning effectiveness, or spin rate and the flight path of a Frisbee.

For some problems in science we may have an **a priori** feeling for the outcome. (What do *you* think we would find for our "textbook reader/nonreader" question?) But for most questions we ask about the world, the answers are not at all clear before we make our observations or conduct experiments. Indeed, other researchers studying the same question using alternative samples or somewhat different methods may arrive at divergent conclusions. This does not mean that the previous research was faulty; rather, it tells us that the problem under investigation is more complex than previously thought and requires additional study, new hypotheses, and further samples and data. This is typical for many of the subdisciplines of anthropology that we introduced in Chapter 1. As we shall see, this dynamic "self-regulating" property of the scientific method is what makes it such a powerful tool for investigating a universe of complex physical and natural phenomena.

## What Is Theory?

A **theory** is a coherent framework, supported by a body of evidence, for understanding patterns of relationships among "things" in the world (indeed, the universe). Two examples: Einstein's general theory of relativity explains gravitation (the attraction exerted by objects of differing masses, underlying our everyday experience of "weight"); and Darwin's theory of evolution accounts for **phylogenetic** relationships among living and extinct organisms and how new species may emerge from existing forms. Of course, not all bodies of theory are as grand as general relativity or evolution. Most deal with more specific relationships on a much smaller scale. Life history theory, for example, concerns itself with variation among organisms in developmental and behavioural events that take place from conception to death, such as rate of maturation, gestation length, fertility and longevity, or body and brain size **allometry** (Hemmer 2007). Theory not only derives from research but also also directs future research and allows us to make reasoned predictions about how the world works. These predictions are called hypotheses, and the more such hypotheses are substantiated through repeated observation and testing, the more a theory assumes the character of a scientific law.

## From Hypothesis to Law

Humans are curious creatures, as are many organisms (including Elephant's children!). We wonder at things we do not understand, and we generally feel more comfortable having an explanation—a theory—of some sort to account for the mysteries that surround us. When we use the scientific method to understand a particular mystery, we are seeking an explanation

**a priori**
arguing from cause to effect; deduced from prior knowledge or presumption

**theory**
explanatory statements or arguments related to particular sets of phenomena supported by observation or experiment

**phylogenetic**
relating to evolutionary histories of ancestry and descent; also *phylogeny*

**allometry**
refers to patterns of size and shape change among parts of organisms at different sizes; or among different related organisms either living or extinct

**contingency**
being dependent on the occurrence or existence of a prior event or thing

BOX 2.1

# RETROSPECTION: Arun Bala (2006) and 'Dialogical Science'

*"There is a shared Eurocentric presumption ... that the historical roots of modern science must lie exclusively in Europe simply because modern science developed in Europe. This is wrong. The roots of modern science are "dialogical"—that is, the result of a long-running dialogue between ideas that came to Europe from a wide diversity of cultures through complex historical and geographical routes ... But modern science was not simply the result of a passive accumulation of ideas and practices from non-Western traditions of thought. Rather, it was the outcome of a process of integrating seminal discoveries from many cultures and combining them within Europe into a new synthesis not achieved elsewhere ... There is a ... broader cultural advantage in nurturing a deeper appreciation of the dialogical roots of modern science. An understanding of the way scientific knowledge advanced through the interaction of ideas drawn from different cultures would subvert attempts to use history either to promote the hegemony of one single culture or to make the existence of diverse cultures an excuse for confrontation and conflict."*

When we use the term "science" to describe what we do, it is generally taken to mean "Western (modern) science." However, Arun Bala, a philosophy of science professor at the University of Toronto, contends that this perspective is ethnocentric as well as historically impoverished. It fails to acknowledge the important scientific accomplishments of Asian, Arabic, and Indian cultures

(others could be noted), whose ideas flowed into medieval Europe and into the minds of thinkers such as Copernicus, Galileo, Kepler, and Newton. We highlight Bala's argument to point out that a Eurocentric bias runs contrary to the holistic spirit of anthropology as well as to a central theme of this text: **contingency**. Knowledge and understanding, as with everything that moves from simpler forms to expressions of greater complexity, is contingent on past knowledge, on "cooperation and competition" among existing ideas and perceptions (Boyd 2006). As Bala suggests, recognizing the contingent nature of knowledge has two major implications. First, it undermines any Eurocentric claims to authority or ownership with respect to scientific knowledge and discovery. Second, the fact that Western science developed from diverse indigenous knowledges subverts the accusation that Western science is inherently imperialistic and disdainful of such knowledge—a claim often made within contemporary critiques of science (postmodernism). While this may be true of individual scientists, it is not true of science as a method or way of knowing. It is important that we acknowledge that Western science has a deep history, one that extends far beyond its geographic horizon. It is also important to appreciate that an individual practising within any knowledge tradition (Western, Chinese, Cree, Maori, or any other) will be influenced by that cultural environment. Within any particular culture, individual experiences will vary, adding nuance to our understanding and interpretations of the world (Cassell 2002).

Source: *The Dialogue of Civilizations in the Birth of Modern Science.* 1–5. New York: Palgrave MacMillan.

---

**null hypothesis**

in statistics, a proposition that there is no difference among samples, conditions, outcomes, etc., that can be disproved through experiment or observation

**data**

observations, measurements, facts (known or assumed) that form the basis for a conclusion; singular *datum*

**sample**

a subset of a whole that represents its qualities with regard to the characteristics under study; for example, if three-quarters of a population of university students have a piercing, approximately the same proportion in a sample selected from that population should have a piercing

using observation and evaluation. It is just that: a method. The road to theory begins with curiosity, stimulating a question (called a **null hypothesis**), which can then be tested and either confirmed or falsified. Testing a hypothesis requires the careful collection of observations, facts, or evidence—**data**—from an appropriate experiment or a **sample** of subjects. Statements such as "In Toronto, most people with Facebook profiles are Euro-Canadian women between 20 and 40 years of age," or "There is no difference in the **prevalence** of HIV/AIDS in sub-Saharan Africa and Vancouver's Downtown Eastside" (Figure 2.2), are examples of testable hypotheses. How we state the hypothesis is critical, for it identifies not only the character of the sample to be studied (Canadian Facebook users, people in sub-Saharan Africa and Vancouver's Downtown Eastside) but also the nature of the evidence required (Who uses Facebook? Who has HIV/AIDS?), as well as any **assumptions** that need to be considered (i.e., women of all cultural backgrounds living in Toronto have equal access to Facebook accounts). This evidence—these data—are the variables we

**Figure 2.2** A view of Hastings Street on Vancouver's Downtown Eastside, notoriously known as "Canada's poorest postal code."

The Canadian Press/Jonathan Hayward.

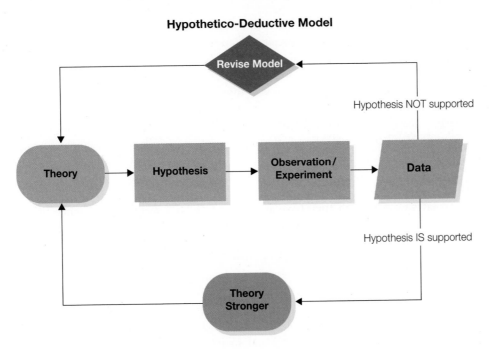

**Hypothetico-Deductive Model**

Revise Model

Hypothesis NOT supported

Theory → Hypothesis → Observation/Experiment → Data

Hypothesis IS supported

Theory Stronger

**Figure 2.3** The scientific method is a self-correcting and self-reinforcing process of discovery.

Richard Lazenby

measure, observe, or describe; they may be explanatory factors (age, sex, ethnicity, residence) or outcomes (disease status, Facebook registration).

From the perspective of scientific discovery, it does not matter so much whether our hypothesis is confirmed or refuted.[1] Both outcomes are informative and lead us to develop new questions, devise new tests, and collect new data, thereby continuing the cycle of discovery (Figure 2.3). This is the nature of science, and it leads to more robust theories, and sometimes even new ones. Note as well that the status of a theory does not hinge on the status of any given prediction—hypotheses come and go all the time! What matters is the balance of evidence over a number of studies that either supports or challenges the current theory. Some theories may be so weakened (found to be more wrong than right) by new findings that they are effectively replaced by new perspectives consistent with these findings. In the 19th century, for example, Darwin's theory of evolution supplanted the one proposed by the French natural historian Lamarck. The reasons why are discussed later in this chapter.

So, theory leads to the formulation of hypotheses that, when tested, either strengthen or weaken the theory at hand and prompt the formation of still more hypotheses. This cycle is the foundation of the scientific method. Our understanding of natural phenomena is always in a state of flux, and vigorous (and healthy!) scientific debate often emerges when hypotheses and data support alternative accounts. An excellent example is the recent controversy over the evolutionary status of a significant fossil discovery from Indonesia, identified as Liang Bua 1 (LB1) but more popularly known as the "Hobbit." Arguments have developed in the recent scientific literature over whether the find was a pathologically deformed member of a recent modern human population, or a relict of an isolated premodern human species (see Chapter 10).[2]

**prevalence**
in the study of disease, the proportion of a population having a condition at any given moment in time

**assumption**
a condition or feature unverified or uncontrolled but taken to be as stated for the purpose of argument

---

1. We talk about falsification/confirmation as either positive/negative results. Because most scientists like to be optimistic about their research, hypotheses are typically worded in such a way that "falsification" is the desired (positive) outcome. Generally speaking, though it may seem counterintuitive, confirmation of a hypothesis amounts to a negative finding!

2. The deeper argument is whether the fossil remains of LB1 represent a contemporary albeit pathologically deformed member of our species, or are in fact representative of a more ancient ancestor whose appearance reflects millennia of isolated evolution. If the latter, as seems to be the case, our existing theories of human phylogeny will have to be significantly modified to accommodate that conclusion.

Over time, a theory's strength builds as the volume of supporting evidence grows, until contradictory arguments are no longer generated. At that point a scientific consensus has been reached and a theory assumes the character of a "law." No doubt you have heard of the "Law of Gravity,"[3] and if you have taken a course in geology you will likewise be familiar with the **Law of Superposition**. In Chapter 3 we will discuss Mendel's Laws of Inheritance, which describe the transmission of genetic information from parent to offspring. As a rule, scientific laws are rare, since declaring a theory to be a "law" has a very particular meaning within science. Essentially, a law states that a relationship or outcome will *always* hold true in a given set of specific circumstances. Apples that break loose from trees will always fall to earth, and sediments in oceans and lakes are always laid down in succession with the oldest layer at the very bottom. It is also true that some well documented theories have yet to be formally rebranded as laws even though they have accumulated such a weight of evidence that their fundamental tenets are seen to be "law-like." The theory of biological evolution is a case in point. Its central premises of variation, selection, and adaptation (discussed later) have been observed and verified time and time again. There are two reasons for a general reluctance to view evolutionary theory as a law. First, we are only able to document the formation of new species[4] retrospectively, by looking to the fossil record (see Chapter 4), which makes speciation a theoretical prediction of Darwinian evolution, not a fact of it. The second reason lies outside science and involves opposing world views. Especially (but not exclusively) in the United States, there is significant political and social resistance from more fundamentalist religious quarters to viewing evolution as a bona fide theory, let alone a law (see Box 2.2).

**Law of Superposition**
layers ("strata", sing. "stratum") within a sedimentary geological deposit are laid down from oldest to most recent, permitting assignment of relative dates to items contained in the deposit

### Normal Science and Paradigm Shifts

Volumes have been written on the nature and history of science, what it is and what it means, and how and why we do it (e.g., Heilbron 2003). In 1962, Thomas Kuhn (1922–1996), a physicist, historian, and philosopher of science, published a **seminal** work titled *The Structure of Scientific Revolutions*. This book is widely acknowledged as an important critique of the practice of what we call "normal" science. For Kuhn, normal science is what scientists do day in and day out: they study nature from within a particular tradition of "conceptual boxes supplied by professional education" (Kuhn 1962, 5). These boxes constitute a **paradigm**—a term you may have heard before and one we guarantee you will hear many times throughout your university career. Paradigms are vital to the practice of science, for without them we would not be able to develop theory and form hypotheses. The essential message of Kuhn's work concerns how paradigms "shift"—that is, how the aforementioned conceptual boxes (scientific traditions) change. In simple terms, a paradigm is transformed when scientists are faced with facts that cannot be ignored or explained by the paradigm in present use. The idea of Darwinian evolution was a form of paradigm shift, in that it replaced the widely held concept of special creation with the origin of species and the understanding of variation. Other examples include the germ theory of disease for understanding infection (see Chapter 14) and plate tectonics as a model for theorizing about the configuration of continents. The rest of this chapter will examine how paradigm shifts during the European Enlightenment changed our understanding of the world generally, and our understanding of biology and human biocultural evolution specifically.

**seminal**
relating to "seed"; in this context, a seminal work is one that becomes a foundation for generations of subsequent ideas and developments

**paradigm**
a conceptual framework within which bodies of theory are developed, directing the course of future investigation

# EVOLUTIONARY THOUGHT FROM PLATO TO DARWIN

Today when we think of *evolution,* it is quite natural to think of *change,* of something new originating from something that existed in the past. We think of ancestors and descendants, each in some way different from the other. However, "change" is a recent idea in Western science. Before the 17th century, the perception of nature had been one of **stasis**. From geographic landscapes to the organisms on them and ultimately to the relationships among them, the idea

**stasis**
a state of equilibrium characterized by the absence of change

---

3. The Law of Gravity was originally derived from Sir Isaac Newton's Second Law of Motion describing the acceleration of objects.
4. Speciation is a fascinating issue that we explore in more detail in Chapter 4; much depends on which concept of species one applies to the question.

In the 18th century the "accepted wisdom" of essence, order, and purpose lent itself to a view of creation known as Natural Theology. Its most articulate proponent was the Reverend William Paley (1743–1805) as expressed in his book *Natural Theology* (1802). Paley's argument is most famously exemplified through his "watchmaker analogy." Highly integrated and complex objects such as pocket watches and people clearly require a designer—that is, a Divine Creator. Such "arguments from design" were not uncommon in the latter days of the Enlightenment (Mayr 1982).

Arguments from design remain with us in the 21st century despite having been discredited in courts of law (Raff 2007). Rising from the ashes of an ideology known as "scientific creationism," the current version, known as Intelligent Design (ID), critiques Darwinian evolution via the concept of "irreducible complexity" (Behe 1996). This argument, simply put, is that anything with multiple interrelated components can only exist and function if all of its various elements were present from the beginning. ID also argues that such complexity could not have developed through slow, gradual evolutionary change. However, this central premise of ID has failed to stand the test of scientific scrutiny. For example, complex structures such as the mammalian eye are not only manifestly imperfect but also have diverse and numerous intermediate forms. As well, some organisms (e.g., bacteria) lack components present in their closely related "irreducibly complex" relatives (Pellan and Matzke 2006).

But it is not so much that ID is conceptually flawed and fails to account for process, history, and relationships among living things. Rather, it is the political and social agenda of ID that is the real story here. Its considerable weight as socially conservative religious ideology is exemplified by two recent newsworthy events. The first was an attempt by members of the Dover, Pennsylvania, school board to insinuate ID into their science curriculum. This action culminated in an acrimonious trial in 2005[5] after a coalition of local parents sued the board. Having heard testimony regarding the scientific merits of both sides (ID and evolutionary biology), Judge John E. Jones ruled for the parents, noting that ID is not science—a position that garnered him "death threats for Christmas" (Raff 2007, 403).

Our second example is in some ways more disconcerting, for it poses disturbing questions as to how the merits of scientific inquiry are judged. In the spring of 2006 Dr. Brian Alters, an education professor at McGill University, learned that his funding application to the Social Sciences and Humanities Research Council of Canada (SSHRC) to study the growing influence of ID in Canada had been refused. In the view of the SSHRC review panel, Alters had not given "adequate justification for the assumption in the proposal that the theory of evolution, and not intelligent design theory, was correct" (Boswell 2006). The implication of this statement is profound, for it sets evolutionary theory and ID on an equal footing when in fact no such parallel exists. The former is based on the rigorous methods of science, the latter on faith; one is an apple, the other an orange! Recall that scientific theory is derived from testable (and tested) hypotheses, predictions, and observations and is subject to constant verification and falsification. Evolutionary theory has the benefit of 150 post-Darwinian years (and counting) of accumulated scientific evidence supporting its fundamental premises. Often lost in the creation—evolution "debate" is the important point that evolutionary theory does not negate religious belief, the practice of faith, or human spirituality, all of which are extremely important aspects of who we are as social and cultural beings. Evolution speaks only to the material, natural world of organic diversity and its history, and it does so fairly, eloquently, and rigorously. Yet ID has a significant number of adherents among Canadians, as a Canadian Press—Decima Research poll released in the summer of 2007 revealed. For example, 26% of respondents agreed that "God created human beings pretty much in their present form at one time in the last 10,000 years or so," while 34% agreed with the statement that "human beings have developed over millions of years from less advanced forms of life, but God guided this process." However, Canadians are comparatively more secular than our neighbours to the south. In a similar poll, 46% of Americans agreed with the first of these statements.

that everything exists as it has always been easily fit with our direct experience of the world. A human life span is short with respect to evolutionary modification, which occurs over generations. And when local geographies were seen to change it was usually in very dramatic fashion (e.g., earthquakes, volcanic eruptions, floods)—a fact that featured prominently in 18th-century attempts to explain extinction and the appearance of new forms in the emerging science of **paleontology**. So far as organisms were concerned, no one had witnessed the appearance of a new species; the dominant view held that animals were **immutable**, or permanent in form. Moreover, it was believed—especially in the West—that humankind was not simply different

http://www.actionbioscience.org/evolution

**paleontology**
the study of fossilized life forms

5. There have been several such trials in the United States, the most famous of which was the Scopes Monkey Trial, which took place in Tennessee in 1925. A full account of this trial can be found at http://www.law.umkc.edu/faculty/projects/ftrials/scopes/scopes.htm.

**immutable**

"not mutable"; an idea traceable to the Greek philosopher Aristotle, stating that forms exist today as they were when created, have not changed in the past, and cannot change in the future

from other animals, but *ordained* to be so. In the following pages we introduce some of the prominent thinkers whose work, intentionally or not, contributed to the development of evolutionary theory as we understand it today. As we shall see, the paradigm of stasis failed to hold up under an accumulating weight of evidence for diversity among both living and extinct organisms.

One thing more—the "revolution" in natural history (biology) that we associate with the development of Darwinian evolutionary theory is really a story that occurred within the Western intellectual tradition. There is good reason for this. In the centuries prior to the European Enlightenment, non-Western scholars had already developed ideas about organic evolution of species and had situated humankind within nature rather than apart from it. Taoist philosophy and modern biological science—including evolutionary thought–have many elements in common (Barnett 1986). The Roman poet Lucretius (c. 99–55 BCE) argued against supernatural intervention in nature and described how new organisms arose and then diverged over time. Islamic scholars, notably Al-Jahiz (c. 776–869 CE), not only had developed a theory of evolution, but also had conceived the principle of natural selection—anticipating Darwin by almost a millennium (Haleem 1995)! It would seem then, that the "revolution" in biology occurred within Europe because it was in the West that there was something to revolt against—an established though erroneous doctrine of stasis and immutability. The question we must first address is this: How and when did such a perspective arise and take hold?

## Essence, Order, and Purpose

Every morning the sun rises in the east, and every evening it sets in the west. Clearly it circles the earth once every day, and what could be plainer than that? So it seemed to most of humanity for most of history. This idea, **geocentrism** (Figure 2.4), is often credited to the Greek astronomer Ptolemy (83–161 CE), though it was widely held by earlier Greek philosophers, including Plato (c. 427–347 BCE) and Aristotle (384–322 BCE). A geocentric view of the world agreed well with emerging Judaeo-Christian world views, in particular accounts of Creation that embraced an earth-and-human-centred perspective.

The philosophies of Plato and Aristotle held particular sway through the ages. Their impact on our understanding of the world was long-standing. Plato proposed a theory of forms that

**geocentrism**

the concept that the earth is the centre of the known universe, around which all other heavenly bodies revolve, attributed to the Greek astronomer Ptolemy but known before his time

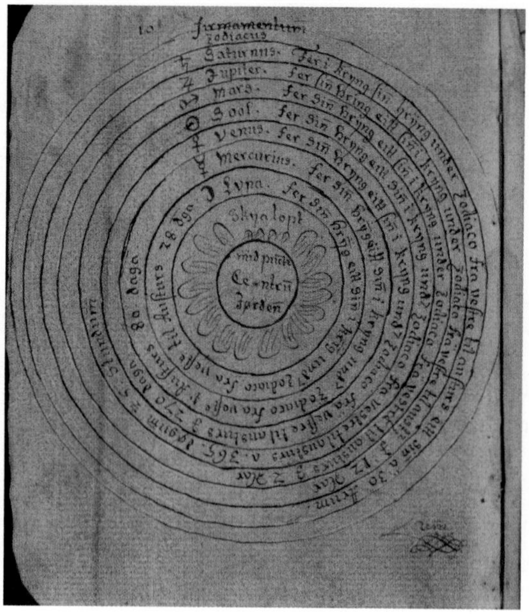

**Figure 2.4** Ptolemy's geocentric model of the universe situated earth at the centre, with all else revolving around it.

Courtesy of the National and University Library of Iceland

separated human perceptions of nature into two aspects. First were the material objects apparent to the senses, which were variable and subject to change. Second were the corresponding "forms" for each of these objects. These forms could be perceived only by the mind and were perfect in every regard as well as unchangeable. For Plato, "reality" existed as the form of a thing, whose immutable *essence* we experience imperfectly through our senses: smell, sight, sound, taste, and touch. Consider this simple example: In your mind you can conjure up an image of a "chair" because you understand the essential qualities of what we might call *chair-ness*. But if you were to go shopping for a chair at your local big box retailer, you would likely find a wide variety of items called chairs, none of which matched the image, the Essence, of "chair" you had constructed in your mind. Of course, today we understand that Plato's imperfect material objects are in fact the very real natural variations present in the world. Unlike Plato, we see the variety of different chairs we have to choose from as real, and the essence of "chair-ness" as imaginary. Plato's belief that there was an underlying unchangeable ideal or essence to all things is referred to now as **essentialism**. If at this moment you are thinking, "So why is this important to evolutionary theory?" ask yourself a simple question: If Plato's perspective on what is real (the immutable form) and what is not (variation) were accurate, how could anything evolve? Indeed, evolution could not occur, because in the Platonic world view the essence remains intact, despite any change in the expression of its imperfections (variation) through time.

Plato also advanced the idea that everything that exists can be ordered hierarchically, as if on a ladder, rung upon rung, from the lowest mineral entity ultimately to the supernatural. In the Judaeo-Christian world view, God rests on the highest rung of all. This idea of a scale in nature (known as the **Great Chain of Being**) was more explicitly developed by Aristotle in his treatise *The History of Animals,* written in 350 BCE. As with Plato's essentialism, the Great Chain of Being presupposes stasis and immutability. It insists that all things exist as they are and where they are, in a fixed position relative to all other things and for all time. Implicit in this hierarchy is the idea—attributed to Aristotle—of a final purpose or direction to creation. The idea that there exists a purposeful order from simple to complex, from least perfect to perfect, is termed **teleology** (from the Greek, *telos*, meaning "end" or "purpose"). However, under such schemes it is not possible to "progress" up the ladder, from simple to complex—stasis rules!

Classical Greek perceptions of nature were rediscovered during the European Renaissance of the 12th and later the 14th through 16th centuries. Incorporated as they were into the doctrine of the Christian Church, and consequently into the learning of all formally educated people, it is not surprising that the dominant view of the world was one of immutable essence, order, and purpose. Ironically, while these ideas were (and are) inherently anti-evolutionary, they came to factor significantly in the development of evolutionary thought during the European Enlightenment (17th to 19th centuries)—a time when natural philosophers (the scientists of the day) began to struggle with the apparent paradox of stasis, having opened their eyes in wonder to the world's natural diversity and complexity.

## From Renaissance to Revolution

In Europe, the Renaissance gave way to the Enlightenment, an era notable for revolutions, ranging from the social and political (the French Revolution), to the economic (the Industrial Revolution). However, both these upheavals were preceded by (in a real sense, were *determined by*) the Scientific Revolution, a transformation touched off by considerations of a very different kind of revolution—that of the earth around the sun. The **heliocentric**[6] view of the

universe, as proposed by Nicolas Copernicus (1473–1543) in *On the Revolutions of the Celestial Spheres*, was a truly profound idea. In effect, it demoted our planet from its hallowed position as "centre of the universe" to that of one among many objects circling one among many stars in the sky (Figure 2.5). Copernicus' book was published the year he died, though his ideas had become widely known throughout Europe before then. Along with Galileo's writings on quantitative experimental methods and Vesalius' study of human anatomy, heliocentrism opened the door to a comparative, rational, and secular study of the natural world, including the place and role of

**Figure 2.5** *Nicolas Copernicus: Conversation with God* by Jan Matejko (1872).

© Paul Almasy/Corbis

**essentialism**

Plato's idea, based on his theory of forms, that what exists in the world and is experienced by the human senses is an imperfect representation of an underlying, perfect, and immutable ideal, or essence, knowable only by the mind

**Great Chain of Being**

Aristotle's ordered, hierarchical, and static view of the world

**teleology**

a perspective proposing that there are end points, or "final causes," toward which natural phenomena are oriented and suggestive of a design, goal, or purpose in the world

**heliocentrism**

the now well-established view that the planets in our solar system revolve about the sun; the Copernican model also incorporates the essential ideas of the daily rotation of the earth on a tilted axis

---

6. The heliocentric model is yet another example of the West following the East; the major elements of Copernican theory can be found in early Vedic Sanskrit texts dating to the 7th century BCE.

"Man" within it. The scientific revolution made it possible to challenge accepted notions of time, geological process, natural history, and organic diversity and complexity—all central to later development of evolutionary theory.

Contributing to this transformation was the European exercise in empire building and colonization. The so-called "voyages of discovery" by Captains James Cook and Louis-Antoine de Bougainville, among many others, filled European "cabinets of curiosity" (Figure 2.6) with thousands of previously unknown plants and animals. Everything from ants to apes, along with "trophies" collected from encounters with newly "discovered" human populations, found their way into European collections (Holmes 2006). The naturalists on board these explorations broadened (indeed, shattered) European perceptions of biological diversity. They also established a tradition that resulted in a young Charles Darwin joining a surveying ship called the *Beagle* as its on-board naturalist. The observations he made during his voyage would forever alter our comprehension of the natural world, both its past and its present.

Despite the changed attitudes toward discovery and knowledge brought about by the Scientific Revolution, the European view of the natural world remained mired in notions of stasis dominated by the paradigms of essentialism and the Great Chain of Being. How is it, then, that in the relatively short span of 200 years, nearly 20 centuries of established and Church-sanctioned doctrine accounting for the Origins of Everything came to be unravelled?

**Figure 2.6** The Cabinet of Curiosity of Ole Worm, 17th c. Danish physician.

Smithsonian Institution Libraries

We can identify three major paradigm shifts that laid the foundations for a new evolutionary approach to biology (a term not even coined until early in the 19th century). The first was a new perspective on time, in particular regarding the age of the earth and the processes that constantly shape it (giving rise to the disciplines of geology and paleontology). The second, noted above, was the increasing awareness of the rich diversity of life, not just in the European countryside, but in distant and very different lands. Out of this awareness came the methods and sciences of **taxonomy**, "ecology," and biogeography. Finally, there was a gradual acceptance of the possibility of biological change—that species were indeed mutable. This central idea took shape in the century before Darwin's birth in 1809, fashioned by the anti-essentialist notion that perhaps there was something *real* about natural variation after all.

**taxonomy**
the method by which organisms are classified and assigned to a group (a taxon; pl. taxa) based on shared biological, ecological, and behavioural relationships

## Time

That the earth is not just thousands of years old, but many hundreds of thousands (indeed, many millions) of years old, is a comparatively recent finding, dating only to the mid-18th century. Before then, chronologies based on biblical events were assumed to be true. The best-known of these was developed by James Ussher (1581–1656), Anglican Archbishop of Armagh, Ireland, from 1625 until his death. Ussher based his chronology on various kinds of information, such the life spans and lineages of named male persons from the Old Testament and the length of the reigns of kings. In this way he arrived at a date for Creation as the eve of October 23, 4004 BCE, which he published in 1650 (Barr 1984–85).[7] The first serious challenge to such chronologies (of which Ussher's was but one) is attributed to James Hutton (1726–1797). Hutton was a Scottish naturalist and geologist who developed the concept of **uniformitarianism**, which argued that the earth is billions of years old (in Hutton's words, "infinitely old"). His study of volcanic and sedimentary deposits in the Scottish Highlands, with their record of upheaval, erosion, and replacement of sedimentary strata, led him to believe that these features formed gradually, as a result of forces that continued to be active and observable—in other words, forces uniform in time and space. Thus, in the past as in the present, wind and water erode landscapes, sediments build up at the bottom of oceans and lakes, and volcanoes emerge from the earth's mantle. Hutton published his ideas in a massive, 2,100-page three-volume treatise in 1794.

**uniformitarianism**
a philosophy in geology which argues that the natural processes affecting the earth and observable today have remained constant (uniform) through geologic time

It is quite likely that the sheer size of Hutton's work hindered early acceptance of his ideas. Wider recognition of the concept of uniformitarianism is generally credited to the eminent 19th-century English geologist Sir Charles Lyell (1797–1875). Lyell authored the highly influential *Principles of Geology*, published in several editions between 1830 and 1875. He firmly established Hutton's uniformitarian thesis, which demanded a considerable antiquity for the world. Yet at the same time, Lyell expressed disdain for notions of organic evolution, and in the second volume of his *Principles* he promoted the concept of "centres of creation" to account for the diversity of species (an idea possibly borrowed from the great French naturalist Buffon, who held similar views). Lyell argued that any perception in the fossil record that older deposits contained only simpler forms while later deposits harboured more complex ones could be explained by "imperfection" of the record. He firmly (and erroneously) believed that the fossil remains of contemporary mammals would one day be found in the most ancient fossil localities. Nonetheless, Lyell's work on the formation and transformation of landscapes had a strong impact on a young English naturalist, Charles Darwin, during his five-year voyage aboard *HMS Beagle*.[8] In later years, Lyell came to accept that species could evolve. In 1863 he published his final book, *Geological Evidence for the Antiquity of Man*.

Uniformitarianism, which required that the earth be of great age, was an important element in the development of evolutionary theory, as it afforded sufficient time for the gradual transformation of species. By the mid-18th century it was already well established that geological

---

7. It is often erroneously stated that Ussher calculated his age for the Earth using all of the "begats" in the Old Testament.
8. Indeed, in a letter dated August 29, 1844, to Leonard Horner, a geologist (and Lyell's father-in-law), Darwin wrote of the impact of the *Principles* on his own thinking: "I always feel that my books come half out of Lyell's brains & that I can never acknowledge this sufficiently" (Burkhardt 1996, 83).

**CHAPTER 2** Science and the Development of Evolutionary Theory

**comparative method**

understanding relationships among organisms by examining the similarities and differences present in various aspects of their biology

**correlation of parts**

the idea that organisms are integrated wholes and that change in one part cannot occur without altering the whole (usually by rendering it dysfunctional)

**extinction**

the complete disappearance of a particular species from a local habitat owing to factors that may be internal (related to the organism's biology) or external (related to environmental change over which the organism has no influence)

**Figure 2.7** Cuvier's comparison of mammoth and living Indian elephant mandibles provided support for the concept of extinction.

Georges Cuvier (1799). "Mémoire sur les espèces d'éléphans vivantes et fossiles, lu le premier pluvôse an 4 [21 January 1796]." Mémoires de l'Institut National des Sciences et des Arts, sciences mathématiques et physiques (mémoires) 2: 1-22, pls. 2-6.

deposits contained many kinds of life forms no longer present in the same region. The systematic study of fossils is due in great part to the work of the French natural historian Georges Cuvier (1769–1832). Cuvier, a professor of animal anatomy at the National Museum of Natural History in Paris, is generally considered the "father of vertebrate paleontology." He contributed much to the development of the **comparative method** in natural history, though he did not subscribe to evolutionary ideas, which were becoming widely discussed in his day. Indeed, his insistence that organisms are functionally integrated wholes (an idea known as the principle of **correlation of parts**) presented a barrier to accepting the possibility of evolutionary development, as Cuvier could not imagine how a single part of an organism can change without rendering the whole animal dysfunctional and thus unable to survive.

Cuvier, however, did establish the fact of **extinction**—a subject of much speculation for at least the previous century—through his careful comparative analyses of fossil and living forms (Figure 2.7). Of course, extinction posed a problem for Cuvier: if species are immutable, and if they eventually die out, how can we still have species at all? Cuvier reconciled the fact of extinction with the absence of evolution by proposing that through geological time, some plants and animals in a given region are lost to creation through intermittent cataclysms—that is, large-scale natural disasters such as earthquakes or floods. Such events were not unknown to recent European experience, as evidenced by the great Lisbon earthquake of 1755 (Figure 2.8), and may well have influenced Cuvier's thinking. The living forms lost through such disasters were replaced by the in-migration of organisms from adjacent regions not affected by these events.[9] To Cuvier's way of thinking, eradication and replacement would give the impression

**Figure 2.8** The Lisbon earthquake of 1755 was a powerful reminder of how natural events could alter landscapes, providing for Cuvier's account of local extinctions.

Courtesy of PEER-NISEE, University of California, Berkeley

9. Cuvier did not resort to notions of special creation to explain the repopulation of areas inundated by natural disaster, nor did he ascribe any particular cataclysmic change to specific biblical events, such as the Noahic flood.

of "evolutionary change" within stratigraphic deposits. In 1832 the English theologian and historian of science William Whewell coined the term **catastrophism** to describe Cuvier's theory of cyclical geologic revolutions. It is important to understand that while catastrophism and uniformitarianism were considered to be opposing ideas in the 19th century (the former associated with religious doctrine, the latter with scientific method), they are in fact not mutually exclusive. Indeed, a number of mass extinctions in the course of geologic history have been tied to catastrophic events, such as extraterrestrial impacts (Firestone et al. 2007) or climate change (Twitchett 2006).

**catastrophism**

Cuvier's notion that fossil forms are produced through series of cataclysmic events and that changes from one kind to the next in succession result from new forms arriving from areas not affected by the event

## Diversity

While the question of the earth's antiquity was slowly being settled from the vantage point of science in the 18th and 19th centuries, the issue of what to make of the burgeoning strangeness of never-before-seen plants and animals displayed in public and private museums was taking shape. Toward the end of the Renaissance, the emerging field of natural history was a gentleman's pastime; it was what (typically) men of means did as leisure. But it was leisure undertaken with serious intent. Amateur naturalists of the day meticulously described the flora and fauna of their local fields and streams. They formed societies, founded journals, and held scientific meetings (Mayr 1982). As Mayr notes, modern biology would be a narrow, lab-centred discipline, and Darwin would likely have had little to talk about, were it not for the "amateur" natural historians who preceded him.

A central challenge to describing the world, however, is labelling it. Think about how difficult it would be to talk to your friends about the last book you read if it had no title, or if in fact the word "book" did not exist. Not a simple task at all! Now think how you would tell your friends about all of the different books your professors have assigned for your courses, or the great variety of MP3s you have downloaded on your iPod™, if they lacked names. Where would Google™ be without the URL? Now you have a sense of the challenge faced by natural historians confronted with myriad kinds of organisms, both familiar and exotic. Fortunately, humans have a long history of living in close relationship with plants and animals, in the endless quest of both getting food and avoiding becoming food. In this endeavour, identifying the natural world becomes crucial to daily living. As a result all human cultures have developed **classification** systems—called folk taxonomies—that are meaningful to them (Medin and Atran 2004).

**classification**

the act of arranging or sorting objects according to features held in common; assigning such objects to a proper class

The English naturalist John Ray (1627–1705) was born to common parents, his father a blacksmith and his mother a healer and herbalist. Ray trained at Cambridge University, where he excelled in languages, mathematics, and natural history, especially botany (no doubt inspired by his mother's herbalist interests). Ray produced several works on the classification of plants and animals and in 1693 published the first formal classification of animals based on sound scientific reasoning. Ray is credited with several major accomplishments that unintentionally moved the study of the natural world closer to an evolutionary account of origins and relationships. For example, though Aristotle had used the terms "genus" and "species" two millennia earlier, Ray was the first to employ these concepts in terms of descent—that is, with regard to reproduction (Mayr 1982). He also supported the argument that fossils represented once living forms; he even produced a classification of nonhuman primates as they were known at the time (the *Anthropomorpha*, though he excluded humans). However, Ray was also a devout Christian and a founder of **Natural Theology**, a philosophy that sought to explain the diversity of organisms as exemplars of Divine Creation. He presented these ideas in his treatise *The Wisdom of God Manifested in the Works of the Creation* (1691), which would be reprinted for several decades after his death in 1705, and which greatly influenced Natural Theology's strongest advocate, William Paley (see Box 2.2, p. 31).

**Natural Theology**

a philosophy of theology founded on principles of observation of the world in a context of Creation, rather than on arguments from divine revelation

While we credit John Ray for laying the groundwork for reasoned arguments based on comparative morphology as an approach to cataloguing the world, it was Carolus Linnaeus (1707–1778), a Swedish botanist, physician, and zoologist, who founded the modern method of taxonomy. Today, Linnaeus is viewed as a giant in 18th-century natural history, having written numerous volumes and dissertations. But he is best known for his monumental work, *Systema naturae* (Systems of Nature), first published in 1735 and subsequently revised through

**Figure 2.9** Frontispiece from *Systema naturae*, 6th ed. 1748.

Courtesy of Michael Philip, Wikipedia Commons

**binomial nomenclature**

a "two-name" system developed by Linnaeus to identify all plants and animals according to genus and species

13 editions (Figure 2.9). According to Linnaean taxonomy, all plants and animals can be uniquely assigned to a category denoted by class, order, genus, and species. You, for example, are a member of the Class Mammalia, Order Primates, Genus *Homo*, and Species *sapiens*. In the 10th edition of this work (1758), Linnaeus proposed that a method of **binomial nomenclature** serve as the unique identifier of organisms, labelled according to the latter two ranks in his system: genus and species. This edition forms the foundation of modern taxonomy[10] (though the categories proposed by Linnaeus have been expanded considerably—see Chapter 4). Linnaeus' system was both practical and logical and brought order to an emerging chaos as natural history expanded its geographic and temporal horizons. But it was also essentialist and very much in line with Divine Creation. In Linnaeus' view, a taxonomist did not produce the "genus" but merely discovered and named those immutable forms originally created through Divine intervention. Nonetheless, we acknowledge Linnaeus for devising the first "modern" classification of humankind, in the 1735 edition of *Systema naturae*. Initially this was based solely on biological criteria, but he later (in the 1758 edition) expanded it to include cultural, behavioural, and cognitive traits. At that time he also assigned humans the taxonomic label *Homo sapiens*. Linnaeus ranked four varieties[11] of *Homo sapiens,* consistent with his belief in Aristotle's Great Chain of Being (Table 2.1).

## Mutability

While new ways of thinking about the age of the Earth, about fossil forms and extinction, and about how to classify and study natural diversity were fundamental to the development of evolutionary theory, none of the historical figures we have introduced so far were "evolutionists." All were devout men, and all accepted that species once created were thereafter immutable; the paradigms of essentialism and the Great Chain of Being continued to hold

**Table 2.1** Linnaeus' classification of *Homo sapiens*, 10th Ed. *Systema naturae* (1758)

| Variety | Skin colour | Temperament | Character | Vestments | Governed by |
|---|---|---|---|---|---|
| Americanus | red | choleric | obstinate | paint | custom |
| Europæus | white | sanguine | capricious | close-fitting | laws |
| Asiaticus | lurid | melancholic | haughty & avaricious | loose | opinion |
| Afer | black | phlegmatic | indolent | grease | caprice |

Source: Adapted from e.g., Gunnar Brøberg in Spencer, 1997, Vol I, p. 617.

---

10. Today the *Systema naturae* has been supplanted by the International Code on Zoological Nomenclature (ICZN).

11. Linnaeus identified a number of other varieties or species within the genus *Homo*, either fanciful (*H. sapiens monstrous* and *H. sapiens ferus*, "monstrous man" and "wild man"), or in order to capture reports from travellers of human-like creatures in distant lands (the designation *H. troglodytes*, "cave-dwelling man," was applied to the Asian ape, orangutan).

sway. A major step toward a theory of evolution was made by the inspired writings and mentorship of a prominent French naturalist, Georges-Louis Leclerc, le comte de Buffon (1707–1788). Buffon was an aristocrat and thus was able to pursue a life's work in natural history (though he also studied mathematics, mechanics, and law). His magnum opus, the 44-volume *Histoire naturelle, générale et particulière,* appeared over several decades, with contributions by a number of his contemporaries. The importance of Buffon's work cannot be understated. Within it lie the origins of cell theory (eventually leading to modern concepts of reproduction and development) as well as a theory of heredity termed **pangenesis**, borrowed from Hippocrates and later adopted by Charles Darwin. (In the manner of science discussed earlier, pangenesis proved to be an incorrect notion—see Chapter 3.) Buffon is credited as the founder of **zoogeography**. Recognizing that there must be strong links between biology and geography, he proposed that organisms are capable of being transformed ("degenerated") as their environmental circumstances alter through time or migration. Taken in combination, these ideas represented a theory of **microevolution**—a concept accounting for much of the diversity we observe within species today. Though shocking by current standards, Buffon even proposed that one could test his theory that environmental circumstances modify species characters by charting how long it would take for Senegalese natives to "turn white" if moved to Denmark (Marks 1997)! However, he did not accept the possibility of **macroevolution**; species per se remained immutable, and geographic differences in species composition represented different "centers of creation." Nonetheless, Buffon was the first to formally articulate a modern **biological species concept** (see Chapter 4) based on reproductive isolation (Mayr 1982).

Somewhat ironically, while Buffon himself did not accept that species were mutable, his patronage and support of Jean Baptiste Pierre Antoine de Monet, le chevalier de Lamarck (1744–1829), eventually gave us the first modern theory of species evolution. The youngest of eleven children, Lamarck came to natural history rather indirectly following a sojourn in a Jesuit seminary and brief stints as a soldier (in the family tradition) and a bank clerk. His interest in natural history led him to the study of botany and medicine, and in 1779 he published a volume on the plants of France. Following this, and with Buffon's support, he gained a position at the Royal Botanical Garden in Paris. After the French Revolution, the garden was transformed into the National Museum of Natural History, and Lamarck was named professor of invertebrate zoology—a somewhat incongruous appointment, for at that time he knew nothing about invertebrates. This was, however, a fortuitous event as it afforded him the opportunity to organize and catalogue the large collections of "insects and worms" kept by the museum (he even coined the term "invertebrate" to distinguish these forms from the "higher" animals). Lamarck's research on the diversity of these lower organisms contributed to his theory of evolution, most fully described in *Philosophie zoologique,* published in 1809. In contrast to both his predecessors and his contemporaries, Lamarck viewed organisms and their environmental circumstances as interacting dynamically to produce ever-increasing complexity and "perfection." This perfection was pursued according to Lamarck's two "laws" (more appropriately seen as rules): the **Law of Use and Disuse**, and the **Law of Inheritance of Acquired Characters**.

What do these "laws" mean? Lamarck's First Law derives from his perception that organisms do not proceed uniformly toward a state of perfection but must constantly adjust to changes in their circumstances. In Lamarck's scheme, the adjustment of organism to environment is the culmination of a cascade of events: (1) as environments change, the needs of animals change to maintain harmony with these new circumstances; (2) these new needs are satisfied by changes in an organism's behaviour and habits (termed "efforts"); (3) these behavioural changes redirect "subtle fluids" to physiologically alter—develop, enlarge, or reduce as necessary—some aspect of the organism's structure. However, it is in Lamarck's Second Law that we encounter the truly evolutionary component of his theory. The Law of Inheritance of Acquired Characters proposes that when both parents possess a particular adjustment acquired during their own lifetimes, they will pass that feature on to their offspring. In this way, acquired features are inherited. The long neck of the giraffe is the most often cited example of Lamarckian inheritance, but let us return to our

**pangenesis**
a theory of heredity arguing that particles in body cells and organs can be influenced by their environment, and once transferred to the sex cells pass on these influences to the next generation

**zoogeography**
the study of the geographic distribution of animals and the ecological communities to which they belong

**microevolution**
small-scale evolutionary events occurring within a population over the span of a few generations, affecting the frequency of specific characters and not involving species formation

**macroevolution**
large-scale evolutionary events, typically viewed over geological time, leading to speciation and the formation of higher taxonomic categories

**biological species concept**
species defined on the basis of reproductive inclusion within its membership and reproductive isolation from other species

**Law of Use and Disuse**
that component of Lamarckian evolution which suggests that the use or disuse of parts, reflecting an organism's needs and circumstances, will cause that part to develop or reduce accordingly

**Law of Inheritance of Acquired Characters**
Lamarck's Second Law stipulates that those changes resulting from use and disuse will, if occurring in both parents, be transmitted to offspring

**Figure 2.10** Could Lamarckian inheritance explain the elephant's trunk?

Henk Bentlage/Shutterstock.com

Elephant's Child's long trunk (Figure 2.10). Without recourse to crocodiles, how do we explain such an appendage? Erasmus Darwin (Charles' grandfather) believed that it resulted from an elephant's "need" to eat grasses but it had difficulty bending its knees! As the grasses were shortened by constant browsing, the trunk would "need" to develop further. For his part, the Italian naturalist Giuseppe Gautieri thought it was a matter of the elephant having a "desire" to smell that it was unable to indulge because its head was too distant from the soil (Corsi 2005). Lamarck did not specify the mechanism or process by which this "acquired" information was passed from one generation to the next. Lamarck viewed evolution as the consequence of imperceptible changes in circumstances, behaviour, and morphology over extended periods of time. Furthermore, he did not believe that environment directly caused structures to alter or to appear anew: the organism's "needs" and "behaviours" were always intermediaries in Lamarck's evolutionary scheme.

Lamarckian ideas of evolutionary change have been largely dismissed.[12] Indeed, they had become so within many (though not all) scientific circles during his lifetime—so much so that Lamarck died in relative obscurity and poverty. Cuvier, for example, was vehemently opposed to Lamarck's evolutionism, as was much of English academia. Yet Lamarck's ideas had profound significance for evolutionary thought. He viewed the organic world as subject to change, he seriously challenged the notion immutability, and he provided—for the first time—mechanisms by which species could be transformed from one form into another. The idea of the "evolution" of diversity, complexity, and adaptation, hinted at in scholarly writing of the 17th and 18th centuries, was now becoming more accessible *and* acceptable to a populace whose appreciation of the consequences of "change" had been fuelled by larger events in society—for example, the French and Industrial Revolutions and the slow transformation of universities from places dominated by church doctrine into secular, knowledge-seeking institutions.

## DARWIN, WALLACE, AND THE "MEANS OF NATURAL SELECTION"

Having read some of the history of ideas leading toward Darwinian evolution, we suggest that you stop for a moment. On your computer or PDA (or, as a more novel idea, a piece of paper!), write out in your own words what you think Darwinism, the term widely applied to the modern theory of evolution, is all about. (This is not a frivolous exercise—we invite you to

---

12. Lamarckian ideas persisted in Soviet Russia well into the 20th century under the guise of Lysenkoism, a doctrine named for Trofim Lysenko, the politically powerful director of the Soviet Institute for Agricultural Sciences. Lysenko believed that one could use Lamarck's Law of Inheritance of Acquired Characters to enhance plant yields, and applied it in an attempt (which failed) to revive an agricultural system in collapse under the Stalinist regime. In Chapter 4 we discuss an interesting and controversial argument that Lamarckian evolution actually does occur and indeed plays a significant role in the formation of species diversity and adaptation.

look ahead to Group Discussion Questions at the end of the chapter.) Has your understanding changed? Has it been influenced by what you have read so far? And do you have a sense from this brief history that it was almost inevitable that someone somewhere in the course of the 19th century would "discover" the ideas we now credit to Charles Robert Darwin? Indeed, by the mid-19th century two English naturalists—Darwin and Alfred Russel Wallace—had reached essentially the same conclusions regarding the origin and evolution of species captured by the term Darwinism. Theirs is as an intriguing story, often viewed as one of the rare "accidents of serendipity" that occur in science from time to time. But really, it is *not* surprising that they reached similar conclusions: evolutionary ideas about the history of life had been taking shape for some time. As Corsi notes (2005, 81): "Books and people, ideas and specimens travelled throughout Europe to a far greater extent than we have cared to investigate."

Notions of species transmutation were becoming more acceptable, especially in French, Italian, and German scientific circles. This acceptance owed much to Darwin's grandfather, Erasmus Darwin (1731–1802), author of *Zoonomia* (1796). In this work, widely read by European naturalists, the elder Darwin discussed the transformation of species through successive adaptations (though he still attributed their first appearance to an act of Creation). In his native England, however, from the 1820s to the 1840s, the scientific establishment was giving evolution a cool reception: the influential Charles Lyell fiercely dismissed Lamarck's theory. Natural Theology was widely accepted with little comment (Mayr 1982), for its premise that there was an omnipotent designer accorded well with the British class structure, the power of the Church of England, and the relative political stability of Victorian times. In 1844, however, this contentment was shattered by the anonymous publication of *Vestiges of the Natural History of Creation*, in which the author (now known to be Robert Chambers, a Scottish book publisher, journalist, and amateur geologist) laid out a theory for the progressive evolution of everything from the solar system to humankind. The book was widely denounced as a threat to the status quo, especially among the ruling classes, the scientific elite, and the clergy.[13] But it was also widely read[14] and embraced by the middle classes and political radicals, including the Chartists, a liberal political movement seeking significant social reforms in post–Industrial Revolution England. *Vestiges* did not disavow Creation (only the active hand of the Creator afterwards); it did, though, expound a central theme (though not a mechanism) that would reappear a decade later in the evolutionary theories of Darwin and Wallace—namely, that organisms evolve through geological time in a slow, gradual progression toward increasing complexity. So it seems fair to ask: How has Charles Darwin's name become synonymous with organic evolution when others before him had been writing about species transformation, and when one of his contemporary countrymen (Wallace) independently arrived at not only the same theory, but the same mechanism, **natural selection**?

**natural selection**
the nonrandom preservation or elimination of variants through competition within and between species promoting differential reproductive success

## Voyages to Natural Selection

Charles Darwin and Alfred Russel Wallace were both English, both naturalists by vocation, and both of questionable health. Beyond that, they had little in common (Hull 2005). Darwin (1809–1882) was born into prosperity; his father and grandfather had built successful careers in medicine, and his maternal grandfather was the wealthy Josiah Wedgwood (of pottery and china fame). It was presumed that Charles would continue the tradition of medicine, but he showed little affinity for it while studying at the University of Edinburgh. Nor did he find himself especially suited for the clergy, for which he trained at Cambridge. At each of these universities, he allowed his studies to lapse while he pursued his real passions, which were

---

13. The rhetoric was quite astounding. Adam Sedgwick, President of the Geological Society, wrote of *Vestiges*: "If our glorious maidens and matrons may not soil their fingers with the dirty knife of the anatomist, neither may they poison the strings of joyous thought and modest feelings by listening to the seductions of this author, who comes before them with ... a fake philosophy" (cited in Mayr 1982, 382).

14. In the first decade of publication, *Vestiges* sold 24,000 copies, far more than Lyell's *Principles of Geology* or *Darwin's Origin of Species* over a comparable period.

natural history and geology. At Cambridge he studied with the mineralogist and botanist John Henslow, whose mentorship had a profound impact that would continue for much of Darwin's life. It was Henslow who, through botanical research, taught Darwin that the key to understanding variation *between* species was to understand geographic variation *within* species (Kohn et al. 2005),[15] and it was Henslow who secured for Darwin the position of naturalist on the second survey voyage of *HMS Beagle*. This was, of course, a momentous occurrence in the history of biology, even though when Darwin boarded ship in 1831, he was very much cast in the Creationist mould and accepted the stability of species. Yet by the time he disembarked five years later, Darwin had embraced an evolutionary perspective and had established the fundamental premise of his theory—namely, that geographic varieties are **incipient species**.

Darwin, however, was a careful and thorough naturalist, and he would spend the following two decades amassing evidence to support his theory, during which time he composed—but did not publish—two short outlines of his theory (in 1842 and 1844).

Alfred Russel Wallace (1823–1923) was born into far more modest circumstances, the eighth of nine children. Though respectable and middle-class, his father was not an astute businessman, and when family affairs turned dire, Wallace was forced to withdraw from school at age 13. He began a long series of apprenticeships (including surveying and map making), all the while educating himself, especially in natural history. Having read other naturalists' accounts of travels afar, including Darwin's, Wallace was inspired to leave London in 1848 at the age of 25, joining an expedition to South America as naturalist. Unlike Darwin, when Wallace embarked on his journey he was already entertaining ideas of species mutability, developed in part from Chambers and in part from his association with the atheistic social reformer Robert Owen, who, in speaking of the class system, argued that people were shaped by their environment. The four years that Wallace spent charting the waters and collecting specimens in and around the mouth of the Amazon were not entirely successful (his ship burned and sank on its return voyage to England, taking with it the plant and animal collections he had hoped to sell). However, the book he published on his return gained the attention of the Royal Geographical Society. With the Society's support, Wallace set out on a series of travels through the Malay Archipelago between 1854 and 1862, reporting on natural history, geography, and local cultures. It was during this time (reportedly through the fog of a malarial "fit") that he arrived at the conclusion that a process such as natural selection could account for the formation of new species.

Despite their different backgrounds, Darwin and Wallace came to have much in common. Both men were naturalists; both had travelled to distant lands and encountered new species in new environments; both were familiar with the efforts of breeders who produced new varieties of species by artificially selecting for particular traits at the expense of others (Figure 2.11); both had read widely, including Lyell's *Principles of Geology* and Chambers' *Vestiges*; and both were recognized in British scientific circles—albeit Darwin much more so because of the class to which he was born.

Perhaps most important, both men had read *An Essay on the Principle of Population,* a slim book published in 1798 by a Scottish economist, the Reverend Thomas Robert Malthus (1766–1834).[16] Malthus' essay is as relevant today as it was in 1798—perhaps very much more so (see Chapter 16). Historians of science contend that it was Malthus who provided the key to unlocking the mechanism of natural selection. Concerned with the plight of Scottish farmers and working people, he observed that population growth always had and always would exceed growth in the resources necessary to sustain it. If left unchecked, populations growing to excess would, without exception, be subject to misery, pestilence, famine, and warfare. The key that both Darwin and

---

15. Henslow maintained a creationist perspective. Much like Buffon before him, he advocated that geography could produce variation within species but that species themselves were immutable.

16. There is some question as to the impact that Malthus had on either Darwin or Wallace. Malthus is not accorded prominence in the writings of either man—indeed, he is mentioned only twice in Darwin's *The Origin of Species* (Hull 2005). As Hull observes, both men were living and writing during the rise of competitive, dog-eat-dog laissez-faire economics in Victorian England. In this regard the Scottish free trade economist Adam Smith may have had as much to do with the development of evolutionary theory as his countryman Malthus!

**Figure 2.11** Breeders artificially select for particular features, "creating" novel forms as a result.

Charles Darwin (1868). *Variation of Animals and Plants Under Domestication.* Image courtesy of Wikipedia Commons

http://www.esp.org/books/
malthus/population/malthus
.pdf

Wallace stumbled upon was as simple as it was elegant: individuals within populations are *not* equally likely to suffer from deprivation or failure to thrive. By virtue of differences in endowment (health, intellect, morphology, prowess, etc.), some would always be more successful in competing for those resources necessary for survival *and reproduction* (food, friends, mates, etc.). Thus they would be *naturally* selected in the "struggle for existence" and would leave more offspring similar to themselves, at the expense of less fortunate and less competitive members of their species. In other words, they would have greater **reproductive fitness**.[17]

In a nutshell, Darwin had come to realize as early as 1838 (Mayr 1982), and Wallace some years later, that evolution by natural selection consisted of four elements:

1. All populations vary, individual by individual; often noticeably in terms of size and shape, but also in smaller and more subtle yet no less important ways, such as in shades of colour or expressions of behaviour.
2. All populations have the potential to reproduce at a rate in excess of the rate at which necessary resources (food, space, mates, and so on) increase.
3. Competition for limited resources occurs not just *between* members of difference species, but, more important, *among* individuals *within* species.
4. At any given moment and in any given circumstance, heritable characteristics possessed by individual "X" increase the likelihood of successful reproduction and survival of offspring, relative to those of individual "Y." (Note that "circumstance" matters immensely. Change the situation, and individual "Y" may be "more fit" than individual "X"! How would you compare your fitness in an isolated Arctic landscape with that of an Inuit hunter? Or an Inuit mother compared to her Aborigine counterpart in the Australian outback?)

To many people today, these four elements seem self-evident—indeed, simplistic. Of course individuals vary! And of course some are more adept than others at acquiring the necessities of life. How could it be otherwise? But in English scientific circles of the mid-19th century, to bring these ideas together as an argument for the evolution of species amounted to an astonishing declaration. Darwin was well aware of the impact his theory would have.

**reproductive fitness**
a measure of the success of an individual in the production of offspring across generations; your children, and their children, and so on all constitute your reproductive success

17. It is important to distinguish between fitness as an "expected" outcome versus fitness as a "realized" outcome. We explore this contrast in Chapter 4.

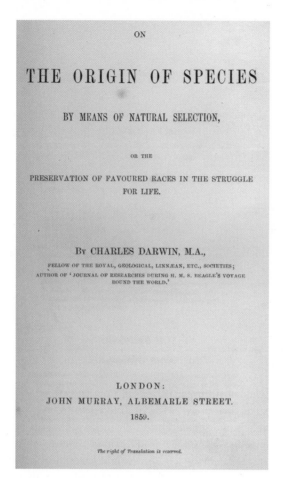

ON

# THE ORIGIN OF SPECIES

BY MEANS OF NATURAL SELECTION,

OR THE

PRESERVATION OF FAVOURED RACES IN THE STRUGGLE FOR LIFE.

By CHARLES DARWIN, M.A.,

FELLOW OF THE ROYAL, GEOLOGICAL, LINNÆAN, ETC., SOCIETIES;
AUTHOR OF 'JOURNAL OF RESEARCHES DURING H. M. S. BEAGLE'S VOYAGE
ROUND THE WORLD.'

LONDON:
JOHN MURRAY, ALBEMARLE STREET.
1859.

*The right of Translation is reserved.*

**Figure 2.12** Darwin's *Origin* is arguably the most influential book ever published in the field of natural history (biology).

Charles Darwin (1868). *Variation of Animals and Plants Under Domestication*. Image courtesy of Wikipedia Commons

He had, after all, witnessed the reaction to the publication of Chambers' *Vestiges*—a reaction that in part underlay his reticence to publish. This changed dramatically in 1855, with the appearance of a short article in the *Annals and Magazine of Natural History* titled "On the Law Which Has Regulated the Introduction of New Species" by A.R. Wallace. The story of the impact this paper had on Darwin, and on the efforts made by his confidantes and supporters (most notably Charles Lyell and the botanist Joseph Hooker) to get him to publish, is fascinating and full of intrigue.

Darwin wrote to Wallace on May 1, 1857: "By your letter & even still more by your paper in Annals, a year or more ago, I can plainly see that we have thought much alike & to a certain extent have come to similar conclusions" (in Burkhardt 1996, 172). Wallace subsequently produced an unpublished paper (*On the Tendency of Varieties to Depart Indefinitely from the Original Type*) in which he outlined not only his ideas concerning evolution but also the essence of natural selection as the mechanism (though he did not use that term). What else was he to do but mail it to Darwin for comment? Darwin, naturally, was stunned by this further coincidence, and for good reason—the focus of all his 20 years' work was laid out before him, described in detail by a self-taught layman of lesser social standing! On June 1, 1858, Darwin wrote to Lyell, who had been pleading with Darwin to publish lest he be upstaged: "Your words have come true with a vengeance that I sh$^d$. be forestalled ... I never saw a more striking coincidence. if Wallace had my M.S. sketch written out in 1842 he could not have made a better short abstract! Even his terms now stand as Heads of my Chapters" (ibid. 1996, 188). The solution contrived by Lyell and Hooker—and with Darwin's consent—was to have a joint paper read at the Linnaean Society on July 1, 1858—an arrangement with which Wallace himself was satisfied, deferring to Darwin's eminence as a naturalist.[18] A little more than a year later, Darwin published what he considered an abstract of his theory, some 700 pages in length—*The Origin of Species by Means of Natural Selection, Or the Preservation of Favoured Races in the Struggle for Life*—a book that is arguably the most significant ever published in the history of biology (Figure 2.12).

### What Is Natural Selection?

Biologists have documented many examples of natural selection through which populations have adapted to their circumstances of life. You can Google landmark examples such as "Industrial melanism" and "Galapagos ground finch beak size and drought." Regarding humans, there

---

18. In fact, the "joint paper" consisted of Wallace's manuscript, which he had sent to Darwin, an extract from Darwin's *The Origin of Species* manuscript, and a letter written by Darwin to the American botanist Asa Gray attesting to Darwin's priority.

are classics such as James Neel's "thrifty genotype" hypothesis for the increased incidence of Type II diabetes among indigenous populations, and Frank Livingstone's work on *Plasmodium falciparum* malaria and sickle cell anemia. The re-emergence of drug-resistant infectious diseases such as tuberculosis reflects adaptation of the pathogen to the selective force of antibiotics—a significant public health concern at the global level today (see Chapter 14). Developments in molecular biology have opened new avenues for identifying the effects of natural selection at the genetic level (Wooding 2004), in terms not only of the presence or absence of particular genetic variants, but also of the manner in which those variants are expressed. For example, many African populations have a higher frequency of a genetic variant known as *A(-6)*, which promotes salt retention—an adaptive feature in hot, humid climates, where sweating removes electrolytes such as sodium (a component of salt) necessary for normal cellular metabolism and neuronal function. Non-African populations with less need to retain salt have recently evolved a different variant, *G(-6)*, to reduce salt retention. This is adaptive in contexts where lifestyle factors (diet, activity) increase the risk of high blood pressure (hypertension), a risk that is raised even further by high levels of sodium in the body.

The core feature of natural selection is that it acts on variation that is normally present in a population. If a particular variant—such as *G(-6)*—provides an advantage to those individuals who have it, then the likelihood is that the variant will increase in frequency in the population over time and that less advantageous variants of a trait will decrease in frequency. The selective forces in the "salt retention" example are (1) heart disease in non-African populations, which leads to higher frequencies of *G(-6)* promoting salt excretion; and (2) the need to maintain normal cellular function in African populations, which increases the occurrence of the *A(-6)* variant aiding in salt retention. Trait frequencies are continually modified across generations at different rates in different populations and may, given sufficient time and isolation, lead to the formation of new species (see Chapter 4).

## Missing Links

Darwin and Wallace provided a theory and a mechanism by which species could evolve by adapting to their circumstances of life, grounded in variation and natural selection. Neither, though, was able to supply a mechanism of inheritance by which such adaptations could actually be passed from one generation to the next. It was clear that selected variation was heritable—plant and animal breeders had shown it to be so time and time again. Neither man had much sympathy for the Lamarckian idea of inheritance of acquired characters (especially following Lyell's rebuke of Lamarck in Volume II of *Principles of Geology*). Darwin conceived of inheritance working through a process (pangenesis) whereby each body cell type created particles called gemmules which were transported to the germ cells (sperm and egg) and brought together at conception to form a new individual.[19] To Darwin's credit, he knew that any theory of inheritance would have to account for all possible outcomes—for example, why offspring sometimes appeared as a "blend" of both parents, and sometimes expressed a feature that occurred only in one and not the other, and sometimes bore a trait that appeared in neither parent. Unfortunately, pangenesis was not that mechanism, a fact of which Darwin was aware at his death in 1882, but for which he could offer no alternative.

Yet the alternative had been published in a European journal in 1866, in a short paper outlining the results of a series of experiments documenting inheritance in pea plants. These experiments had been carried out by a somewhat reclusive Austrian biologist and Augustinian monk, Gregor Mendel (see Chapter 3), now considered the father of the science of genetics. Some debate exists as to whether Darwin was ever aware of Mendel's work. Most likely he was not, and in any case he might not have given Mendel's ideas much credence, for Darwin viewed variation as the product of natural selection, whereas Mendel saw it as the outcome of hybridization (Sclater 2006). Darwin was not alone in his ignorance of Mendel's paper. Indeed, it received very little attention, and as a consequence, the vital "link" tying variation to natural selection and inheritance would remain "lost" until the end of the 19th century.

---

19. Pangenesis was another idea deeply rooted in Greek philosophy, notably Hippocrates in the 5th century BCE.

# SUMMARY

The history of evolutionary thought is part of the larger history of Western science, the origin of which many tie to the adoption of Copernicus' heliocentric model of the universe in place of the geocentric perspective handed down from the ancient Greeks. In truth, its roots are much deeper and more widely spread, extending several millennia into Islamic, Indian, and Asian scholarship. But it was the development of the scientific method that opened doors to new ways of thinking about the organic world, with its emphasis on hypothesis and observation, reason and fact. This transformation occurred rapidly throughout the European Renaissance and Enlightenment (Figure 2.13). In this chapter we have presented only a handful of the ideas and individuals who shaped these developments. By the time Darwin's *The Origin of Species* was published in 1859, the theme of "essence, order, and purpose" (also traceable to ancient Greek philosophy), in which species were seen as created and immutable, had given way to one of variation, diversity, and evolution over long spans of geological time. The rise of evolutionary biology in the 19th century must also be viewed in the larger context of the social, political, and economic transformation of Europe, highlighting notions of competition, class, and change. As we explore in Part IV, this ongoing relationship between (human) biology and political economy is as fascinating as it is it is, at times, disheartening.

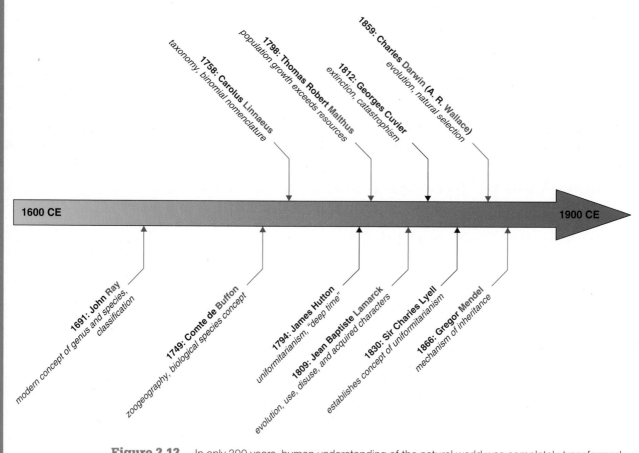

**Figure 2.13**    In only 300 years, human understanding of the natural world was completely transformed from one grounded in early Greek philosophy and church doctrine, to one based on a secular, scientific world view.

Richard Lazenby

# CORE REVIEW

**What is Western science? How does science differ from other world views?**

Western science developed in Europe and is often associated with a post-Copernican emphasis on reason, observation, and experiment. Modern scholars now recognize the deep historical ties that Western science has with non-Western traditions as were practised in the Near East and Asia for many hundreds of years prior to Copernicus. In contrast to other world views (e.g., Christianity, Confucianism), Western science invokes the scientific method, in which a current interpretation (theory) raises questions (hypotheses), which are answered through the structured collection of information (data), which either supports or refutes the hypothesis. As a consequence the original theory is modified (strengthened or weakened). The scientific method is a self-correcting enterprise oriented to concepts of reason, testability, and reproducibility.

**How did early Greek philosophy constrain the development of evolutionary thought?**

In the two millennia prior to the Copernican Revolution, Platonic essentialism and Aristotle's notion of the Great Chain of Being held sway and were absorbed into the orthodoxy of Church doctrine. Essentialism proposes that only the "form" is real and that variation is abstract and a degradation from that "ideal." The "Great Chain" situated all "forms" in a natural order, a progression, from the most simple to the most complex—an order that was static and unchanging. Evolutionary thinking requires precisely the opposite perspective: an appreciation of the reality of variation, and the possibility that forms can "progress" from more simple to more complex, from ancestor to descendant.

**What scientific advances of the 15th to 18th centuries led to the development of evolutionary theory?**

Roughly coincident with the Renaissance and the Enlightenment periods in Europe, these four centuries witnessed the emergence of new ways of thinking about the universe, the earth, and nature. Ptolemy's geocentric model of the universe was replaced by Copernicus' heliocentrism; and mathematics and physics re-emerged as serious subjects of study, leading to an understanding of gravity and planetary motion. In natural philosophy, three developments paved the way for new thinking regarding evolution: (1) a radical new perspective on time, with the earth viewed as significantly old and as subject to uniformitarian processes; (2) a greater regard for biological diversity and geographic variation; and (3) the emerging sense that species were at least potentially mutable, as evident from the fossil record and from recognition that the environment can modify populations within species.

**What fundamental insights did Darwin bring to his theory of evolution by natural selection?**

Darwin realized that the origin of species by natural selection required four elements: (1) heritable variation must be present in the population; (2) population growth must exceed the increase in resources required for survival and reproduction; (3) individuals within a population or species must compete among themselves for access to those resources; and (4) some individuals compete more successfully, and thus the advantageous characteristics conferring that success will be selected to appear in greater frequencies in future generations.

# CRITICAL THINKING QUESTIONS

1. The eminent American population geneticist Theodosius Dobzhansky once wrote that "Nothing in biology makes sense except in the light of evolution" (*American Biology Teacher*, March 1973 [125–29]). Given your appreciation of the fundamental nature of evolution, adaptation, and selection, how would *you* construct an argument that would support Dobzhansky's assertion? Why would you argue against his position?
2. Michael Ruse, a philosopher of science and Darwinian scholar, once observed that "Darwinism is a term much like Christianity or Marxism, in that everybody 'knows' what it means, and yet on not very close inspection it turns out that everybody's meaning is slightly different" (Ruse 1992, 74). Is Ruse correct? How different from or similar to that of your classmates is your understanding of Darwinism? Discuss how and why such differences and similarities might arise.

# GROUP DISCUSSION QUESTIONS

1. Early in this chapter we suggested that the statement "There is no difference in the prevalence of HIV/AIDS in sub-Saharan Africa and Vancouver's Downtown Eastside" constituted a testable hypothesis. How would such a test be carried out? What kinds of data would be required, and from what sample of subjects? While this statement is testable, do you think it might in fact be an unreasonable claim as we have stated it? Why?
2. Scientific progress does not occur independently of the social and political climate. In recent years in North America (in both Canada and the United States) there has been a resurgence of neoconservative politics and religious fundamentalism within an increasingly culturally and ethnically diverse society. If a proposal were made to your local school board that the tenets of intelligent design be taught alongside evolutionary theory, would you respond for or against it? How would you justify and support your decision?

# RESOURCES AND READINGS

"The Complete Works of Charles Darwin." **http://darwin-online.org.uk/darwin.html**
A. Petto and L. Godfrey, eds., *Scientists Confront Intelligent Design and Creationism* (New York: Norton, 2007).

# Chapter 3

# The Biological Basis of Human Variation

## OVERVIEW

In order to understand the mechanisms underlying human evolution and variation, we need to have a thorough understanding of genes and how traits are inherited. This chapter introduces you to the basics of genetics, starting with the blueprint of life, DNA (deoxyribonucleic acid). We explore the role of DNA in protein synthesis, the nature of chromosomes, the mechanisms by which cells divide, sources of variation, and how our understanding of genetics came about. We also examine the genetic basis of common human traits and explore some of the controversial applications of genetics research. As you will learn in this chapter, the integration of genetics and biological anthropology has allowed researchers to address a diversity of anthropological questions.

## CORE CONCEPTS

- heredity, mechanisms of inheritance, heritability, genetic determinism

## CORE QUESTIONS

- What is DNA? What functions does it serve, and how does it differ from RNA?

- What are mitosis and meiosis, and how do they differ?

- What are some of the sources of variation on which natural selection acts?

- What are proteins, and how are they synthesized?

- How are traits transmitted from one generation to the next, and how did our knowledge of this process come about?

- What are polygenic traits, and how do they differ from monogenic traits?

- What is behavioural genetics, and what are some of the challenges that behavioural geneticists face?

- What can the study of ancient DNA tell us about past populations, and what are the main limitations of this area of research?

The capacity to blunder slightly is the real marvel of DNA.
Without this special attribute,
we would still be anaerobic bacteria
and there would be no music.

Lewis Thomas (1913–1993)

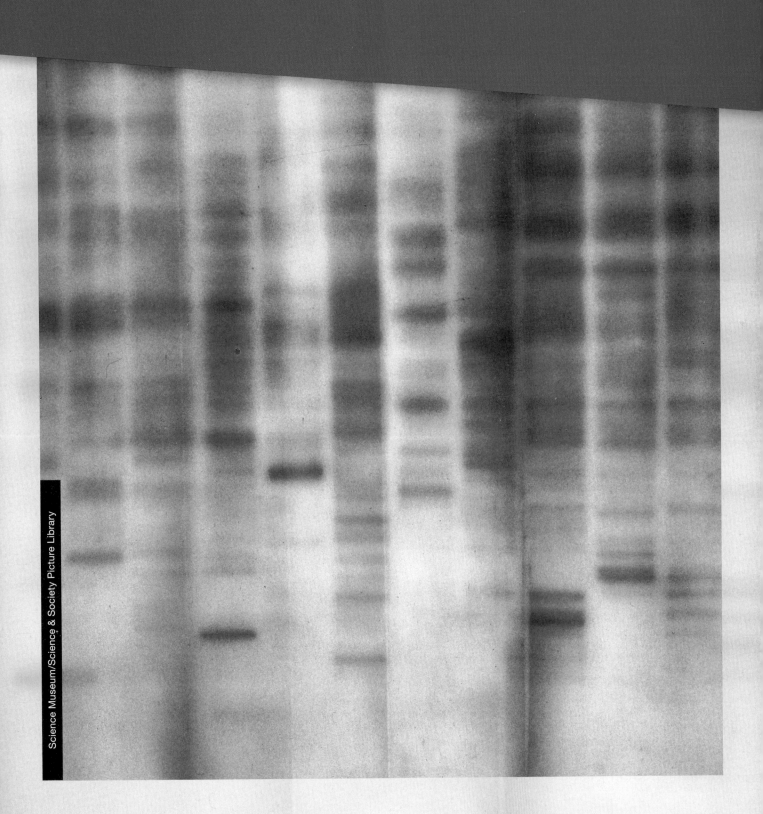

**genetics**

the study of genes and how
traits are transmitted from
one generation to the next

**genes**

sequences of DNA that
code for proteins

**stem cells**

unspecialized cells that have
the ability to differentiate into
specialized cells in the body

**nucleus**

a structure in eukaryotic
cells that contains the
genetic material

**prokaryotes**

organisms that lack a cell
nucleus

http://www.stemcellnetwork.ca

http://www.cihr-irsc.gc.ca

**pluripotent**

having the ability to differentiate into different tissue
types

# PROLOGUE: THE GENE SCENE

The past few decades have seen tremendous advances in the field of **genetics**. In the 1980s, British geneticist Sir Alec Jeffreys developed a method of DNA fingerprinting for use in crime scene investigations, producing the first DNA fingerprint in 1984 (see opening photo). As any of you who have watched *CSI* or *Law and Order* know, DNA has become a key tool for iden-tifying perpetrators and victims of crimes. It has also found its way into many other aspects of our society. Genetic testing is now being used to identify paternity, to predict inherited dis-orders such as Huntington's disease, and to locate the **genes** that may predispose an individual to cancer, among other diseases. Indeed, this sort of testing has become a multimillion-dollar business. Now that the human genome map has been completed, we have a complete blue-print of our own genetic makeup, and we are currently awaiting completion of genome maps for other primates, including earlier hominins (see Chapters 5 and 11). In the meantime, sci-entists are madly searching for genes that might extend our lives, prevent obesity, and protect us from disease. At the same time, though, ethical and moral concerns about genetic testing and manipulation in the form of cloning remind us of past abuses (see Chapter 13).

# THE BUILDING BLOCKS OF LIFE

Cells are the basic building blocks of life. There are a number of different kinds of cells, including those that make up various tissues in the body (e.g., bone, skin, nerve, and muscle cells), sex cells (sperm and ovum), and **stem cells**, which are unspecialized cells that can dif-ferentiate into any type of specialized cell (see Box 3.1). Except for the sex cells and red blood cells, every cell in the human body contains the same genetic information.

The earliest organisms appeared some 3.7 billion years ago. They had DNA in their cell walls but lacked a **nucleus**. Known as **prokaryotes**, these organisms had limited capabilities and reproduced by splitting in two. Even today, the most diverse and successful life forms on the planet—such as bacteria—are prokaryotes! Between 1.5 and 1 billion years ago, the first

---

| **BOX 3.1** | **FOCUS ON... Stem Cell Research in Canada** |
|---|---|

Stem cells are found in all tissues and play a crucial role in growth, development, and maintenance of the body. Humans and other mammals possess two different types of stem cells: embryonic and adult. Embryonic stem cells, created four to five days after conception, are able to develop into any type of specialized cell in the body, ranging from blood cells to those found in con-nective tissues and vital organs. Sources of these **pluripotent** cells include embryonic and fetal tissue, as well as blood from the placenta and umbilical cord. In contrast, adult stem cells, derived from a variety of adult tissues, repair and regenerate these tissues by constantly reproducing themselves.

Stem cells were discovered in the 1960s by two Can-adians, biophysicist James Till and physician Ernest McCul-loch, while they were conducting research on radiation. Over the past decade, Canadian scientists have played a leading role in stem cell research, and in 2001 the Stem Cell Network was established by 80 scientists from universities and hospi-tals across Canada to promote this research, with the ultimate goal of developing therapies to treat a variety of diseases and conditions. Potential applications of stem cell therapy include

creating tissues for transplantation; treating degenerative diseases such as Alzheimer's, Parkinson's, diabetes, heart disease, and muscular dystrophy; and developing and testing new medications. Current research projects in Canada include investigating the potential of using stem cells to repair brain injury resulting from stroke; damaged heart muscle resulting from cardiac arrest; and spinal chord injuries.

Despite its potential to improve the lives of millions of people in Canada and around the world, no other area of med-ical research has generated as much controversy as stem cell research. Heated debates have arisen regarding the ethical, legal, and social implications of that research. At issue is the creation and use of embryos as a source of stem cells, and the fear that this might lead to human cloning. Canada currently does not have legislation regulating the use of embryonic stem cells in research; however, in 2002 the Canadian Institute for Health Research (CIHR) established strict guidelines for the use of stem cells, and scientists are increasingly focusing on adult stem cells in order to avoid the ethical issues associated with using embryonic ones.

multicellular organisms appeared, known as **eukaryotes**. These possessed a nucleus containing DNA (Figure 3.1) and had the ability to perform a greater number of functions, grow larger, and produce more energy than prokaryotes.

DNA is a macromolecule consisting of smaller molecules called **nucleotides**, which are composed of a sugar, a phosphate, and one of four nucleic acid **bases**: adenine (A), guanine (G), cytosine (C), and thymine (T). DNA is found in the nuclei of cells (**nuclear DNA**, or nDNA) on long strands called **chromosomes** (Figure 3.2). Genes are made up of segments of DNA, and their location on the chromosomes is referred to as their **locus**. DNA is also found in **mitochondria** (**mitochondrial DNA**, or mtDNA), which are structures that generate energy for the cell. Mitochondrial DNA contains fewer genes (only 37), and unlike nuclear DNA, it is passed only through females.[1] Thus both males and females get their mtDNA from their mother. While much smaller overall, mtDNA is more plentiful than nDNA because each cell contains hundreds or even thousands of mitochondria and hence a similar magnitude of mtDNA.

The double helix structure of the DNA molecule was published in 1953 by James Watson and Francis Crick, who in 1962, along with Maurice Wilkins, received for their work the Nobel Prize for Medicine. However, it was an X-ray image of the molecule, taken in 1952 by a young British scientist named Rosalind Franklin, that provided them with the necessary clues to its structure (Figure 3.3). Tragically, Franklin died of ovarian cancer before the Nobel Prize was awarded.[2]

DNA has the ability to replicate—that is, make copies of itself. This process of **replication** takes place before new cells are produced. The action of **enzymes** causes the strands of the molecule to separate. The bases of free nucleotides join up with the corresponding bases on the separated strands (A with T and C with G) to form new duplicate strands (Figure 3.4). The result is two copies of the DNA molecule, each carrying the same genetic information.

Usually, DNA replicates without any difficulties, but occasionally **mutations** occur, altering the sequence of bases. These mutations are, variously, **point mutations**, in which there is a change in one base of the gene sequence (say, an A–T pair for a G–C pair); **deletions**, resulting in missing segments of DNA; **insertions**, characterized by the addition of extra DNA; or **inversions**, which involve the reversal of a section of DNA. A variety of factors can cause mutations, including exposure to chemicals, sunlight, and radiation. This explains why

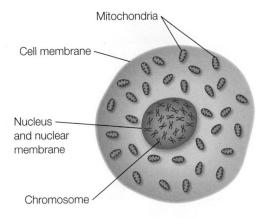

**Figure 3.1**  DNA is found in all cells with the exception of mature red blood cells.

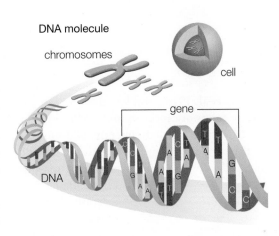

**Figure 3.2**  The DNA molecule has a double helix structure that allows it to replicate, or make copies of itself.

**eukaryotes**
organisms that have within their cells a nucleus containing DNA

**nucleotide**
the basic structural unit of a DNA or RNA molecule, consisting of a phosphate, sugar, and base

**base**
a chemical unit making up part of a DNA and RNA molecule. There are four bases in DNA: adenine, thymine, guanine, and cytosine. In RNA, thymine is replaced with uracil

**nuclear DNA (nDNA)**
DNA found within the nucleus of a cell

**chromosome**
a structure composed of DNA and found in the nucleus of cells

**locus**
the location of a gene on a chromosome

**mitochondria**
structures within a cell that generate energy for that cell

**mitochondrial DNA (mtDNA)**
DNA found within the mitochondria of a cell

**replication**
the process whereby a duplicate copy of a molecule (i.e., DNA) is made

**enzyme**
a protein that acts as a catalyst for chemical reactions in the body

**mutation**
an alteration to a gene or chromosome

**point mutation**
a change in one base pair of a gene sequence

**deletion**
a type of mutation characterized by the loss of DNA

**insertion**
a type of mutation characterized by the addition of DNA

**inversion**
a type of mutation in which a section of DNA is reversed

1. In mammals and other sexually reproducing organisms, mitochondria in sperm are usually destroyed by the egg after fertilization. They may also be lost during fertilization.
2. A documentary of her discovery, titled "Secret of Photo 51," was produced by Nova in 2003. Several books have also been written about her life and work (see below).

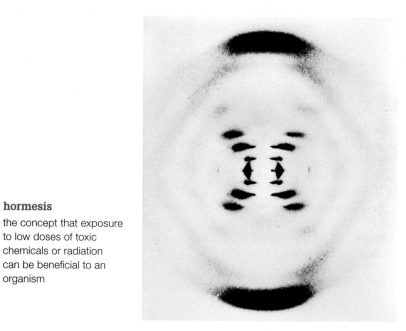

**Figure 3.3**   This X-ray diffraction photograph of DNA provided clues to its double helix structure.

Science Photo Library

you put on a lead apron before you have radiographs taken at the dentist's office, and why you slather on sunscreen during the summer months (though usually not nearly enough). Interestingly, research has revealed that exposure to low levels of these agents may actually be beneficial because they stimulate growth and strengthen the immune response. Put another way, "whatever doesn't kill you might make you stronger" (Renner 2003, 28). This concept, known as **hormesis**, was first described in 1888 by the German pharmacologist Hugo Schulz, who observed that exposure to small doses of poisons stimulated the growth of yeast (Kaiser 2003, 376). Hormesis has recently become the subject of renewed interest: over the past few decades, the data have begun to indicate that low-level exposure to toxic chemicals or radiation may in some cases *benefit* an organism. For example, minute concentrations of **dioxins** fed to rats have been found to inhibit tumour growth (Kociba et al. 1978), and low doses of radiation have been found to delay the development of certain forms of cancer in mice (Mitchel et al. 2003).

Mutations occur frequently, and most of them are neutral—that is, they have no effect on the organism. Some mutations can actually be beneficial. One example relates to the gene that codes for the CCR5 protein, a receptor used by HIV to gain entry into target cells.

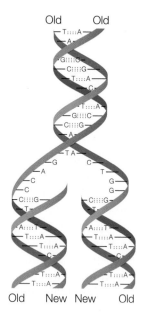

Old       Old

Old   New   New   Old

**Figure 3.4**   DNA replicates before a cell divides. This means that each new cell contains the same genetic material.

One mutated form of this gene, *CCR5-Δ32,* is characterized by a deletion of a segment of 32 base-pairs. This damages the receptor, thus preventing HIV from entering cells. As a consequence, individuals who carry two copies of the mutated allele are generally immune to HIV infection; and individuals who carry one copy have some protection from infection, or experience slower progression of the disease if they do become infected (Marmor et al. 2001).[3] Harmful mutations can also occur, such as the one that results in sickle cell anaemia, a common disease in sub-Saharan Africa and parts of Asia (see Chapter 4).

In some cases, the effect of a mutation on an organism depends on the environment in which that organism lives. A classic example involves the English peppered moth, of which two varieties exist: light and dark. The story, as revealed by British ecologist H.B.D. Kettlewell, who conducted the original study, goes like this. Before the Industrial Revolution, the dark-coloured variety was rare. With the advent of coal-burning factories in the 18th and 19th centuries, the darker variety became more common and the lighter variety less so. Why? A darkening of tree bark by pollution meant that the darker moth became more difficult for predators to spot, and the lighter variety, once well camouflaged, became more visible. Consequently, the lighter variety was targeted and their frequency declined. With improvements in air quality, the situation reversed itself and the lighter variety again

---

3. This mutation has been linked not only to HIV but also to smallpox, malaria, and multiple sclerosis.

became more common. Thus a mutation that gave rise to two different colours of moths was beneficial to dark moths during the Industrial Revolution but deleterious to them at other times. Despite criticisms of Kettlewell's experiments, this phenomenon of **industrial melanism** remains a good illustration of natural selection in operation.[4]

Genetic variations arising from mutation are attracting considerable attention for how they affect our susceptibility to diseases such as Alzheimer's, diabetes, asthma, and schizophrenia. The simplest types are **single nucleotide polymorphisms (SNPs)**, which are genetic variations produced by a point mutation—for example, the substitution of thymine for adenine. Occurring in at least 1% of the population, SNPs also appear to play a role in how people respond to medication.

## Mapping the Human Genome

In the late 1980s, researchers began work on mapping the human **genome**. By the end of 2000, a rough draft had been completed by the International Human Genome Sequencing Consortium (IHGSC 2001) and by Celera Genomics (Venter et al. 2001); a final map was completed in 2003. As a result of this endeavour, we now know that the human genome contains 3.2 billion nucleotide bases and 20,000 to 25,000 genes (IHGSC 2004); this is vastly less than previous estimates, derived from the central dogma of molecular biology, which suggested that the human genome needed about 120,000 genes in order to produce the diversity of proteins that build tissues and regulate biological processes. One of the most significant results of this map has been the discovery that most of our DNA is noncoding. In fact, less than 2% of our DNA codes for proteins. The remaining DNA, often referred to as "**junk DNA**," was at first thought to have no function at all. We now know, however, that this material may serve a number of important functions, including the repair of broken strands of DNA and the regulation of gene expression (Gibbs 2003).

A common misconception is that the human genome that has been mapped represents *the* human genome. In fact, the International Human Genome Sequencing Consortium derived its map using the DNA of only 24 individuals, and Celera Genomics from only five individuals, all of whom were Caucasian. To address this gap, a second project was launched in 1991 by a group of prominent population geneticists. Known as the Human Genome Diversity Project (HGDP), the goal of this initiative is to map global genetic diversity by collecting DNA from hundreds of different populations. Such a sample would permit scientists to explore the evolutionary histories of these populations and identify genes that may play a role in their susceptibility or resistance to particular diseases. This project has generated vehement opposition, especially from indigenous peoples, who have characterized it as an example of "scientific colonialism" whose underlying objective is to patent this genetic data for commercial purposes, such as developing medical cures for wealthy individuals in industrialized countries. Concerns have also been expressed about how informed consent would be obtained and how this research would affect these populations psychologically, socially, and economically. At the very (and unlikely) extreme, it has been claimed that the genetic data thereby collected will be used to develop biological weapons against indigenous populations. Perhaps the most important issues arising from HGDP relate to ownership and human rights.

Other large-scale projects involving the collection and analysis of genetic data have been initiated. In 2002 the International HapMap Project was launched to develop a **haplotype** map of the human genome. This will be used to identify genes associated with disease. In 2005 the National Geographic Society, together with IBM, geneticist Spencer Well, and

**industrial melanism**
increased pigmentation resulting from human modification of the environment, such as occurred during the Industrial Revolution

**single nucleotide polymorphisms (SNPs)**
genetic variations that are produced by the substitution of a single nucleotide in a sequence. SNPs are point mutations that occur in at least 1% of the population

**genome**
all genes carried by an organism or species

**junk DNA**
multiple copies of a base sequence, which may be repeated on the same chromosome or dispersed throughout the genome; most junk DNA has no known coding function

http://www.hgalert.org/topics/personalInfo/hgdp.htm

**haplotype**
a group of closely linked alleles present on a chromosome that tend to be inherited together

---

4. In her recent book *Of Moths and Men: Intrigue, Tragedy, and the Peppered Moth* (2003), Judith Hooper contends that Kettlewell's experiments were likely fraudulent, noting that he released his moths, which are normally active at night, during the day; that these moths do not normally land on tree trunks; that bats, not birds, are their main predators; and that Kettlewell demonstrated the camouflaging effect of colour by reportedly photographing dead moths that he had pinned or glued to tree trunks himself! Her claims have been vigorously attacked.

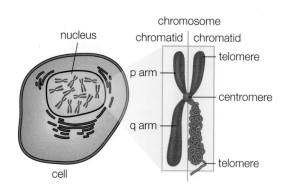

**Figure 3.5** Chromosomes are made up of genes that code for various proteins in the body. Humans have 23 pairs of chromosomes.

the Waitt Family Foundation, launched the Genographic Project to investigate the migratory history of our species using DNA donated by hundreds of thousands of people from around the world. Over the past few years the genomes of other species, including several primate species (see Chapter 5) and Neandertals (see Chapter 11), have been or are being mapped.

## Telomeres and the Search for an Anti-Aging Gene

Biological anthropologists have become increasingly interested in human aging (see Chapter 14). The field of molecular genetics has the potential to make a valuable contribution to our knowledge of this universal phenomenon. Possible anti-aging genes have been found in mice (Kurosu et al. 2005), and a similar version of one of these genes exists in humans (Arking et al. 2002). A number of genes and genetic pathways that may be linked to human longevity and aging have been identified (Browner et al. 2004). One chromosomal region that has received a great deal of attention for its possible role in aging is the **telomere**, located at the tips of the **chromatids** that are joined together at the **centromere** (Figure 3.5). Consisting of highly repetitive DNA sequences, telomeres play an important role in maintaining chromosomal integrity by preventing the loss of genes each time a cell divides. They do so by allowing for the replication of DNA at the very ends of the chromosomes without the latter sustaining any damage.

A correlation has been observed between telomere length and life span. Cawthon and colleagues (2003), for example, found that individuals with longer telomeres lived longer than those who had shorter ones. This finding suggests that the human life span could be extended if telomere length could be maintained. The key may lie in an enzyme known as **telomerase**, which adds nucleotide bases to the ends of the telomeres. Laboratory experiments indicate that telomerase can be used to prolong the life of cells beyond their normal limit (Bodnar et al. 1998).

While the question remains whether telomere shortening is a cause or consequence of aging, it appears to have other important impacts as well. For example, telomere shortening has been found to be correlated with increased insulin resistance in humans (Gardner et al. 2005), and animal studies indicate that telomerase may inhibit the formation of malignant tumours (Gonzalez-Suarez et al. 2000; Rudolph et al. 2001).

## The Functions of DNA

The most important function of DNA is **protein synthesis**. All **proteins** are made up of **amino acids**, of which there are 20 in all. The differences between the many proteins that exist lie in the number of amino acids they contain and how they are arranged. Protein synthesis occurs outside the nucleus in structures called **ribosomes**. Because the DNA molecule cannot travel

**telomere**
a region of DNA located at the end of a chromosome

**chromatid**
one of two identical copies of DNA that make up a chromosome

**centromere**
a region in the middle of the chromosome where the two chromatids are joined together

**telomerase**
an enzyme that adds bases to the ends of telomeres

**protein synthesis**
the process by which amino acids are assembled to form proteins

**protein**
organic compounds made up of chains of amino acids

**amino acids**
molecules that make up proteins

**ribosomes**
structures found in cells that are involved in the assembly of proteins

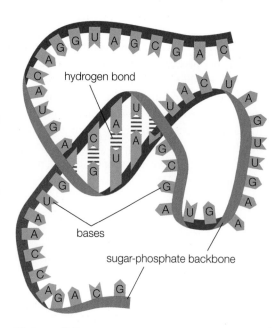

**Figure 3.6** Unlike DNA molecules, RNA molecules are usually single-stranded.

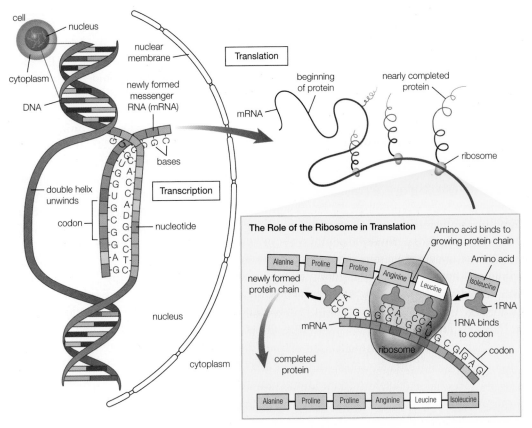

**Figure 3.7** The genes that make up chromosomes provide instructions for the synthesis of proteins—large molecules made up of amino acids.

**The Role of the Ribosome in Translation**

Amino acid binds to growing protein chain

Amino acid

Alanine — Proline — Proline — Anginine — Leucine — Isoleucine

newly formed protein chain

1RNA

1RNA binds to codon

mRNA

completed protein

ribosome

codon

Alanine — Proline — Proline — Anginine — Leucine — Isoleucine

---

through the nucleus membrane, its message must be copied into a form that can be carried to the ribosome. This is accomplished through the formation of **RNA**. Unlike DNA, the RNA molecule is single-stranded and has uracil instead of thymine as one of its bases. It also contains a different type of sugar (Figure 3.6).

In the first stage of protein synthesis, the two strands of the DNA molecule separate and free nucleotides arrive and join together with the corresponding bases on the separated strands to form **messenger RNA**—a process known as **transcription** (Figure 3.7). The messenger RNA then leaves the nucleus and travels to the **cytoplasm**, where its message is translated with the assistance of the ribosome. Facilitating this process of **translation** are **codons** on the messenger RNA that specify particular amino acids. These amino acids are carried by **transfer RNA** to the ribosome, where they are joined together to form a **polypeptide** chain.

## CELL DIVISION

### Mitosis

As noted above, DNA has the ability to replicate and does so prior to cell division—a process required for growth as well as maintenance of tissues. The division of **somatic cells** is known as **mitosis**. Each cell in the human body contains 46 single-stranded chromosomes. The first step in mitosis is the replication of these chromosomes, resulting in 46 double-stranded chromosomes (Figure 3.8). These duplicate pairs line up at the centre of the cell and then diverge so that the strands are separated. The individual strands move toward opposite ends of the cell, the cell membrane constricts in the middle, and two new cells are formed, each containing 46 single-stranded chromosomes. The end result is two identical **diploid** cells.

**RNA**
ribonucleic acid

**messenger RNA (mRNA)**
a form of RNA that carries the genetic instructions of a DNA molecule to the site of protein synthesis

**transcription**
transfer of genetic information carried by DNA to RNA

**cytoplasm**
the substance found within the cell membrane and surrounding the nucleus

**translation**
synthesis of a chain of amino acids based on a message carried in RNA

**codon**
a unit of three bases/nucleotides that code for a particular amino acid

**transfer RNA (tRNA)**
RNA molecules that carry amino acids to ribosomes, where they are used in protein synthesis

**polypeptide**
a chain of amino acids

**somatic cells**
all cells in the body with the exception of the sex cells

**mitosis**
division of the somatic cells resulting in the production of two identical daughter cells

**diploid**
having a full set of paired chromosomes; in humans, each somatic cell contains 23 pairs of chromosomes

**CHAPTER 3** The Biological Basis of Human Variation

## Meiosis

The sex cells (**gametes**) also divide, in a process known as **meiosis**. Unlike mitosis, however, this process involves *two* cell divisions and the production of *four* daughter cells, each containing only 23 chromosomes (Figure 3.8). The reason for this should (we hope) be obvious—male and female gametes pair up at conception to form a new individual with the full complement of 46 chromosomes, half from mom and half from dad.

In the first stage of meiosis, which occurs within ovarian cells called **oogonia** and testicular cells called **spermatogonia**, 46 single-stranded chromosomes replicate to produce 46 double-stranded chromosomes (Figure 3.9). These paired chromosomes arrange themselves and line up at the centre of the cell. The pairs separate, members of each pair move to opposite ends of the cell, and the cell divides to produce two new daughter cells, each containing 23 double-stranded chromosomes. So far, the process is a match to mitosis; however, there are some important differences on the female side of things. The initial division in the female ovary produces two **primary oocytes**, but (unlike male spermatocytes) they are not created equal. One oocyte sequesters most of the contents of the cytoplasm. If this were mitosis, it would end here. However, the goal is to produce functional eggs and sperm, and to be so they need to go through one more reduction division, to produce viable **haploid** gametes. As before, things are a bit different in females. The primary oocyte does not divide equally: through the process of unequal cytoplasmic cleavage, one of the haploid cells—the ovum—receives the majority of the cytoplasm. Thus, while all four of the resultant sperm cells are viable, only the ovum is in females. The other female daughter cells, termed **polar bodies**, are resorbed.

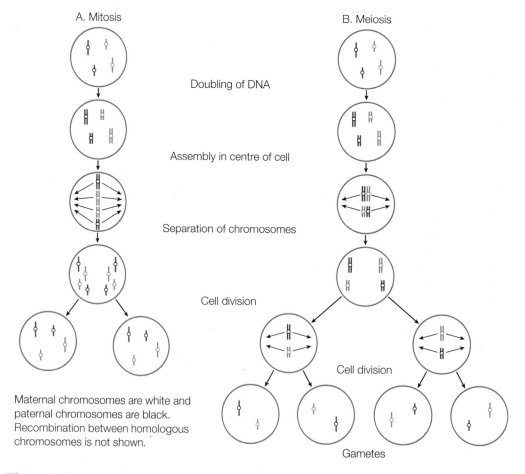

**Figure 3.8** Mitosis involves one cell division and results in two identical daughter cells that are identical to the parent cell. Meiosis, in contrast, involves two cell divisions and results in four daughter cells, each containing half of the genetic material of the parent cell.

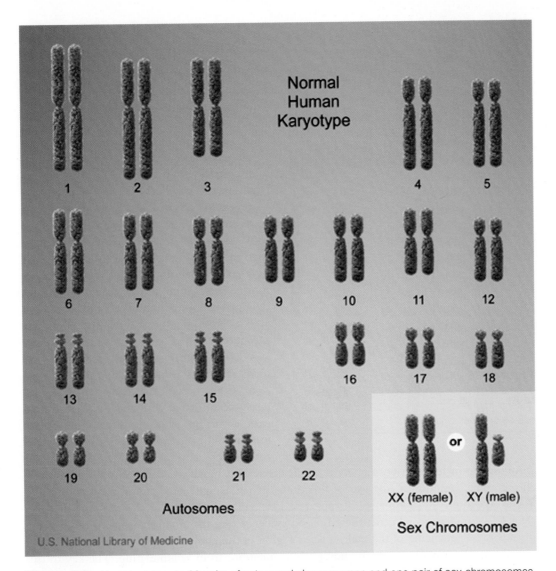

**Figure 3.9** Humans possess 22 pairs of autosomal chromosomes and one pair of sex chromosomes.

US National Library of Medicine

There is another very significant difference between men and women. While men produce sperm throughout their adult lives, women have a limited supply of eggs, most of which are produced during fetal development. And most of these (perhaps as many as 1 million) are recycled. At puberty, a human female has perhaps four hundred primary oocytes; over her reproductive lifespan of perhaps 35 years, these are released "monthly" in hope of being fertilized.

We mentioned earlier that mutation is an important source of variation. Meiosis increases variation through a process called **recombination** (Figure 3.10). Also referred to as "crossing over," this occurs when genetic material is exchanged between **homologous** chromosomes during cell division. Problems can occur during meiosis in such a way that chromosome strands fail to separate properly during the final division. The end result of this **nondisjunction** is fewer or more chromosomes than normal; the cell receiving the extra chromosome is referred to as trisomic. The best-known example of **trisomy** is Down syndrome (named after the 19th-century British physician John Langdon Down, who first described the condition), which results from nondisjunction of the ovarian 21st chromosome. Thus, at fertilization, Down syndrome children have three rather than the normal two copies of chromosome 21. **Monosomy**, where an individual has fewer than the normal complement of chromosomes, may also occur. Females with Turner syndrome, for example, are missing an X chromosome and consequently have sexual characteristics that are usually underdeveloped.

**recombination (crossing over)**

the exchange of genes between homologous chromosomes during meiosis

**homologous**

chromosomes that go together in a pair

**nondisjunction**

the failure of chromosome pairs to separate properly during meiosis

**trisomy**

a condition characterized by an extra chromosome

**monosomy**

a condition characterized by fewer than normal chromosomes

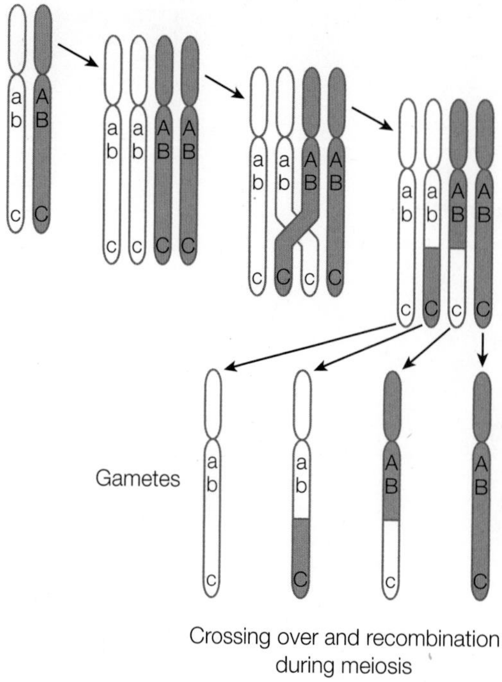

Gametes

Crossing over and recombination during meiosis

**Figure 3.10** The process of recombination or crossing over involves the shuffling of genetic material from one chromosome to another. It is a source of genetic variation.

**karyotype**

arrangement of the full set of chromosomes by numbered pairs

**autosome**

a chromosome other than the sex chromosomes

## Is the Y Chromosome Doomed to Extinction?

The Y chromosome is often overshadowed because it is the smallest in the entire human **karyotype**. Once considered a "genetic wasteland" whose only function—though admittedly a pretty important one—is to stimulate the development of the testes in the embryo and the release of male hormones, its composition has recently been revealed with the help of new genetic techniques. A debate has arisen in recent years over the fate of the Y chromosome. To understand the issue, we need to turn the geological clock back some 300 million years, when the X and Y chromosomes, which arose from an ancestral **autosome**, diverged from each other (Lahn and Page 1999). Researchers estimate that since its inception, the Y chromosome has lost as many as 1,000 of its original genes, leaving only 78 today (Skaletsky et al. 2003). The explanation lies in the fact that the Y chromosome rarely recombines with the X chromosome except at its tip. This means that it has largely lost the ability to repair itself—an ability that homologous chromosomes (including the X chromosome in females) possess. As a result, deleterious mutations can accumulate in the Y chromosome, resulting in the loss of functional genes. Despite predictions by some that the Y chromosome could ultimately disappear and be replaced by another chromosome that also carries a sex-determining gene, there is good evidence that the Y chromosome is not, in fact, in jeopardy. Sequencing of the male-specific region of the chromosome has revealed a mechanism by which it maintains itself and prevents mutations from accumulating. The key to this mechanism is the fact that it stores copies of its most important genes as mirror images or "palindromes," so that the bases read the same way in each direction (like the word "madam" or the sentence "madam I'm Adam"). Continuous recombination between the arms of the palindromes allows the chromosome to repair genes damaged by mutation through a process known as gene conversion (ibid. 2003). Thus there is no danger of the chromosome shrinking away to nothing. Not surprisingly, this same gene repair mechanism has also been documented in the Y chromosome of chimpanzees (Rozen et al. 2003).

## MECHANISMS OF INHERITANCE

As you learned in Chapter 2, Darwin did not know the source of variation on which natural selection acted or how traits were transmitted from parent to offspring. He was influenced by the theory of pangenesis and believed that offspring were somehow a blend of the traits of the parents. It was not until the early 20th century that scientists became aware of the work of Gregor Mendel, who identified the source of variation and the mechanisms of inheritance. An Augustinian monk who lived in what was then Austria, Mendel was trained in physics but developed an interest in botany, and spent eight years of his life conducting hybridization experiments on plants. He presented the results of his experiments at the 1865 meeting of the Brünn Natural History Society and published his report the following year (Mendel 1866).[5]

http://www.mendelweb.org

5. While Mendel is widely recognized today as the founder of genetics, his work has generated controversy, with some contending that he falsified his data (Fisher 1936)—claims that have been vehemently denied (Hartl and Fairbanks 2007).

Mendel's scientific training served him well, for he chose the garden pea plant (*Pisum sativum*) for his studies, noting that it exhibited traits that were either present or absent (referred to today as **discrete** or **Mendelian traits**). The pea plant also has the ability to self-pollinate, which gave Mendel effective control over which plants could become the parents of the next generation—in particular, self-fertilized versus **cross-fertilized** plants. After carrying out a series of breeding cycles to produce pure-breeding plants (i.e., ones that give rise to plants with the same physical characteristics in each successive generation), Mendel crossed pea plants with different characteristics (e.g., tall vs. short height, yellow vs. green seeds, smooth vs. wrinkled seeds; Figure 3.11) and observed the physical appearance (i.e., the **phenotype**) of the next generation of plants. He found that all exhibited the same characteristics. In the case of height, all of the plants were tall; in the case of seed colour, all were yellow. Thus the tall and yellow factors were visible and the short and green factors were hidden. He concluded from this that every plant carried two factors for each trait, one provided by each parent. We refer to these factors today as **alleles**—alternate forms of a gene that occur at the same location on homologous chromosomes. The allele that is expressed is the **dominant** allele; that which is hidden is **recessive**.

In his second set of experiments, Mendel crossed all of the offspring produced by his initial experiments, referred to as the $F_1$ generation,[6] and studied the appearance of the second or $F_2$ generation. In the case of height, when all $F_1$ tall plants were crossed, the result was three tall plants and one short plant. This can be represented schematically in a **Punnett square** (see Figure 3.12). If you remember that all $F_1$ tall plants carry two different alleles—one for the dominant tall trait, which we will represent as "T," and one for the recessive short trait, which we will represent as "t," the **genotype** of all of these first-generation plants will be Tt. In contrast, one-quarter of the second-generation plants will have the genotype TT, one half will be Tt, and one quarter will be tt. In other words, the recessive trait is expressed only when both recessive alleles are combined in an offspring. When the two alleles are identical (e.g., TT or tt), an organism is said to be **homozygous** for that gene ("homo" = "same"), while those with different alleles (e.g., Tt) are said to be **heterozygous** ("hetero" = "different").

The traits that Mendel observed in his pea plants were **monogenic traits**—that is, controlled by a single gene. An excellent illustration in humans is the ABO blood group system. If you have ever given or received blood, more than likely you know what "type" you are. Our blood type is determined by the inheritance of one of three alleles (A, B, or O) from each parent. A and B are dominant alleles; O is recessive. However—and this is an added wrinkle—because the A and B allele are "equally dominant," there are six possible genotypes and four possible phenotypes. In this case, A and B are considered **co-dominant**. Thus individuals with "type A" blood are either AA or AO, those with "type B" blood are BB or BO, those with type O blood can only be OO (since "O" is recessive), and those with type AB blood are AB, thanks to co-dominance.

One of the most studied Mendelian traits is the ability to taste phenylthiocarbamide (PTC), a bitter synthetic compound that some people can taste and others cannot. The ability to taste PTC is determined by a dominant allele, and about 75% of the world's population can taste this substance. The discovery of this difference in taste sensitivity came about in the early 1930s, when a chemist accidentally released some of the powder into his lab, leading one of his coworkers to complain of a bad taste in his mouth, while he himself could taste nothing (Fox 1932). Scientists have pondered the significance of the ability to taste PTC, and believe that the trait may have evolved in order to prevent humans from eating toxic plants (Boyd 1950). More recent studies have explored the relationship between taste sensitivity and other phenotypic traits such as cigarette smoking. Several studies, for instance, have demonstrated that among humans, the ability to taste PTC is less prevalent in smokers than in nonsmokers (Enoch et al. 2001; Cannon et al. 2005). Interestingly, chimpanzees also vary in their ability

**discrete (Mendelian) traits**
traits that are controlled by genes at a single locus; also referred to as monogenic traits

**cross-fertilized**
plants (or animals) that are fertilized by fusing the reproductive cells of two different organisms belonging to the same species

**phenotype**
the observable characteristic of an organism

**allele**
alternate form of a gene

**dominant**
the allele or trait that is expressed

**recessive**
the allele or trait that is hidden

**Punnett square**
a way of graphically representing the crossing of organisms with the same or different genotypes

**genotype**
the genetic makeup of an organism

**homozygous**
having two identical alleles at a single genetic locus

**heterozygous**
having two different alleles at a single genetic locus

**monogenic traits**
traits that are controlled by genes at a single locus

**co-dominant**
a trait in which both alleles are expressed

---

6. In this terminology, "F" refers to "filial," a term meaning "offspring"; thus, F1 are the 1st generation offspring, F2 the second, and so on.

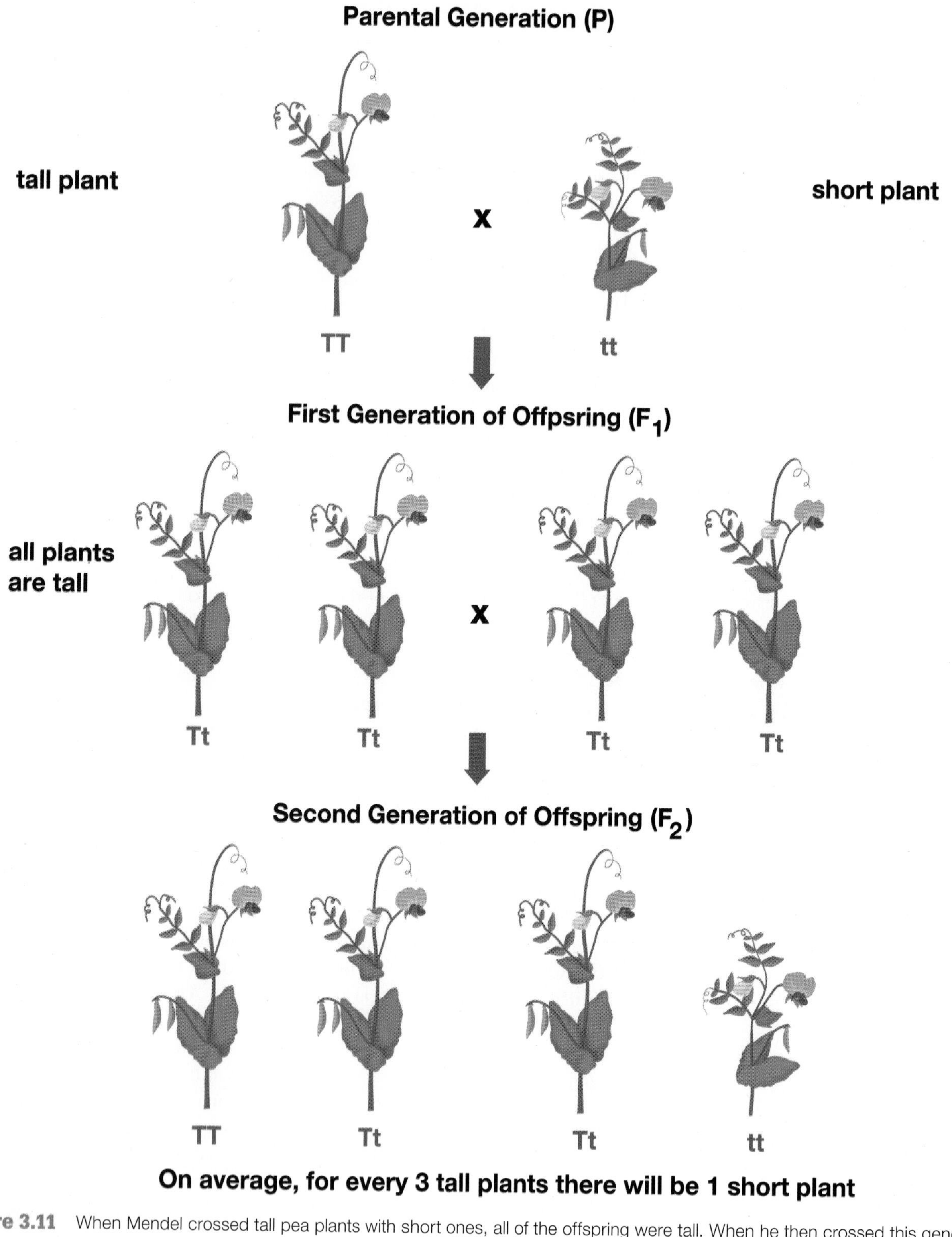

## Parental Generation (P)

**tall plant**                                           **short plant**

TT          X          tt

## First Generation of Offpsring (F₁)

**all plants
are tall**

Tt          Tt          X          Tt          Tt

## Second Generation of Offspring (F₂)

TT          Tt          Tt          tt

**On average, for every 3 tall plants there will be 1 short plant**

**Figure 3.11**   When Mendel crossed tall pea plants with short ones, all of the offspring were tall. When he then crossed this generation, three-quarters of the offspring were tall and one-quarter was short.

to taste PTC, an observation first reported in 1939 (Fisher, Ford, and Huxley 1939). This ability appears to have developed through a separate mutation that occurred after humans and chimps diverged (Wooding et al. 2006). As with humans, it too may have evolved to enable chimpanzees to avoid eating toxic plants (ibid.); if so, this would be an excellent example of convergent evolution (see Chapter 4).

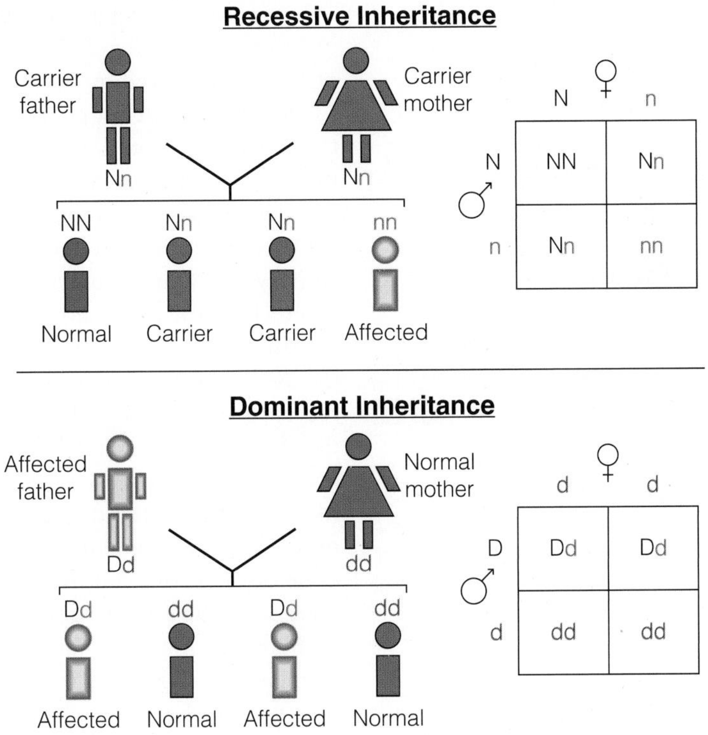

## Recessive Inheritance

## Dominant Inheritance

**Figure 3.12** Mendel's experiments revealed that two factors, or alleles, are responsible for each trait. The dominant allele is expressed as a capital letter (e.g., N), and the recessive allele is expressed as a lower-case letter (e.g., n). Dominant traits are therefore expressed in individuals who are NN or Nn, and recessive traits are only expressed in individuals who are nn.

As a result of his experiments, Mendel formulated two principles of inheritance known as the **principle of segregation** and the **principle of independent assortment**. According to the first of these, which we now know arises during meiosis, traits are transmitted by a large number of independent units (genes). These occur in pairs—that is, every individual has two copies, which may be the same or variant (alleles). These copies are randomly separated during the production of sex cells so that each sex cell contains only one allele from each parent. In other words, each of us inherits one allele from each parent. According to the principle of independent assortment, the segregation of any given pair of genes during meiosis does not influence the segregation of any other pair. In other words, the genes are not linked. Returning to our pea plants, this means that yellow seeds are not always found with tall height. The main reason for this outcome is that these two genes are not located on the same chromosomes. While this is the case for many genes, there are, in fact, some traits that are linked together (i.e., they are found on the same chromosome) and that tend to be inherited together, especially if their coding sequences are close to each other. A special case of linkage occurs with respect to the X chromosome, and most **sex-linked** genes are carried on this chromosome.

One of the best-known examples of an **X-linked** trait is red–green colour blindness. Individuals with this feature have difficulty distinguishing colours in the red–green wavelength range. Around 6 to 8% of humans today express this trait, and most of them are males. Because it is a recessive trait, individuals who carry the normal gene on the X chromosome lack this trait, and females who have one dominant gene and one recessive gene are **carriers** with normal colour vision (Figure 3.13). However, females who inherit the recessive allele from both parents and males who inherit the recessive allele from their mothers are red–green colourblind, as illustrated in this **pedigree** diagram.

**principle of segregation**
the separation of alleles during the production of sex cells such that each sex cell contains only one allele from each parent

**principle of independent assortment**
the distribution of one pair of alleles into the sex cells does not influence the distribution of another pair

**sex-linked**
traits that are controlled by genes located on one of the sex chromosomes

**X-linked**
traits that are controlled by genes located on the X chromosome

**carrier**
an individual that is heterozygous for a recessive trait and that does not physically manifest the trait

**pedigree**
a diagram that illustrates the transmission of a genetic trait from one generation to subsequent generations of a family

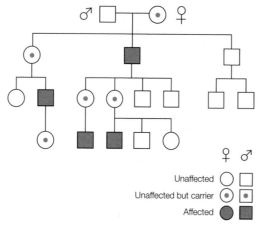

**Figure 3.13** Red–green colour blindness is an X-linked trait. Males who inherit the recessive allele from their mothers, and females who inherit the recessive allele from both parents, are colourblind. In contrast, females who inherit the recessive allele from only one parent are carriers.

Another well-known example of an X-linked trait is hemophilia, a genetic disorder characterized by the inability of blood to clot. As with red–green colour blindness, this recessive trait is far more common in males than females, though about 10% of females who are carriers of the recessive allele will exhibit reduced blood-clotting activity (they are protected from the most severe form of the condition). As the gene for this disorder is carried as a recessive on the X chromosome, males who inherit the recessive gene from their mother will have the disease, while females who inherit one defective X chromosome will be carriers. Males who have the disease will always pass on the recessive gene to their daughters, but none of their sons can inherit the gene from their dad. The disorder can also result from a spontaneous mutation (about 30% of cases).

Hemophilia is known to have affected the British monarchy. Queen Victoria transmitted the gene to her son, who in turn passed it on to his descendants (Figure 3.14).

Sex linkage may also occur with regard to the Y chromosome, in which case only males will express the trait and fathers will pass it to all their male offspring. However, because the

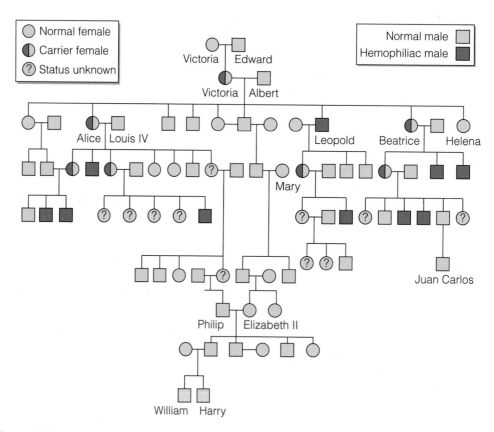

**Figure 3.14** Hemophilia was once known as the "royal disease" because of its high frequency in European royal families.

Y possesses very few genes, the proportion of sex linkage through Y is very small. At one time the "male hairy ear" trait (hypertrichosis pinnae auris) was thought to be transmitted through Y linkage; this has since been shown not to be the case (Lee et al. 2004).

## Pleiotropy

A single gene can influence multiple phenotypic traits. These genes are known as **pleiotropies**. One of the best-known examples relates to **phenylketonuria** (PKU), a genetic disorder characterized by the body's inability to convert the amino acid phenylalanine to another amino acid, tyrosine, due to the lack of an enzyme called phenylalanine hydroxylase. In individuals who lack this enzyme, phenylalanine increases to toxic levels in the blood and other tissues, leading to mental and developmental disabilities, among other symptoms. PKU is inherited as an autosomal recessive gene, which means that an individual must have both recessive alleles to develop the disorder. The pleiotropic effect of this gene lies in the fact that phenylalanine also plays a role in the production of melanin, the pigment that gives skin and hair its colour. Individuals with PKU do not produce sufficient melanin and consequently exhibit lighter hair, skin, and eyes. Today, screening newborns for PKU is routinely done, and elevated levels of phenylalanine can be treated with proper dietary measures (see Chapter 14).

**pleiotropy**
a gene that influences more than one trait

**phenylketonuria (PKU)**
a genetic disorder characterized by a deficiency in the enzyme phenylalanine hydroxylase, resulting in the accumulation of excessive amounts of phenylalanine

## Polygenic Traits

In contrast to monogenic traits such as the ABO blood group system, a multitude of human physical characteristics are controlled by many genes that interact with one another and with the environment. **Polygenic traits** (also known as continuous traits) include hair and eye colour, stature, and body weight (see Box 3.2). Given our current knowledge of genetics, one might assume that the genes underlying these traits have all been identified, especially now that the human genome has been mapped. However, scientists have yet to identify the genes underlying many basic physical characteristics. Skin colour, for example, is thought to be controlled by perhaps as many as half a dozen genes, but the exact number and the mutations responsible for light and dark pigmentation remain unknown, though a "freckle gene" associated with red hair and fair skin has been identified (Bastiaens et al. 2001). Similarly, three genes that control eye colour have been identified (those for green, blue, and brown eyes), but the genetic basis of other eye colours remains unknown, and we do not yet know the precise mechanisms of inheritance or how exactly eye colour changes over time.

**polygenic traits**
traits controlled by genes at more than one locus; also known as continuous traits

**quantitative trait locus**
a section of DNA associated with a particular phenotypic trait

---

### BOX 3.2    FOCUS ON... Do Genes Make Us Fat?

The most common forms of human obesity result from the interaction of numerous genetic, environmental, and behavioural factors (Comuzzie and Allison 1998, 1374). The significant medical, social, and economic implications of obesity have prompted geneticists to accelerate their search for the genes that contribute to this trait. The complexity of this phenotype means that identifying the specific genes underlying obesity is extremely challenging. Nevertheless, great strides have been made in identifying genes and genetic markers associated with obesity. The latest version of the *obesity gene map*—first presented in the 1990s by a group of Canadian scientists from Quebec—tells us that 127 candidate genes and 253 **quantitative trait loci** have been linked to obesity-related phenotypes (Rankinen et al. 2006). These include a common variant of the FTO gene (Frayling et al. 2007).

Much of the current research on obesity focuses on the biology of appetite. We know that certain chromosomal abnormalities are linked to excess eating and weight gain. A good example is Prader-Willi syndrome, a rare genetic disorder characterized by an insatiable appetite and slow metabolism, such that the consumption of only a small number of calories leads to weight gain. In addition, research is being directed at the genes that control where in the body fat is stored. Fat on the trunk, for example, is an important risk factor for diseases such as diabetes and cardiovascular disease. Therefore, recognizing these genes may one day lead to treatments that alter the location of fat storage. Researchers have also begun using nonhuman primates—baboons in particular—as models for the study of the genetics of obesity because of their close similarities to us (Comuzzie et al. 2003).

---

**CHAPTER 3** The Biological Basis of Human Variation

# BEHAVIOURAL GENETICS

Researchers have long recognized that a number of human behaviours have a genetic component. We know, for example, that some behaviours run in families and that we share certain behavioural patterns with our closest living relatives, the chimpanzees. However, determining the **heritability** of human behaviours such as homosexuality (see Box 3.3), aggression, and intelligence has proven to be extremely challenging, and considerable debate has arisen regarding the extent to which genes ("nature") vs. environment ("nurture") underlie such behaviours. Indeed, the nature–nurture controversy has shifted back and forth over the past century between viewing genes as the primary determinants of human behaviour and recognizing the crucial role played by cultural and environmental factors in shaping such traits.

A good example of a complex behaviour that appears to have a genetic component is aggression. If you have ever seen the classic 1956 movie *The Bad Seed*, you will know that the main premise is that violent behaviour can be inherited, showing up in seemingly innocent-looking children who unleash a reign of terror on those around them. Research in the field of psychiatric genetics, in particular, has focused on the ways in which genes may be linked to aggressive behaviour, and a large number of biological agents are now known to influence aggression, including hormones, enzymes, and growth factors (Nelson and Chiavegatto 2001).

Researchers in behavioural genetics face a number of challenges, including the fact that behaviours are difficult to define and quantify. As complex traits, they involve multiple genes, and deciphering whether genes are a cause or an influencing factor is difficult. In addition, the field of behavioural genetics has generated considerable controversy with respect to the ethical, moral, legal, and social implications of assigning genetic causes to human traits such

**heritability**
the proportion of phenotypic variation that can be ascribed to genotypic variation in a specific population

---

## BOX 3.3 — FOCUS ON... Is There a Gay Gene?

Homosexual behaviour is widespread in the animal kingdom. Among primates, it occurs not only among humans but among a number of other species as well (Vasey 1995). In our own species, family and twin studies have suggested that about 50% of the variance in sexual orientation is genetic, and scientists have begun searching for genes responsible for homosexuality. A number of studies have indicated that the X chromosome plays a role, at least among males. In 1993, geneticist Dean Hamer and colleagues published a paper in the journal *Science* in which they reported finding a genetic marker for homosexuality (Hamer et al. 1993). Based on interviews with 76 gay brothers and their families, and comparisons of their X chromosomes, they identified a fragment of DNA called *Xq28* that was shared by 64% of the sibling pairs tested. It was dubbed the "gay gene" by the media. This finding was repeated in a subsequent study, which found that the marker was shared among 67% of gay brothers (Hu et al. 1995). More recent studies have also found a link between the X chromosome and homosexuality. Sven Bocklandt and colleagues, for instance, found that the frequency of extreme skewing of X chromosome inactivation was significantly higher in mothers of gay men than in mothers of heterosexual men (Bocklandt et al. 2006). To put this in simpler terms, inactivation of one of the X chromosomes normally occurs in females early in embryonic development in order to compensate for the fact that males inherit only one X chromosome. This means that males and females express equivalent levels of genes on this chromosome. While most females have approximately equal numbers of cells with inactivated X chromosomes, some women have a much greater proportion of cells with an inactivated X (skewing).

Despite the findings cited above, the role of the *Xq28* region in male homosexuality remains uncertain. Research by George Rice and George Ebers, neurologists at the University of Western Ontario, and their colleagues failed to find a link between male homosexuality and *Xq28* in 52 gay male sibling pairs (Rice et al. 1999). In addition, other chromosomes have been implicated in male homosexuality, which suggests that the *Xq28* is only one of many factors influencing sexual orientation. A full scan of the human genome, for example, revealed that 60% of gay brothers shared identical stretches of DNA on three other chromosomes (Mustanski et al. 2005). While molecular research has yet to produce conclusive evidence for specific genes underlying homosexuality, the consensus today is that sexual orientation is the result of a complex interaction of biological and environmental factors. The search for genes continues, but other biological factors have also been considered, including hormones and brain structure. Perhaps the more interesting question to ask is why genes associated with homosexuality are present in humans in the first place.

as homosexuality and aggression. For example, the identification of "susceptibility genes" for aggressive behaviour could potentially lead to abuses such as the implementation of measures designed to oppress certain segments of the population. In recent years, a new paradigm in behavioural genetics has emerged that emphasizes a balanced view, one that recognizes that while much of our behaviour is rooted in our genes, we have the capacity to modify and change our behaviour (Drew 1997, 48).

## TAMPERING WITH MOTHER NATURE: THE ETHICS OF GENETIC MANIPULATION

If you could determine your child's genetic profile, would you? Should you? It is one thing to manipulate genes in an attempt to cure a disease such as cystic fibrosis or sickle cell anaemia; it is quite another to alter genes to change an individual's physical appearance or personality. Such genetic manipulation might take the form of germ-line gene therapy, in which genetic alterations are made to the sex cells, or somatic-cell gene therapy, in which changes are made to the somatic (or body) cells. Transferring a new gene into a cell is a complicated process involving several steps. The ultimate goal of gene therapy is to replace a damaged or faulty gene by inserting a healthy version into the same location on a particular chromosome. While some degree of error can be tolerated with respect to somatic cells, any error in the sex cells could potentially have devastating consequences, and there is great potential for abuse of this technology. For example, the technique of germ-line gene therapy to cure a genetic disorder could be appropriated by a cosmetics company to change an individual's skin colour. For now, the greatest potential of gene therapy lies in its ability to treat chronic infectious and degenerative diseases.

The development of recombinant DNA technology in the 1970s allowed scientists to insert pieces of DNA from one organism into the DNA of another. This technique has allowed for the manufacture of insulin and other substances that can be used for medical treatments, as well as the production of hardier strains of plant and animal products. While the principle behind this technique is not that different from altering plants and animals through selective breeding—which humans have been doing for thousands of years—it has generated tremendous controversy. Critics have highlighted the dangers of such practices, including the possibility of prompting allergic reactions and more serious medical conditions in individuals who consume genetically modified foods.

Issues have also arisen surrounding genetic screening. Such screening is normally done at fertility clinics in order to avoid implanting embryos with genetic disorders such as Down syndrome. However, a survey of in vitro fertilization clinics in the United States revealed that some prospective parents have requested screening to select for embryos that *have* a particular disease or disability such as deafness in order to ensure that their children will have the same condition as themselves (Baruch et al. 2008).

Cloning, the creation of an exact genetic copy of a molecule, cell, or organism, has also generated considerable controversy.[7] Since Dolly the sheep was cloned in 1997 (Figure 3.15), numerous other animals have been cloned, and serious concerns have been raised about human cloning. We know from animal experiments that clones are often

**Figure 3.15** Dolly the sheep with her first offspring.

AP Photo/John Chadwick

---

7. Clones are only genetically identical. Phenotypic variation exists owing to epigenetic and environmental factors.

born with birth defects or develop significant health problems leading to early death. You may recall, for instance, that Dolly suffered from the early onset of arthritis. Opponents of cloning also warn that this technology could be used to harvest organs from cloned humans.

# ANCIENT DNA

**ancient DNA (aDNA)**
DNA in ancient (i.e., nonmodern) remains

In the 1980s a new subfield of biological anthropology focusing on the extraction and analysis of **ancient DNA (aDNA)** emerged. Ancient DNA (aDNA) was first derived from human remains in 1985, when scientists retrieved DNA from a 2,400-year-old Egyptian mummy (Pääbo 1985). Since that time, it has been recovered from a variety of tissues, including bones, teeth, mummified remains, and preserved brain tissue (Doran et al. 1986; for an excellent review of aDNA research, see Mulligan 2006). Applications include examining the origins of anatomically modern humans and the position of Neandertals in our evolutionary history (Krings et al. 1997), identifying genetic diseases such as thalassemia (Yang 1997), detecting and diagnosing infectious diseases such as tuberculosis and leprosy (Spigelman et al. 2002; Donoghue et al. 2005), determining biological relationships within skeletal samples (Dudar et al. 2003), and determining sex (Stone et al. 1996; Faerman et al. 1998). Most of these studies have utilized mitochondrial DNA, for its greater quantity in cells means that it is more likely to survive than nuclear DNA in very old specimens. In Canada, facilities devoted to ancient DNA research include the Paleo-DNA Laboratory at Lakehead University, the McMaster Ancient DNA Centre, and the Ancient DNA Lab at Simon Fraser University.

**polymerase chain reaction (PCR)**
a technique used to amplify or make copies of DNA

One of the problems with early attempts to extract DNA from archaeological remains was that there was often very little remaining and what did survive was fragmentary and degraded, especially in very old specimens. A major breakthrough came in the mid-1980s with the development of a technique known as **polymerase chain reaction (PCR)**. This technique revolutionized the study of aDNA because it enabled scientists to amplify (i.e., make millions of copies of) DNA from only a single molecule. This development provides more DNA for researchers to analyze. This technique has come at a cost, however, as any modern DNA that may have contaminated ancient specimens is amplified as well. Indeed, contamination has been a major stumbling block in the analysis of ancient DNA. Sources of modern DNA include dead skin cells, sweat, saliva, dandruff, and blood, and contamination can occur at a number of stages, including during the excavation itself and in the laboratory afterwards. Because of the high potential for contamination, strict precautions must be taken when preparing archaeological samples for DNA analysis. Contamination controls include working in a laboratory dedicated specifically to the study of aDNA, wearing protective gowns, gloves, and masks, performing multiple extractions, and extracting and sequencing samples in more than one laboratory (Cooper and Poinar 2000; Yang and Watt 2005).

# SUMMARY

In this chapter we introduced you to the structure of cells and the genetic material contained within them, the mechanisms of cell division, and the way in which traits are transmitted from parent to offspring. DNA is the universal code of life and functions not only to synthesize proteins but also to regulate other important processes such as growth and development. As you will learn in Chapters 11 and 12, genes have played a fundamental role in the evolutionary history of our species, and genetic evidence has provided valuable clues to the origins of modern *Homo sapiens* and the evolutionary relationship between modern humans and Neandertals. Genes also play a critical role in the development of such chronic diseases as diabetes and hypertension. While the field of genetics is diverse, encompassing such areas as molecular, population, medical, and behavioural genetics, new disciplines such as biomedical anthropology (see Chapter 14) are beginning to emerge from the integration of some of these subfields with biological anthropology.

# CORE REVIEW

### What is DNA? What functions does it serve, and how does it differ from RNA?

DNA, or deoxyribonucleic acid, is a double-stranded molecule consisting of a sequence of bases that code for the synthesis of proteins and that regulate biological processes such as growth and development. RNA, by contrast, is a single-stranded molecule that plays an important role in protein synthesis. Messenger RNA carries the genetic message coded by the DNA to the ribosome in the cell where it is translated. Codons on the messenger RNA code for specific amino acids, which are brought to the ribosome by transfer RNA. These amino acids join together to form polypeptide chains that make up proteins.

### What are mitosis and meiosis, and how do they differ?

Mitosis refers to the division of somatic, or body cells. It involves the replication of genetic material and the division of a cell to produce two identical daughter cells, each containing the full complement of DNA. Meiosis, by contrast, refers to the division of the sex cells. It involves the replication of genetic material and two cell divisions producing four nonidentical daughter cells, each containing half the genetic material of the original parent cell.

### What are some of the sources of variation on which natural selection acts?

Mutation and recombination, or crossing over, are major sources of variation on which natural selection acts. Mutations may occur at the level of the gene (point mutation) or at the level of the chromosome (chromosomal mutation), and can be caused by a variety of agents, including ultraviolet radiation and chemicals. Some mutations occur randomly, and some genetic regions appear less stable (more prone to mutation) than others. While the vast majority of mutations have no effect on an organism (i.e., they are neutral), some may be harmful and others beneficial.

### What are proteins, and how are they synthesized?

Proteins are molecules made up of chains of amino acids. They are the basic building blocks of the various tissues found in organisms. They are synthesized in cells in a process that involves the separation of the two strands of a DNA molecule, the construction of a strand of messenger RNA, the transfer of the genetic message coded for by the DNA to the cytoplasm of the cell, and the construction of a chain of amino acids brought to the ribosome by transfer RNA.

### How are traits transmitted from one generation to the next, and how did our knowledge of this process come about?

Gregor Mendel's experiments on the common pea plant provided us with the mechanism by which traits are transmitted from one generation to the next. He demonstrated that traits are transmitted by a large number of independent units that we now call genes. These occur in pairs (i.e., every individual has two alleles), and these alleles are randomly separated during the production of sex cells so that each sex cell contains only one allele from each parent. He also demonstrated that the distribution of one pair of genes into the sex cells does not influence the distribution of another pair. In other words, traits are not inherited together unless the genes for those traits are located on the same chromosome.

### What are polygenic traits, and how do they differ from monogenic traits?

Polygenic traits are controlled by genes found at more than one locus. They include traits such as stature and obesity, which reflect the interactions among both genetic and environmental factors. Monogenic traits, by contrast, are controlled by genes at a single locus. They are also influenced by the environment (e.g., not all tall plants are equally tall), but to a lesser extent than are polygenic traits.

**What is behavioural genetics, and what are some of the challenges that behavioural geneticists face?**

Behavioural genetics is the study of the genetic basis of human behaviours—for example, homosexuality and aggression. It seeks to identify the genes that underlie such behaviours; but at the same time, it recognizes the important contribution of environmental factors. Behavioural geneticists face a number of challenges in their work, including the difficulty of defining and quantifying behaviours, identifying the genes that contribute to different behaviours, and determining their precise role. Their research has generated considerable controversy with respect to the ethical, moral, legal, and social implications of assigning genetic causes to human traits.

**What can the study of ancient DNA tell us about past populations, and what are the main limitations of this area of research?**

The extraction and analysis of DNA from archaeological remains dating back thousands of years can provide valuable insight into the origin of modern humans and the degree to which our earlier ancestors contributed their genes to modern humans. The study of ancient DNA has also allowed scientists to identify genetic and infectious diseases in skeletal remains, determine biological relationships within skeletal samples, and determine sex from ancient remains. The most significant limitations for this area of research are the degradation of DNA over time and contamination with modern DNA.

# CRITICAL THINKING QUESTIONS

1. What are some of the ways in which genetic abnormalities can be repaired or prevented?
2. Why haven't traits such as poor eyesight been selected out of the population by now?

# GROUP DISCUSSION QUESTIONS

1. Should federal agencies provide grants for research on "gay genes"? What are the ethical implications of providing funding for this kind of research? Why are we looking for homosexual genes as opposed to heterosexual, bisexual, or transgendered genes?
2. Who owns your genes? Who has the right to decide how they may be studied or manipulated?
3. The use of embryonic stem cells has provoked a variety of opinions on the appropriate ways in which such stem cells may be obtained. Options include creating embryos specifically for research purposes, using excess embryos created by in vitro fertilization for fertility treatments, and using fetal tissue obtained from elective abortions. In your opinion, are any of these options acceptable?

# RESOURCES AND READINGS

- M.H. Crawford, ed., *Anthropological Genetics: Theory, Methods, and Applications* (Cambridge: Cambridge University Press, 2006).
- A.H. Goodman, D. Heath, and M.S. Lindee, eds., *Genetic Nature/Culture: Anthropology and Science Beyond the Two-Culture Divide* (Berkeley: University of California Press, 2003).
- B. Herrmann and S. Hummel, eds., *Ancient DNA: Recovery and Analysis of Genetic Material from Paleontological, Archaeological, Museum, Medical, and Forensic Specimens* (New York: Springer, 1994).
- G. Pálsson, *Anthropology and the New Genetics* (New Departures in Anthropology) (Cambridge: Cambridge University Press, 2007).
- A. Sayre, *Rosalind Franklin and DNA* (New York: Norton, 2000).
- J.D. Watson and A. Berry, *DNA: The Secret of Life* (New York: Knopf, 2003).

# Chapter 4 From Variant to Species

## OVERVIEW

In this chapter we examine how evolutionary theory has advanced through the 20th century to adopt a more expansive view of variation, selection, and adaptation. We explore ways in which biologists have grappled, with some success and a great deal of frustration, with the fundamental questions of "what is a species?" and "what is speciation?" We wrap up this chapter, and this opening section to *A Human Voyage*, by contrasting two models used to classify biological diversity—*clade* and *grade*—that enable researchers to draw comparisons among different species and understand their evolutionary history. This will set the stage for subsequent chapters as we chart our course through the history of ourselves and our nearest primate relatives.

## CORE CONCEPTS

- variation and variability, neo-Darwinism, evolutionary developmental biology, epigenetics, modes of selection, non-Darwinian mechanisms, species and speciation, modes of evolution, classification, evolutionary systematics, cladistics

## CORE QUESTIONS

- What is the relationship between variant and variation?

- How has the paradigm of evolutionary developmental biology challenged Darwinism?

- What is a species, and in what theoretical and practical ways is the traditional concept of the biological species limited?

- In what ways can natural selection alter phenotypes within a population?

- Is the fossil record of biological variation better explained by gradual evolution or punctuated equilibrium?

*Modification of form is admitted to be a matter of time.*

Alfred Russel Wallace (1823–1913)

# PROLOGUE: SWEET ACCIDENTS OF HISTORY

Between 1663 and 1673, the French monarch Louis XIV sent over 700 "filles du roy" (King's Daughters) to New France. His intent was to provide wives for the men of the recently established colonies and to foster permanent settlement. Prior to 1663 the ratio of men to women had reached 169:100, and the king had taken it upon himself to "adopt" young girls of childbearing age (mostly orphans or women lacking family support), provide for their transport to the New World, and supply each with a dowry. They brought little else with them. However, one of these women arrived with something slightly different, slightly unique. She debarked at Québec, possibly more than a little bewildered, and carrying a genetic mutation responsible for Leber Hereditary Optic Neuropathy (LHON), a disorder affecting mostly young adult males and resulting in progressive loss of central vision in one or both eyes. Recently, geneticist Anne-Marie Laberge and her colleagues at the Université de Montréal identified this young King's Daughter using pedigree analysis and genealogical records (Laberge et al. 2005a). Three different mutations within the mitochondrial genome cause LHON, the most common of which is G11778A, responsible for 52 to 92% of cases worldwide. However, though LHON is relatively rare among French Canadians, 86% of those with the condition carry a much less common mutation called T14484C—the one that arrived, complete with a king's dowry, in 1669. In evolutionary biology, this event is known as a **founder effect**.

**founder effect**

the potentially biased sampling of the genetic variation in a species due to the isolation of a small number of its members

Charles Darwin was unaware of founder effects (though he had unknowingly documented their outcome in describing his famous finches); nor was he aware of the many other processes beyond natural selection that are implicated in shaping human biological diversity through the ages.

Interestingly, though our LHON *fille du roy* founder was married in Québec City almost 350 years ago, her granddaughters and great- (and great-great-) granddaughters migrated to southwestern Québec, near Montréal, where LHON is most common today (Figure 4.1). As it happened, the high degree of cultural, linguistic, and religious isolation characteristic of the 8,500 or so French colonists who established New France between 1608 and 1759 is recognized as a major factor determining the high prevalence of as many as 30 known genetic disorders among modern Québécois families (Laberge et al. 2005b). Through the study of such population differences, here and elsewhere, we have gained new insights into

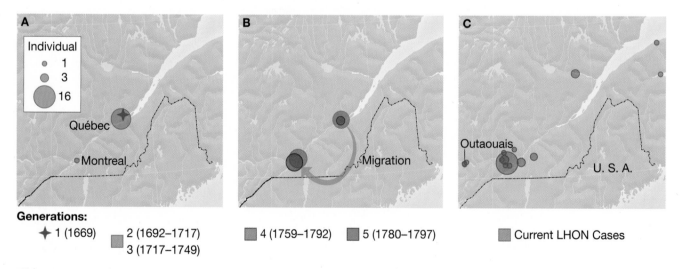

**Generations:**
✦ 1 (1669)    ■ 2 (1692–1717)    ■ 4 (1759–1792)    ■ 5 (1780–1797)    ■ Current LHON Cases
■ 3 (1717–1749)

**Figure 4.1** A single female founder married in Quebec City in 1669 is credited with establishing the hereditary disorder LHON in New France; migration of her descendants to the Montreal region is responsible for the current geographic distribution of cases.

Anne-Marie Laberge, Michele Jomphe, Louis Houde, Helene Vezina, Marc Tremblay, Bertrand Desjardins, Damian Labuda, Marc St-Hilaire, Carol Macmillan, Eric A. Shoubridge and Bernard Brais, A "fille du roy" introduced the T14484C Leber Hereditary Optic Neuropathy Mutation in French Canadians, *The American Journal of Human Genetics*, Vol. 77, no. 2 (August 2005). Copyright © 2005 The American Society of Human Genetics Published by Elsevier Inc. Reprinted with permission.

not only the biology of human diversity, but also the historical and cultural factors that have shaped its geography.

# VARIANT, VARIATION, VARIABILITY

As you learned in Chapter 2, the differences among individuals are central to Darwin's theory of evolution, published in 1859. In fact, it is impossible to imagine how evolutionary change could occur if every member of a sexually reproducing species was alike in all respects, since differential reproductive success presumes that some individuals have an advantage over others in seeking and acquiring necessities such as food, space, and mates. These competitive benefits exist because individuals (**variants**) have a tendency to differ (**variability**), which can be characterized along a continuum of expression (**variation**) (Figure 4.2).

Darwin's "Big Book" (as *The Origin of Species* has come to be known) was filled with examples of variation within and between species, illustrating his principle of natural selection. However, he was unaware of the source of that variation and of how it was transmitted from one generation to the next. Our modern understanding of these missing elements took shape in the late 19th century with the "rediscovery" of Gregor Mendel's principles of inheritance by the Dutch botanist Hugo de Vries (1848–1935) and, independently, by the German botanist Carl Correns (1864–1933). While de Vries and Correns explored patterns of inheritance in the tradition of Mendel, credit for situating the "gene"[1] as the locus of variation, and the founding (and naming) of the science of genetics, belongs to the British biologist William Bateson (1861–1926). Indeed, in the first decades of the 20th century, genetics was a field ripe with innovations and experiments that investigated the mechanisms and products of inheritance and that clarified notions of dominant and recessive traits, heterozygosity, homozygosity, **heterosis**, and mutation. Early geneticists (including Bateson in England, Wilhelm Johannsen in Denmark, and T.H. Morgan in the United States) experimented with organisms that were able to reproduce quickly and that could be managed efficiently in a laboratory environment—plants, algae, and insects. Enabling this flurry of genetic discovery were developments in probability theory and in statistical methods for detecting patterns of variation. Darwin's half-cousin, Sir Francis Galton (1822–1911), made significant contributions in this area, describing the normal probability distribution and developing linear regression analysis.

The field of **population genetics** emerged during the 1920s and 1930s, though in its early days there was much disagreement as to whether natural selection acting on population variation was a more important evolutionary force than mutation as the original source of that variation (Mayr 1982). This debate was more or less settled in 1942, when Sir Julian Huxley published his important work *Evolution: The Modern Synthesis.*[2] That book was based on three guiding principles: (1) selection is the paramount force in evolution; (2) evolution entails gradual change over many generations; and (3) evolution

**variant**

individuals within populations having different expressions of a trait

**variability**

the tendency for members of a population to exhibit different versions of a particular trait

**variation**

the range of expression for a trait evident among all members of a population or a subgroup within it; e.g., the group as a whole, or all males, or all children aged 2 to 10

**heterosis**

also known as heterozygote advantage; the tendency for offspring of genetically distinct individuals to have increased vigour as they are less likely to express deleterious recessive alleles, which increase in frequency when males and females with similar genetic background mate

**population genetics**

a science concerned with variation in gene frequencies within populations and the forces that modify them over time

%

Height (cm)

**Figure 4.2** Variability in height reflects the interaction of inheritance and development. Most variants (individuals) are somewhat "average" in height, but some are short and others comparatively tall; collectively, variation in height can be plotted as a normal distribution (bell curve, represented by the dashed line).

m.bonotto/Shutterstock.com

---

1. The term "gene" was coined by the Danish geneticist W.L. Johannsen in 1909 as a disambiguation of de Vries notion of "pangenes."
2. An eminent biologist in his own right, Julian Huxley (1887–1975) was also the grandson of Thomas Henry Huxley, a 19th-century British biologist and perhaps the staunchest defender of Darwin's evolutionary theory. Julian was also the brother of the writer Aldous Huxley and half-brother of the Nobel laureate biologist Andrew Huxley. Julian received a knighthood in 1959, the centenary of publication of *The Origin of Species*. Huxley's "modern synthesis" reflected the culmination of efforts by a number of eminent biologists and population geneticists, including George Gaylord Simpson, Ronald Fisher, and Sewell Wright, whose research brought statistical rigour to the study of variation in populations.

occurs within populations. These principles form the core of what many biologists now refer to as neo-Darwinism—the marriage of mutation as the source of variation with natural selection as the mechanism that determines whether a mutation is helpful (i.e., adaptive) or otherwise.

## A New Synthesis in the Making?

An important lesson to take away from this brief account is that Darwinism today is a very different theory of evolution from that originally proposed in the 19th century. As you learned in Chapter 2, theories are constantly subject to change, often dramatically, as new insights are made. And while a theory's general premises might be widely held, vigorous debate over finer points is often the norm. Indeed, Darwinian evolutionary theory as shaped over the past 50 years is considerably different from what Huxley proposed in 1942. For that reason we find it more appropriate to drop the prefix "Neo" and simply refer to modern evolutionary theory as Darwinism. These more recent understandings—regarding, for example, the roles of *non*-Darwinian mechanisms of change (Kimura 1983; discussed later in this chapter), the **epigenetic** origin of novel variation through development (Hall 2007), and gene function and regulation underlying the emerging field of **genomics** (Bartel 2004)—have greatly expanded how we view variation within and between species as well as the process of **speciation** itself.

### Evolutionary Developmental Biology

In much the same way that Huxley's *Modern Synthesis* combined laboratory genetics with field biology, one of the more significant developments in the past 20 years has been the fusion of evolutionary theory with developmental biology. This merging of evolution with development (known familiarly as evolutionary developmental biology, or "**evo-devo**") is not a new idea—its central premise can be traced back to studies of comparative embryology in the 19th century and to Ernst Haeckel's (1834–1919) notion of recapitulation.[3] That said, evo-devo has emerged in modern form as a powerful paradigm unifying two fundamental biological realities. On the one hand, we see a fantastic range of variability in living organisms; on the other, we have a highly conserved genome, by which we mean that significant fractions of DNA sequences are shared, more or less unchanged, among these varied life forms. Recent estimates are that less than 3% of the human genome codes for proteins that build tissues and control physiological processes. The remaining 97% or so are *noncoding* sequences consisting of either redundant "**junk**" **DNA** or regulatory genes that control cellular processes (see Chapter 3). Evolutionary developmental biology helps us understand how such small quantities of coding DNA can produce such vast amounts of biological variation.

Considerable amounts of human noncoding DNA are shared by species as diverse as mice, fish, and fruit flies. In fact, the same species of fruit fly, *Drosophila melanogaster*, studied by early geneticists such as T.H. Morgan to shed light on the role of mutation in inheritance, are now being used to comprehend the genetic basis of a range of human illnesses, from autism to addiction to sleep disorders (e.g., Yuan et al. 2006). But why is so much of the same DNA found across such a broad range of organisms, and how do we account for the fact that we have such an amazing variety of outcomes? Well, when you think about it, we actually have a lot in common with most flies and fish: we all have a head-end and a tail-end, we all have a bilateral body plan built on the notion of symmetry, we all have light-sensitive organs for perception, and we all have appendages, be they wings, fins, or legs. In short, it makes good evolutionary sense to not continually reinvent a wheel, but rather to tinker with it—turning genes on and off at different intervals during development or increasing or decreasing their activity—to reach different end points (Veraska et al. 2000).

Brian Hall, emeritus professor[4] of evolutionary biology at Dalhousie University, notes that evo-devo aims to understand how, in the absence of mutation, modifying the process of development can create new phenotypes, and how "ecology impacts on development

**epigenetic**

genetic and nongenetic influences on gene expression resulting in increased phenotypic complexity during development and evolution

**genomics**

the study of the genome of a species, including both mapping sequences and identifying gene function

**speciation**

the formation of new species from pre-existing forms

**"evo-devo"**

evolutionary developmental biology; a branch of evolutionary theory that invokes a prominent role for embryonic development and epigenetic mechanisms in the ontogeny and phylogeny of phenotypes

**"junk" DNA**

in genetics, refers to multiple copies of a base sequence that may be repeated on the same chromosome or dispersed throughout the genome. Most junk or redundant sequences have no known coding function, though others, such as the "Alu" gene family, constitute about 11% of the mass of the human genome and have been implicated in a number of diseases, including breast cancer, hemophilia, and type II diabetes

---

3. Ernst Haeckel was a 19th-century German zoologist. In 1866 he proposed a "biogenic law" that the development of an organism repeated its evolutionary history. The literal version of this had been rejected by the early 20th century.

4. Students often view their instructors as "professor this" or "professor that." In fact, there is a formal hierarchical system in universities. The progress through the ranks is from instructor to lecturer to various levels of professor (assistant, associate, full), with much depending on years of service and accomplishments. The distinction "emeritus professor" is offered to a distinguished scholar, often at retirement, to recognize an academic life of significant contributions and international recognition.

to modulate evolutionary change" (Hall 2001, 177). How, then—and this is a key issue for evo-devo—can the external environment ("ecology") affect the growth and development of an embryo to arrive at new *heritable* variation? Biologists have long appreciated that phenotypes are "plastic" and are products of the interaction of genes and environment (**phenotypic plasticity** is a topic explored in depth in Chapter 14). However, the products of biological plasticity—say, for example, growing taller because you have a better source of nutrition—are not heritable. That is, your children will not necessarily be taller as a result of your increased stature. In evo-devo, a concept called **transgenerational epigenetic inheritance** (Jablonka and Lamb 2007) argues that in some circumstances, environmentally mediated development can result in new phenotypes that may be passed on to the next generation.

## From Germ Plasm Theory to Epigenetic Inheritance Systems

The notion of transgenerational epigenetic inheritance stands in contradiction to one of the fundamental tenets of Darwinian evolutionary theory—namely, that germ cells (sperm and egg) and somatic (body) cells are independent. Put another way, after fertilization occurs, germ cells produce more germ cells as well as body cells, as the zygote develops into the fetus, the fetus into the infant, and so on. However, body cells only produce more body cells. This principle was set in place over a century ago by the German biologist August Weismann (1834–1914), who in 1893 published his "germ plasm theory." Weismann aimed to debunk Lamarck's notion of the inheritance of acquired characters (see Chapter 2) by arguing that only changes (by mutation or recombination) in the sperm and egg were heritable.

We now know that there are a number of ways in which information can be passed from one generation to the next irrespective of changes in DNA base sequences. These are termed epigenetic inheritance systems (EIS; see Jablonka and Lamb 2005), of which there are several. The best understood EIS is associated with chromatin markers such as histones and methyl groups—proteins that assist in maintaining chromosome structure and gene expression. Chromatin markers can be established by the cell's environment as well as by external conditions (e.g., nutrition). As such, these markers can vary from one cell to the next, even though the underlying genetic base-pair sequences in all of the cells remain stable and unchanged. In a manner of speaking, differences in chromatin marks form genetic phenotypes, which, as recent studies in rodents have shown, can be inherited over a number of generations (Whitelaw 2006). The existence of epigenetic inheritance systems can have profound effects, both in the short term (establishing human disease patterns; see Box 4.1) and in an evolutionary context. Again, rodent studies have demonstrated an EIS effect for male fertility (reduced sperm count and motility) following exposure to pesticides—an effect that lasted for several generations (Anway et al. 2005). Similar concerns have been raised regarding recent fertility declines in humans (Perry 2008).

Aside from epigenetic inheritance systems, there are other ways that developmental processes can affect phenotypic variation. The concepts of **morphological integration** and **modularity** are important in this regard (Hallgrímsson et al. 2002). Morphologically integrated traits share common developmental pathways and thus exhibit correlated growth patterns. Through the action of pleiotropy, which occurs when a single gene influences a number of traits (see Chapter 3), morphologically integrated characters combine to form modules that serve a common function; when integrated with other modules, they contribute to the emergence of higher levels of complexity (Mitteroecker and Bookstein 2008). The significance of a modular genotype-phenotype is that it permits parts of an organism to evolve independently—an idea known as **mosaic evolution** and one that is well documented in our own evolutionary story. Importantly, relatively small changes in one module can have a major influence on adjoining modules. As we will explore in Chapter 8, the evolution of the human cranium is a particularly interesting example of morphological integration and modularity, given our unique combination of relatively large brains, small faces, and complex cranial base structure (Lieberman, McBratney, and Krovitz 2002).

**phenotypic plasticity**
a potential for individuals to adapt to variation in external conditions in order to maintain homeostasis and function

**transgenerational epigenetic inheritance**
the transmission of novel phenotypic features from parent to offspring acquired without recourse to modification in DNA gene sequences

**morphological integration**
a tendency for related structures governed by common developmental pathways to covary in a predictable manner

**modularity**
the tendency for components of organisms to develop as independent entities; nesting of modules contributes to higher-order complexity

**mosaic evolution**
different parts of an organism evolve at different rates; in humans, change followed a different evolutionary trajectory in our neurological system than in our locomotory system

BOX 4.1     **FOCUS ON... Programming the Fetus**

In the 1990s, British researchers noticed a rather unusual geographic distribution of adult male mortality and morbidity for heart disease, hypertension, and diabetes (Barker 1998), a pattern which mimicked that for infant mortality. Intrigued, David Barker and his colleagues sought out old medical records to see if they could find a link in the health history of the affected individuals. They were surprised to find that the strongest correlation was with birth weight: full-term babies born with low birth weight (LBW) were more likely to die in infancy; furthermore, if they survived, they were at increased risk for heart attack, stroke, and impaired glucose metabolism as older adults. Barker proposed that the fetus was responding to poor maternal nutrition by economizing on the use of nutrients received across the placenta. Development of less important organs (e.g., kidney and pancreas) was in this way compromised to ensure adequate nutrition for essential organs such as the brain. The outcome was, in effect, a program for late-onset chronic diseases, earning Barker's hypothesis the name "fetal programming." Over the past decade, numerous studies have confirmed and expanded this association in other countries, as well as in women. In a recent review, De Boo and Harding (2006) list seven well-documented diseases related to fetal programming, and almost a dozen others with weaker associations.

A fascinating extension to the fetal programming hypothesis is the recent recognition of significant intergenerational effects. A classic "natural experiment" occurred during the Second World War with the Dutch Hunger Winter of 1944–45. The occupying forces of Nazi Germany placed an embargo on food supplies to the western Netherlands, leaving citizens without adequate nutrition. By February 1945 the average energy intake was less that 600 calories per day, and as many as 18,000 people died from malnutrition or related causes by the time the embargo was lifted in May 1945. But the Hunger Winter also left a rich scientific legacy, one that documented the disease epidemiology of starvation over several generations. Among the findings of the Dutch Famine Birth Cohort Study was that women who were pregnant during their first trimester through the Hunger Winter gave birth to children of normal birth weight, whereas the daughters of these women subsequently gave birth to LBW babies. Christopher Kuzawa (2005) has labelled this effect **intergenerational phenotypic inertia**, and its implications are profound. Intergenerational phenotypic inertia is an epigenetic phenomenon whereby a fetus is able to regulate its own development in utero by predicting the nutritional environment into which it is likely to be born, based on "epigenetic signals" received from its mother and her mother, grandmother, and so on. This matrilineal character of phenotypic inertia occurs because the uterine environment provided by a mother is derived in part from her own experience of her mother's uterine environment. The evolutionary logic is quite simple, in fact. Fast growth and large size in a fetus leads to greater nutritional demands during gestation and after birth. If a mother was temporarily receiving more than adequate nutrition while pregnant, even though the typical situation was one of chronic food shortages, giving birth to larger babies and children would be potentially disastrous, as there would not be sufficient resources for it after birth! Conversely, a fetus should not limit its growth in utero if the mother is nutritionally deprived only in the short term.

# SPECIES NOW AND THEN

**intergenerational phenotypic inertia**
the regulation of fetal growth rate based on matrilineal nutritional history

**microevolution**
a change in gene frequency or chromosome structure over a few generations affecting the distribution of phenotypes (expressed traits) within species

**macroevolution**
the origin of new species over long periods of geologic time

In the previous chapter we argued that the ultimate source of new *genetic* variation occurs as either point or chromosomal mutation—that is, through a change or rearrangement of one or more base-pairs coding for the synthesis or regulation of proteins. Mutations are not uncommon, and some chromosomes and loci are more likely to mutate than others. For example, mutation occurs at a higher rate in noncoding junk DNA, and the vast majority of genetic errors are selectively neutral (see Chapter 3), having no great impact on the development, function, or (for that matter) evolution of organisms. However, genetic variation also occurs elsewhere in the genome, which leads us to ask: Under what conditions do new kinds of organisms evolve? How do we proceed from the small changes that alter gene frequencies and their developmental expression within populations from one generation to the next (**microevolution**) to the larger-scale shifts over many generations that result in the formation of new species (**macroevolution**)?

This is the great challenge of evolutionary biology, and while we understand much more today than did Darwin and his contemporaries, it remains very much an elusive and vexing question, for at least three reasons (Searle 1998). First, biologists have had a difficult time agreeing on what is meant by the term "species" (a definitional problem); second, speciation events are notoriously difficult to study (an operational problem); and finally, little is understood about species formation and genetic evolution (a knowledge deficit problem). As a first step in exploring this challenge, we need to address a fundamental question: What is a species, and how do we know one when we see one?

## Species and Species Concepts

The idea of "species" as a collection of organisms (**demes** or populations) bound together by a shared morphology, ecology, genome, reproduction, and behaviour is central to fields as diverse as **biogeography**, evolutionary biology, paleontology, classification, and conservation. Yet which of these common features takes precedence in the definition of a species has been debated hotly within biology. Though use of the term has considerable antiquity (see Chapter 2), the most commonly cited definition of "species" in the modern era is attributed to the evolutionary biologist and historian of science Ernst Mayr (1942, 120), who wrote that species are "groups of actually or potentially interbreeding natural populations which are reproductively isolated from other such groups." Known as the biological species concept (BSC), this view hinges on the notion of reproductive isolation, which applies fairly well to wild-living **sympatric** populations but is inappropriately applied to **allopatric** species. For example, it is illogical to invoke the BSC to argue that the common marmoset (*Callithrix jacchus*), a New World monkey native to Brazil, is a species distinct from *Galago moholi*, a form of lesser bush-baby living in southern and eastern Africa. These two allopatric primates are neither "actually or potentially interbreeding" by virtue of nothing less than the Atlantic Ocean! Yet in the case of the sympatric bushbaby species *Galago moholi* and *Galago senegalensis* (Figure 4.3), reproductive isolation becomes a relevant and defining feature, as these species overlap both geographically and ecologically.

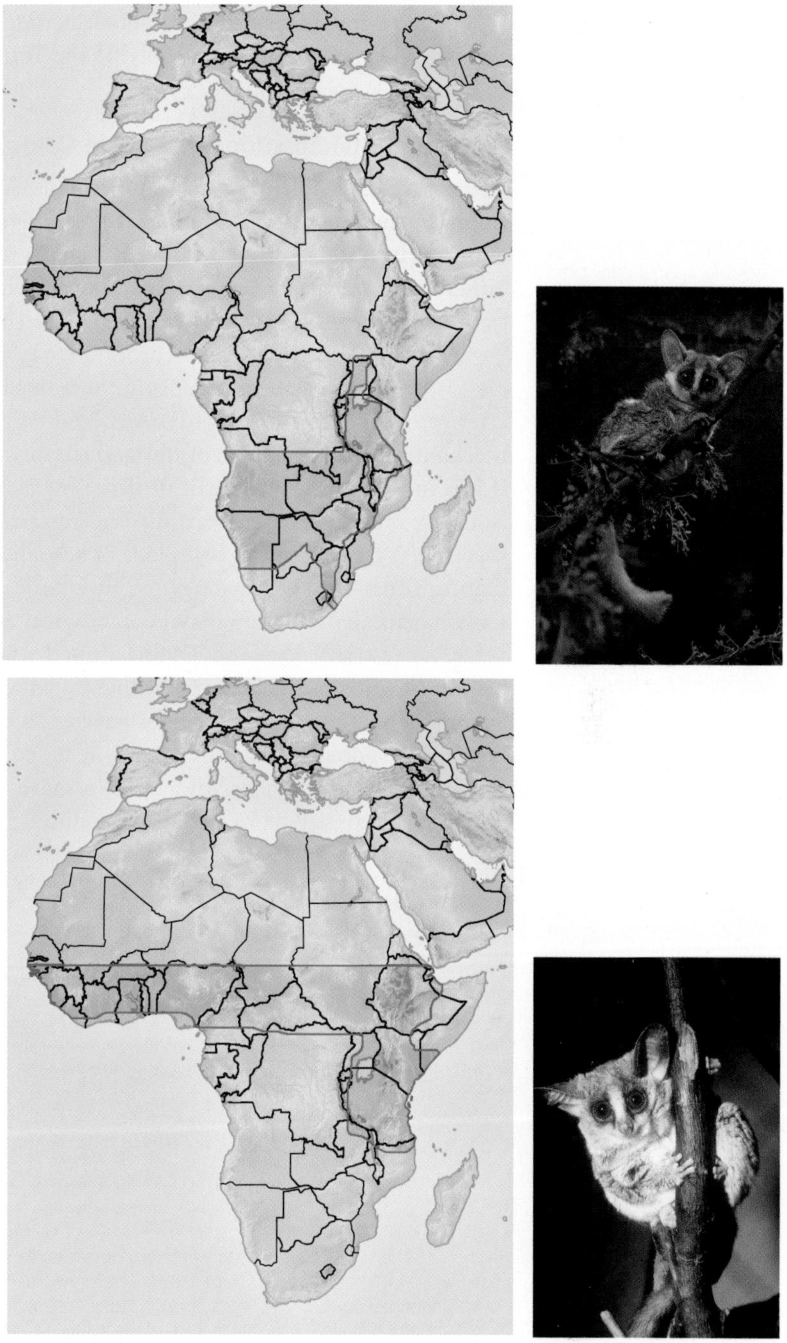

The BSC can also be problematic in cases of **parapatric** species, whose ranges abut one another, thus affording the potential for reproduction. The Hamadrayas and Olive baboons are a good example. These distinctive species of Old World monkey are known to interbreed along their shared geographic borders. Yet other baboon species, such as the Chacma and Yellow baboon, whose ranges also share a boundary, do not. In fact, hybridization is not uncommon among primates in the wild and is known to occur among macaques, gibbons, capuchins, orangutans, and red-tailed and blue monkeys. Typically, the offspring of interspecific hybrid crosses tend to be sterile or to suffer reduced fertility or survivorship, and thus are effectively reproductively isolated (see below). That such interspecific crosses produce offspring at all suggests a geologically recent evolutionary divergence. Patterson and colleagues (2006) have proposed that our earliest hominin ancestors of ca. 6.5 mya continued to interbreed with members of the emerging chimpanzee lineage for a million years or so *after* the initial divergence of these evolutionary lines (see Chapter 9). Indeed, based on genetic evidence from the Y chromosome and mtDNA, Tosi and colleagues

**Figure 4.3** The utility of the biological species concept rests on the potential for interbreeding to occur, which in turn requires geographic proximity. *Galago moholi* (top) and *Galago senegalensis* (bottom) are sympatric species.

Photos: Volkmar K. Wentzel/National Geographic Stock (top); Gary Retherford/Photo Researchers, Inc. (bottom)

**deme**

a local breeding population; that subset of a species within which most members find a mate

**biogeography**

the study of the geographic distribution of organisms, habitats, and evolutionary history as it relates to landscape and ecology

**sympatry**
refers to species that coexist in the same geographic region

**allopatry**
species that "live apart" and do not occupy the same geographic locale; allopatric species are presumed to exist in genetic isolation

**parapatry**
refers to species whose ranges are contiguous but not overlapping; gene flow is possible

**recognition species concept**
a concept of the species as a group whose members, according to particular cues, identify potential mates with whom they might successfully interbreed (in contrast, the BSC emphasizes an absence of breeding potential)

(2000) have argued that the Stumptail macaque of Southeast Asia is a viable species that arose through a hybridization event involving the Toque macaque and the Crab-eating macaque during the Pleistocene glaciations.

## Are Other Species Concepts More Useful?

If the BSC is problematic in some instances, are there other ways to define "species" that might be more useful? A number of alternatives have been proposed—as many as 24, by some counts (Hey 2001). Groves (2007) has characterized the differences among species concepts as either "theoretical" or "operational," depending on whether reproductive isolation or potential for interbreeding is a key feature of the concept.[5]

As you might expect, for reproductive isolation to be maintained between sympatric species, isolating mechanism(s) of some sort must have developed that act either before (pre-) or after (post-) mating (Table 4.1). As noted earlier in the context of hybridization, *post*-mating mechanisms ensure failure of the gamete or developing zygote, the early death of the hybrid if it is indeed born, or infertility if the hybrid manages to survive to adulthood.[6] *Pre*-mating isolating mechanisms are various and tend to prevent individuals of different species from meeting or mating in the first place. These mechanisms may be behavioural (such as different mating rituals, e.g., bird songs) or mechanical (such as differently sized or shaped male and female genitalia), or they may be ecological (such as differences in habitat use, e.g., arboreal versus terrestrial). Paterson (1985) argued some time ago that "species" are maintained not by post-mating mechanisms but rather by who chooses to mate with whom (pre-mating mechanisms). He suggested that species have evolved in such a way that they know how to identify appropriate potential mates. On this, he based his **recognition species concept** (RSC). The RSC posits that members of a species share a Specific Mate Recognition System (SMRS), which may consist of calls, facial or body markings, chemical signals, or movements. An

**Table 4.1** Reproductive isolating mechanisms may assume a variety of forms which either prevent current, or restrict future, mating between species.

| Type | Acts Through |
| --- | --- |
| Pre-Mating: Space | Mating is prohibited by physical barriers such as rivers or by occupation of different zones within habitats (ground versus tree dwelling) |
| Pre-Mating: Time | Mating is prohibited by activity cycles (day versus night) or seasonality (spring versus fall mating) |
| Pre-Mating: Behaviour | Members of different species are unresponsive to mating rituals (e.g., displays) or signals (songs, pheromone) |
| Pre-Mating: Function | In sexually reproducing species, male and female genitalia are not mechanically suited by virtue of size, shape, or other attributes of form |
| Post-Mating: Gamete incompatibility | Though mating may occur, the sperm and egg are not biochemically compatible, preventing fertilization |
| Post-Mating: Inviability | Though mating and fertilization may occur, the organism is inviable and dies during development (as a zygote or fetus) or immediately after birth if carried to term |
| Post-Mating: Sterility | Hybrid offspring are born but are infertile when mated with like hybrids. |

5. Of the 24 versions listed by Hey (2001), 10 refer to "biological processes"—such as reproduction or competition—that occur among members of a species and that contribute to "a shared process of evolution."

6. In some cases, hybrids may successfully produce offspring if they mate with one of the parental forms. A liger, for example, results from a cross between a male lion and a female tiger (tigons result from the opposite cross). Female ligers and tigons are fertile when mated with a male lion or tiger, but male ligers and tigons are infertile. Consequently, ligers and tigons remain simply hybrids, not species in their own right.

interesting example is the galago, a small nocturnal primate native to Africa (see Figure 4.3). In recent years, a number of new species have been identified by "splitting" previously known forms into separate groups. Galagos are nocturnal animals and in the dark of night rely on vocalizations and odours in order to communicate with **conspecifics** to find appropriate mates. Ambrose (2003) has recently proposed that three separate species be distinguished within Allen's galago (*Galago alleni*), found in Central Africa, based on a distinctive auditory SMRS used in both contact and alarm situations.

**conspecific**

belonging to the same species

## What about Species in the Fossil Record?

Of course, concepts such as the BSC and the RSC are not particularly helpful when all we have to examine are patterns of variation rather than the processes that gave rise to and have maintained those patterns (such as reproduction or behaviour; Groves 2007). The fossil record represents the classic situation where we need to distinguish among diverse forms but—save for inventing a time machine—have no recourse to criteria based on concepts such as the BSC or RSC. And there are numerous interesting questions that rest on being able to make a reasonable, parsimonious identification of extinct species. We might want to know, for example, how many species of early hominin lived more or less contemporaneously in Africa ca. 2 mya, at a time when our own genus, *Homo*, was becoming established. For that matter, how many hominin species were roaming throughout Europe and the Near East only 250,000 years ago? Which in turn summons this broader question: Who—or what—were the Neandertals (Weaver et al. 2007)? And how can we know, when we study the beginning of this human voyage of ours, which dates back some 6 million years, whether we are looking at a human ancestor or that of the chimpanzees? In cases like these we need to resort to Groves' (2007) "operational" species concept. In this way, fossil species can be defined in such a way as to include—along with an analysis of what the skeletal remains might look like—various presumptions regarding ancestral and descendent relationships, ranges of variability, and (reproductive) behaviour.

Essentially, the task is one of dividing the fossil record into meaningful segments. To that end, we have two dimensions with which to work—morphology and time (Wood and Lonergan 2008). Morphological species (**morphospecies**) is an operational species concept which argues that if things appear sufficiently different in shape or appearance, they qualify as different species, irrespective of time. Clearly, cows are not horses and chickens are not eagles. While the morphological species concept might seem self-evident and simplistic, it is likely the oldest of all species concepts, given the human inclination to organize the world into neat and tidy categories. No doubt our recent ancestors found being able to distinguish cows from horses quite handy! On a more serious note, were Neandertals different enough from us in appearance to qualify as a species distinct from us? Should we designate them *Homo neanderthalensis* rather than *Homo sapiens* (see Chapter 11)? Basically, we are asking whether fossil phenotypes are clearly distinguishable. Do they have

**morphospecies**

designation of species in the fossil record according to similarity in form irrespective of time

features that set them apart from other fossil forms? Do they produce clusters of supposedly related kinds? The crux of the morphospecies concept is this: What constitutes "sufficiently different" (Figure 4.4)? A wide variety of sophisticated statistical methods have been brought to bear on this issue; generally, these aim to identify the "smallest cluster of individual organisms that is 'diagnosable' on the basis of the preserved morphology" (Wood and Lonergan, 2008, 366).

The concept of **chronospecies** relies instead on a temporal framework to distinguish one species from another. Thus, if two fossils are separated by a significant passage

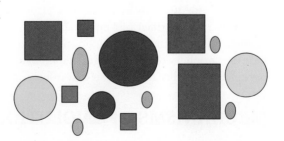

**Figure 4.4** In paleontology, fossils are assigned to a morphospecies on the basis of a shared morphology that distinguishes them from other such groups. How many morphospecies are represented by this collection of 'fossils'? Would the number change if you used only colour (or only shape) to make your decision?

**chronospecies**

designation of species identity by virtue of the passage of time; two fossils may be deemed species if separated by sufficient time

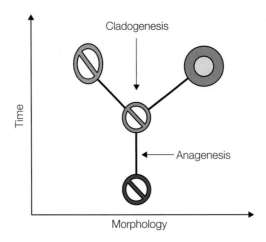

of time—which may include an apparent gap during which they do not overlap—they are usually considered distinct species. This approach is often used in conjunction with the morphospecies concept if one of the fossils possesses one or more characteristics not evident in the other.

## How Do New Species Evolve?

Though evolutionary biologists might disagree over definitions, they do not dispute that species exist. This implies that one or more processes exist through which one kind of organism gives rise to another over time. We often ponder the **tempo and mode** of evolution: At what rate does it proceed? What pattern of diversity arises from it? These questions can only be asked with regard to the fossil record, because no one can predict the rate or pattern of future evolution. Metaphors invoking images of trees and bushes are common (see Darwin's own depiction at the beginning of Chapter 2).

**Figure 4.5** The linear model of phyletic gradualism (anagenesis) differs from the branching model of punctuated equilibrium (cladogenesis). The latter is defined by periods of relatively little change, with short bursts of relatively rapid change as new clades arise through a splitting of the previous lineage.

**tempo and mode**
refers to the pace and manner of evolutionary change

**anagenesis**
a pattern of slow, continual evolutionary change, also known as Darwinian gradualism

**phyletic evolution**
an alternative term for anagenesis, with "phyletic" denoting a line of direct ancestor–descendant relationship

**cladogenesis**
a pattern of evolution characterized by branching, in which a single species may give rise to one (or more) "daughter" species that subsequently diverge; also known as horizontal speciation

**clade**
a group of species sharing a closer ancestry among themselves than any of them do with species of other clades

**punctuated equilibrium**
a pattern of evolution characterized by periods of stasis interrupted by rapid evolutionary change; more commonly found in small, peripheral populations on the edge of a species range

As we have seen, Darwin and Wallace proposed natural selection as the principal force driving organismic evolution with a tempo of slow, gradual change—a mode of evolution termed **anagenesis** (also known as Darwinian gradualism, or **phyletic evolution**). New adaptive variants appearing through mutation and recombination (see Chapter 3) confer greater reproductive fitness in the "struggle for life." Individuals carrying these traits would leave greater numbers of offspring; thus the traits would appear more frequently in subsequent generations. Those traits that reduced fitness would be selected against, their bearers reproducing less or not at all. Given sufficient time, the entire species would eventually express the new phenotype of adaptive characters, and the previous form would disappear, effectively becoming an extinct ancestor.

Speciation might also occur through a mode of evolution known as **cladogenesis** (also known as branching evolution). In paleontology, cladogenesis is characterized by a splitting event whereby an evolving lineage divides to form two distinct **clades**, or separate lineages (Figure 4.5). Unlike the case in anagenesis, there is no presumption of rate of change for cladogenesis, though it is often associated with a theory known as **punctuated equilibrium** (or PE for short; Eldridge and Gould 1972). The defining features of PE are long periods of phenotypic stasis in which little or no change occurs, followed by a comparatively rapid "burst" of significant morphological evolution. For this reason, PE is often referred to as "horizontal evolution," for it seems as if the new clade has materialized out of nowhere. This sudden appearance is an artifact of paleontological time scales, which tend to be quite coarse "in the ground." As expressed by Eldridge and Gould, speciation by way of PE will most likely occur near the periphery of a species' geographic range, which is often a zone of ecological transition occupied by smaller demes, one that offers unique evolutionary opportunities.

## MECHANISMS OF EVOLUTION

Whether one is speaking of microevolution or macroevolution, the question at hand is how the frequency with which a given phenotype is present in a population changes from one generation to the next. In the traditional view of Darwinism, this change is considered an outcome of natural selection. However, as we noted earlier, there are other, non-Darwinian[7] mechanisms

---

7. Though designated as non-Darwinian, forces such as gene flow and genetic drift are not inconsistent with Darwinism; rather, they should be viewed as extensions or elaborations of the theory.

that can exert profound changes on the incidence of different phenotypes, often over relatively short periods of time. These mechanisms act at the level of either the population (**gene flow**, **genetic drift**, and founder effect) or the individual (the epigenetic inheritance systems noted earlier in this chapter). In the following section we look at the different ways in which natural selection acts on population variation, and then turn our attention to non-Darwinian factors.

## How Does Selection Operate to Produce Adaptation?

Adaptation refers to a thing (e.g., the hominin pelvis is an adaptation for bipedal locomotion), a process (e.g., people adapt to increased exposure to sunlight by tanning), or a state of being (e.g., animals with stockier bodies are better adapted to conserve heat in cold environments). Natural selection is often understood as a "sorting" mechanism through which adaptive features useful for survival are favoured and less adaptive traits are found wanting. There are, in fact, several distinct patterns through which selection can affect trait frequencies: directional, stabilizing, and diversifying selection.

Under **directional selection**, one expression of a phenotypic character is favoured at the expense of all other forms—a pattern commonly observed in living populations. Over relatively short periods of time, directional selection can shift trait frequencies within a species, thus acting as an agent of microevolution. The peppered moth's transition from a light to a dark variety in 19th-century England (see Chapter 3) is an example of directional selection. In humans, the recent evolution of **lactase persistence** in European and African populations at some point in the past 8,000 years is an excellent example of directional selection. Lactase is an enzyme that humans require in order to convert the milk sugar lactose, a disaccharide, into two more readily digestible monosaccharides ("simple sugars"), glucose and galactose. In many populations, the body loses its ability to produce lactase in early childhood (see Chapter 14). However, some human groups have evolved single nucleotide polymorphisms (SNPs) within the gene coding for the lactase enzyme; this allows for that enzymes continued production into adulthood (Tishkoff et al. 2007). Notably, these populations have a cultural history of cattle herding and dairy consumption, which would have exerted positive directional selection favouring the lactase-persistent SNP.

Recent ancient DNA analysis of European Neolithic peoples indicates that the SNP associated with this geographic population, labelled T/C 13910, appeared sometime *after* the adoption of dairy farming in southern Europe, ca. 8800 years ago (Burger et al. 2007). This suggests that while cattle may have been herded by these early European Neolithic farmers, fresh milk was likely not a major part of their diet until after they had acquired the T/C 13910 mutation. This example also reminds us that, when it comes to looking at humans as exemplars of evolutionary processes, one needs to always be cognizant of the role that culture (in this case, dairy farming) plays in shaping selective forces. This is a very important point that you should always bear in mind; as we emphasize throughout this text, humans are very much a biocultural species. Directional selection has been implicated in the evolutionary history of a variety of species, from horses to humans. For example, using a number of phenotypic characters of teeth and jaws, Kimbel and colleagues (2006) proposed that directional selection was responsible for the anagenetic transition among our early hominin ancestors in Africa, from 4.2 to 3.0 mya (see Chapter 9).

Natural selection can also act to stabilize variation within a population under conditions where the average phenotype has an adaptive advantage relative to more extreme expressions of a character. Or it can disrupt one distribution of phenotypes so that two distinct distributions result. Each of these cases—**stabilizing selection** and **diversifying selection**—has particular micro- and macroevolutionary implications.

An interesting example of the former is the argument that human populations have evolved a pattern of stabilized fertility around an average value below the maximum possible (Kaplan 1996). The argument here is that maximizing fertility over a woman's reproductive life span is likely to reduce survivorship for any given child, given finite access to resources. Thus, limiting the number of children per family is adaptive. Theoretically, this strategy balances the cost of raising children against their individual chances of surviving as the number of "mouths to feed" increases. However, humans being complicated biocultural creatures, Kaplan (1996)

**gene flow**
the movement of genes with or without the movement of individuals over geographic space

**genetic drift**
random changes in allele frequencies in small populations independent of selection

**directional selection**
a form of positive or negative selection resulting in a shift in phenotypes toward one end of the distribution, typically occurring in dynamic and changing environments

**lactase persistence**
in humans, the continued production of the enzyme lactase necessary for digesting the milk sugar lactose, past childhood

**stabilizing selection**
a form of selection favouring the most common phenotype at the expense of extreme expressions of a character

**diversifying selection**
a form of positive selection favouring the extremes of the distribution of phenotypes and/or negative selection against the most common expression; may result in sympatric speciation

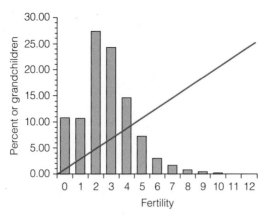

**Figure 4.6** Reproductive fitness as measured by number of grandchildren (solid line) increases with size of family, though most families stabilize fertility around a lower value to avoid economic hardship.

From H. Kaplan, (1998). A theory of fertility and parental investment in traditional and modern human societies. *American Journal of Physical Anthropology* 101 (S23): 91-135. Reprinted by permission of John Wiley and Sons

From H. Kaplan, (1998). A theory of fertility and parental investment in traditional and modern human societies. *American Journal of Physical Anthropology* 101 (S23): 91-135. Reprinted by permission of John Wiley and Sons

**adaptive radiation**

the opportunistic and relatively rapid diversification of new forms into new ecological zones through a series of speciation events

**model organism**

an extensively studied and well-understood species from which new insights into human biology and disease might be obtained; examples range from bacteria such as *E. coli* to mammals such as mice

**constraint**

genetic or functional limitation on the activity or expression of a characteristic

**adaptationist**

a perspective that commonly seeks an adaptive explanation or mechanism for the presence or form of a particular phenotypic character

**biological reductionism**

a method of analysis which argues that biological complexity can be explained in terms of physical laws applied to individual parts

**holism**

in contrast to reductionism, holism argues that complex systems such as organisms possess properties not evident within their separate parts

reported that while the most common number of children in her sample was indeed stable around a relatively low level of two per family, maximum reproductive fitness as measured by the number of grandchildren was actually realized by those families having the most children (Figure 4.6). The outcome of maximizing fertility was a reduction in standard of living within the larger families; in other words, the cost was a cultural (economic) one, not necessarily a biological (survivorship) one.

Diversifying selection describes a process whereby less common variants within a population are favoured at the expense of the more frequent average phenotype. This form of natural selection has been implicated most famously in the **adaptive radiation** of "Darwin's finches" of the Galapagos Islands (Sato et al. 2001). The 15 different finch species differ primarily in terms of beak size and shape; this reflects diversifying selection acting on an original population[8] driven by dietary adaptation to exploit different food resources defined by seed size and hardness. Recently, Abzhanov and colleagues (2004) argued that selection may have acted on developmental timing rather than beak structure per se (i.e., by modifying epigenetic pathways). Using the **model organism** *Gallus gallus* (the domestic chicken) they showed that differences in the expression of *Bmp 4* genes coding for bone morphogenetic protein 4 could produce a range of different beak types. Interestingly, variation in beak shape within finches has been shown to affect song production (Huber and Podos 2006), which suggests that diversification within finches may have been promoted by pre-mating isolation consistent with the recognition species concept discussed earlier.

It must be remembered that individuals are complex amalgamations of a great many phenotypic characters (morphological, physiological, and developmental), many of which are integrated and modular, as noted earlier. This raises the important issue of **constraint**, which limits selection to achieving solutions that work as opposed to something that might be theoretically optimal. Indeed, all adaptations should be viewed as compromises—as subtle adjustments constrained by a need to retain function in related features. This raises one last important consideration: not every feature of an organism may, in fact, be an adaptation per se. Many years ago, Harvard University biologists Stephen J. Gould and Richard Lewontin (1979) argued against the **adaptationist** approach of dissecting an organism into its constituent parts—a practice known as **biological reductionism**—in order to discover a particular feature's singular contribution to fitness. Some features, they argued, may simply exist in their current form as a result of selection acting on a related attribute, or as a consequence of changes in body size. The important thing to remember here is that an organism *is* greater than the sum of its parts, and a complete appreciation of its evolutionary and developmental history requires a more **holistic** perspective.

## Beyond Natural Selection

Whenever we hear of significant political or natural upheavals (such as terrorist attacks, earthquakes, flu pandemics, and the like), we are reminded that our success or failure in the evolutionary enterprise is often determined by random events quite unrelated to the adaptive value of our unique phenotype. Sometimes we are just in the wrong (or right) place at the wrong (or right) time. Alternatively, commitment to a chosen career, a desire to explore new economic opportunities,

---

8. Using mtDNA analysis, Sato and colleagues (2001) have identified a putative ancestral species, the dull-coloured grassquit (*Tiaris obscura*), now found in Ecuador. *T. obscura* likely arrived on the Galapagos Archipelago and nearby Cocos Island about 2.3 mya. It is certain that Darwin's finches on the Galapagos Islands are all descended from a single common ancestor, for there is greater similarity among them than exists between any of these and their continental relatives.

or simply a wish to travel the world may take us hundreds or thousands of kilometres from our birthplace. As a result we transfer our particular version of the human genome from a deme with which we share many features in common, to one with which we do not. Or consider the possibility that we choose to run away to a beautiful desert island with a few dozen like-minded individuals, start a cult, and eschew any contact with the world we have left behind. Most likely our little group will have brought along only a portion of the genetic variation of our former gene pool, in which case any changes (mutations) that occur within our new gene pool could have a larger impact owing to its smaller size. Each of these scenarios constitutes a force of evolution, but none were anticipated by Darwin, nor do they necessarily invoke the operation of natural selection. All have had a significant impact in shaping the geographic diversity of humankind.

## Gene Flow

Gene flow refers to the transfer of genes from one geographic location to another, but it is important to note that gene flow does not necessarily imply that an individual has moved—only his or her genes. Such exchanges of genetic information occur quite often where adjacent demes share a border; when mating crosses that border, so do alleles. That being said, we do tend to think of gene flow as the movement of individuals from place to place. When someone moves into or leaves a population, the relative proportion of alleles for any given gene necessarily changes (albeit very slightly; Figure 4.7); however, when wholesale migrations occur,

Population A

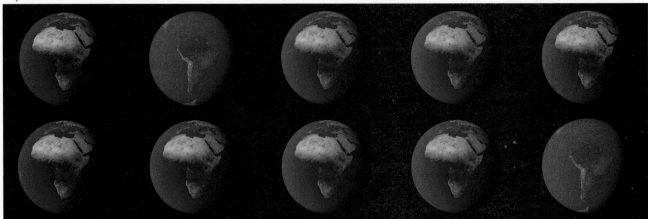

Frequency of Africa allele = 8/10 = 80%; of South America allele = 2/10 = 20%

Population B

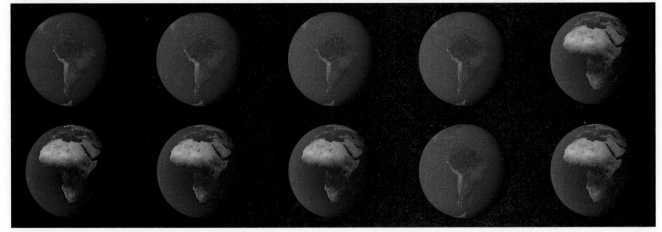

Frequency of Africa allele = 5/10 = 50%; of South America allele = 5/10 = 50%

**Figure 4.7** In population A there are more 'African' alleles than 'South American' alleles. If individuals carrying the African allele left, and were replaced by incoming 'South American' alleles, the relative proportions can change dramatically (as in population B).

**CHAPTER 4**  From Variant to Species

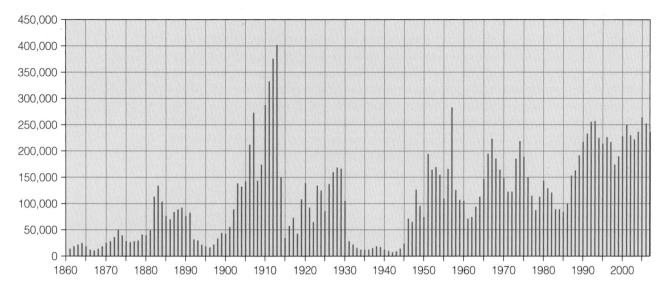

**Figure 4.8** Immigration has always been a major source of population growth in Canada. Declines are associated with major political and economic events, such as the First and Second World Wars, the Great Depression, and changes to law (e.g., the *Immigration Act*).

Citizenship and Immigration, (2007). Facts and Figures: *Immigration Overview*; available at http://www.cic.gc.ca/english/pdf/pub/facts2007.pdf, page 4. Reproduced with the permission of the Minister of Public Works and Government Services Canada, 2009

the impact can be quite profound. Human history abounds with mass migrations of peoples, often through acts of force—the term "diaspora" may be familiar to you. In recent history, globalization and increasing disparities of wealth and opportunity among social classes within and between developed and developing nations have resulted in a significant increase in the movement of people. Even within countries, rural to urban migration (or vice versa) is commonplace as people look to improve their quality of life.

Canada is a nation defined by over five centuries of immigration.[9] Today, people from other nations are arriving—along with their genes—as visitors, students, temporary workers, immigrants, refugees, asylum seekers, or adoptees. As of 2008, almost 1,000,000 people from around the world were awaiting approval to immigrate to Canada; in 2006, over a quarter of a million arrived as permanent residents. In recent years (Figure 4.8), the majority of permanent and temporary residents have been native to the Asia-Pacific region (Citizenship and Immigration Canada 2008), and have settled in major urban centres such as Vancouver, Calgary, Toronto, and Montreal.

The impact of such significant levels of gene flow will likely not be known for some time, perhaps several generations. Theoretically, an influx of new genetic variation is considered a good thing, conforming to a concept best known from plant studies as **heterosis**, or heterozygote advantage. Heterosis is the opposite of **inbreeding depression**, which argues that continued reproduction among closely related individuals leads to greater homozygosity (see Chapter 3) and an increased likelihood that harmful recessive traits will appear more frequently in the phenotype, with detrimental effects on health and survival (Meagher, Penn, and Potts 2000).

Heterozygote advantage proposes just the opposite: mating among individuals with different genetic backgrounds increases heterozygosity and reduces the expression of harmful recessive characteristics. In humans, a classic example of heterosis relates to sickle cell polymorphism and malaria resistance. In regions of the world where malaria caused by the parasite *Plasmodium falciparum* is endemic, a heterozygote person carrying both the dominant normal ("HbA") and recessive sickle cell ("Hbs") hemoglobin alleles (genotypically "As") has a fitness advantage over homozygous AA *and* ss individuals (see Chapter 14).

**heterosis**

also known as heterozygote advantage; the tendency for offspring of genetically distinct individuals to have increased vigour as they are less likely to express deleterious recessive alleles, which increase in frequency when males and females with similar genetic background mate

**inbreeding depression**

reduced vigour in an organism by virtue of increased homozygosity resulting from mating between related individuals

---

9. Of course, the original immigrants to Canada were the ancestors of today's living Native peoples.

Heterozygote advantage also accounts for patterns of variation for cystic fibrosis, or CF. CF is a genetic disorder that impairs the mucous glands of several organs and is the most common lethal single-gene disorder in European-derived populations, with an incidence of 1 in 2,500 live births. CF is much less frequent—indeed, sometimes unknown—in other groups. Heterozygous carriers of the recessive allele were thought to have increased resistance to cholera and typhoid fever, though recent research combining genetic, clinical, and historical-geographic evidence now points to tuberculosis as the selective agent (Poolman and Galvani 2007). Individuals with the recessive CF allele[10] have reduced capacity to produce an enzyme, arylsulphatase B, that the TB bacterium requires in a host in order to produce its own cellular walls. The maintenance of deleterious recessive alleles in a population as a result of heterosis is termed **balanced polymorphism**.

Original population

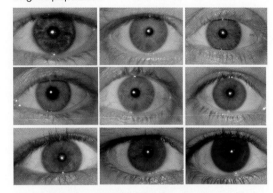

Founder population

**Figure 4.9** Founding populations typically underrepresent the degree of genetic diversity present in the parent population. In this example, only three variants of iris pigmentation form the founder population.

Richard A. Sturm and Tony N. Frudakis. 2004. "Eye color: Portals into pigmentation genes and ancestry," *Trends in Genetics* 20(8). Copyright © 2004 Elsevier Ltd. All rights reserved. Photo courtesy of Richard A. Sturm.

**balanced polymorphism**

polymorphism means "many types" and in genetic terms denotes phenotypes established at proportions that do not require mutation to maintain their existence. Balanced polymorphism occurs when a heterozygote has a selective advantage over alternative homozygotes, thereby maintaining allele diversity within the population

**polydactyly**

a congenital condition in which an individual has more than five fingers or toes on one hand or foot

**Tay-Sachs**

a genetic disease affecting neurological development caused by a mutation on chromosome 15. The most common form occurs in infancy and early childhood and is fatal within the first five years of life

**genetic screening**

a practice in medical genetics involving identification of potentially harmful genotypes

## Founder Effect and Genetic Drift

Earlier we mentioned that the 15 species of Darwin's finches on the Galapagos Islands most likely originated from a single finch species arriving from Central or South America. As a subset of their original deme, this founding group of birds would have brought with them a limited sample of the genetic diversity present in the continental population, which explains why Darwin's finches are more similar to one another than any one of them is to the parent population. The reduction in genetic diversity and resulting phenotypic similarity associated with such events is known as founder effect (Figure 4.9) and has been well documented in human populations as a result of a long history of migration (Cavelli-Sforza 1997). For example, the complete absence of blood types A and B among the indigenous peoples of Central and South America suggests that the founding colonizers migrated from Asia carrying only the allele for blood type O.

Many founder effects of which we are aware concern diseases of diverse origin, as these are the kinds of outcomes that are noticeable in society (e.g., **polydactyly** among the Amish) or otherwise of medical—and anthropological—interest (e.g., **Tay-Sachs** disease among Québécois). A recent study by the University of British Columbia's Genetic Pathology Evaluation Lab (Kaurah et al. 2007) investigated whether a disease known as hereditary diffuse gastric cancer (HDGC) occurred due to common ancestry or independent mutation. They found that in 15 of 38 families studied with a history of HDGC, four of them—all from the southeast coast of Newfoundland—had a novel mutation and a common haplotype, suggesting a founder effect. An unfortunate sidebar to this story is that **genetic screening** is as yet not very effective at identifying whether an individual carries the mutation responsible for the disease—in the above study the detection rate was only 40%. Even within families that have experienced two cases of hereditary diffuse gastric cancer, it is unlikely that a family member will be diagnosed before age 50, while the disease can appear as early as the second decade of life.

---

10. Of the 1,400 identified mutations resulting in cystic fibrosis, the most common is ΔF508, estimated to be 600 generations old, which closely approximates the time frame for global endemicity for *Mycobacterium tuberculosis*.

As a result, as-yet-undiagnosed members of families having a history of HDGC have chosen radical prophylactic gastrectomy (surgical removal of the stomach) as a preferred alternative to the possibility of developing gastric cancer.

Assuming no additional migration, increases in genetic variation within a founding population are the result of mutation. These mutations may achieve polymorphic frequencies (i.e., constitute at least 1% of all alleles for a gene) through one of two processes. One is positive natural selection, as we suspect occurred with regard to finch beak morphology. The other is through random fluctuations in allele frequency from one generation to the next. Kimura (1983) argued that most mutations are selectively neutral and are neither an advantage nor a disadvantage with respect to the bearer's fitness. The significant redundancy found in the genome (junk DNA) supports this argument. Many single nucleotide polymorphisms code for the same amino acid in the production of proteins and thus are inconsequential. For example, the DNA sequences GAA and GAG both specify the amino acid known as glutamic acid; thus a mutation in the third position from A to G (or G to A) has no impact—that is, it is selectively neutral. This leads us to ask: in the absence of either positive or negative selection, which we know can increase or decrease allele frequencies, how do selectively neutral mutations spread through a population?

In Kimura's model, a process known as genetic drift plays a prominent role in shaping human genetic diversity. Drift refers to the probability that gene frequencies will change from one generation to the next simply as a matter of chance. There are numerous factors—in humans, many of them biocultural, as we have already seen—that conspire to bring potential mates together. The classic Mendelian heterozygote cross, with its hypothetical genotype frequencies (calculable in a Punnett square; see Chapter 3), is exactly that—hypothetical. The expected "AA—Aa—Aa—aa" outcome for a single-gene, two-allele trait might occur on average, but not with certainty. While less likely, two heterozygous parents could produce all aa, all AA, or all Aa children, strictly by chance. In large populations, such random deviations from expectations tend to have a negligible effect—the gene pool is simply too large. In small populations, random events can have greater impact. This is especially true when generation time is short and genetic diversity is low; in which case, a novel mutation can quite easily become established at polymorphic levels, or reach "fixation" (meaning that all members of the population will eventually have it).

A phenomenon combining features of both founder effect and genetic drift is known as a **genetic bottleneck** (Figure 4.10). Bottlenecks occur much as they sound: through relatively sudden constrictions on the transfer of genetic diversity from one generation to the next. Such occurrences are commonly associated with a rapid reduction in population size through increased mortality. Natural disasters, political unrest, and particularly virulent diseases are well-known causes. Recent human history is full of examples of all of these, and the differential impact of such agents within and between populations along lines of class, race, and gender is a critical element in understanding the impact of these "constricting" events (see Chapters 14 and 15). For example, Herring and Sattenspiel (2007) note that, while the Spanish influenza pandemic of 1918–19 killed at least 50,000,000 people worldwide, the geopolitical distribution of death was very uneven. In Canada as a whole, flu mortality was estimated at 0.6%, but it reached 3% for Aboriginal populations nationally, 18% among the Aboriginal population in the northern Manitoba community of Norway House, and as high as 70% in two Labrador Inuit

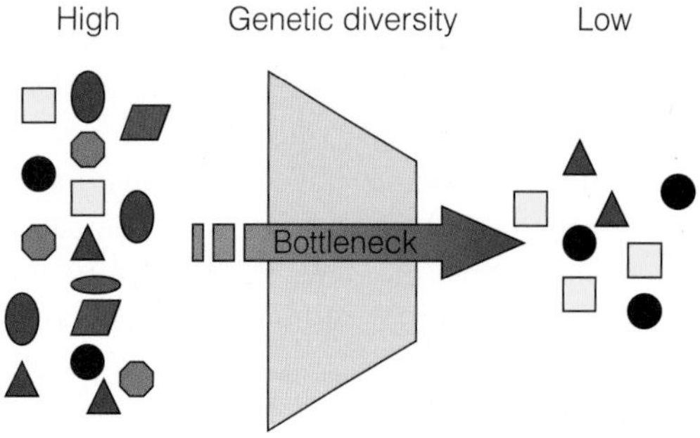

**genetic bottleneck**

a sudden constriction on the genetic diversity appearing in a generation, commonly associated with a reduction in population size

**Figure 4.10** Genetic bottlenecks restrict the transfer of alleles, with the result that the population following the event has much less genetic diversity.

communities. This variation in mortality reflects numerous underlying social factors, the presence of coexisting diseases (e.g., tuberculosis), and access to resources such as health care and adequate nutrition. The outcome of a bottleneck event is the loss of genetic diversity, and in this regard it mimics a founder effect. If the event also involves a significant reduction in population size, there is potential for drift to affect future genetic variance.

## Is Macroevolution Simply the Sum of Microevolution?

It seems logical that we should link the small changes occurring within a population from one generation to the next with the much larger changes over protracted periods of time that result in speciation. That is, macroevolution is the sum of microevolution (or, conversely, accumulated microevolutionary change produces macroevolution). Certainly, genetic and epigenetic mechanisms exist that in theory might ultimately lead to isolation and species differentiation. However, two caveats stand in the way of this overly simplistic notion. The first is that microevolutionary (Darwinian or non-Darwinian) adjustment of allele frequencies, developmental pathways, or phenotypes is not predictive of future macroevolutionary events. There is no rule in evolutionary theory which says that X amount of microevolution equals a new species! It is therefore erroneous to presume that microevolution inexorably leads to macroevolution.

Our second caveat is that the ultimate test of macroevolution in wild-living populations is the existence of pre- or post-mating reproductive isolation, which may be effected with little or no microevolutionary (genetic or epigenetic) alteration. A classic example is that of the common chimpanzee (*Pan troglodytes*) and its nearest relative, the bonobos *(Pan paniscus)*. Bonobos are thought to have become *geographically* isolated as a small founding population south of the Congo River (Myers Thompson 2003) about 1 mya (Hey 2009). Apes as a rule avoid water, and rivers are known to impede gene flow in bonobos and chimpanzees (Eriksson et al. 2004). Though considered separate species and having interesting morphological and behavioural differences, genomic analysis (Becquet et al. 2007) shows that chimpanzees and bonobos differ genetically by only 0.3%. Moreover, the range of genetic variation within chimpanzees and bonobos collectively overlaps that seen in humans, who are, of course, a single species with even greater behavioural and morphological differences than occurs in *Pan*. In other words, the species distinction between chimpanzees and bonobos is based on geographic rather than biological events.

http://www.talkorigins
.org/faqs/macroevolution
.html

# WRESTLING WITH DIVERSITY

In Chapter 2, you learned that the 18th-century Swedish botanist, Carolus Linnaeus, devised the first modern system for cataloguing and naming plants and animals. Classification (part of the discipline of **biological systematics**) is an essential aspect of biology, and no doubt also an essential element of the human psyche, bringing at least a semblance of order to what would otherwise appear as a chaotic assortment of living things. In the absence of classification, making comparisons among these "living things" would be at most an amusing pastime, and little if anything could be said of their evolutionary relationships (phylogeny). Since Linnaeus, biological systematics has become a science in its own right; taxonomies and classifications are not created willy-nilly, but follow a particular methodology as set out under the auspices of the International Commission on Zoological Nomenclature (ICZN), including specification as to the spellings of Latin and Greek terms. Systematics also provides the basis from which hypotheses regarding evolutionary relationships among organisms can be proposed and tested.

**biological systematics**
the formal science of classification and taxonomy, specifying a set of rules and guidelines for categorizing biological diversity and deriving phylogenies

As a group, primates have been a particularly vexatious and fascinating project for systematists, owing in part to the complicated biogeographic and evolutionary history of this group (see Chapters 5 and 7). In no small measure, the fact that humans are one of the Primate

Order's more prominent and problematical members has also created some concern, though not so much with our placement in the grand scheme of things, as with public acceptance of the fact of that placement. Stating that we are related to animals such as chimpanzees or bushbabies has not sat well with some factions of human society since Darwin first asserted that claim (Browne 2001). As we explore in the following chapters of *A Human Voyage*, there are many reasons not just to embrace this reality but to celebrate it! But before we follow that current, it will be useful to develop a classificatory framework through which we can trace and talk about our family ties.

## The Name Game

Organisms are formally identified according to genus and species, two of the four levels of relatedness developed by Linnaeus (the others being class and order). Modern Linnean taxonomy recognizes nine major ranks (Table 4.2), and within these are "higher" and "lower" divisions (identified by the prefixes "super," "sub," or "infra," respectively). For example, between the major taxonomic ranks of order and family, one can identify the descending arrangement of suborder, infraorder and superfamily. Such intermediary levels reflect the existence of features (biological, ecological, geographic, and/or phylogenetic) shared by taxa

**Table 4.2**  Linnean classification of *Homo sapiens*.

| | | |
|---|---|---|
| Kingdom | Animalia | Do not make their own food, but depend on intake of living food |
| Phylum | Chordata | Have at some stage gill slits as well as notochord (a rodlike structure of cartilage) and nerve chord running along the back of the body |
| Subphylum* | Vertebrate | Notochord replaced by vertebral column ("backbone") to form internal skeleton along with skull, ribs, and limb bones |
| Class | Mammalia | Maintain constant body temperature; young nourished after birth by milk from mother's mammary glands |
| Order | Primates | Hands and feet capable of grasping; tendency to erect posture; acute development of vision rather than sense of smell; tendency to large brain relative to body size |
| Superfamily | Hominoidea | Rigid bodies, broad shoulders, and long arms; ability to hang vertically from arms; no tail |
| Family | Hominidae | As above but 98% identical at genetic level |
| Subfamily | Homininae | Ground-dwelling with bipedal locomotion |
| Genus | *Homo* | Large brain; reliance on cultural as opposed to biological adaption |
| Species | *sapiens* | Brains of modern size; relatively small face |

* Most categories can be expanded or narrowed by adding the prefix "sub" or "super." A family could thus be part of a superfamily, and in turn contain two or more subfamilies.

Source: From Haviland. *Human Evolution and Prehistory*, 6E. © 2003 Wadsworth, a part of Cengage Learning, Inc. Reproduced by permission.

**cladistic**

a taxonomic method emphasizing phylogenetic relatedness and based on the existence of *clades* composed of members of evolving lineages such that they can be "nested" into meaningful ranks within the larger framework. For example, the infraorder distinction for New versus Old World monkeys recognizes a unique evolutionary history as well as their significant separation.

The classification adopted in this text follows what is known as a **cladistic** approach, which emphasizes shared evolutionary history, rather than a **gradistic** model, which focuses on morphological or ecological similarities. The related concepts of *clade* and *grade* are important to distinguish, as they factor into discussions not only of living primate diversity, but also of our evolutionary history (Wood and Lonergan 2008; see Chapter 9). While grade-level taxonomies provide meaningful heuristic models for discussing major events in primate evolution,[11] they are in the end categories whose descriptive boundaries find transitional forms such as the Southeast Asian tarsier (see Chapter 7) difficult to accommodate. A cladistic taxonomy, on the other hand, takes into account degrees of biological (phylogenetic) relatedness, assessed by field observation, morphology, and analyses of molecular and DNA data.

Morphological and/or genetic traits that are shared by many different forms across a number of taxonomic ranks reflect a deep evolutionary history. These "primitive" or **pleisomorphic** traits can be contrasted with features that have only recently evolved (called **apomorphic** or "derived" traits); the latter are shared by only a few closely related forms and do not extend deep into the taxonomic hierarchy. An analysis of pleisomorphic and apomorphic variation results in a structure called a **cladogram** (Figure 4.11), a branching "tree" that groups forms together based on their shared phylogenetic history (Wood and Lonergan 2008; Pilbeam and Young 2004).

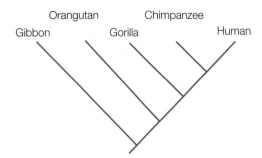

**Figure 4.11** Recent genetic analyses clearly identify humans and chimpanzees/bonobos as the most closely related, with gorillas somewhat more distant, followed by the Asian apes: orangutans and gibbons.

**gradistic**

a taxonomic method that groups forms into named categories (the major units of which are termed *grades*) based on similarity of form, behaviour, and/or ecology; also known as phenetics

**pleisomorphic**

primitive; a pleisomorphic trait is one held in common by a wide range of forms across a number of ranks within a classification; e.g., a tail is a pleisomorphic character within the primate order

**apomorphic**

derived; an apomorphic trait is recently evolved and shared by relatively few members of closely related forms; it distinguishes them from other members within a classification; e.g., lack of a tail is a derived feature of apes with respect to monkeys

**cladogram**

a branching depiction of relationships among taxa based on proximity of evolutionary descent

# SUMMARY

In this chapter we introduced the nature of biological variation at the population or species level as the product of an individual's (the variant) potential to differ (variability) from other members of its group. Such variation can arise through a number of mechanisms and processes, which, besides mutation, include various modes of natural selection (directional, stabilizing, and diversifying), non-Darwinian factors such as genetic drift and gene flow, and modified and integrated developmental pathways (e.g., epigenetic inheritance systems). Variation underlies current concepts of species both past (e.g., morphospecies and chronospecies) and present (biological species and recognition species), as well as our understanding of how new species arise over time, thus creating a vast amount of biological diversity. Comprehending this diversity, its evolution and relationship patterns, falls to the scientific endeavour known as biological systematics, through which taxonomic categories are created and organisms are assigned names reflecting their biological heritage. Such relationships may be organized using concepts such as clades (based on phylogeny) or grades (based on functional and/or ecological similarity), both of which provide useful models for understanding and reconstructing evolutionary history.

---

11. Examples of such events discussed in subsequent chapters include the transition from prosimians to anthropoids (Chapter 7) and the development of very large back teeth in late Pliocene hominin evolution (Chapter 9).

# CORE REVIEW

**What is the relationship between variant and variation?**

Variants refer to individuals within populations (or to particular traits expressed by those individuals). Collectively, the distribution of variants (the range of expression of a trait) constitutes population variation. In short, a variant is observed within individuals, and variation within populations.

**How has the paradigm of evolutionary developmental biology challenged Darwinism?**

Darwinian evolutionary theory proposes that selection acts on variation produced through mutation in DNA, which is then inherited by succeeding generations. Evo-devo proposes that novel phenotypes can be produced through non-DNA changes to development that are subsequently heritable. Evo-devo constitutes an expansion of current Darwinian theory.

**What is a species, and in what theoretical and practical ways is the traditional concept of the biological species limited?**

Species are groups of organisms sharing a common ancestral history and having the potential to reproduce in a coherent fashion. According to the BSC, reproductive isolation by pre- or post-mating mechanisms is the ultimate test of species identity, though this criterion may be a moot point when applied to allopatric species and is of little use when applied to the fossil record.

**In what ways can natural selection alter phenotypes within a population?**

Selection can act to direct change in the distribution of variants by favouring one tail of a distribution, or it can stabilize the range of variation around an average phenotype. It can also produce two distinct distributions by favouring either tail more or less equally. It is important to remember that similar outcomes can result from negative selection acting against particular phenotypes as much as positive selection favouring others.

**Is the fossil record of biological variation better explained by gradual evolution or punctuated equilibrium (PE)?**

Both gradual evolution and PE can be documented in the fossil record, and neither is necessarily a better explanation. It has been argued that the relatively rapid tempo of PE better accommodates the existence of gaps in the fossil record, since rapid evolution would effectively mask the absence of transitional forms. Using the model of Darwinian gradualism, the absence of transitional forms is explainable only by stating that we have not found them yet—a relatively weak argument!

# CRITICAL THINKING QUESTIONS

1. Increasingly, our understanding of variation in nature—including that of humans—is originating from the field of molecular genetics. What are the implications for disciplines such as anthropology and medicine of learning more and more about smaller and smaller parts of ourselves?
2. Organismic variability at the species level and biological diversity at the global level are inextricably linked. What impact(s) do you think a reduction in either would have for the other?

# GROUP DISCUSSION QUESTIONS

1. The American primatologist Matt Cartmill once wrote (1994, 5) that "everything human has to be understood as the historical product of a [biological] reality antecedent to human hopes and fears and politics ... People are animals and the descendents and cousins of animals, and ... the seemingly unbridgeable gulf that separates us from other animals is an illusion due to the accidents of history." Do you agree with this assessment? Are the only meaningful differences between ourselves and other animals cultural in nature?

2. The suggestion has been made that the genetic similarity between humans and chimpanzees is so close that hybridization might be possible. Do you think that scientists should be allowed to pursue this possibility? What are the implications for society at large if such an experiment proves successful?

# RESOURCES AND READINGS

- B. Hallgrímsson and B.K. Hall, *Variation: A Central Concept in Biology* (New York: Academic Press, 2005).
- International Commission on Zoological Nomenclature, **http://www.iczn.org**
- For more on the fascinating story of the Dutch Hunger Winter, visit **http://www .dutchfamine.nl/index_files/study.htm**.

# Chapter 5

# What It Means to Be a Primate

## OVERVIEW

In the previous two chapters we introduced you to the biological building blocks of all life forms and the mechanisms by which organisms evolve. An understanding of our evolutionary history requires not only a good knowledge of the biological basis of human variation but also knowledge of how we compare with our closest living relatives, the nonhuman primates. This chapter introduces you to the features that characterize the Order Primates. It discusses how these features may have originated, classifies primates according to morphological and biochemical evidence, and describes their habitats, dietary adaptations, feeding strategies, and locomotor patterns. It also provides a survey of the major groups of living primates, including their distinguishing characteristics and biological and behavioural adaptations. While we share many features with our closest living relatives, we remain unique in a number of important ways.

## CORE CONCEPTS

■  prosimians, anthropoids, hominoids, adaptation, diversity

## CORE QUESTIONS

■  In what ways do primates differ from other mammals?

■  How might these characteristics have evolved?

■  Where do primates live, how do they move about, and what do they eat?

■  What types of social groups do they live in?

■  What distinguishes prosimians from monkeys, and monkeys from apes?

■  What are some of the differences between New World and Old World monkeys?

■  In what ways are humans unique as primates?

■  What does genetic evidence tell us about our relationship to other primates?

*How like us is that ugly brute, the ape!*

Quintus Ennius, 239–c. 169 BCE

Courtesy of Lisa Gould

# PROLOGUE: THROUGH THE LOOKING GLASS

When you were a child, your parents no doubt took you to the zoo, where you found yourself pressed up against a glass window peering into the gorilla enclosure or watching intently as gibbons swung from branch to branch or baboons jostled with one another for food. Non-human primates, particularly the great apes, have long attracted our attention for their close anatomical and behavioural resemblance to humans. Beginning in the 1930s, Hollywood capitalized on our fascination with our primate cousins by featuring them in films such as the Tarzan series, former U.S. President Ronald Reagan's *Bedtime for Bonzo* (1951), and Clint Eastwood's *Every Which Way But Loose* (1978). In the 1940s, scientists recognized the potential of using nonhuman primates to test the safety of space travel for humans—in particular, the effects of prolonged weightlessness. In 1948 a rhesus monkey was launched into space, and in the years that followed, additional monkeys were rocketed into the atmosphere (see http://history.nasa.gov/animals.html). The first chimpanzee in space, a four-year-old named Ham, successfully completed a suborbital flight in January 1961; four months later, the first American astronaut, Alan B. Shepard, followed his path. Many thousands of nonhuman primates have been used in medical research, including the development and testing of drugs, the treatment of neurological diseases such as Alzheimer's, and immunological studies. Of course, the fact that we can learn so much about ourselves, including our origins and biological and behavioural complexity, is but one reason to study primates. We also investigate primates because they are innately interesting, socially and behaviourally complex mammals. Moreover, many primates occupy key positions within their habitat and are thus under great pressure from human activity and habitat loss (see Chapter 15 for a discussion of primate conservation). To appreciate primates as unique members of the taxonomic Order Primates, and as models for understanding more about ourselves, we need to first be aware of what makes a primate different from, say, a gazelle or a ground sloth.

## DEFINING A PRIMATE

**Mammalia**

the class to which all mammals belong; this includes placental, egg-laying, and marsupial mammals

Primates belong to the Class **Mammalia** and are members of the placental subgroup of mammals. All primates have a suite of characteristics that they share with other placental mammals, including body hair, mammary glands, increased brain size, a relatively long gestation period, and the ability to maintain a constant body temperature. The majority of primates are generalized compared to many other mammals, meaning that they lack specialized features—for example, hooves (as in horses) or high, pointed cusps on the molar and premolar teeth (as in dogs).

Shared primate features reflect a common evolutionary history characterized by environmental adaptation. To date, over 300 species of primates have been identified, most of them in tropical and subtropical areas of the world.[1] Ranging in size from the pygmy mouse lemur (30 g) to the gorilla (200 kg), primates share a number of characteristics not seen in other mammals. That said, the degree of expression of these characteristics varies greatly among different species, and not all primates possess the same ones. In fact, one of the difficulties in defining primates as a group is that they have no single characteristic that distinguishes them from other orders of mammals. So what *does* distinguish them from other mammals? Primates share a set of characteristics that can be divided into those related to locomotion, sensory adaptations, dietary adaptations, and behaviour.

### Locomotory Features

**quadrupedal**

walking on all four limbs

Primates retain a generalized skeletal structure that resembles that of their early mammalian ancestors (Figure 5.1). Because it is generalized, it allows great flexibility in movement. While all nonhuman primates are **quadrupedal**, there is great variation in the way in which they

---

1. The number of reported primate species is constantly changing as new species are uncovered. Within the past few years, for example, a previously unknown species of uakari monkey in the Amazon and at least 20 new species of lemur in Madagascar have been identified.

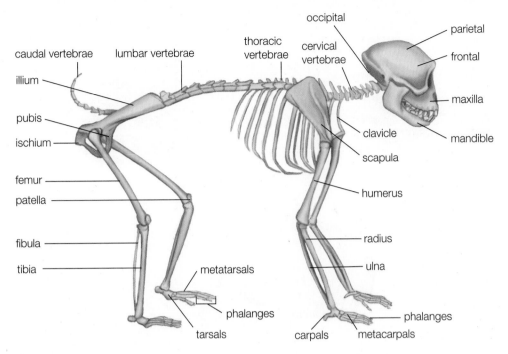

Figure 5.1  The basic skeletal structure of a monkey is similar to that of a human.

move about, and many species use more than one form of locomotion. All primates exhibit a marked tendency toward upright posture in the upper body and have flexible shoulder joints and clavicles (collarbones). Like many other mammals, most primates have five functional digits on each hand and foot (**pentadactyly**). What sets them apart from other mammals, however, is their grasping (**prehensile**) hands with **opposable** thumbs, which allow for a variety of grips (Figure 5.2). Another general characteristic of nonhuman primates is a grasping hindfoot as a result of having an opposable big toe. In addition, all primates have flattened nails and tactile pads on at least one digit; some species retain a claw on certain digits as an adaptation for feeding.

## Sensory Adaptations

Primates have greater reliance on vision than other mammals. This is reflected in their forward-facing eyes, which result in overlapping fields of view, giving primates **stereoscopic vision**—that is, the ability to see things in three dimensions. Because of the importance of vision, the eyes are partly or completely enclosed in a bony orbit that provides protection. This takes the form of a **postorbital bar** in prosimians and a postorbital plate or cup in monkeys, apes, and humans (Figure 5.3). Many primate species have colour vision (Box 5.1), though most of the prosimians lack this feature as they are **nocturnal** and therefore do not need to be able to see colour. Associated with the increased reliance on vision in primates is a decreased reliance on smell, reflected in a reduction in the size of the snout and the **olfactory** areas of the brain.

Figure 5.2  Opposable thumbs allow primates to use both precision and power grips.

**pentadactyly**
having five digits on each hand and foot

**prehensile**
grasping

**opposable**
the thumb or big toe can make contact with the tip of each of the other digits on the same hand/foot

**stereoscopic vision**
characterized by overlapping fields of view, allowing humans and other primates to see in three dimensions

**postorbital bar**
the bony ring that separates the eye orbit from the back of the skull

**nocturnal**
active during the night

**olfactory**
relating to the sense of smell

**CHAPTER 5**  What It Means to Be a Primate

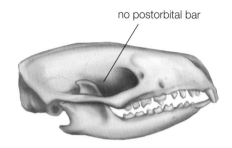
no postorbital bar

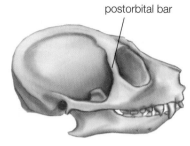
postorbital bar

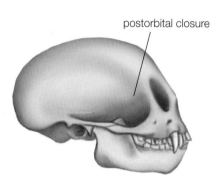
postorbital closure

**diurnal**

active during the day

**trichromatic**

a condition in which an animal possesses three light-sensitive pigments in the cones in the retina of the eye, making it possible to see blue, green, and red

**dichromatic**

a condition in which an animal possesses two light-sensitive pigments in the cones in the retina of the eye, making it possible to see blue and green

**estrus**

period of sexual receptivity in females, correlated with ovulation

**Figure 5.3** Primates have a postorbital bar or closure that protects the eyes. A bar is typically seen in prosimians such as lemurs and lorises, whereas complete closure characterizes monkeys, apes, and humans.

---

**BOX 5.1**    **FOCUS ON... The Evolution of Colour Vision**

The ability to see colour varies greatly among the primates. Not surprisingly, **diurnal** species have the best colour vision, while nocturnal species have none. Humans, apes, and all Old World monkeys can differentiate among blues, greens, and reds (i.e., they are **trichromatic**), while diurnal prosimians can differentiate only between blues and greens (i.e., they are **dichromatic**). New World monkeys are either trichromatic or dichromatic (only one New World monkey is nocturnal). Interestingly, the ability to discriminate between colours also varies by sex. Among the New World marmosets and tamarins, for example, males are dichromatic but some of the females are trichromatic (Smith et al. 2003).

At what point in primate evolutionary history did selection for the ability to see reds occur, and why might this trait have been selected for? It is generally assumed that all early prosimians were monochromatic or dichromatic. Andrew Smith has hypothesized that a mutation in the X chromosome allowing for the ability to see red colours likely occurred after the separation between Old and New World monkeys and probably occurred more than once. According to Smith and colleagues (2003), trichromatic colour vision would have provided an important advantage to fruit-eating primates by allowing them to spot ripe orange and red fruits. In fact, it has long been argued that trichromacy evolved as an adaptation for frugivory. But what about trichromatic species that eat mainly leaves? Research by Dominy and Lucas (2001) on primates living in Kibale National Park in Uganda suggests that trichromacy likely evolved in order to allow them to detect more nutritious young leaves, which are distinguished by their red colour. Liman and Innan (2003), on the other hand, suggest that trichromacy may have been selected for to allow males to see the reddish sexual swellings of females in **estrus**. Alternatively, it may have been selected for in order to allow primates to determine the emotional state of their kin and enemies by being able to detect colour changes in their skin (Changizi, Zhang, and Shimojo 2006). Support for this hypothesis lies in the fact that primates with bare skin on their faces and rumps have highly evolved colour vision whereas those with fur-covered skin do not. So what is the adaptive significance of trichromacy? All of the above hypotheses are plausible, and it is likely that a variety of environmental factors selected for colour vision in primates (recall our discussion of convergent evolution in Chapter 4).

---

## Dietary Adaptations

Primates have **diphyodont** and **heterodont** dentition consisting of two sets of different kinds of teeth that serve a variety of functions, reflecting their generally **omnivorous** diet. In adults, there are four kinds of teeth: incisors, canines, premolars, and molars. The incisors are used for cutting, the canines for piercing, and the premolars and molars for crushing and grinding. The number and type of teeth in each quadrant of the jaw is expressed as a **dental formula**. So, for example, a dental formula of 2.1.2.3 (such as your own) means that in each quadrant of the mouth there are two incisors, one canine, two premolars, and three molars. An individual with this dental formula has a total of 32 teeth, while an individual with a dental formula of 2.1.3.3 has four extra premolars, or 36 teeth in total. In contrast, most early mammals possessed a dental formula of 3.1.4.3, or 44 teeth in total. Thus there has been a reduction in the number of teeth in primates. When dealing with fossilized remains, the number of teeth can be very useful in identifying the different taxa—for example, for distinguishing between early prosimians and anthropoids. Some primate species have unusual dental formulae. The aye-aye, for example, has a specialized dental formula of 1.0.1.3 for the upper jaw and 1.0.0.3 for the lower jaw.

## Behavioural Features

Compared to other mammals, primates have large brains, especially the **neocortex**, that portion of the brain controlling higher brain functions such as memory, problem solving, and abstract thought. They also display longer gestation periods and a low reproductive rate, resulting in a reduced number of offspring. Unlike other mammals who give birth to large numbers of offspring at a time (**r-selection strategy**), primates follow what is referred to as a **K-selection strategy**. This is an adaptive strategy in which individuals have fewer offspring but invest greater parental care, thereby giving them a greater chance of survival. With the exception of marmosets and tamarins, which give birth to twins, all primates (usually) give birth to only one offspring at a time. Primates also have a longer period of infant dependency, which allows for a greater period of learning. Finally, primates have an extended life span, ranging from less than 10 years in some tamarin species to 50 years or more in some of the great apes. Many other animals live longer than primates; what distinguishes primates from other animals is the lengthened period of each stage of their life cycle (i.e., infant, juvenile, adult), again reflecting the importance of learned behaviour.

## THE ORIGIN OF PRIMATE CHARACTERISTICS

How did the suite of characteristics seen in primates come about? In the 1920s, two British anatomists, George Elliot-Smith and Frederic Wood-Jones, hypothesized that primate features such as forward-facing eyes and grasping hands with nails instead of claws evolved as adaptations to an arboreal way of life. Critics of this **arboreal hypothesis** noted that other mammals such as squirrels are also well-adapted to life in the trees yet do not possess these characteristics. In response to these criticisms, primatologist Matt Cartmill (1972, 1992) proposed an alternative hypothesis to explain the origin of primate characteristics. His **visual predation hypothesis** argues that forward-facing eyes and grasping hands arose as adaptations to insect predation. According to this hypothesis, such features allowed the earliest primates, which closely resembled modern insectivores, to exploit insects in the bushy forest undergrowth in which they lived. Randall Sussman's (1991) **angiosperm radiation hypothesis**, in contrast, argues that primate characteristics evolved as adaptations to a diet of flowers and nectar. It fails to explain, however, why such a diet would have necessitated the visual specializations seen in primates, or the fact that the molar teeth of the earliest primates do not exhibit features seen in other species known to eat nectar. More recently, a fourth hypothesis has linked the evolution of primate visual characteristics to the presence of predators, snakes in particular (Isbell 2006). Specifically, features such as forward-facing eyes initially evolved to enable primates to detect

---

**diphyodont**
having two sets of teeth: permanent and deciduous, or baby teeth

**heterodont**
having different kinds of teeth e.g., molars, premolars, incisors, canines

**omnivorous**
eating a variety of different foods, including both plants and animals

**dental formula**
the number of each type of tooth in one quadrant of the mouth

**neocortex**
the outer part of the brain that is involved in higher functions such as reasoning, abstract thought, and language

**r-selection strategy**
a reproductive strategy in which females have many offspring and invest little parental care in those offspring

**K-selection strategy**
a reproductive strategy in which females have few offspring and invest greater parental care in those offspring

**arboreal hypothesis**
the hypothesis that primate features evolved as adaptations to a life in the trees

**visual predation hypothesis**
the hypothesis that primate features evolved as adaptations to insect predation

**angiosperm radiation hypothesis**
the hypothesis that primate features evolved as adaptations to flowering plants

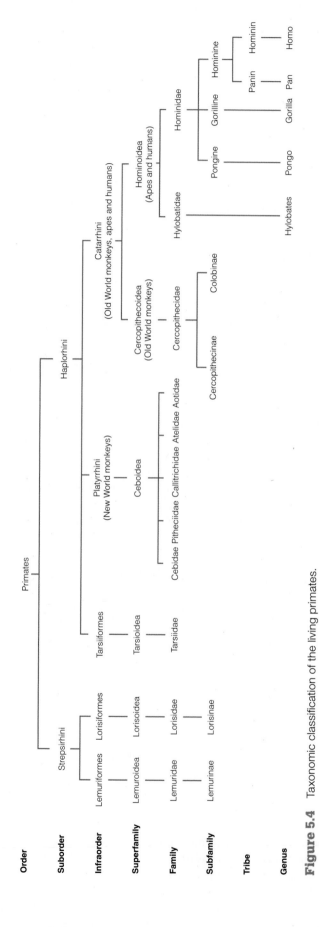

**Figure 5.4** Taxonomic classification of the living primates.

constricting snakes before they struck. Further modifications then occurred with the evolution of venomous snakes. While the mechanisms that led to the evolution of the defining characteristics of primates remain uncertain, there is increasing recognition that not all primate characteristics evolved together and that they likely arose at different times in response to varying environmental conditions.

# CLASSIFYING PRIMATES

As you learned in Chapter 2, the science of classifying organisms is known as taxonomy. This system of classification was developed by Linnaeus, who grouped organisms together based on shared characteristics. The Order Primates has traditionally been divided into two suborders: **Prosimii**, encompassing lemurs, lorises, and tarsiers, and **Anthropoidea**, consisting of monkeys, apes, and humans. One problem with classifying organisms based on physical similarities is that groups of species that are not closely related may be grouped together. Recognizing this limitation, researchers now use biochemical evidence to examine evolutionary and biological relationships among species. For example, comparisons of amino acid sequences of various proteins, and of DNA strands from different species, have revealed that chimps are our closest living relatives (Sibley and Ahlquist 1984). Consequently, anthropologists have increasingly been classifying chimps and humans within the Subfamily **Hominine** (see Chapter 8 for further discussion of this classification scheme). Biochemical data have also revealed that tarsiers, formerly classified as prosimians, are actually more closely related to anthropoids. As a result, the Prosimii, excluding the tarsiers, have been reclassified as the Suborder **Strepsirhini**, and tarsiers, monkeys, apes, and humans have been grouped together in the Suborder **Haplorhini** (Figure 5.4). It is this classification scheme that we will follow in this text.

# PRIMATE BIOGEOGRAPHY

Nonhuman primates are distributed in tropical and subtropical regions of the world. They occupy diverse ecological niches, ranging from the swampy forests of Borneo and Sumatra to the snowy mountains of Japan. Some species are restricted to lowland areas; others are found at higher elevations. Some species remain relatively isolated from humans; others live among them. As with many other mammals, nonhuman primates use space in different ways from day to day and season to season. The total area exploited over the course of a year is called the **home range**, which can vary in size from less than 1 square kilometre in the case of prosimians to many square kilometres in the case of monkeys and apes. Overlapping home ranges may lead to hostile encounters, and some species actively defend their **territory** against neighbouring populations. Chimpanzee males, for example, are known to participate in border patrols (Goodall 1986); these can lead to violent interactions resulting in injury and death if they come upon members of neighbouring groups. The home range is actually the sum of all of the group's **day ranges**, over which they travel from waking up until sleeping, often in search of the next available food resource. Day ranges that emphasize particular zones within the home range, and in which they spend most of their foraging time, define the **core area**.

## Primate Locomotion

Most primates are arboreal and spend the majority of their time in the trees. Some species have adapted to a terrestrial way of life, but no nonhuman primate species is fully terrestrial, and all of them spend at least some of their time in the trees. Gorillas, because of their large body size, are almost completely terrestrial. Primates use four different methods of locomotion, with many species using more than one form. This flexibility in locomotor patterns is possible because of their generalized skeletal structure. The basic form of primate locomotion is quadrupedalism, or movement on all four limbs, and most primates utilize this form of movement on at least some occasions. Primates that exhibit this pattern have an **intermembral index** of over 70, meaning that their forelimbs and

**Prosimii**
the suborder that includes lemurs, lorises, and tarsiers

**Anthropoidea**
the suborder that includes monkeys, apes, and humans

**Hominine**
the subfamily that includes modern humans and our earlier ancestors, as well as chimpanzees and bonobos

**Strepsirhini**
the suborder that comprises the lemurs, lorises, and galagos

**Haplorhini**
the suborder that comprises the tarsiers, monkeys, apes and humans

**home range**
the entire area exploited by an animal or group of animals

**territory**
an area that is defended against conspecific members of neighbouring groups

**day range**
the distance a primate moves in one day

**core area**
the portion of the home range that contains the greatest concentration of resources and that is most heavily used by a group

**intermembral index**
a measure of the relative lengths of the upper and lower limbs, calculated as (humerus length + radius length) x 100 / (femur length + tibia length)

**knuckle-walker**

a form of locomotion characterized by walking on all four limbs with the body weight partially supported by the middle phalanges of the hands

**vertical clinging and leaping**

a form of locomotion characterized by leaping using the hindlimbs and clinging to branches and tree trunks using the forelimbs

**brachiation**

a form of locomotion characterized by arm-over-arm movement

**semibrachiator**

an animal that combines arm-over-arm movement with other forms of locomotion

**bipedalism**

moving on two legs

**monogamous**

characterized by one adult male, one adult female, and their offspring

**sexual dimorphism**

differences in physical characteristics between males and females of the same species

**single-male/multifemale**

consisting of a single adult male and several adult females and their offspring

**polygynous**

a type of mating pattern in which one male mates with more than one female

**polyandry**

a type of mating pattern in which one female mates with more than one male

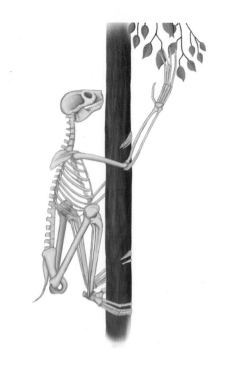

Skeleton of a vertical clinger and leaper (Indri)

**Figure 5.5** Vertical clingers and leapers have longer hindlimbs than forelimbs.

Courtesy of Stephen D. Nash

hindlimbs are of similar length (Figure 5.1). Quadrupeds include arboreal species such as macaques, terrestrial species such as baboons, and **knuckle-walkers** such as chimps and gorillas. A second form of locomotion, utilized by many of the prosimians, is **vertical clinging and leaping**, whereby strong hind limbs propel the body and the forelimbs grasp tree trunks and branches. Species that utilize this mode of locomotion exhibit longer hind limbs than forelimbs (Figure 5.5) and consequently have a low intermembral index. **Brachiation**, a mode of locomotion characterized by arm-over-arm movement, is seen in gibbons and siamangs. Brachiators have extremely flexible shoulder joints and longer forelimbs and shorter hindlimbs (Figure 5.6), giving them a high intermembral index. Researchers have hypothesized that these anatomical traits may have evolved to allow apes to hang from branches while feeding on fruit. Among New World primates, spider monkeys and muriquis are **semibrachiators**, meaning that they combine leaping with arm-over-arm movement. They also use their strong prehensile tails as a fifth hand. Humans are the only primates to display habitual **bipedalism**, though other primate species have been observed moving bipedally over short distances.

## Social Structure and Residence Patterns

Primates are social animals and exhibit a variety of different types of social organization. The size and type of their social groups are influenced by a number of factors, including the number of predators in their environment and the availability and distribution of food resources. Larger groups, for example, are typically found in areas with a greater number of predators. In contrast, smaller groups tend to be found in areas where food resources are widely dispersed. Different types of social groups have been documented within a single species.

A number of species such as gibbons and siamangs are **monogamous**— that is, they form social units characterized by one adult male, one adult female, and their immature offspring. Within these units, the adult male and female form long-term mating partnerships and there is little **sexual dimorphism**, reflecting the decreased need by males to compete for females. Males also tend to invest more time and energy caring for their offspring than they do in other types of social groups. **Single-male/multifemale** communities consist of a single adult male, several adult females, and their offspring.[2] This type of social group, which has a **polygynous** mating pattern, is characteristic of howler monkeys, langurs, geladas, and some gorilla populations. A less common form of social structure, seen in marmosets and tamarins, is **polyandry**, characterized by groups consisting of one adult female, several adult males, and their offspring.[3] Unlike other primate species, where females are the primary caregivers of infants, males within these social units take an active role in looking after infants during the first few months of their life.

---

2. This type of social group was formerly referred to as a harem.

3. There may be more than one adult female in this type of group, but usually only one is sexually active.

The most common type of social group is the **multimale/multifemale** group characteristic of species such as savanna baboons and macaques. Comprising a number of adult males and females and offspring, these groups can number in the hundreds and are typically found in areas where predation pressure is high. Mating activity is promiscuous, and sexual dimorphism is marked. A form of multimale/multifemale group seen among chimpanzees is the **fission–fusion** group. The most flexible type of social group, it is characterized by fluid membership, with frequent movement of members to and from the group. Promiscuous sexual activity and moderate to high sexual dimorphism are characteristic of this type of community, reflecting the need for males to compete with one another for mating partners. Finally, several species of primates, most notably orangutans, are mainly solitary, spending most of their time foraging for food on their own and interacting with one another only occasionally for the purpose of mating.[4]

Primate social groups are dynamic entities, and adolescents often leave the group of their birth (their **natal group**) to join another group or form one of their own. This strategy ensures that inbreeding does not occur. Among many primate species, males emigrate while females remain in their natal group for life (i.e., they are **philopatric**). Good examples are Japanese macaques and rhesus monkeys, in which females form **matrilineal** kin groups. In contrast, female gorillas, chimpanzees, and bonobos leave the group of their birth when they reach sexual maturity to join other established groups.

Skeleton of a brachiator (gibbon)

**Figure 5.6** Brachiators have longer forelimbs than hindlimbs.

Courtesy of Stephen D. Nash

**multimale/ multifemale**

consisting of a number of adult males and females and their offspring

**fission–fusion**

a type of multimale/ multifemale social group whose membership changes frequently

**natal group**

the group in which an individual is born

**philopatric**

remaining in one's birth group

**matrilineal**

groups in which descent is traced through the female line

## Feeding and Foraging

As noted earlier, primates typically have a generalized rather than specialized dentition, reflecting their mainly omnivorous diet. Teeth can, in fact, provide very useful information on diet. The cusp pattern, for example, can tell us whether a primate's diet is composed primarily of fruit or leaves, while the degree of wear on the enamel can tell us how coarse their diet is. This is particularly helpful when we are dealing with fossil remains rather than living animals. While all primates are omnivorous to some extent, most species favour certain types of foods. **Folivorous** primates rely mainly on a diet of leaves, and some, such as colobus monkeys, have specialized digestive systems to process such a diet. Most primates prefer fruit when it is available (i.e., they are **frugivorous**) and detect it on the basis of colour and scent.[5] Many strepsirhines are insectivores, relying heavily on a diet of insects.

Some primates occasionally kill and eat small mammals, including other primates. Male chimpanzees, for example, engage in cooperative hunting and often share meat with one

**folivorous**

leaf-eating

**frugivorous**

fruit-eating

---

4. Some primatologists prefer to call these species semisolitary, as females usually forage with their offspring.

5. The presence of ethanol in fruits appears to be an important cue for detecting and selecting these foods (see Dominy 2004).

another and with nonhunting members of their social group, including females. Differences in hunting strategies have been observed among chimpanzees living in Gombe versus the Taï Forest. Hunting behaviour among the former, for instance, tends to be more opportunistic, and immature red colobus are the primary prey. In contrast, male chimpanzees of the Taï Forest organize cooperative hunting parties that target mature red colobus monkeys. (Boesch and Boesch 1989).

A number of foraging strategies have been observed among primates. The search for food may take up a substantial part of an individual's daily activities, and the responsibility for finding food falls largely on females, who need to feed not only themselves but also their dependent offspring. The distribution of food influences the size of a foraging group. Small groups, for instance, are typical of habitats characterized by a low density of resources. Seasonal availability of food resources also affects foraging behaviour.

Complex feeding strategies have been observed among many primate species. An interesting dietary adaptation has been documented among red colobus monkeys on the island of Zanzibar. It appears to have arisen from an increase in the human population on the island and a reduction in the natural habitat of the monkeys as a result of logging. Despite living in an environment characterized by various exotic fruit trees, the monkeys appear to have taken up the habit of eating charcoal left over from the destruction of the forests. What might be the advantage of eating this substance? As it turns out, the leaves of the fruit trees on which they subsist contain toxic compounds. Eating charcoal allows the monkeys to consume the protein-rich leaves. In this way, they absorb the toxins and eliminate them from the body, at the same time retaining the vital proteins in the leaves (Struhsaker et al. 1997).

As primatologists have discovered, diet, physiology, brain size, and activity levels are all directly linked. Katharine Milton's (1981) long-term study of two sympatric New World primates, spider and howler monkeys, has revealed significant differences between the two species with respect to feeding strategies and types of foods consumed. Howler monkeys rely primarily on a diet of leaves and forage collectively in relatively small areas. Spider monkeys, in contrast, eat mainly fruits and often forage over much larger ranges in small groups or by themselves. Observations of their digestive patterns have revealed that it takes howler monkeys five times longer to digest their food than it does spider monkeys. An examination of their intestinal tracts has also revealed that howlers have considerably larger colons than spider monkeys. As a result, food remains in the gut longer in howlers and they are thus able to derive energy-rich fatty acids from the fermenting masses of leaves, whereas spider monkeys with their smaller digestive tracts can process their high-energy fruit diet quickly and easily. Milton also found correlations among diet, physiology, and brain size, and hypothesized that the larger brains of spider monkeys compared to howlers are a product of their high-energy diet.

Knowledge of primate diets can also be useful in providing insight into disorders that affect humans. For example, observations of primates who appear to become intoxicated as a result of eating ripe fruit have prompted researchers to investigate how we may have developed a taste for, and ultimately, in some cases, an addiction to alcohol (Stephens and Dudley, 2004).

## THE LIVING PRIMATES

### Strepsirhini

The Suborder Strepsirhini comprises the prosimians, of which there are roughly 50 species in the world today. This suborder is further divided into two infraorders: Lemuriformes, which includes lemurs, indris, sifakas, and aye-ayes, and Lorisiformes, which includes lorises and galagos, or bushbabies. Prosimians (or "pre-apes") are often described as more closely resembling the earliest primate forms (see Chapter 7). Their characteristics include the following:

- Small body size. They are the smallest of the primates, ranging in size from the pygmy mouse lemur (30 g) to the indri (7 kg), the latter about the size of a large housecat.
- Primarily nocturnal. This is reflected in their large eyes and lack of colour vision.

- A **tooth comb** formed by the lower incisors and canines (Figure 5.7). These teeth are joined together and protrude outward. The function of this feature varies among prosimians, with some species using it for grooming, others for feeding. The lesser galago, for example, uses its tooth comb to extract sap from tree bark.
- A **grooming claw** on one digit.
- A well-developed sense of smell, reflected by an elongated or protruding snout and the presence of a **rhinarium**.
- A tail in some species, such as lemurs.

## Lemuriformes

This infraorder encompasses about 60 species of lemurs, as well as indris, sifakas, and aye-ayes. All of these species are restricted to the island of Madagascar off the eastern coast of Africa. Among the most diversified of the primates, these animals occupy a variety of ecological niches and consequently exhibit a wide range of adaptive behaviours. Some species, such as the dwarf lemur and the aye-aye, are nocturnal, while others are diurnal. All are primarily arboreal, though some are more terrestrial than others. They use quadrupedal or vertical clinging and leaping modes of locomotion to get around, and they exhibit various forms of social organization, ranging from solitary to large groups. The males of some species, such as ring-tailed lemurs, mark their territories with chemicals produced by scent glands in their wrists. The fat-tailed dwarf lemur is the only primate species to hibernate during the winter months, when ambient temperatures fluctuate significantly (Dausmann et al. 2005). What is the adaptive significance of this behaviour? Primatologist Kathrin Dausmann suggests that it may be a way of coping with food scarcity during the winter months by reducing the amount of energy spent on body-temperature regulation (ibid.). Another unusual member of this infraorder is the aye-aye, the only member of its genus. Occupying a similar environmental niche to woodpeckers, aye-ayes are distinct in having an elongated bony finger, which they use to tear at tree bark to extract insects.

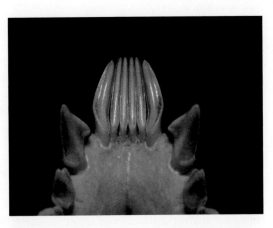

**Figure 5.7** Tooth combs are formed by the anterior teeth and are used by strepsirhines for grooming and foraging.

William K. Sacco, specimens courtesy of Yale Peabody Museum

## Lorisiformes

This infraorder includes about eight species of lorises and six to nine species of galagos, or bushbabies (Figure 5.8). Found in Africa and Southeast Asia, lorises resemble lemurs in having a dental comb and a grooming claw. Nocturnal and largely solitary, they are quadrupedal and rely on a diet of insects, fruit, eggs, snails, and lizards. Galagos are distributed over much of sub-Saharan Africa and are known for their excellent leaping abilities. Their diet includes fruit, insects, and gum from trees. Another member of the Lorisidae family is the potto. Found in the rainforests of Africa, pottos are nocturnal and arboreal.

**Figure 5.8** Galagos, also known as bushbabies, are nocturnal and are primarily insectivorous.

© Gallo Images/Corbis

## Haplorhini

The Suborder Haplorhini includes tarsiers, monkeys, apes, and humans. More than 200 species of monkeys have been identified. These include New World monkeys (Infraorder Platyrrhini) and Old World monkeys, apes, and humans (Infraorder Catarrhini). Tarsiers, being unique in having both strepsirhine and haplorhine features, have been assigned to the Infraorder Tarsiiformes. Characteristics of haplorhines include:

- Larger body size than the strepsirhines.
- Diurnal. The two exceptions are the New World owl or night monkey (*Aotus*) and the Old World tarsier, which are nocturnal.
- A tail in most species.
- Nails on all digits (with the exception of marmosets and tamarins).
- No rhinarium.
- Decreased reliance on sense of smell and increased reliance on vision compared to the strepsirhines. This is reflected in the complete closure of the back of the orbits with a bony plate.
- Larger brain relative to body size than the strepsirhines.

## Platyrrhini

**Platyrrhines**

New World monkeys

The **Platyrrhines**, or New World monkeys, derive their infraorder name from their broad, flat noses with outward-facing nostrils. About 70 species live in the tropical and subtropical forests of Central and South America. All are diurnal except for the owl monkey (*Aotus*). They are mainly arboreal and range in size from marmosets and tamarins (100 g) to howler monkeys (10 kg). Divided into five families (Garber et al. 2008)—Cebidae, Atelidae, Callitrichidae, Pitheciidae, and Aotidae—they display the following characteristics:

- Smaller body size than Old World monkeys.
- A prehensile or grasping tail in some species. This feature facilitates locomotion; it is also a feeding adaptation that allows monkeys to hang from branches while reaching for food.
- Dental formula of 2.1.3.3 for most species.

The Family Cebidae consists of capuchin monkeys (like Marcel on the television show "Friends"!) and squirrel monkeys. Occupying the rainforests of Central and South America, these primates rely on an omnivorous diet and live in multimale/multifemale groups. The Family Atelidae includes the howler, spider, woolly, and woolly spider monkeys. Among the largest of the New World monkeys, howlers (Figure 5.9) are known for their loud vocalizations, which serve to warn other members of their group and to help defend them against predators. Spider monkeys (Figure 5.10), so named for their long, thin limbs and long, prehensile tails, are highly agile. One species of woolly monkey is currently critically endangered due to the destruction of its habitat by ranchers (see Chapter 15 for a discussion of some of the major threats to primates). The Family Callitrichidae comprises the tamarins and marmosets, the tiniest of which is the pygmy marmoset. Both these primates use **scent markings** to claim food resources within their territories. They are also rather unusual in giving birth to twins. The Family Pitheciidae consists of the sakis, titis, and uakaris. One species of uakari is distinctive in having a red face

**scent markings**

a form of communication characterized by the deposition of chemicals such as urine or pheromones to mark territories

**Figure 5.9** Howler monkeys are known for their loud vocalizations, which can be heard over long distances.

Courtesy of Kayla Hartwell

and a partly bald head. Finally, the Family Aotidae comprises the night (or owl) monkeys, the only nocturnal anthropoid.

## Catarrhini

The Infraorder Catarrhini encompasses the most widely distributed of all primates: Old World monkeys, apes, and humans. So named for their narrow noses with downward-facing nostrils, the **Catarrhines** are divided into two superfamilies, the Cercopithecoidea (Old World monkeys) and the Hominoidea (apes and humans).

The Old World monkeys, of which approximately 80 species have been identified, are grouped into one large family, the Cercopithecidae, and are further divided into two subfamilies: the Cercopithecinae and the Colobinae. Occupying a wider variety of habitats than New World monkeys, they can be found in tropical and subtropical forests of Africa and Asia, as well as savannah and grassland environments of Africa. Most species of Old World monkeys are arboreal, but some spend a considerable amount of time on the ground, where they move about quadrupedally. Features seen in catarrhines include:

**Figure 5.10** Spider monkeys have prehensile tails that allow them to grasp branches.

Courtesy of Kayla Hartwell

**Catarrhines**
Old World monkeys

- **Ischial callosities**
- Greater size range and a greater degree of sexual dimorphism than New World monkeys.
- Dental formula of 2.1.2.3.

**ischial callosities**
patches of hardened skin on the rear end that facilitate sitting

### Cercopithecinae

Included in this subfamily are macaques, baboons, and mandrills. Anatomically more generalized and more omnivorous than the colobines, they possess cheek pouches for the temporary storage of food. Among the cercopithecines, the macaques are the most widely distributed, being found from Morocco to the snowy mountains of Japan (Figure 5.11).[6] All of them are both arboreal and terrestrial. Some species (such as baboons) show marked sexual dimorphism in body size and/or canine size. The females of some species display pronounced swellings and colour changes to the genital area to signal estrus. Barbary macaques are the only Old World monkeys without tails, as well as the only wild-living nonhuman primate in Europe (Gibraltar). Mandrills live in the forests of West Africa; the males have brightly coloured swellings on their snouts that may also function to attract females.

### Colobinae

This subfamily encompasses the Genus *Colobus*, a group of leaf-eating species that live in the forests of Africa and Asia. Colobus monkeys have specialized stomachs to facilitate the digestion of large quantities of leaves, as well as molars with sharp cusps for cutting and slicing leaves. Colobines are arboreal quadrupeds and semibrachiators, and their absent or greatly reduced thumb allows them to swing quickly and easily from branch to branch. They tend to be less sexually dimorphic than the cercopithecines and to live in small groups. African colobus monkeys are frequent prey of chimpanzees, especially those of the Ivory Coast, who hunt in groups. Proboscis monkeys of Borneo are easily recognized by their large, pendulous nose, which may act as a sexual signal for females. They are also known to be very good swimmers—unusual among nonhuman primates. About 16 species of langurs occupy the forests of India, Southeast Asia, and Indonesia. One of these species, the Hanuman langur, is revered in India.

---

6. One recently discovered species of macaque, *Macaca munzala*, lives at altitudes of 1600 to 3500 metres above sea level, higher than any other nonhuman primate species (Cachel 2006).

**Figure 5.11** Japanese macaques relaxing in volcanic hot springs.

Koichi Kamoshida/Getty Images

**Figure 5.12** Tarsiers have huge eyes that allow them to see in the dark. Each eyeball is the size of its brain.

Tom McHugh/Photo Researchers, Inc.

## Tarsiers

The five species of tarsiers (Figure 5.12) living today are restricted to Southeast Asia. As noted above, tarsiers were long categorized in the Suborder Prosimii but have recently been shifted to the Suborder Haplorhini. While they have a number of prosimian characteristics, including a nocturnal way of life, a grooming claw, and a vertical clinging and leaping mode of locomotion, they also display anthropoid features, including the lack of both a rhinarium and a dental comb. They are also more closely related biochemically to anthropoids than to prosimians. Known as outstanding leapers owing to the mechanical advantage of elongated tarsal bones in the ankle (from which they get their name), they can jump vertically up to 4 metres (Swindler 1998, 39). They are also the most carnivorous of all nonhuman primates, relying on a diet of insects, frogs, and lizards. Their eyes are unusual not only in their very large size relative to the size of the head, but also for their inability to move. To compensate for this, tarsiers can rotate their head 180 degrees. They are generally solitary though some species are known to form monogamous pair bonds.

## Hominoidea

This superfamily consists of humans and the apes. It comprises two families: Hylobatidae (the so-called lesser apes, the gibbons and siamangs), and Hominidae (great apes, including humans), and three subfamilies: Pongine (orangutans), Gorilline (gorillas), and Hominine (chimpanzees/bonobos and humans). Hominoids share the following features:

- Largest of the primates (with the exception of the gibbons and siamangs)
- Diurnal
- No tail
- Nails on all digits
- More complex behaviour
- More complex brain and cognitive abilities
- Increased period of infant development and dependency

## Hylobatidae

The eight species of gibbons and siamangs that make up this family are also referred to as lesser apes because of their smaller size compared to the other apes. Confined to the tropical rainforests of Southeast Asia, they exhibit a number of characteristics that reflect their arboreal way of life, including a locomotor pattern characterized by brachiation. This is reflected in their long arms relative to body size; long, curved fingers with reduced thumbs; and highly mobile shoulder joints designed for suspension and arm-over-arm movement. The most impressive brachiators of all nonhuman primates, gibbons and siamangs can move through the trees at speeds of over 50 km an hour! They rely heavily on fruit and show little sexual dimorphism. Males and females form monogamous pair bonds; males are actively involved in rearing their young, and females participate in territorial defence using distinct vocalizations, which have been described as songs (Marshall and Marshall 1976).

## Hominidae

Orangutans are found only in Borneo (*Pongo pygmaeus*) and Sumatra (*Pongo abelii*). The largest of the Asian apes, and in fact the largest living arboreal mammal, they are mainly solitary. Unlike the other great apes, they move quadrupedally along the ground on their fists, and move slowly and cautiously through the trees using both arms and legs. They are mainly frugivorous and show pronounced sexual dimorphism. Dominant males have large fat pads on their faces as well as large **laryngeal sacs** that enable them to make loud vocalizations. Currently numbering approximately 50,000, wild orangutans may face extinction within the next ten to twenty years (http://www.orangutanrepublik.org/index_threats.htm).

**laryngeal sac**
an expanded larynx or voice box used to produce vocalizations

Gorillas are the largest of the primates and inhabit the forests of western and central Africa. They are divided into two species (*Gorilla beringei* and *Gorilla gorilla*) and four subspecies: the western and eastern lowland gorilla, the mountain gorilla, and the Cross River gorilla. These subspecies differ from one another with respect to a number of features, including the colour and length of their hair and the size of their jaws and teeth. Their large body size—ranging up to 200 kg or more in males—means that they spend most of their time on the ground, where they walk on their knuckles. They are almost exclusively vegetarian and rely heavily on a diet of leaves. Mature adult males (Figure 5.13) are referred to as **silverbacks** because of the saddle of white hair across their backs. They have large **sagittal crests** on the top of their skulls that serve to anchor their powerful jaw muscles. They live in groups consisting of one or occasionally two adult males, a number of adult females, and their offspring.

Chimpanzees (*Pan troglodytes*), the best known of all nonhuman primates thanks to the extensive field studies of Jane Goodall and others, live in equatorial regions of eastern, central, and western Africa. Though they are arboreal, they spend most

**silverback**
a mature adult male gorilla characterized by a saddle of white hair across his back

**sagittal crest**
a large ridge of bone running along the sagittal suture of the skull; it serves to anchor the muscles involved in chewing

**Figure 5.13** Primatologist Dian Fossey's research on mountain gorillas was featured in the film *Gorillas in the Mist.*

Courtesy of Pascale Sicotte

**CHAPTER 5** What It Means to Be a Primate

of their time on the ground and exhibit a variety of locomotor patterns, including knuckle-walking, semibrachiation, and occasional bipedalism. They are omnivorous and eat a wide range of foods, including small game and other primates, which some groups hunt collectively. Males are larger and heavier than females, but their degree of sexual dimorphism is less pronounced than in gorillas and orangutans. They live in large, fluid communities, and the females leave the group of their birth when they become sexually mature. Their complex social behaviour has been the focus of numerous studies, and they have been used as models for early hominin behaviour.

Bonobos (*Pan paniscus*) (Figure 5.14), sometimes referred to as pygmy chimpanzees, are, in fact, similar in height to the common chimpanzee *Pan troglodytes* but are more slightly built. They also differ from chimps in having smaller heads and dark skin on their face. Restricted to the forests of the Democratic Republic of Congo, they have not been as well studied as chimpanzees—owing, in part, to political instability in the Congo. They live in large communities and exhibit slight sexual dimorphism. Like chimpanzees, they are omnivorous and eat a variety of foods, including small mammals. They are well known for their frequent use of non-reproductive sex to facilitate group cohesion and to reduce stress (de Waal 1990).

**Figure 5.14**   Bonobos are one of the few species of primates that engage in face-to-face copulation.

Martyn Colbeck/Photolibrary/Getty Images

Humans and our earlier human ancestors (hominins) are members of the Tribe Hominini (see Chapter 8), a distinct taxonomic category that recognizes a number of anatomical and behavioural characteristics that distinguish us from other members of the Primate order. Unlike other primates, we live in virtually every environment on the planet, and now even off of it! We eat pretty much every food available to us, and we are the only primates who are **obligate** bipeds. As such, we have some unique skeletal adaptations related to our mode of locomotion (see Chapter 8). The phases of our **life history**—which differ from those of the other primates—include a longer gestation period, a prolonged period of infant dependency, a later period of sexual maturation, and a longer life span, as well as a lack of estrus and a much longer postreproductive phase in human females. We also have a larger and more complex brain and are the only primates capable of spoken language. Our most distinctive feature is our complete reliance on material culture for survival.

## The Nonhuman Primate Genome

In Chapter 3 we talked about the human genome project. The first call for an international primate genome project to map the genome of nonhuman primate species came in 2000 (McConkey and Varki 2000; Vandeberg et al. 2000). The rationale behind this initiative is the close genetic, metabolic, and physiological similarity of some nonhuman primates to humans. As such, detailed knowledge of their genome has tremendous potential to contribute to our understanding of human disease, evolution, and population genetics. The genomes of two nonhuman primate species—rhesus macaques (Gibbs et al. 2007) and chimpanzees (Chimpanzee Sequencing and Analysis Consortium 2005)—have already been mapped, and efforts are

**obligate**

by virtue of necessity; our recent ancestors of the past 2–3 million years had developed a number of adaptations that effectively obliged them to adopt a terrestrial, bipedal form of locomotion

**life history**

the occurrence (timing, duration, etc.) of specific events and traits characteristic of a species. Common life history variables include gestation length, interbirth interval, age at sexual maturity, and maximum life span currently under way to map the genomes of additional species, including marmosets, orangutans, gibbons, and gorillas (Marques-Bonet, Ryder, Eichler 2009). What have the results of these studies revealed so far? Humans and chimpanzees share 99% of their genes. At the same time, however, a number of differences are apparent with respect to the genes involved in olfaction (i.e., smell), speech, digestion, hearing, inflammatory and immune responses, and resistance to disease (Clark et al. 2003; Varki and Nelson 2007; Chimpanzee Sequencing and Analysis Consortium, 2005). Chimpanzees, for example, have a significantly higher number of functioning olfactory receptor genes compared to humans (Varki and Nelson 2007).

http://www.genome
.gov/11509418

## Primate Cloning

Reports of the first primate to be cloned utilizing a method involving splitting an embryo appeared in newspapers worldwide in January 2000. Employing a technique different from that used to clone Dolly the sheep, researchers split an eight-cell embryo of a rhesus macaque into four genetically identical two-cell embryos and implanted them into surrogate mothers, one of whom gave birth to a healthy female offspring (Chan et al. 2000). Why are scientists so keen to clone primates? Unlike mice, on which medical treatments are typically tested, monkeys are much more closely related to humans and make excellent models for testing new drugs and other treatments. The hope is that such clones can be used to develop treatments for life-threatening diseases such as diabetes and Parkinson's. Having genetically identical monkeys would also allow researchers to evaluate more accurately their responses to different treatments.

# SUMMARY

As you have seen in this chapter, primates are quite generalized compared to other mammals and share a set of characteristics that reflect not only their common evolutionary history but also their adaptation to similar environments. Primates share a number of anatomical and behavioural features, but they also exhibit considerable morphological and behavioural diversity. You have been introduced to the major groups of primates and the characteristics that distinguish them from one another. New genetic evidence has led to revisions in primate classification, and analyses of the genes of our closest living relatives, the chimpanzees, have revealed some important differences between this species and humans. Many primate species are critically endangered; sadly, some will likely become extinct within your lifetime. Studies of living primates are vital, especially if we are to develop strategies to save them from disappearing forever. In the next chapter we will discuss various aspects of primate behaviour and explore how those behaviours may have evolved.

# CORE REVIEW

### In what ways do primates differ from other mammals?

Primates share a set of characteristics that include a generalized skeletal structure allowing for great flexibility in movement, a marked tendency toward upright posture in the upper body, and flexible shoulder joints and clavicles. They also have grasping hands and feet with opposable thumbs and big toes that allow for a variety of grips. In addition, all primates have flattened nails and tactile pads on at least one digit. They rely to a greater extent on vision than do other mammals, as reflected in their forward-facing eyes and overlapping fields of view, and their decreased reliance on smell is reflected in a reduction in the size of the snout and the olfactory areas of the brain. Primates have diphyodont and heterodont dentition consisting of two sets of different kinds of teeth that serve a variety of functions, reflecting their generally omnivorous diet. Finally, they have a larger neocortex than other mammals, longer gestation periods, lower reproductive rates, a longer period of infant dependency, and an extended life span.

### How might these characteristics have evolved?

Several hypotheses have been proposed to explain the evolution of primate characteristics. The arboreal hypothesis posits that primate features such as forward-facing eyes and grasping hands with nails instead of claws evolved as adaptations to an arboreal way of life. The visual predation hypothesis posits that these features arose as adaptations to insect predation. A more recent hypothesis, termed the angiosperm radiation hypothesis, argues that primate characteristics evolved as adaptations to a diet of flowers and nectar. The origin of these traits has also been linked to the presence of predators, specifically snakes. Many primatologists today argue that primate characteristics likely arose in response to a variety of different environmental factors.

### Where do primates live, how do they move about, and what do they eat?

Most nonhuman primates live in tropical and subtropical regions of the world. They occupy a wide diversity of habitats ranging from the swampy forests of Borneo and Sumatra to the snowy mountains of Japan. Most primates are arboreal and spend the majority of their time in the trees; however, some species have adapted to a terrestrial way of life. They use a variety of different methods of locomotion, including quadrupedalism, bipedalism, brachiation, and vertical clinging and leaping. Primates have a primarily omnivorous diet that includes fruits, leaves, insects, and small mammals. Most species tend to favour certain types of foods, and some have specialized digestive systems to process the foods they consume.

### What types of social groups do they live in?

Primates live in a variety of social groups. These include monogamous, single-male/multifemale, polyandrous, and multimale/multifemale groups. A few species, such as orangutans, tend to be solitary, though males and females interact for the purpose of mating, and females usually forage with their offspring.

### What distinguishes prosimians from monkeys, and monkeys from apes?

Prosimians are smaller than monkeys, possess a tooth comb and grooming claw, have a well-developed sense of smell, and are primarily nocturnal. Monkeys are smaller than apes. Also, the latter are distinctive for their more complex behaviour, more complex brain, greater cognitive abilities, and increased period of infant development and dependency.

### What are some of the differences between New World and Old World monkeys?

New World monkeys are smaller than Old World monkeys. Most species have a dental formula of 2.1.3.3, and some species have a prehensile tail. In contrast, Old World monkeys exhibit a greater size range and a greater degree of sexual dimorphism. They also possess a dental formula of 2.1.2.3., and some species have ischial callosities.

### In what ways are humans unique as primates?

Among primates, humans are unique in a number of ways. We are the only primates who are obligate bipeds. We also have a longer gestation period, a prolonged period of infant dependency, a later period of sexual maturation, a longer life span, and a lack of estrus. Human females also experience menopause. In addition, we are the only primates capable of spoken language. Our most distinctive feature is our complete reliance on material culture for survival.

**What does genetic evidence tell us about our relationship to other primates?**

Molecular studies have revealed the close genetic relationship between humans and other primates, most notably chimpanzees, with whom we share nearly 99% of our DNA. These studies have also revealed interesting differences between human and chimp DNA with respect to genes involved in olfaction, speech, digestion, hearing, inflammatory and immune responses, and resistance to disease.

## CRITICAL THINKING QUESTIONS

1. What allows different species of primates to live in the same environment?
2. What makes Old World monkeys among the most successful of all primates, apart from humans?

## GROUP DISCUSSION QUESTIONS

1. Considerable efforts have been made to map the chimpanzee genome. Is this species the best choice for an international primate genome project, or would other primate species be better candidates?
2. Should nonhuman primates be used in medical research? Should we clone nonhuman primates? Why or why not?

## RESOURCES AND READINGS

- F. Ankel-Simons, *Primate Anatomy: An Introduction*, 3rd ed. (New York: Academic Press, 2007).
- C.J. Campbell, A. Fuentes, K.C. MacKinnon, M. Panger, and S.K. Bearder, eds., *Primates in Perspective* (Oxford: Oxford University Press, 2006).
- B.M.F. Galdikas, N.E. Briggs, L.K. Sheeran, G.L. Shapiro, and J. Goodall, eds., *All Apes Great and Small: Volume I: African Apes* (Netherlands: Springer, 2002).
- C. Groves, *Primate Taxonomy* (Washington: Smithsonian, 2001).
- S.M. Lehman and J. Fleagle, eds., *Primate Biogeography: Progress and Prospects* (New York: Springer, 2006).
- R.W. Sussman, *Primate Ecology and Social Structure: New World Monkeys* (New York: Pearson Prentice Hall, 2003).
- D.R. Swindler, *Primate Dentition: An Introduction to the Teeth of Non-human Primates* (Cambridge: Cambridge University Press, 2002).
- P.F. Whitehead and C.J. Jolly, eds., *Old World Monkeys* (Cambridge: Cambridge University Press, 2000).

# Chapter 6 | Primate Behavioural Ecology

## OVERVIEW

You have now been introduced to our closest living relatives, the nonhuman primates. As you have seen, they exhibit a great deal of diversity in appearance, habitats, locomotor patterns, feeding strategies, and dietary adaptations. Similarly, their behaviours vary greatly and carry a wide range of meanings. This chapter introduces you to primate behavioural ecology—that is, the study of the ways in which primates adapt behaviourally to their environments. We begin by briefly outlining the history of primatology. We then explore what it means to live in social groups; examine aggressive, affiliative, and sexual behaviours/reproductive strategies; and consider whether nonhuman primates possess culture and language. By the end of this chapter you will appreciate the many similarities we share with our primate cousins. At the same time, you will see that certain behaviours remain unique to humans.

## CORE CONCEPTS

■ behavioural ecology, dominance, altruism, kin selection, sexual selection, reproductive strategy, infanticide

## CORE QUESTIONS

■ What are the advantages and disadvantages of studying primates in captivity versus in the wild?

■ What benefits do primates derive from living in social groups?

■ What types of reproductive strategies do primates utilize? How do male and female strategies differ?

■ In what contexts does tool use occur among nonhuman primates?

■ What strategies do primates use to maintain social stability and cohesion?

■ How do primates communicate? What purposes does their communication system serve?

*If you are studying an animal, or a people, or even a language
that is struggling for survival, how can you not interfere?
To turn your back on your subject is to turn your
back ... on what it means to be human.*

Biruté Galdikas, Primatologist

Courtesy of Sylvie Colquhoun

# PROLOGUE: PRIMATES "R" US

The study of our nearest relatives, the nonhuman primates, is carried out as often as not by researchers in non-anthropological disciplines (e.g., psychology, medicine), and primatologists publish in journals dedicated solely to that field of study, attend meetings emphasizing primatological themes, and are members of various professional societies devoted to the science of primatology. All of that said, it is also true that primatology maintains a unique relationship with anthropology generally, and with biological anthropology in particular. The reasons are matters not simply of history, but also of pedagogy. Humans are primates, and our understanding of human origins and human patterns of social and sexual behaviour is enriched when we examine primate origins and behaviours; indeed, our understanding would be poorer without that examination. In the following pages we explore a number of facets of nonhuman primate **behavioural ecology**. We urge you, as you read, to reflect on both the differences and the similarities—on the ways that primate behaviours are distinct with respect to our own, but also on the ways they parallel human patterns. But be aware of what has been called the "trap of the present": the diversity of primate and human behaviour that can be observed today represents millions of years of independent evolution. Thus, behavioural similarities among primate species (and ourselves) may say nothing about evolutionary connections (**homology**) and everything about how two (or more) species converged on the same "solution" in similar ecological circumstances (**homoplasy**).

## THE ROOTS OF PRIMATOLOGY

The first studies of nonhuman primates date back to the 17th century, when scientists dissected primates to examine their anatomical similarities to humans and other animals. While primate anatomy continued to be a major research focus well into the 20th century, studies of the behaviour of **captive** primates were also undertaken. At the same time, scientists became increasingly aware of the need to provide a constant supply of animals for medical research. This led to the establishment of colonies of **provisioned** primates, including the first major primate breeding facility in the United States, established in 1930 by psychologist Robert Yerkes in Florida,[1] and a colony of **free-ranging** rhesus macaques established in 1938 by psychologist Clarence Ray Carpenter on Cayo Santiago Island off the coast of Puerto Rico. In the early 1970s, a troop of Japanese macaques (*Macaca fuscata*) were relocated from their home range of Arashiyama, near Tokyo, to a colony in Texas. This colony, known as the Arashiyama West group, has been the focus of considerable study by University of Calgary primatologists Mary Pavelka and Linda Marie Fedigan (see Box 6.1, p. 125).

The first field studies were also initiated during this time period to document the behaviours exhibited by species in their natural habitats. Following the Second World War, Japanese primatologists began collecting data on *Macaca fuscata*, and their long-term studies have produced an impressive body of data on the behaviour of these animals and many other primate species. Experimental studies of primates in laboratory settings also became popular during the 1950s and 1960s. These included social deprivation experiments conducted by psychologist Harry Harlow on rhesus macaques and the attempt to teach American Sign Language to a chimpanzee named Washoe. The 1960s also marked the launch of three extraordinary field studies: Jane Goodall's study of chimpanzees (Goodall 1986) (Figure 6.1), Dian Fossey's research on mountain gorillas

**behavioural ecology**

the study of the ways in which primates adapt behaviourally to their environments

**homology**

Similarity by virtue of evolutionary decent from a common ancestor

**homoplasy**

Similarity by virtue of convergent evolution, rather than an ancestor-descendant relationship

**captive**

housed in environments such as zoos and colonies where movement is restricted

**provisioned**

supplied with food

**free-ranging**

animals whose movements are not hindered by humans

http://www.janegoodall.ca

**Figure 6.1** Jane Goodall has studied the chimpanzees of Gombe Stream National Park, Tanzania, for over 40 years.

© Bettmann/Corbis

---

1. This colony has since relocated to Georgia and is now known as the Yerkes Regional Primate Centre.

(Fossey 1983), and Biruté Galdikas's study of orangutans (Galdikas 1995) (Figure 6.2). These and other long-term field studies allowed researchers to examine life histories, demographic shifts, and the impact of environmental changes on behavioural patterns; they also turned upside down many of our notions about nonhuman primates. Canadian primatologists have made significant contributions to our knowledge of nonhuman primates, including variation in demography and life-history in ring-tailed lemurs (Gould, Sussman, and Sauther 2003) (Figure 6.3), the impact of predation on activity patterns (Colquhoun 2006), and predictors of reproductive success in capuchins (Fedigan, Carnegie, and Jack 2008).

There are disadvantages to studying captive primates. A schedule of regular provisioning means that their natural foraging patterns may not be observable. Captivity may alter their activity levels so that animals normally active during the day become active at night instead. Confined spaces may alter locomotor patterns and increase the

**Figure 6.2**  Biruté Galdikas teaches primatology at Simon Fraser University and has spent the last 40 years studying orangutans.

Rodney Brindamour/National Geographic Stock

http://lemur.duke.edu

**Figure 6.3**  Primatologist Lisa Gould observing a ring-tailed lemur in Madagascar.

Courtesy of Lisa Gould

level of aggression within a group. The lack of seasonal changes can affect reproductive schedules so that birth rates are either increased or decreased. Captive primates, such as those imported for biomedical research, have been known to carry pathogens that can be transmitted to humans.[2]

There are also disadvantages to studying primates in the field. Working in remote places can be expensive and dangerous. It takes time to locate the subjects and for the animals to become **habituated**.[3] It takes still more time to identify all the individuals in a group, map out their relationships to one another, and recognize their various behaviours. While field studies of unprovisioned animals can provide better information about foraging patterns, researchers working in the field may occasionally give food to their study subjects in order to more closely observe group dynamics. Interestingly, the provisioning of Japanese macaques with sweet potatoes during field studies in the 1950s resulted in the adoption and spread of a unique behaviour in which one of the animals, an adult female, began washing the potatoes to remove sand, a practice that subsequently spread to other members of the group.

Primate behavioural ecology—a field that emerged in the 1970s—has moved away from emphasizing description toward the use of standardized methods of data collection, allowing primatologists to conduct broader comparative studies and to test hypotheses about the adaptive significance of various behaviours. More attention is also being directed toward primate conservation, and many primatologists are actively involved in efforts to protect these animals (see Chapter 15).

## SOCIAL LIVING

In Chapter 5 we talked about the various forms of social organization exhibited by contemporary nonhuman primates (Figure 6.4), and it is reasonable to assume that their ancestors lived in a variety of different social groups as well (Müller and Soligo 2005). Living in a group provides a number of benefits to its members. It maximizes food exploitation, for a greater number of individuals are more likely to find food than a smaller number. This is especially important where food resources are unevenly distributed and hard to find. Primates living in social groups can share information on feeding sites and defend food resources. Social groups provide members with a greater number of mating partners, thereby increasing their reproductive fitness. Such groups offer protection from predators as well as from primates in other groups. Help in caring for offspring is available. Finally, groups allow for the transmission of behaviours from one member to another.

Group living also has drawbacks. Those of you who have shared a house or apartment know that living in groups can lead to conflict. Larger groups are associated with increased competition for food and mating partners, as well as increased stress, as reflected in lower birth rates and greater incidence of aggression.[4] Furthermore, increased group size may also facilitate the spread of infectious diseases (Caillaud et al. 2006).

In most primate societies, individuals are organized into **dominance hierarchies**. In this structure, some individuals are of higher **rank** than others. These hierarchies are more pronounced in singlemale/multifemale and multimale/multifemale groups, in which males must compete with one another for access to females, a notion grounded in Darwin's theory of **sexual selection** (discussed later in this chapter). These hierarchies serve an important function—they provide social stability and reduce conflict within a group. **Dominant** individuals generally have greater access to food resources and mating partners, though higher rank is not invariably associated with greater reproductive success: in species among which female choice plays an important role in mating strategies, **subordinate** males may succeed in gaining mates (see below). Males may attain their rank through physical strength, aggression, and the ability to mobilize support within their group by forming alliances, often with related

**habituated**
accustomed to the presence of humans

**dominance hierarchy**
a social structure in which males or females hold positions of rank determined either through competition or inheritance

**rank**
the social position or status of an individual within a group

**sexual selection**
a theory proposed by Charles Darwin to explain why males of some species adopt behaviours or morphologies that may not appear adaptive in terms of natural selection, but that in fact enhance reproductive opportunities as a result of successful competition with other males and their subsequent selection by females as potential mates

**dominant**
a higher ranking individual

**subordinate**
a lower ranking individual

---

2. A well-known case occurred in 1989 and involved a research lab in Reston, Virginia, where a group of macaques imported from the Philippines was found to carry a strain of the Ebola virus. Fortunately, the virus proved to be fatal only to the monkeys.

3. Unhabituated animals are likely to run away or stop what they are doing when humans are near.

4. One of the ways in which stress can be investigated in primates is by measuring hormone levels in body fluids.

**Figure 6.4**  Social living provides baboons and other primates with mating partners and protection from predators.

Courtesy of Travis Steffens

males. Rank may also be inherited from the mother, as happens among Japanese macaques and savannah baboons. Top-ranking individuals in a group are typically referred to as **alpha** males or females.

Separate dominance hierarchies may exist for males and females, and males are usually dominant over females. In a small number of species such as monogamous gibbons, however, the two sexes are codominant; in still other species—notably lemurs—females are dominant over males. Female dominance hierarchies tend to be more stable; male hierarchies can change rapidly depending on age, body size, kinship, and other factors.

Rank within a dominance hierarchy can affect an individual member's health by influencing susceptibility to stress-related diseases (Sapolsky 2005). Also, dominance rank can affect reproductive success by influencing the survival of offspring, the age at which offspring reach sexual maturity, and the rate of reproduction. Among the Gombe chimpanzees, for instance, higher ranking females were found to have higher infant survival rates, more rapidly maturing female offspring, and reduced **interbirth interval** resulting in higher fertility rates, collectively reflecting preferential access to better foraging areas (Pusey, Williams, and Goodall 1997). An interesting example of delayed sexual maturation is exhibited by orangutans, among whom the presence of a dominant male can lead to the arrested development of subordinate males so that they fail to develop secondary sexual characteristics, such as the classic "cheek-flange" (Maggioncalda, Czekala, and Sapolsky 2002; Winkler, 2005).

**alpha**
the highest ranking individual in a group

**interbirth interval**
the length of time between successive births

## DO NONHUMAN PRIMATES HAVE CULTURE?

Perhaps no other primate behaviour has garnered as much attention as tool use. Indeed, the use of tools is what has made primates—the great apes in particular—such attractive models for studying early hominin behaviour (though this approach has been critiqued recently; see Sayers and Lovejoy, 2008). The first observation of tool use among primates in the

**Figure 6.5** East African chimpanzees have been observed using sticks to fish for termites.

Stan Osolinski/Photolibrary/Getty Images

**Figure 6.6** Chimpanzees of the Taï Forest in West Africa use hammerstones to crack open nuts.

Michael Nichols/National Geographic/Getty Images

wild dates back to the 1960s, when Jane Goodall witnessed Gombe chimpanzees modifying and using twigs to extract termites from mounds (Figure 6.5). Since then, numerous incidents of tool use have been recorded among both captive and wild primates, and considerable variation has been observed within and between species. For instance, chimpanzees living in the Taï Forest of West Africa typically use hammerstones to crack open nuts (Figure 6.6), while those living in the savannah woodlands of western Tanzania use sticks to dig for tubers, roots, and bulbs—an activity they engage in during the rainy season, when other foods are also abundant (Hernandez-Aguilar, Moore, and Pickering 2007). In Senegal, chimpanzees have been observed fashioning spears from twigs to capture prosimians (bushbabies) in the hollows of tree trunks and branches (Pruetz and Bertolani 2007), while a chimpanzee population from the Congo Basin uses two distinct sets of tools to extract termites from their nests depending on whether the nests are subterranean or above ground (Sanz, Morgan, and Gulick 2004).

A synthesis by Whiten and colleagues (1999) of data derived from seven chimpanzee field studies revealed significant variation in behavioural repertoires among communities in East and West Africa. More specifically, 39 different behavioural patterns were documented, suggesting the existence of chimpanzee 'cultures' that are socially learned and are exhibited by multiple members of a group (ibid.). A subsequent study provided additional evidence that behavioural differences observed among chimpanzee groups are cultural rather than genetically determined (Lycett, Collard, and McGrew 2007). Furthermore, female chimpanzees, who leave their birth group on reaching sexual maturity, appear to be primarily responsible for transmitting cultural traits (Lind and Lindenfors 2010).

Archaeologist Julio Mercader of the University of Calgary has recently conducted a fascinating study of the antiquity of tool use among chimpanzees. He and his team investigated a collection of what appeared to be stone tools recovered from the Taï Forest (Figure 6.7). Dating to 4,300 years ago, the tools had traces of starch residue, suggesting that they had been used to process the same species of nuts exploited by chimpanzees in that region today. The data also indicate that chimpanzees transported stones from other locations to areas where they were used repeatedly (Mercader, Panger, and Boesch 2002; Mercader et al. 2007). This finding has important implications for the origins of tool use among humans (see Chapter 9).

Tool use has also been observed among captive and wild orangutans (Figure 6.8). Biruté Galdikas (1982), for example, recorded several incidents in the field during which individuals used sticks to scratch their backs or scare off wasps. More recently, primatologist Carel van Schaik observed orangutans of the Suaq Balimbing swamp in Sumatra using and modifying tools to extract fruit, honey, and insects. He and his team also documented the transmission of this behaviour to other members of the group (van Schaik et al. 2003). Interestingly, other orangutan populations in Borneo and Sumatra do not appear to use tools, leading to speculation that tool use by the Suaq orangutans may reflect their insect-rich environment.

**Figure 6.7** Anthropologist Julio Mercader of the University of Calgary has found evidence of chimpanzee stone tool use dating back 4,300 years.

Courtesy of Ken Bendiktsen

It is also possible that tool use has not yet been acquired by other orangutan groups. Whatever the case, van Schaik argues that the common ancestor of apes and humans likely used tools and that great ape cultures may have existed for at least 14 million years (ibid.).

Among chimpanzees and gorillas, tool use is typically related to food procurement and processing. Recent observations of wild gorillas in northern Congo, however, have revealed the use of tools for other purposes. In one case, a gorilla was observed using a stick to test the depth of a pool of water before wading through it (Figure 6.9). In another case, a gorilla used the trunk of a small shrub as a bridge to cross a swampy area (Breuer, Ndoundou-Hockemba, and Fishlock 2005). Incidents of tool use have also been reported in captive bonobos (Hohmann and Fruth 2003). One individual, a captive male named Kanzi, acquired the ability to make and use stone tools by observing humans doing the same. Kanzi also independently developed his own technique of making tools by throwing stones against a hard surface to fracture them (Toth, Schick, and Savage-Rumbaugh 1993; Schick et al. 1999). Wild bonobos have been observed using leaves as sponges to soak up water, throwing sticks and branches at other bonobos and at humans, and using twigs to scratch their back or fend off aggressive bees (Hohmann and Fruth 2003).

Tool use is not restricted to the great apes. Several species of monkeys have been observed using tools in the wild. For example, capuchin monkeys in the Caatinga forests of Brazil have been seen using stones to dig for grubs and tubers and to crack open seeds, as well as twigs and branches to probe for insects and honey. This behaviour, though, was restricted to the dry season, when food resources were scarce (de A. Moura and Lee 2004). One study reported a total of 31 incidents of tool use and 8 different types of tool use behaviour in capuchins in Santa Rosa National Park, Costa Rica (Chevalier-Skolnikoff, 1990).

## Primate Medicine: Is There a Doctor in the Forest?

The observation that primates sometimes consume or anoint themselves with plants, insects, and soils that have little or no nutritional value has led to speculation that some of these items serve medicinal purposes. Self-medication by animals, also known as **zoopharmacognosy**, is attracting increasing attention among primatologists as well as other scientists searching for

**Figure 6.8** Orangutans have recently been observed using tools in the wild.

Courtesy of Dennis O'Neil

**Figure 6.9** A gorilla uses a stick to test the depth of the water.

AP Photo/Wildlife Conservation Society, Thomas Breuer

**zoopharmacognosy**
the self-medication by animals with plants, soils, and other natural substances

**CHAPTER 6** Primate Behavioural Ecology

natural substances that could be used to develop drugs for human use. Employing plants and insects as treatments for ailments such as parasitic infections and gastrointestinal upsets has been documented in a number of primate species (Huffman 1997). Capuchin monkeys in Costa Rica, for example, have been observed rubbing themselves with oranges, lemons, and limes, which are known to contain antibacterial compounds. They have also been observed rubbing their fur with the same plants often used by local indigenous people to treat skin conditions (Baker 1996), which raises the interesting possibility that humans are adding to their own traditional knowledge by borrowing from their nonhuman relatives. Wedge-capped capuchins in Venezuela intentionally rub themselves with millipedes known to contain compounds that act as insect repellents, especially against mosquitoes that transmit botflies (Valderrama et al. 2000). Pregnant and lactating female sifakas in western Madagascar consume greater amounts of tannin-rich plants than other members of their group. The consumption of tannins has been linked to increased body weight and increased milk secretion. In addition, tannins have antiparasitic properties (Carrai, Borgognini-Tarli, and Huffman 2003). Chimpanzees of Tanzania's Mahale Mountains National Park increased consumption of plants with known medicinal properties during the rainy season, when rates of nematode infection were higher than normal (Huffman et al. 1997). Similarly, bitter pith chewing[5] has been linked to parasite-related diseases in the same group of chimpanzees (Ohigashi et al. 1994). The use of medicinal plants to treat parasitic infections and gastrointestinal upsets has been documented in bonobos and gorillas as well (Huffman 1997).

**Geophagy**, the intentional consumption of soil, has been observed in many primate species (including humans). This practice appears to serve a variety of functions, including neutralizing plant toxins, treating gastrointestinal disorders and diarrhea, providing nutrients, and protecting against malaria (Burton, Bolton, and Campbell 1999; Glander 1994; Krishnamani and Mahaney 2000). For example, the practice of eating soil together with clumps of leaves, documented in chimpanzees in Kibale National Park, appears to enhance the antimalarial properties of the leaves (Klein, Fröhlich, and Krief 2008). Zoopharmacognosy is a fascinating area of study, which leaves us to wonder about the antiquity and evolutionary origin of such behaviours and the degree to which they may have been practised by early hominins.

**geophagy**
the intentional consumption of soil

## AGONISTIC BEHAVIOURS

**agonistic**
threatening behaviour that is directed toward an opponent or adversary

Acts of aggression, or **agonistic** behaviours, are common in many primate communities. They occur between individuals of the same sex or the opposite sex; between related or unrelated individuals; and between individuals of different rank. The frequency of these acts depends on a number of factors, including the availability of food resources, mating partners, and space. Aggressive behaviours may take the form of threats conveyed by facial expressions and gestures, such as baring the canine teeth; or they may rise to the level of physical fighting resulting in serious injury and occasionally death. Different forms of aggression characterize males and females: males tend to have brief face-to-face encounters, whereas female encounters tend to be more prolonged.

The first observations of intergroup conflict among chimpanzees were made in the 1970s, when Jane Goodall and her colleagues observed attacks between neighbouring groups that resulted in the death of a number of individuals (Goodall et al. 1979). Initially thought to be a rarity, these acts of aggression are now known to be a common feature of chimpanzee society and to occur in the context of defending territories, food resources, and females (Wrangham and Peterson 1996). Intragroup conflict has also been documented in many primate species. In chimpanzee as well as olive baboon communities, for instance, attacks by males on females have often been recorded. Estrous females are often targeted, suggesting that males use violence and physical coercion in order to gain sexual access. Aggressive encounters associated

---

5. Pith refers to the soft, spongy substance in the centre of the stems of many plants.

with competition for mating partners and territory have also been documented among male orangutans. Similarly, acts of intrasexual aggression in the context of mating have been observed among wild bonobos (Hohmann and Fruth 2003).

One of the interesting results of long-term field studies that have been conducted on gorillas has been the finding that these animals are much less aggressive than previously believed. Indeed, gorillas have long been portrayed as ferocious animals. One of the most colourful descriptions of their reportedly fierce nature comes from the account of a 19th-century American missionary named Dr. Savage, who wrote: "When confronted with a gorilla the hunter must stand his ground while listening to the horrifying cries and watching the onrushing monster, and then as the animal gets closer and closer, the courageous hunter steps forward and puts the barrel of the gun in the gorilla's mouth and pulls the trigger. If the gun fires the gorilla drops dead but if the gun does not fire, the gorilla crushes the barrel between its teeth reversing the intended order of events" (Savage 1847, 423, quoted in Swindler 1998, 13).[6]

# AFFILIATIVE BEHAVIOURS

## Grooming

Among primates, one of the most common **affiliative** behaviours is grooming (Figure 6.10). A type of **altruistic** behaviour, it serves a number of important functions, including removing **ectoparasites**, reducing stress, reinforcing social bonds, currying favours such as food, sex, and protection, and gaining access to infants. Grooming occurs between lower and higher ranking individuals, males and females, related and unrelated individuals, and parents and their offspring. Its frequency and duration depend on a number of factors, including group size, sex ratio, and female dispersal patterns. For example, primates living in larger groups tend to spend more time grooming than those in smaller groups,[7] whereas those living in small groups may spend very little time engaged in this activity. Females who remain with their natal group spend a greater amount of time grooming than females who leave their birth group upon maturity (Lehmann, Korstjens, and Dunbar 2007). Rank and kinship also play an important role in the distribution of grooming within social groups (Schino 2001).

**affiliative**
amicable behaviours that promote social cohesion

**altruistic**
behaviour that benefits other members of a group but is either of no benefit to the individual engaged in it or is harmful to that individual

**ectoparasites**
parasites on the outside of the body, i.e., in the fur

## Alliances

Cooperation is a vital component of primate social groups. Primates depend on one another for their survival, and affiliative behaviour has been observed in virtually all primate species (de Waal 1990). It has been hypothesized that this behaviour evolved indirectly through **kin selection**—that is, the tendency of primates to direct beneficial behaviour toward their relatives, thereby contributing to the survival of some of their alleles.[8] Indeed, kinship plays an important role in primate society by fostering alliances and strong social bonds. Kin selection may also explain why primates engage in altruistic behaviour such as grooming and providing care and protection for related members of their group.

**Figure 6.10** Grooming is a pleasurable activity that reduces tension and reinforces social bonds.

AP Photo/Shuji Kajiyama

**kin selection**
the tendency of individuals to direct beneficial behaviour toward relatives living within the same social group

---

6. Savage believed not only that the gorilla was an aggressive carnivore, but also that it was a species of orangutan!

7. Members of large groups may spend as much as 20% of their day grooming.

8. The kin selection hypothesis was originally proposed in the 1960s by British evolutionary biologist William Hamilton.

**CHAPTER 6** Primate Behavioural Ecology

Within primate societies, individuals often form alliances for the purpose of getting access to food resources and mating partners, gaining protection from other members of the group, or launching an attack against a third party. Alliances may be formed between members of the same sex, members of the opposite sex, biologically related individuals, unrelated individuals, and individuals of different ages and social ranks. Some of these alliances, such as mating **consortships**, may be short-term; others may last for years (Chapais 1995).

In some cases, predation by other animals may help forge an alliance between two different primate species. In the Taï forest, for example, red colobus and Diana monkeys peacefully coexist because they rely on different foods. When threatened by predators such as chimpanzees, however, the monkeys are drawn together. The smaller and faster-moving Diana monkeys act as guards, uttering alarm calls when they spot chimpanzees, while the colobus monkeys, who occupy higher areas in the trees, protect the Diana monkeys from birds of prey (Bshary and Noë 1997).

Female alliances typically occur in the context of food competition, though female bonobos may form alliances to dominate males. In contrast, male alliances occur in the context of competition for mates, hunting, the sharing of meat, and territorial defence. Alliances between male chimpanzees are usually interpreted as reflecting kinship, since males stay in the group of their birth while females leave their group when they reach sexual maturity. A recent genetic study of chimpanzees in Kibale National Park, however, has demonstrated that males who spend time together are not closely related to one another (Mitani, Merriwether, and Zhang 2000).

Continued conflict can be detrimental to a group, and the maintenance of group cohesion depends on cooperation among its members. In order to deal with conflicts arising within groups, primates have developed effective methods of conflict resolution. **Reconciliation** can take a number of forms, including approaching the victim of aggression after the conflict has ended and sitting beside them, making gestures such as touching, kissing, and embracing, grooming one's opponent, and vocalizing (de Waal 1989; Silk 2002).

## SEXUAL BEHAVIOUR AND REPRODUCTIVE STRATEGIES

For most primate species, sexual activity takes place when females are in estrus, a period of sexual receptivity correlated with ovulation. For many species this is signalled by various cues, including **proceptive behaviours** such as presenting hindquarters to males, visual cues such as swelling and pink coloration of the skin in the genital region, and olfactory cues such as **aliphatic acids** secreted within the vagina, the odour of which varies over the course of the reproductive cycle (Grammer, Fink, and Neave 2005). There is considerable variation among primates in the length of the reproductive cycle and its constituent phases (e.g., menstruation, receptivity; Hrdy and Whitten 1987), from as few as 15 days in the common marmoset to 50-plus days for the mouse lemur. Among anthropoids (including humans), reproductive cycles generally fall within a relatively narrow range of 28 to 32 days, though exceptions do occur. Primates differ in other aspects of reproductive timing, such as the interbirth interval (also known as birth spacing). Monogamous gibbons, for example, abstain from sexual activity for several years until a female's most recent offspring is weaned and she comes into estrus again. Galdikas and Wood (1990) found that among great apes, birth spacing varied from $45.5 \pm 1.2$ months for gorillas to $66.6 \pm 1.3$ months for chimpanzees and $92.6 \pm 2.4$ months for orangutans. Such differences reflect many factors, including variations in environment, social organization, and parental investment. With respect to the latter, as male investment in rearing increases, the interbirth interval decreases: male gorillas are active participants in caring for related offspring, while orangutan males offer virtually no assistance. Researchers have also speculated that some nonhuman primate females experience menopause, just as human females do (see Box 6.1).

**consortship**

among primates, a temporary affiliation of male and female for the purposes of mating and reproduction; in some species (e.g., chimpanzees), males may forcibly coerce females into a consortship

**reconciliation**

the process of making peace after an altercation

**proceptive behaviour**

actions, typically on the part of females, to initiate a sexual interaction; may include facial gestures, limb and body postures or movements, and sounds

**aliphatic acids**

a group of fatty acids which, secreted by a sexually receptive female, act as chemical messengers (pheromones) to alert males to her reproductive status

Courtesy of Mary Pavelka

As a species, humans are unique in experiencing the universal termination of menses and hence reproductive ability in all women who live past middle age. The maximum life span of *Homo sapiens* is 100 to 120 years, and less than halfway through this life span all women stop reproducing. Conversely, in the other primates, the vast majority of females continue to reproduce until very old age and then die within a normal interbirth interval. In orangutans, for example, females live on average about three years after having their last baby, but the normal interval between births for this species is seven to nine years. Think of Flo, from Jane Goodall's chimpanzee study. Among other things, Flo is famous for the sad tale of the difficulties she had dealing with her final infant Flame and her unweaned juvenile son Flint when Flo herself was a very old lady. This is the norm for the other primates: to continue reproducing until death or close to it. Termination of reproductive capability does occur occasionally in some individual monkeys

and apes, but even then it is much closer to the end of the life span. It occurs as part of the overall advanced aging of the individual, not in healthy middle age, as it does for women.

Why do human females experience universal termination of reproductive ability so far in advance of their ability to maintain life? How can natural selection favour phenotypes that do not reproduce? There are two possible explanations for this pattern in humans. Both human and great ape females stop reproducing by around age 50. The difference is that the great apes' maximum life span is also about 50 years, whereas humans continue to live as much as double that. This increase in the maximum human life span is a species-level characteristic and not an artifact of recent modernization (which affects local average life span or life expectancy, not maximum life span). Menopause is thus a by-product of selection for longer life span in humans. It is not clear why the reproductive system could not be extended along with the other systems—possibly 50 years is an inherent limit on primate (or even mammalian) female reproduction. Another possibility is the grandmother hypothesis: that over the course of human evolution, natural selection favoured females who stopped reproducing themselves and instead invested their efforts in the survival and reproductive success of their "children and grandchildren." Perhaps it is related to the high costs of labour and delivery in humans due to the obstetrical dilemma posed by our narrow birth canal (a consequence to bipedalism) and large brain size.

As a species characteristic, no, nonhuman primate females do not experience menopause. But the answer to the question partly depends on whether the term menopause is regarded simply as cessation of menses at the level of the individual, or whether it refers to a life history characteristic of a species.

For further reading, see Fedigan and Pavelka (2007), Pavelka et al. (2002), Fedigan and Pavelka (2001), Pavelka and Fedigan (1999), Pavelka (1999), Fedigan and Pavelka (1994), Pavelka and Fedigan (1991), Pavelka (1991).

Source: Written by Mary Pavelka and Linda Fedigan, Department of Anthropology, University of Calgary

The sexual behaviour of *Pan paniscus* has garnered particular attention because of the frequency, diversity, and contexts in which it occurs. Sexual activity takes place not only between males and females but also between members of the same sex, and between both related and unrelated individuals. It may be characterized by face-to-face copulation, genital rubbing, and oral–genital sex. Unlike other primate species, for whom sexual activity is linked to reproduction, sex for bonobos serves many different purposes, including facilitating the female transfer between troops, reinforcing social bonds, reducing tension, and establishing power alliances (de Waal 1982). Until recently, humans and bonobos were believed to be the only primates to engage in face-to-face copulation; however, this behaviour has recently been observed among Western gorillas, though this may be an individual rather than population-level phenomenon.

Among primates, only humans and *P. paniscus* engage in extended sexual activity outside the ovulatory cycle (estrus). In contrast to bonobos and other primates, however, ovulation in humans is not marked by demonstrable visual cues, and this has led some to suggest that humans have evolved a form of "concealed ovulation." This observation has led to considerable speculation as to how and why this may have occurred. Primatologists Frederick Szalay and Robert Costello have hypothesized that concealed ovulation in human females may have resulted from the adoption of obligate bipedalism (Szalay and Costello 1991). According to their argument, locomotion on two legs meant that any physical signs of sexual receptivity—such as sexual swelling—would have been a hindrance. However, studies reviewed recently by Grammer, Fink, and Neave (2005) suggest that human females signal their ovulatory status in ways other than developing marked visual cues. These ways may include chemical signals (pheromones) to attract potential mates. Behaviours known as **mate guarding**, common among nonhuman male primates, have been shown to occur in humans when the female in a relationship is ovulating (Gangstad, Thornhill, and Garver 2002).[9] Gangstad and colleagues note, for example, that men will call their female partner by cell phone more often when she is ovulating in order to "keep tabs" on her whereabouts. Recently, Miller, Tybur, and Jordan (2007) analyzed the success of lap dancers at obtaining tips from male clients of "gentlemen's clubs" and found that tip earnings nearly doubled for dancers who were ovulating compared to those in their menstrual phase. Miller and colleagues proposed that human females may use pheromones to elicit economic benefits from wealthy males by "leaking" cues of their fertility status—a strategy with clear evolutionary significance. They also admitted, however, that several other mechanisms known to signal ovulation could also be acting (including changes in facial attractiveness, increased soft-tissue body symmetry, and lower waist–hip ratios). Thus, human females may not in fact have concealed their ovulatory status so much as shifted cues from visual to olfactory.

**mate guarding**

actions by dominant male primates aimed at restricting sexual access to receptive females

## Sexual Strategies

When Darwin proposed his theory of sexual selection in 1871, he aimed to explain two distinctions between males and females within species. First, the two sexes often differed in morphology—and in very conspicuous ways. In particular, males tended to be larger in a number of features and often sported quite flashy adornment—the male peacock with his spectacular tail comes to mind (Figure 6.11a), and so does the male mandrill's more colourful muzzle (Figure 6.11b). Second, the two sexes employed very different strategies to solicit mates, involving distinct patterns of mate competition and mate choice (Swedell 2006). In most instances, these strategies manifested themselves as male–male competition and female choice, which Robert Trivers (1972) ascribed to the stark asymmetry between males and females in degree of **parental investment** (often calculated as the "energy cost" of reproduction). This inequity is readily apparent: a male's investment in producing low-cost sperm pales in comparison to a female's burden as entailed in egg production, gestation, birth, and lactation. According to Trivers, this imbalance leads to fundamentally different approaches employed by each sex to attain reproductive success, often dichotomized as quantity of females (male) versus quality of offspring (female). In other words, males seek to impregnate as many females as possible, while females strive to be impregnated by the most appropriate male in order to ensure a healthy infant likely to survive to adulthood.

**parental investment**

a model describing the apportionment of resources (time, food, protection, caregiving, etc.) by males and females into the successful rearing of offspring

### Female Strategies

A female primate may employ a number of different tactics as part of an overarching strategy to maximize the quality of her offspring. She may incite males to compete though direct agonistic encounter or via sperm competition (see below); she may choose dominant males on the presumption that this will translate into high-quality infants; she may choose males who demonstrate affiliative behaviours, which may then translate as rearing assistance or protection of infants from other aggressive males; she may mate with multiple

---

9. "Mate-guarding" would include greater attentiveness and vigilance, as well as proprietary behaviour on the part of the male in the relationship when the female partner was in estrus.

**Figures 6.11a and b** Darwin's sexual selection theory accounts for conspicuous dimorphism between males and females.

Left: ultimathule/Shutterstock.com; Right: Adam Jones/Digital Vision/Getty Images

males so as to confuse paternity, thereby soliciting aid from males who believe the offspring is theirs (Stumpf, Thompson, and Nott 2008); she may compete with other females for access to better food resources; and she may even synchronize ovulation with other females in the group (Ostner, Nunn, and Schülke 2008), or time birth to seasons of high resource availability.

**Reproductive Timing** Female primates living in habitats with seasonal fluctuations in resource abundance often time conception so that birth and/or lactation occur when food is sufficient to maximize survivorship. Lewis and Kappeler (2005), for example, found that Verreaux's sifaka, a species of lemur from Madagascar, timed conception to coincide with high or declining food resources. This enabled them to store energy as fat mass. Also, they gave birth during the lean season (thus relying on the stored energy) and timed mid-to-late lactation and weaning to increasing food abundance, which facilitated the survival of the newly weaned offspring. Females within a group may synchronize their estrus cycles to coincide with seasonal variations in resources (Anderson, Nordheim, and Boesch 2006). But they may also do so independent of variations in food energy availability. This latter form of synchrony would increase male parental care, as males would be less likely to abandon a new mother in favour of an estrous female. Ovulatory synchrony would also reduce the ability of a single male in a multimale group to sequester all receptive females. Finally, synchrony with regard to birth would reduce the likelihood of one or a few young infants being targets of harassment or even death by older (usually) males in the group (Swedell 2006).

**Female Mate Choice** Female choice plays an important role in the reproductive success of males, and studies of this behaviour abound in the literature. Unfortunately, identifying the factors underlying female choice of mating partners is confounded by the difficulty in distinguishing between behaviours that are merely social and those that are related specifically to reproduction (Wolfe 1991). As well, female mating choices may change over their lifetime (Strier 2003). So it has been difficult to draw solid conclusions about this aspect of reproductive behaviour.

Having said this, a number of factors appear to influence female choice of mating partners, including protection, access to food, and assistance in caring for offspring. For instance, males may act as allies and provide females with protection from other members of their group or from predators. They may also defend food resources and participate in infants' care by grooming and protecting them and sharing food with them. In multimale/multifemale social groups, mating tends to be promiscuous, with both males and females having numerous sexual partners (though a dominant male may enjoy preferential access through consortship with an estrous female at the peak of her cycle, when she is most likely to conceive). As noted, such behaviour may be advantageous to females by enabling them to confuse males about the paternity of offspring and thereby reduce the likelihood that those males will harm their offspring. We know that among humans, promiscuous behaviour carries the risk of sexually transmitted diseases. Does the same apply to nonhuman primates? Interestingly, an analysis of blood samples taken from healthy females representing over 40 different primate species housed in zoos revealed that, on average, the white blood cell counts of promiscuous species were 50% higher than those of monogamous species (Nunn, Gittleman, and Antonovics 2000).

A female's rank can also play a role in mating choice. Among marmosets, for instance, the dominant female has the ability to suppress ovulation in subordinate females through the use of pheromones, visual cues, and physical bullying. This strategy provides benefits to both the mother and the lower ranking females. The mother gets help from other members of her group in guarding and feeding her young, and the subordinates gain protection so that they may one day produce offspring of their own (Barrett, Abbott, and George 1993).

An important consideration is to distinguish between female choice (an action) and female preference (a motivation or desire) (Swedell 2006). A female may prefer to mate with a particular male for a variety of reasons, but may be kept from doing so by the actions of other members of the group and thus will choose an alternative and perhaps still desirable mate. Meredith Small (1989) observed that in some species, females often prefer to mate with unfamiliar males, who may be new immigrants. This may be to avoid the negative effects of inbreeding (i.e., increased genetic homozygosity), or it may simply be a tactic to maximize partners (again with the effect of confusing paternity).

## Male Strategies

**sperm competition**
when a female mates with multiple partners over a short period of time, males who are able to deposit a larger volume of higher quality sperm further into the female reproductive tract should succeed in impregnating more females; sperm competition is facilitated in multi-male social systems by large testes, large penises, and longer tailed sperm

**infanticide**
the killing of infants, in this context as a reproductive strategy to solicit reproductive opportunity by the adult male

The limiting factor for male reproductive success is access to receptive females, and as the majority of nonhuman primates do *not* live in monogamous pair-bonded social units, some form of intermale competition is the rule. Aggressive competition for females is part of life for a male living in single-male/multifemale or multimale/multifemale social group. The point of engaging in that competition is to maximize the number of females with whom he is able to mate and/or the number of copulations achieved with any given receptive female. In the latter regard, a phenomenon known as **sperm competition** can play a significant role, if the female involved is able to solicit sexual encounters from multiple males within a single estrous cycle. A number of factors comprise a male's competitive strategy, including body and canine size, dominance rank, ability to coerce females, and male mate choice. The practice of **infanticide** (see below) can also contribute to a given male's reproductive success.

**Size Matters** Some primates (e.g., hamadryas and gelada baboons, and gorillas) form single-male/multifemale (polygynous) units by actively excluding other adult males within the larger band structure, relying on features such as body and canine size to defend their harem at all times from solitary (usually young adult) males who might seek to usurp the leader. Vigilance is key, and often costly in terms of energy, for it detracts from time spent foraging. Males living in multimale/multifemale groups (e.g., savannah baboons, macaques) compete only in the presence of estrous females.[10] Dominance hierarchies are common in such cases, with the alpha male typically attaining high rank through competitive bouts. Their social rank influences their reproductive success, with high rank often leading to greater mating and reproductive success, often through formation of temporary consortships with estrous females at the peak of their ovulatory cycle. While a strong correlation exists between rank and reproductive success, high-status males are not always successful. Among chimpanzees and baboons (other than hamadryas), lower ranking males may form alliances to gain access to females. Using DNA genotyping in captive bonobos, Marvan and colleagues (2006) found that dominance rank was not associated with mating success; both infants tested in their study had been sired by the lowest ranking male in the group, even though the dominant male formed exclusionary consortships with the estrous females.

Male reproductive success also depends heavily on social skills. Lower ranking males and older males may befriend females and thereby increase their chances of mating with them. Long-term studies of baboons, for instance, have found that a large percentage of copulations occur between females and their male friends, even when these males are low in rank (Smuts 1985). Physiological changes also influence male reproductive behaviours. Testosterone levels fluctuate over the course of a year, and elevated levels increase the chance of aggressive interactions related to mating.

**Infanticide** Groundbreaking research by primatologist Sarah Blaffer Hrdy has demonstrated that infanticide is common in many primate species. Hrdy (1977) documented numerous cases of infanticide in Hanuman langur communities, in which males from outside groups moved in, replaced the resident males, and proceeded to kill the offspring of those males. According to the sexual selection hypothesis, such events would result in the mothers of the killed infants coming into estrus; the new males would thus be able to father their own offspring, thereby increasing their reproductive success. Infanticide in this case is seen as an adaptive strategy that allows males to father as many offspring as possible. While most documented cases of infanticide involve males (van Schaik and Janson 2000), the killing of infants by females has been observed among chimpanzees at Gombe; this may reflect increased competition for resources (Goodall 1986). More recently, several cases of female-led infanticide have been documented in chimpanzee groups in the Budongo Forest in Uganda. In two of these cases, the attacks were launched by resident females against the offspring of immigrant females (Townsend et al. 2007).

The sexual selection hypothesis for infanticide has come under fire based on claims that there is little evidence for the intentional killing of infants among wild primates, that infant deaths are generally the consequence of more general aggression, that there is no genetic basis for this practice, and that no benefit from infanticidal behaviour has ever been demonstrated (i.e., it has not been shown that males who kill infants have greater reproductive success over their lifetime than those who do not; Sussman, Cheverud, and Bartlett 1995). Responding to these claims, Hrdy, Janson, and van Schaik (1995) note that infanticide is, in fact, widespread and has been recorded in both captive and wild primates, including chimpanzees, gorillas, colobus monkeys, and red howler monkeys. Teichroeb and Sicotte (2008), for example, documented cases of infant killing among colobus monkeys living in the Boabeng-Fiema Monkey Sanctuary in Ghana. In all cases, infants were attacked by unrelated males, who consequently gained access to the mother for mating. The same pattern has been observed among other primate species. Furthermore, analyses of DNA extracted from the feces of wild Hanuman langurs have demonstrated that males were unrelated to their infant victims but were, in fact, the likely fathers of subsequent offspring (Borries et al. 1999). Hrdy and colleagues (1995) also note that among red howler monkeys, females who have lost their offspring to infanticide have shorter interbirth intervals than those who have not, increasing the likelihood that incoming males will father offspring and thus increase their reproductive success.

---

10. "Estrous" is the adjectival form of the noun "estrus."

It should not be assumed that females respond passively to the occurrence or potential occurrence of infanticide, though active defence against an infanticidal male is unlikely to succeed due to disparities in body size. However, other options are available. For example, because infanticide is often associated with a takeover event, the presence of a new or unfamiliar male may cause a resident female to develop post-conception sexual swellings and pseudoestrous behaviours as a means to manipulate the usurper's assessment of his paternity (Swedell 2006). Alternatively, a female may indeed permit her infant to be killed, as a "loss-minimizing" tactic, knowing that she will have opportunities to become impregnated sooner by the incoming male.

## LANGUAGE AND COMMUNICATION

http://www2.gsu .edu/~wwwlrc/

Communication is a vital component of the behavioural repertoire of all social animals, and nonhuman primates exhibit a rich array of gestures, vocalizations, facial expressions, and olfactory signals, all of which carry some form of meaning. The type of communication a primate uses is influenced by a number of factors, including habitat, sex, age, and rank. Primates who spend most of their time in the trees, for example, rely more heavily on auditory (vocal) signals, whereas more terrestrial species rely more heavily on visual signals, which can easily be seen by other members of their group. Forms of communication may also differ between males and females.

Primates utilize four modes of communication: visual, auditory, olfactory, and tactile. Visual forms of communication include gestures, facial expressions (Figures 6.12a and b), postures, eyelid flickering, lip smacking, tongue flicking, and exposing canine teeth. Primate vocal communication systems are equally varied, even within the same species. Howler monkeys, for example, have a vocal repertoire that includes 15 to 20 different sounds, and their loud calls, which can be heard more than a kilometre away, are facilitated by an enlarged voice box. Some species, such as gibbons, are known for their song-like territorial calls. Others use a variety of calls to signal predators or food resources. Vervet monkeys, for instance, have different alarm calls corresponding to different types of predators, while chimpanzees may utter different sounds corresponding to different types of food (Slocombe and Zuberbühler 2006). In recent years, fascinating research on primate vocal patterns has revealed evidence of what have been interpreted as local "dialects" among chimpanzees (Mitani et al. 1992). Some species also use a variety of olfactory signals to convey meaning. These may take the form of scent marking to mark territories, urine washing, and "stink fighting," seen in ring-tailed lemurs. Finally, tactile forms of communication include grooming, touching, embracing, and hand clasping. These may be used to convey interest in a mating partner, to avoid aggression, or to reconcile with a former opponent.

**Figures 6.12a and b** Chimpanzees express many of the same feelings we do.

Left: © DLILLC/Corbis; Right: © DLILLC/Corbis

Given the complexity of primate communication systems, considerable debate has surrounded the question of whether nonhuman primates possess language. In this regard, particular attention has been paid to our closest relatives, the great apes. Ape language studies date back to the 1950s, when psychologists Keith and Catherine Hayes attempted to teach a chimpanzee named Vicki how to speak. Though Vicki was able to utter four human words, the experiment ultimately failed because chimpanzees, like other nonhuman primates, lack the vocal apparatus necessary for human speech. Subsequent studies focused on teaching American Sign Language (ASL) to chimps (Figure 6.13) and other apes, beginning with an experiment launched by psychologists Beatrice and Allen Gardner to teach ASL to a young chimpanzee named Washoe. Not only did Washoe learn to sign more than a hundred words, but she was also able to put words together and teach signs to other chimpanzees. Since then, gorillas and orangutans have also been taught to use sign language. More recently, bonobos have been taught to communicate using special computer keyboards.

**Figure 6.13** Primatologist Roger Fouts spent much of his academic career teaching chimpanzees to communicate using sign language.

Time & Life Pictures/Getty Images

Considerable criticism has been directed toward the ape language studies that have been conducted to date, including charges that the animals were simply mimicking their instructors. Do these studies indicate that great apes possess language? That depends largely on how one defines language. If we define language as characterized by grammar and syntax, then the answer is no. Even so, it is clear that the line between human and nonhuman cognitive abilities is much less distinct than once thought.

A fascinating study of primate artistic expression by Anne Zeller of the University of Waterloo found some intriguing similarities between human children and the great apes in their choices of colour and pattern. In a study of over 300 paintings done by chimpanzees, gorillas, orangutans, and children, Zeller (2007; see opening image in Chapter 1) discovered an almost universal preference for the colour yellow as their first choice, and the frequent use of diagonal lines. These results suggest that ape drawings are not simply random scribbles but reflect conscious choices.

# SUMMARY

Though they are mostly tropical-dwelling species, nonhuman primates occupy a diverse range of habitats and ecologies, from dense forest to savanna woodland to open scrub grassland. Some are seldom seen by humans; others appear quite comfortable sharing an urban landscape with dense human populations. This ecological diversity has translated into an equally varied repertoire of social and reproductive behaviours. As we have seen in this chapter, primates develop complex relationships within groups, between males and females, and among adults, juveniles, and infants. These relationships are influenced by extragroup features such as seasonality, predation, and the distribution of resources, as well as consort formation and intragroup dynamics leading to affiliative and agonistic interactions. These latter factors are associated with attributes such as established dominance hierarchies, sexual dimorphism, and female choice, all of which play significant roles in maintaining the integrity and cohesiveness of primate society. This cohesion is dependent on effective forms of communication, be they calls, gestures, or (among higher primates) complex facial expressions. A particularly interesting facet of primate behavioural ecology—one that has become a major focus of research—is the degree to which primates manipulate the environment in a manner entirely suggestive of culture, and researchers today are promoting the notion of primate ethnicity, as argued for *Pan* species. Both natural selection and sexual selection act to shape this complex arena of primate lives. Another exciting area of research attracting considerable attention is the application of molecular genetics to the study of primate behaviour. We have already provided some examples in this chapter—for instance, the use of DNA to investigate the relationship between dominance rank and mating success. Other applications include assessing the influence of kinship on social behaviour, examining diet and feeding strategies, and investigating dispersal patterns (Di Fiore 2003).

# CORE REVIEW

**What are the advantages and disadvantages of studying primates in captivity versus in the wild?**

Studying primates in captivity enables researchers to closely monitor individuals and alter their environments to suit their research objectives. In contrast, studying primates in the wild allows researchers to observe the interaction between the animals and their natural habitat and to examine seasonal changes in behaviour. Studies of captive primates are hindered by the fact that natural foraging patterns cannot be observed, activity levels can be altered, and certain behaviours such as aggression and reproduction can be reduced or amplified. Field researchers also face a number of challenges, including the costs and dangers of conducting fieldwork in remote places and the time it takes to locate and habituate subjects. The individuals in a group must then be identified, including their various behaviours, and their relationships mapped out.

**What benefits do primates derive from living in social groups?**

Group living allows individuals to share information on feeding sites, defend food resources, gain access to mating partners, gain protection against predators and attacks by other primates, rely on others for assistance when caring for offspring, and learn and transmit behaviours from one member to another.

**What types of reproductive strategies do primates utilize? How do male and female strategies differ?**

Reproduction (mating system) is a determining factor in how primates organize and maintain social groups. Male strategies focus on access to adult females (quantity); females tend to focus on producing the best baby possible (quality). The ratio of adult males to adult females is a paramount feature underlying residence pattern; this in turn is a decisive aspect of mating systems. A few species form one-male, one-female bonds, but more common systems are multimale, multifemale groups and one-male, multifemale groups. In these latter cases, success in reproduction may reflect a variety of factors, including dominance, degree of dimorphism, female choice, and practices such as infanticide.

**In what contexts does tool use occur among nonhuman primates?**

Tool use typically occurs in the context of food procurement and processing. Chimpanzees, for example, modify and use sticks to extract termites from mounds, dig for tubers, roots, and bulbs, and catch small mammals. They also use stones to crack open nuts. Orangutans use sticks to extract fruit, honey, and insects. Gorillas have been observed using a stick to test the depth of a pool of water before wading through it, and using the trunk of a small shrub as a bridge to cross a swampy area.

**What strategies do primates use to maintain social stability and cohesion?**

Dominance hierarchies found in many primate species provide social stability and reduce conflict within a group. Affiliative behaviours such as grooming, establishing alliances, and engaging in conflict resolution also serve to reduce stress and reinforce social bonds. Kinship plays an important role in primate societies by fostering alliances and strong social bonds, and may explain altruistic behaviours seen in some primates.

**How do primates communicate? What purposes does their communication system serve?**

Primates utilize four modes of communication: visual, auditory (vocal), olfactory, and tactile. These include a wide variety of gestures, vocalizations, facial expressions, and olfactory signals, all of which carry some form of meaning. Purposes of such signals include marking territories, warning other members about potential predators, conveying interest in a mating partner, drawing attention to food resources, threatening or avoiding aggression, and reconciling with a former opponent.

# CRITICAL THINKING QUESTIONS

1. A greater degree of sexual dimorphism in body size exists in primate societies that emphasize competition among males for access to sexually receptive females. How would you account for the fact that, as a species, humans exhibit comparatively low levels of dimorphism yet still maintain relatively high levels of intermale competition for mates?

2. To what extent do you think genetic versus environmental (i.e., social) factors influence primate behaviour?

# GROUP DISCUSSION QUESTIONS

1. Nonhuman primates have long been used as models for early hominin behaviour. In what ways do primates make good models? Which species do you think most closely represents the behaviour of our earlier ancestors, and why?

2. Given that many nonhuman primates live in multimale/multifemale groups and are promiscuous, do you think that there is any basis for the argument made by some people that humans are not naturally monogamous?

# RESOURCES AND READINGS

- B. Chapais and C.M. Berman, eds., *Kinship and Behavior in Primates* (Oxford: Oxford University Press, 2004).
- L.M. Fedigan, *Primate Paradigms: Sex Roles and Social Bonds* (Chicago: University of Chicago Press, 1992).
- B.M.F. Galdikas, 1995. *Reflections of Eden: My Years with the Orangutans of Borneo* (Boston: Little, Brown, 1995).
- L. Gould and M.L. Sauther, eds., *Lemurs: Ecology and Adaptation* (New York: Springer, 2006).
- J.D. Patterson and J. Wallis, eds., *Commensalism and Conflict: The Human-Primate Interface* (Norman, OK: American Society of Primatologists, 2005).
- M.M. Robbins, K.J. Stewart, and P. Sicotte, eds., *Mountain Gorillas: Three Decades of Research at Karisoke* (Cambridge: Cambridge University Press, 2001).
- K.D. Strier, *Primate Behavioral Ecology*. 3rd ed. (Boston: Allyn and Bacon, 2006).
- S.C. Strum and L.M. Fedigan, *Primate Encounters: Models of Science, Gender, and Society* (Chicago: University of Chicago Press, 2002).

# Chapter 7 Primate Evolution

## OVERVIEW

This chapter focuses on the evolution of nonhuman primates. We begin by exploring how once-living primates ended up as fossils, the methods used to determinate the age of these fossils, and what we can learn from these remains about fossil primate behaviour. We also place the fossil evidence for primate evolution in the context of the evolution of mammals and the environmental and climatic changes that accompanied the appearance and radiation of the primates. Major events in primate evolution are highlighted, beginning with the appearance of mammals directly preceding the first true primates and ending with the origin of apes. The anatomical characteristics of these primates are described, and their possible phylogenetic relationships are outlined.

## CORE CONCEPTS

■ absolute dating, relative dating, adaptive radiation, plesiadapiforms, adapids, omomyids, anthropoids, hominoids

## CORE QUESTIONS

■ When did the first true primates appear, and what characteristics did they possess that made them primates?

■ How does one distinguish between prosimians, anthropoids, and hominoids in the fossil record?

■ What hypothesis best explains the origin of New World monkeys, and what evidence supports this hypothesis?

■ What factors allowed the Miocene apes to diversify into so many different species?

■ What can we learn about the behaviour of extinct primates from studying their fossilized remains?

*Man still bears in his bodily frame the indelible stamp of his lowly origin.*

Charles Darwin (1809–1882)

# PROLOGUE: THE FAMILY TREE

According to Fleagle (2000, 87), three defining periods characterize the study of primate evolution. The first began with the publication of Linnaeus' *Systema Naturae*, in which humans and other primates were classified together based on physical similarities. The second began with the discovery, in the 1830s, of the first primate fossils in Europe, South America, and India, demonstrating the existence of extinct forms of this group of mammals. The third followed the publication of Darwin's *Origin of Species*. As you learned in Chapter 2, implicit in Darwin's theory of evolution by natural selection was the idea that humans had evolved from an ape-like ancestor; indeed, he ended his book with the comment that "in the distant future ... light will be thrown on the origin of man and his history." His strong supporter, the anatomist Thomas Huxley, demonstrated the close anatomical similarities between humans and the African great apes in *Man's Place in Nature* (1863), confirming Darwin's belief that Africa was the birthplace of humans. As we explore in this chapter, primate evolution is a vibrant field of study and has provided us with the context in which to situate our own evolutionary history, which we cover in Part III, Ancient Currents.

# HOW PRIMATES BECOME FOSSILS

When we talk about the fossilized remains of extinct primates, we are typically referring to remains that have been preserved for many millions of years. Fossils can exist in different forms, but most of the evidence we discuss in this chapter consists of the remains of bones and teeth. In what circumstances are these elements preserved? When an organism dies, its soft tissues begin to decompose. The rate of decomposition varies with a number of factors, including temperature, humidity, and the location of the body (e.g., whether it is buried or exposed). Once the soft tissue has decomposed completely, the exposed skeleton begins to break down and may be lost completely unless conditions are favourable for its preservation. For example, bones covered by volcanic ash or deposited in water and covered with sediments will undergo fossilization as minerals in the surrounding sediments or groundwater infiltrate the bones and turn them into stone, preserving them for millions of years (see Chapter 8). Because fossilization occurs only under very specific conditions, however, fossils are extremely rare, which means that there are large temporal and geographical gaps in the fossil record. In addition, not all elements of a skeleton may be preserved. Many fossil primates, in fact, are represented only by teeth and jaw fragments, making it difficult to draw any conclusions about locomotor patterns or body size. A further difficulty is that the earliest primates were small and are therefore much less likely than larger mammals to have been fossilized. It is also important to keep in mind that the fate of some evolving lineages is extinction. Thus their remains do not make any further contributions to the story of evolution. Finally, fossils must be brought to the surface by geological activity, erosion, or some other process before we can discover them. Despite all these limitations, paleontologists have been able to extract a tremendous amount of information from the remains that have been uncovered.

## Dating Primate Fossils

In order to explore evolutionary relationships between different fossil primates, it is necessary to establish the time frame in which these primates lived. Before this can be done, the exact location from which a fossil came—that is, its **provenience**—must be identified. Once this has been established, the age of the fossil can be determined. Methods of dating fossilized remains can be divided into two categories: **relative dating** and **absolute** or **chronometric dating**. The choice of method depends on a variety of factors, including the nature of the material to be dated and the geological context of the site. Because both these methods are prone to **dating error**, dates are reported as a value plus or minus some measure of error, whether one is using an absolute or relative technique. Another factor to consider is the precision of the particular method used. For early primate and hominin deposits, error on the order of tens or hundreds of thousands of years is typical.

**provenience**
the original location of a fossil or artifact

**relative dating**
a method of dating that identifies objects as being younger or older than other objects

**absolute (chronometric) dating**
a method of dating that assigns a specific age and estimated error to a fossil or site (e.g., 1.6 ± .23 million years)

**dating error**
the degree to which a date derived from an absolute or relative technique differs from the actual date

## Relative Dating Methods

Relative dating methods involve determining whether a fossil is older or younger than something else without assigning an exact age to the fossil. The most common method of relative dating uses the principle of **stratigraphy** (see Figure 7.1). This method is based on the **law of superposition**, which states that fossils buried in lower (i.e., deeper) strata or layers are older than those buried closer to the surface. This method works well on sites that have not been disturbed; however, alterations in stratigraphy resulting from geological processes such as folding and uplifting can disturb a site in such a way that older layers of sediment may come to lie above younger layers. Closely related to stratigraphic dating is **biostratigraphic dating**, also known as *faunal correlation*. This technique involves dating a fossil based on associated faunal remains. For example, a primate fossil found with the remains of an extinct species of pig known to have lived between 35 and 40 mya would, by association, be considered to fall within the same time range. **Fluorine dating** also provides relative dates based on the amount of fluorine in bones. Underlying this method is the fact that when an organism dies, its bones and teeth absorb fluorine from the surrounding groundwater. As a general rule, the longer the remains have been buried, the more fluorine they contain. Thus if bones found at the same site have different amounts of fluorine in them, we can conclude that those with greater amounts are older. Finally, relative dating by **paleomagnetism** involves examining shifts in the earth's magnetic field. These shifts, which involve a reversal of the magnetic field from north to south, have occurred periodically over the millions of years of the earth's history and are recorded in sedimentary rocks. By comparing the reversals documented at one site with those from other sites that have been securely dating using methods of absolute dating, we can obtain an approximate age.

## Absolute Dating Methods

Methods of absolute (chronometric) dating provide specific dates to fossils and sites. Some of these methods are based on the decay of radioactive elements contained in organic or inorganic material. Using the knowledge that unstable **radioactive isotopes** decay into more stable forms at a constant rate, researchers can date objects by measuring the relative proportion of stable and unstable forms. The best-known of these **radiometric dating** methods is **carbon-14 (radiocarbon) dating**, which is based on the decay of the radioactive form of carbon, $^{14}C$. All living organisms possess carbon-14, which they obtain from their environment. When an organism dies, it stops taking in radioactive carbon and the carbon-14 decays into stable nitrogen-14 ($^{14}N$). The amount of time it takes for half the $^{14}C$ to decay is 5,730 years—a figure referred to as its **half-life**. Thus it takes 5,730 years for half the $^{14}C$ in an organism to decay, and another 5,730 years for half of *that* amount to decay, and so on. This method is used to date organic materials such as wood, charcoal, and bone. Unlike other methods of absolute dating discussed below, however, carbon-14 dating is only useful for dating sites within the past 50,000 years or so. Therefore it cannot be used to date primate fossil evidence extending earlier than this date.

In the late 1970s a new method of radiocarbon dating was developed called **accelerator mass spectrometry (AMS) dating**. Like carbon-14 dating, this technique is used on organic

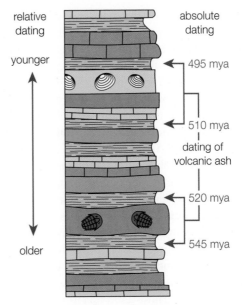

**Figure 7.1** Relative dating involves determining whether something is older or younger than something else. Absolute dating, in contrast, involves assigning a specific age to something.

**stratigraphy**

the study of the different layers (strata) that have been deposited over time

**law of superposition**

the rule that lower deposits are older than higher ones

**biostratigraphy**

a method of relative dating that involves dating a fossil based on associated faunal remains that have been securely dated using other methods

**fluorine dating**

a method of relative dating that involves comparing the amount of fluorine that has accumulated in fossils found at the same site

**paleomagnetism**

a method of relative dating that involves comparing reversals in the earth's magnetic field

**radioactive isotopes**

unstable isotopes that decay, emitting radioactivity

**radiometric dating**

an absolute method of dating based on the radioactive decay of isotopes

**carbon-14 (radiocarbon) dating**

a method of absolute dating based on the radioactive decay of $^{14}C$ into $^{14}N$

**half-life**

the amount of time it takes for half the original radioactive material to decay

**accelerator mass spectrometry (AMS) dating**

a method of radiocarbon dating used to date very small samples

**CHAPTER 7** Primate Evolution

materials such as charcoal, seeds, pollen grains, and hair, and can provide dates ranging to 40,000 or 50,000 years ago. Unlike carbon-14 dating, however, it has the advantage of requiring only very tiny samples of organic material (1 mg of carbon or less).

Another method of absolute dating that has been widely used to date fossil sites is **potassium–argon dating** (or K-Ar dating), which is based on the decay of the radioactive isotope of potassium-40 ($^{40}$K) into argon gas ($^{40}$Ar). As $^{40}$K has a half-life of 1.3 billion years, this method is most suitable for dating samples older than 100,000 years. A related method, developed more recently, is **argon–argon dating**, which involves measuring the ratio of argon-40 ($^{40}$Ar) to argon-39 ($^{39}$Ar). While this method also requires volcanic rock, it can be used on much smaller samples than potassium–argon dating.

Other methods of absolute dating have been used to date fossils extending back millions of years. Several of these rely on the decay of one or more of the radioactive isotopes of uranium. **Fission-track dating** is based on the observation that when uranium-238 ($^{238}$U) in materials such as obsidian decays by fission, it produces small tracks in the rock. These can then be counted to determine the specific age of the rock. **Uranium–lead dating**, performed on zircon and other minerals, looks at the radioactive decay of $^{238}$U to $^{206}$Pb and $^{235}$U to $^{207}$Pb, whereas **uranium–series dating** of carbonate materials such as coral focuses on the decay of thorium-230 ($^{230}$Th) to uranium-234 ($^{234}$Ur).

Two methods of absolute dating based on the accumulation of trapped electrons in certain materials have also been used to date ancient fossils. The **electron spin resonance (ESR)** technique involves measuring electrons trapped in materials such as shell and bone, and is based on the observation that the greater the number of trapped electrons, the older the object. The method of **thermoluminescence (TL)** involves measuring the amount of light produced by the release of electrons trapped in objects such as metals and ceramics when they are heated. The more light given off, the older the sample is. Finally,

**potassium–argon dating**

a method of absolute dating based on the radioactive decay of potassium ($^{40}$K) into argon gas ($^{40}$Ar)

**argon–argon dating**

a method of absolute dating that measures the ratio of $^{40}$A to $^{39}$A

**fission-track dating**

a method of absolute dating that involves counting the number of tracks produced by the decay of the uranium isotope $^{238}$U by fission

**uranium–lead dating**

a method of absolute dating that looks at the radioactive decay of $^{238}$U to $^{206}$Pb and $^{235}$U to $^{207}$Pb in minerals

**uranium–series dating**

a method of absolute dating that looks at the decay of thorium-230 ($^{230}$Th) to uranium-234 ($^{234}$Ur)

**electron spin resonance (ESR)**

a method of absolute dating that involves measuring electrons trapped in materials such as shell and bone

**thermoluminescence (TL)**

a method of absolute dating that involves measuring the amount of light produced by the release of electrons trapped in objects such as metals and ceramics when they are heated

| ERA | PERIOD | EPOCH | Million years ago |
|---|---|---|---|
| Cenozoic | Quaternary | Holocene | |
| | | Pleistocene | 0.10 |
| | Tertiary | Pliocene | 1.8 |
| | | Miocene | 5 |
| | | Oligocene | 24 |
| | | Eocene | 34 |
| | | Paleocene | 55 |
| Mesozoic | Cretaceous | | 65 |
| | Jurassic | | |
| | Triassic | | |
| Paleozoic | Permian | | 225 |
| | Carboniferous | | |
| | Devonian | | |
| | Silurian | | |
| | Ordovician | | |
| | Cambrian | | 570 |

**Figure 7.2** The evolution of the primates occurred during the Cenozoic era.

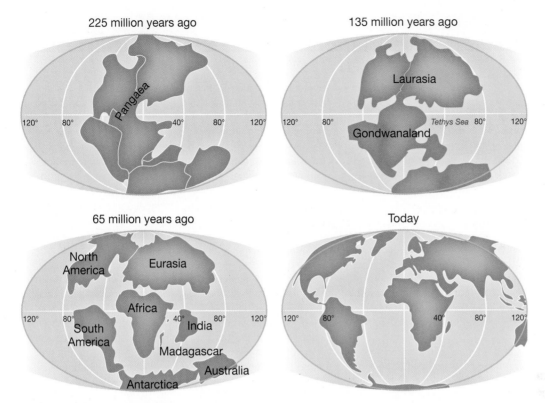

225 million years ago

135 million years ago

65 million years ago

Today

**Figure 7.3** The continents that exist today derive from larger land masses that existed more than 100 mya.

Boaz, Noel T.; Almquist, Alan J., *Biological Anthropology: A Synthetic Approach to Human Evolution*, 1st, © 1997. Electronically reproduced by permission of Pearson Education, Inc., Upper Saddle River, New Jersey

a recently developed method of dating, known as **cosmogenic nuclide dating**, looks at the radioactive decay of aluminum-26 ($^{26}$Al) to beryllium-10 ($^{10}$Be) in quartz sand crystals.

## Geological Time Scale

When we talk about the evolution of primates, we are talking about a period of time spanning tens of millions of years. The **geological time scale** is based on geological divisions as defined by fossilized remains of extinct organisms and by evidence of climatic changes (Conroy 2005). The interval of geologic time during which mammals, including primates, evolved is known as the **Cenozoic era**, also referred to as the "age of mammals." It is further subdivided into smaller intervals of time called **epochs**, of which there are seven: Paleocene, Eocene, Oligocene, Miocene, Pliocene, Pleistocene, and Holocene (see Figure 7.2).[1]

## THE EARTH AT A GLANCE

In order to understand the conditions in which primates evolved, it is necessary to examine the geological events that were taking place during the Cenozoic era. If you were to go back in time for a moment to the beginning of the Mesozoic era (225 mya), you would see that the continents as we know them today did not exist. Instead, they were joined together to form one giant supercontinent known as **Pangaea** (see Figure 7.3). Beginning around

**cosmogenic nuclide dating**

a method of absolute dating that looks at the radioactive decay of aluminum-26 ($^{26}$Al) to beryllium-10 ($^{10}$Be) in quartz sand crystals

**geological time scale**

the division of the Earth's geologic events into time periods such as eras and epochs

**Cenozoic era**

the geological era in which mammals, including primates, evolved

**epochs**

a measure of geologic time that partitions periods (e.g. Tertiary) into smaller units, defined with regard to major climatological/ environmental events

**Pangaea**

the original land mass made up of the seven continents we know today

---

1. The date of the Pliocene–Pleistocene boundary has recently been changed from 1.8 million to 2.6 million years ago based on paleoclimatic data. However, we will use the 1.8 mya date here as it is most widely recognized among paleoanthropologists.

## BOX 7.1 FOCUS ON... Adaptive Radiation on Madagascar

The island of Madagascar, off the east coast of Africa, is distinctive for its high degree of **biodiversity**. Considered a "global biodiversity hotspot" (Conservation International 1999), Madagascar is home to a total of 105 species of mammals (Groombridge and Jenkins 1994), many of which have restricted geographical ranges. The explanation for the high degree of **endemism** seen on this landmass is still a mystery. The separation of Madagascar from Africa more than 150 mya and its resulting isolation certainly explain, in part, its rich biodiversity. The island's geographic features appear also to have played a major role in the explosive speciation that has occurred there. Based on an examination of watersheds and climate change, Wilmé, Goodman, and Ganzhorn (2006) have hypothesized that cooler and drier conditions during periods of glaciation had a more pronounced effect on watersheds with sources located at relatively low elevations, leading to greater levels of habitat isolation and speciation in those places than at higher elevations.

What about the origin and adaptive radiation of strepsirhines on the island? Several hypotheses have been proposed to explain the colonization of Madagascar by early prosimians. Some researchers have suggested that lemurs rafted across from mainland Africa on floating masses of vegetation (Charles-Dominique and Martin 1970). Others have hypothesized that they originated in India and rafted from there to the island (Gingerich 1975). A third hypothesis suggests a migration across one or more land bridges that may have connected the island to mainland Africa periodically (Tattersall 1982). While the date and manner of lemur colonization of Madagascar remains unclear, a recent genetic study points to a single origin for all Malagasy primates.[2] Estimates are that these animals reached Madagascar by about 54 mya (Yoder et al. 1996).

Fleagle (1999, 91) has characterized the strepsirhines of Madagascar as "a natural experiment in evolution." Isolated on the island with no competition from other animals, these primates spread into a variety of environments in much the same way that Darwin's finches radiated across the Galapagos Islands and adapted to new ecological niches (though without flying, of course!). Recall from Chapter 5 that the Malagasy strepsirhines display a wide variety of adaptations, including several forms of locomotion and social organization, dietary specializations, and activity patterns.

2. The name used to refer to primates that live on the island of Madagascar.

---

**biodiversity**
variation in life forms within a given ecosystem

**endemism**
the state of being found exclusively in a particular place

**continental drift**
the movement of the plates that make up the earth's continents

**Laurasia**
the land mass consisting of North America, Europe, and Asia

**Gondwanaland**
the land mass consisting of South America, Africa, Antarctica, Australia, Madagascar, and India

135 mya, the plates on which the continents sit began to slowly move apart in a process known as **continental drift**. Floating on a fluid layer underneath, these plates eventually split to form two major landmasses, a northern one called **Laurasia** and a southern one called **Gondwanaland**. By 65 mya, Laurasia had split to form North America and Eurasia, and Gondwanaland had broken apart to form South America, Africa, Antarctica, Australia, Madagascar, and India.

What, then, are the implications of continental drift in terms of the evolution of mammals—and primates in particular? As we will see later in this chapter, many of the early primate fossils have been found in North America and Europe. This might seem puzzling, given the northern latitudes and temperate climates of these continents today. But it is not surprising that primate fossils have been found on these continents if you consider that they were once situated much closer to the equator. Similarly, the discovery of related primate species on two different continents, as in the case of Old and New World monkeys, makes sense when you consider that Africa and South America were once closer together. The island of Madagascar is home to a huge diversity of primate species, due in part to its separation from Africa (see Box 7.1).

## RECONSTRUCTING ANCIENT ENVIRONMENTS

Climate change has had a profound impact on primate evolution and has been the catalyst for a number of significant events, such as the radiation and diversification of primate species. We have heard a great deal about global warming in recent years, but fluctuations in global temperatures have occurred numerous times in the evolutionary history of the primates. For example, the movement of the continents altered ocean currents so that warm water from tropical regions could no longer move to temperate and polar regions, leading to a reduction in global temperatures. The building of mountain ranges along the edges of continental plates affected patterns of precipitation. In turn, climatic changes resulting from these processes produced changes in vegetation, which took the form of an expansion or reduction in the size of forests, grasslands, and deserts. Changing temperatures also had an impact on the movement of mammals. Reductions in temperature, for example, led to a drop in sea levels and the consequent exposure of land bridges, which allowed mammals to migrate to other regions. Conversely, the disappearance of land bridges and the separation of continents resulted in the isolation of populations.

To understand how primates evolved, it is necessary to examine the kinds of environments in which they lived. Reconstructing ancient environments—a field of study known as **paleoecology**—is a multidisciplinary endeavour that applies techniques developed in archaeology, chemistry, biology, geology, and other disciplines. **Paleobotanists**, for example, study the fossilized remains of ancient plants in order to determine the type of habitat in which early primates lived. As you learned in Chapter 5, one hypothesis

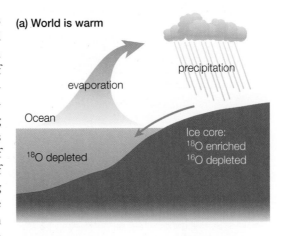

(a) World is warm

precipitation

evaporation

Ocean

$^{18}O$ depleted

Ice core:
$^{18}O$ enriched
$^{16}O$ depleted

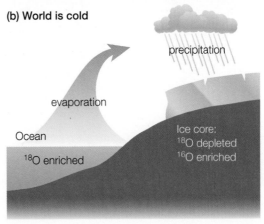

(b) World is cold

precipitation

evaporation

Ocean

$^{18}O$ enriched

Ice core:
$^{18}O$ depleted
$^{16}O$ enriched

**Figure 7.4** The ratios of the stable isotopes of oxygen, $O^{18}$ to $O^{16}$, measured in ice cores and deep-sea sediments, provide us with valuable information on climate change.

**paleoecology**
the study of ancient environments

**paleobotany**
the study of ancient plants

to explain the origin of primates, the angiosperm hypothesis, is based on the observation that the appearance of the earliest primates coincided with the appearance and radiation of flowering plants, as determined by analyses of fossilized plant remains. Information on plant remains can also be gathered by **palynologists**, who study the distribution of various pollen species; the analysis of faunal remains found in association with primate fossils is the focus of **paleontologists**.

A number of methods can be used to reconstruct paleoclimates. The most important of these for studying long-term climate change is **oxygen isotope analysis** of ice cores taken from polar icecaps and sediment cores taken from the ocean floor. Oxygen isotope analysis is based on the fact that the ratio of the two **stable isotopes** of oxygen in seawater, $^{18}O$ and $^{16}O$, varies according to temperature. Because $^{16}O$ is lighter than $^{18}O$, when water evaporates, more of the heavier $^{18}O$ isotope is left behind in seawater, while the precipitation that falls is more enriched in $^{16}O$ (Figure 7.4). During glacial periods, this precipitated $^{16}O$ is locked up in glaciers. As a result, ice cores that exhibit lower $^{18}O{:}^{16}O$ ratios indicate colder periods, while those that exhibit higher $^{18}O{:}^{16}O$ ratios indicate warmer periods. The reverse holds true for deep-sea cores, which represent the continuous deposition of sediment, including the remains of marine organisms that incorporate oxygen into their shells. During colder periods, the shallow waters in which these organisms once lived would have been enriched in $^{18}O$, resulting in higher $^{18}O{:}^{16}O$ ratios in these organisms. As illustrated in Figure 7.5, significant climatic fluctuations have occurred over the span of primate evolution.

**palynology**
the study of pollen

**paleontology**
the study of the fossilized remains of extinct life forms

**oxygen isotope analysis**
the use of stable oxygen isotopes to reconstruct ancient climates; it can also be used to examine the geographic origins of organisms such as humans

**stable isotopes**
different forms of an element that have different atomic mass and that are not radioactive

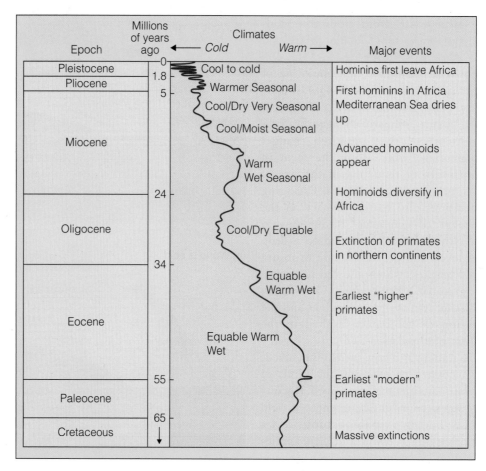

**Figure 7.5** Major events in primate evolution and patterns of climate change during the Cenozoic era.

# CLASSIFYING FOSSIL PRIMATES

Once fossil primates have been uncovered, the next step is to determine what type of taxon is represented by the fossil. Teeth can be very useful in distinguishing between primates and other mammals, and between primate taxa such as strepsirhines and haplorhines. For example, as we noted in Chapter 5, primates have only two incisors per quadrant of the mouth whereas other mammals have three. Among the haplorhines, fossil catarrhines and platyrrines, like their modern counterparts, have dental formulae of 2.1.2.3 and 2.1.3.3 respectively. Primates also vary in terms of the number and pattern of cusps. Strepsirhines have upper molars with three cusps, monkeys have a **bilophodont** molar pattern (Figure 7.6) characterized by four cusps, and hominoids have a **Y-5 pattern** formed by the presence of five cusps on the lower molar teeth (Figure 7.7).

Recall from Chapter 4 that the most widely accepted modern definition of species is a group of interbreeding organisms that are reproductively isolated from other such groups. When we are dealing with fossil remains, we obviously do not know whether early primates were able to interbreed or not. One of the ways in which species can be identified in the fossil record is by examining the morphology of fossils—size, for example—and comparing it to that of **extant** species. If the range of variation seen in the fossils falls within the range seen in similar modern species, researchers can conclude that the fossils most likely represent one species. If, on the other hand, the fossils exceed the range of variation exhibited by modern forms, they most likely represent more than one species. This approach has several limitations, and there has been considerable debate over the number of primate species represented in the fossil record. For example, fossils have, on occasion, been classified as representing more than one species when in fact, they represent males and females of a single sexually dimorphic species. The choice of extant group

**bilophodont**

molar teeth characterized by four cusps connected by two ridges of enamel

**Y-5 pattern**

cusp pattern formed by five cusps on the lower (mandibular) molar teeth of hominoids

**extant**

still existing

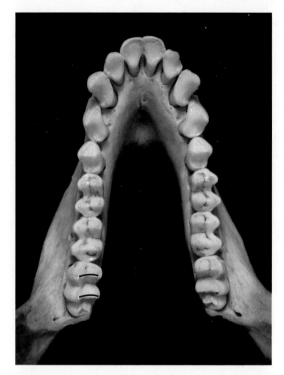

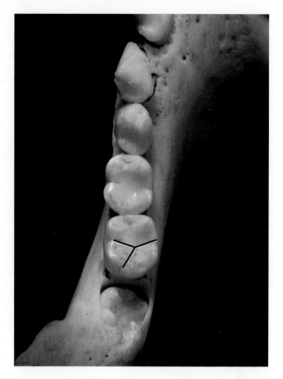

**Figure 7.6** Monkeys possess a bilophodont molar pattern.

William K. Sacco, specimens courtesy of Yale Peabody Museum

**FIGURE 7.7** Hominoid molars have a Y-5 cusp pattern.

William K. Sacco, specimens courtesy of Yale Peabody Museum

with which to compare the fossil evidence can also lead to inaccurate classifications. We now know from the fossil record that many early primate species had no living counterparts. This raises the question of whether we can compare the degree of diversity in fossil primates with that of modern species (Begun 2004a, 501). These difficulties are compounded the further back in time you go, because the fossil finds become fewer and more fragmentary.

# RECONSTRUCTING EARLY PRIMATE DIETS AND SOCIAL BEHAVIOUR

Within the past three decades, **paleobiology**, the reconstruction of the behaviour and ecology of fossil primates, has become an increasingly popular field of study (Fleagle 2000, 90). Using data derived from biomechanical and ecological studies of living primates as well as paleoenvironmental and paleoclimatic research, primate paleontologists have been able to reconstruct many aspects of early primate behaviour, including their diet, patterns of locomotion, and social behaviour. Reconstructing the behaviour of fossil primates is a challenging task, however, and the reliability of such reconstructions can be affected by a number of factors, including the choice of extant primate with which to compare the fossil evidence. Compounding these difficulties is the fact that many behaviours are impossible to reconstruct from fossil remains, and morphological differences between living and extinct species of primates make it difficult to infer behaviours.

**paleobiology**
the study of the behaviour and ecology of fossil primates

## Dietary Reconstruction

As you learned in previous chapters, extant primates are omnivorous, though some species rely more heavily on some foods than others. When it comes to examining fossil evidence, how do we go about determining what early primates ate? A variety of techniques have been used to reconstruct the diet of fossil primates. These include estimating body mass, analyzing

**CHAPTER 7** Primate Evolution

dental microwear
microscopic wear on the enamel surfaces of the teeth

**dental microwear**, examining tooth morphology, and measuring enamel thickness. When we look at extant primates, for example, we can see that smaller species such as the strepsirhines tend to be more insectivorous whereas large species such as orangutans are usually folivorous. How do we estimate body mass from fossilized remains? A number of indicators have been used, including tooth size and tarsal bone size (Conroy 1987; Dagosto and Terranova 1991). A recent study of body mass and molar morphology of late Eocene anthropoid primate remains from the Fayum region has revealed that these anthropoids were likely frugivorous. In contrast, late Eocene prosimians appear to have had remarkably diverse diets. This finding suggests that an adaptive shift to fruit eating was not the major impetus for the origin of the anthropoids (Kirk and Simons 2001).

Information on the diet of early primates can be obtained by looking at dental microwear. The proportion of pits and scratches on the surfaces of teeth reflect the type of diet on which an animal relied. A coarse diet of leaves, for example, is reflected in a greater number of pits and scratches, while a softer diet of fruits manifests as less wear. The results of such studies have revealed evidence of a wide diversity of diets among European Miocene primates (Ungar 1996).

Diets have also been inferred from tooth cusp morphology. Among living primates, for example, frugivores have rounded tooth cusps whereas folivores and insectivores have more pointed cusps used for slicing through cellulose and exoskeletons, respectively. Another method that has been used to reconstruct diet involves measuring the lengths of the crests connecting the molar tooth cusps as well as the tooth length to calculate a **shearing quotient** (SQ), which can then be used to assess the potential of the teeth to shear foods between the edges of their crests (Kay 1984). Folivores and insectivores, for instance, typically have higher SQ values than frugivores, reflecting their longer shearing crests and more **occlusal** surface relief relative to fruit-eaters.

shearing quotient
a measure of the relative shear potential of molar teeth

occlusal
the chewing surface of a tooth

Measurement of tooth enamel thickness can also provide clues to the diet of fossil primates (see Chapter 8). Thicker enamel observed in some hominoid species suggests a diet of harder, more abrasive food items; thinner enamel points to softer foods such as fruits.

## Social Behaviour

Fossilized remains of early primates can also provide information on their social organization and mating systems. The degree of sexual dimorphism in body size and canine teeth has been used as an indicator of social behaviour in early primates based on observations of extant primates. As you learned in Chapter 5, sexually dimorphic species tend to live in multimale/multifemale groups (like baboons) or in single-male/multifemale groups (like gorillas). In contrast, species that lack sexual dimorphism, such as the gibbons, tend to be monogamous. Among fossil primates, sexual dimorphism in canine and/or body size of many species has been used to argue that such animals lived in social groups similar to those of baboons and gorillas (Ross 2000, 183), while the lack of sexual dimorphism in other species has been interpreted as suggesting a monogamous way of life (Swindler 1998, 224). It is important to emphasize, however, that the relationship between sexual dimorphism and social behaviour is not always straightforward, and that more than one mating system may be associated with a particular degree of sexual dimorphism (Begun 2004).

## PALEOCENE: AGE OF THE PLESIADAPIFORMS

The earliest fossils that have been identified as primate date back to the Eocene epoch, which began 55 mya. However, the common ancestor of primates likely appeared millions of years before that. To get an idea of what this primate ancestor might have looked like, we need to go back even further in time to the **Paleocene** epoch, 65 to 55 mya. The climate during this time period was much warmer than it is today, and the landscape of North America and Europe was dominated by savannas and woodlands. By this time Gondwanaland had split into South America, Africa, Antarctica, Australia, India, and Madagascar.

There is a general consensus today that primates evolved from a small, insectivorous mammal that resembled a tree shrew. Radiating into ecological niches previously occupied by dinosaurs, these early mammals, known as **plesiadapiforms**, were widespread throughout Europe and

Paleocene
the first epoch of the Cenozoic era, dating from about 65 to 55 mya

plesiadapiforms
a group of primate-like mammals that lived during the Paleocene epoch

North America; indeed, 25 genera and over 70 species have now been recognized (Fleagle 1999). Once referred to as "archaic" primates because of dental similarities to later strepsirhines, they exhibit a number of features not seen in primates of modern aspect (**euprimates**), including a dental formula of 3.1.3.3 or 3.1.4.3, large **procumbent** central incisors resembling those of rodents, a long snout, laterally facing eyes, claws instead of nails, and no postorbital bar.

Among the best known of the plesiadapiforms are *Purgatorius* and *Plesiadapis*. Recovered from early Paleocene deposits in Montana, the fossilized remains of *Purgatorius* consist primarily of teeth and jaw fragments. Estimated to have been the size of a mouse, this mammal had a dental formula of 3.1.4.3, and its molar teeth reflect a reliance on a diet of insects and fruit. *Plesiadapis,* which is represented by both cranial and postcranial remains, was somewhat larger and possessed claws on all digits and non-opposable thumbs.

The plesiadapiforms were a very successful group of mammals that were adapted to a wide range of different environments. Yet by the end of the Paleocene, most of them had become extinct, likely due to competition from rodents as well as environmental and climatic changes at the end of the Paleocene. Of the few that survived into the Eocene, it is not clear which, if any, gave rise to the euprimates. One possible candidate, the late Paleocene taxon *Carpoletes simpsoni,* whose remains have been found in Wyoming, possessed a divergent, opposable big toe with a nail—a feature characteristic of euprimates (Bloch and Silcox 2006; Bloch et al. 2007).

# EOCENE: AGE OF THE PROSIMIANS

The adaptive radiation of the first true primates (the euprimates) occurred during the **Eocene** epoch. During the early Eocene, North America was still connected to Europe, a global warming event led to a significant increase in temperatures, and tropical forests covered much of North America, Africa, and Eurasia. These conditions facilitated the appearance and spread of many new mammals, including primates. Possessing characteristics similar to those of living strepsirhines (see Chapter 5)—including forward-facing eyes, a postorbital bar, and a reduced snout compared to the plesiadapiforms—these early primates consisted of two major families: the Omomyidae and the Adapidae. Most of the fossil evidence for these primates comes from North America and Europe, where they inhabited a wide range of habitats. The common ancestor of **omomyids** and **adapids** has not yet been identified, though several possible candidates have been proposed, and there is growing consensus that the strepsirhines, tarsiiforms, and anthropoids diverged shortly before the beginning of the Eocene (Rasmussen 2007).

The omomyids such as *Necrolemur* closely resembled living tarsiers in having a small body size (less than 500 g), large eyes reflecting a nocturnal way of life, and long tarsal bones. Some species were insectivorous; others relied more heavily on a frugivorous diet. Most had a dental formula of 2.1.3.3, and their postcranial skeleton appears to have been adapted to a vertical clinging and leaping mode of locomotion. One omomyid from China, *Teilhardina asiatica,* dated to 55 mya, has recently been identified by Canadian scientist Xijun Ni and her colleagues as the oldest known true primate (Ni et al. 2004). The spread of *Teilhardina* from Asia to North America may have been facilitated by an episode of rapid global warming some 55 mya (Smith, Rose, and Gingerich 2006).

The adapids resembled modern-day lemurs and had longer snouts than the omomyids (Figure 7.8). Among the best-known adapids are *Notharctus* and *Adapis*. They were larger than the omomyids and were diurnal. Their diet consisted mainly of fruits and leaves, and their postcranial skeleton displayed features characteristic of arboreal quadrupeds. They had a dental formula of 2.1.4.3 for both the upper and lower jaw, and some species had sexually dimorphic canines, suggesting a variety of mating systems.

The Eocene was also marked by the appearance of the first anthropoids. The fossil record has yielded few clues to the identity of their ancestors, but some intriguing evidence has come to light in Asia which suggests that anthropoids originated on this continent and later migrated to Africa. One of these **basal anthropoids** is *Eosimias*, whose 45-million-year-old remains were discovered in 1994 in China. A tree-dwelling primate, it displays a number of tarsier-like features in its ankle bones, suggesting that it moved in much the same way as tarsiers (Beard et al. 1994, 1996). More recently, the dental remains of what may be the oldest

**euprimates**
primates of modern aspect; also referred to as true primates

**procumbent**
forward-projecting

**Eocene**
the second epoch of the Cenozoic era, dating from about 55 to 34 mya

**omomyids**
tarsier-like primates from the Eocene epoch

**adapids**
lemur-like primates from the Eocene epoch

**basal anthropoids**
the earliest anthropoids

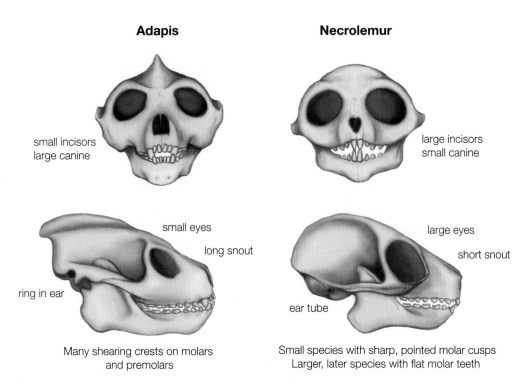

**Adapis**

small incisors
large canine

small eyes

long snout

ring in ear

Many shearing crests on molars
and premolars

**Necrolemur**

large incisors
small canine

large eyes

short snout

ear tube

Small species with sharp, pointed molar cusps
Larger, later species with flat molar teeth

**Figure 7.8** The adapids more closely resembled lemurs; the omomyids more closely resembled tarsiers.

anthropoid in the world, a tiny primate named *Anthrasimias*, have been uncovered in India from deposits dating to nearly 55 mya (Bajpai et al. 2008). Both these taxa have been assigned to the Family Eosimiidae.

By the late Eocene, North America and Europe had separated completely, global temperatures had dropped significantly, and most of the omomyids and adapids had disappeared. Insufficient fossil evidence currently makes it impossible to identify the precise nature of the relationship between the Eocene primates and later primates, but the strepsirhine, tarsiiform, and anthropoid lineages were clearly distinct by the end of this epoch.

## OLIGOCENE: AGE OF THE ANTHROPOIDS

From 55 to 34 mya, global temperatures declined. The transition from the Eocene to the **Oligocene** epoch was marked by a reduction in the amount of forest, the extinction of many land mammals in Europe—including the almost complete disappearance of primates from the northern hemisphere—and the appearance of primates in equatorial regions as we recognize them today. Numerous Oligocene primate fossil remains have been found. Our knowledge of primate evolution during this epoch comes primarily from fossils found in a region of Egypt known as the **Fayum**, located about 150 km southwest of Cairo. To date, this region, has yielded the remains of over 17 genera, including both haplorhine and strepsirhine fossils (Simons 1995; Kirk and Simons 2001). A desert today, this area was once a warm tropical environment characterized by trees and swamps. It was home to a variety of mammals, such as mastodon and hyrax (Simons 2008), animals possibly related to elephants.

The radiation of the anthropoids continued during the Oligocene, and three families have been identified in the fossil record from Fayum: Parapithecidae, Propliopithecidae, and Oligopithecidae. The most primitive of the anthropoids recovered from this region are the **parapithecids**, primates that more closely resembled monkeys than the other Oligocene anthropoids. Like New World monkeys, they had a dental formula of 2.1.3.3, and the low rounded cusps on their molar teeth indicate a frugivorous diet. Their small eye sockets point

**Oligocene**
the third epoch of the Cenozoic era, dating from about 34 to 24 mya

**Fayum**
a fossil-rich region of Egypt once home to many Oligocene anthropoids

**parapithecids**
the most primitive Oligocene anthropoids

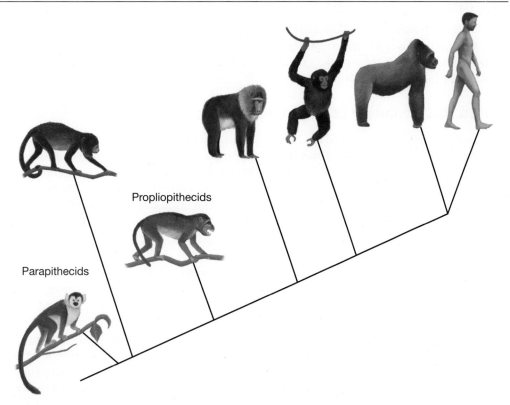

| New World monkeys (platyrrhines) | Old World monkeys (cercopithecoids) | Gibbons and Siamangs (hylobatids) | Great apes and humans |
| --- | --- | --- | --- |

Propliopithecids

Parapithecids

**Figure 7.9**  Proposed evolutionary relationships among Oligocene and extant anthropoids.

to a diurnal way of life, and their postcranial skeleton was adapted to a quadrupedal mode of locomotion. One of the best-known parapithecids is **Apidium**, a small arboreal quadruped with strong leaping abilities (Conroy 1990). While *Apidium* and other parapithecids share similarities with some of the New World monkeys, they also retain a number of primitive features seen in extant prosimians. Current consensus is they are stem anthropoids that predate the platyrrhine–catarrhine split (Figure 7.9).

The **propliopithecids** were the largest of the Oligocene anthropoids and were more ape-like than the parapithecids. Like modern-day catarrhines, they had a dental formula of 2.1.2.3, and many species had sexually dimorphic canines. The largest and best known of the propliopithecids, **Aegyptopithecus** (Figure 7.10) weighed 6 to 8 kg, exhibited a Y-5 pattern on its lower molars, and was an arboreal quadruped. Despite its anthropoid status, *Aegyptopithecus* was still rather primitive, possessing a long snout, a relatively small brain, and limb bones that resembled those of prosimians and New World monkeys. Based on these characteristics, this anthropoid was likely a primitive catarrhine that predated the divergence of Old World monkeys and apes (Fleagle 1999; see Figure 7.9).

*Apidium*
a parapithecid from the Oligocene epoch

**propliopithecids**
the largest Oligocene anthropoids

*Aegyptopithecus*
a propliopithecid from the Oligocene epoch

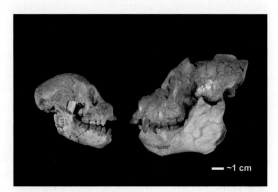

**Figure 7.10**  *Aegyptopithecus* females (left) were smaller than males (right).

Courtesy of Dr. Elwyn Simons

**CHAPTER 7**  Primate Evolution

Much less is known about the late Eocene oligopithecids. Resembling both adapids and anthropoids, their relationship to other primates is unresolved. They most likely also represent basal anthropoids that diverged prior to the platyrrhine–catarrhine split (Beard 2004).

The Fayum region has also yielded fossil evidence of a possible ancestor of the tarsiers. An early Oligocene lower jaw fragment, identified as belonging to the genus *Afrotarsius*, has been tentatively assigned to the Family Tarsiidae and may represent the oldest tarsiiform primate from Africa (Simons and Bown, 1985).

## Origin and Evolution of New World Monkeys

The earliest fossil evidence of New World monkeys in South America comes from late Oligocene (26 mya) deposits in Bolivia and consists of two genera: *Branisella* and *Szalatavus* (Fleagle, Kay, and Anthony 1997). Like extant New World monkeys, these anthropoids possessed a dental formula of 2.1.3.3. One of the most hotly debated questions in primate evolution concerns the origin of New World monkeys in South America. By the beginning of the Oligocene, Africa and South America were separated by a vast expanse of ocean, and North and South America were also separate continents. For the ancestors of New World monkeys to have reached South America, they had to have originated in either North America or Africa and travelled across water. While some have hypothesized that the ancestors of New World monkeys arose from North American strepsirhines and migrated to South America (Swindler 1998, 229), the hypothesis best supported by the fossil evidence holds that the ancestors of New World monkeys arose from an African anthropoid and spread to South America by rafting across the southern Atlantic on floating masses of vegetation (Hoffstetter 1974, 1980). While such a suggestion may seem ludicrous, lower sea levels during the Oligocene would have resulted in the exposure of numerous islands in the southern Atlantic, making travel from one continent to the other easier. Morphological similarities between African anthropoids and those found in South America provide strong support for this hypothesis (Fleagle 1985). In addition, tests of the **floating island model**, which assumes an average body weight of 1 kg and the ability, based on studies of water deprivation, to survive without water for nearly two weeks, indicate that small primates could have crossed the Atlantic on floating islands in 8 to 15 days (Houle 1999).

## Origin and Evolution of Old World Monkeys

Fossil evidence for Old World monkeys from the early Miocene (24 to 16 mya) is rare. Our knowledge of these monkeys comes from fossil remains uncovered at sites in Egypt, Libya, and Kenya. As you learned in Chapter 5, Old World monkeys are divided into two subfamilies: cercopithecines and colobines. In the Miocene, the earliest Old World monkeys belonged to the Family **Victoriapithecidae**, which consisted of two genera: *Victoriapithecus*, known mainly from 15-million-year-old deposits on Maboko Island in Kenya, and *Prohylobates*. Ranging in size from 3 to 5 kg (Harrison 1989), *Victoriapithecus* possessed bilophodont lower molars adapted to a diet of hard fruits and seeds, and a postcranial skeleton adapted to a quadrupedal mode of locomotion. Their facial structure resembled that of colobines, while their dental morphology resembled that of cercopithecines (Conroy 1990). Sexually dimorphic canines suggest that they may have had a multimale/multifemale social organization similar to that of modern macaques (Benefit 1999).

By the late Miocene, victoriapithecids had become extinct and had been replaced by cercopithecids. By this time, the cercopithecines and colobines had diverged from each other. An adaptive radiation of these monkeys coincided with the extinction of many hominoid species in Africa and Eurasia. This may have been prompted by climatic changes that led to a reduction in forest habitat to which Miocene hominoids were adapted. We will examine these hominoids in more detail below.

**floating island model**
the hypothesis that the ancestors of New World monkeys rafted across the Atlantic from Africa to South America on floating islands of vegetation

**Victoriapithecidae**
the family to which the earliest Old World monkeys belong

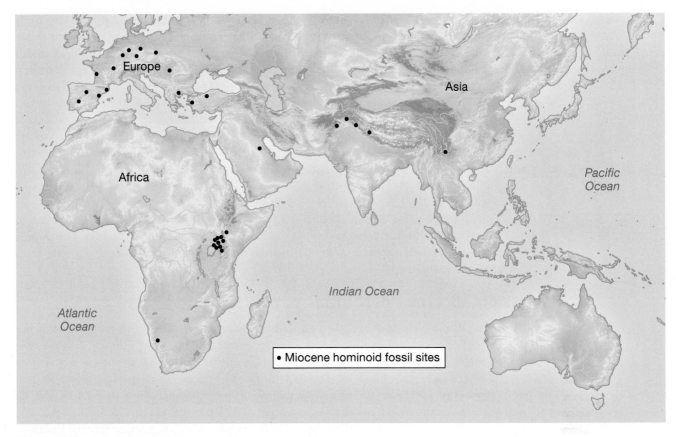

**Figure 7.11** Miocene hominoid fossil sites.

# MIOCENE: PLANET OF THE APES

The **Miocene** epoch is commonly referred to as the age of the hominoids—that is, primates that include apes (and humans) but exclude monkeys. During this time period, significant geological, climatic, and environmental changes transformed the landscape. By this time the continents had assumed roughly the positions they have today, but the continued movement of the tectonic plates altered ocean currents, and the formation of a land bridge between Africa and Asia allowed for the movement of animals between the two continents. Temperatures increased considerably in the early Miocene, and heavy tropical forests were common. These conditions provided an ideal setting for the diversification of hominoids, with dozens of genera and as many as 100 species distributed across the Old World (Begun 2003). Thousands of hominoid fossils have been recovered from sites in Africa, Europe, and Asia (Figure 7.11), and many of these have been well studied. While the evolutionary relationships of these hominoids are becoming clearer, many questions remain unanswered and there are still significant gaps in the fossil record, particularly with respect to the direct ancestors of modern apes.

**Miocene**

the fourth epoch of the Cenozoic era, dating from 24 to 5 mya

## Early Miocene (24–16 mya)

During the early Miocene, hominoids were restricted to forest and woodland environments of Africa. Many of the early Miocene taxa fall within the Superfamily Proconsuloidea, and a number of these taxa are considered to represent primitive hominoids (Begun 2007). Ranging in size from about 10 to 50 kg, the **proconsulids** possessed a number of derived characteristics seen in modern apes, such as the absence of a tail and a larger brain relative to body size than that of monkeys. Unlike extant apes, however, they did not have the highly flexible limbs used in suspensory

**proconsulids**

primitive hominoids from early Miocene Africa

**CHAPTER 7** Primate Evolution

locomotion; rather, their limbs were better suited for arboreal quadrupedalism. Most likely evolving in Africa from an Oligocene catarrhine, they exhibited a number of significant dental traits, including upper molars with a **cingulum** on the lingual (or tongue) surface and lower molars with a Y-5 pattern—a feature that distinguishes hominoids from Old World monkeys (though it is present in some propliopithecids, such as *Aegyptopithecus*). The morphology of the teeth indicates that the proconsulids were adapted to a diet of soft fruits. One of the best-known of these proconsulids is *Proconsul heseloni*, a medium-sized catarrhine that lived in Kenya about 18 mya.

Besides the proconsulids, other early Miocene taxa attributed to Hominoidea include *Afropithecus* and *Morotopithecus*. The former, dating to about 17 mya, had a mosaic of primitive and derived features. Its cranial morphology displayed some similarities to that of *Aegyptopithecus*, and it possessed the thick tooth enamel seen in later Miocene hominoids (Begun 2007). *Morotopithecus*, whose remains have been found at the site of Moroto in Uganda, may date to 21 mya, though other estimates put it at 15 mya. With an estimated body weight of 36 to 54 kg, it possessed lumbar vertebrae similar to those of living hominoids, as well as a scapula indicative of a mobile shoulder joint, which may have enabled it to hang and swing from branches like modern apes (Gebo et al. 1997).

## Middle Miocene (16–12 mya)

By the end of the early Miocene, the climate had cooled and sea levels had dropped, reducing the amount of forest and exposing a land bridge between Africa and Eurasia. This allowed many species of mammals, including hominoids, to move out of Africa into new environments, where they diversified into myriad forms. The oldest Eurasian hominoid, known from remains recovered in Turkey and Germany, is *Griphopithecus*, which shares a number of characteristics with African middle Miocene apes. The latter include the 15-million-year-old *Equatorius africanus* and the 14-million-year-old *Kenyapithecus wickeri*, a semiterrestrial knuckle-walker. While these hominoids retain features seen in the earlier proconsulids, they display a number of characteristics resembling those seen in the living apes, including large, flat molar teeth with thick enamel, which enabled them to exploit new food resources, particularly hard food items. Another African hominoid was the 13-million-year-old *Otavipithecus namibiensis*, whose remains have been found in Namibia (Conroy et al. 1992), making it the first African Miocene hominoid to be found south of the equator.

In 2002 the partial skeleton of a new middle Miocene ape named *Pierolapithecus catalaunicus* was discovered in Spain. While its postcranial skeleton displays a number of primitive monkey-like characteristics, including short phalanges of the hand indicating little, if any, suspensory locomotion, it also possesses modern ape-like features of the thorax, lower vertebrae, and face, suggesting that this hominoid, rather than the known middle Miocene African taxa, may have been close to the last common ancestor of great apes and humans (Moya-Sola et al. 2004). Similarities have been noted between *Pierolapithecus catalaunicus* and another middle Miocene hominoid, *Dryopithecus fontani*, whose contemporaneous remains have been found in France and Austria. The two may in fact be synonymous (Begun 2007).

More recently, deposits in Spain have also yielded the remains of a middle Miocene ape named *Anoiapithecus brevirostris* (Moya-Sola et al. 2009). Like *Pierolapithecus*, its skeleton displays a combination of primitive and derived features. What makes this hominoid remarkable, however, is its strikingly flat face. At the same time, its teeth display features similar to *Kenyapithecus*. This evidence, together with the *Pierolapithecus* fossils, strengthens the argument that members of the Family Hominidae first evolved in Eurasia from hominoids who left Africa at the end of the Early Miocene and subsequently returned to Africa as hominines (Begun 2007).

## Late Miocene (12–5 mya)

By the end of the middle Miocene, hominoids with clear affinities to the hominine and pongine clades had emerged. Climatic changes during this time period—specifically, a shift to colder and drier conditions—led to a reduction in forest environments in Europe and Asia and an increase in open grassland areas, prompting the movement of hominines into tropical regions of Africa, and of pongines south into Southeast Asia (Begun 2007). The best-known genus of the hominine clade was **Dryopithecus**, of which three late Miocene species have been identified in the fossil record. Much of our knowledge of *Dryopithecus* comes from the work of David Begun, a University of Toronto paleoanthropologist, whose excavations at the site of Rudabánya in Hungary (Figure 7.12) have yielded a large number of fossils identified as *Dryopithecus brancoi* (Kordos and Begun 2002). Analysis of a complete cranium of this species, which lived approximately 10 mya, has revealed a number of similarities to the African great apes, including a large brain comparable in size to that of chimpanzees, thin tooth enamel suggesting a soft fruit diet, and a face that tilts downward when viewed from the side—a feature referred to as **klinorhynchy** (Kordos and Begun 2001). Studies of the postcranial skeleton of *Dryopithecus* indicate that this hominoid was arboreal with a suspensory mode of locomotion.

**Dryopithecus**
a genus of large-bodied hominoids that lived in Europe during the Miocene epoch

**Figure 7.12** Excavations by the University of Toronto of the late Miocene hominoid site of Rudabánya in Hungary have yielded the remains of *Dryopithecus*.

Courtesy of David Begun

**klinorhynchy**
downward bending of the face relative to the cranial base; an increase in klinorhynchy is related to the origin of the hominines

Besides *Dryopithecus*, other late Miocene hominoids include *Oreopithecus* and *Ouranopithecus*. The former, whose remains have been found at the site of Mount Bamboli in Italy dating to 6 to 7 mya (Begun 2002), is rather unusual in having a combination of both ape and monkey features. Like *Dryopithecus* and African apes, it has molar teeth with thin enamel and a postcranial skeleton characterized by highly mobile shoulder joints and long arms and hands, allowing for suspensory locomotion. In contrast, its dental morphology, which points to a folivorous diet requiring heavy chewing forces, resembles that of Old World monkeys. Given its unusual combination of traits, the phylogenetic position of this genus is currently unclear.

Remains of *Ouranopithecus macedoniensis*, consisting mainly of jaw fragments, have been uncovered in Greece. Its body size is estimated to have been about 50 to 70 kg (Begun 2002), and its cranial anatomy shows a number of similarities to *Dryopithecus*. It differs from the latter, however, in having large jaws, broad, flat molars, and thick tooth enamel adapted to a diet of hard foods. It has been interpreted as most likely representing a late member of the *Dryopithecus* clade (Begun 2007).

The best-known genus of the pongine clade is **Sivapithecus**, whose fossils have been recovered from deposits in India and Pakistan dating between 12 and 8 mya. Analysis of its dentition has revealed thick enamel and relatively low cusps on the molar teeth, indicating a diet consisting primarily of hard food items. Its facial morphology closely resembles that of modern orangutans (Figure 7.13). Its postcranial bones, however, differ from *Pongo* in a number of respects. Specifically, *Sivapithecus* possesses a postcranial morphology characteristic of arboreal quadrupedalism but without the suspensory adaptations seen in modern orangutans. Given these differences, *Sivapithecus* was most likely a sister clade to *Pongo* (Begun 2005).

**Sivapithecus**
a genus of large-bodied hominoids that lived in Asia during the Miocene epoch

One other late Miocene hominoid, *Gigantopithecus*, deserves mention. Known primarily from fossils found in India, Pakistan, China, and Vietnam, remains of this pongine first appear in the fossil record around 9 mya (Ciochon, Olsen, and James 1990). Its massive teeth first came to light in the 1930s in a Chinese apothecary shop, where they were being sold for their reputed medicinal properties. Based on the size of these teeth as well as its jaws, *Gigantopithecus* is estimated to have weighed over 500 kilograms (ibid.). One species, *Gigantopithecus blacki*, was named after Canadian anatomist Davidson Black, who is best known for his identification of *Homo erectus* fossils in China (see Chapter 10).

We have introduced you to only a small number of Miocene hominoids. In fact, more than 40 genera are now known to have existed (Begun 2007). In contrast, only 5 genera of apes exist today. The relationship between late Miocene hominoids and extant apes has been

**CHAPTER 7** Primate Evolution

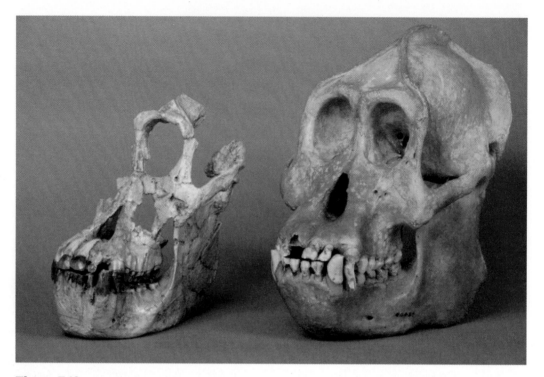

**Figure 7.13** The face of *Sivapithecus* closely resembles that of modern orangutans.

Courtesy of Ian Tattersall

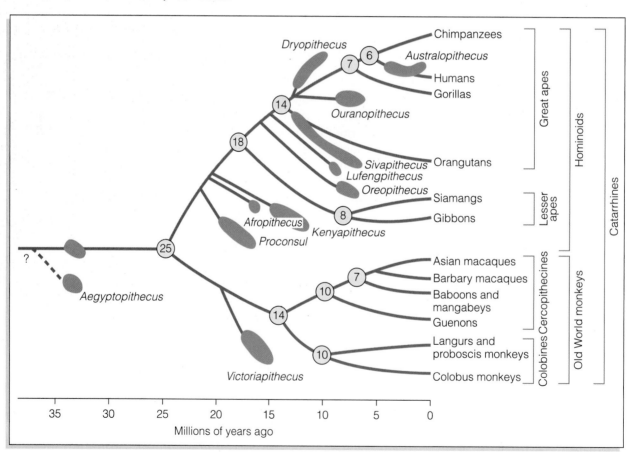

**Figure 7.14** This phylogenetic tree illustrates possible relationships among Miocene and extant primates.

Reprinted from *Current Biology*, Vol. 8, no. 16, Caro-Beth Stewart and Todd R. Disotell, Primate evolution - in and out of Africa, R582-R588, 1998, with permission from Elsevier

the subject of intense debate, and various genera have been proposed as possible ancestors of chimpanzees, gorillas, and orangutans. Unfortunately, large gaps in the late Miocene fossil record have made it impossible to directly link fossil hominoids to extant species.[3] This gap is particularly evident in Africa, where almost no fossils dating from 12 to 5 mya have been found. Consequently, the relationship between late Miocene hominoids and the living apes remains unclear (see Figure 7.14 for one possible phylogeny). As you will learn in Chapter 9, however, the recent discovery of the remains of several possible hominin ancestors attests to our rapidly expanding knowledge of this important stage of primate evolution.

# MOLECULAR SYSTEMATICS

One of the most significant advances in the study of primate evolution in the past 50 years has been the development of **molecular systematics**, the use of molecular data to reconstruct primate phylogeny. Underlying this technique is the assumption that species that share similarities in their amino acid sequences and thus in their DNA most likely shared a common ancestor. Between-species comparisons have been made using amino acid sequences in a variety of proteins. For example, Sarich and Wilson's (1967) comparison of serum proteins in humans and great apes demonstrated a close genetic relationship between African great apes and humans. From this, they estimated that the two groups shared a common ancestor as recently as 5 mya.

Another technique for investigating biological relationships between primate species is **DNA hybridization**, a method pioneered by biologists Charles Sibley and Jon Ahlquist to investigate phylogenetic relationships among birds. Recall from Chapter 3 that a DNA molecule consists of two strands of nucleotides. When the molecule is heated, the strands separate; when they cool down, they reattach to each other. DNA hybridization involves heating DNA molecules from two different species until the strands separate, then mixing together two of the strands—one from each species. The more closely related the species, the more closely their DNA will match, producing a stronger bond between the two strands. It follows that the more closely related the species, the higher the temperature required to break the bonds. This technique has revealed that chimpanzees and humans are more closely related to each other than either is to gorillas (Sibley and Ahlquist 1987). On this basis, some researchers have argued that humans and chimpanzees should be placed in the same genus (Wildman et al. 2003).

Biomolecular data have also been used to determine how long ago different primates diverged. Based on a concept called the **molecular clock**, divergence times can be estimated by comparing DNA from different living species, counting the number of genetic differences, and assuming a constant rate of change in each lineage. The date at which two lineages diverged can then be calculated based on the number of differences between the two. Utilizing mitochondrial DNA, divergence times have been calculated for Old and New World monkeys as well as for humans and apes. Based on this technique, Old and New World monkeys appear to have split around 35 mya, a date that is consistent with the hypothesis that New World monkeys originated in Africa and migrated to South America (Schrago and Russo 2003). With respect to the great apes, molecular data indicate divergence times of approximately 14 mya for orangutans, 8 mya for gorillas, and 5 to 6 mya for chimpanzees (Gagneux et al. 1999; Goodman 1999) (see Figure 7.15).

Comparisons of phylogenetic relationships derived from molecular data with those derived from the fossil record have yielded a high degree of concordance (Fleagle 2000, 89); this demonstrates the value of using molecular data to study primate evolution. There is increasing recognition, however, that estimates of divergence times may vary with the type of molecule used. It has also been suggested that mutations may not occur at the same rate in all lineages and that some lineages may have evolved more quickly than others (ibid., 90). As a consequence, calculated divergence times are not always consistent with the fossil evidence. Even so, molecular systematics has the potential to provide information about primate

**molecular systematics**
the use of molecular data to reconstruct the evolutionary history of early primates and determine the time of divergence of different species

**DNA hybridization**
a method used to assess phylogenetic relationships by splitting strands of DNA from two separate species, then mixing together one strand from each species

**molecular clock**
a concept involving the use of molecular data to estimate the sequence and timing of divergence of various evolutionary lineages

---

3. The first fossil chimpanzee, found recently in Kenya, dates to 545,000 years ago (McBrearty and Jablonski 2005).

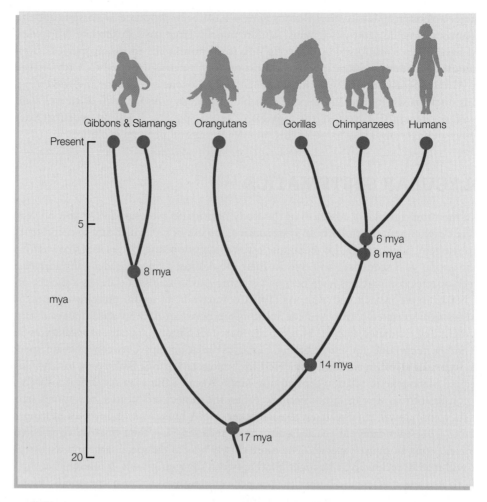

**Figure 7.15** Molecular data have been used to calculate the date of divergence of living hominoids.

From *Primate Diversity* by Dean Falk. Copyright © 2000 by W.W. Norton & Company, Inc. Used by permission of W.W. Norton & Company, Inc.

evolution that is not available from the fossil record—for example, about the relationship between late Miocene hominoids and the African great apes.

## SUMMARY

To date, thousands of primate fossils representing close to 200 genera have been identified (Fleagle 2000, 87). These finds have resulted in a significant increase in our knowledge of the evolutionary history of these animals and their biological and behavioural adaptations. As this chapter has illustrated, sorting out the relationships between the diversity of species that once existed is no easy task. The fragmentary nature of the fossil evidence and the significant temporal and geographical gaps that exist in the fossil record have made it difficult to determine ancestor–descendant relationships and to connect fossil primates with extant species. Nevertheless, researchers have been able to obtain a great deal of information about the habitats, dietary and locomotor adaptations, and social behaviour of early primates. In addition, biomolecular data have allowed us to examine phylogenetic relationships among primates that previously could be determined only by fossil evidence. These data have also made it possible to calculate dates of divergence of separate lineages. We now have a much clearer picture of the evolutionary history of the primates. As Fleagle (ibid., 97) points out, it is ironic that just as new fossil primates are being discovered, we are on the verge of losing living ones.

# CORE REVIEW

**When did the first true primates appear, and what characteristics did they possess that made them primates?**

The first primates of modern aspect appeared during the Eocene epoch, a period sometimes referred to as the "age of prosimians." These mammals possessed a suite of characteristics seen in living primates, including forward-facing eyes, a reduced snout, nails instead of claws, and generalized dentition.

**How does one distinguish between prosimians, anthropoids, and hominoids in the fossil record?**

Prosimians and anthropoids can be distinguished by their dentition. For example, fossil strepsirhines have a dental formula of 3.1.4.3, while fossil catarrhines and platyrrines, like their modern counterparts, have dental formulae of 2.1.2.3 and 2.1.3.3 respectively. The number and pattern of the cusps also varies among these primates. Strepsirhines have upper molars with three cusps, while monkeys have a bilophondont molar pattern characterized by four cusps on upper and lower molars. Distinguishing hominoids from anthropoids in the fossil record is more difficult, especially when dental remains are all that exist. Hominoids and many of the catarrhines, for example, have Y-5 molars. The postcranial skeleton of the former, however, exhibits features characteristic of an orthograde (i.e., semi-erect) posture, as well as highly flexible and mobile arm and shoulder joints.

**What hypothesis best explains the origin of New World monkeys, and what evidence supports this hypothesis?**

The divergence of Old and New World monkeys occurred during the Oligocene epoch. Early platyrrhines arose from an anthropoid ancestor in Africa and are believed to have migrated from Africa to South America by island hopping on floating masses of vegetation.

**What factors allowed the Miocene apes to diversify into so many different species?**

Climatic and environmental changes during the Miocene led to the opening up of new ecological niches, into which hominoids moved. These niches varied from woodland environments to open grasslands. Lack of competition from other mammals allowed hominoids to exploit new environments.

**What can we learn about the behaviour of extinct primates from studying their fossilized remains?**

The study of primate fossils can reveal information about their diet, mode of locomotion, and social organization. Tooth morphology and wear, for example, can tell us whether the diet was primarily insectivorous, frugivorous, or folivorous. The relative lengths of the limb bones and morphological features of the shoulders, hands, and feet can tell us about their mode of locomotion. Estimates of body size and the presence or absence of sexual dimorphism can provide clues to the type of social organization—for example, whether a particular species lived in monogamous or multimale/multifemale groups.

# CRITICAL THINKING QUESTIONS

1. In what ways did climatic and environmental changes play a role in the adaptive radiation of the anthropoids and hominoids?
2. Large gaps in the fossil record mean that we currently know nothing about the direct ancestors of the gorilla and chimpanzee. Based on your knowledge of Miocene hominoids and African apes, what might the ancestor of these apes have looked like?

# GROUP DISCUSSION QUESTIONS

1. What is the relevance of primate evolution to the study of human evolution? How can information derived from fossil primates help us understand how humans evolved?
2. Scientists working at a late Oligocene site in Egypt have discovered an assemblage of fossils that they interpret as representing an anthropoid species that lived in multimale/multifemale groups. How would they have arrived at this assessment?

# RESOURCES AND READINGS

- F.C. Anapol, R.Z. German, and N.G. Jablonski, *Shaping Primate Evolution: Form, Function and Behavior* (Cambridge: Cambridge University Press, 2004).
- D.R. Begun, D.V. Ward, and M.D. Rose, *Function, Phylogeny, and Fossils: Miocene Hominoid Origins and Adaptations* (New York: Plenum, 1997).
- S. Cachel, *Primate and Human Evolution* (Cambridge: Cambridge University Press, 2006).
- J.G. Fleagle, *Primate Adaptation and Evolution* (London: Academic Press, 1998).
- W.C. Hartwig, ed., *The Primate Fossil Record* (Cambridge: Cambridge University Press, 2002).
- J.M. Plavcan, R.F. Kay, W.L. Jungers, and C.P. Van Schaik, eds. *Reconstructing Behavior in the Primate Fossil Record.* (New York:Kluwer Academic/Plenum, 2002).
- M.J. Ravosa and M. Dagosto, eds., *Primate Origins: Adaptations and Evolution* (Netherlands: Springer, 2006).
- C.F. Ross and R.F. Kay, *Anthropoid Origins: New Visions* (Netherlands: Springer, 2004).

# Chapter 8

# What It Means to Be a Hominin

## OVERVIEW

Somewhere between 5 and 7 million years ago (mya) the evolutionary line leading to modern humans diverged from that of the chimpanzee. The challenge for paleoanthropology has been to identify those features that are distinctive for the hominin clade. These features result from adoption of a unique form of locomotion, bipedalism; a unique type of dental anatomy, including smaller front teeth and thick molar enamel; and a brain larger than expected for our body size. All of these developments are linked to new ways of doing things (behaviour) in a new kind of habitat (ecology); more travel over open ground, carrying objects (food, tools); more cooperative group interaction (less agonistic episodes and more conciliatory behaviours); more foresight, planning, learning; and new foraging strategies. As a result of these developments, by 4 mya, hominins had arrived on the primate stage—indeed, they were becoming the principal actors.

## CORE CONCEPTS

■ hominin and protohominin, bipedalism, nonhoning chewing complex, enamel thickness, encephalization, relative brain size, expensive tissue hypothesis

## CORE QUESTIONS

■ What is the significance of the category "hominin"?

■ What adaptive advantages have been suggested for the shift to bipedal locomotion?

■ How is diet implicated in the evolution of hominin bipedalism?

■ Why are teeth so useful in reconstructing hominin evolution?

■ How is relative size and organization significant in the evolution of the hominin brain?

■ What role does energetics play in hominin evolution?

*You scream, scratch, and throw coconuts, apparently, and then having another inch or so on top of the skull, you produce the dialogues of Plato, Macbeth, the Ninth Symphony, and the catalogue of the Museum of the Royal College of Surgeons. In short, when the skull is the right size, it immediately begins to put itself in museums. I am sorry, but there is something here that eludes me.*

John Boynton Priestley (1894–1984)

# PROLOGUE: A LOOK IN THE MIRROR

As the previous few chapters have illustrated, it is not a difficult task to describe the differences that set modern humans apart from our closest living relatives, though some of the genetic, morphological, and behavioural similarities might seem downright eerie. Compared to chimpanzees and bonobos, we appear to be relatively hairless, more or less vertical, bulbous-headed, dentally diminutive, multilingual, culturally complex, and technologically sophisticated creatures. How we got to be that way is what this book is about. But when it comes to cataloguing the fossil record of ancestors and descendants, things become less certain, and exceedingly so the deeper in time we travel. With rare exceptions, the remains of our extinct forebears come out of the ground as bits and pieces, typically broken and often distorted by the pressures of soil and time. In other words, rather shoddy! This is one reason why it is both possible and logical for two different paleoanthropologists to arrive at dissimilar conclusions about how our evolution unfolded (see Chapter 9 for examples). Might both be correct in every aspect? Probably not. Might both be mistaken, at least in part? Most likely yes.

Several considerations factor into deciding which among various interpretations of **protohominin** and hominin (Box 8.1) evolution may be "best" in the sense of being most plausible. Of course, it begins with the fossils—how do we determine whether a particular bit or piece belongs to the hominin lineage or some other? Aside from this fundamental exercise in classification (see Chapter 4), we also need to be able to situate the remains in their proper context with a good degree of confidence. (Context includes all aspects of time, geology, ecology, and behaviour.) Fortunately, the unique complex of biological adaptations and modifications alluded to above, acquired over 6 million years of hominin[1]

**protohominin**

referring to a number of fossil forms dating between 4.5 and 6.5 mya that show some derived hominin features but also many panin-like or goril-line-like characteristics

---

## BOX 8.1  FOCUS ON... Hominid or Hominin?

Before molecular genetics was applied to questions of phylogeny, classification was based on a Linnean framework in which morphologically similar forms were grouped together in inclusive and ever broader hierarchies, from genus to kingdom (see Table 4.2). In this system, all living apes (and their respective ancestors) belong to the taxonomic superfamily of Hominoidea, subsuming separate families for hylobatids (gibbons), pongids (orangutan, chimpanzee/bonobo, and gorilla), and hominids (humans). In the past two decades, increasingly refined genetic analyses have forced a reappraisal of how close the different living apes, ourselves included, are to one another. We now know, for example, that humans and chimpanzees/bonobos are more closely related[2] to each other than either group is to gorillas, with orangutans and gibbons more distant "second cousins." These analyses have led to a new taxonomic scheme (Figure 8.1) in which the genera *Pan* and *Homo* are classified as distinct Tribes (Panini and Hominini) within the subfamily of Hominine, distinct from the subfamilies of Gorilla and Orangutan.

Many authorities advocate the morphologically inspired term "hominid" rather than its genetic counterpart "hominin,"

arguing that the former is more pertinent historically (i.e., "hominid" is more commonly found in the literature) or is more appropriate in discussing adaptation with respect to the paleontological record. In this text we have chosen the term "hominin" for two fundamental reasons. First, it more accurately reflects our understanding of the genetic—and thus evolutionary—history of humankind with respect to our primate relatives. As such, the label "hominin" has gained widespread acceptance among scientists in both lab and field research. Second, there is nothing in either the derivation or application of a genetic taxonomy that precludes it from being employed in discussions of morphology or adaptation (Whitcome, Shapiro, and Lieberman 2007; Wood and Lonergan 2008). Indeed, recent morphological analyses agree with the genetic phylogeny, supporting the concept of a human–chimpanzee clade distinct from gorillas (e.g., Lockwood, Kimbel, and Lynch 2004).

---

2. One often sees figures of 98% to 99% similarity for shared regions of human and chimpanzee DNA; recent studies suggest that 95% commonality may be more accurate as there are important elements of the genome not shared between *Homo* and *Pan* (Wooding and Jorde 2006).

---

1. A number of earlier forms, dating between 4.5 and 6.5 mya, are still ambiguous, with a mélange of hominin and panin features (see Chapter 9). Until more remains are discovered, many refer to these fossils as "protohominins."

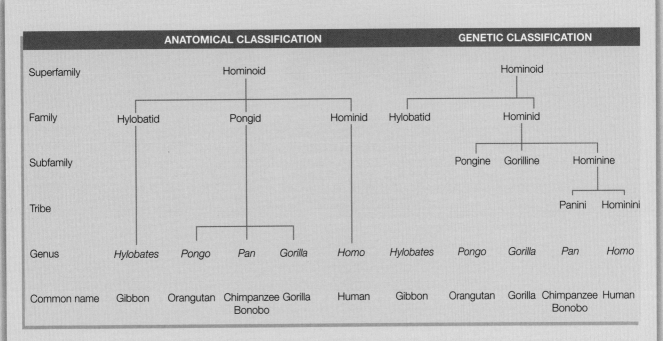

**Figure 8.1** The molecular genetic classification emphasizes the similarity of the greater apes, including all of the Family Hominid, and in particular the closeness of humans and chimpanzees/bonobos, combining these forms within the same subfamily (Hominine) distinguished at the level of tribe. The implication is that a molecular genetic classification permits a more fine-grained approach to evolutionary relationships than does morphology.

evolution, has left some revealing anatomical signatures in bones and teeth. Scientific fields as diverse as physics, chemistry, ecology, primatology, and psychology (among others) provide valuable contextual data. When all of these lines of evidence are brought together, the field of paleoanthropology is able to produce fascinating pictures of the past, even though parts of the canvas have to be repainted now and then as new discoveries come to light (Figure 8.2).

In this chapter we explore some of the important signatures and signposts that have guided us in our attempts to reconstruct, with a fair degree of certainty, at least some parts of this human voyage. In this exploration we need to consider the biocultural impact of becoming highly **encephalized**, dentally generalized, **obligate bipeds** adapting to climate change and embarking on an inconceivable cultural and technological odyssey (Figure 8.3). It begins with an examination of those ubiquitous anatomical features that signify our adoption of bipedal locomotion. Given the fundamental nature of this transition, we explore some of these ideas in detail. We then move on to discuss dental adaptations— what teeth look like in relation to what they do. Hominins have acquired some unique dental characteristics and, given that teeth form a considerable portion of the early hominin fossil record, their contribution to interpretations of evolutionary history is substantial.

**Figure 8.2** Vignettes depicting early hominin lifeways are based on information obtained from a wide range of scientific disciplines.

Mauricio Anton/Science Photo Library

**encephalized**

having a high brain size to body size ratio

**obligate biped**

in biology, obligate denotes a condition of necessity; an obligate biped therefore *must* walk on two limbs

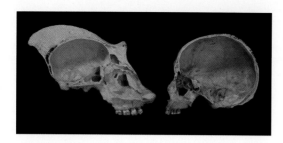

**Figure 8.3** A capacity for reasoning reflected in an increasing brain size relative to body size is one of the hallmarks of hominin evolution. Compare the relative size of the brain case in a human skull (right) and that of a gorilla (left).

William K. Sacco, specimens courtesy of Yale Peabody Museum

Though a somewhat later development, it also behooves us to introduce some major issues relating to increasing relative brain size (which we pursue further in Chapters 9 and 10), as reasonable arguments can be made that these evolutionary trends are inextricably linked.

So here we are: two legs, small teeth, big brains—a triumvirate of seemingly innocuous changes, but each profound in its own right and even more so when considered together. No other species ever evolved on this planet having features put together in just this way. In part because of this, we are to date the only species capable of asking—and answering—why.

## WHAT MAKES A HOMININ A HOMININ?

This heading might seem somewhat blasé, but it is in fact an earnest question and one that has deep historical roots. Scholars of various stripes—anthropologists, psychologists, primatologists, biomechanicians, and philosophers alike—have struggled with this question: What criterion best captures the essence of human uniqueness? What sets us apart from other primates, most particularly chimpanzees? What might have been that kernel of difference that set one group of apes on a separate evolutionary trajectory eventually leading to you and me, somewhere in an African forest 6 million years ago? Many candidates have been proposed over the years: large brains, language, culture and tool use, reproductive behaviour, bipedalism, and dental anatomy, to name a few. Some have lost prominence over time with new fossil discoveries. For example, the evolution of brains relatively larger than those of living chimpanzees, once considered the *conditio sine qua non* of hominin status, occurred millions of years after the panin–hominin divergence. Furthermore, the study of living primates has nixed the claim that only hominins fashion tools for specific purposes; in fact, modern chimpanzees arguably possess complex local cultural traditions (Whiten 2007) analogous to human ethnicity (as discussed in Chapter 6). Bonobos are sexually adventurous and like ourselves engage in sexual relations for nonreproductive purposes. One famous bonobo, Kanzi, long adept at American Sign Language, is now vocalizing words such as "milk" and "grape" (Pilcher 2005) as well as comprehending moral judgments of "right" and "wrong" (Lyn, Franks, and Savage-Rumbaugh 2008).

While many of the apparent differences between humans and our nonhuman primate relatives have become blurred in recent years, two realms have (so far) stood the test of time as hallmarks of our clade: bipedal locomotion (Figure 8.4; Zollikofer, Ponce de León, and Lieberman 2005) and dental morphology (Lucas, Constantino, and Wood 2008). Interestingly, both can be linked to a source of strong selective pressure—namely, food acquisition and processing—and it is not unreasonable to suppose that it was a shift in one or more aspects of getting and eating food that provided a fundamental opportunity for evolution of the earliest hominins.

### Four Legs Good, Two Legs Better?

As you learned in Chapter 5, the most common form of primate locomotion is quadrupedalism, though many primates are quite capable of standing upright and lumbering (or dancing) around on two legs occasionally—a capacity known as **facultative bipedalism**. You also might recall that primates often sit with an upright **orthograde** posture while feeding

**conditio sine qua non**

A Latin term meaning 'without which there is nothing'. In this context, large brains were once thought to be the preeminent hominin feature from which all else followed. We know now that this is not the case.

http://elucy.org/Main/WhatIs Bipedalis.html

**facultative bipedalism**

adopting a two-legged posture only under particular circumstances as an exception to a habitual non-bipedal form of locomotion

**orthograde**

indicating upright or erect posture, notably with regard to the trunk or grooming, whether on the ground or on a tree limb. But among the primates, only humans normally and naturally move from place to place on two limbs. Though when you think about it, we are really bipedal only when we are *not* moving (unless we are jumping on the spot!). When humans walk or run, we are actually unipeds—one foot on the ground (stance phase) and one in motion (swing phase).[3] This fact has resulted in a major restructuring of human skeletal anatomy, literally from head to toe, associated with erect posture, the effective weight transfer from trunk to legs, maintaining stability and balance, and increased mechanical efficiency (Table 8.1). The significance of having the many changes to anatomy resulting from bipedal behaviour distributed through the skeleton is that paleoanthropologists can find evidence for it even in the partial or fragmentary remains that are characteristic of the fossil record.

A really good question is why hominins are not constantly falling over during the swing phase of bipedal walking, when only one leg contacts the ground and the other is in motion. The answer is a nifty piece of biomechanical engineering. Your pelvis differs from that of a quadrupedal ape: the large blade-like ilium, for example, is shorter and directed to the side rather than to the back (Figure 8.5). The effect of this change is to redirect the actions of the three gluteal muscles (gluteus maximus, g. medius and g. minimus) that attach from the ilium to the femur. In apes, these muscles extend the leg, pulling it rearward, but in bipedal hominins they act not only as extensors, but also as rotators (g. maximus), and abductors (g. medius and g. minimus)—meaning that these muscles not only pull the leg backward, but also turn it inward or outward and help to keep it positioned under the torso. Importantly, contraction of these muscles on the side of the body that is in stance phase pulls the centre of mass away from the midline of the body, thus repositioning it over the supporting limb and slightly rotating the trunk counterclockwise. In this way, with each step, balance and stability are constantly adjusted from side to

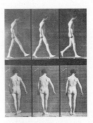

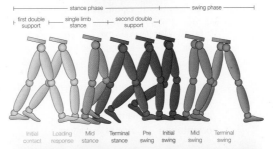

**Figure 8.4** The analysis of human gait has a long history. In the late 19th century, Eadweard Muybridge photographed humans (and other animals) walking, running, jumping, climbing, and carrying objects from multiple angles against a standardized gridded backdrop. Modern kinematic analyses help us understand the evidence for the evolution of bipedal gaits left some 3.7 mya by hominins walking over cooling volcanic ash in East Africa.

(top) © CORBIS (centre) Reprinted by permission of Gideon Ariel, Ph.D., Ariel Dynamics, www.arielnet.com (bottom) John Reader/Science Photo Library

---

3. As running speed increases, both feet will be off the ground simultaneously, comparable to a canter or gallop in quadrupeds such as horses or dogs.

**Table 8.1** Anatomical features associated with bipedal locomotion contrasted with chimpanzee (entries in bold are illustrated).

| Functional Objective | Trait | Human | Chimpanzee | Significance in Hominins | |
|---|---|---|---|---|---|
| 1. Orthograde (vertical) trunk | | | | | |
| a | **Foramen magnum position** | **Beneath cranium** | **Back of cranium** | **Balance of head for forward vision** | |
| b | Shape of spine | S curve with lumbar lordosis | C curve lacking lumbar lordosis | Balance of trunk and head | |
| c | **Shape and orientation of iliac blades of pelvis** | **Short, wide, and curved, mediolateral orientation** | **Long, narrow, and flat, anteroposterior orientation** | **Supports trunk** | |
| 2. Weight transfer | | | | | |
| a | Vertebral body size | Larger, esp. lumbar | Smaller | Assists weight transfer from trunk to pelvis | |
| b | Size of hip joint | Large | Small | Assists weight transfer from trunk to legs | |
| c | Cortical bone distribution in neck of femur | Thicker inferiorly | Even throughout | Assists weight transfer from trunk to legs | |
| 3. Balance | | | | | |
| a | **Bicondylar angle of femur** | **Valgus** | **Absent/varus** | **Places lower leg closer to midline of body** | |
| b | Anterior inferior iliac spine | Present | Absent or weak expression | Attachment for strong iliofemoral ligament preventing thigh from overextending | |
| c | **Longitudinal arches of foot** | **Two, one medial and one lateral** | **Only medial** | **Increases shock-absorbing capacity and rigidity through stance phase** | |
| 4. Efficiency | | | | | |
| a | Humerofemoral index; i.e., the ratio of arm to thigh length (also true for total upper and lower limb lengths) | Low | High | Increase in leg length relative to arm length results in greater stride length | |
| b | Relative tarsus length in foot | Long | Short | More efficient power arm in foot | |
| c | Relative lengths of metatarsals and phalanges | Shorter | Longer | More efficient lever arm in foot | |
| d | **Opposability of large toe** | **Absent** | **Present** | **Efficient "toe-off" initiating swing phase of stride** | |

Human    Great Ape

Top four pairs of illustrations (skeletal): From Jumain/Kilgore/Trevathan. *Essentials in Physical Anthropology*, 7E. © 2009 Wadsworth, a part of Cengage Learning, Inc. Reproduced by permission. www.cengage.com/permissions.

Bottom pair of illustrations (foot soles): From Jumain/Kilgore/Trevathan. *Introduction to Physical Anthropology*, Media Edition (with Basic Genetics for Anthropology CD-ROM and InfoTrac®, 10E. © 2006 Wadsworth, a part of Cengage Learning, Inc. Reproduced by permission. www.cengage.com/permissionsom/permissions.

**Human**                                                           **Great Ape**

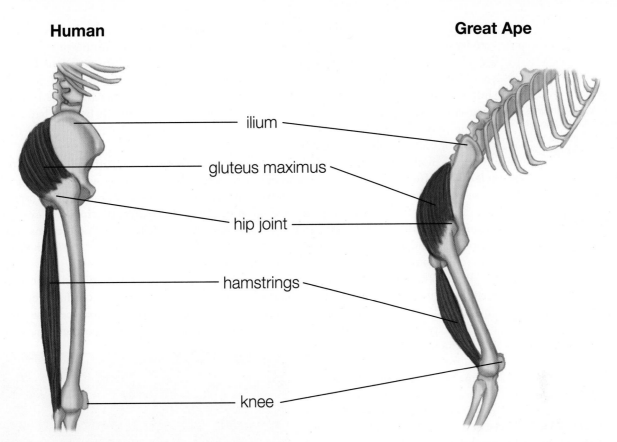

— ilium —

— gluteus maximus —

— hip joint —

— hamstrings —

— knee —

**Figure 8.5** Reorientation of the gluteal muscles of the thigh changes their function from primarily locomotion (great ape) to stability (human).

side. Think of it as an almost imperceptible mini-ballet, repeated over and over, keeping you moving forward without falling over.

## What Are the Benefits of Bipedal Locomotion?

One can make the logical assumption that bipedalism occurred because it was adaptive, having conferred one or (more likely) more advantages in terms of reproductive fitness to those primates who adopted the behaviour over those who did not. It must also have been the case that those benefits outweighed any negative consequences (costs) of being bipedal. And as you can also imagine, this transformation would not have occurred overnight (see Chapter 9), but rather would have accrued over time as the advantages and behaviours facilitated by this unique form of locomotion reinforced the shift from facultative to obligate status.

Chimpanzees today occupy a variety of habitats, from the tropical forests of central Africa to the more open savannah woodlands of eastern Senegal. While the latter populations have received less scientific scrutiny over the years, they also occupy a habitat most likely consistent with that of our earliest hominin ancestors in the later Miocene (see below). Tree cover is patchily distributed save for gallery forests following river courses and is interspersed with open grassland and brush—perfect conditions for stealthy predators such as lions and cheetahs. Surveillance has long been argued as one of the fundamental adaptive benefits of bipedal locomotion in such a habitat—being able to see farther over the grasses and low scrub within which danger might lurk. Researchers have often observed chimpanzees crossing open spaces stop and stand upright in order to reconnoitre the landscape and then, reassured of no present danger, resume traversing the ground with their classic knuckle-walking gait. Clearly, not becoming a big cat's dinner has fitness value!

Modern African apes have often been seen carrying objects from place to place. These items range from foods such as fruits or small animals to branches or stones, the latter used in displays or for cracking nuts. While an archaeological (stone tool) record of technological activity does not appear until ca. 2.5 mya, long after the advent of hominins, it is not unreasonable to suppose that object carrying was part of the logic for a shift from four-limbed to two-limbed locomotion early in hominin evolution. Kelly (2001) has proposed that such a shift moved through an evolutionary stage of **tripedalism** motivated by a need for these open-country Miocene apes to carry stones on their backs supported by one hand while moving across the ground. These stones might have been used as defensive objects—that is, thrown or used as clubs (Young 2003).

While both surveillance and carrying are arguably adaptive, it is difficult to evaluate the **selective differential** of those animals performing such behaviours consistently compared to those that do so less often or not or all. Two explanations for the evolution of bipedalism have been proposed, both pointing to physiological benefits: **thermoregulation** and **energetic efficiency**. Both are mechanistic in nature; as such, it is possible to model predictions of these hypotheses under laboratory conditions (Sockol, Raichlen, and Pontzer 2007) or through computer simulations (Sellers, Dennis, and Crompton 2003).

Peter Wheeler of Liverpool's John Moores University has argued (Wheeler 1994) that, relative to quadrupeds, an effectively hairless, savannah-foraging bipedal hominin would have enjoyed a significant benefit in terms of managing environmental heat load because upright posture exposes much less surface area to solar radiation during the hottest time of day. Furthermore, breezes are stronger away from the ground surface, leading to increased **convective** and evaporative cooling. With these advantages, a hominin walking on two limbs could search for scattered food resources at greater distances from shade or water, though access to the latter would remain a significant constraint on activity. It is not clear that this argument can account for the origins of bipedal behaviour in the earliest hominins, since they most likely evolved in a semiforested habitat (see Chapter 9). That said, thermoregulatory benefits would certainly reinforce this form of locomotion once adopted, besides facilitating exploration of equatorial savannah environments.

For some time, researchers have debated whether bipedalism was more efficient in terms of energy use than quadrupedalism, especially at slower walking speeds (e.g., Rodman and McHenry 1980). In other words, are two legs metabolically cheaper than four? A recent comparison of chimpanzees and humans walking on treadmills found that human bipedalism was about 75% less costly in energy use than either quadrupedal or bipedal walking in chimpanzees (Sockol, Raichlen, and Pontzer

**tripedalism**

a theoretical model proposing that early Miocene hominins may have adopted a three-limbed gait prior to bipedalism, in order to carry objects such as stones

**selective differential**

a measure of the probability that a given phenotype will reproduce compared to an alternative phenotype

**thermoregulation**

the adjustment of body temperature in the normal range achieved physiologically or behaviourally

**energetic efficiency**

the assessment of the relative metabolic (i.e., caloric) cost of performing a given task

**convective cooling**

reduction of body temperature by air movement

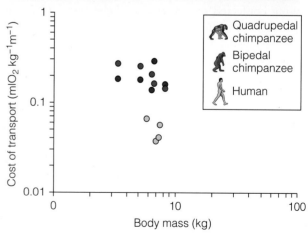

**Figure 8.6** Experimental studies of chimpanzees indicate that they are less efficient as bipeds than humans.

(top) Cary Wolinsky/Aurora/Getty Images (bottom) Sockol, M.D., et al., (2007). Chimpanzee locomotor energetics and the origin of human bipedalism, *Proceedings of the National Academy of Sciences* 104: 12265-12269. Copyright © 2007 National Academy of Sciences, USA. Reprinted with permission

2007; Figure 8.6). Differences in anatomy and gait are implicated in this advantage. Karen Steudel-Numbers and her colleagues (Steudel-Numbers and Tilkins 2004; Steudel-Numbers, Weaver, and Wall-Scheffler 2007) used a similar experimental model to investigate the impact of body size proportions on the energy expended in bipedal locomotion. Human subjects of varying body size and relative limb length walked or ran on treadmills, and metabolic costs (oxygen consumption and carbon dioxide production) were measured. In both scenarios, significant energetic efficiencies were achieved only for participants having legs that were long relative to body mass. Because our earliest hominin forebears were actually quite diminutive, with small bodies and relatively short legs (Chapter 9), it is unlikely that energetic considerations played a major role in the adoption of bipedalism.

### Bipedalism Also Has Significant Drawbacks

While paleoanthropologists have postulated several adaptive scenarios to explain how this unique form of locomotion might have evolved, it is also true that bipedalism has entailed various costs. Many of these are associated with significant medical conditions that plague modern humans. For example, the heart has to circulate blood against gravity to a much greater degree in bipeds, contributing to the likelihood of heart attack and stroke. Musculoskeletal problems such as "fallen arches" in the feet, prolapse of intervertebral discs in the lower back, patellofemoral syndrome (a condition often seen in athletes resulting in chronic pain in the knee joint), and inguinal hernia have all been linked to upright posture and locomotion.

The most significant negative consequences associated with walking on two limbs relate to childbirth. The adoption of this gait entailed a fairly radical restructuring of the pelvis and a reshaping of the birth canal through which the fetus passes (Figure 8.7). Birth is actually a somewhat torturous journey for recent hominin infants, made more difficult by a fairly rigid shoulder anatomy and a larger brain. Moving from "top" to "bottom," the human birth canal consists of three components—inlet, midplane, and outlet. The transition from one to the next sees the widest dimension rotate from side-to-side to front-to-back, which means that so, too, must the newborn. Indeed, unlike nonhuman primates, a human baby enters the world facing rearward![4] Just when this particular pattern of birth evolved is unknown, though it is likely a derived feature, appearing first in the genus *Homo*. Earlier bipedal hominins (members of the genus *Australopithecus*) had a somewhat differently configured pelvis and birth canal, one that is a mosaic of derived and pleisomorphic characters (Lovejoy 2005); the latter are associated with the lower portions of the pelvis (bony structures known as the pubis and ischium). Fetal rotation would not have been necessary for australopithecine babies, given that the pelvis was fairly wide and did not change orientation from inlet to outlet. Perhaps more important, their brains were likely not appreciably larger than in modern chimpanzees.

### Do We Know Why Hominins Adopted Bipedal Behaviour?

A very short answer to this question is "absolutely not." But we do have some interesting conjecture regarding this fundamental development in hominin evolution. Central to this inquiry is the locomotory status of the creature commonly referred to as the **Last Common Ancestor**[5] (LCA) of panins and hominins, which is as yet unknown (or at best poorly known; see Chapter 9). On the ground, living chimpanzees typically travel quadrupedally using a form of movement known as **pronograde knuckle-walking** (Figure 8.8). It seems logical to presume that the LCA of humans and chimpanzees was also a knuckle-walker (Begun 2004b), though this conclusion implies that knuckle-walking is a primitive trait for hominines,[6] and

**Last Common Ancestor**
a term designating that species from which diverging clades evolved

**pronograde**
a posture in which the trunk is held more or less horizontal and approximately parallel with the surface on which the animal moves

**knuckle-walking**
a form of locomotion seen in living chimpanzees, bonobos, and gorillas, in which body weight is borne on the forelimb through contact of the flexed "second knuckle" of the hand

---

4. Rosenberg and Trevathan (2003) argue that this form of emergence of the neonate, known medically as occiput anterior, may have led to the development of assisted birth, since the mother would be unable to "catch" the newborn, remove obstructions from the airway, deflect the umbilicus from the neck, etc.

5. There can be any number of "last common ancestors" depending on the clades contrasted: of ourselves and chimpanzees, of African apes and Asian apes, or of elephants and flatworms, for that matter.

6. Remember: hominines include the gorillas, chimpanzees, bonobos, and ourselves, whereas hominins specify only the bipedal apes (humans and our ancestors), distinct from panins and gorillans (see Chapter 4).

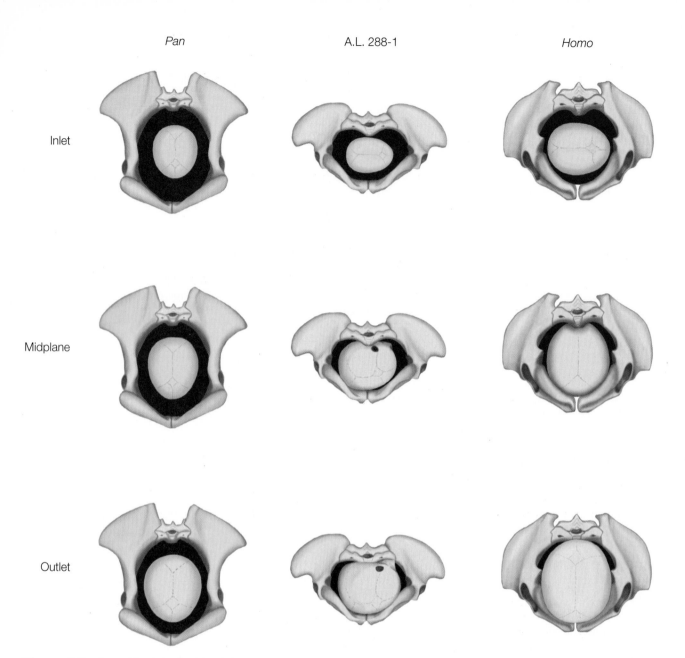

|  | Pan | A.L. 288-1 | Homo |
|---|---|---|---|
| Inlet |  |  |  |
| Midplane |  |  |  |
| Outlet |  |  |  |

**Figure 8.7** A combination of pelvic shape and large brain requires modern infants to rotate 90° through the midplane of the birth canal and emerge facing backward. The mosaic nature of the australopithecine pelvis as seen in AL 288-1 ("Lucy") likely resulted in a unique pattern of birth.

Lovejoy, C.O., (2005). The natural history of human gait and posture. Part 1: Spine and pelvis, *Gait and Posture* 21: 95-112. Copyright © 2004 Elsevier B.V. All rights reserved.

**orthograde clamber**
a form of arboreal hand-assisted bipedal locomotion applied specifically to orangutans, involving extension at the knee, hip, and shoulder

not one derived within the panin clade after it parted ways with hominins. Given that the more distantly related gorilla is also a knuckle-walking ape, a "primitive" assessment seems a reasonable position to adopt. However, others argue against this view. Crompton, Vereecke, and Thorpe (2007) propose that our *terrestrial* bipedality can be traced to an earlier *arboreal* bipedality present in the LCA, the two modes of locomotion sharing a common element of orthograde posture and leg extension. Using the orangutan as a model, Crompton and coworkers suggest that hand-assisted extended hind-limb movement over flexible[7] branches, termed **orthograde clamber**, constitutes a behaviour lending itself to a transition from tree

7. "Flexible" is a central aspect of their model, since a stable branch greater than 10 cm in diameter poses less challenge (i.e., selective pressure) for travel or feeding. Orangutans are the only living great ape that lives and travels predominantly in trees.

to ground. In support of their idea, they note that the earliest hominins predating 2.5 mya lived in more wooded habitats and retained long, grasping arms with curved fingers (see below and Chapter 9). Recent evidence of distinct anatomical differences in the chimpanzee and gorilla wrist (Kivell and Schmitt 2009) support the arboreal origins model for hominin bipedalism. These authors argue that the form of knuckle-walking found in these two apes is demonstrably different, with chimpanzees having a more flexible wrist adapted to greater arboreality and the gorilla a more rigid structure reflecting its more columnar forelimb posture and greater terrestriality. This model would argue for independent evolution of knuckle-walking behaviour in these closely related apes.

**Figure 8.8** If not carrying an object in their hand or arm, chimpanzees knuckle-walk while on the ground, with the first joint of the fingers flexed and bearing weight.

Clive Bromhall/Photolibrary/Getty Images

However, David Begun and his colleagues (Begun, Richmond, and Strait 2007) are critical of the "arboreal origins" hypothesis as it does not fit neatly with a number of aspects of the comparative anatomy of either living hominoids or extinct ancestral hominins (see Box 8.2).

http://www.chass.utoronto.ca/anthropology/Faculty/Begun/index.htm

Leaving aside the debate as to whether bipedalism arose from a terrestrial knuckle-walking or an arboreal orthograde clamber heritage (or some other ancestral locomotive form), we are still left with a fundamental question: Why? We have considered a few of the benefits of walking upright, but what behaviour(s) motivated the adoption of this unique gait? If carrying was so important, what were they carrying, why, and to where? If managing body temperature was a factor, in what conditions did this necessity acquire so much significance? In effect (as David Begun notes in Box 8.2), we need to ask: What was the locomotor and behavioural ecology of the last common ancestor?

## CARRYING: WHAT AND WHY?

A phrase that has long endured in any hypothesis germane to the origin of bipedalism is "freeing of the hands." Even Darwin in *The Descent of Man* (1871) invoked the idea that hands no longer committed to movement could be otherwise gainfully occupied manipulating objects. But freed for what purpose? Early views (e.g., Washburn 1960) implicated technology—the manufacture, use, and transport of tools—which is not an unreasonable proposition. However, bipedal adaptations predate the archaeological record for stone tools by several millions of years, and living chimpanzees have a rich (mostly nonlithic) technological tradition, yet remain quadrupedal. The magnitude of change involved in transitioning from a four- to two-legged gait is so profound that it must have involved selection favouring extended periods of upright walking (Harcourt-Smith 2007). Such pressures would have been rooted in ongoing environmental changes. At that time, the continuous forest cover was slowly being replaced by woodland and woodland savannah. It is likely that traditionally exploited food resources became more patchily distributed, necessitating a shift in food-getting strategies and/or the adoption of new foods. As a result, at least some Miocene hominoids spent increasing amounts of time travelling over more open ground, though how far and to what degree are unanswered (perhaps unanswerable) questions.

A number of hypotheses associating bipedal behaviour with food transport have been proposed, based on interpretations of the fossil and early archaeological record, comparative anatomy, and primate analogy. Perhaps the most ambitious among these has been Owen Lovejoy's (1981) "male provisioning" hypothesis. We say ambitious because Lovejoy attempted to synthesize aspects of behaviour, physiology, and sociology into one overarching idea and contentious in the context of an emerging feminist anthropology in the 1970s and 1980s, which rightly took

BOX 8.2    PROFILE... Out On A Limb? Not!

*David Begun is Professor of Anthropology at the University of Toronto specializing in Miocene hominoid evolution.*

Bipedalism in humans is a remarkable adaptation that defines our lineage. We are not sure when bipedalism evolved, though indications are that it was at least 7 mya (Brunet et al. 2002a, b). The big question is this: Why did bipedalism evolve in humans in the first place? To understand this, we need to know from what the first human bipeds evolved—that is: What was the positional behaviour (posture and locomotion) of the ancestors of the first bipeds (Begun, 1992, 2004c; Richmond, Begun, and Strait 2001)? There are two main views on this question. Probably the most widely accepted hypothesis is that human bipedality evolved from a form of positional behaviour that emphasized climbing and vertical postures in the trees. We humans share numerous characteristics with our highly arboreal close relatives, the great apes, including highly mobile shoulder joints, wrists with a limited contact with the ulna, and many detailed features of the wrist and fingerbones. The ulna is one of two bones in the forearm; with reference to the hand, it is found on the side away from the thumb—that is, nearest the little finger. Try this: with your palm facing you, try to tilt your wrist in the direction of your pinky finger, then toward your thumb. There is a much looser connection on the pinky side, so it is much more mobile. Also, the vertical position of our backbone comes from upright postures adopted by our ancestors as they climbed tree trunks (Stern 1975). The other theory is that humans went through a terrestrial phase such as that seen today in living African apes, who are knuckle-walkers (they move with their wrists extended, bearing weight on the middle of the three bones of the fingers). The arboreal characteristics of the human upper limb, which are undeniable, have been superimposed on a second set of features that we see only in living knuckle-walkers, which of course also spend a lot of time in the trees. The most striking of these features is the fusion of two bones of the wrist. Nearly all primates have nine bones in their wrists, among which are two called the centrale and the scaphoid. Hominoids such as orangutans and gibbons, as well as almost all other primates (a few exceptions exist among Malagasy prosimians) have these nine wristbones. But African apes, along with living and fossil humans, have only eight bones, the centrale and the scaphoid having become fused together (Richmond, Begun, and Strait 2001; Begun 2004c). How can we reconcile these two opposing theories to understand how bipedalism in humans evolved?

There is no doubt that humans evolved from an ancestor that was dependent on trees. Nearly all primates are, even the most terrestrial ones, such as gorillas and baboons. But did we go through a knuckle-walking phase on our way to a fully terrestrial lifestyle? In the past, the fossil evidence has been interpreted to indicate that humans moved into a savanna environment, away from the trees, and that bipedalism evolved as an efficient mode of locomotion on the ground. Indeed, we humans are highly efficient in our terrestrial locomotion, using less energy than other primates to move about. Yet the fossil evidence tells a different story. We now know from the fossil record that all humans from before the appearance of our genus, *Homo*, lived in environments with forests of one type or another. So it is entirely plausible that humans descended from the trees gradually, perhaps in response to changing ecological conditions in Africa that were leading to a breaking up of the continuous forest cover around the equator.

Recent evidence from behavioural studies of orangutans in Indonesia supports the view that humans transitioned from arboreal to terrestrial without going through a knuckle-walking phase (Thorpe, Holder, and Crompton 2007). Orangutans in this study were observed to practise extended periods of bipedal behaviour in the trees; this was taken as a model for the precursor to the evolution of human bipedalism. But in most cases, the orangutans were also supporting themselves with their arms, which led the researchers to call this behaviour "hand assisted bipedalism," though others called it "foot assisted suspension" (Begun, Richmond, and Strait 2007). The fact is that all primates are occasionally bipedal, so the observation that orangutans do it in the trees is not surprising. Is it a good model for the origin of human bipedalism? Probably not. We need to explain the sharing among African apes and humans of the centrale fused to the scaphoid, as well as more than a dozen features of the arm and wrist that seem to be present to limit extension (bending the wrist toward the back of the forearm) and to strengthen resistance to shear (forces that cross from the thumb to the pinky side of the wrist). Why would humans share these features with African apes if we did not also share with them a style of locomotion requiring these features? Otherwise, since humans and chimps are more closely related to each other than are chimps and gorillas, and if humans do not share a knuckle-walking ancestry with African apes, gorillas and chimps would have to have evolved knuckle-walking independently, and humans would have to have evolved the 20-plus features of the forelimb that we share with African apes independently as well, for some other reason (Begun 2004c). Both scenarios seem highly unlikely. In the end, there is nothing about the story of the origin of bipedalism that precludes an arboreal chapter. But the multitude of bony features we share with living knuckle-walkers can really only be explained by the hypothesis that humans passed through a knuckle-walking phase on our way to becoming fully committed terrestrial bipeds.

Source: Written by Dr. David Begun, Department of Anthropology, University of Toronto.

exception to the more or less passive role that Lovejoy assigned to females. The male provisioning model argued that bipedalism had a selective advantage in a more open, expansive habitat in which males could range widely carrying tools and weapons and return with food (especially hunted or scavenged meat) to a **home base**. Once "home," males would share resources with a monogamously pair-bonded female and their offspring. This bond was ensured by the evolution of **concealed ovulation** in females: since males could no longer visually identify sexual receptiveness in females, their guaranty of paternity was effectively purchased with food. The success of this arrangement was enhanced by a reduction in **birth spacing** permitted by the high energy of animal protein, which in turn allowed for fairly rapid population increase.

There are many errors and inconsistencies in Lovejoy's 1981 account, not the least of which is that monogamous pair bonding is rare among primates generally, and in humans in particular (though some would characterize humans as "serially monogamous," moving from one committed relationship to the next). In those animals that do bond for life, sexual dimorphism tends to be reduced, which we know is not the case for the hominin fossil record (see Chapter 9). We know that females, hominin and panin alike, assume significant roles in nearly all aspects of social life and are not limited to a dependent existence of childbearing, childrearing, and contingent foraging (see Hager 1997). Lovejoy (2009) has recently produced a refreshed, more nuanced model of early hominin life history and social behaviour following the publication of the analysis of the *Ardipithecus ramidus* remains from Ethiopia (see Chapter 9). He has retained, however, his original model's central features: bipedality, vested male provisioning, concealed ovulation, and reduction of sexual size dimorphism. Lovejoy links such changes to habitat expansion, cooperative foraging among males, and the advent of female choice for nonaggressive males (also seen among some living nonhuman primates). At this point in time, we await the critique of Lovejoy's updated model. Having noted this, we must also observe that a female's reproductive commitments are a very real biological reality that cannot be discounted when we are considering how bipedal adaptation evolved (see Box 8.3).

# FEEDING: HOW AND WHEN?

Food is fundamental. Second only to sex as an organizing feature of primate social structure and intragroup behaviour (Chapter 6), it ranks first from the perspective of **time allocation** and **energy budget** among most if not all primate species, including panins (Lehmann et al. 2007). We have already seen that food is implicated in a number of scenarios regarding bipedal origins, either as an object carried or in terms of efficient travel on the ground between food resource patches. However, as noted earlier, energetic efficiency was not a feature of walking in the earliest hominins, and furthermore, these forms retained certain forelimb characters associated with climbing or grasping in trees (discussed more fully in Chapter 9). This combination of features suggested to Kevin Hunt (1994) that habitual bipedal *walking* developed around 3 to 4 mya from an earlier *positional* adaptation for bipedal foraging. Hunt noted that among panins at two sites in Tanzania, 80% of all bipedal events were related to food getting (others being vigilance, display, etc.), and of these, 95% were postural rather than locomotory. Chimpanzees either stood upright on the ground to reach into the lower branches of trees, or they balanced erect on branches, supported by one hand, while collecting fruit with the other. Hunt suggested that such behaviours in early hominins would have selected for an anatomy of the foot, pelvis, and trunk that would be "pre-adaptive" for a shift from standing to walking. In this model, then, bipedal walking was contingent on a prior phase of bipedal standing.

Which of these various hypotheses and adaptive advantages seems most able to explain bipedalism? Bits and pieces of each is a reasonable answer. Two things are certain: bipedality did not evolve over a short period time. The required anatomical and behavioural changes are simply too profound and too extensive to argue otherwise. Evidence for bipedalism is found in protohominins as old as 6 million years (Richmond and Jungers 2008), whereas anatomy associated with arboreal climbing persists until at least 3 million years ago

**home base**
an area likely associated with shelter and water to which hominins would repeatedly return from foraging

**concealed ovulation**
ovulation occurs during that stage in a placental female mammal's reproductive cycle (estrus) during which she is receptive to sexual intercourse (either physiologically or induced through copulation); it may be signalled with swelling and reddening of the genital area. Thus, concealed ovulation refers to the absence of visual signalling, such that the male is unable to detect when a female may be likely to conceive

**birth spacing**
the amount of time that passes between life births, e.g., birthdate to birthdate. In primate life history, birth spacing is correlated with a number of variables, including female rank. Access to food resources is a primary determinant of birth spacing

**time allocation**
in the study of life history, time allocation studies document how much time is spent during a given time period (day, season, age stage, etc.) performing particular tasks

**energy budget**
a compendium of the sources and expenditures of energy, typically measured in calories or kilojoules

**BOX 8.3** **FOCUS ON... Babies On Board**

Carrying has long been touted as one factor in the evolution of bipedalism (Robinson 1972; Watson et al. 2009), and some items are difficult if not impossible to put down. Take a fetus, for example: wherever mom goes, it goes! This reality prompted Whitcome, Shapiro, and Lieberman (2007) to ask whether the lower spine in women was somehow adapted to this increased

burden and forward displacement of the centre of mass (COM) during pregnancy. As noted in Table 8.1, a lower curve in the spine (lordosis) is normally present in humans of both sexes, facilitating positioning of the COM in line with the axis of weight transfer through the hips to the lower limbs. This curve, which develops in children in response to the shift from crawling to

Reprinted by permission from Macmillan Publishers Ltd: *Nature*, K.K. Whitcome, L.J. Shapiro, D.E. Lieberman, (2007). Fetal load and the evolution of lumbar lordosis in bipedal hominins, 450: 1075-1078. Copyright © 2007 Nature Publishing Group.

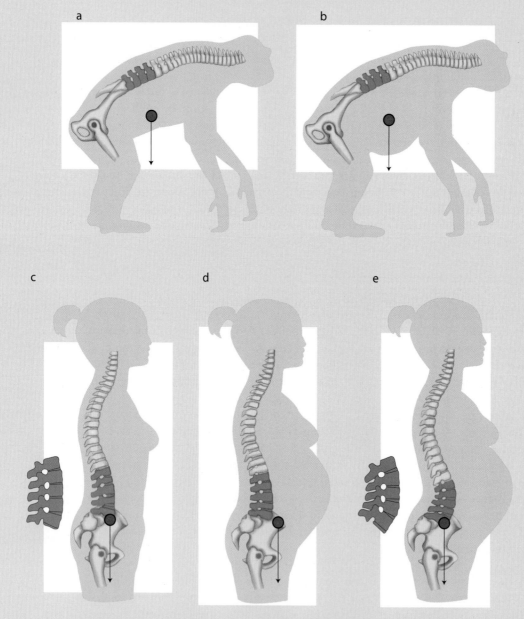

**Figure 8.9** Lumbar lordosis is adaptive in bipeds for effective weight transfer, balance, and stability, and must be realigned in pregnant human females to offset the forward placement and weight of the fetus.

**Figure 8.10** While travelling, infant apes ride on the mother's back, aided by prehensile hands and feet and the chimpanzee's coarse hair.

After birth, of course, infant apes are not able to get around on their own. Newborn chimpanzees are as helpless as human babies. They do not begin to travel on their own until about age three (Pontzer and Wrangham 2006) and are usually carried on their mother's back, clinging to her body hair (Figure 8.10). This strategy would not work for bipedal hominins, whose evolution can be characterized by the loss of two necessary features: effective body hair and a grasping foot. Amaral (2008) suggests that hair loss may have evolved very early in a forested habitat to cope with heat stress associated with high activity levels. If so, this would have placed a high selective pressure, especially on females, to adopt bipedal behaviour enabling infant carrying. Alemseged and colleagues (2006) note that a 3.3-million-year-old juvenile hominin discovered in Ethiopia lacks a prehensile foot structure, indicating a long history of infant carrying by mothers.

Wall-Scheffler, Geiger, and Steudel-Numbers (2007) note that ethnographic studies of modern human hunter-gatherers reveal that a mother typically carries her infant for the first years of life in an adjustable sling, allowing her to shift the child to different body positions (e.g., back, hip) as necessary in order to perform various tasks. They argue that devices such as slings may have been an early technological development, since arm carrying increases the energy cost of locomotion and reduces mobility by shortening stride length (i.e., we walk with longer steps if we can swing our arms). These costs are especially true for hominins with relatively narrow hips – an evolutionary development appearing around 2 million years ago (see Chapter 10). Recent experimental studies suggest that the energetic efficiency of "sling carrying" is realized only if the load (infant) is borne on the mother's front or back; an asymmetric load (hip carrying) actually consumes more energy (Watson et al. 2008).

upright walking, is never present in quadrupedal forms such as chimpanzees. Whitcome and colleagues found that during pregnancy women compensate for the weight of the fetus by shifting the lower back rearward. They effectively adjust their posture so that their "pregnancy centre of mass" is aligned for appropriate weight transfer and stability (see Figure 8.9). A change in the size and shape of the three lower lumbar vertebrae in females accommodates this behavioural response. In females, these vertebrae are more wedge-shaped toward the back, with larger and stronger articulating surfaces. Interestingly, in two well-preserved lumbar spines recovered from hominin ancestors from South Africa, this adaptation is present in the one considered female (known as Sts 14), and absent in the one deemed male (Stw 431)!

(Alemseged, Spoor, and Kimbel 2006). Most researchers now accept a gradual transition in the evolution of bipedal locomotion, from an *occasional* behaviour as seen in the earliest protohominins between 4.5 to 7.0 mya, to *habitual* bipedality persisting until ca. 2.0 mya, ending in an *obligate* commitment to bipedalism with the appearance of the first members of the genus *Homo* (Harcourt-Smith 2007). Interestingly, Videan and McGrew (2001) studied bipedal posture and locomotion in captive chimpanzees and bonobos and found that both species exhibited various bipedal behaviours with about the same frequency. However, there were some fascinating differences. Immature individuals in both species were more prone to bipedal locomotion than adults. Adult chimpanzees were more likely to use bipedalism for display; in bonobos it was for vigilance and carrying. Such studies tell us we should be wary of seeking a "best explanation" for the evolution of bipedalism, as it clearly serves a multitude of useful purposes.

## Tales Told by Teeth

Teeth are unique warehouses of information. The different kinds of teeth that make up a dentition—incisors, canines, premolars, molars[8]—vary in size and shape (i.e., height,

---

8. These tooth classes are found in the adult ("permanent") dentition. Subadults have fewer teeth: deciduous incisors, canines, and molars. These latter teeth are replaced by the permanent premolars in the adult dentition.

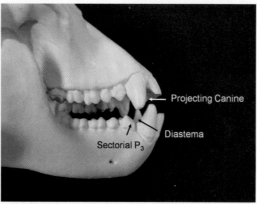

**Figure 8.11** Diagnostic features of hominin dentition include reduction or absence of C/P3 honing mechanism with loss of the sectorial P3.

Courtesy of Richard Lazenby

breadth, width of crowns and roots), structure (cusp pattern, enamel thickness), and pattern of wear (surface flattening, sharpening, damage). This variation reflects a tooth's evolutionary history as well as its function during life—its clade as well as its grade (Begun 2004b see Chapter 4 for discussion of clade and grade). Also, because they are extremely durable, teeth are "overrepresented" in the fossil record; historically, they have been the most commonly discovered type of fossil remains. Consequently, volumes have been written, and numerous debates engaged, regarding what teeth tell us about hominin evolution. Often single teeth—even fragments—can alter our interpretations of fossil taxonomy and diversity, especially for early protohominins, for which we have comparatively few remnants (Haile-Sellassie, Suwa, and White 2004; Begun 2004b).

Two features are often cited as distinctive of hominin versus hominid (panin and gorilline) dentitions.[9] The first is canine size reduction with loss of the C/P3 honing mechanism and decreased canine sexual dimorphism (Figure 8.11); the second is increasing molar enamel thickness. These changes have implications for social behaviours within and between sexes as well as for dietary adaptation, in terms of foods eaten and their mechanical properties (i.e., how hard and tough individual food items might be) (Lucas, Constantino, and Wood 2008).

## Canine Honing

Primate canines are large, sharp teeth that project beyond the **occlusal plane**. These teeth serve a variety of functions, both passive (processing food) and aggressive (agonistic displays, fighting). For species in which male–male competition is a significant aspect of social life, canines tend to exhibit greater levels of sexual dimorphism beyond that expected owing to body size differences (Plavcan 2003). These projecting canines are accommodated in the opposing jaw by a **diastema**; the large upper canine, for example, fits into the space (diastema) between the lower canine and third premolar (P3) when the mouth is closed. In fact, when apes close their mouths, the **distolingual** surface of the maxillary (upper) canine slides along the **mesiobuccal** surface of the mandibular (lower) P3, effectively **honing** (sharpening) the canine and creating what is known as a **sectorial P3**. In hominins and some protohominins (Haille-Selassie, Suwa, and White 2004), reduction in the size of the upper canine is associated with progressive loss of the C/P3 honing mechanism, reduction or closure of the diastema in the lower mandible, and blunting rather than sharpening of the tips of the canines as they occlude with the teeth in the opposing jaw—remember these concepts as they will return in Chapter 9.

We are not yet sure of the evolutionary timing of these dental modifications; indeed, we may have great difficulty pinpointing these (as other) transitions associated with the hominin–panin divergence (Cobb 2008; we discuss why this is so in Chapter 9). But we *can* make some inferences regarding their significance. For example, if large, projecting canines are most expressive in males living in competitive multimale primate societies in which aggression plays an important role in establishing and maintaining rank and thus preferred access to estrous females, then canine reduction suggests important changes in early hominin social organization. It might be suggested that a behavioural hallmark of hominin evolution associated with canine reduction

**occlusal plane**

The occlusal plane reflects the orientation of the chewing (i.e., occlusal) surfaces of the upper and lower dentitions

**diastema**

a space between adjacent teeth in the dental row into which the canine from the opposite jaw fits in a closed mouth

**distolingual**

the conjunction of the rearward (distal, away from the midline of the mouth) and inner (lingual, or tongue-facing) surfaces of a tooth

**mesiobuccal**

the conjunction of the forward (mesial, toward the midline) and buccal (outer, cheek-facing) surfaces of a tooth

**honing**

sharpening, in this instance of one tooth through repeated contact with another

**sectorial P3**

in Old World primates, a lower third premolar in which the mesiobuccal surface appears as a long, sloping surface due to contact with the upper canine

---

9. Here we focus on teeth, but in actuality a holistic view of dental adaptation would include properties of the supporting skeletal structures of the upper (maxilla) and lower (mandible) jaws. These aspects are considered in Chapters 9 and 10.

is decreased male–male competition and an increase in relations emphasizing cooperation and coalition (Begun 2004a). Having said this, we also need to account for canine reduction in females. Canine teeth in most female primates are not as large as in conspecific males, but they are nonetheless fairly large and projecting, and they are used as weapons in agonistic encounters with males, predators, and other females. Some time ago, Greenfield (1992) proposed a "dual selection" hypothesis to account for male and female canine reduction, in which less **intrasexual** competition and a shift to using canines as "modified incisors" to process food selectively favoured smaller canines. Others see little comparative evidence for the "dual selection" dietary explanation for female canine reduction (e.g., Plavcan and Kelley 1996), suggesting that it can be viewed as a direct outcome of fewer female aggressive encounters or as a **correlated response**—that is, a change in a supposedly independent feature (such as male and female facial **prognathism**) produced a change in canine dimensions.

## Enamel Thickness

Enamel thickness refers to the depth of the outer layer of a tooth overlying the supporting dentin relative to the size of the tooth (Figure 8.12a). As discussed in Chapter 7, enamel thickness has historically played an important role in reconstructing primate evolutionary history. For example, middle Miocene fossil hominoids such as European *Dryopithecus* have thin-enamelled molars, whereas more recent forms such as *Ouranopithecus*, discovered in Greece and dating to ca. 8 mya, have the thick-enamel trait seen in most hominins. However, the degree to which this classic dental attribute reflects clade (phylogeny) versus grade (function) is open to debate. Begun (2004b) notes, for example, that this feature tends to distinguish higher order taxonomic categories (i.e., genus and above) rather than species-level ones, and thus will have limited utility in pointing us in the direction of the LCA, since this creature would have been very closely related to both its hominin descendants and its panin ones.

Enamel thickness is also an indicator of dietary adaptation, with thick-enamelled species exploiting harder, more abrasive foods and thinner enamelled species exploiting softer items such as fruits. Lucas, Constantino, and Wood (2008) have suggested that the **microstructure**

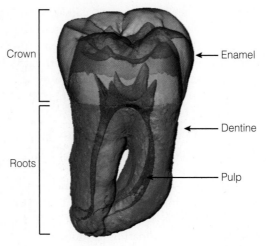

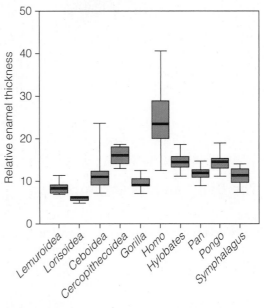

**intrasexual**

"intra" means within; thus intrasexual variation refers to differences that exist within males or females separately

**correlated response**

changes that occur in one feature are consistently associated with changes occurring in another

**prognathism**

projection of the lower face; the gnathic portion of the face is that which contains the upper and lower jaws

**Figure 8.12** (a) Teeth are composed of an enamel crown (light blue) supported by an underlying dentin layer that also contributes to the roots, which are embedded in bone. Enamel thickness in hominoid teeth may be an indicator of phylogeny, but it also reflects adaptation to particular diets adopted by several taxa that may or may not be closely related. (b) The variation in enamel thickness within living primates is large, especially in ourselves. Thus, while humans on average have the greatest enamel thickness, there is overlap with other species, including panins, suggesting limited utility of enamel thickness for phylogenetic inference.

(top) Courtesy of Matthew Skinner (bottom) Reprinted from the *Journal of Human Evolution*, Vol. 54/2, Anthony J. Olejniczak, Paul Tafforeau, Robin N.M. Feeney, Lawrence B. Martin, Three-dimensional primate molar enamel thickness, pp. 187–195, 2008, with permission from Elsevier

**microstructure**

the arrangement of cells and their associated structures that contribute to the material properties of a tissue; usually, microstructure is only viewable with the use of instruments such as microscopes and CT scanners

of thick enamel helps prevent damage to a tooth by restricting the propagation of cracks from deep within the tooth to the outer surface. Among the early protohominins, the degree of enamel thickness varies, though generally it is always thicker than in living chimps and gorillas. However, studies of living primates, including humans, suggest a greater range of enamel thickness variation than previously appreciated (e.g., Suwa and Kono 2005; Olejniczak et al. 2008; Figure 8.12b). As such, enamel thickness may not be as reliable an indicator of phylogeny as we once believed.

## WHY IS MY FOREHEAD SO LARGE?

As we outlined in Chapter 5, one of the defining features of primates with respect to other mammals is an increase in **relative brain size**. That is, primates have a higher ratio of brain mass to body mass. In the course of hominin evolution, brain/body **scaling** has been taken to an extreme, culminating in modern humans. Though this is highly variable, on average your brain is about three times larger than expected for a hominine of your body size. In the following chapters we will be considering how these changes are manifested in the hominin fossil record. Still, there are several issues germane to distinguishing the hominin from the nonhominin brain that merit our attention at this time. The first of these is organization. It is not overall size alone that sets the hominin brain apart, but how various structures *in* the brain have changed with respect to one another. This reorganization reflects the ways in which some functional capacities of the hominin brain have been emphasized or expanded at the expense of others over time (Holloway, Broadfield, and Yuan 2003). We also need to consider how we "feed" this ever-expanding brain—what behavioural changes would have provided for the increased energy demands of this most complex and least understood organ?

### The Brain and Its Organization

The hominine brain is a tiered, bilateral, lobular, and fissured mass with the consistency of unset gelatine, the outer layer of which is intricately folded (Figure 8.13). The major divisions of the brain include the hindbrain (cerebellum, pons, medulla), midbrain (tectum, tegmentum), and forebrain (cerebrum, thalamus, hypothalamus). The cerebrum is divided into two hemispheres, each further partitioned into four lobes: frontal, parietal, occipital, temporal.[10] These lobes are distinguished by folds (gyri) and fissures (sulci). In evolutionary terms, the forebrain is most recent, the hindbrain most ancient—indeed, our hindbrain resembles the entire brain of creatures such as reptiles or birds. Among hominins, the cerebrum—also known as the cerebral cortex—is highly convoluted compared to that of panins.

As we will discuss in the following chapters, hominin evolution is characterized by fundamental shifts in geography and ecology, social and cultural dynamics, technological achievement, and communication. All of these together suggest accompanying transformations in the central nervous system (CNS). It is fair to surmise that increasing social and technological complexity has placed a selective premium on those brain functions responsible for features such as fine motor control, long-term memory, reasoning/planning, and verbal/visual communication,

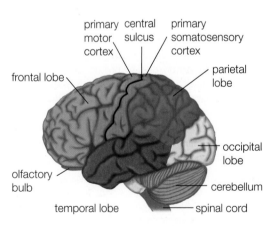

primary central primary
motor sulcus somatosensory
cortex cortex

frontal lobe

parietal lobe

occipital lobe

olfactory bulb

cerebellum

temporal lobe

spinal cord

**Figure 8.13** The brain is a complex arrangement of layers, lobes, folds, and fissures.

10. Lobes are named according to the bone of the cranium against which they lie; thus the temporal lobe of the brain lies under the temporal bone of the cranium.

among others (including distinctions related to gender) (Lindefors, Nunn, and Barton 2007). While the relative volume of some compartments of the **neocortex**, such as the frontal lobe, appears similar among hominoids (Semendeferi and Damasio 2000), the degree of convolution—and thus the surface area and neuronal density of the neocortex within lobes—shows a gradient within mammals, including primates (Zilles et al. 1988), associated with brain functionality (Toro and Burnod 2005).

**Endocasts**, whether natural or reconstructed (Figure 8.14), provide unique insights into brain evolution, forming the basis for the science of **paleoneurology**. They provide information pertaining only to the outer surface of the cerebral cortex; even so, the relative positions of major features and the volumes of cortical areas can both be determined. One of these features, the **lunate sulcus (LS)**, has been the subject of considerable debate over the years, especially regarding its placement in the brains of earlier hominins such as the australopithecines (Holloway, Broadfield, and Yuan 2003). The LS, which demarcates the primary visual cortex of the occipital lobe, is readily seen in anthropoid primates but less commonly in modern humans. When it is present in the human brain, it occupies a position more to the back of the brain than in species such as chimpanzees, suggesting relative reduction of the primary visual cortex in ourselves. Adjacent areas of the brain, such as the parietal and temporal lobes, have been shown to be somewhat larger than expected in humans (Rilling and Seligman 2002). This presumably reflects an emphasis on the brain functions of these regions, such as language capacity. Recently, Holloway, Clarke, and Tobias (2004) have observed a posterior placement of the LS in a small-brained early hominin from South Africa dated to ca. 2.5 mya, suggesting that brain reorganization occurred prior to significant increases in volume. They argue that the implied reduction in the primary visual cortex in these (and possibly earlier) hominins would have allowed increases in adjacent areas of the brain as previously noted—areas associated with the integration and analysis of information facilitating tool making and use (e.g., throwing), long-term spatial memory, facial recognition of self and others (including predators), and social communication. Such interpretations are by their nature speculative, but they are grounded in our current understanding of brain function. All of the features mentioned are present in panins to some degree, but they are most highly developed in ourselves, and the qualitative and quantitative differences could well be associated with the neural reorganization noted by Holloway and colleagues.

Besides endocasts, another avenue advancing our understanding of brain evolution is primate comparative neuroanatomy. Recently, Carol MacLeod, a paleoneurologist at Vancouver's Langara College, applied magnetic resonance imaging and histology to compare size and complexity in the cerebellums of anthropoids, hominoids, and humans in relation to cognitive functioning (see Box 8.4).

**neocortex**
the outer portion of the mammalian brain in which higher functions such as memory, reasoning, language processing and production, and problem-solving occur

**endocasts**
impressions of the inner surface of the cranium and outer surface of the brain, which may occur naturally as "fossils" or from moulds created in the laboratory

**paleoneurology**
the study of the evolution of the brain and its functions

**lunate sulcus**
a fissure found in the anterior portion of the occipital lobe that demarcates the primary visual cortex; readily visible in nonhuman primate brains, the LS is often not seen in humans

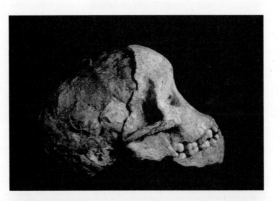

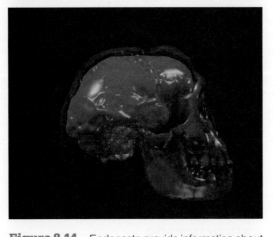

**Figure 8.14** Endocasts provide information about the external configuration of the brain, including relative size and position of lobes, gyri, and sulci. (a) One of the most famous natural endocasts, associated with a young *Australopithecus africanus* specimen from the site of Taung, South Africa. (b) Modern medical imaging now allows creation of virtual endocasts, such as that of the controversial Liang Bua 1 specimen from Indonesia. (Not to scale.)

(top) Javier Trueba/MSF/Photo Researchers, Inc. (bottom) Courtesy of Kirk E. Smith, Electronic Radiology Laboratory, Mallinckrodt Institute of Radiology, Washington University at St. Louis, MO.

## PROFILE... Thinking Outside the Box

Courtesy of Carol MacLeod.

*Dr. Carol MacLeod teaches Anthropology at Langara College in Vancouver, BC. Her research has focused on evolution and comparative anatomy of the primate cerebellum.*

How does one go about studying one of the most fascinating of questions about human origins—why and how humans became so smart? What is special about our brains? How are our brains different from the brains of chimpanzees, macaques, or lorises? Are our brains organized differently from the brains of our closest relatives, the great apes, or are we simply all genius chimpanzees because we have huge brains?

One way of answering these questions is to measure primate neuroanatomical structures and to compare them with one another to see if there have been significant increases in particular structures in certain taxa. Not all brain structures increase at the same rate; the neocortex and neocerebellum increase at a higher rate than earlier developing structures when these structures are regressed against whole brain volume (Finlay and Darlington 1995). Multiple regression analysis shows this exponential increase clearly and can reveal unexpected increases in some structures when the primate sample size is examined in detail.

For my research, I collected as many measures from primate brains as I could, using both magnetic resonance brain scans and preserved brains of monkeys, apes, and humans. My ape sample was large enough to analyze apes and humans against monkeys to see if there was differential expansion of some structures, reflecting a grade shift (Martin 1980) in brain proportions of hominoids to monkeys. My particular interest is the cerebellum, that cauliflower-like appendage at the base of the brain. Until recently, the cerebellum was thought to be concerned uniquely with movement and balance. This is true of the oldest part of the cerebellum, the vermis (medial cerebellum). Now neuroscientists are showing great interest in the lateral part of the cerebellum, the neocerebellum. This is important in the planning of movement, visuospatial problem solving, procedural learning (learning how to do something), working memory ("remembering" several things at once when executing a task), attention switching, and even language in humans. In other words, the lateral cerebellum participates in thinking.

I was not surprised to see that the neocerebellum was larger than expected in apes over monkeys, but I was surprised at the magnitude of this increase. The hominoid lateral cerebellum, when regressed against the vermis, is 2.7 times larger than the monkey lateral cerebellum with a vermis of the same size (MacLeod et al. 2003). The neurological structure has undergone selection, and a whole taxonomic category has acquired a new outlook on the world as a result. The skills of the lateral cerebellum noted earlier were probably important to the early hominoids as they acquired finesse in exploiting the frugivorous niche as suspensory feeders. With the increase in brain size of the ancestors to great apes and humans, these cerebellar skills were augmented, perhaps to facilitate tool using and making, as well as complex feeding strategies characteristic of the great apes and early hominins.

An intrinsic love of anatomy drives many a physical anthropologist. Collecting volumes of brain structures is time consuming and meticulous work, but it is a pleasure for me to measure volumes from such a beautiful and complex structure as the cerebellum. There is much more to learn about its evolution in the primate order.

Source: Written by Dr. Carol MacLeod, Department of Anthropology, Langara College, Vancouver

## ENERGETICS

Physiologists studying the modern adult human brain tell us that it forms about 2% of our body mass yet demands 15% of cardiac output, 20% of oxygen consumption, and 25% of glucose utilization. Under resting conditions (awake or asleep) the brain relies almost entirely on the simple sugar glucose as its energy source, and whole-brain and regional[11] studies show increases in glucose utilization with normal neuronal activity. The brain "burns" approximately 4.2 kilojoules of energy per minute (about 1 calorie)—anyway you look at it, the brain

---

11. Such studies focus on specific functions of the brain, such as motor tasks or various sensory stimulations (visual, auditory). Recently Kemppainen and colleagues (2005) showed that as the level of physical exercise and thus brain activity increases, the brain "switches" from glucose to lactate as a source of metabolic energy.

is not an economical organ to keep running! Of course, size is a factor here, both phylogenetically (evolution) and ontogenetically (growth). Early hominins were smaller in both body size and brain size, with the latter not much larger than those of living panins. Significant increases in body and relative brain mass have occurred only within the past 2.3 million years with the transition from the genus *Australopithecus* to *Homo* (see Chapter 10). Aiello and Wells (2002) estimate that this evolutionary development increased resting metabolic energy requirements by about 39%, more so for females than for males due to the added costs of pregnancy, gestation, and lactation. Furthermore, the costs are even greater for subadults (infants and children especially), for whom the brain forms a higher proportion of body mass and can consume up to 70% of total energy requirements (ibid.).

Growing bigger bodies and brains must have been accompanied by changes in how these larger, "brainier" hominins captured energy (e.g., by hunting) and used it for growth, maintenance, and reproduction. Possibly they shifted to higher quality, energy-dense foods, reallocated energy from one metabolic need to another, or simply changed activity levels to reduce energy requirements. Some combination of these is a reasonable if not probable conclusion. The paleontological record for these early members of the genus *Homo* indicates a continuation of the trend toward reduced jaw and tooth size, increased lower-limb length, and decreased body breadth (the adaptive value of these changes is explored in Chapters 10 and 11). These modifications imply a significant dietary change: a shift away from hard, tough foods, which require larger teeth and jaws (Lucas, Constantino, and Wood 2008), toward resources more readily digestible with a smaller gut (which would fit into a narrower trunk). In particular, this means more meat and fat, accompanied by items with high carbohydrate content such as tubers and seeds (Aiello and Wells 2002). This dietary transition is captured by an idea proposed in the 1990s called the "expensive tissue hypothesis," ETH for short (Aiello and Wheeler 1995). This hypothesis argues that the body's essential organs bear 'fixed costs'—that is, they have specific energy demands that must be met in order to maintain function. These organs include the brain, liver, heart, kidneys, intestinal tract, and lungs. Aiello and Wheeler calculated that of these, only the size of the intestinal tract was smaller than expected for an average 65 kg human. They concluded that this tradeoff—a shift of energy resources from intestinal tract size to brain size—was achieved by adopting the kind of diet described above: more meat and fewer fibrous, plant-based resources, which require a large gastrointestinal tract for processing. This would have been accomplished by a shift in foraging strategy to increase the proportion of hunted game; this in turn would have been realized most effectively by cooperative hunting facilitated by an increase in group size required to provide the necessary "hominin power."

Support for the ETH has been slow in coming (Gibbons 2007). However, over the past few years studies of primates and other animals have confirmed the general premise of energy tradeoffs among "expensive" tissues. For example, Isler and Van Schaik (2007) did not find a negative correlation[12] for brain and gut size in birds, but they did find one for brain and pectoral muscle size. On average, pectoral muscles comprise 18% of a bird's body mass and are energy-expensive tissues, given that they must generate sufficient power for liftoff. In other words, larger bird brains mean smaller pectoral muscles. Among primates, capuchin monkeys in Central America have relatively large brains and small guts and eat a high-quality diet that includes insects and bird's eggs, whereas sympatric howler monkeys have relatively small brains and large guts, which they require in order to digest fruit and leaves.

As suggested earlier, hunting and the reallocation of resources among tissues are two possible avenues to feed an expanding brain. Another is by changing the amount of energy we use, and this can be achieved in two ways. First, we can conserve energy by limiting activity. Contemporary human populations adopt this strategy when resources are scarce; similarly, primates generally spend a good deal of the day resting when not feeding or travelling. However, for a mobile forager whose life depends on tracking wild game, resting is not an especially viable option.

---

12. A negative correlation exists if one variable increases in response to the other decreasing.

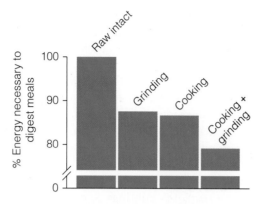

**Figure 8.15** Cooking and grinding is the most "cost-effective" way to acquire nutrients from meat.

Another option is to modulate growth rate.[13] Humans grow in three phases (see Chapter 14). From birth to about two years, growth is fairly rapid; then it drops off until puberty, after which it picks up again until maturity is reached at around 18 years of age. This fast–slow–fast pattern differs from that of panins, who match humans in the first two years but then accelerate growth until just before achieving maturity at 12 years, when growth slows. These different growth trajectories result in lower energy costs for human infants and children. Chimpanzees use 50 kcal per day versus 27 kcal per day for humans during the first 10 years; subsequently they use on average 11 kcal per day and humans 42 kcal per day until maturity (Aiello and Wells 2002). The benefits are twofold: brain growth continues until later childhood in humans, and reduced demand for body growth at this time means more energy can be given over to growing brains. Furthermore, children are typically not self-sufficient during this period; thus lower energy demand during the first 10 years represents less of a burden for those who are providing food.

A final wrinkle in the "expensive tissue–energy tradeoff" story has recently been argued by primatologist Richard Wrangham and his colleagues (Boback et al. 2007). In an experimental study using Burmese pythons, they measured the **specific dynamic action** (SDA) for four different diets: intact raw beef, ground raw beef, intact cooked beef, and ground cooked beef. They found that the least costly diet in terms of digestion and nutrient capture was meat that had been ground and cooked; this reduced SDA by almost 24% compared to the intact raw meal (Figure 8.15). Grinding reduces the energy required for digestion by disrupting tissue integrity; cooking reduces food toughness, which saves energy for species that masticate their food. For a standard human diet including cooked food, the SDA is relatively low: about 6 to 8% of the energy ingested is used to process it. The implication for hominin evolution, and for encephalization in particular, is that the advent of cooking, or cooking and grinding combined, would have further enhanced the energy equation: for every unit of energy captured, less would have been required for getting nutrients into the body so that more could be used for (brain) growth. The open question—and a large one—is when in the past did our ancestors begin to process their food—meat in particular—in this way? That we do not yet know.

**specific dynamic action**

a measure of energy consumed in digesting, absorbing, and assimilating nutrients from a meal

# SUMMARY

In this chapter we have examined a number of features that distinguish hominins from our nearest relatives, the chimpanzees. These include (1) the adoption of upright gait, considered the essential characteristic of our lineage; (2) reduction in anterior dental structures (incisors and canines especially), accompanied by changes in certain characteristics such as enamel thickness; and (3) larger body size and in particular a high ratio of brain to body mass. These changes are profound not only in terms of shaping our expectations of the paleontological record, but also in terms of how we understand and reconstruct past social behaviours in the context of shifting ecologies and adaptive strategies of food getting, group formation, intra- and intersexual relations, communication, and mobility.

---

13. Patterns of growth are explored in greater detail in Chapter 14.

Becoming bipedal confers a number of advantages, both physiological and behavioural. We keep cooler, we forage farther, and we manipulate objects with increasing dexterity. Dental changes imply that the divergence of our clade from that of panins included significant shifts in dietary options, and the energy costs of an expanding brain hint at one such change: the inclusion of energy-dense, high-quality animal proteins and fats. These changes did not happen overnight, even in geological terms. The **stem hominin** lived about 5 mya, was occasionally bipedal, had fairly large anterior teeth, was small of brain and body, and (we suspect) appeared not too dissimilar from living bonobos. Most of the features we consider definitively hominin are not really manifested in the fossil record until the last 2 to 3 million years. The events that occurred in the preceding 3 million years are the subject of the following chapter.

Understanding what it is to be a hominin not only sets the stage for piecing together our evolutionary story, but also helps us ask the bigger question: In what ways are we truly different from nonhominins—the panins especially—and what does that mean for who we are today? As we explore hominin evolution in the next four chapters, perhaps one overarching lesson should be front and centre—the "what" is generally well appreciated. By this we mean that we have a rich documentation of fossils and a robust understanding of their geological and ecological context. We can describe and measure even small tooth fragments in exacting detail using highly sophisticated technologies. It is the "why" that remains both elusive and fascinating. Most of our evolutionary scenarios are to some degree speculative, gaps remain in the fossil record (and likely always will), and healthy debate exists regarding which evidence is most noteworthy, reliable and informative.

**stem hominin** in phylogeny, a stem species is the first member of an emerging clade; the stem hominin would be that member of our lineage appearing after the divergence with panins

# CORE REVIEW

## What is the significance of the category "hominin"?

Historically, paleoanthropology has referred to ourselves and our immediate ancestors as hominids, a label grounded in the morphological similarities and differences that distinguish us from the African apes. Recent genetic analyses suggest that the degree of difference among all of the apes, including ourselves, does not neatly conform to a hominoid-versus-hominid distinction, and a new taxonomy is required. This system places ourselves and our ancestors in a tribe separate from that of the chimpanzees (hominin versus panin), which together constitute a subfamily, the hominines, which is distinct from gorillas (gorillines) and orangutans (pongines). Collectively, all of the apes (ourselves, chimpanzees, gorillas, orangutans, and the gibbons and siamangs) retain the superfamily designation of hominoid.

## What adaptive advantages have been suggested for the shift to bipedal locomotion?

Bipedal locomotion has several benefits: it allows us to look out over greater distances (surveillance); it allows us to manipulate and carry objects (tool manufacture, use, and foraging); it enhances thermoregulation in a more open habitat (less exposure of surface area to solar radiation and greater exposure to cooling breezes); and it boosts energy efficiency for long-distance travel. Some of these benefits would have accrued with the evolution toward obligate as opposed to facultative bipedalism, such as increasing lower-limb length, and would not have been an immediate benefit promoting the adoption of this behaviour in the earliest protohominins.

### How is diet implicated in the evolution of hominin bipedalism?

Several scenarios suggest that food gathering played a crucial role in the shift from quadrupedalism through various stages toward obligate bipedalism. Gathering fruit from low-hanging branches would place a selective advantage on a foot and shoulder anatomy facilitating walking, and open country foraging from a central location near a water source would be assisted by an ability to carry items efficiently over longer distances.

### Why are teeth so useful in reconstructing hominin evolution?

Teeth are durable and thus are often found in the fossil record. Their number, size, shape, and wear reveal much about social dynamics (sexual dimorphism, competition) and diet (foods requiring grinding versus slicing). In hominin evolution, loss of the canine honing complex, for example, has been interpreted as indicating more conciliatory behaviour in male–male and female–female interactions within groups.

### How is relative size and organization significant in the evolution of the hominin brain?

Relative size refers to the size of the brain in relation to overall body size. Hominins have large relative brain size compared to all other primates (and mammals generally), indicating greater neuronal density. Size is only one aspect of hominin paleoneurology—in addition, several important changes have occurred in the organization of the various parts of the brain. Hominins have emphasized those areas of the brain associated with cognitive abilities such as foresight, planning, spatial analysis, memory, and language.

### What role does energetics play in hominin evolution?

Energy, derived solely from food, is critical to growth, development, body maintenance, reproduction, and activity. Efficient capture and use of energy contributes to reproductive fitness. Different parts of the body have different energy requirements, as do individuals at different life stages. Children especially have relatively large energy needs, both to facilitate growth and to provide for an energy-expensive brain that forms a larger proportion of body mass than it does in adults. In hominin evolution, development of efficient bipedal locomotion and a tradeoff of energy shunted from the gut to the brain are two significant developments associated with the advent of the genus *Homo*—developments that conferred a large selective advantage over competing forms.

# CRITICAL THINKING QUESTIONS

1. The fact that hominins are bipedal suggests that the selective benefits outweighed the costs. We also know that this form of locomotion required almost 2 million years to develop from an occasional to a habitual activity. Given this, would you expect that the principal selecting factor(s) would have been biological or cultural?
2. Significant conclusions regarding hominin evolution have been drawn based on relatively small amounts of evidence (e.g., a handful of teeth or fragments of bone, often separated in time by tens of thousands of years). Given that variation within a species may result from growth and development, health and disease, sexual dimorphism, environmental circumstances, and so forth, are such determinations warranted?

# GROUP DISCUSSION QUESTIONS

1. As we saw in the case of bipedal origins, we often use studies comparing the behaviours and anatomies of living nonhuman primates to develop interpretations about events in hominin evolution several millions of years in the past. What advantages and limitations accompany this approach to reconstructing evolutionary histories?

2. A large relative brain size is a defining feature of hominins, presumably associated with higher cognitive functioning (in conjunction with neural reorganization). In modern humans, *absolute* brain size averages around 1400 cc, but ranges from just under 1000 cc to over 1800 cc. What does this degree of variation suggest about using *relative* brain size as a marker of cognitive capacity in our ancestors? What additional information is required to evaluate this feature?

# RESOURCES AND READINGS

- An excellent survey of the relationship of brain evolution and nutrition can be found in Leonard, Snodgrass, and Robertson (2007).
- For a superb introduction to primate, human, and fossil skeletal and dental anatomy, see Paul Whitehead, William Sacco, and Susan Hochgraf, *A Photographic Atlas for Physical Anthropology* (Englewood: Morton, 2005).
- Interesting perspectives on current debates and discoveries in human evolution can be found at John Hawks's website, **http://johnhawks.net/weblog**.

# 9 Hominin Origins: From Ape to Australopithecine

## OVERVIEW

This chapter traces the evolution of species comprising the lineage leading from the last common ancestor (LCA) that humans shared with chimpanzees to the origin of the genus *Homo*. At least four genera and perhaps as many as 13 species are documented in eastern, southern, and most recently west-central Africa, though the precise evolutionary relationships among them remain unclear. Though all of the species prior to the advent of *Homo* remain relatively small of brain and body, at least two major trends develop over this ca. four-million-year history: (1) the exploitation of more diverse habitats, ranging from savannah to forest, facilitated by an increasingly efficient bipedal adaptation; and (2) an increasing capacity to exploit a more diverse range of food resources, processed either through the evolution of large posterior teeth (megadontia) or by way of prelithic and lithic technologies, the initial evidence of the latter possibly associated with the fossil remains of *Australopithecus*.

## CORE CONCEPTS

- biogeography, protohominin, divergence, hominin, australopithecine, megadontia, phylogeny

## CORE QUESTIONS

- What rationales support the splitting or lumping approaches in hominin systematics?

- What impact does recent molecular (DNA) research have on the status of the protohominins *Sahelanthropus* and *Orrorin?*

- How do we account for the fact that late Miocene and Pliocene hominins were adapted to both terrestrial and arboreal locomotion?

- What role might early *Homo* have played in the evolution of robust, megadont australopithecines?

- Why is it possible to construct several different scenarios for the evolution of hominins during the Pliocene?

calida/Shutterstock.com

*Ancient bones from Olduvai*
*Echoes of the very first cry*
*Who made me here and why*
*Beneath the copper sun?*

Johnny Clegg

# PROLOGUE: WE ARE ALL AFRICANS

**missing link**

a popular phrase referring to transitional fossils, which typically bear a combination of pleisomorphic and apomorphic traits linking them with earlier and later forms within a clade

**speciose**

literally, "full of species"; a taxonomy consisting of many rather than fewer named species

**Single Species Hypothesis**

the idea that all hominins through time belong to a continually evolving set of populations exploring different geographic and ecological niches but maintaining reproductive potential through intermittent interbreeding

In *The Descent of Man* (1871), Darwin pointed to the African continent as the birthplace of humanity. His reasoning was based on the similarities he perceived between humans and the African apes housed at the London Zoo. This proposition was not at all well received in Victorian England (see Chapter 2); nonetheless, it had been proven correct by the mid-20th century as more and more "**missing links**" connecting humans with their forebears were discovered and described. The earliest hominins and their lifeways—the subject matter of paleoanthropology—are the focus of this chapter. These ancestors lived over a period spanning ca. 4.5 million years from the last common ancestor (LCA) of the hominin and panin clades to the appearance of the genus *Homo*. This time period encompasses the terminal Miocene and the entire Pliocene geological epochs. It is a story not only of biological evolution but also of geological and environmental transformation during which physical and ecological landscapes alike were altered.

Keeping in mind that the divergence of hominins was accompanied by significant morphological and behavioural changes (outlined in Chapter 8), it should not be too surprising that there is considerable difference of opinion regarding the meaning and significance of these modifications. This is perhaps most evident in the various taxonomies proposed for these fossil forms, labelled as "**speciose**" versus "less speciose" by Wood and Lonergan (2008)—or, more prosaically, as "messy versus clean" by David Begun (2004b). Just how many ancestors have occupied our family bush since we parted ways with chimpanzees is one of the central questions in paleoanthropology, and the answer we give depends on how we interpret the variation expressed in the fossil record (see Box 9.1). Wood and Lonergan's recent review lists 4 (clean) to 13 (messy) different hominin taxa leading up to the origin of the genus *Homo*.

Cleanliness taken to the extreme amounts to the **Single Species Hypothesis**, which maintains that hominins evolved "as a single, phenotypically diverse, reticulating evolving species" (Hunt 2003, 485). This view, which is not widely held, argues that populations of hominins would continually split up (geographically or ecologically), form again, hybridize (and thereby share any small modifications they may have acquired) split up again, and so on through time, capturing the notion of reticulating, or interweaving. In this model, re-forming and hybridization maintains that essential quality of a biological species—namely, fertility. The single species hypothesis may or may not be an accurate depiction of the past; however it is important to remember that how we "split" or "lump" species in the fossil record will have a significant impact on our interpretations, not only of hominin phylogeny but also of particular aspects of the life history of the various taxa (Skinner and Wood 2006). For example, calculating the brain size or body size of a species, or the degree of sexual dimorphism represented, depends entirely on which forms you include within that taxon.

In the following pages you will be introduced to some very peculiar names representing fossils and their discovery locales. These will no doubt tie up your tongue and clog up your brain. You may well wonder how paleoanthropologists are able to piece anything together when it comes to reconstructing the fossil record (figuratively and literally!). At this point you may wish to review the section in Chapter 4, "Wrestling with Diversity", since many concepts introduced there are central to appreciating some of the current arguments swirling around studies of early hominin evolution. If, at the end of this chapter, you feel a need to wash your hands of the whole thing, we have good news for you: the protohominin and hominin genera identified prior to *Homo* can be condensed to the acronym SOAAP (Table 9.1; Figure 9.1): *Sahelanthropus, Orrorin, Ardipithecus, Australopithecus,*[1] and *Paranthropus.* See, it is getting a bit easier already!

---

1. We lump *Australopithecus* and *Kenyanthropus* in this category. The taxonomic status of the latter is subject to ongoing debate (see text), due mostly to a significant degree of distortion in the cranial remains recovered.

BOX 9.1    FOCUS ON... A Splitting Headache?

When a fossil is discovered and described, one of the first goals of the researcher is to name it, thereby placing it within a framework in which species are grouped according to scientific principles of classification and taxonomy (referred to as **biological systematics**). Taxonomies enable scientists to talk about biological diversity generally and to test hypotheses regarding how this diversity may have evolved (Ohl 2007). In effect, a taxonomy is an explicit hypothesis about phylogeny—the name assigned to a fossil is a statement about its place in the evolutionary history of a lineage. Like all hypotheses, it is testable through observation, measurement, and comparison.

In a classic hierarchical Linnaean taxonomy, all hominins (living or extinct) are members of the Order Primates, Suborder Anthropoidea, Superfamily Hominoidea, Family Hominidae, Subfamily Homininae, and Tribe Hominini (see Chapter 4). But we do not know them by these labels; instead, we talk of genus and species and employ binomial nomenclature: *Orrorin tugenensis*, for example, or *Paranthropus robustus*. These names have been proposed in accordance with rules laid out in the International Code of Zoological Nomenclature. This code requires that the designation of genus be unique; however, a species name need only be unique within the genus of which it is a member. If you discovered a new species of australopithecine you could name this **holotype** *Australopithecus erectus* if you had reason to, even though the species *erectus* already exists within the genus *Homo*. But you could not name a new kind of giraffe *Homo camelopardalis*.

Taxonomic names are not necessarily permanent. In the middle of the 20th century, there were several more genera and species of recent human ancestors than recognized by most paleoanthropologists today: Pithecanthropus erectus, Sinanthropus pekinensis, and Telanthropus capensis, among others. These taxa have all been "sunk" into the category *Homo erectus*, now that additional discoveries of that ancestor have broadened our understanding of its geographic distribution, time depth, and morphological variation. If that was not confusing enough, names having been sunk can be revived. The megadont southern African australopithecines were named *Paranthropus robustus* back in 1938 when they were first described; then they were sunk into the taxon *Australopithecus robustus* based on similarities identified with the

smaller-toothed *A. africanus*. Today, most researchers once again see the robust forms as distinctive at the genus level, and as a result the taxon *P. robustus* is back in vogue.

Determining what to name an organism is no easy task, even when dealing with living species for which soft parts and reproductive behaviours can be observed. In the case of extinct forms the difficulties are compounded, since all that (usually) remain are bones and teeth, geological and paleoenvironmental reconstructions, and inferences about unobservable behaviour. Many factors come into play. For example, how much of the original skeleton is present, and how informative are the pieces recovered? Some parts of the skeleton carry more "information content" than others. Also, what condition are they in? Fossils are typically fragmented and distorted; furthermore, they may be encrusted with mineral deposits that obscure details of morphology, or, in the case of teeth, they may be worn from a lifetime of use (but see Box 9.5). How old is a fossil in relation to other discoveries, and what is its context? And, not least important, what mindset is motivating the researchers who discovered it? Considerable renown and sometimes even celebrity can be attached to naming a fossil deemed sufficiently unique to be a never before described species, especially if it is thought to occupy an esteemed place in a lineage (i.e., first in the line). Some scientists place more emphasis on the differences they see in a discovery when compared to known fossil species ("splitters"), and messy classifications are the outcome. Other researchers (called "lumpers") place more emphasis on similarities observed among fossils, which results in cleaner classifications with fewer members. And, of course, still others are somewhere in between. Effectively, it comes down to how one interprets biological variation and the importance of one collection of traits relative to another. These decisions require that a number of examples of a prospective taxon be available for analysis. When only one specimen is discovered, creating a new species or genus is tricky. It needs to have derived features not evident in known taxa to which it might be related, or features that lie outside the range of known variation. *Ardipithecus ramidis*, for example, was split from its original inclusion in the genus *Australopithecus* by White, Suwa, and Asfaw (1995) when they determined that size differences in some of the dental features made *Ardipithecus* more likely a **sister taxon**, and not on the direct line leading to *Homo* (a position they have since reversed).

---

To appreciate not only why the hominin–panin divergence took place but also a host of subsequent evolutionary developments requires that we consider the context in which these events played out. What was the climate like between 8 and 2 mya? What changes in local ecologies—the limits of forest cover or structure of animal communities—can be discerned? In what ways has the geographic landscape been modified, including the size of lakes, the courses of rivers and streams, and the impact of volcanic, seismic, and tectonic activity? All such events, both short and long term, establish the **biogeographic** framework within which evolutionary change occurs (Andrews 2007), and this is where we begin this chapter.

**biological systematics**
the formal science of classification and taxonomy, specifying a set of rules and guidelines for categorizing biological diversity and deriving phylogenies

**holotype**

the specimen that serves as the "name-bearer" of a fossil species and from which a description of the salient features of the taxon are obtained. It need not be the sole source of information for identifying a member of the taxon, nor does the holotype need to be a typical example

**sister taxon**

in systematics, sister taxa are those forms which are related by virtue of a divergence event and that share a last common ancestor; panins and hominins are sister taxa, as are *Australopithecus* and *Ardipithecus*

**biogeography**

the study of the geographic distribution of organisms, habitats, and evolutionary history as it relates to landscape and ecology

**basal**

a qualitative term distinguishing the earliest widely accepted hominins from those forms later assigned to the genus *Homo*

**megadont**

literally, large teeth; these forms are characterized by expansion of the posterior teeth, i.e., premolars and molars.

**Table 9.1** Hominin diversity from the late Miocene to the advent of the genus *Homo* is considerable though also depends upon one's approach to taxonomy and phylogeny.

| Grade | Speciose Taxonomy[1] | Date (mya) | Locality | Less Speciose Taxonomy |
|---|---|---|---|---|
| Possible or probable hominins | *Sahelanthropus (S.) tchadensis* | 7.4—6.5 | Toros-Menalla, Chad | *Sahelanthropus (S.) tchadensis* |
| | *Orrorin (O.) tugenensis* | 6.0—5.7 | Tungen Hills, Kenya | *Orrorin (O.) tugenensis* |
| | *Ardipithecus (Ar.) ramidus* | 4.4 | Middle Awash, Ethiopia | *Ardipithecus (Ar.) ramidus* |
| | *Ar. kadabba* | 5.8—5.5 | Middle Awash, Ethiopia | *Australopithecus (A.) afarensis* |
| **Basal** hominins | *Australopithecus (A.) anamensis* | 4.2—3.9 | Middle Awash, Ethiopia; Kanapoi and Allia Bay, Kenya | *as above* |
| | *A. afarensis* | 3.9—3.0 | Middle Awash, Hadar and Omo in Ethiopia; Koobi-Fora in Kenya; Laetoli, Tanzania | *as above* |
| | *Kenyanthropus (K.) platyops* | 3.5 | Lomekwi, Kenya | *as above* |
| | *A. bahrelghazali* | 3.6 | Koro Toro, Chad | |
| | *A. africanus* | Ca. 3.0—2.0 | Taung, Sterkfontein, and Makapansgat, South Africa | *A. africanus* |
| | *A. gahri* | 2.5 | Middle Awash, Ethiopia | *as above* |
| **Megadont** hominins | *Paranthropus (P.) aethiopithecus* | 2.6—2.3 | West Turkana, Kenya | *Paranthropus (P) boisei* |
| | *P. boisei* | 2.1—1.1 | Olduvai Gorge, West Turkana, and Koobi Fora, Kenya | *as above* |
| | *P. robustus* | Ca. 2.0—1.5 | Swartkrans, Drimolen, and Kromdraai, South Africa | *P. robustus* |

1. The accepted abbreviation of the genus name is given in parentheses; by convention and for the sake of convenience, scientists often use this form rather than the unabbreviated name; e.g., *Ar. kadabba* rather than *Ardipithecus kadabba*, or for modern humans, *H. sapiens* rather than *Homo sapiens*.

Source: Adapted from Wood and Lonergan (2008)

We then ask several fundamental questions of the fossil record: (1) Can we identify the last common ancestor shared with panins, and if so, what kind of creature are we talking about? (2) What do we know about the most ancient members of our clade, the so-called proto-hominins living between 4.5 and 7 mya? How confident can we be in their status as human ancestor? And (3), how do we make sense of the taxonomic diversity of early hominins, at

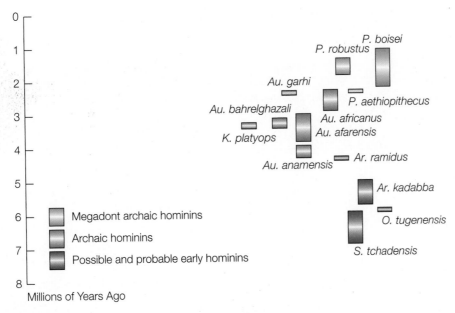

**Figure 9.1** A timeline of early hominin evolution (adapted from Wood and Lonergan 2008).

Adapted from B. Wood and N. Lonergan, (2008). The hominin fossil record: taxa, grades and clades, *Journal of Anatomy* 212: 354–376. Reprinted by permission of John Wiley and Sons

http://www.becominghuman.org

times **synchronic** and sympatric, living between 4 and 2 mya? And (4) which of these gave birth to the genus *Homo*? This last question is an especially important one because, even though *Homo* expanded its geographic and ecological boundaries far beyond Africa into diverse selective landscapes in Europe and Asia (see Chapters 10 and 11), it has remained the principal hominin genus living on the planet over the past 2 million years.[2] Reduction in taxonomic diversity is a characteristic feature of adaptive radiations, since proliferation of species is generally accompanied by high extinction rates (Eldridge 1989). Thus, it is normal to proceed from many competing forms early on as the radiation "blooms," to one or two surviving branches as natural selection culls those varieties that do not quite make the grade. We conclude this chapter by looking at different ways in which paleoanthropologists have reconstructed hominin phylogeny to reflect this process of species expansion and contraction.

**synchronic**

at the same time; thus synchronic species coexist in time

## A PLACE IN TIME

Recall from Chapter 1 that biological anthropology is very much a multidisciplinary and interdisciplinary field in which numerous scholars contribute different scientific expertise to understanding who and what we are as a particular kind of species. This approach is readily evident within the subfield of paleoanthropology (Henke and Tattersall 2007; see Table 9.2), which demands not only that fossil bones and teeth be accurately described and their variations documented, but also that they be situated in time and placed in the context of landscape and habitat. This contextual information is essential to understanding aspects of social behaviour (e.g., arboreal primates look different from terrestrial species and behave differently), diet (e.g., food resources vary by climate and vegetation), predation (e.g., different carnivores inhabit forests versus savannah woodlands), and life history (e.g., body size, longevity, fertility, and other traits are all impacted by habitat variability). As we learned in the previous chapter, to

---

2. As many as nine different species of the genus *Homo* have been identified, including our own, though many paleoanthropologists would opt for a smaller number, in the range of three or four. One genus of pre-*Homo* hominin, *Paranthropus*, long considered a side branch not directly ancestral to ourselves, did coexist with *Homo* until ca. 1 mya.

**Table 9.2** Many scientific disciplines contribute to the field of paleoanthropology. Our understanding of hominin phylogeny requires a synthesis of this knowledge to interpret the evolution of species diversity, both morphological and behavioural.

| Discipline | Relevant Area(s) of Expertise | Principal Applications |
|---|---|---|
| Skeletal biology | Bone and tooth variation | Quantitative and qualitative description of fossils; functional anatomy; classification |
| Primatology | Behaviour and evolution of living nonhuman primates | Modelling hominin behaviour and social dynamics |
| Cultural anthropology | Human social and cultural interactions | Modelling hominin behaviour and social dynamics |
| Archaeology | Manufacture and use of technology and resource exploitation | Modelling the evolution of tools and landscape use (e.g., capture and processing of food resources) |
| Psychology | Comparative neuroanatomy and brain function | Encephalization, cognition, and language development |
| Geology/geography | Composition and structure of the planet and the processes by which it changes | Reconstruction of local, regional, and continental landscapes and paleoclimate, volcanic activity, glaciers, erosion, lakes and rivers, etc. |
| Chemistry | Organic and inorganic chemical properties | Isotopic reconstruction of diet and paleoenvironment; absolute dating of fossil sites; ancient DNA |
| Physics | Material properties, motion, energy, time | Absolute dating of fossil sites; biomechanical modelling of hominin behaviour (e.g., locomotion; mastication) |
| Zoology | Animal ecology and evolution | Predator—prey interactions, community structure, hominin diet, paleoenvironmental reconstruction, faunal dating |
| Botany | Plant ecology and evolution | Community structure, hominin diet, paleoenvironmental reconstruction |
| Statistics | Probability theory, sampling methods, hypothesis testing, and predictive modelling | Evaluation of hypotheses based on qualitative or quantitative observation of sample variation |

understand evolutionary change in locomotion and encephalization, we need to place these early hominins in a geological and ecological framework. In this vein, climate change has long been considered an important factor in hominoid migrations and speciation (e.g., Bobe and Behrensmeyer 2004; Andrews 2007).

## Hominoids, Habitats, and Hypotheses

Scientists reconstruct paleoenvironments at various levels, from the global and continental to the regional and local (Elton 2008). Large-scale climate change is linked to planetary events such as cyclical shifts in the earth's orbit and major geographic transformations such as mountain building and continental drift. These events alter oceanic and atmospheric circulation, which in turn impacts regional and local climate and ecology, including precipitation, seasonality, vegetation, and the structure of animal communities. During the **Neogene period**, spanning the Miocene and Pliocene geological epochs from ca. 23 to ca. 1.8 mya, changes in the North Atlantic and Indian Ocean circulation (Cane and Molnar 2001), as well as tectonic uplift of the East African Rift system in Kenya and Ethiopia (Sepulchre et al. 2006; see Figure 9.2), were major forces in the trend toward cooler climates, increasing **aridification**, contraction of rainforests, and expansion of woodland and grassland habitats in Africa and Eurasia. These changes began around 15 mya and quickened toward the end of the Miocene epoch at 5.5 mya, culminating in the series of glacial advances and retreats that have marked the last two million years of the earth's history. These transformations had profound effects on biodiversity and community ecology—and, it follows, on hominin evolution.

**Neogene period**
a geological time period comprising the Miocene and Pliocene epochs, associated with global climate change and diversification of a number of avian and mammal species, particularly open woodland and grassland forms

**aridification**
a drying trend resulting from lower seasonal or annual precipitation levels

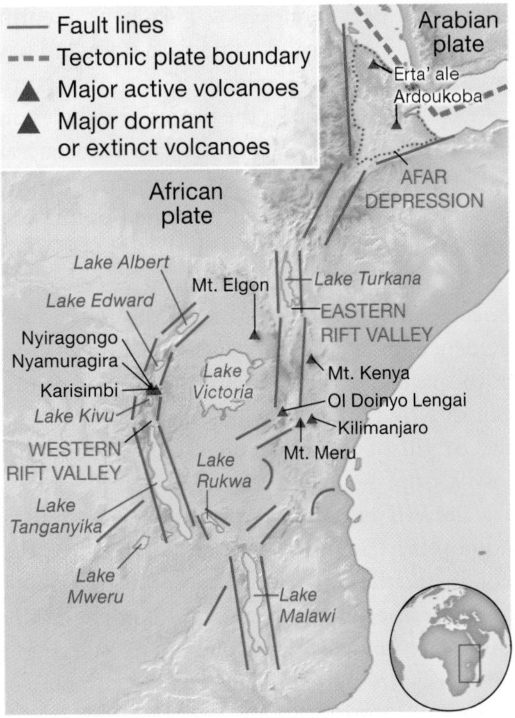


**Figure 9.2** The African continent was transformed during the Miocene by several significant geologic events, including uplifting along a major fault recognized today as the Great Rift Valley, which extends from Ethiopia in the north to Malawi in the south. Numerous hominin fossil localities are associated with the Rift Valley.

As you learned in Chapter 7, the adaptive radiation of apes in Africa and Eurasia took place during the early to middle Miocene (23 to ca. 10 mya). Migration between these two continents occurred throughout that period while tropical and subtropical forests were still available to support these arboreal primates (Andrews 2007). University of Toronto paleoanthropologist David Begun has hypothesized that the last common ancestor of the panin and hominin clades originated in Eurasia among the Dryopithecines and migrated into Africa during the late Miocene epoch around 8 to 6 mya as extensive continuous forests began to disappear at higher latitudes (Begun 2005). Paleoenvironmental data from Miocene and Pliocene fossil sites in East Africa suggest ongoing climate change. Variations in the timing and magnitude of precipitation cycles and the expansion or contraction of lakes and rivers and their subterranean water sources produce **mosaic habitats** of forest, mixed woodland, and savannah grasslands (Reed 2008). However, in reconstructing paleoenvironments we need to remember that taphonomic processes can alter fossil deposits and produce "mixed messages" regarding what happened and when. Recall that taphonomy includes all of the events that affect biological remains after they have become part of the geological record—that is, after death. These events include soil compaction, upheaval, wind or water erosion, and mixing; any or all of these might artificially create the appearance of a mosaic habitat (Elton 2008). While reliable evidence does indicate that large areas of grassland habitat appeared in tropical Africa as early as 8 mya (Jacobs 2004), it is likely that our earliest ancestors continued to rely heavily on forest and woodland habitat near lakes or rivers, as a food source or refuge, well into the Pliocene. This is indicated by both paleobotanical and fossil data (see below).

**mosaic habitat**
an area characterized by a range of habitat types, from forest to grassland

## Climate, Habitat, and Selection

In what ways might these changes in habitat and climate have impacted hominoids living in central and eastern Africa in the late Miocene? The transition from closed forest to woodland/grassland was not abrupt, and changes occurred at different times in the past and at different rates, depending on factors such as latitude. We also know that climate fluctuated during the Neogene period into the Pleistocene epoch, creating **faunal turnover** events. In East Africa,

**faunal turnover**
the historical transition in species composition within a geographic region associated with changes in vegetation and other climate variables

Bobe and Berhensmeyer (2004) have identified four major changes in mammalian fauna beginning 3.4 mya and ending 1.8 mya, and have documented the transition from forest habitat (with resident pigs, elephants, and monkeys) to grassland (with ruminants such as gazelle and antelope). Even though the overall trend was one of gradual cooling and aridification, warming episodes did occur during the late Miocene and Pliocene. Given this temporal and regional variation in environment, it is important to ask some fundamental questions. What selection pressures might have been presented by these newly emerging habitats? How might they have impacted the last common ancestor (LCA) and influenced subsequent hominin evolution?

In addressing these questions, we need to keep a few things in mind. First, for this stage in the evolution of African hominoids ca. 5–7 mya, we have very little in the way of fossil evidence for gorillines, panins, or hominins; the bits and pieces are few and far between in both space and time and are the subject of much controversy (Suwa et al. 2007). At best we can only hypothesize what adaptations and selective forces[3] could have been paramount for the origin of the hominin clade. Definitive statements must await discovery of additional fossils from new localities in order to clarify which features (morphological, behavioural) are derived rather than primitive, and which may be a product of homology rather than homoplasy (Begun 2007; see Chapter 4). Recent arguments that bipedal locomotion may not in fact be an especially useful criterion for assigning hominin status to fossil remains (e.g., Crompton, Vereecke, and Thorpe 2008; see Chapter 8) point to some of the difficult issues faced by paleoanthropologists studying our origins. Also, as discussed in Chapter 6, we know that living panins have fairly complex cultural behaviours; however, it is unlikely that some very significant selection pressures (e.g., predation) would have been lessened until our ancestors had developed some form of defensive technology such as stone tools, or learned to control fire (Pawlowski 2008). This means that early hominins would have been subject to the same kinds of selection pressures as other larger bodied mammals. This fact actually works in the paleoanthropologist's favour, for it strengthens the use of analogy from the life-ways of living apes such as chimpanzees and bonobos when we are trying to infer how early hominins might have behaved.

Nonetheless, we can come to some fairly sound conclusions regarding the paleoenviron-ment and ecology of the LCA and early hominins. For example, the long-held **savannah hypothesis** proposing that hominin origins were linked to loss of forest habitat and expansion of grasslands, effectively "forcing" adoption of new lifeways (including bipedalism), is no longer tenable. First postulated in the early 20th century, the savannah hypothesis gained prominence in the decades prior to the 1970s when paleoanthropologists had little evidence of hominins much older than ca. 3.0 mya. Those fossils that *were* known had been discovered at sites suggestive of savannah-like environments. Since then—and in particular over the past 20 years—the hominin fossil record has grown in both quantity and complexity (see below), and may extend as far back as ca. 6–7 mya. Most of these early sites have been found in habitats that are either mixed woodland (e.g., *O. tugenensis* from Kenya), **gallery forest** (e.g., *S. tchadensis* from northern Chad), or woodland–grassland mosaic (e.g., *Ardipithecus* and *Australopithecus* from the Middle Awash study area in northeastern Ethiopia). Also, the presence of **lacustrine paleosols** and fossil remains of aquatic species tell us that these early hominins kept close to water sources. These recent developments have led to the **forest hypothesis**, which argues that hominins diverged from panins while still occupying a treed habitat; thus the derived features of hominins (bipedalism, dental changes, etc.; see Chapter 8) arose in a forested rather than open-country environment. The savannah grassland habitat may not have played a key role in our history until the later divergence of the genus *Homo* ca. 2.5 mya (Bobe and Behrensmeyer 2004). But we should not rule out the possibility that the first hominins evolved in a more open habitat, in some locality as yet undiscovered. The fact that

**savannah hypothesis**
the now discredited idea that the development of open savannah grassland created conditions leading to the evolution of hominins

**gallery forest**
dense, canopied forest found along water courses such as rivers and lakeshores

**lacustrine paleosols**
ancient soils associated with lake sediments

**forest hypothesis**
a recent proposal based on paleoenvironmental data from fossil localities that the hominin clade diverged from panins while still occupying a wood-land/forest habitat

---

3. We must also not lose sight of the possibility that non-Darwinian forces such as genetic drift or founder effect could have played a role in early hominin origins, or that certain aspects of morphology seen in fossil remains and thought to be important may be pleiotropic by-products of selection for some other characteristic.

a putative early hominin, *S. tchadensis*, is found some 2,500 km *west* of the loci of hominin evolution in East Africa (Ethiopia and Kenya) suggests that the range within which our forebears roamed was actually quite extensive, and early fossil localities associated with savannah habitat may not yet have been discovered.

It has also been suggested that early hominin divergence was not driven by the stable conditions offered by forest or savannah habitats, but rather by the increasing unpredictability of climate and environment during the late Miocene and Pliocene. This is the **variability selection hypothesis** (Potts 1999), whose main tenet is that fluctuating conditions created a diversity of adaptive conditions to which species needed to respond. This was achieved not by acquiring habitat-specific adaptations, but by selection favouring morphologies and behaviours that would work in complex, changeable "multi-habitat" situations (Pawlowski 2007). The variability selection model is appealing because it accounts for the locomotory *and* dietary flexibility suggested by the fossils themselves (see below). However, we must remember that natural selection tends to happen "in the moment," as it were—organisms adapt to immediate or recent conditions, not to changes that may take hundreds or thousands of years to take hold. It is more likely that early hominines, including the LCA, would have experienced reasonably stable environmental conditions and trends from one generation to the next.

**variability selection hypothesis**
a model which suggests that the operating factor in hominin evolution was environmental disparity, rather than stability, which promoted adaptive flexibility in hominin traits, including locomotion, dental adaptations, and technology

# A PLETHORA OF PROTOHOMININS

The basal hominins immediately preceding our own genus *Homo* are known as the australopithecines. The first of these appeared about 4.2 mya in eastern Africa. There are several species assigned to the genus *Australopithecus* (Table 9.1, p. 188), representing at least two sister clades, commonly referred to as the "robust" and "gracile" lineages. Australopithecines are themselves preceded by several earlier forms, and in this text we use the term "protohominin" to refer to these pre-australopithecine fossil taxa. Known from east and central Africa and dating to between 7 and 5 mya, they include *S. tchadensis*, *O. tugenensis*, *Ar. ramidis*, and *Ar. kaddaba*. Each of these taxa exhibit morphology suggesting facultative bipedality, but they also retain attributes that are adaptive for arboreal settings. All have dental traits linking them with both earlier hominoids and later hominins, and all are found in sites indicative of woodland habitat. So why do we choose to call them "protohominins"? Recent DNA studies point to a hominin–panin divergence time of 4 to 5 mya (Hobolth et al. 2007), and that event may have been a complex, drawn-out affair (see Box 9.2). This evidence raises some questions regarding the phylogenetic status of these "pre-australopithecines," which remain open to some debate (Wood and Lonergan 2008). So at this time it is best to adopt a more conservative "wait and see" position. The nature of paleoanthropology is such that, between the time we make this assertion and the time you read it, the state of things may well have changed!

Protohominins exhibit a mixture of primitive and derived features, which we describe in the following sections. This mixture should not surprise you. Indeed, the closer we get to the LCA, the more we should expect to find fewer and fewer derived traits unique to the emerging hominin or panin lineages, as less evolutionary change would have occurred since their initial divergence (Cobb 2008). There is also the real possibility of hybridization between the two clades as divergence ensues (Box 9.2). In other words, gene flow and proximity in time would conspire to keep the LCA and its immediate panin and hominin descendants looking pretty much alike.

## *Sahelanthropus tchadensis*—First Twig on the Bush?

In 2001 and 2002, several fossils were discovered at a number of sites in the Toros-Menalla area in northern Chad by members of the research team Mission Paléoanthropologique Franco-Tchadienne (MPFT), led by Michel Brunet of the Université de Pontiers, France. These were all attributed to a new hominin taxon, *Sahelanthropus tchadensis* (Brunet et al. 2002a, 2005; Figure 9.5). The holotype is known formally as "TM 266-01-060-1"—more

**BOX 9.2**     **FOCUS ON... The Long Good-Bye**

Depictions of speciation events tend to give the impression that they are abrupt and somewhat instantaneous (Figure 9.3). In fact, they are vague, generally clouded in mystery, and of completely uncertain duration. Fossil morphology is generally not helpful in this regard. While it can suggest that speciation occurred at some point in the past, it usually cannot tell us precisely when or over what span of time. The combination of dating error and the expectation that sister taxa will look very similar immediately following divergence constrains estimations of speciation dates. Prior to the 1970s, the origin of the hominin lineage was placed in the range of 10 to 15 mya as a rough but educated estimate based solely on fossil remains—in particular, those of a middle Miocene Asian ape called *Ramapithecus*, which had a short face and small canines (now considered *Sivapithecus*). The development of "molecular clocks" such as radioimmunoassay and DNA hybridization has allowed researchers to estimate divergence times for living hominoids based on accumulated differences in gene sequences and protein structures. These methods suggested a much more recent date for the separation of hominins from African apes, in the range of 6 to 8 mya (Wilson and Sarich 1969). This has generated a debate—"early or late divergence?"—that remains with us to this day. However, many paleoanthropologists are beginning to see a consensus emerging between the fossil and genetic approaches at around 5 to 7 mya (Wolpoff et al. 2006).

Recently, Patterson and colleagues (2006) have added a new wrinkle to the question of timing for the hominin–panin split. They studied close to 20 million autosomal and X chromosome base pairs of **aligned sequence** DNA data from humans, chimpanzees, gorillas, orangutans, and macaques, correcting for aberrations such as neutral and **recurrent mutation** rate variation within the genome. Using **genetic divergence** estimates

for chimpanzees and humans, they calculated a **species divergence** time of 5.4 to 6.3 mya—which, clearly, is problematic for forms such as *Sahelanthropus,* dated close to 7 mya, and possibly even for *Orrorin,* dated at around 6 mya. More surprisingly, for *Pan–Homo* they found a larger than expected reduction in genetic divergence time for the X chromosome, on the order of 1.2 million years—something that was not observed in the *Gorilla–Homo* data. What does this mean? Their "provocative explanation" (as they put it) is that the emerging hominins continued to exchange genes with panins for perhaps as long as 1 million years, and that final speciation did not occur until perhaps as recently as 4 mya. As you learned in Chapter 4, hybridization is not uncommon between closely related species, and population genetic studies of both insects and mammals have shown that hybrid sterility is most closely associated with X-linked genes. Thus, hybrid males with their single X chromosome would be sterile more commonly than homogametic (XX) females, and natural selection would intensely select against any X-linked alleles reducing fitness. This would tend to conserve genetic divergence times for the X chromosome compared to those of the autosomes (i.e., the X chromosome remains similar between diverging species, and differences accumulate more readily in autosomes within each lineage). Perhaps even more provocative is their suggestion that later hominins may actually have emerged from *within* the hybrid zone (Figure 9.4). The implications of this argument are profound both for the early divergence hypothesis and for our interpretations of the protohominin fossil record. Recently, Hobolth and colleagues (2007) have calculated a recent species divergence time of 4.1 ± 0.4 mya for humans and chimpanzees, as well as a lower genetic divergence estimate for the X chromosome, supporting Patterson et al.'s findings.

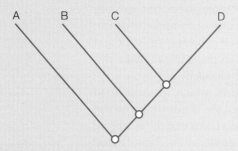

**Figure 9.3**   Though rigorously determined, graphic depictions of speciation events give the impression that they occur rather abruptly, which is not the case

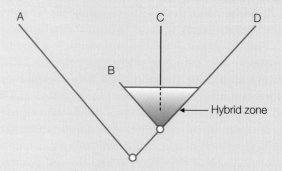

**Figure 9.4**   Patterson et al.'s 2006 model of hominin origins may be traced to a surviving hybrid population.

colloquially as "Toumaï."[4] Toumaï consists of a distorted yet mostly complete cranium with several dental attributes, including fragmented teeth and **alveoli**. The remaining finds are isolated teeth or lower jaw fragments. The 6 to 7 mya date for *Sahelanthropus* is based

4. In the local Goran language, Toumaï means "hope of life," a name often given to babies born prior to the dry season, when circumstances become considerably harsher and survival less certain.

on faunal association with eastern African **assemblages**, including forest-dwelling pigs and elephants, as well as fish species and crocodilians. Toumaï may well have lived in woodland or gallery forest adjacent to a lake.

This discovery is very significant for several reasons. In the first place, it is rare to find specimens as complete as this cranium, however distorted. Then there are the added factors of its early date and geographic location. Toumaï predates all previously known protohominins by as much as a million years and is found roughly 2,500 km west of the East African Rift Valley, where all previous protohominin and many hominin discoveries have been made since the late 1950s (Figure 9.5). It is even further removed from southern Africa, where australopithecines were first discovered (see Box 9.3). The addition of *S. tchadensis* to the hominin clade means that we can identify—at present—three independent loci for hominin evolution, reflecting a geographic range larger than for any living African hominine (i.e., chimpanzee or gorilla).

## Why a New Hominin and Why a New Taxon?

As to be expected for a protohominin at such an early date, *Sahelanthropus* combines primitive and derived features (Brunet et al. 2002b). On the primitive side, it has a massive browridge (relatively larger and thicker than in living gorillas) projecting from a small, chimpanzee-sized brain case (with an estimated capacity of 320 to 380 cm$^3$) and evidence of a sagittal crest on top of the vault. It also has an expansive area at the back of the head for the attachment of neck muscles. Derived features include a relatively short face—unusual for Miocene apes as well as for later hominins such as *Ardipithecus* and the australopithecines. Dental traits seen in Toumaï include small canines that wear at the tip and little in the way of a diastema in the mandible, indicating that it lacked a canine honing complex. Enamel thickness is moderate (more than in *Pan* but less than in australopithecines). Importantly, according to Brunet and colleagues (ibid.), the **foramen magnum** is located closer to the face as in bipeds; it is also longer than wide, unlike the shape seen in chimpanzees.

Brunet and his colleagues argue that the presence of bipedality[5] combined with the absence of canine honing establish Toumaï as the earliest member of the hominin clade. Recall from Chapter 8 that most paleoanthropologists regard these two features as essential criteria for hominin status. At the same time, some characteristics of the dentition and face are distinctive even compared to later forms such as *Ardipithecus* and *Orrorin*—especially the large browridge and the shape and surface relief of the upper incisors. These traits have been used

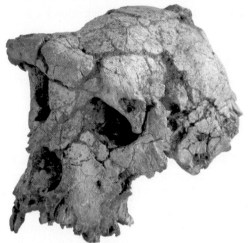

**Figure 9.5** Site locality in Chad of *Sahelanthropus tchadensis*

(bottom) AFP/Getty Images

**aligned sequence**

in molecular genetics research, sequences of DNA (or RNA) derived from homologous sites within the genome are literally arranged or aligned to identify similarities and differences between species, the latter resulting from e.g., point mutations, insertions, or deletions

**recurrent mutation**

a mutation that tends to occur repeatedly at the same locus; a number of genetic disorders are maintained at high frequencies through recurrent mutation (e.g., Marfan syndrome in humans, leading to impaired collagen formation)

**genetic divergence**

an estimate of the time since two genomes diverged, based on the number of differences observed and assuming a constant rate of mutation

**species divergence**

an estimate of time since speciation; because genetic differences are constantly accumulating within lineages, estimates of genetic divergence time will always be older than species divergence time

**alveoli**

the bony sockets for teeth present in the upper and lower jaws

**assemblages**

the collection of all remains of plants or animals from paleontological contexts

**foramen magnum**

"large passage," the foramen magnum is the largest hole in the cranium, through which the brain stem passes to become the spinal cord

5. Bipedality is inferred for *S. tchadensis* from the anterior position of the foramen magnum as no infracranial remains are known.

stem hominin

a stem species is pro-
genitor of all later species
within a clade, arising from
the last common ancestor

to justify a new taxon. This mixture of primitive (hominoid-like) and derived (hominin-like) traits, considered alongside their antiquity, suggests that *S. tchadensis* may be very close to what taxonomists refer to as the **stem hominin**.

This claim has invited skepticism. Not everyone was quick to jump on board the "*Sahelanthropus* as hominin" ship. University of Michigan paleoanthropologist Milford Wolpoff, among others (including Brigette Senut and Martin Pickford, the discoverers of *Orrorin tugenensis*), has questioned the hominin claim for Toumaï, suggesting instead that it was in all likelihood a late Miocene ape adapting to a tough diet (Wolpoff et al. 2002, 2006). They note that thicker enamel is in fact a pleisomorphic characteristic common to earlier Miocene hominoids (thin enamel is derived in panins), so it is not surprising to find it in Toumaï. Reduced, apically worn canines, which Brunet and colleagues argue indicate loss of the honing mechanism, are to be expected if the specimen is a female. This canine condition has been recognized in some earlier middle Miocene female fossil apes such as *Ramapithecus*. Wolpoff and colleagues also argue that the foramen magnum occupies a more posterior, chimpanzee-like position, based on distance from the position of the third molar tooth. Finally, the expanded posterior brain case, the sagittal crest to which chewing muscles attach, and the massive browridge could be explained as responses to diet and posture. Heavy chewing generates large biomechanical forces, which a large browridge can absorb, especially in a flat-faced, small-brained animal. If the foramen magnum is indeed more posteriorly placed, the large neck muscles would assist in balancing the head in a species that moves about quadrupedally.

So, is Toumaï hominin or hominine? Currently, the consensus favours the former, though this issue will likely only be settled with the discovery of infracranial remains unambiguously establishing it to be a biped, like the eastern African protohominins.

## *Orrorin tugenensis*—Sound on the Ground and at Ease in the Trees

In 2001, Brigette Senut and members of the Kenya Palaeontology Expedition described 13 new hominin fossils from the Lukieno Formation, a ca. 6 mya lacustrine (lake) and fluvial (river) deposit in the Tugen Hills near Lake Baringo, Kenya. Both dental and infracranial material was found, and a new taxon—*Orrorin*[6] *tugenensis*—was proposed (Senut et al. 2001a). The associated fauna, including impala, elephants, and monkeys, indicate an open woodland habitat with gallery forest along the lake margins (ibid.). The infracranial fossils, including the top (**proximal**) portion of several femora, the lower (**distal**) part of the right humerus, and a hand **phalanx**, suggest that *Orrorin* was an adept climbing biped. Using the preserved femora as a guide, Nakatsukasa and colleagues (2007) have conservatively estimated body size in this species at around 1.2 m tall and 35 to 50 kg, comparable to modern bonobos.

proximal

in anatomy, a position
closer to the midline of the
body

distal

in anatomy, a position
farther from the midline of
the body

phalanx

one of a series of short
bones that make up the
fingers in the hand, or toes
in the foot

muscle markings

impressions on a bone
surface that define the
point of origin or insertion
of a muscle; activities that
build up muscles can also
create more prominent
muscle markings

### Why a New Hominin and Why a New Taxon?

*Orrorin* exhibits several primitive features, such as chimpanzee-like upper incisors and canines (including some suggestion of a honing complex). The lower molar is chimp-like in some respects and human-like in others. But *Orrorin* also has thick enamel, as in later hominins, and the overall size of the (molar) teeth is reduced. *Orrorin*'s status as a hominin is assured by its femoral anatomy. The parts recovered articulate with the pelvis, and even though no pelvic fossils have been found, the bony features of the femur and the size and shape of the impressions left by the hip muscles point toward a bipedal adaptation (Figure 9.6). But *Orrorin* also retains primitive features in its skeleton that tell us that climbing was still very much part of its locomotor behaviour. The humerus preserves **muscle markings** for forearm flexion that are more similar to those of chimpanzees, and the handbone is curved, consistent with a strong grasping ability (both features are also found in australopithecines, discussed later in this chapter).

---

6. In the local Tugen language, *Orrorin* means "original man."

As you might have guessed, *O. tugenensis* has not been accepted without debate. Senut and colleagues (2001) have created a new taxon for these remains, arguing that it was unlike later australopithecines in having relatively small and differently shaped molar teeth and more *Homo*-like proximal femora. It also differed from *Ardipithecus* (see below) in having thicker enamel. However, it was their assertion that *Orrorin* was ancestral to *Homo* that caused more than a little controversy (White 2006), since this constituted a major restructuring of commonly held interpretations of hominin phylogeny on the basis of comparatively little fossil evidence. Senut and colleagues' assertion has not been generally accepted, and the suggested *Homo*-like features of the femur have been questioned (Begun 2004c). Recently, Richmond and Jungers (2008) compared the size and shape of the most complete of the *Orrorin* femora with a large sample of great apes, australopithecines, early *Homo* specimens and modern humans, and found that *Orrorin* most likely had a bipedal gait comparable to the australopithecines, but very different from *Homo*.

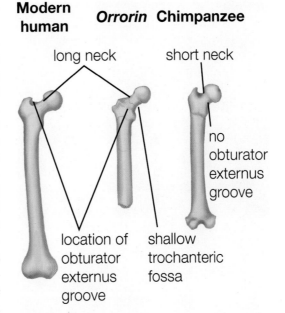

**Modern human**    *Orrorin* **Chimpanzee**

long neck    short neck

no obturator externus groove

location of obturator externus groove    shallow trochanteric fossa

**Figure 9.6** The *Orrorin* proximal femur is more like that of humans and less like that of chimpanzees in features such as longer neck (a), a shallow trochanteric fossa (b), and the presence of a groove for insertion of the obturator externus muscle (c), which chimpanzees lack.

## The Ardipithecines—Hominins, Yes, But Whose Ancestor?

Ethiopia, in the Horn of Africa, has suffered a very difficult and in many ways tragic social and political history during the 20th century. Yet geographically, it may well be the womb of humankind—an irony that should not be lost on us. No other region of this planet has offered such an ancient, rich, and significant fossil record of our Human Voyage. Since the 1970s, Ethiopia's Afar Depression has yielded a treasure trove of fossil remains, from protohominins to early modern *Homo sapiens*, spanning several million years. Among the Afar sites, Aramis in the Middle Awash Study Area has provided evidence of the transition from the LCA to protohominins, and from protohominins to the basal hominins known as australopithecines (White et al. 2006; and see Table 9.1, p. 188). The first of these transitions is represented by two species attributed to a new genus: *Ardipithecus kadabba* (5.8 to 5.2 mya) and *Ar. ramidus* (4.4 mya) (White et al. 1994, 2009).[7]

### Why a New Hominin and Why a New Taxon?

*Ardipithecus* is represented by **craniodental** and infracranial remains exhibiting a mixture of primitive and derived traits (as we saw with *Sahelanthropus* and *Orrorin*), but also by unique attributes not present in any other known hominin. Not surprisingly, the older species *Ar. kadabba* is considered the more primitive of the two, especially in having a larger crowned and more pointed canine and a C/P3 honing complex similar to the condition seen in smaller bodied (e.g., female) chimpanzees. However, the canine in *Ardipithecus* shows some wear on the tip, typical of later hominins, indicating its use in chewing. Predictably, this apical wear is more evident in the more recent species *Ar. ramidus,* whose canines are somewhat smaller. The

**craniodental**

a descriptive term referring to the hard tissues, bone, and teeth comprising the skull

---

7. In the local Afar dialect, "Ardi" means "floor," "ramid" means "root," and "kaddaba" is the term for "basal family ancestor." *Ar. kadabba* was initially identified as a subspecies of *Ar. ramidus* (i.e., *Ar. r. kadabba*) but was elevated to species status following description of additional dental remains (Haile-Selassie, Suwa, and White 2004).

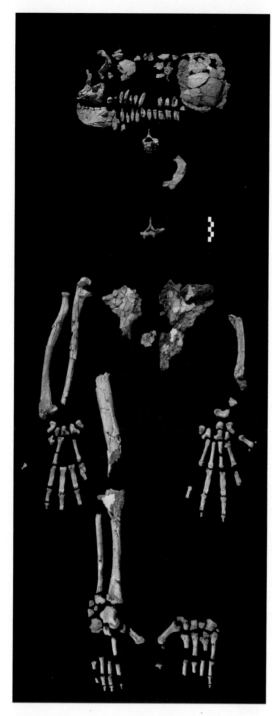

**Figure 9.7** Interpretation of the partial skeletal of *Ar. ramidus* has cast new doubts as to the nature of the last common ancestor of hominins and panins, and subsequent hominin evolution.

Fossil credit: Housed in National Museum of Ethiopia, Addis Ababa. Copyright protection notice: Photo © T. White 2009, From *Science* Oct. 2 issue./Brill Atlanta

most striking feature in both species is the presence of thin enamel on the molar teeth, unlike any other known hominin species and more like the condition seen in living hominoids (Smith et al. 2008). However, White and colleagues (2009) have suggested that the pattern and distribution of thin enamel in *Ar. ramidus* differs from that of extant apes.

In the fall of 2009, White and colleagues published a series of 11 papers in the journal *Science* describing the remains of *Ar. ramidus*, totalling 110 specimens, including a very fragmented and fragile partial skeleton that required a number of years to carefully extract from the sediments (Figure 9.7). These publications, covering all aspects of fossil anatomy, adaptation, environment/ ecology, dating, geology, and behaviour garnered worldwide attention. The focus of this attention was the authors' conclusion as to *Ar. ramidus*' adaptive grade, which challenged long-held views that the basal hominin leading to later australopithecines (and ultimately to *Homo*) derived from a chimpanzee-like suspensory/knuckle-walking ancestor (as discussed in Chapter 8). Rather, they assert that *Ar. ramidus* was rather un-chimp-like in many respects: it had low levels of sexual dimorphism (including canines), as well as a cranial anatomy reminiscent of *Sahelanthropus* from Chad. In this regard *Ar. ramidus* lacked the derived features chimpanzees acquired after their divergence from the hominin lineage. Its dentition suggests omnivory, yet it does not have the larger teeth seen in later australopithecines (discussed below), and it offers no evidence for the C/P3 honing mechanism.

Most interesting, though, are these authors' views as to *Ar. ramidus*' locomotor habits. Its remains (e.g., pelvis, upper and lower limbs) suggest facultative bipedality, yet the foot structure reveals (somewhat surprisingly) a fully opposable large toe. The infracranial fossils include curved handbones and ape-like upper limbs, which tell us that these species were still efficient climbers—what White and colleagues refer to as palmigrade clambering. Missing is any indication of knuckle-walking or suspensory locomotion, as seen in extant chimpanzees. Palmigrade clambering is in fact more reminiscent of earlier Miocene apes, though it does agree well with the paleontological evidence (e.g., plant remains such as seeds and fossil monkeys and pigs) indicating that they lived in woodland habitats. The bipedal status of *Ardipithecus*, and thus its hominin affinity, is established by the presence of a diagnostic dorsal slant of the proximal joint surface of the **pedal phalange**. This derived trait is associated with "toeing off," the action that propels the leg forward into the "swing phase" of bipedal walking as the heel is lifted from the ground  (see Figure 8.4). This trait is not found in any of the living quadrupedal African hominoids but is present in both *Ar. kadabba* (Haile-Selassie 2001) and in *Ar. ramidus* material discovered at the Middle Awash site of Gona, Ethiopia, dating to ca. 4.6 mya  (Semaw et al. 2005). In this respect, *Ardipithecus* conforms to the flexible locomotor pattern already seen in preceding protohominins, *Sahelanthropus* and *Orrorin*. Indeed, White and colleagues (2009) contend that the similarities between *Ar. ramidus* and these earlier protohominins are such that the genus names *Sahelanthropus* and *Orrorin* should be "sunk" (see Box 9.1) and replaced by *Ardipithecus*.

This series of papers presents a fascinating account of the discovery, recovery, and interpretation of the fossils, touching on their locality and behaviour (diet, locomotion, and life history; see also Chapter 8). As is common in the field of paleoanthropology, such sweeping revision of commonly held positions invites scrutiny by other researchers. It remains to be seen how much of this new interpretation of *Ar. ramidus* will hold up over the next few years. As noted in one of these articles (Lovejoy et al. 2009, 73) "[*Ar. ramidus*] is so rife with anatomical surprises that no one could have imagined it without direct fossil evidence."

**pedal phalange**

referring to the series of bones forming the toes of the foot, analogous to the fingers of the hand (manual phalanges)

# THE AUSTRALOPITHECINES

The australopithecines are a diverse group of hominins, distributed across as many as nine different species and at least two (if not three) genera from 4.2 to 1.1 mya (Table 9.1). The best known of these, called *Australopithecus*, has pinpointed Africa as the birthplace of humankind (confirming Darwin's assertion), though not without controversy (see Box 9.3). Australopithecines are distinguished for their wide geographic distribution, having been found at a number of sites in eastern and southern Africa (Figure 9.8). Though several hundred fossils assigned to the various australopithecine species have been discovered, the evolutionary relationships among them and later hominins (genus *Homo*) are still the subject of considerable debate.

A number of developments characterize australopithecine evolution. First, though overall body size does not increase appreciably—they remain about the size of common chimpanzees (40 to 50 kg; McHenry and Coffing 2000)—australopithecines are notable in that the various species fall into one of two morphological variants—one more slightly built and gracile, the other somewhat larger and robust. Second, the differences between the **gracile** and **robust** variants are most pronounced in the craniodental remains (face, skull, teeth), earning the robust variant the label of megadont hominins. This significant increase in the size of the posterior teeth (premolars and molars) is taken to an extreme in the more recent robust form, *Paranthropus boisei*. Third, the sample size for several australopithecine species, including the earliest forms, is sufficiently large that we can document variation in sexual dimorphism in both body and canine size, though the degree to which such dimorphism reflects australopithecine mating behaviour and/or competition (as known for living hominoids) is not clear (Plavcan 2000). Fourth, canine reduction continues, resulting in the complete absence of a C/P3 honing complex and no diastema. Fifth, though still comparatively small-brained, the trend toward increasing encephalization (brain size scaled to body size)—which as you learned in Chapter 8 was a defining feature of hominin evolution—begins with *Australopithecus*. Sixth, while the protohominins *Sahelanthropus*, *Orrorin,* and *Ardipithecus* were at least facultatively bipedal, and the early australopithecines retain a facility for climbing in trees, the transition to obligate bipedality likely occurred among later members of the gracile lineage ca. 3.0 to 2.5 mya, presaging the arrival of our own genus, *Homo*. And finally, the production of stone tools with cutting edges around 2.6 mya, attributed to the gracile species *Australopithecus gahri*, marks a momentous development in technology and challenges the assertion that *Homo* was the earliest maker of **percussive stone tools**.

**gracile**

small or slightly built; among australopithecines, refers to those species lacking the skeletal features associated with extreme megadontia

**robust**

rugged or strongly built; several australopithecine species possess skeletal and dental features associated with large chewing muscles and crushing and grinding of hard foods

**percussive stone tools**

implements fashioned by purposefully striking one stone against another to produce a cutting edge

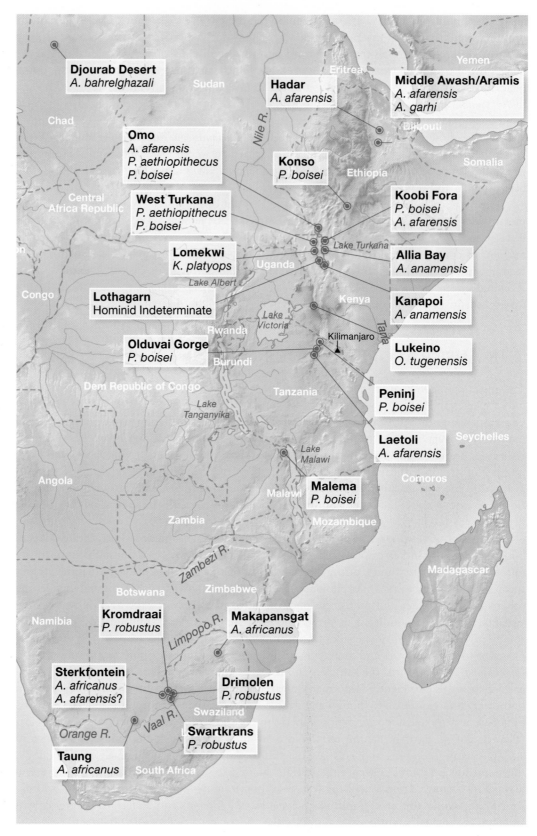

**Figure 9.8** Australopithecine sites extend ca. 5,000 km from northeastern to southern Africa, though comparatively little research has been conducted between Tanzania and South Africa.

From Ann Gibbons, (2002). Becoming human: In search of the first hominids, *Science* 295: 1214–1219. Reprinted with permission from AAAS

BOX 9.3

# RETROSPECTION: Raymond Dart and the Man-Ape of South Africa

*In manipulating the pieces of rock brought back by Prof. Young, I found that the larger natural endocranial cast articulated exactly by its fractured frontal extremity with another piece of rock in which the broken lower and posterior margin of the left side of a mandible was visible. After cleaning the rock mass, the outline of the hinder and lower part of the facial skeleton came into view . . . Apart from this evidential completeness, the specimen is of importance because it exhibits an extinct race of apes intermediate between living anthropoids and man . . . It is manifest that we are in the presence here of a pre-human stock, neither chimpanzee nor gorilla, which possesses a series of differential characters not encountered hitherto in any anthropoid stock. This complex of characters exhibited is such that it cannot be interpreted as belonging to any living anthropoid . . . It is therefore logically regarded as a man-like ape. I propose tentatively, then, that a new family of Homo-simidae be created for the reception of the group of individuals which it represents, and that the first known species of the group be designated Australopithecus africanus, in commemoration, first, of the extreme southern and unexpected horizon of its discovery, and secondly, of the continent in which so many new and important discoveries connected with the early history of man have recently been made, thus vindicating the Darwinian claim that Africa would prove to be the cradle of mankind.*

In this article, Raymond Dart was describing a small, ape-like partial cranium and a natural endocast of the animal's fossilized brain, discovered at the site of Taung, South Africa. The find was that of a child, between three and six years of age when it died. The proposal for a new family of primates intermediate between ape and human (Homo-simidae is no longer recognized), and for a new genus and species as a root stock from which humans evolved, stunned the still young discipline of paleoanthropology. The assertion that human origins lay in Africa and not in Asia or Europe (as had been proposed in the early years of the 20th century) was an outrageous claim. Surely, humans must have evolved from a large-brained ancestor, one capable of generating descendants able to produce Western civilization and all which that entails. The so-called Piltdown Man, "discovered" in 1912 in England, had been contrived from fragments of a modern human cranium associated with an intentionally modified partial jaw of an orangutan; it was not exposed as a hoax until 1953 (though some scientists, notably American, were suspicious of its authenticity from the outset). But the tenacity with which Eurocentric scholars clung to its primacy in human ancestry, and the extent to which they criticized Dart's claim for *A. africanus*, is an interesting history of politics, race, and class (Spencer 1990). To the intellectual aristocracy of Europe, it was unfathomable that "man" (i.e., White Europeans) could have his lowly origins in a geography and landscape populated by peoples they had subjugated and colonized. It was bad arithmetic that did not add up! But Dart held to his view, and the unearthing of additional australopithecine fossils from several cave sites in South Africa over the next several decades (continuing to this day) built the case for an African origin of humankind. With Piltdown exposed, and with the discovery of yet more australopithecine fossils in eastern Africa by Mary and Louis Leakey in 1959, the case was settled. Darwin and Dart had been proved right—led by a little child.

Source: *Nature* (1925) 115: 195–199

## Australopithecine Origins

From 4.2 to 3.0 mya, two gracile australopithecine species are recognized from eastern Africa: *A. anamensis* and *A. afarensis,* which are thought to form a **phyletic sequence** originating in *Ar. ramidus* (White et al. 2006; see Figure 9.9). These speciation events are thought to be tied to ecological niche expansion and diversification. We saw earlier that protohominins occupied closed forest or woodland habitats, and a fundamental australopithecine adaptation seems to have been exploitation of more open savannah grasslands, bushlands, and aquatic fringes in addition to woodland and gallery forest zones. This broadening of habitat use does not seem to be linked to any major change in climate, habitat, or mammalian species turnover (White et al. 2006), all of which are believed to have had an impact on the later evolution of *Homo*. Just why the first australopithecines decided to venture into more diverse habitats than had been exploited by protohominins remains an unanswered question. If we adopt a speciose classification, the ensuing million years of australopithecine evolution (from 3.0 to 2.0 mya) witnessed a profusion of species, including branching events leading to additional gracile and robust forms evolving in both eastern and southern Africa. It is thought that one of these gracile branches, possibly represented by *A. garhi,* gave rise to the genus *Homo* ca. 2.3 mya.

**phyletic sequence**
an unbroken lineage of ancestor-descendant species

The origin of australopithecines has been dated to ca. 4.2 mya with the discovery of *Australopithecus anamensis*[8] at the sites of Kanapoi and Allia Bay on the shores of Lake Turkana, Kenya (Leakey et al. 1995). Additional remains attributed to *A. anamensis* found at two localities in Ethiopia—Asa Issie and Aramis (also dated to ca. 4.2 mya)—were recently described by Tim White and colleagues. These latter discoveries extend both the range and the habitat diversity of this species, as the Ethiopian environment comprised more closed woodland than the Kenyan sites. White and colleagues (2006) argue that *A. anamensis* evolved from *Ar. ramidus* over a span of only 200,000 years—an event they term **punctuated anagenesis**, in which a slowly evolving lineage is suddenly marked by a rapid speciation event. In this case, these authors suggest that a shift toward increasing tooth size in *Australopithecus* relative to *Ardipithecus* led to a rapid "ecological breakout"—that is, an opportunistic expansion into the more diverse habitats that were now appearing in eastern Africa's landscape as a result of climate change. At the same time, craniodental and infracranial remains indicate that *A. anamensis* had clear affinities to the earlier *Ar. ramidus* and to later *A. afarensis*. For example, at Asa Issie, *A. anamensis* canine shape is broadly similar to that of *Ar. ramidus*, but a proximal femur fragment is quite similar to that of the more recent *A. afarensis* in terms of shaft curvature and muscle attachment relief. *A. anamensis* craniodental traits associated with upper and lower jaw form and the C/P3 complex show changes that would be predicted if *A. anamensis* were ancestral to *A. afarensis* (Kimbel et al. 2006).

It seems that *A. anamensis* had barely arrived on the evolutionary stage before it gave way to *A. afarensis*, the earliest evidence for which occurs at 3.7 mya. *A. afarensis* is known principally from major fossil localities in Tanzania (Laetoli, 3.7 to 3.5 mya) and the Afar Depression (Hadar, 3.4 to 3.0 mya); the type specimen is an adult mandible containing nine teeth discovered at Laetoli in 1974 (known as LH 4). These two regions have yielded numerous remains of this species, sampling over 300 individuals of various ages, including the most ancient hominin child yet discovered—a three-year-old found at the Dikka locality in Hadar and dating to 3.3 mya (Figure 9.10).

**punctuated anagenesis**
speciation has two tempos, slow and gradual (anagensis), or rapid followed by stasis (punctuated equilibrium); punctuated anagenesis combines these into a pattern of rapid change within a continually evolving lineage; the possibility of punctuated anagenesis is not universally held among evolutionary biologists

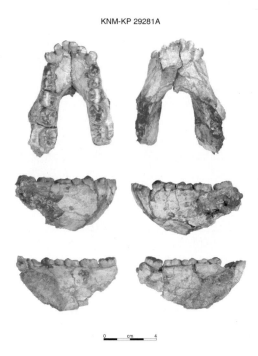

KNM-KP 29281A

**Figure 9.9** *A. anamensis* from East Africa is the first of a number of basal hominin species.

(bottom) Fossil image: Ward, C.V., Leakey, M.G., and Walker, A. 2001. Morphology of *Australopithecus anamensis* from Kanapoi and Allia Bay, Kenya. *Journal of Human Evolution* 41: 255-368. Copyright © 2001 Academic Press. All rights reserved. Image courtesy of C.V. Ward.

8. In the local Turkana language, "anam" means lake; all of the initial *A. anamensis* finds are associated with a lacustrine environment.

The relationship of *A. anamensis* and *A. afarensis* has remained somewhat cloudy due to the absence of fossil materials in the half-million year gap between the two forms, though the recent discovery of dental (tooth and jaw) and fragmentary postcranial remains from the site of Woranso-Mille, Ethiopia, offers some intriguing clues (Haile-Selassie et al. 2010). This locality has been dated 3.57 to 3.8 mya, and the dental remains show plesiomorphic affinities with the older *A. anamensis* forms as well as some derived features found in the later *A. afarensis* material. The Woranso-Mille fossils are, unfortunately, too sparse and fragmentary to support a definitive taxonomic assignment to either of these species; however, their transitional morphology supports the argument that *A. anamensis* and *A. afarensis* comprise a phyletic lineage. In fact, Haile-Selassie and colleagues suggest that these two forms may not represent separate species. If this proves to be the case as future discoveries are made, it will likely result in "sinking" the taxon *A. anamensis* into *A. afarensis*, since the latter has priority owing to its earlier discovery.

Among paleoanthropologists, Laetoli and Hadar have garnered as much contro-

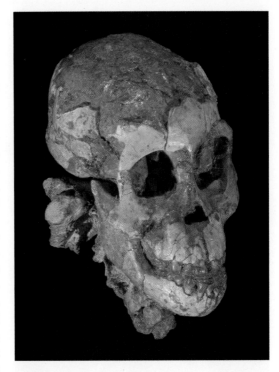

**Figure 9.10** The discovery of a three-year-old fossil at the site of Dikka, Hadar Locality, was embraced by the media as "Lucy's Child.", in reference to the famous partial skeleton nicknamed "Lucy" discovered in 1974.

Vilem Bischof/AFP/Getty Images

versy as celebrity. The older Laetoli site is best known for the rare preservation[9] of hundreds of animal trails, from insects to elephants—and, remarkably, for the 24 metre long tracks of two (possibly three) bipedal hominins (Figure 9.11). The Laetoli trails have been studied intensely and debated hotly since they were discovered in 1978 (Leakey and Hay 1979). At that time they were the oldest record of hominin bipedality. Debate swirled around whether these tracks had been produced by *A. afarensis* or a more modern (*Homo*) species, and how similar the bipedal adaptation of the track makers was to that of modern humans in terms of posture, foot structure, and locomotory biomechanics (e.g., stride length and walking speed). A recent comparison of the Laetoli imprints with impressions in wet sand made by modern humans and chimpanzees (Berge, Penin, and Pellé 2006) has concluded that the Laetoli hominins shared locomotor features in common with both humans and chimpanzees but were much more like the former than the latter. Details of arch structure and weight-transfer pattern (determined from heel and toe impressions), the relatively short stride length, and the narrow foot gap (i.e., distance between left and right foot) clearly align the Laetoli trails with a human-like pattern of relatively slow walking with heel strike and toe-off. However, a comparable experimental study has found that the Laetoli trails could have been produced by hominins walking with either a human-like extended knee or a panin-like bent knee posture, and at a speed higher than usually thought (Raichlen, Pontzer, and Sockol 2008). What is generally accepted within the

---

9. The Laetoli tracks are preserved in carbonatite, a rare igneous rock of volcanic origin. Presently, the East African Rift Valley is home to the only active carbonatite volcano in the world, known as Ol Doinyo Lengai ("Mountain of God" in the local Maasai language), which dominates the Tanzanian landscape. Carbonatite volcanoes are unusual in releasing very low-temperature lava, which cools quickly, preserving excellent detail, though it is also quickly weathered when exposed to the elements. The Laetoli tracks were produced by the now dormant Sadiman volcano, about 20 km distant. The fine detail of their preservation is owed to their having been rapidly covered with further layers of volcanic ash. Since their exposure, they have been the subject of major conservation efforts.

**Figure 9.11** Early hominin tracks found at Laetoli, Tanzania, provided tantalizingly early evidence for bipedality.

John Reader/Science Photo Library

http://www.elucy.org

**intermembral index**

the ratio of the length of the upper and lower limbs, expressed as a percentage. An IM index greater than 100 indicates relatively long arms, as in chimpanzees, while smaller IM indices suggest lengthening of the lower limb, as in the genus *Homo*

paleoanthropological community is that the fossil tracks were produced by hominins, most likely from the *A. anamensis–A. afarensis* lineage,[10] but with a bipedal adaptation not yet like our own in some respects.

The Hadar locality in Ethiopia made headlines worldwide when an almost 40% complete skeleton of a ca. 1.1 m tall hominin (Figure 9.12) was discovered in November 1974 by members of the International Afar Research Expedition (IARE), led by the French geologist Maurice Taieb and paleoanthropologists Donald Johanson and Yves Coppens. Nicknamed "Lucy" (more formally designated AL 288-1),[11] this fossil discovery and other startling finds made soon after (including 333 fossil pieces from 13 individuals thought to have perished together) challenged then accepted views of hominin evolution. Lucy was an old (3.2 mya), small-brained (ca. 380 cc), bipedal hominin with reduced canines—an unexpected combination of traits for human ancestors as we understood them in the early 1970s. Up until then, based on known species such as the 1.9 mya ER 1470 cranium of *Homo rudolfensis* from Kenya (see Chapter 10), the belief was that hominin evolution had been initiated with brain expansion, followed by features such as bipedal locomotion. Preservation of the sacrum and the left half of Lucy's pelvis as well as her knee joint (resembling one found a year earlier by Johanson only a few kilometres away) established this species' status as an obligate biped; it also generated much speculation concerning other life history attributes, such as childbirth (discussed in Chapter 8). Compared to living hominoids, Lucy and her *A. afarensis* relatives had a reduced **intermembral index** (calculated as the ratio of upper to lower limb length) and shorter hand and foot bones. However, while their upper and lower limbs were nearer the same length (unlike in living apes with longer upper limbs), *A. afarensis* still had arms that were relatively long, combined with curved hand and foot phalanges—traits attesting to adeptness in climbing. It is possible that hominins such as Lucy were accomplished terrestrial foragers during the day and retreated to the relative safety of trees in the evening (see Box 9.4).

## More Skeletons in the Australopithecine Closet

A number of other australopithecine species have been identified from the middle to late Pliocene, though except for *A. africanus* in South Africa, all are known from single localities and one or but a handful of fossil remains (see Figure 9.8). For example, *A. bahrelghazali*, discovered at the site of Koro Toro in Chad in 1993 and recently dated to ca. 3.6 mya by cosmogenic nuclide dating (Lebatard et al. 2008), consists of a partial mandible with seven teeth, including canines and premolars. Many paleoanthropologists see *A. bahrelghazali* as a western version of

---

10. Footbones from a South African gracile australopithecine, *A. africanus*, named "Little Foot" (STS 573), have been suggested as a good match for the kind of foot structure possessed by the Laetoli hominins (Clarke 1998). The circumstances of discovery make the dating of Little Foot problematic, but a recent claim of over 4 mya has been made (Partridge, Granger, and Caffee 2003; see text for discussion).

11. The well-known anecdote has it that "Lucy" acquired her name from the 1967 Beatles song "Lucy In The Sky With Diamonds," which was played frequently in the IARE camp. Formally, AL 288-1 refers to Afar Locality 288, with "Lucy" being the first discovery at that site. Lucy was not an inappropriate moniker, as the morphology of the pelvic bone identified AL-288-1 as female.

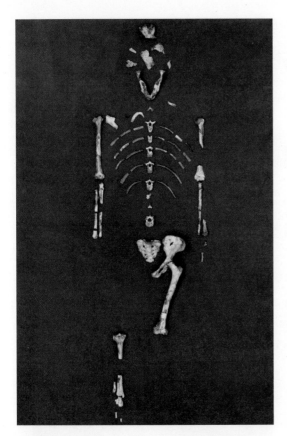

**Figure 9.12** Lucy is perhaps the best-known hominin outside the field of paleoanthropology. The completeness of her skeleton challenged many long-held interpretations of early hominin evolution within the field.

Courtesy of the Institute of Human Origins

A. *afarensis*, though Guy, Mackaye, and Likius (2008) have shown that the cross-sectional shape of the **mandibular symphysis** can discriminate taxa among living hominoids (including humans) and that this trait confirms *A. bahrelghazali's* status as a new species. Caution must be exercised, however, until more remains of this form are discovered.

Another contemporary of *A. afarensis* was described by Meave Leakey and colleagues (Leakey et al. 2001) from the ca. 3.5 mya site of Lomekwi, west of Lake Turkana in Kenya. These fossils, given the name *Kenyanthropus platyops* ("flat-faced man from Kenya"), consist of a number of isolated teeth, mandibular and cranial fragments, and—most important—a nearly complete albeit distorted cranium. Leakey and colleagues argue that the small-crowned molar teeth and **orthognathic** features of this fossil are evolutionarily derived with respect to *Australopithecus* (whose lower faces protrude from under the nasal region), justifying its attribution to a new genus. However, *K. platyops'* brain size is similar to *A. afarensis*, and other dental traits such as enamel thickness are comparable with *A. anamensis*. Given the significant distortion of the cranium, some paleoanthropologists are reserving judgment, considering *K. platyops* a variant of *A. afarensis*.

**mandibular symphysis**
the midline of the lower jaw, where the left and right dental arcades meet

**orthognathic**
"ortho" refers to vertical or flat, and "gnathic" to the jaws; thus orthognathic means "flat-face"

The discovery of a new australopithecine species, *A. garhi*,[12] from the site of Bouri in Ethiopia (Asfaw et al. 1999; Figure 9.13) represents a significant addition to the story of hominin evolution in eastern Africa, as it is situated both chronologically (at ca. 2.5 mya) and morphologically between earlier *A. afarensis* and later *Homo* species. Compared to the previous million years, the pre-*Homo* fossil record of gracile hominins after 3.0 mya is rather sparse, though it is of critical importance in untangling that most central of questions: Which species gave rise to the genus *Homo*? *A. garhi* in part answers that question. Cranial, dental, and infracranial remains representing more than one individual are known, including a partial skeleton with upper and lower limbs and footbones. While distinguished from *A. afarensis* by absolutely larger posterior teeth, it does not share the suite of derived craniodental features of the megadont complex (see below) characteristic of *Paranthropus*, a sister clade not considered ancestral to later hominins. Cranial capacity is still small and comparable to *A. afarensis*, at around 450 cc. Asfaw and colleagues (1999) remark that while the infracranial material cannot be attributed to this taxon with certainty (none were found with the craniodental remains), they exhibit both human-like and *A. afarensis*-like features. They provide the earliest example of a derived *Homo*-like intermembral index, though the relative lengths of the upper (humerus) and lower (ulna) armbones remain primitive and ape-like. The foot phalanx recalls *A. afarensis* in terms of size and curvature.

As significant as *A. garhi* may be in terms of hominin phylogeny, its putative behavioural and technological adaptations are equally so. Bouri is located in the Middle Awash study area, which, as noted earlier, is associated with an open woodland and lakeshore grassland habitat. Fossil remains of catfish, suids, and bovids occur in the Bouri deposits, and bones of the latter

12. In the local Afar language, "garhi" means "surprise."

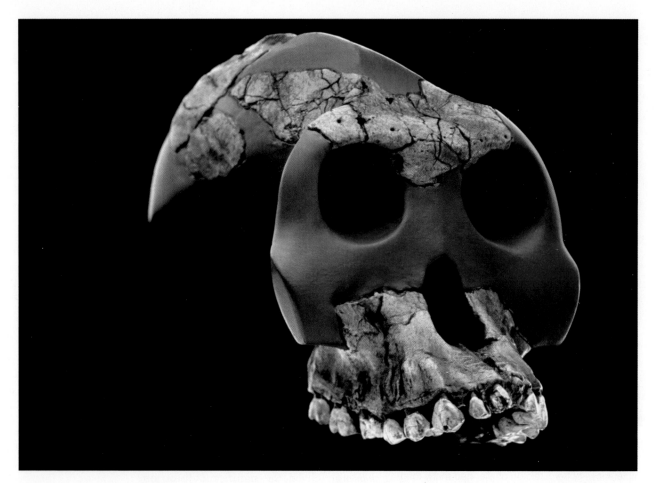

**Figure 9.13**   *A. garhi* represents an important link between *A. afarensis* and early *Homo*, which some believe reflects an ancestor-descendent relationship.

Fossil credit: Original housed in National Museum of Ethiopia, Addis Ababa. Copyright protection notice: © 1999 David L. Brill/Brill Atlanta

show evidence of cutmarks and intentional breaking made by stone tools (Figure 9.14). A few stone artifacts have been located near the discovery site, apparently having eroded out of the hominin-bearing sediments. Artifacts belonging to the earliest known lithic technology (the Oldowan; see Chapter 10) have been reported at the 2.6 mya Gona site just 96 km north of Bouri, though these lack association with hominin remains.[13] While tentative, the implication is that the original maker and user of lithic percussive technology was not *Homo*, as has always been presumed, but *A. garhi*. It is salient here that the raw materials for manufacturing Old-owan tools are not readily available at Bouri and must have been intentionally carried to the site to scavenge an animal carcass; furthermore, the comparative absence of tools in the sediments may indicate that these early hominins had already learned to **curate** stone tools.

Although eastern Africa has provided a wealth of Pliocene remains of gracile australopith-ecines, the original discoveries of this variant were made in southern Africa beginning in 1925. Several sites have yielded remains of this hominin, known as *A. africanus*, including Taung, Sterkfontein/Jacovec Cavern, and Makapansgat (see Figure 9.8). In many respects, *A. africanus* resembles *A. afarensis* from eastern Africa in being a small-bodied, bipedal, thick-enamelled hom-inin. Other features appear more derived, however, including a slightly larger average brain size (452 cc vs. 438 cc; McHenry and Coffing 2000), a less prognathic face, and slightly smaller teeth. *A. africanus* has generally been viewed as having originated as a population(s) of *A. afarensis* that migrated south toward the end of the Pliocene, and dates of between 3.0 and 2.0 mya are often cited. Dating has long been an issue for the South African sites, which consist of sedimentary

**curate**

to care for; in archaeology, a curated tool is one that is stored for later use at a given site, or transported in order to be used at different locations

---

13. Remains of *Ar. ramidus* have been found in the Gona study area, but east of the archaeological deposits and ca. 1.8 million years older.

**Figure 9.14** Faunal remains recovered in association with *A. garhi* show clear evidence of butchering and hammering to acquire meat and bone marrow.

From J. Heinzelin, et al., (1999). Environment and behaviour of 2.5 million year old Bouri hominids, *Science* 284: 625–629. Fossil credit: National Museum of Ethiopia, Addis Ababa. Copyright protection notice: © 1999 David L. Brill/Brill Atlanta

dolomitic limestone cave deposits—a geological context in which the classic radiometric methods used in eastern Africa (e.g., $^{40}K/^{40}Ar$ or $^{40}Ar/^{39}Ar$; see Chapter 7) are not applicable. Sites such as Sterkfontein, from which more than 500 hominin fossils have been recovered, have historically been dated using biostratigraphic (faunal) association with eastern African localities whose antiquity has been determined using radiometric techniques (Partridge et al. 2003). Recent development of methods such as cosmogenic nuclide dating, which tracks the decay of $^{26}Al$ and $^{10}Be$ (isotopes of aluminum and beryllium) in buried quartz sand crystals, have allowed researchers to obtain absolute dates for cave deposits. Using this approach, Partridge and colleagues (2003) have obtained a date of ca. 4.0 mya for the partial skeleton StW 573 ("Little Foot"; Figure 9.15) and for remains attributed to *Australopithecus sp. indet.* from Jacovic Cavern,[14] which include a partial cranium, two proximal femora, and isolated teeth. (The label "species indeterminate"—or *sp. indet.*—is used when researchers are confident in assigning a fossil to a particular genus, but are not sure to which species it should be assigned.) The Jacovic fossils appear to sample both gracile and robust (discussed below) australopithecine species. The proposed early date for these remains is remarkable and would suggest that the southern African species are descended from either *Ar. ramidus* or *A. anamensis*, not *A. afarensis*. However, Walker and colleagues (2006) recently dated deposits above and below the sediments in which Little Foot was recovered using the radiometric method $^{238}U/^{206}Pb$ and obtained a date of only ca. 2.2 mya. This may be a more reasonable estimate for the antiquity of this fossil, as the uranium (U)–lead (Pb) dates agree well with the biostratigraphic *and* paleomagnetic records of the deposits, and the method requires fewer assumptions regarding depositional history than cosmogenic nuclide dating.

---

14. StW stands for "Sterkfontein West," the locality within the Sterkfontein complex where remains of Little Foot were discovered.

## BOX 9.4 PROFILE... Bones and Behaviour

*Courtesy of Michelle Drapeau*

*Michelle Drapeau is an associate professor in the Department of Anthropology at the Université de Montréal. She serves as codirector of field operations in the Bala Paleoanthropological Research Area of southern Ethiopia.*

I have many research interests, and though they may appear unrelated, they are in fact different ways of improving our understanding of human origins. My interest in bone biology stems from a curiosity about how bone responds to loads incurred during life. I am intrigued by the differences between modelling (macroscopic bone changes, usually occurring during growth) and remodelling (the replacement of bone at the microscopic level, which usually has little or no visible effect on shape changes)—more specifically, by the interaction between the two and how each provides us with different pieces of the same puzzle: What can a skeleton tell us about what that individual did during his or her life? Often, one of the limitations of studies that compare the bones of different individuals is the difficulty of sorting the influence of factors such as sex, age, ethnicity, medical history, and so on from that of physical activities.

Luckily, humans are unique in that they tend to favour one upper limb over the other. Apes tend to be much more symmetrical in the general use of their limbs. The human asymmetry of upper-limb use provides a perfect context in which to test hypotheses relating to bone modelling and remodelling in response to physical activities. By comparing the upper limbs of the same individuals, we have "two" samples (right side and left side) that are perfectly concordant in terms of potential influence of age, sex, and other factors noted above. The only difference between the two sides is related to the differences in the type of activities and their intensity. In that context, I compared the asymmetry of muscle markers in humans and great apes. I was able to show that the morphology of muscle insertions is influenced by activity in all species and that, as expected, humans have a much more asymmetric expression of these markers.

Understanding how bone responds to loads is elemental, but understanding why bones are shaped the way they are is rather fascinating. For example, I am interested in understanding the differences between the elbow of humans and great apes. They appear very similar, particularly when compared to those of other primates or mammals. However, they also have subtle differences that reflect the very different use of the upper limbs in African apes (knuckle-walking and forelimb-dominated climbing), orangutans (predominantly forelimb-dominated climbing and below-branch suspension), and humans (manipulation). African apes have an extension of the distal part of the articulation to better resist loads when knuckle-walking with the arm in full extension, whereas orangutans have a more crested articulation in order to better resist the shearing stress generated by their strong wrist and finger flexors.

These comparisons of extant hominoid species and the investigation of bone responses to individuals' activities have an ultimate goal: to better understand how to interpret skeletal shape of individuals for whom no direct knowledge of behaviour exists—that is, that are known only through fossils. I am particularly interested in our early ancestors of the late Pliocene. Though we believe that bipedality had already appeared at the dawn of our lineage, there is still much debate about the degree of retention of arboreality. Analysis of the skeleton of *Australopithecus afarensis* has shown that it had hands that were more mobile—most likely an adaptation to some manipulation—and had therefore relinquished some stability, which is better suited for arboreality. Also, *A. afarensis* had short hands, not particularly long arms, and feet that were clearly derived from the arboreal hominoid form. All of this indicates that selection for manipulation and efficient bipedality was more important than maintaining important adaptations for arboreality in *A. afarensis*.

Source: Written by Dr. Michelle Drapeau, Department of Anthropology, Université de Montréal.

## Robust Australopithecines and the Megadont Adaptation

As we have seen, the jaws and teeth of the australopithecines provide crucial data regarding not just the phylogeny of these various species, but also levels of sexual dimorphism, aspects of social behaviour, and dietary habits. New research methods are greatly extending the quality of information we can glean from dental remains (Skinner et al. 2008; see Box 9.5). For example, the shape of the dental arcade measured in terms of palate length to width (Cobb 2008) is transitional between panins (U-shape) and later hominins (parabolic) (Figure 9.16). Smaller canines suggest reduced male–male competition, and thicker enamel points toward a reliance on tougher foods. However, one of the most salient features of the craniodental complex within australopithecines is a trend toward postcanine megadontia, which is taken to an extreme in that sister clade known as the robust australopithecines (Figure 9.17).

Three species of robust australopithecines are known, belonging to the genus *Paranthropus*.[15] These include *P. aethiopithecus* and *P. boisei* from eastern Africa (2.6 to 1.1 mya) and *P. robustus* from southern Africa (2.0 to 1.5 mya; see Figure 9.8). Widely presumed to have become extinct by 1.0 mya and not to be ancestral to later hominins, their origins are somewhat more ambiguous. Some researchers link all robust species to a still unknown eastern African progenitor (possibly *A. afarensis*); others see separate origins for the eastern and southern African lineages, the latter derived from *A. africanus*. This view would suggest that the megadont adaptation evolved independently in these two geographic locales. Differences do exist between the two eastern African species, as well as between the more recent (post-2.3 mya) eastern and southern African species of *Paranthropus*. For example, the earlier form

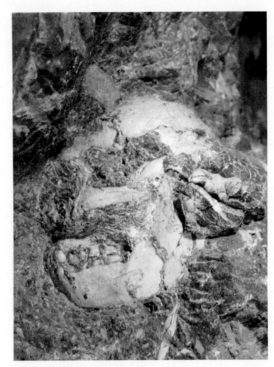

**Figure 9.15** StW 573, Little Foot, is one of the most complete partial skeletons of *Australopithecus* yet found, though much of it remains encased in limestone breccias requiring painstaking efforts to recover.

Greg Marinovich/Getty Images

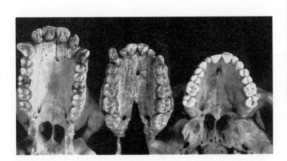

**Figure 9.16** A defining feature of the transition from panin to hominin relates to the shape of the dental arcade, which is associated with modification of the facial skeleton. Hominoids (left) have a parallel U-shaped tooth row, and humans (right) a parabolic shape. Australopithecines (centre) are somewhat transitional, though still more ape-like.

Courtesy of Dr. William Kimbel/Institute of Human Origins

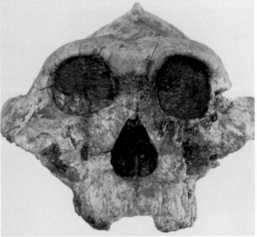

**Figure 9.17** Three species of robust australopithecines are recognized, two from eastern Africa (including *Paranthropus boisei* depicted here) and the third from southern Africa.

John Reader/Science Photo Library

15. Considerable debate exists regarding the systematics of the robust forms. *Paranthropus* was the original taxon created by Robert Broom in 1938 for the South African species *P. robustus*. However, when similar forms were discovered in East Africa—originally called *Zinjanthropus boisei* by the Leakeys—they were later assigned to the genus *Australopithecus*. Some researchers consider the megadont adaptation and the behaviour implied by it to be sufficient to indicate an adaptive shift worthy of a generic distinction, and refer all robust species to *Paranthropus*. This is the position taken in this text. Collectively, however, all of the Plio-Pleistocene hominins not ascribed to *Homo* are casually referred to as "australopithecine."

**BOX 9.5** **PROFILE... What Lurks Within ...**

*Dr. Matt Skinner is a postdoctoral fellow at the Max Planck Institute in Leipzig, Germany. His primary area of research is dental evolution in early hominins.*

Almost half a century ago the development of the scanning electron microscope revolutionized a number of scientific fields, including biology, allowing scientists to see structures at unprecedented levels of magnification. The last decade has seen a similar revolution in imaging with the development and widespread use of micro-computed tomography (microCT). Like tomographic scanners used in hospitals to examine the internal structures of the human body, micro-computed tomography allows visualization of internal structures of hard tissues (such as bones and teeth) at very high resolution. Increasingly, paleoanthropologists are able to scan rare fossils and see into them in ways never before possible. This access to internal structures of the hard tissues of living and extinct animals (which, importantly, does not damage museum specimens and fossils) has revealed unseen aspects and prompted new questions about the biology of fossil hominins.

Along with my colleagues at the Max Planck Institute for Evolutionary Anthropology, located in Leipzig, Germany, I have applied micro-computed tomography to the study of the internal structures of the teeth of fossil hominins. But why are teeth so important to paleoanthropologists? In fact, being able to study the internal and external structures of teeth allows us to address many important questions. The shape

Courtesy of Richard Lazenby

of teeth can help us decide whether a newly discovered fossil represents a new species of hominin or whether it is another example of a species that has already been discovered. We are also interested in the processes by which fossil hominins grew their teeth. Did early hominins grow their teeth more like living chimpanzees? And when during human evolution do we first see hominins that grew their teeth like us? Tooth shape and structure can also provide information about what kind of foods a fossil hominin might have eaten. Did it tend to eat hard foods like nuts, tough foods like tubers, or soft foods like fruit?

Of course, hominins used their teeth before they died and became part of the fossil record, and this means that much of the original shape of the tooth can be worn away. This makes it much more difficult to compare the fossil to others that have been found previously. However, after we microCT scan a fossil tooth we can remove the partially worn enamel and reveal a structure that is called the enamel-dentine junction, or EDJ (see Figure 8.12). This junction is the interface between the enamel cap, which you can see when you look at your teeth in a mirror, and the underlying dentine core of the tooth. The shape of the EDJ forms early during tooth development and is primarily responsible for the shapes of your incisors, canines, premolars, and molars. So, by looking at the shape of the EDJ in worn fossil teeth, we can recover hidden information about the original shape of the tooth, which helps us decide which species the tooth belongs to and whether or not two species, whose teeth may look similar from the outside, actually have very different internal structures and grew their teeth in different ways. In addition to examining EDJ shape, we can also use microCT to examine the thickness of enamel on the teeth used for chewing, as well as the shape of their roots, which are often hidden inside fossilized jaws. These provide important information as to how the tooth functions when it breaks down food.

But paleoanthropologists are not just studying the teeth of fossil hominins. Ongoing research using microCT scanning includes the study of inner ear morphology to help us understand how hominins moved, the size and shape of the brain to trace the evolutionary changes of this most important of organs, and the internal structures of the bones of the skeleton to improve our understanding of what kind of activities fossil hominins habitually practised during their lives.

Source: Written by Dr. Matthew Skinner, Department of Human Evolution, Max Planck Institute for Evolutionary Anthropology, Leipzig

**prognathic**

refers to the degree to which the lower face projects forward

*P. aethiopithecus* has a more **prognathic** face, larger incisors, and a smaller mandible than *P. boisei* (Wood et al. 1994), and as a rule the eastern African robust species are exceptional in the degree to which they express the major craniodental features defining this clade (Wood and Chamberlain 1987). In spite of these distinctions, it is reasonable to see them as geographic variants sharing a common ancestor.

Though comparable in body size to their gracile "sisters" such as *A. afarensis* and *A. africanus* (ca. 30 to 45 kg for females and males), robust australopithecines are exceptional for having massive postcanine teeth, estimated between 600 to 700 mm$^2$ in occlusal (chewing) surface area, in contrast to 450 to 500 mm$^2$ in gracile forms (McHenry and Coffing 2000). This of course is the source for the label "megadont." The transition to megadontia is associated with a number of cranial modifications that accommodate a substantial muscle mass providing large chewing forces, including well-developed sagittal and nuchal crests and expansive cheekbones. Researchers initially concluded that this anatomy reflected an adaptation to a diet of tough, fibrous foods, which earned *P. boisei* the nickname "Nutcracker Man" when the first cranium was discovered by Mary Leakey in 1959.

Web link http://www.leakey .com/index.html

These features are so derived relative to the earlier gracile australopithecines that scientists quite naturally viewed the robust species as dietary specialists living in open grassland habitats and surviving on hard-to-chew foods as a result of ecological factors or possibly through **competitive exclusion** vis-à-vis tool-using australopithecines or early species of *Homo*. However, paleoenvironmental reconstruction of robust australopithecines locales indicates habitat diversity, from open, arid grassland to lakeshore margins to closed, wet woodlands. Ungar, Grine, and Teaford (2008) recently studied dental microwear on the molar teeth of several *P. boisei* specimens from various sites and time periods and found that the pattern of wear was not consistent with a constant diet of tough, fibrous foods. This finding challenges the notion of dietary specialization and points to an interesting discrepancy between what an animal's morphology suggests it *could* eat based on biomechanical considerations and what it may *actually* have eaten as revealed in tooth wear patterns. In biology, this is known as **Liem's Paradox**: a species may evolve a specialized phenotype in order to access secondary **fallback foods** when preferred resources are less available. At the same time, this adaptive morphology in no way impedes its ability to consume more easily processed preferred foods when they are available. What this means is that *Paranthropus* was actually more of a dietary generalist, able to eat pretty much anything, and not a specialist at all! Interestingly, Ungar and colleagues (2008) also found that *P. robustus* in southern Africa had a dental microwear pattern more in keeping with biomechanical expectations; that is, this species most likely relied more heavily on fallback foods than eastern African *P. boisei*. While deriving from a gracile species such as *A. afarensis* or *A. africanus*, the robust australopithecines were for the most part contemporaries with members of early *Homo*, including the species *H. habilis* and *H. ergaster*. Neither of these forms exhibits a megadont adaptation, but both are likewise associated with a varied range of habitats. As we explore in the following chapter, exploitation of diverse food resources by early *Homo* (including fallback foods) was made possible not by teeth, but by tools.[16] A review of models for the extinction of this last-surviving member of the australopithecine clade (Wood and Strait 2004) also tested the presumption that *Paranthropus* was too much of a dietary specialist to survive the regime of climate change (cooling and drying) in eastern and southern Africa established in the late Miocene. These authors examined 11 different criteria providing direct (e.g., dental wear, carbon isotope analysis) and indirect (e.g., paleoecology, tooth size and shape) evidence for specialization, principally regarding diet. Their results were not sufficiently compelling to conclude that *Paranthropus* was more specialized than the earliest members of the genus *Homo*. Thus, while it is clear that extinction was the ultimate fate of this enigmatic genus, the factors which led to the disappearance of *Paranthropus* remain a mystery.

**competitive exclusion**
a phenomenon in which two species closely related in phenotype and ecology come into direct competition for resources. In these cases one species will either become extinct or adopt a new phenotype (morphology and/or behaviour), allowing it to exploit other resources.

**Liem's Paradox**
a model in biology that describes the apparent paradox between a specialized phenotype and a generalized behaviour; the paradox is resolved if the specialized phenotype does not restrict an organism from nonspecialized behaviours

**fallback foods**
resources on which a species relies when its preferred, more easily acquired and processed foods are unavailable

# FROM BUSH TO BRANCH: RECONSTRUCTING PLIOCENE HOMININ PHYLOGENY

If nothing else, this discussion of early hominin evolution should convince you that paleoanthropology is a complex discipline in which fieldwork, fossil data, analysis, and personalities produce competing interpretations. For example, sound arguments can be made that

---

16. Some paleoanthropologists have argued for many years that *Paranthropus* had sufficient manual dexterity to fashion Oldowan-type tools. Recent research of the internal structure of a handbone attributed to this species (Lazenby et al. 2008) suggests that while it is human-like in some respects, *Paranthropus* may have had limited dexterity.

*Sahelanthropus, Orrorin,* and *Ardipithecus* are all members of the hominin lineage. However, even though they comprise a temporal sequence, their morphological differences make it unlikely that they form an evolutionary sequence, and each discoverer has claimed that "their fossil" is the most likely stem hominin species. Unravelling the earliest history of the human lineage is further complicated by three realities. First, molecular data place the hominin–panin divergence somewhere within the 2 million-year time frame occupied by these protohominins. Second, many of the most significant discoveries (such as *Sahelanthropus*) are fairly recent, and analyses are still in early stages. As these progress, considerable revision to existing interpretations is likely to occur. Third and finally, the discipline is plagued by a still extremely poor late Miocene/Pliocene fossil record for African hominoids (e.g., ancestors of chimpanzee and gorilla). These challenges will only be overcome by further fossil discoveries in the 4 to 7 mya time range and by continued cooperation and sharing of data among researchers.

It does not get much easier untangling relationships among the diversity of hominin species between. 4.0 and 2.0 mya (Figure 9.18). Prior to 3.0 mya, the lineage *Ar. ramidus–A. anamensis–A. afarensis* is the only game in town (assuming, of course, that we reject both *Kenyanthropus* as a valid genus and the putative 4.0 mya date for *A. africanus* in southern Africa). The rest of it remains a bit of a muddle. Is *Homo* derived from *A. gahri* or *A. africanus?* Are the robust eastern African forms linked phyletically (by linear descent) or cladistically (branching evolution) with *A. afarensis?* Do the eastern and southern African robust species form a sister clade, or do they belong to separate and geographically isolated lineages? These are all important and as yet unanswerable questions. It may be that the reality is something quite different from any these alternatives; Asfaw and colleagues (1999) have noted that their four models (Figure 9.18) do not exhaust the possibilities. The take-home message here is that the volumes of data we have about our early hominin forebears remain small compared to what we do not yet know. The problem is that we can never *know* what we do not know.

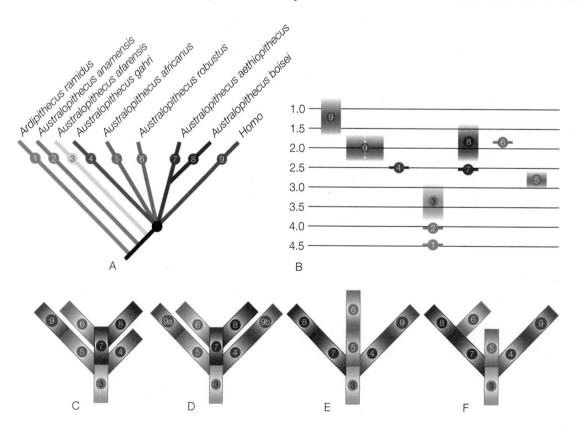

**Figure 9.18** The complexity of hominin diversity in the Pliocene and early Pleistocene is such that a number of possible phylogenetic reconstructions are possible.

From B. Asfaw, T. White, O. Lovejoy, et al., (1999). Australopithecus gahri: A new species of early hominid from Ethiopia, *Science* 284: 629-635. Reprinted with permission from AAAS

**Table 9.3**  Developments in early hominin evolution

| Development | Suggested by | Implications |
|---|---|---|
| Facultative bipedalism | Forward position of foramen magnum in the base of the skull (*Sahelanthropus*); size and shape of the head and neck of the femur (*Orrorin*); foot bones adapted to "toeing off" during swing phase (*Ardipithecus*); femur curvature and muscle attachment relief (*Australopithecus anamensis*) | Adoption of bipedal loco-motion for some activities, though all four genera lived in woodland habitats and retained climbing ability, as evidenced by shoulder, forelimb, and hand anatomy |
| Obligate bipedalism | Restructured pelvis, reduced intermembral index, and valgus (oblique) angle between knee and shaft of the femur (*Australopithecus afarensis; A. gahri*) | Exploration of diverse habitats, open-country terrestrial food resources and greater geographic distribution; ability to exploit arboreal environ-ment retained in these species (e.g., curved pha-langes) |
| Canine reduction and loss of C/P3 honing | Apical wear of tip of canine and reduction or loss of diastema between the canine and P3 (*Ar. ramidus* and later australopithecines) | Reduced emphasis on male–male or male–female competition and use of teeth in display or aggres-sion |
| Parabolic dental arcade | Ratio of palate length to breadth at the 2nd molar (*Australopithecus afarensis*) | Reduction of facial projec-tion subsequent to ante-rior tooth reduction |
| Increasing molar enamel thickness | Thickness of enamel layer relative to tooth size (*Sahelanthropus; Orrorin,* and later australopithecines; absent in *Ardipithecus* species) | Shift to harder, more abra-sive diets |
| Megadontia | Increased size (relative and absolute) of pos-terior dentition (premolars and molars) and associated cranial architecture associated with chewing musculature (*P. aethiopithecus, P. boisei, P. robustus*) | Increased reliance and exploitation on tough, abrasive fallback foods |
| Encephalization | Increase in brain/body mass ratio relative to living hominoids, e.g., chimpanzees (*Australopithecus afarensis*) | Speculative; possibly reflective of changing social and behavioural environment, or chal-lenges of exploiting new habitats |

Nonetheless, the picture is clearer now than it has ever been (Table 9.3), though still not nearly clear enough. This confusing picture reflects the fact that paleoanthropology is a highly active and deeply fascinating field of study.

# SUMMARY

It is likely that hominins originated somewhere in eastern Africa and sometime between 4 and 7 mya. Several candidate fossils exhibiting a mix of derived and primitive features have been found in this time frame that may represent a stem species close to the LCA shared by homi-nins and panins; none of these, however, are definitive and are thus considered protohominins.

A reasonable case can be made linking *Ardipithecus ramidus* in eastern Africa with the succeeding species, *Australopithecus anamensis* and subsequently *A. afarensis*, the first well-known bipedal hominin. Still, all of the late Miocene and Pliocene species are small-brained and relatively large-toothed, and while having at least facultative bipedality they retained an adept arboreal climbing capability as evidenced by relatively long arms and curved hand and foot bones. These features accord well with paleoenvironmental data, which suggest that these species exploited a diverse range of habitats, from open savannah to woodland and closed forest. In the late Pliocene, australopithecines diversified into several varieties, including a robust megadont sister clade, *Paranthropus*, known for its massive cheek teeth and pronounced cranial features. This genus likely derived from *A. afarensis* in eastern Africa, though the possibility remains that the southern African variant, *P. robustus*, evolved independently of the southern African gracile species, *A. africanus*. Most paleoanthropologists link the emergence of *Homo* with the eastern African form *A. afarensis*, with the possibility that the 2.6 mya species *A. gahri* forms an intermediary link. The possibility that *A. gahri* rather than *Homo* was the first maker of stone tools is a provocative but not unreasonable claim, one that challenges decades of anthropogenic hubris.

# CORE REVIEW

### What rationales support the splitting or lumping approaches in hominin systematics?

Taxonomic "splitters" emphasize the differences they see in a sample of fossils; "lumpers" emphasize the similarities. Both consider the passage of time—large differences in fossils separated by only a relatively short period of time would suggest that different species are present, supporting a splitting event, whereas small differences in forms separated by several hundreds of thousands of years would suggest that one is looking at within-species population variation, suggesting that "lumping" is in order.

### What impact does recent molecular (DNA) research have on the status of the protohominins *Sahelanthropus* and *Orrorin*?

Genetic divergence times derived from molecular differences suggest that the last common ancestor of chimpanzees and humans lived ca. 4.0 to 5.0 mya. Both *Sahelanthropus* and *Orrorin* predate this estimate and thus would likely be excluded from consideration as the stem hominin from which all later members of our lineage derived. This would further suggest that one of these protohominins could, in fact, be the LCA of panins and hominins.

### How do we account for the fact that late Miocene and Pliocene hominins were adapted to both terrestrial and arboreal locomotion?

There are two considerations here—morphology and behaviour. The fossil evidence (e.g., curved hand and foot bones) suggests that these hominins, while bipedal, still possessed a good grasping ability associated with climbing. Behaviourally, it would be entirely reasonable to expect that early hominins that still lived in treed habitats would avail themselves of that protection and/or foraging opportunity.

### What role might early *Homo* have played in the evolution of robust, megadont australopithecines?

While it is not clear that *Homo* was the first maker of stone tools, the appearance of early *Homo* is closely associated with that of stone tools. We assume that this would have afforded considerable benefit in competition for resources with other (non–tool using?) hominins, who may have been forced to exploit fallback foods (tougher, more fibrous items) with greater frequency. In this case, selection would favour a megadont adaptation that would nonetheless still allow the robust australopithecines to take advantage of high-quality foods when available.

**Why is it possible to construct several different scenarios for the evolution of hominins during the Pliocene?**

Several factors come into play here. In the first place, we have the vagaries of the fossil record. Many forms are represented by very little evidence, and these may be separated by several hundreds of thousands of years. Paleoanthropologists must ask themselves: At what point does variation within a species translate into variation between species? There is also the matter of which morphological variables we should give greater credence to in terms of sorting out different species and their ancestor–descendant relationships. These are tough questions, and the slightest difference in answer might produce a different (and equally reasonable) phylogeny! Finally, we have to understand that paleoanthropologists are also human. They have their own understandings and biases (as do we all) and should be expected to favour those fossils with which they are most closely tied.

# CRITICAL THINKING QUESTIONS

1. In reconstructing hominin phylogeny, paleoanthropologists consider what fossils look like as well as when and where they were found. How much emphasis do you think each of these factors should be given in sorting out the fossil record of ancestor–descendant relationships?
2. How do you account for the fact that there may have been two (if not more) contemporaneous species of hominins living side by side in Africa?

# GROUP DISCUSSION QUESTIONS

1. You are a group of famous alien paleoanthropologists visiting this planet. When given a tour of a biological anthropology lab, you see replicas of crania of a Bantu pygmy from Africa, an Australian aborigine, and a member of the Swedish 1970s disco/pop band ABBA. You are convinced they are in fact different species and that they could not all be members of *Homo sapiens*. How did you reach this conclusion? What features did you find most compelling in your argument, and why? What would it take to convince you otherwise?
2. *Australopithecus afarensis* seems to have inhabited a diverse range of habitats in the late Pliocene, as do living chimpanzees today. Given such flexibility, what selective factors (ecological? behavioural? social?) do you think might have been central to the evolutionary transition to a form such as *A. garhi*, and eventually early *Homo*?

# RESOURCES AND READINGS

- A. Gibbons, *The First Humans: The Race to Discover Our Earliest Ancestors* (New York: Doubleday, 2006).
- R. Lewin, *Bones of Contention: Controversies in the Search for Human Origins* (Chicago: University of Chicago Press, 1997).
- V. Morell, *Ancestral Passions: The Leakey Family and the Quest for Humankind's Beginnings* (New York: Touchstone, 1996).
- Additional background and discussion on a variety of topics dealing with hominin evolution in general can be found at the following sites: **http://iho.asu.edu**, and **http://www.nationalgeographic.com/outpost**.

# 10 Plio-Pleistocene Transitions: The Emergence of the Genus *Homo*

## OVERVIEW

As you learned in the previous chapter, a number of different species of hominins coexisted in eastern and southern Africa during the late Pliocene epoch. Around 2.5 million years ago one of these species gave rise to the first members of the genus *Homo*, hominins that possessed a larger brain and body size than their predecessors, had a more sophisticated stone tool technology, hunted large game, and used fire. One of these species was the first to leave Africa and disperse to other regions of the Old World, where it endured for well over a million years. This chapter reviews the fossil evidence for these hominins, examines their anatomical characteristics, explores the ways in which they adapted behaviourally to their environments, and addresses some of the debates surrounding the taxonomic status and phylogenetic position of members of this genus.

## CORE CONCEPTS

■ experimental archaeology, bioenergetics, life history, stable isotope analysis, Oldowan, Acheulian, migration, hunting

## CORE QUESTIONS

■ In what ways did early members of the genus *Homo* differ morphologically from the australopithecines?

■ What behavioural adaptations characterized early *Homo*?

■ What are the anatomical characteristics of *Homo erectus*? In what ways did these hominins differ from *Homo habilis* and *Homo rudolfensis*?

■ Why do some paleoanthropologists think that there are separate African and Asian species—*Homo ergaster* and *Homo erectus* respectively?

■ What accounts for the success of *Homo erectus*? Why did this species endure for such a long period of time with few morphological changes?

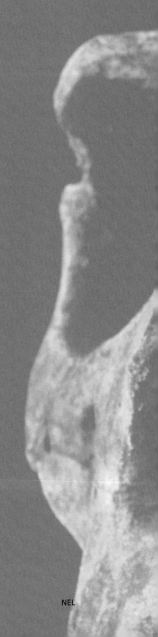

*I was taught that the human brain was the crowning glory of evolution so far,
but I think it's a very poor scheme for survival.*

Kurt Vonnegut (1922–2007)

# PROLOGUE: 35% MAKES ALL THE DIFFERENCE

Is a 35% increase really meaningful? If you were talking about the annual change in your investment portfolio or home heating bill, it certainly would be! But perhaps not so meaningful in the case of the price of a single iTunes download or the number of unmatched socks in the family laundry bin. However, in the history of our genus it turns out to have pretty significant import, as 35% is the difference between the average brain size for early *Homo* compared to *A. africanus*. What explains this dramatic increase, which took place over as little as half a million years and is still the subject of much debate (as we discussed in Chapter 8)? Diet is certainly implicated, and so are various aspects of sociality and spatial organization (i.e., group living and movement). Brain expansion is by many accounts the defining feature of the transition from Australopithecine to *Homo*.

The one demonstrable event that can be situated within the time frame of brain expansion is the development of an established stone tool industry. Even though the very earliest occurrence of these Oldowan-type tools predates the first appearance of the forms we ascribe to the genus *Homo*, it is certain that this new mode of interacting with the environment (more specifically, killing and/or butchering animals) became a large part of the behavioural niche carved out by our lineage. The implications are nothing short of profound (we can say this retrospectively with much confidence!). The development and evolution of a percussive stone tool technology has been linked to functional asymmetry (handedness), neural asymmetry, language development (including grammar and syntax), foresight, elaboration of the frontal cortex and its executive functions (including recognizing future consequences of current actions; see Semendeferi et al. 2002), and eventually, migration out of Africa. As we will see in this chapter, the advent of the genus *Homo* was accompanied by accelerating changes in morphology, technology, subsistence, life history, and social behaviour. Humankind had entered a new adaptive milieu unlike that experienced by any of our ancestors (or known from living hominoids, for that matter)—one that would forever, and unrelentingly, chart the course for all subsequent human evolution—the ascendancy of material culture.

## OUR ANCESTORS COME TO LIGHT

http://www.leakeyfoundation.org

The first fossils attributed to early *Homo* were discovered in 1960 when excavations by Louis Leakey and his team at Olduvai Gorge (Figure 10.1) uncovered hominin fossils consisting of a nearly complete left parietal bone, a partial right parietal bone, a partial mandible, 14 teeth, and a number of hand bones. The age at death of this individual was estimated to have been 12 to 13 years based on the degree of eruption of its teeth. Dating between 1.8 and 1.6 million years ago, the remains were recovered from the same deposit as the *Zinjanthropus* fossil (now recognized as *P. boisei*) discovered by Mary Leakey in 1959. Given the catalogue number OH 7 for Olduvai Hominid 7, its large cranial capacity (680 cc) compared to "Zinj" prompted Leakey and his colleagues to assign it the taxonomic name *Homo habilis* ("handy man"), reflecting their belief that it

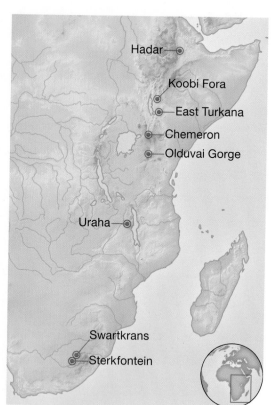

**Figure 10.1** Early *Homo* sites in Africa.

Based on Schrenk, F., Kullmer, O., Bromage, T. (2007). The earliest putative Homo fossils, *Handbook of Paleoanthropology*, edited by Henke, W. and Tattersall, I. Berline: Springer Verlag, p. 1613; Jurmain, R., Kilgore, L., Trevathan, W., (2005). *Introduction to Physical Anthropology*, 10e. Belmont, Calif: Wadsworth, p. 189.

had made the stone tools found nearby. Six additional specimens representing adults, adolescents, and juveniles were also recovered during this excavation (Leakey et al. 1964). More recent finds include a cranium (OH 24), a maxilla with a complete set of teeth (OH 65), and a partial female skeleton (OH 62).

The initial reaction from many people was that the hominins represented by these fossils were not significantly different from the australopithecines to warrant identification as a new species. Hindering acceptance of these fossils as distinct from earlier hominins was the fact that the sample size was small, the remains were very fragmentary, and there were few infracranial bones. This view changed in the early 1970s, however, with the discovery of additional early *Homo* fossils at the site of Koobi Fora on the eastern shores of Lake Turkana.[1] Dating between 1.9 and 1.4 mya, these remains resemble those from Olduvai, and many are currently interpreted as representing *Homo habilis,* though the taxonomic status of some of these fossils has been questioned (see below). In more recent years, the *Homo* lineage in East Africa has been extended to 2.3 mya with the discovery of a maxilla (A.L. 666–1) from Hadar, Ethiopia (Kimbel et al. 1996). A number of early *Homo* fossils have also been found in South Africa, including a fragmentary skull (Stw 53) at the cave site of Sterkfontein (Tobias 1991).

http://anthropology.si.edu/humanorigins

## The Anatomy of Early Homo

The key defining feature of the genus *Homo* is its larger brain relative to body size compared to the australopithecines (Leakey, Tobias, and Napier 1964; Tobias 1991; Figure 10.2). The cranial capacity of *Homo habilis* ranged from just over 500 cc, close to that measured in some

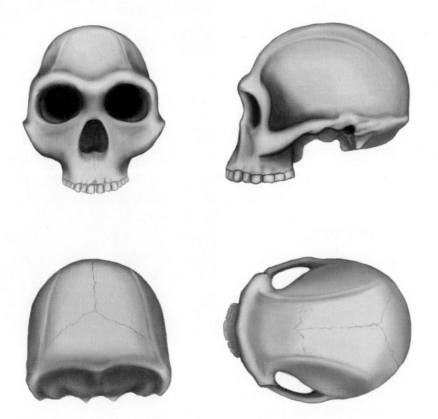

**Figure 10.2** Compared to the australopithecines, early *Homo* had a larger cranial capacity, a more rounded braincase, a smaller and less projecting face, and smaller molars.

Courtesy of Richard G. Klein

---

1. These fossils were labelled KNM-ER for "Kenya National Museum East Rudolf," indicating that the site is located on the east side of Lake Rudolf (renamed Lake Turkana in 1975).

*Australopithecus* fossils (452 cc for *A. africanus*, 521 cc for *A. boisei*, and 530 cc for *A. robustus*), to over 650 cc, with an average of 612 cc (McHenry and Coffing 2000). Besides a larger brain, *Homo habilis* had a more rounded braincase, and casts of its endocranium display evidence of enlargement of the frontal and parietal lobes of the brain (Tobias 1991). In modern humans, these lobes house three language centres: **Broca's area**, which is responsible for language processing, speech production, and language comprehension; **Wernicke's area**, which is involved in the understanding and comprehension of spoken language; and the **angular gyrus**, which plays a role in a number of processes related to language and cognition. Thus the enlargement of these areas of the brain in early *Homo* suggests that this hominin may have been capable of some form of rudimentary speech. We will discuss language origins further in the next chapter.

The face of *Homo habilis* was smaller and less projecting than that of the australopithecines. Its dental characteristics included a parabolic dental arcade (palate), large incisors, large canines relative to the premolars, and smaller molars than those of some australopithecines, though some early *Homo* fossils had relatively large molars.

Our knowledge of the infracranial anatomy of early *Homo* comes from studies of only a small number of preserved infracranial skeletons. Its limb proportions reflect both ape-like and more human-like features (Haeusler and McHenry 2007). An analysis of the relative limb strength of OH 62 indicates that *Homo habilis*, while fully bipedal when on the ground, engaged in frequent arboreal locomotion (Ruff 2008). Similarly, analysis of the left foot of OH 8, originally uncovered in 1960, has revealed that while *Homo habilis* was an obligate biped, it retained some features characteristic of arboreal adaptation (Susman 2008).[2]

As noted above, the first *Homo habilis* fossils were found in deposits that also yielded stone tools, and it is generally agreed that they were the makers of these tools, an assumption based primarily on their larger brain. Hand bones have been recovered from Olduvai, though uncertainty remains regarding whether they belonged to *Homo habilis* or *A. boisei* (Tocheri et al. 2008). Morphological studies of these bones have revealed a combination of primitive and derived features, suggesting that these hominins did not manipulate objects in the same way that we do (Tocheri et al. 2003).

## One Species or Two?

Fossils discovered in the early 1970s at Koobi Fora were initially interpreted as representing *Homo habilis* based on similarities with fossils found at Olduvai. One of the most complete skulls (KNM-ER 1470; Figure 10.3), however, stood out as having what appeared to be a larger cranial capacity (752 cc) than other early *Homo* fossils from Koobi Fora and elsewhere. This led to speculation that more than one species of *Homo* was represented in the

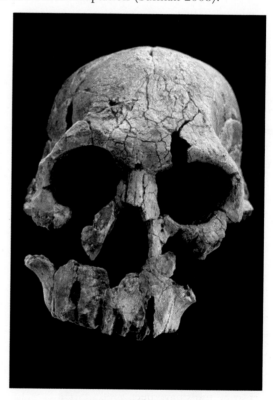

**Figure 10.3** A recent reconstruction of KNM-ER 1470 has revealed that this individual had a cranial capacity of about 700 cc.

**Broca's area**
a portion of the frontal lobe responsible for language processing, speech production, and language comprehension

**Wernicke's area**
a portion of the parietal and temporal lobes involved in understanding and comprehending spoken language

**angular gyrus**
a portion of the parietal lobe involved in a number of processes related to language and cognition

2. This fossil has recently been identified as belonging to the same individual as OH7 (Susman 2008).

fossil record from East Africa. This observation led to its identification as *Homo rudolfensis* (Groves 1989; Wood 1991, 1993),[3] and additional fossils have since been assigned to this taxon based on their larger cranial capacities and other features (see Schrenk et al. 2007 for a summary of this evidence). While the majority of *Homo rudolfensis* fossils uncovered to date come from Koobi Fora and date to approximately 1.8 mya, fossilized remains of this species, including the body of a mandible (UR 501) found in a "corridor" known as the Malawi Rift (Schrenk et al. 1993) and a temporal bone (KNM-BC 1) uncovered at the site of Chemeron in Kenya (Hill et al. 1992; Prat et al. 2005), extend its time range back to nearly 2.5 mya. As for KNM-ER 1470, a more recent reconstruction of this fossil suggests that this particular hominin had a cranial capacity of about 700 cc, not 752 cc as originally estimated, placing it closer to *Homo habilis* (Bromage et al. 2008). Nevertheless, this specimen is still considered by many to represent *Homo rudolfensis*, and it is this taxonomic designation that we will use here.

# BEHAVIOURAL ADAPTATIONS

## The First Stone Tools

As noted earlier in this chapter, *Homo habilis* was so-named because its remains were first found in a deposit that also yielded stone tools. Representing the **Oldowan industry**, the earliest of these **Lower Paleolithic** tools come from the 2.6 mya site of Gona in Ethiopia (Semaw et al. 2003). Consisting of pebble tools and choppers made of quartz, chert, or flint (Figure 10.4), their method of manufacture was by percussion, which involved striking one stone with another to make a cutting edge. Flakes chipped off during this process were also used as tools.

To an untrained eye, some of these implements look like any other rock or pebble. Indeed, naturally shaped stones have often been mistaken for tools. To the trained eye, however, a number of clues

**Figure 10.4** Oldowan tools resembled these chopper tools, found at the Isimila Acheulean site in southern Tanzania.

Courtesy of Pamela R. Willoughby

**Oldowan industry**
the earliest stone tool industry, characterized by pebble and chopping tools made and used by early hominins

**Lower Paleolithic**
the period associated with the Oldowan and Acheulian stone tool industries

indicate that these stones were, in fact, modified and used by hominins. In the Hadar region of Ethiopia, for example, stone tools have been found in association with early *Homo* remains (Kimbel et al. 1996). At other sites such as Olduvai, dense concentrations of stones suggest that human activity such as food processing or tool manufacturing may have taken place at these locations. Some of these sites have been interpreted as home bases, to which hominins returned repeatedly with tools and carcasses (Isaac 1978). In addition, tools made of stone not local to the area suggest that hominins intentionally transported the material from elsewhere, indicating planning and foresight. **Quarrying sites** characterized by a large number of stone tools have been identified archaeologically in East Africa.

Attempts have been made to determine how these tools were used through **experimental archaeology**. More specifically, paleoanthropologists have endeavoured to make and use stone tools in order to understand how early hominins may have done the same. Louis Leakey himself butchered animals using tools he had made (Jones 1980). Also, microscopic wear on the cutting edges of tools has been examined to assess tool use. Such studies suggest

**quarrying sites**
sites from which hominins obtained raw materials to make stone tools

**experimental archaeology**
a field of archaeology that uses a number of different methods to test hypotheses about how artifacts and structures may have been made and used

---

3. The name *rudolfensis* was coined by Russian paleontologist V.A. Alexeev, who identified KNM-ER 1470 as *Pithecanthropus rudolfensis* (Alexeev 1986).

that Oldowan tools were likely used to process carcasses and to extract marrow from the bones of animals that had been either hunted or scavenged. At some butchering sites tools have been found in association with animal bones exhibiting cut marks.

Unfortunately, our knowledge of the role of tools in food acquisition and processing is limited, as tools made of perishable materials such as wood have not been preserved in the Lower Paleolithic archaeological record (Ungar et al. 2006a, 219). Based on our observations of modern great apes, however, early hominins would almost certainly have used such tools for acquiring and processing food. Perhaps they also used sticks to fish for termites or capture small mammals, as some chimpanzees do today.

## A Taste for Meat

Hunting and the consumption of meat have long been viewed as playing a significant role in human evolution. In the 1960s and 1970s, hunting models emphasizing the role of males were pervasive in the literature (see Chapter 8). Such models presented scenarios in which the introduction of stone tools led to the increased consumption of meat. This in turn resulted in the expansion of the brain and, consequently, more sophisticated tool kits, more efficient hunting techniques, and further expansion of the brain. We have already mentioned that Oldowan tools have been found with animal bones at a number of early *Homo* sites, pointing to the consumption of meat. As you learned in Chapter 6, chimpanzees in the wild today form intentional hunting parties and capture a variety of small mammals, including other primates. Similarly, archaeologists have long assumed that hominins obtained animals through hunting. Microscopic studies of animal bones found at early *Homo* sites, however, have revealed evidence consistent with scavenging in the form of hominin-made cut marks superimposed on carnivore tooth marks, and cut marks located on bones that would have yielded little meat (i.e., those left behind by carnivores) (Shipman 1986).

Challenges to the "Man the Hunter" model have also come from studies of modern-day hunter-gatherers. Among such groups, a greater proportion of their diet consists of plant foods than meat, and most of these plant foods are gathered by women. This observation has prompted researchers to develop alternatives, termed "Woman the Gatherer" models, that emphasize plant consumption among early hominins. O'Connell and colleagues (1999), for example, have argued that underground plant resources such as roots and tubers[4] may have been a key component of the diet of early *Homo* and would have been more abundant over the last 2.5 million years. Similarly, Wrangham and colleagues (1999) argue that plants would have been a vital food resource, especially in times of food shortages, as fallback foods.

Direct evidence for what early *Homo* actually consumed comes from the fossils themselves. In Chapter 7 we talked about the various ways in which the diet of fossil primates can be reconstructed. These include examining tooth size and shape, enamel thickness, and dental microwear. As noted above, early *Homo* had larger incisors and smaller molars than the australopithecines. These differences suggest that their diet involved greater use of the anterior teeth and the consumption of foods that required lighter chewing forces, though this dental trend is difficult to evaluate without larger sample sizes and more precise estimates of body weight (Ungar et al. 2006a, 219). Tooth shape—more specifically, the amount of relief on the chewing surfaces—can also provide information on the types of foods consumed. Species that rely on tough foods such as leaves, for example, tend to have greater occlusal relief than those that rely on hard foods such as nuts and seeds. Tooth shape can be examined using **dental topographic analysis**. This technique involves using a laser scanner to generate 3D models of teeth and geographic information system (GIS) software to measure features on the surface of those teeth. The application of this method to the teeth of *A. afarensis* and early *Homo* has revealed that the latter had greater occlusal relief than the former, suggesting that *Homo* relied on tougher, more elastic (i.e., deformable) foods than their predecessors (Ungar 2004; see also Box 9.5 in Chapter 9).

**dental topographic analysis**

a method of analysis that involves using a laser scanner to generate 3D models of teeth and GIS to measure features on the surfaces of those teeth

---

4. Also known as "underground storage organs."

The use of dental microwear to reconstruct diet (see Chapter 7) is based on the observation that the consumption of hard objects such as nuts and seeds tends to produce large pits on the enamel surfaces, whereas the consumption of tough foods such as leaves tends to result in smaller pits and more striations. In contrast, species that consume soft fruits tend to have microwear patterns that fall somewhere in between (Teaford and Walker 1984; Teaford 1988). Ungar and colleagues (2006b) examined dental microwear in a sample of 18 molar teeth from Plio-Pleistocene hominins in East and South Africa (6 from *Homo habilis*, 7 from early *Homo*, 5 from *Homo erectus*) and compared those data with observations of five extant primate species and two protohistoric human foraging groups. Their analysis revealed that the early *Homo* specimens had a higher prevalence of intermediate microwear pits than the other groups, pointing to the consumption of a more varied diet.

Chemical analysis of early *Homo* fossils has also pointed to a generalized diet for these hominins. One type of analysis that has been used to reconstruct the diet of past populations, including hominins, is **stable isotope analysis** of the carbon and nitrogen atoms in bones and teeth. In contrast to traditional sources of dietary information such as faunal remains, which provide information on the range of animal foods available, stable isotope analysis of **collagen** (the major organic component of bone) and **carbonate** (a component of the mineral of bones and teeth) provides direct evidence of the types of foods that were actually eaten. This technique is based on the fact that the **isotopic signatures** of foods consumed are reflected in the tissues of the consumer and thus provide a record of their dietary intake over a period of time. More specifically, isotopic analysis of collagen provides information on an individual's intake of dietary protein over a period of 10 years or more, whereas isotopic analysis of carbonate provides a profile of the carbon isotopes in the total diet (i.e., fats, proteins, and carbohydrates). Underlying the use of stable carbon isotope analysis to reconstruct diet is the fact that the ratio of the stable carbon isotopes $^{13}$C and $^{12}$C, expressed as a $\delta^{13}$C value in parts per thousand, or per mil (‰), differs among different types of plant foods (Figure 10.5). Individuals who consume primarily $C_3$ plants (most temperate region plants) have lower $\delta^{13}$C values than those who consume a diet rich in $C_4$ plants (e.g., maize and millet). In addition, individuals who rely primarily on terrestrial resources have lower $\delta^{13}$C values than those who consume a predominantly marine diet. In contrast, dietary reconstruction using stable nitrogen isotope analysis looks at the ratio of the stable isotopes $^{15}$N to $^{14}$N, expressed as a $\delta^{15}$N value in per mil (‰). These values principally reflect trophic level, or the position of an organism in the food chain. Thus carnivores have higher $\delta^{15}$N values than herbivores. Also, humans who obtain most of their dietary protein from high trophic-level marine foods (large fish, seals, etc.) have higher $\delta^{15}$N values than those who rely primarily on terrestrial protein sources (Figure 10.5). With respect to early *Homo*, stable isotope analysis of tooth enamel taken from three specimens from Swartkrans has revealed a predominantly $C_3$ diet that may have included fruits, nuts, leaves, and animals that feed on these foods, with the addition of some $C_4$ foods such as grass-eating vertebrates and insects—a pattern also seen in *A. robustus* (Lee-Thorp et al. 2000).

In summary, data derived from the fossil and archaeological record and from paleoenvironmental reconstructions point to increasing dietary versatility with the appearance of *Homo* (Ungar et al. 2006a). The use of tools made of stone and other materials, along with changes in dentition, would have allowed them to exploit a broader range of food

**stable isotope analysis**
a type of chemical analysis that looks at stable isotopes of certain elements in bones and other tissues of the body; it can tell us something about the diet and residential history of an individual

**collagen**
a type of protein that forms the main organic component of bone

**carbonate**
a component of the mineral of bones and teeth

**isotopic signature**
the ratio of stable isotopes of a particular element, for example, $^{13}$C/$^{12}$C; this is expressed as $\delta^{13}$C in per mil (‰)

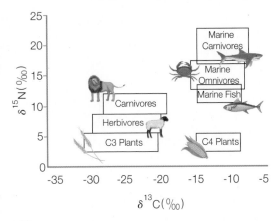

**Figure 10.5** Reconstructing the diet of past populations involves comparing isotope values measured in humans with those derived from a range of plants and animals from the environment in which those humans lived.

Courtesy of Tracy Prowse

resources than the australopithecines, and this flexibility would have been beneficial in allowing them to adapt to changing environmental conditions during the Late Pliocene, including the spread of grasslands across East Africa.

# HOMO ERECTUS: ENIGMA OR ARCHETYPE?

## An Anatomy for All Occasions

The end of the Pliocene epoch some 1.8 mya marked the emergence in Africa of a third species of *Homo* that possessed a larger brain and body and a more modern-looking infracranial skeleton than *Homo habilis* and *Homo rudolfensis*. Known as **Homo erectus**, this species had a cranial capacity ranging from 700 to 1200 cc, with an average of 871 cc (McHenry and Coffing 2000)—an increase of more than 40% over early *Homo* (Figure 10.6). This larger brain was housed in a skull that was uniquely *Homo erectus*. Cranial characteristics included a long, low vault, a low sloping forehead, a pentagonal shape when viewed from the rear, a somewhat projecting face, a heavily built jaw with small molars, **shovel-shaped incisors**, a **sagittal keel**, a heavy **supraorbital torus** or browridge, an **angular torus** on the parietal bone, occipital angulation, and an **occipital torus** that served to anchor large neck muscles (Figure 10.7).

Far fewer infracranial remains belonging to *Homo erectus* have been recovered than crania, so our knowledge of the infracranial anatomy of these hominins comes mainly from only a handful of specimens. These suggest that *Homo erectus* had a significantly larger body than earlier hominins, as well as modern body proportions with longer legs that would have allowed them to expand their foraging range and cover greater distances more efficiently. Body mass estimates derived from hindlimb joint size range from an average of 52 kg for females to 63 kg for males (Aiello and Wells 2002); stature estimates range from 148 cm to

**Homo erectus**
a hominin that first appeared in Africa around 1.8 mya and subsequently spread to Eurasia and the Far East

**shovel-shaped incisors**
front teeth with marginal ridges of enamel on the lingual (tongue) surface

**sagittal keel**
a raised area of bone running along the sagittal suture

**supraorbital torus**
a ridge of bone running across the top of the eyes; also referred to as the browridge

**angular torus**
a ridge of bone running across the posterior part of the parietal bones

**occipital torus**
a horizontal ridge of bone running across the occipital bone

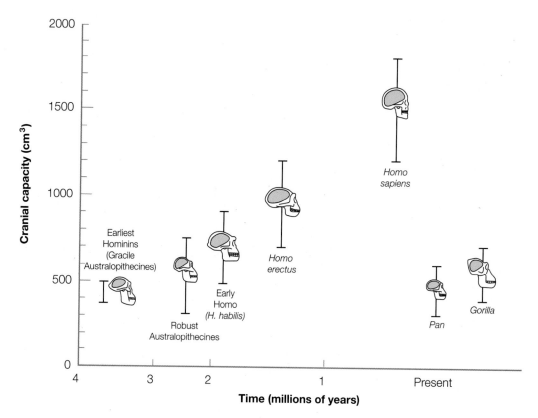

**Figure 10.6**   A trend toward increasing brain size over the past 2 million years is evident in the hominin fossil record.

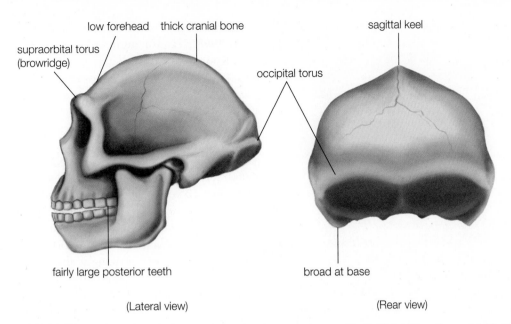

low forehead  thick cranial bone  sagittal keel

supraorbital torus
(browridge)

occipital torus

fairly large posterior teeth

broad at base

(Lateral view)

(Rear view)

**Figure 10.7** *Homo erectus* had a larger cranial capacity than earlier hominins as well as cranial features that included a large supraorbital torus, a sagittal keel, and an occipital torus.

From Jurmain/Kilgore/Trevathan. *Essentials of Physical Anthropology*, 7E. © 2009 Wadsworth, a part of Cengage Learning, Inc. Reproduced by permission. www.cengage.com/permissions

185 cm (Antón 2003, 156). This transition to a larger body size occurred rapidly and likely reflects a shift to a more nutritious diet that included greater amounts of meat. A major *disadvantage* of increased body size would have been the increased need for energy to fuel such a body (see Chapter 8).

## One Species or Two?

*Homo erectus* was remarkable not only for its significantly larger brain and body compared to earlier hominins, but also for the fact that it was the first hominin to disperse from Africa into other parts of the Old World (see below). Given the widespread geographic distribution of *Homo erectus*, it is not surprising that considerable regional variation is evident in the fossils that have been found to date. Some paleoanthropologists (e.g., Jacob 2001) have argued for the identification of *Homo erectus* fossils from Africa as a separate species, *Homo ergaster* (Groves and Mazek 1975), distinct from *Homo erectus* in Asia (Wood 1991). This argument is based largely on morphological differences between African and Asian specimens, including smaller cranial capacities, thinner cranial bones, smaller and less prognathic faces, and less pronounced supraorbital and occipital tori in the African crania, though some of the latter display features that more closely resemble those seen in Asian *Homo erectus* (see below). In contrast, other scholars argue that while differences exist between African and Asian specimens, these differences reflect geographic variation within a single species (Rightmire 1998; Antón et al. 2007). In this text we will consider the African forms as *Homo ergaster* and the Asian forms as *Homo erectus*.

## Homo ergaster

*Homo ergaster* fossils have been recovered in both East and South Africa (Figure 10.8; Tattersall 2007). They include a 1.89 mya occipital fragment (KNM-ER 2598), uncovered at Lake Turkana; a 1.8 mya skull from Koobi Fora (KNM-ER 3733); a 1.5 mya mandible (KNM-ER 992), also found at Koobi Fora; and a 1.5 mya partial cranium (SK 847) recovered from Swartkrans in South Africa. Other fossils labelled *Homo ergaster* include the "Daka" partial cranium from Bouri, Ethiopia, dated to 1.0 mya (Asfaw et al. 2002); another 1.0 mya

**Figure 10.8** Locations where *Homo ergaster* fossils have been found.

From Jurmain/Kilgore/Trevathan. *Essentials in Physical Anthropology*, 7E © 2009 Wadsworth, a part of Cengage Learning, Inc. Reproduced by permission. www.cengage.com/permissions

cranium (UA 31) from Buia, Eritrea (Abbate et al. 1998);[5] and a number of specimens from Koobi Fora dating between 1.9 and 1.5 mya. Fossils identified as *H. ergaster* have also been found at Olduvai Gorge, among them a 1.5 mya partial cranium bearing spectacular supraorbital tori (OH 9).

The best-known *Homo ergaster* fossil found to date is the nearly complete skeleton (KNM-WT 15000)[6] of an adolescent male estimated to have been about 12 years of age when he died (see below) (Figure 10.9). Found at the site of Nariokotome on the western shore of Lake Turkana, the skeleton, nicknamed "Turkana Boy," has been dated to 1.6 mya, making it among the oldest *Homo ergaster* fossils found to date in Africa (Walker and Leakey 1993). Besides being in an excellent state of preservation, a particularly striking feature of this individual is his stature; he was around 160 cm tall when he died (Ruff and Walker 1993), and it is estimated that he would have reached 180 cm had he lived to adulthood.[7] Also, the body proportions of this individual more closely resemble those of later *Homo*. In particular, a lengthening of the lower limbs points to a more efficient striding gait, meaning that *Homo ergaster* would have been able to cover long distances more efficiently. The long, linear body build and increased surface area from which to dissipate heat (see Chapter 14) also indicate that *Homo ergaster* was well adapted to the hot African climate and may have been more active during the mid-day.

The discovery of the Nariokotome skeleton also provided scientists with a rare opportunity to study the life history of *Homo ergaster*. An analysis by Dean and colleagues (2001) of the timing of formation of the anterior tooth crowns of this adolescent revealed a rate of growth closer to that of great apes than to modern humans, suggesting that this individual developed more rapidly than we do. Similarly, Smith's (2004) examination of skeletal and dental indicators of growth in the skeleton, including the length of the **diaphyses**, the degree of fusion of the **epiphyses**,[8] and the degree of formation of the teeth, revealed a marked difference between the skeletal and dental age of this individual, also pointing to a more rapid rate of development than that seen in modern humans.

**diaphyses**

the shafts of the long bones

**epiphyses**

the caps at the ends of the long bones; bone growth ceases when the epiphyses fuse to the diaphysis

## HOMO ERECTUS

### Indonesia

The discovery of *Homo erectus* fossils in Indonesia dates back to 1891, when a young Dutch physician named Eugène Dubois came to Java to look for the remains of early humans, whom he believed had originated in Asia. His excavations near the village of Trinil on the

---

5. The identification of the Daka and Buia fossils as *Homo ergaster* has not been accepted by everyone.

6. KNM-WT denotes Kenya National Museum West Turkana.

7. Various stature estimates have been calculated for this individual, some of them less than 150 cm (Ohman et al. 2002).

8. The growth of the long bones occurs in the region between the epiphysis and the diaphysis. Once the epiphysis fuses to the diaphysis, growth ceases.

Solo River (Figure 10.8) yielded a skullcap with a low, sloping forehead and a heavy browridge, as well as a modern-looking femur that he thought belonged to the same individual. In 1894 he announced his new species, *Pithecanthropus erectus* ("erect ape-man"), more popularly known as Java Man. The Trinil fossils were subsequently classified as *Homo erectus* (Mayr 1950).

The earliest *Homo erectus* remains in Asia come from the site of Mojokerto, which has yielded a juvenile cranium dating to 1.8 mya (Swisher et al. 1994).[9] Other early *Homo erectus* fossils, including the most complete cranium found in Java, have been uncovered at the site of Sangiran, from deposits dating between 1.7 and 1.0 mya. The site of Ngandong, first excavated in the early 1930s, has also yielded a rich array of *Homo erectus* fossils, including twelve crania initially labelled *Homo soloensis*. Their remarkably late date, ranging from 46,000 to 27,000 years ago (Swisher et al. 1996) suggests that *Homo erectus* survived in Java long after they had disappeared elsewhere in Asia, perhaps due to their relative isolation and differing subsistence base.

## China

The earliest Chinese fossils identified as *Homo erectus* come from the site of Gongwangling in Lantian county, Shaanxi province (Figure 10.8), and date to 1.2 mya, though the recent discovery in northern China of stone tools and modified bones may extend the range of *Homo erectus* to nearly 1.7 mya (Zhu et al. 2004). Dental remains dating to 1.8 mya have been recovered from deposits at the site of Longgupo Cave (Huang et al. 1995), but their taxonomic status is uncertain (Schwartz and Tattersall 1996). Later *Homo erectus* fossils include the Hexian cranium, with an estimated age of approximately 412 ky (Grün et al. 1998).

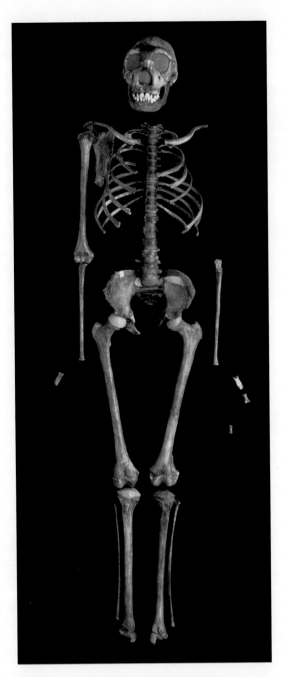

**Figure 10.9** The *Homo ergaster* specimen KNM-WT 15000 is remarkable for its state of preservation and degree of completeness.

Artifact credit: National Museums of Kenya, Nairobi. Copyright protection notice: © 1985 David L. Brill/Brill Atlanta

The largest and best-known sample of *Homo erectus* fossils comes from the site of Zhoukoudian (also referred to as Choukoutien) near Beijing. First excavated in 1921, the site has yielded the remains of approximately 40 individuals and more than 100,000 stone tools and other artifacts spanning hundreds of thousands of years. Detailed studies of the fossil assemblage were made by Canadian anatomist Davidson Black, who assigned the taxonomic name *Sinanthropus pekinensis* to the fossils (Black 1931; see Box 10.1). These studies were continued by his successor, the eminent German anatomist Franz Weidenreich, who produced a series of superb descriptions and casts of the fossils (Figure 10.10). The Zhoukoudian remains, commonly

---

9. Originally labelled *Homo mojokertensis*, this specimen is now recognized as *Homo erectus*.

BOX 10.1    PROFILE... Davidson Black

Courtesy of Julie Cormack

Black was born on July 25, 1884, in Toronto, Ontario. As a young man he was a keen naturalist, spending many hours exploring and later working (with the Hudson's Bay Company) in the lake districts north of Toronto, or wandering the forests and valleys of the city's hinterlands identifying and collecting zoological specimens, especially birds. He was a skilled artist, having earned three drawing certificates from the Provincial Art School—a talent that prepared him well for his eventual training in medicine and later for a career in anthropology. He suffered from the same congenital weak heart as his father (who died at age 49, when Davidson was two years old), an ailment that became further stressed one winter when Davidson contracted rheumatic fever. During his extended convalescence, he realized that his career path would be medicine and not the family profession—law—that his mother wished of him.

In 1906 he graduated from the University of Toronto with a bachelor's degree in medicine (M.B.). He immediately returned to that university to acquire a Bachelor of Arts (B.A.) degree, which he was awarded in 1911 (after a slight delay because he had not completed his German language classes). Before graduating, Davidson accepted a post as lecturer at Western Reserve University in Cleveland, Ohio, where he taught neurology. During a sabbatical visit to Europe, just as the clouds of the First World War were beginning to darken, he had the pleasure of handling the newly discovered Piltdown Man fossils from southern England, today known to be forgeries (a human cranium with an orangutan lower jaw). That experience convinced him that anthropology, not medicine, would be an exciting field to pursue. In 1918 he was offered a teaching post at the newly established Rockefeller-funded Peking Union Medical College (PUMC) in Beijing, China, and he and his wife left Canada for an unknown future. Black had been hired as Professor of Embryology and Neurology but quickly found himself engrossed in the analysis of numerous human skeletal finds made by his Swedish colleague, J.G. Andersson. He was slowly leaving behind his medical teaching responsibilities in order to explore local caves in search of human remains. In 1922 he joined Roy Chapman Andrews's Central Asiatic Expedition to Mongolia.

Since 1919, animal fossils had been found at limestone quarries in the Western Hills southwest of Beijing. Within a couple of years, Andersson had arranged a small excavation there. Three teeth were found, and Black, as the resident anatomist, was asked to identify them. He recognized them as "human," and with a German-American geologist, Amadeus Grabau, he assigned them the name *Sinanthropus pekinensis* ("China man from Peking"). The discovery of human fossils and (later) thousands of stone artifacts and animal bones placed the Zhoukoudian caves on the world's anthropological map. Black was responsible for identifying and publishing descriptions of the Zhoukoudian human remains, today known as our 500,000-year-old direct human ancestor—*Homo erectus*.

Black was very comfortable with the Chinese community, and he collaborated with Chinese scientists such as Wong Wenhao and Ding Wenjiang of the National Geological Survey of China to establish the Cenozoic Research Laboratory (the foundations of the present-day Institute of Vertebrate Paleontology and Paleoanthropology). Black was also the administrative liaison between the Rockefeller Foundation that funded the Zhoukoudian program and the international multidisciplinary research team (of Chinese, Swedish, French, Austrian, and one Canadian expert) that was responsible for excavation and scientific analyses. But Black's contributions were cut short: on March 15, 1934, at the height of his work at Zhoukoudian, he died at age 49 of congenital heart failure. Within a year, his position at the PUMC had been taken up by a German-American anthropologist, Franz Weidenreich. Then in 1937, during the Japanese invasion of Manchuria, excavations stopped. In 1941, with hostilities worsening, attempts were made to transfer the Peking Man fossils out of the capital. After leaving the PUMC's vaults, they vanished. Their location remains unknown to this day. (For further details, see Cormack 2000, 2003; Tobias et al. 2000, 2001.)

Source: Written by Julie Cormack, Mount Royal University, Calgary. Dr. Cormack is writing the authorized biography of Dr. Davidson Black, who participated in the world's first international multidisciplinary archaeological project: the excavation and analysis of one of humanity's earliest ancestors—*Homo erectus* from China.

referred to as "Peking Man," were later reclassified as *Homo erectus* and have been dated from about 300,000 to 600,000 years ago using electron spin resonance, palaeomagnetism, and biostratigraphy. While the *Homo erectus* crania from China resemble those from Indonesia with respect to vault size and shape, differences are evident in the shape of the supraorbital torus and the degree of facial prognathism. Specifically, the Chinese specimens possess supraorbital tori that are straighter when viewed from above and less prognathic faces (Antón 2003).

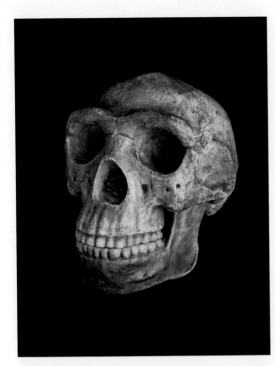

One of the greatest mysteries in paleoanthropology concerns the disappearance of the Zhoukoudian fossils prior to the outbreak of the Second World War. The Japanese invasion of China in 1937 prompted researchers to pack up the fossil remains in preparation for shipping to them to the United States for safekeeping. Somewhere along the route, however, the precious cargo disappeared, and their whereabouts remain unknown to this day. Fortunately, the detailed descriptions, drawings, and casts made by Weidenreich of all the original *Homo erectus* fossils found at the site have enabled continued study of this material. Still, the mystery has been the subject of great speculation as well as fodder for popular culture.[10]

**Figure 10.10**  This *Homo erectus* skull, recovered from the site of Zhoukoudian, was reconstructed in 1937 by anatomist Franz Weidenreich.

Natural History Museum, London/GetStockphotos.com

### Georgia

Early *Homo erectus* remains dating to 1.7 mya have been recovered from an early Pleistocene site lying below medieval ruins at the site of Dmanisi in the Republic of Georgia. These include four partial crania, four mandibles, and infracranial remains (Gabunia et al. 2000; Gabunia and Vekua 1995; Vekua et al. 2002). Thousands of faunal bones and a large number of Oldowan-like stone tools have also been found at this site. Resembling early *Homo ergaster* specimens from Africa, the Dmanisi fossils exhibit smaller cranial capacities (less than 800 cc), thinner cranial bones, and a less pronounced supraorbital torus than their Asian counterparts.

The morphological heterogeneity of the Dmanisi assemblage has resulted in a lack of consensus—even among those who have excavated and studied them—regarding the taxonomic status of these fossils. Similarities between these specimens and those from the Turkana Basin in Kenya have prompted Gabunia and colleagues (2000) to label them *Homo ergaster*. A more recent analysis, however, has revealed some resemblance to *Homo erectus* fossils from Sangiran, which suggests that the Dmanisi hominins may belong to this taxon (Rightmire, Lordkipanidze, and Vekua 2006).

## BEHAVIOURAL ADAPTATIONS

### Technological Leaps and Bounds

The earliest *Homo erectus* fossils are associated with Oldowan tools. About 1.5 mya, a new Lower Paleolithic stone tool industry known as the **Acheulian** appears in the African archaeological record. Characterized by a greater variety of types, Acheulian tools were **bifacial**, meaning that flakes were removed from both sides of the tool, resulting in a much greater cutting edge than the earlier Oldowan tools. The principal Acheulian tool was the **hand axe** (Figure 10.11), a teardrop-shaped tool whose functions may have included digging, chopping, and cutting. The Acheulian toolkit also included cleavers and scrapers, which may have been used to butcher carcasses and remove meat from the bones. *Homo erectus* also appears to have used fire (see Box 10.2).

Earlier in this chapter we distinguished between *Homo erectus* in Africa, which we have referred to as *Homo ergaster*, and *Homo erectus* in Asia, based on morphological differences between the two. Behavioural differences also characterized these species, most notably a difference in tool technology between western Eurasia/Africa and East Asia, identified by

**Acheulian**
a Lower Paleolithic stone tool industry usually associated with *Homo erectus*

**bifacial tool**
a stone tool that has had flakes removed from opposite sides to produce a cutting edge

**hand axe**
a teardrop-shaped stone tool characteristic of the Acheulian industry

---

10. Canadian writer Robert J. Sawyer won Canada's top science fiction award for his 1996 short story "Peking Man," which links the disappearance of the fossils to Bram Stoker's Dracula.

**Figure 10.11** Acheulian stone tools included hand axes and cleavers. The reproduction hand axe seen here measures approximately 12 cm in length.

Courtesy of Anne Keenleyside

**Movius Line**

a hypothetical line drawn by archaeologist Hallam Movius to mark the boundary between Acheulian and non-Acheulian stone tool industries

the **Movius Line**. More specifically, simple Oldowan-like choppers and flake tools, such as those found at Zhoukoudian, characterize most Asian *Homo erectus* sites, whereas Acheulian hand axes are virtually absent in China and Southeast Asia, though hand axe–like tools have recently been discovered in southern China (Yamei et al. 2000). Some paleoanthropologists have viewed this difference in tool types as indicative of cognitive differences between *Homo erectus* and *Homo ergaster;* others see it as more likely reflecting environmental differences—notably, the presence in the Far East of dense forests of bamboo, which may have provided *Homo erectus* with material suitable for making tools (Pope 1989).

The more advanced cognitive abilities of *Homo erectus* compared to earlier hominins are also reflected in their presumed presence on islands separated from the mainland by large bodies of water. Stone tools and faunal remains dating between 800,000 and 880,000 years ago have been recovered from deposits on the island of Flores. At that time, the island would have been separated from the mainland by at least 19 km of water. This suggests that these hominins must have had some type of watercraft in order to reach Flores (Morwood et al. 1998).[11]

## The First Big-Game Hunters?

The evolution and dispersal of *Homo erectus* has long been linked to big-game hunting. Archaeological evidence commonly cited as proof of hunting by these hominins is the association of stone tools with the remains of large animals, many of them with cut marks. At the 400,000-year-old sites of Torralba and Ambrona in Spain, for example, the presence of stone tools together with the bones of dozens of elephants and other large mammals—many of them with apparent cut marks—have been interpreted as evidence of cooperative hunting by *Homo erectus*. Similarly, the Kenyan site of Olorgesailie, dating between 600 kya and 1 mya, has yielded

---

11. The ability to make and use watercraft has generally been attributed to modern humans, who are believed to have used them to colonize Australia some 40,000 to 60,000 years ago (see Morwood et al. 1998).

**FOCUS ON... The Use of Fire**

The use of fire is generally linked to the appearance of *Homo erectus*. Early reports of the archaeological excavations at Zhoukoudian in China noted the presence of ash deposits, which were interpreted as evidence for the use of fire (Black 1931). Subsequent analyses of these deposits, however, have revealed that while there is evidence of fire at the site in the form of burned bones, there is "no direct evidence for in situ burning" (i.e., hearths) by hominins (Weiner et al. 1998, 253).[12] Thermally altered patches of clay, stone artifacts, and/or animal bones have been found at Koobi Fora (Bellomo 1994), Chesowanja (Gowlett et al. 1981), and Swartkrans (Brain 1993), suggesting the use of fire by *Homo ergaster* by 1.6 mya. Evidence of fire has also been found at the 700,000-year-old site of Kao Poh Nam in Thailand in the form of fire-cracked basalt cobbles associated with stone tools and animal bones. But there is no archaeological evidence

that *Homo ergaster/erectus* had the ability to make fire, and we do not see any evidence for this until much later in time, after the appearance of *Homo sapiens*. So it is likely that these hominins made use of fires resulting from lightning strikes, volcanic activity, and other natural processes (Bellomo 1994).

Fire would have had numerous benefits for *Homo erectus*. It would have provided them with light, heat, and protection from predators; it would also have allowed them to cook their food. This has important implications in terms of morphological and behavioural changes (see Chapter 8). Because cooked foods are easier to digest than raw foods, cooking may have contributed to a reduction in tooth and gut size among *Homo erectus*. It may also have allowed these hominins to expand the range of plant foods in their diet (Wrangham et al. 1999, 568). Fire was also likely an important factor in allowing *Homo erectus* to disperse into more northern latitudes.

concentrations of Acheulian tools together with the bones of baboons, elephants, hippos, and other mammals, suggesting that such tools were used to kill and butcher these animals. Some of the evidence for big-game hunting prior to 500,000 years ago has been re-evaluated, and taphonomic alterations and/or hominin scavenging appear to account for some of the assemblages seen at these sites. For instance, most of what were initially believed to be cut marks on the bones found at Torralba and Ambrona were later found to be scratches resulting from soil abrasion (Shipman and Rose 1983). Evidence for the importance of meat in the *Homo erectus* diet is certainly more compelling than it is for *H. habilis* and *H. rudolfensis*, and meat would have provided some of the calories needed to fuel the larger brain and body size of these hominins. As noted in the discussion of "Energetics" in Chapter 8, however, high-carbohydrate foods such as tubers and seeds would likely have comprised additional sources of energy.

## The First Voyager: Hominins Out of Africa

It is widely assumed that *Homo ergaster* was the first hominin to leave Africa. This is based on features that would have allowed it to migrate out of Africa, including long limbs, modern body proportions, and a larger brain than earlier hominins. The discovery of *Homo erectus* fossils in Indonesia dating to 1.8 mya and in the Republic of Georgia dating to 1.7 mya suggests that this migration occurred far earlier than previously thought and that these hominins dispersed rapidly across Asia (Figure 10.12). Dispersal rates have been calculated for *Homo erectus* based on demographic and reproductive variables derived from extant mammals and fossil taxa (human and nonhuman) from Europe, Africa, and Asia (Antón, Leonard, and Robertson 2002). Among mammals, a strong correlation exists between body size, diet, and home range size such that larger body size and greater consumption of meat are associated with a greater home range. The latter, in turn, is related to dispersal capability. Using data on body weight, dietary quality, and home range size in modern nonhuman primates and human hunter-gatherers, Antón, Leonard, and Robertson (2002) have argued that changes in foraging strategies and an increased reliance on meat resulted in an increase in body and home range size, and consequently the rapid dispersal of these hominins. A recent computer simulation model points to rapid multiple dispersals from Africa prior to 1.7 mya and to rapid colonization of Southeast Asia by 1.6 mya (Mithen and Reed 2002). The periodic advance of glaciers in the northern hemisphere during the Pleistocene meant that the sea level would have been significantly lower than it is today, thus allowing these hominins to walk to Java from the mainland via exposed land bridges.

---

12. Chemical analysis of the so-called ash layers revealed no evidence of silica particles that would be found if wood had been burned (Weiner et al. 1998).

**CHAPTER 10** Plio-Pleistocene Transitions: The Emergence of the Genus *Homo*

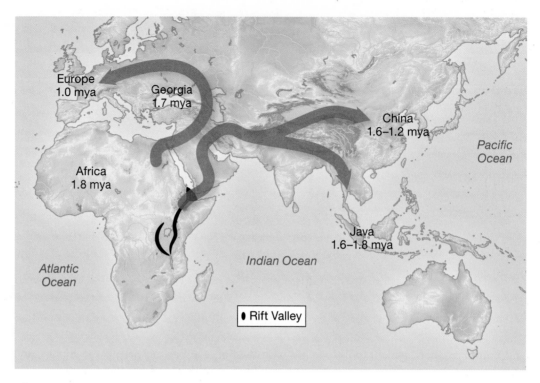

**Figure 10.12** Map showing possible routes of dispersal taken by *Homo erectus*.

Based on Mithen and Reed (2002) and Stanford, et al. (2009)

Factors that may have precipitated this dispersal have been debated, and it is now generally believed that technological advances are unlikely to have been the catalysts, as the migration of *Homo ergaster* out of Africa postdates the appearance of the earliest stone tools (i.e., Oldowan tools) and predates the emergence of Acheulian tools (Antón, Leonard, and Robertson 2002, 773). Instead, biological and ecological factors—including fully developed bipedalism and a global cooling trend that resulted in the eastward migration of mammalian fauna and the opening up of new ecological niches for hominins and other animals to exploit—appear to have played a more important role.

## THE HOBBITS OF FLORES ISLAND

In 2003 a remarkable discovery was made in a limestone cave on the island of Flores in eastern Indonesia. The partial skeleton of a tiny adult female hominin (LB1), nicknamed the "hobbit" because of her small body size and large feet, was uncovered from deposits that have been dated to 18 to 95 kya (Roberts et al. 2009). These deposits also yielded a variety of stone tools and animal bones representing Komodo dragon and a dwarf species of Stegodon.[13] What is so striking about this skeleton is its unique combination of primitive and derived features never before seen in any hominin. Its cranial capacity, estimated at only 380 to 410 cc, falls within the range of early australopithecines. Similarly, its small stature (estimated at only 1 m), its body proportions, and its primitive wrist resemble those of *Australopithecus* (Tocheri et al. 2007; see Box 10.3). Yet the shape of its brain, as revealed by three-dimensional reconstructions (see Figure 8.14), resembles that of *Homo erectus*, suggesting that it possessed higher cognitive abilities than *Australopithecus* (Falk et al. 2005). Similarly, its facial morphology and dental characteristics link it more closely to *Homo* than *Australopithecus*.

**microcephaly**

a congenital condition characterized by an abnormally small head

A variety of interpretations have been proposed to explain the unique mosaic of features seen in this individual. Claims that it represents a modern human with **microcephaly** or a modern pygmy have been rejected by most researchers, and detailed analyses of the fossils

---

13. An extinct mammal similar to an elephant.

BOX 10.3    PROFILE... The Hobbits

Courtesy of Matthew Tocheri

When I was working toward my undergraduate degree in anthropology at Lakehead University during the late 1990s, I had no idea of the adventure that awaited me within a few years. After graduating from Lakehead, I headed to Arizona State University (ASU) to begin my new life as a physical anthropology graduate student. Though I went to ASU with a focus on bioarchaeology, I soon found myself more interested in research about human evolution and functional morphology. These new interests led to my doctoral dissertation research, which focused on the evolution of the wrist in hominids (humans and great apes), especially in relation to the evolution of behaviours involving tools in hominins (humans and our close fossil relatives). Through my research, I learned that modern humans and Neandertals have differently shaped wrist bones compared to great apes and other primates. Even the handful of wrist bones from early hominins, such as *Australopithecus* and *Homo habilis*, show more similarities to African apes than they do to us and Neandertals. But just as I was preparing for my doctoral defence, something extraordinary and unexpected happened. I suddenly found myself in the same room as casts of wrist bones from *Homo floresiensis*—the so-called "hobbits" of human evolution discovered on Flores, Indonesia, in 2003. The "hobbit" remains had sparked a huge controversy in paleoanthropology, and the debates over them both at professional meetings and in the literature were extremely intense and volatile. Some researchers considered the "hobbit" remains to represent a tiny species of human that went extinct roughly about 17,000 years ago; others were adamant the remains represented nothing more than modern humans with some sort of pathology or growth disorder.

As I slid the lid off the container that held the casts, little did I realize that I was about to be transported figuratively into "Mordor" and literally into the centre of one of the biggest and most heated debates in human evolution for more than a century. What I saw inside the container is illustrated below (Figure 10.13). It was obvious: these wrist bones did not belong to a normal or pathological modern human; instead, they resembled the bones of African apes and "Lucy" (*Australopithecus afarensis*)—exactly like what you would expect the wrist bones of a primitive human species to look like. The hobbits were for real: another human species that had survived at least until 17,000 years ago, sharing this world with us as close evolutionary cousins. So there I was, joining a fellowship with a hobbit. In return for promising to tell a part of her species' story as I now understood it from her wrist, she would help emphasize the importance of the wrist for understanding the recent evolutionary history of our own species.

This unexpected meeting soon led to a comparative study of the "hobbit" wrist bones, published in Science (Tocheri et al. 2007). Those bones provided a key piece of evidence to support interpretations that *Homo floresiensis* was a human species distinct from modern humans and Neandertals. Presently, I am preparing to return to Indonesia for the third time in 18 months to work with my Indonesian, Australian, and American colleagues as we continue to piece together the evolutionary history of *Homo floresiensis*. Without doubt, we are in for more surprises and debates as far as the "hobbits" are concerned. I can hardly wait.

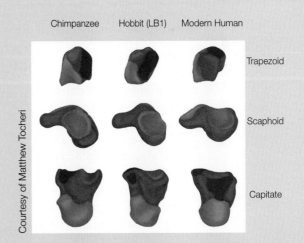

Courtesy of Matthew Tocheri

**Figure 10.13**   A visual comparison of three of the hobbit's (LB1) wristbones scaled to the same size as those of a chimpanzee and a modern human. The colours indicate the anatomically comparable articular and nonarticular bone surfaces (see Tocheri et al. 2007 for details).

Source: Written by Matthew Tocheri, Human Origins Program, Department of Anthropology, National Museum of Natural History, Smithsonian Institution, Washington, D.C.

**insular dwarfism**
a process by which a
founding population
becomes isolated in a
small environment such
as an island and con-
sequently undergoes a
reduction in size

support the identification of this hominin as a new species, *Homo floresiensis* (Brown et al. 2004; Argue et al. 2006). Its unique morphology has prompted Brown and colleagues to suggest that it evolved from an ancestral *Homo* population that became isolated on the island and consequently underwent a process known as **insular dwarfism**. This process, which occurs when a founding population becomes reproductively isolated in a small environment such as an island, has been documented in a number of mammalian species. The reduction in body size that results from this isolation is believed to be the result of decreased availability of food resources (smaller bodies require less food) and fewer predators (smaller individuals therefore have less chance of being eaten). Alternatively, *Homo floresiensis* may have descended from an unknown small-bodied hominin that arrived on the island much earlier in time. In addition to its uncertain ancestry, it remains a mystery how such a population was able to survive alongside *Homo sapiens* as recently as it did. Unfortunately, the archaeological record provides no clues to the nature of the interaction between *Homo floresiensis* and *Homo sapiens* (Morwood et al. 2004).

Does biological anthropology include the study of "hobbits"? For Dr. Matthew Tocheri, a Canadian paleoanthropologist at the Smithsonian Institution's Human Origins Program, it most certainly does (see Box 10.3).

## ANOTHER PIECE OF THE PUZZLE, BUT WHICH PIECE?

By now you are probably feeling rather overwhelmed by all the various fossils we have introduced you to in this chapter. You are not alone: the taxonomic status of early *Homo* and its relationship to other Plio-Pleistocene hominins is one of the most contentious issues in paleoanthropology today. Among the questions that have yet to be resolved is whether *Homo habilis* is indeed a valid taxon. Early analyses of *Homo habilis* remains emphasized the resemblance between this hominin and later humans. Within the past decade, however, the emphasis has shifted to highlighting the similarities between *Homo habilis* and the australopithecines. These similarities have prompted some paleoanthropologists to call for the inclusion of this species within the genus *Australopithecus* (Wood and Collard 1999). Further support for this argument comes from analyses of the rate of dental development in early *Homo*, which more closely resembles that of fossil and extant African apes than later humans (Dean et al. 2001).

Also unresolved is the number of species represented by the Plio-Pleistocene fossil record. As you learned in Chapter 4, the identification of fossil species is based on the degree of morphological variation seen in the fossil record (i.e., morphospecies) and the amount of time separating various fossil forms (i.e., chronospecies). With respect to Plio-Pleistocene hominins, considerable debate has surrounded the interpretation of morphological variation seen in fossils identified as *Homo habilis*. Some experts view this variation as representing a single polytypic species, with variation representing sexual dimorphism or differences due to growth and development; others view it as evidence for more than one species. Complicating the identification of *Homo* in the fossil record is the fact that at least one australopithecine species, *A. garhi*, coexisted with early *Homo* between 2.4 and 1.6 mya.

Most paleoanthropologists today agree that *Homo* evolved from *Australopithecus* in eastern Africa but disagree on which australopithecine species was the mostly likely ancestor. Separate origins have been hypothesized for *Homo habilis* and *Homo rudolfensis*, the former arising from *A. africanus* and the latter from *A. afarensis* (Schrenk et al. 2007), the same species postulated to have given rise to the *Paranthropus* lineage by 2.5 mya. As we discussed in the previous chapter, *Australopithecus garhi* has been identified as a possible ancestor of early *Homo*.

If indeed several species of early *Homo* existed, as is becoming increasingly apparent, we are left to ponder which one gave rise to later species of *Homo*. If we accept the existence of *Homo habilis*, *Homo rudolfensis*, and *Homo ergaster* in Africa during the Pliocene and into the Pleistocene, a number of phylogenies are possible (Figure 10.14). Based on its more modern-looking cranio-facial morphology, *Homo habilis* may, according to some paleoanthropologists, represent the ancestor of *Homo erectus/ergaster*, with *Homo rudolfensis* simply a side branch that became extinct around 2.0 mya. Alternatively, based on its larger cranial capacity, *Homo rudolfensis* may represent the ancestor of *Homo erectus/ergaster*, with *Homo habilis* constituting a separate lineage that eventually disappeared. Support for this latter view comes from two recent fossil finds at the site of

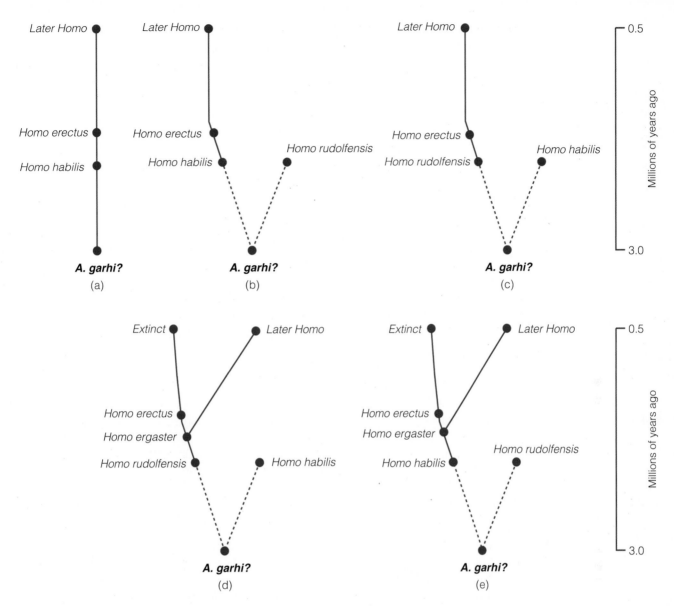

**Figure 10.14**   Various phylogenies have been proposed for early *Homo*.

Ileret in northeastern Kenya, suggesting that *Homo habilis* and *Homo erectus* coexisted in eastern Africa for nearly 500,000 years (Spoor et al. 2007). As you will recall from previous chapters, the coexistence of species can occur if they have differing diets and foraging behaviours.

## SUMMARY

Significant climatic changes during the Late Pliocene transformed the African landscape to one of reduced forested habitats and increased open grassland savannah, with associated changes in mammalian fauna. In response to these changes, hominins underwent an adaptive shift reflected in a larger brain, a larger body size, a change in limb proportions, and a reduction in the size of the molar teeth. The first members of the genus *Homo* appeared in eastern Africa about 2.5 mya, and there is increasing consensus that at least three species of early *Homo* (*Homo habilis*, *Homo rudolfensis*, *Homo ergaster*) coexisted in Africa between 1.9 and 1.6 mya, a time when robust australopithecines still occupied parts of the continent. *H. habilis* and *H. rudolfensis* retained a number of features seen in the australopithecines but at the same time shared some unique features with later species of *Homo*, most notably a larger brain size relative to body size. These hominins were also capable of advanced, human-like behaviour, including making and using stone tools and hunting. Some have suggested that they may even have possessed some form of rudimentary speech. By 1.7 mya, *Homo ergaster* had ventured out of Africa and a new species, identified as *Homo erectus*, had reached Indonesia. One of the most successful hominin species that ever lived, *Homo erectus* had a larger brain and body size than earlier hominins, made and used more sophisticated tools, engaged in hunting, and used fire.

# CORE REVIEW

**In what ways did early members of the genus Homo differ morphologically from the australopithecines?**

Early members of the genus *Homo* had a larger brain, a more rounded brain case, a smaller, less projecting face, and smaller molars than the australopithecines. Their limb proportions exhibited a mosaic of ape-like and human-like features, and analyses of their limb and foot bones indicate that while they were fully bipedal on the ground, they also engaged in frequent arboreal locomotion.

**What behavioural adaptations characterized early Homo?**

Early *Homo* made and used stone tools. These took the form of Oldowan choppers and pebble tools, which were likely used to process carcasses and extract marrow from animal bones. Chemical and dental analyses of early *Homo* fossils indicate that, compared to the australopithecines, these hominins consumed a more varied diet that included plant resources such as roots and tubers, and meat.

**What are the anatomical characteristics of Homo erectus? In what ways did these hominins differ from Homo habilis and Homo rudolfensis?**

*Homo erectus* had a larger cranial capacity, a pentagonally shaped skull with thick cranial bones, a heavily built jaw with small molars possessing thinner enamel than earlier hominins, a sagittal keel, a heavy supraorbital torus, an angular torus, and an occipital torus. It also had a larger body size and more modern limb proportions than the latter two species, indicating that it was a fully committed terrestrial biped.

**Why do some paleoanthropologists think that there are separate African and Asian species, labelled Homo ergaster and Homo erectus respectively?**

This distinction is based on both morphological and behavioural differences. Asian *Homo erectus* had a larger cranial capacity, a larger and more prognathic face, thicker cranial bones, and more pronounced supraorbital and occipital tori than African *Homo ergaster*. *H. erectus* also utilized a different stone tool technology characterized by simple choppers and flake tools, in contrast to *Homo ergaster*, who made and used Acheulian hand axes. This difference in tool technologies may reflect environmental differences—notably, the presence in the Far East of dense forests of bamboo, from which *Homo erectus* may have made tools.

**What accounts for the success of Homo erectus? Why did this species endure for such a long period of time with few morphological and behavioural changes?**

The success of *Homo erectus* arose from their larger brain and increased intelligence, reflected in their more sophisticated tool technology and control of fire, their increased reliance on meat, their larger body size and modern limb proportions—which allowed them to cover long distances more efficiently—and their ability to move into and adapt to a wide variety of different environments.

# CRITICAL THINKING QUESTIONS

1. What features, in your opinion, define the genus *Homo*?
2. If we accept that several species of early *Homo* lived in eastern Africa between 1.9 and 1.6 million years ago, what factors might have allowed these species to evolve, let alone coexist?
3. Considerable morphological variability has been observed within and among *Homo erectus* fossil assemblages from Africa and Asia. What might this mean in terms of their evolutionary history?
4. Why do you think *Homo erectus* was able to survive in parts of Indonesia until as recently as 27,000 years ago, a time when modern humans had already made their appearance?

# GROUP DISCUSSION QUESTIONS

1. Why does southern Africa appear to be a dead end for later human evolution until the late Middle Paleolithic?
2. In 2007, officials at the National Museums of Kenya announced plans to ship the famous *Homo erectus/ergaster* skeleton from Nariokotome to the Field Museum in Chicago for a special exhibition. This announcement drew protests from many paleoanthropologists, who feared for the safety of this precious fossil. What are your views on shipping hominin fossils from Africa to other parts of the world for display? What are the advantages and disadvantages of doing so?
3. It is widely assumed that *Homo erectus* emerged in Africa and dispersed from there to Eurasia and the Far East. We know virtually nothing, however, about their route of migration. If you were a paleoanthropologist, how might you go about tracing their migration route? Where would you look for additional fossil evidence?

# RESOURCES AND READINGS

- T.G. Bromage and F. Schrenk, eds., *African Biogeography, Climate Change, and Human Evolution* (New York: Oxford University Press, 1999).
- W.H. Gilbert and B. Asfaw, *Homo erectus: Pleistocene Evidence from the Middle Awash, Ethiopia* (The Middle Awash Series) (Berkeley: University of California Press, 2008).
- M. Morwood and P. Van Oosterzee. *A New Human: The Startling Discovery and Strange Story of the "Hobbits" of Flores, Indonesia* (London: Collins, 2007).
- J.H. Schwartz and I. Tattersall, *The Human Fossil Record: Volume 2—Craniodental Morphology of Genus Homo, Africa and Asia* (New York: Wiley-Liss, 2003).
- P. Shipman, *The Man Who Found the Missing Link: The Extraordinary Life of Eugene Dubois* (London: Weidenfeld & Nicolson, 2001).
- C.B. Stanford and H.T. Bunn, eds., *Meat-Eating and Human Evolution* (Oxford: Oxford University Press, 2001).
- C.C. Swisher III, G.H. Curtis, and R. Lewin, *Java Man: How Two Geologists Changed Our Understanding of Human Evolution* (Chicago: University of Chicago Press, 2001).
- J.L. Thompson, G.E. Krovitz, and A.J. Nelson, eds., *Patterns of Growth and Development in the Genus Homo* (Cambridge: Cambridge University Press, 2003).
- P.S. Ungar, ed., *Evolution of the Human Diet: The Known, the Unknown, and the Unknowable* (Oxford: Oxford University Press, 2006).

# Chapter

# 11 The Advent of Humanity

## OVERVIEW

As you learned in the previous chapter, *Homo ergaster* was the first hominin to leave Africa and migrate to other regions of the Old World. This chapter explores the next stage in our evolutionary history: the emergence of Middle and Late Pleistocene hominins in Africa, Europe, and Asia. We examine the fossil evidence for these individuals and explore their anatomical and behavioural characteristics. We introduce you to the most famous Late Pleistocene hominins, the Neandertals,[1] and highlight their distinctive cranial and infracranial morphology, patterns of growth and disease, and behaviours. We conclude this chapter with an examination of the genetic evidence for these hominins and the reasons for their ultimate demise.

## CORE CONCEPTS

- archaic hominins, Neandertals, thermoregulation, Mousterian, zooarchaeology, symbolic behaviour, language

## CORE QUESTIONS

- In what ways did archaic hominins differ from *Homo erectus*?

- What are the morphological characteristics of Neandertals? In what ways did they differ from modern humans?

- What is the adaptive significance of Neandertal cranial and infracranial morphology?

- What do we know from the archaeological and fossil record about Neandertal lifestyles and behaviours?

- What does the genetic evidence tell us about the position of Neandertals in our evolutionary history?

---

1. We use the spelling *Neandertal* here, but the alternative spelling, *Neanderthal*, is also commonly used in the literature. "Thal" in German means "valley." The 'h' was dropped in the early 20th c. to make the spelling consistent with the German pronunciation, which has no 'th' sound.

> *There was no difference between what Neanderthals
> and modern humans could do [as hunters].
> Both of them were wolves with knives.*
>
> John Shea, Anthropologist

# PROLOGUE: SKELETONS IN THE CLOSET

**Neandertals**

a group of Late Pleisto-cene hominins who lived in Europe and western Asia between approximately 130,000 and 30,000 years ago

In 1911 the French novel *La Guerre du Feu* (Quest for Fire) was published. Set in Europe 80,000 years ago, it tells the story of a violent confrontation between a primitive tribe representing *Homo erectus* and a group of **Neandertals**, as the former attempt to steal a burning ember from the latter. Having lost their valuable flame, three Neandertals set out in search of fire, and their journey brings them face to face with a group of *Homo sapiens,* who possess the ability to make fire. A series of hostile encounters follows. The story ends with the lead character, a Neandertal named Naoh, in a moonlit embrace with his paramour, the anatomically modern Ika. More than 40 years later, British author William Golding, best known for his novel *Lord of the Flies*, published *The Inheritors* (1955), a book about the last Neandertals and their extinction at the hands of anatomically modern humans. In both these novels, Neandertals are portrayed as anatomically and behaviourally inferior, and this theme has been woven into many subsequent books and films on human evolution. More than fifty years later, the academic debate on the distinctiveness of Neandertals is as lively, and as dramatic, as ever. Were these creatures a separate species? Did they contribute to the genome of modern European and Near Eastern populations? Or were they summarily dispatched by encroaching Upper Paleolithic modern forms? Recent archaeological, paleontological, and, most provocatively, molecular discoveries are shedding new light on these questions.

# THE EMERGENCE OF ARCHAIC HOMININS

**archaic hominins**

hominins that show a mosaic of *Homo erectus* and modern human traits

By 500 kya our human voyage had embarked on a new direction with the appearance of **archaic hominins**. These hominins combined features seen in earlier *Homo erectus* fossils with those seen in anatomically modern humans (Figure 11.1). These included smaller teeth, a significantly larger cranial capacity (averaging 1350 cc), and an associated change in the overall shape of the skull from a pentagonal-shaped vault to a more parallel-sided vault with a maximum breadth located higher up on the skull. We will examine the fossil evidence for archaic hominins from each of the three main geographic regions of the Old World and discuss their taxonomic status and phylogenetic relationships.

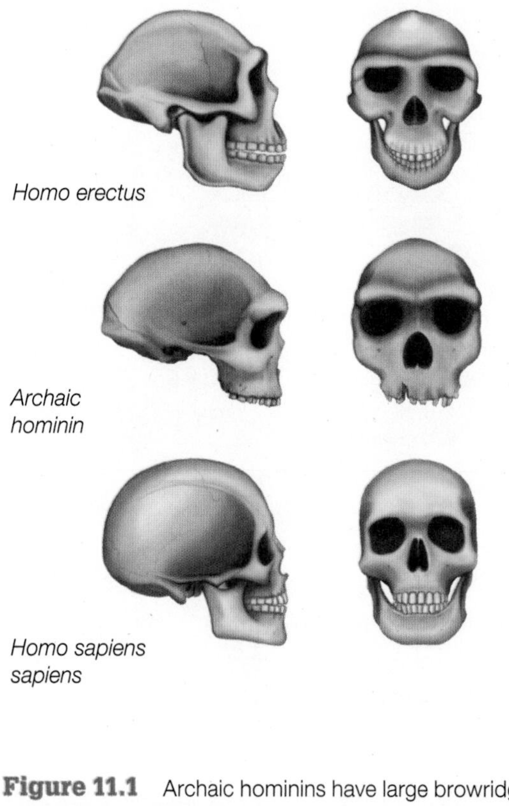

*Homo erectus*

*Archaic hominin*

*Homo sapiens sapiens*

**Figure 11.1** Archaic hominins have large browridges, as seen in *Homo erectus*, but a larger cranial capacity and a more parallel-sided vault more closely resembling that of modern humans.

## African Archaic Hominins

Fossils of archaic humans have been found at a number of sites in East and South Africa (Figure 11.2). One of the earliest of these is a partial cranium recovered from the site of Bodo in Ethiopia. Possibly dating to about 600,000 years ago, it exhibits a combination of *Homo erectus* and modern features—a low vault, a heavy browridge, and thick cranial bones typical of *Homo erectus*, but also a cranial capacity of 1250 cc, within the range of modern humans. This cranium also has cut marks indicating defleshing, though the purpose of that

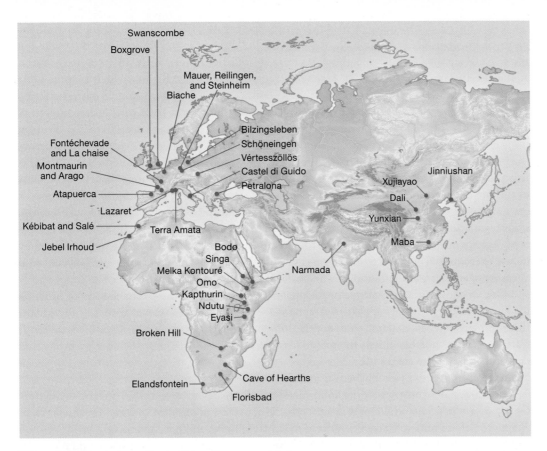

**Figure 11.2** Archaic sites in Africa, Europe, and Asia.

act (cannibalism? mortuary ritual?) remains unknown (White 1986). One of the most complete Middle Pleistocene crania ever found comes from the site of Broken Hill (Kabwe) in Zambia (Figure 11.3). Dating to at least 125,000 years ago, it resembles the Bodo cranium and other African archaic specimens in possessing the low vault, sloping forehead, and heavy browridge seen in *Homo erectus;* but it also has a cranial capacity that exceeds the range for this species.

**Figure 11.3** This cranium from Kabwe was once referred to as Rhodesian Man.

Pascal Goetgheluck/Science Photo Library

## European Archaic Hominins

Archaic hominins are best known from Europe, represented by that most distinctive group, the Neandertals, whom we will discuss later in this chapter. Like their African counterparts, European archaic hominins possessed thick cranial bones, a heavy browridge, a pronounced occipital torus, and a cranial capacity similar to that of modern humans. Early archaic specimens include a mandible recovered from the site of Mauer near Heidelberg, Germany, a tibia and some teeth from the site of Boxgrove in southern England, a partial cranium from the site of Arago in France, a partial cranium from the site of Swanscombe in England, a nearly complete cranium from Steinheim in Germany, and a cranium from Petralona, Greece (Figure 11.2).

**calvarium**
the skull excluding the facial bones and mandible

Over the years a number of Middle Pleistocene fossils have been labelled the first inhabitants of Europe. These include an 800,000- to 900,000-year-old **calvarium** discovered at the site of Ceprano in Italy and the 500,000-year-old Boxgrove fossils. In 1994, excavations at the site of Gran Dolina in the Atapuerca region of northern Spain yielded a remarkable collection of bones belonging to at least six individuals, together with stone tools resembling Oldowan tools, and faunal remains. Recovered from the lowest layer of the site, known as TD6 (for Trinchera Dolina) or the Aurora stratum, these fossils have been dated by electron spin resonance and paleomagnetism to more than 780,000 years ago. Even more tantalizing, the bones of all six individuals—two adults, two adolescents, two infants—display cut marks in a pattern identical to that seen in the faunal remains, prompting claims that the occupants of the site engaged in cannibalism (Fernández-Jalvo et al. 1999). The unique combination of cranial and dental traits displayed by these fossils—including a fully modern midfacial region, slightly enlarged mandibular anterior teeth, reduced posterior teeth, and a gracile mandible—have led Spanish paleoanthropologists to classify them as *Homo antecessor*, a species that they believe probably originated from *Homo ergaster* in Africa and may represent the last common ancestor of modern humans and Neandertals (Bermúdez de Castro et al. 1997).

One of the largest collections of European archaic fossils comes from the site of Sima de los Huesos ("Pit of Bones"), also in Atapuerca. Representing a minimum of 28 individuals, these remains have been dated to over 300,000 years ago and exhibit a number of Neandertal features that are notably absent in archaic fossils from Asia and Africa, including a projecting face and arched browridges (de Castro et al. 2004). These features suggest that the European Neandertal lineage was established by at least 300,000 years ago.

In 2008, paleoanthropologists announced the discovery of yet another archaic fossil consisting of a partial mandible and some teeth. Uncovered at the site of Sima del Elefante in Atapuerca, these remains have been dated to 1.1 to 1.2 mya and have tentatively been assigned to *Homo antecessor* (Carbonell et al. 2008). If this dating is correct, these fossils would represent the earliest occupants of Europe.

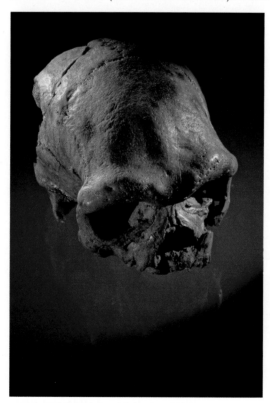

**Figure 11.4** This cranium, excavated from the site of Dali in China, exhibits features characteristic of *Homo erectus* and *Homo sapiens*.

Courtesy of Kenneth Garrett Photography

## Asian Archaic Hominins

Early archaic fossils in Asia (Figure 11.2) also display a mosaic of *Homo erectus* and modern features, though smaller, flatter faces in some of the crania point to regional differences between these specimens and those of Africa and Europe. One of the best-known fossils, a nearly complete skull dating to approximately 200,000 years ago, comes from the site of Dali in China (Figure 11.4). It displays the low vault and massive browridge typical of *Homo erectus*, but it also has facial features that more closely resemble those of modern humans. A partial skeleton from Jinniushan in China, dating to more than 200,000 years ago, has a cranium with a pronounced browridge and sloping forehead but a cranial capacity that exceeds that of *Homo erectus* (Tiemei, Quan, and En 1994). The early dates for this and other archaic specimens are close to those obtained from the latest *Homo erectus* fossils, suggesting that the two species may in fact have coexisted in China (Tiemei et al. 1994), though some paleoanthropologists favour a scenario of continuity between

*Homo erectus* and archaic hominins in this region (see Chapter 12). Archaic hominin remains in the form of a calvarium dating between 150,000 and 125,000 years ago have also been found at the site of Narmada in central India. Its features most closely resemble those of later European hominins, suggesting a European rather than an Asian origin for this particular population (Cameron, Patnaik, and Sahni 2004).

## One Species or Several?

The transitional nature of the archaic fossils described above makes it difficult to classify them, and there has been considerable debate concerning the number of species of archaic humans that existed during the Middle and Late Pleistocene. Some paleoanthropologists prefer to lump all fossils into one category, which they refer to as archaic *Homo sapiens;* others recognize the existence of at least two species. In 1908 the Mauer mandible was given the species name **Homo heidelbergensis** based on its robusticity and lack of a chin (Schoetensack 1908). Since that time, many of the archaic fossils described above (e.g., Boxgrove, Arago, Steinheim, Swanscombe, Petralona) have been assigned to this taxon (Figure 11.5). The picture that is emerging is one of archaic populations arising from their *Homo erectus* ancestors at different times in Europe, Africa, and Asia. Regional and temporal variability is evident in these fossils, with the earlier specimens more closely resembling *Homo erectus* and the later specimens more closely resembling modern humans (as one would expect). Paleoanthropologists who accept *Homo heidelbergensis* as a valid taxon see this species as ancestral to Neandertals in western Eurasia and the earliest *Homo sapiens* in Africa (Rightmire 2007; see Figure 11.6a). In contrast, others view *Homo ergaster* as being ancestral to Neandertals in western Eurasia and *Homo sapiens* in Africa (Figure 11.6b). The taxonomic status of archaic hominins in Asia and their connection with modern Asians remains unresolved. Similarities between the Chinese specimens found at Dali and Jinniushan and those from Africa and Europe raise the possibility that these late Middle Pleistocene humans represent an eastward expansion of *Homo heidelbergensis* (Rightmire 2007). It is hoped that the discovery of additional archaic fossils from China will clarify this issue.

**Homo heidelbergensis**
the name given by some paleoanthropologists to early archaic fossils from Europe and Africa

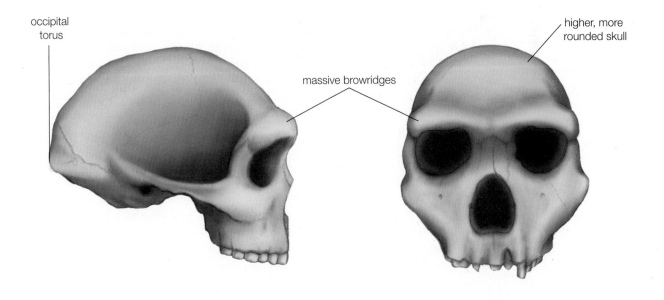

occipital torus

massive browridges

higher, more rounded skull

**Figure 11.5** The cranium of *Homo heidelbergensis* displays heavy browridges and an occipital torus, seen in *Homo erectus*, and a higher, more rounded skull, seen in *Homo sapiens*.

Courtesy of Richard Klein

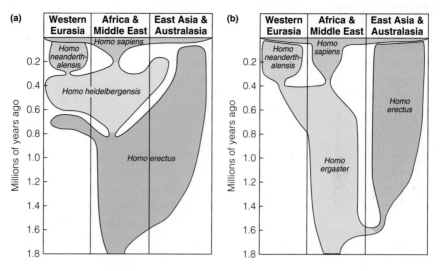

**Figure 11.6** Two possible phylogenies are illustrated here. In the first one (a), *Homo heidelbergensis* gave rise to Neandertals in western Eurasia and anatomically modern humans in Africa. In the second one (b), *Homo ergaster* gave rise to Neandertals in western Eurasia and modern humans in Africa.

From *How Humans Evolved,* 5th edition, by Robert Boyd and Joan B. Silk. Copyright © 2008, 2006, 2003, 2000, 1997 by W.W. Norton & Company, Inc. Used by permission of W.W. Norton & Company, Inc.

## BEHAVIOURAL ADAPTATIONS OF ARCHAIC HOMININS

In Chapter 10 you learned about the Oldowan stone tool industry associated with *Homo habilis* and possibly the australopithecines, and the Acheulian industry associated with *Homo erectus*. Early archaic hominins continued to make and use Acheulian tools, including bifaces and flake tools, but archaeological evidence indicates that these tools were more finely made than those attributed to *Homo erectus*. There was also considerable geographic variability in tool types, with hand axes being common in Africa and Europe and almost non-existent in Asia. In addition to stone tools, archaic hominins also made tools from wood, as indicated by three remarkably well-preserved wooden spears found at the 400,000-year-old site of Schöningen in Germany (Thieme 1997). Unfortunately, organic materials such as these are rarely preserved in the archaeological record; in this case we owe their preservation to the anaerobic environment and the presence of tannic acids in the bog in which they were deposited.

Archaic hominins probably lived in some sort of shelters, but archaeological evidence for these is almost non-existent. Oval or circular arrangements of stones found at the sites of Terra Amata in France and Bilzingsleben in Germany suggest some form of structure, while a linear arrangement of large rocks found in Lazaret Cave in southern France may have supported the poles of a tent (de Lumley 1969). The remains of plants, small and large mammals, birds, and fish have been found at various Middle Pleistocene sites, and some of these resources may have been part of the diet. Faunal remains recovered from several sites have been used to argue for big game hunting, though other activities might also account for the association of these bones with stone tools. Among the most convincing evidence are the remains of mammals found in association with *Homo heidelbergensis* fossils at Boxgrove (Roberts and Parfitt 1999). The association of the Schöningen spears with stone tools and butchered animal bones further bolsters the argument that archaic hominins successfully hunted large game.

## THE APPEARANCE OF NEANDERTALS

When Darwin published his "Big Book" in 1859, very little fossil evidence for earlier humans had been uncovered. Neandertal fossils had been found in 1830 in Belgium and 1848 in Gibraltar, but neither was recognized at the time as representing an earlier human form. In

**Figure 11.7** The geographic range of Neandertals, determined from fossil and mtDNA evidence, spanned western Europe to central Asia (see Krause et al. 2007).

1856, what was to become the Neandertal type specimen was recovered from the Feldhofer cave in the Neander Valley in Germany, from which the name of these hominins derives.[2] Consisting of the top of a skull, some ribs, parts of a pelvis, and some limb bones, it was initially believed to be a modern human with some type of pathological condition. In the decades that followed, however, additional Neandertal fossils uncovered from sites in western and central Europe confirmed their status as ancient humans. Spanning the period from about 130,000 to 30,000 years ago, thousands of Neandertal fossils have been unearthed to date, and their geographic range is now known to have extended into central Asia (Krause et al. 2007; see Figure 11.7). No other group of fossil hominins has been more thoroughly studied.

**Figure 11.8** This image of a Neandertal, based on Marcellin Boule's reconstruction of the skeleton from La Chapelle-aux-Saints, reflected the widely held belief that these hominins were ape-like in appearance.

The Granger Collection, New York

In 1911, French paleontologist Marcellin Boule undertook a reconstruction of the skeleton of an elderly male found in 1908 at the site of La Chapelle-aux-Saints in France.[3] In doing so, he ignored several important features, including the large cranial capacity of this individual (1620 cc) and several pathological conditions affecting his skeleton. Consequently, he portrayed this individual as ape-like in appearance, with stooped posture, bent knees, and a long, low cranium reflecting what Boule believed to be low intelligence. Boule's reconstruction,

http://www.talkorigins.org/ faqs/homs/savage.html

2. This site was revisited in 1997, and excavation of cave sediments discarded in 1856 yielded dozens of artifacts and faunal remains and over 60 human bone fragments, including several that belonged to the original specimen excavated in 1856 (Schmitz et al. 2002).

3. The age at death of this individual was estimated as 40 years; this would have been considered elderly for Neandertals, most of whom died before age 40 (Trinkaus 1995).

which relegated Neandertals to a separate species that eventually became extinct, was widely accepted and gave rise to the stereotypical image of Neandertals that has long been accepted in popular culture (Figure 11.8).

## Neandertal Morphology

Descriptions of Neandertal morphology typically refer to that of the **classic** Neandertals of western Europe and it is important to emphasize that Neandertals living in the Near East did not exhibit many of the extreme morphological features seen in their European

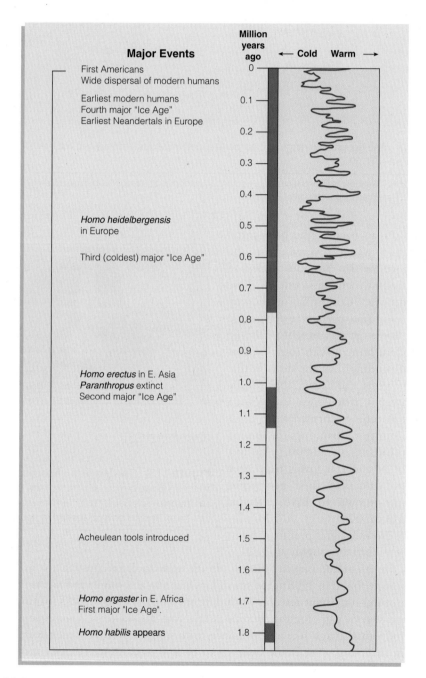

**Figure 11.9** Changing climatic conditions during the Middle and Upper Pleistocene had a major impact on archaic hominins, including Neandertals.

Boaz, Noel T.; Almquist, Alan J., *Biological Anthropology: A Synthetic Approach to Human Evolution,* 2nd, © 2002, p. 320. Reprinted by permission of Pearson Education, Inc., Upper Saddle River, NJ.

counterparts. To appreciate the morphology of European Neandertals, it is useful to examine the environmental conditions in which these hominins lived. Classic Neandertals emerged in Europe at the beginning of the last interglacial period, about 130,000 years ago, when the climate was noticeably warmer than during the previous glacial period (Figure 11.9). About 115,000 years ago, however, climatic conditions deteriorated once again, ushering in the last and most recent glacial period in Europe. Sheets of ice covered much of northern Europe, and most of western and central Europe and Eurasia consisted of tundra. Isolated by these glacial conditions for a considerable period of time, the Neandertals developed a distinctive morphology that has made them unique among hominins.

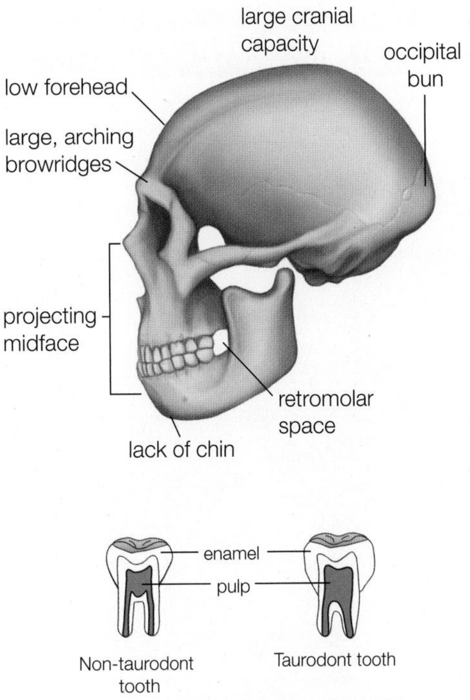

Classic Neandertals possessed the following: a large skull with a low vault and a low, sloping forehead; a cranial capacity that in some cases exceeded that of modern humans (average 1500 cc); a rounded feature at the back of the cranium known as the **occipital bun**; small mastoid processes; **midfacial prognathism**; a large nasal cavity; large rounded orbits; prominent arched browridges; and no distinct chin. Their dental characteristics included relatively large incisors, relatively small molars, a **retromolar space** reflecting the forward shift of the teeth relative to the skull vault, and **taurodontism** (Figure 11.10).

The unique cranial morphology of classic Neandertals has long been viewed as an adaptation to cold temperatures. Researchers have hypothesized that a forward-projecting face would have kept the nasal cavities—and thus the incoming cold air—further away from the temperature-sensitive brain, while the large size of the nasal cavities would have provided greater surface area for warming and humidifying the cold air. More recently, biomechanical explanations have come to dominate the literature. Proponents of the "anterior dental loading" hypothesis (Brace 1964; O'Connor, Franciscus, and Holton 2005; Rak 1986) have argued that the large, prognathic face and large incisors of Neandertals were adaptations to heavy occlusal forces resulting from the use of the teeth as tools. Support for this hypothesis comes from the heavily worn incisors seen in Neandertal fossils as well as degenerative changes to the **temporomandibular joints**. O'Connor and colleagues (2005) tested the anterior dental loading hypothesis by assessing the ability of the Neandertal **masticatory** system to generate heavy occlusal loads (i.e., bite force), using modern humans as a comparison. Their results revealed that compared to modern humans, Neandertals were not capable of generating significantly higher levels of anterior bite force, and that their larger, more heavily worn anterior teeth might instead reflect repetitive use of their teeth. While O'Connor and colleagues agree that some Neandertal craniofacial features are likely masticatory adaptations, they conclude that this hypothesis does not account for *all* of their features.

Compared to modern humans, Neandertals were shorter and stockier, with more robust, heavily muscled, and slightly curved long bones and large, barrel-shaped chests. Stature estimates based on long-bone lengths average 158 cm in females and 166 cm in males (Churchill 2008), and their limb bones were shorter than those of most modern human populations.

**Figure 11.10** The classic Neandertal cranium had a long, low vault, heavy browridges, and an occipital bun. Dental characteristics included a retromolar space and taurodontism.

From Jurmain/Kilgore/Trevathan. *Essentials of Physical Anthropology*, 7E. © 2009 Wadsworth, a part of Cengage Learning, Inc. Reproduced by permission. www.cengage.com/permissions

**occipital bun**
a bulge on the occipital bone of the skull that projects posteriorly

**midfacial prognathism**
forward projection of the nasal region of the face

**retromolar space**
a gap between the third molar and the ascending ramus of the mandible

**taurodontism**
enlargement of the pulp cavity in molar teeth

**temporomandibular joint**
the location on the skull base where the mandible articulates with the temporal bone

**masticatory**
related to chewing

Courtesy of Alan Cross

The potentially fatal consequences of failing to thermoregulate (i.e., maintain a stable core body temperature in response to behavioural and environmental stress) have long been recognized as an important variable in the study of hominin energetics. Decades of research have produced numerous hypotheses regarding the role of thermoregulation in hominin evolution, including in relation to the origins of habitual bipedality, the selection of a larger body size in the genus *Homo*, and the relative proportions of the body and limbs as hominins dispersed ecogeographically.

My colleagues and I (Cross, Collard, and Nelson 2008) recently identified several problems with previous estimates of heat loss during hominin locomotion. We argued that the conventional equations for estimating heat loss have modelled the body as a two-dimensional, undifferentiated mass and, consequently, have not accounted for regional differences in variables known to affect thermoregulation. These variables include skin temperature, surface area, and the rate of movement for each body segment. To better reflect the dynamic, three-dimensional nature of bipedality, we employed a fifteen-segment model of the body. Our segmented method utilized segment-specific data for skin temperature, surface area, and rate of movement. For the latter, we had volunteers walk on a treadmill and used 3D motion capture technology to quantify the displacement of each body segment during normal walking. Using segment-specific data rather than weighted

means allowed us to estimate the role of each body segment in total-body heat loss—something that cannot be done with the conventional method. When we compared the heat loss estimates of the segmented method to those derived through the conventional method, we found that intersegment variability had a significant impact on heat loss estimates. Given that body and limb proportions have differed among hominin species, these new findings are likely to have particular relevance to evolutionary studies.

For example, the unique body and limb proportions of the Neandertals are widely thought to represent adaptations to low temperatures consistent with Bergmann's and Allen's Rules. We have now used the segmented method to test this hypothesis (Cross and Collard, in prep). First, we used published osteometric data to create a segmented model of a Neanderthal. Next, we estimated 3D segment displacement rates and distances for the Neanderthal by scaling values recorded for a sample of modern humans walking at 1.2 m/s. We then used these data to estimate Neanderthal segment-specific and total-body-heat loss when ambient temperature was modelled between 20°C and 35°C. Lastly, the Neanderthal heat loss estimates were compared with those of the modern human sample.

Our results indicate that the conventional method for estimating surface area is not appropriate for use in nonhuman hominins because it cannot account for the proportional differences that exist between species. Furthermore, heat loss estimates showed that the differences between these species are not consistent with the expectations of ecogeographic rules. Though the Neanderthal morphology would have consistently lost less heat than that of modern humans, the former's upper arms were the only segments estimated to consistently lose relatively less heat than those of the latter. Surprisingly, it was estimated that Neanderthal legs would have lost relatively more heat than those of modern humans. While Bergmann's Rule appears to be consistent with the total body surface area / mass pattern identified for these species, that rule fails to account for the interspecies thermoregulatory differences in the axial segments alone. These findings suggest either that interspecies comparisons are not appropriate when attempting to identify the presence or absence of ecogeographic rules in hominins, or that these long-accepted ecogeographic rules do not explain the evolution of limb and body proportions in the genus *Homo*.

This research was funded by SSHRC-CGS# 766-2004-0723, SSHRC-CGS#767-2006-1902, and the Canada Research Chairs Program.

Source: Written by Alan Cross, Laboratory of Human Evolutionary Studies, Department of Archaeology, Simon Fraser University, Burnaby, British Columbia.

These features have been interpreted as adaptations to the cold climatic conditions in which they lived (see Box 11.1). The marked robusticity of Neandertal limbs has also been interpreted as reflecting high activity levels and a physically demanding lifestyle. Researchers have investigated activity levels in Neandertals using a number of approaches, including taking external measurements of limb bones and examining musculoskeletal stress markers. More recently, research on functional adaptations in Neandertals has shifted to examining the **cross-sectional geometry** of their bones. In one such study, a comparison of upper- and lower-limb robusticity in Neandertals, early modern humans, and recent humans using measurements taken from the midshaft of long bones revealed similarities between Neandertals and modern foragers such as the Inuit, suggesting that they shared a similar pattern of mechanical loading (Pearson, Cordero, and Busby 2008). Analyses of Neandertal hand bones have revealed that these hominins, like modern humans, had the ability to produce and use complex tools. A three-dimensional comparison of Neandertal hand morphology with that of modern populations has indicated that Neandertal hands were adapted primarily for power, whereas those of modern humans were adapted to more frequent precision manipulation (Niewoehner 2008).

Detailed studies of the Neandertal pelvis have revealed that compared to modern humans, Neandertals had longer and thinner **pubic rami**. Initially thought to reflect differences between the two groups in the length of gestation (Trinkaus 1984), this difference is now believed to be more likely related to locomotion and posture-related biomechanics (Rak and Arensburg 1987).

## Growing Up Neandertal

Neandertals appear to have buried their dead (see below). As a result, a large number of well-preserved skeletons of infants, children, and adolescents have been recovered from Neandertal sites. These remains have enabled researchers to compare the growth and development of these hominins with that of anatomically modern humans.

Compared to other primates, humans have longer periods of infant and childhood growth, allowing for a greater period of learning. The question of whether Neandertals also had prolonged growth has been addressed using a variety of methods. Computer tomography (CT) has allowed researchers to reconstruct Neandertal skeletons and compare their morphology with that of modern humans.[4] Ponce de Léon and colleagues (2008), for instance, recently used CT scanning to reconstruct the remains of a Neandertal newborn found in Mezmaiskaya Cave, Russia, and two infants found in Dederiyeh Cave in Syria. Their study revealed that Neandertal babies were born with brains as large as those of modern human infants but that their brains grew more rapidly than ours during the first few years of life. They stress that their findings do not imply that Neandertals completed their brain growth earlier than modern humans. Rather, these hominins may have matured later than we do owing to the high metabolic costs to the mother associated with rapid brain growth (ibid.).

Studies of Neandertal dental development have yielded seemingly conflicting results. Ramirez Rozzi and Bermúdez de Castro's (2004) analysis of a sample of Neandertal and anatomically modern human teeth revealed that Neandertal tooth enamel was deposited more rapidly, suggesting that they reached maturity earlier than modern humans. In contrast, a more recent study of anterior tooth growth found it to fall within the range of variation seen in modern populations (Guatelli-Steinberg et al. 2005). As Guatelli-Steinberg (2009) emphasizes, interpreting the rate of dental development among Neandertals hinges on knowing the range of variation in dental development exhibited by modern humans. Furthermore, the rate of dental growth seen in Neandertals may not be an accurate reflection of their overall growth rate. She recommends a multi-faceted approach in which dental development is examined in conjunction with the development of other systems such as the skeleton (ibid.). A small number of studies have addressed Neandertal ontogeny by examining both dental and skeletal growth. Thompson and Nelson (2000), for example, examined data on dental maturation and femoral growth from four Neandertals, five Upper Paleolithic *Homo sapiens* from Europe, and two modern samples, and found that the Neandertal growth trajectory differed from that of the other samples, suggesting either advanced dental development or slow femoral growth compared to modern humans.

**cross-sectional geometry**
the mass and distribution (shape) of cortical bone viewed in a plane perpendicular to the long axis of a tubular bone, such as the femur or metacarpal

**pubic ramus**
the portion of the pubic bone of the pelvis that extends medially

---

4. This method involves using computer software to transform fossil fragments into 3D objects on a computer screen and then to assemble them to form a complete bone.

## Reflections of a Hard Life

Neandertals suffered from a variety of ailments, including traumatic injuries, nutritional deficiencies, and joint disease. Trauma has been documented in many Neandertal skeletons, and a number of these injuries have been interpreted as signs of interpersonal violence. These include the remains of a young adult Neandertal from St-Césaire, who displayed evidence of sharp-force trauma to the cranium (Zollikofer et al. 2002), and of an adult from Shanidar, who exhibited a cut mark on the ninth left rib (Trinkaus 1983). In their review of Neandertal trauma, Berger and Trinkaus (1995) noted the high frequency of traumatic lesions in Neandertal remains and the fact that the healed or partially healed nature of many of them indicates survival of the injury. Interestingly, their examination of the anatomical distribution of these traumatic lesions revealed a pattern similar to that seen in modern-day rodeo riders, and they posit that this high prevalence of head and neck injuries may have resulted from frequent close encounters with large prey animals, as might occur in attempts to hunt them with spears at close distances (Berger and Trinkaus 1995).[5]

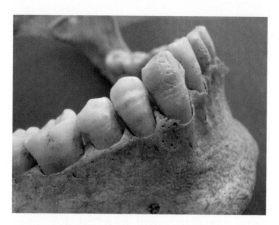

**Figure 11.11** Linear enamel hypoplasia, defects in the surface of the tooth enamel that result from episodes of nutritional or disease stress during childhood, have been documented in Neandertal remains. They are seen here in modern human mandibular teeth.

Courtesy of Anne Keenleyside

Neandertals also experienced episodes of nutritional stress, as revealed in their teeth, many of which exhibit defects known as **linear enamel hypoplasias** (Figure 11.11). These nonspecific indicators of stress, which result from a disruption in enamel formation, provide a permanent record of stress episodes during childhood. A number of studies have revealed high rates of enamel hypoplasia in Neandertals, suggesting that they suffered from high levels of nutritional deficiencies (Ogilvie, Curran, and Trinkaus 1989). A recent comparison of the prevalence of enamel hypoplasia in Neandertals and Alaskan Inuit, however, found that Neandertals were no more stressed than the latter (Guatelli-Steinberg, Larsen, and Hutchinson 2004).

Joint diseases recorded in Neandertal skeletons provide further evidence of a hard life. Osteoarthritis, or degenerative joint disease, has been recorded in a number of Neandertal remains, including the skeleton from La Chapelle-aux-Saints, discussed earlier. Another joint disease, diffuse idiopathic skeletal hyperostosis (DISH), has also been diagnosed in a Neandertal skeleton (Crubézy and Trinkaus 1992). Characterized by excessive bone growth on the vertebrae, the condition is more common in males and in older adults. While its etiology remains unknown, genetics and diabetes have been implicated, among other factors.

Documentation of debilitating conditions such as traumatic injuries and joint disease has led to speculation that such individuals would have required considerable care from other members of their group. One of the best-known examples is Shanidar 1, an adult male Neandertal estimated to have been 30 to 45 years of age at the time of his death. Examination of his skeleton revealed that he had suffered multiple fractures, including an injury to the right humerus that had resulted in paralysis leading to atrophy of the bone (Trinkaus 1983). Solecki (1971) concluded from this that he would have been dependent on others for care. Similarly, healed injuries in other Neandertals have been interpreted as evidence of care and compassion (Trinkaus and Zimmerman 1982). Dettwyler (1991) has challenged the assumption that the survival of disabled individuals is evidence of compassion and support, arguing that skeletal remains tell us nothing about the degree to which an individual was "handicapped" by his or

**linear enamel hypoplasias**

horizontal defects in tooth enamel that represent episodes of physiological stress that occurred while the teeth were forming

---

5. In the 1980s, Dr. Valerius Geist, Professor Emeritus of Environmental Science at the University of Calgary, proposed that Neandertals were "close quarter hunters"; see his 1981 paper "Neanderthal the Hunter" in *Natural History* 90(1): 26–36.

her disability, or the way in which that individual was treated. It is hard to imagine, however, how any individual incapacitated by injury or disease would have survived for any length of time in the wild without help.

# NEANDERTAL BEHAVIOURAL ADAPTATIONS

## Technology

In Europe, Neandertals are most often associated with the **Mousterian** stone tool industry (Figure 11.12), named after the site of Le Moustier in France. This **Middle Palaeolithic** industry was characterized by a number of methods of manufacturing, including the **Levallois**, or prepared core technique, which involved preparing disc-shaped cores from which flakes were knocked off and made into tools. In contrast to Acheulian assemblages, Mousterian toolkits encompassed a greater variety of tool types, and the variability in these toolkits has led to considerable discussion and debate about their significance. In the mid-20th century, the well-known French archaeologist François Bordes identified four (later five) major types of assemblages, hypothesizing that they represented different cultural groups (Bordes 1961). In contrast, archaeologist Lewis Binford interpreted them as indicating different behavioural complexes—that is, different toolkits used for different functions (Binford and Binford 1966). As Mellars (1996) points out, however, other factors such as temporal changes in stylistic attributes perhaps contributed to this variability. So it is important to consider the interaction of multiple factors when attempting to explain the diversity seen in Middle Palaeolithic assemblages. More recent Neandertal sites such as Saint-Césaire and Arcy-sur-Cure in France, are associated with a tool industry known as the **Châtelperronian**, which consisted of blade and bone tools and personal ornaments.

**Mousterian**
a stone tool industry generally associated with Neandertals

**Middle Palaeolithic**
the period dating from about 125,000 to 40,000 years ago and associated with Mousterian tools

**Levallois**
a tool-manufacturing technique that involved making tools from a prepared core

**Châtelperronian**
an Upper Paleolithic tool industry associated with late Neandertals

**Figure 11.12** The Mousterian stone tool industry was characterized by a greater variety of tool types than the Acheulian industry. These included scrapers and points, such as those seen here.

Courtesy of Anne Keenleyside

A particularly interesting artifact, interpreted as the oldest musical instrument in the world, came to light in 1995 in a cave in Slovenia. Dating between 82,000 and 43,000 years ago, it consisted of the partial femur of a cave bear that had been punctured on one side with four holes, forming what appeared to be a small flute (Turk 1997). This interpretation has not been accepted by everyone, however, and the holes may have been made by carnivore teeth (Chase and Nowell 1998).

A variety of behavioural strategies enabled Neandertals to cope with the cool climate in which they lived. These included the occupation of caves and rock shelters and the use of fire, as indicated by deposits of ash and charcoal at a number of sites. They also likely wore clothing made from animal hides. There is no evidence in the archaeological record of sewing implements, but heavy anterior tooth wear and wear patterns on some of their stone tools may point to the preparation of hides for clothing and/or shelters.

There has been considerable debate about the degree to which Neandertals moved during their lifetime, with some researchers arguing for a limited range and others for longer distances. Most of our information on Neandertal mobility comes from raw materials, some of which have been found to originate from locations over 100 km away (Mellars 1996), though the majority come from distances of less than 5 km. Recent strontium isotope analysis of a Neandertal third molar from the 40,000-year-old site of Lakonis in Greece points to the movement of this individual over a fairly wide geographic area (over 20 km) during his or her lifetime (Richards et al. 2008).

## Diet and Subsistence Practices

Like their *Homo erectus* ancestors, Neandertals and other archaic hominins exploited a variety of food resources, including large and small game and a variety of plants. Recently, stable isotope and dental microwear analyses have been used to investigate Neandertal diet. Stable carbon and nitrogen isotope analyses of Neandertal skeletal remains recovered from several sites have revealed that in Europe at least, they derived almost all of their dietary protein from meat (Fizet et al. 1995; Bocherens et al. 1999, 2005; Richards et al. 2000; Richards and Schmitz 2008). Furthermore, their $\delta^{15}N$ values are higher than those measured in contemporaneous carnivores such as cave hyenas, suggesting that these hominins were top predators (Bocherens et al. 2005). These findings are consistent with **zooarchaeological** evidence obtained from Neandertal sites, which points to a heavy reliance on medium to large herbivores such as reindeer, red deer, bison, and horse.

> **zooarchaeological**
>
> nonhuman, typically used to refer to animal bones

The question of whether Neandertals hunted or scavenged has long been the subject of debate, though it is now widely recognized that Neandertals were capable of hunting a variety of game, while also likely scavenging on occasion. In general, archaeological evidence for *scavenging* consists of faunal assemblages containing primarily cranial and foot bones, the presence of carnivore tooth marks on the bones, and a lack of cut marks on fleshier parts of the skeleton (Marean and Kim 1998; Marean 1998). Archaeological evidence for *hunting* includes a focus on one or two species of large mammals, evidence of butchery in the form of cut marks on bones that would have yielded a considerable amount of meat, and the presence of weapons such as spears. At Combe Grenal, for instance, the faunal assemblage consists of predominantly horse and large bovid (e.g., bison) remains, greater representation of meat-bearing upper limb bones than lower limb bones, and clear patterns of cut marks on the limb bones—evidence consistent with hunting (Chase 1986). A number of other Neandertal sites have also yielded the remains of large game. At the site of Umm el Tlel in Syria, for example, the fragment of a broken point was found embedded in the bones of a wild ass (Boëda et al. 1999). As well, the presence in Neandertal male humeri of asymmetry of the deltoid tuberosity—a bony feature to which the deltoid muscle used to abduct the arm (i.e., move it away from the body) is attached—has been cited as evidence for the use of thrusting spears (Schmitt, Churchill, and Hylander 2003). This evidence, together with the presence of traumatic injuries in some Neandertal skeletons, as discussed earlier in this chapter, points to the practice of hunting game at close proximity.

Reports of the postmortem modification of Neandertal remains, possibly for the purpose of consumption, date back to 1899 when excavations at the site of Krapina in Croatia uncovered a large number of broken, burned, and cut bones scattered around fire pits. More recently, a Neandertal skull with an enlarged base was recovered from the Guattari cave in Italy and was interpreted as reflecting removal of the brain for consumption. Subsequent reanalysis of this and the Krapina specimens has since revealed that the observed damage is more consistent with postdepositional processes, including scavenging by carnivores and the postmortem preparation of bodies for burial (see below, as well as Russell 1987; Trinkaus 1985; White and Toth 1991). The cannibalism theory has recently been revived by the discovery of cut marks on the bones of six Neandertal skeletons recovered from the site of Moula-Guercy (Defleur et al. 1999). Neandertal and deer bones found at the site exhibited similar cut marks, and the bones of both species had been broken open, presumably to extract the marrow. Cut marks on the lingual (inner) surface of a juvenile Neandertal mandible suggest that its tongue had been cut out (ibid.). While this evidence is certainly convincing, the question remains as to why Neandertals engaged in this activity in the first place.

## Ritual and Symbolic Behaviour

Neandertals are often referred to as the first humans to practise intentional burial. Indeed, numerous Neandertals have been found buried in caves. Archaeological evidence commonly cited as proof of deliberate burial includes articulated skeletal remains, an unusual positioning of the body, the presence of presumed grave goods such as tools and animal bones, and the presence of floral and burned remains possibly reflecting funerary rituals. As critics point out, however, the preservation of articulated skeletal remains may occur as a result of natural depositional processes in caves and rock shelters (Gargett 1989, 1999). There are few if any convincing examples of grave goods associated with Neandertal remains, and pollen discovered in the famous Shanidar burial from Iraq, and interpreted as evidence of burial with wildflowers, may have blown into the cave or been carried into the grave by burrowing rodents (Sommer, 1999). Nevertheless, the consensus today is that these burials are real and that they reflect deliberate actions. Neandertals also used red ochre and other natural pigments, possibly for artistic purposes (D'Errico 2003), and they made objects such as pendants and engravings that are suggestive of artistic expression (Figure 11.13).

## The Origins of Language

Whether or not Neandertals possessed spoken language has been the subject of considerable debate. Some researchers believe that language as we know it today emerged late in human evolution and coincided with the appearance of anatomically modern humans. Others argue that language evolved at a much earlier stage in our evolutionary history. When we are dealing with fossil evidence, none of the soft tissues that make up our vocal structures have been preserved. We can, however, get some insight into the language capabilities of earlier hominins by looking at several features of the skull, the size and shape of which often reflect soft tissue anatomy. In Chapter 10 we noted that early *Homo* endocranial casts show enlargement of the frontal and parietal lobes, regions that in the modern human brain house the language centres. Other cranial

**Figure 11.13** Pendants similar to these have been recovered from the site of Arcy-sur-Cure in France.

Courtesy of Kenneth Garrett Photography

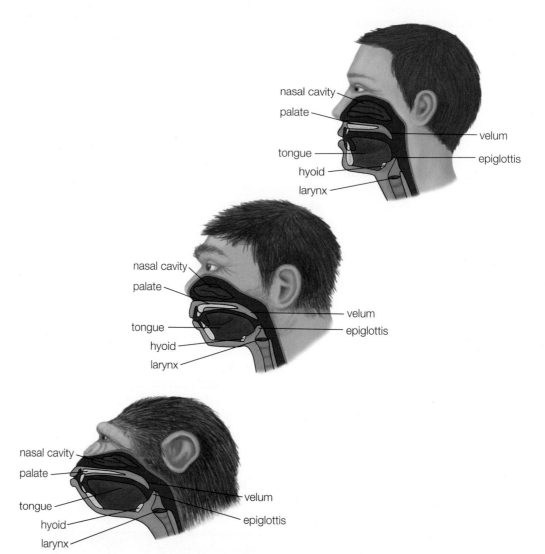

**Figure 11.14** Compared to chimpanzees, Neandertals have a lower larynx and a longer pharynx, as indicated by the angle of the base of their skull.

**larynx**

an organ in the neck responsible for the production of sound; also known as the voice box

**pharynx**

part of the neck and throat located superior to the larynx that modifies sounds made by the larynx

**basicranial flexion**

the degree of angling of the base of the skull from which the position of the larynx and size of the pharynx can be inferred

**vowel space**

The space within the oral cavity in which vowel sounds are created by altering the relative position of tongue and pharynx

**hyoid bone**

a bone in the neck that supports the tongue and provides attachment for muscles that connect to the larynx

**hypoglossal canal**

a bony canal in the occipital bone through which passes the hypoglossal nerve that controls the movement of the tongue

features may also provide clues to the emergence of language in our earlier ancestors. A low **larynx** and large **pharynx**, for example, have long been considered "anatomical prerequisites for producing the full range of human speech" (Lieberman and Crelin 1971, 220). Sound generated in the larynx, or voice box, is modified by the pharynx, the cavity above the larynx that creates our familiar vowel sounds. The position of the larynx and the size of the pharynx can be inferred from the degree of flexion of the base of the skull (**basicranial flexion**) (Figure 11.14). Based on their reconstruction of the vocal anatomy of Neandertals—most notably, a higher positioned larynx and smaller pharynx compared to modern humans—Lieberman and Crelin (1971) concluded that they were incapable of making the full range of sounds made by modern humans. The accuracy of this reconstruction has been questioned, however, and a recent study has revealed that the Neandertal **vowel space** was comparable in size to that of modern humans, meaning that they could potentially have made the same range of sounds we can (Boë et al. 2002). The 1988 discovery, in the Kebara Cave in Israel, of a 60,000-year-old Neandertal **hyoid bone** almost identical in size and shape to that of modern humans has also been used to argue that Neandertal vocal capabilities were very similar to our own (Arensberg et al. 1990). Similarly, a comparably sized **hypoglossal canal**, which carries the main nerve supply for the tongue, has been cited as evidence that Neandertals had the same degree of motor control of the tongue and thus the same vocal abilities as we do (Kay, Cartmill, and

Balow 1998). This claim, however, has been disputed based on the finding that earlier hominins and some nonhuman primates have hypoglossal canals that are as large as ours, yet cannot speak (DeGusta, Gilbert, and Turner 1999).

New genetic evidence has recently provided additional clues to Neandertal language capabilities in the form of a genetic variant called *FOXP2*, which is found in modern humans and which plays a role in speech and language.[6] Initially thought to have originated in modern humans less than 200,000 years ago (Enard et al. 2002), this variant has recently been detected in two Neandertal specimens from Spain dating to approximately 43,000 years (Krause et al. 2007), raising the possibility that they possessed language abilities similar to those of modern humans.

# DECIPHERING THE NEANDERTAL GENOME

The taxonomic status of Neandertals and their relationship to modern humans has been the topic of some of the most heated debates in paleoanthropology. On the one hand, many have argued that the Neandertals were morphologically too specialized to have contributed to the modern human gene pool and that they represent a different species, *Homo neanderthalensis*. This view is supported by some of the growth studies that were discussed earlier in this chapter. Opponents, however, argue that Neandertals were not so distinct from modern humans and should therefore be classified as a subspecies, *Homo sapiens neanderthalensis*. As you will learn in Chapter 12, skeletal remains exhibiting a mosaic of Neandertal and modern human features have in fact been found in Portugal, lending support to the argument that the two groups interbred.

Within the past decade, genetic data have provided a new means of addressing the position of Neandertals in our evolutionary history. In 1997, scientists announced that they had sequenced mitochondrial DNA from the Neandertal type specimen discovered in 1856 (Krings et al. 1997). To verify the results, the mtDNA was extracted and analyzed at two different labs, one in Europe and one in the United States. Comparison of the Neandertal mtDNA with that of modern humans revealed that the Neandertal sequence showed three to four times the number of differences than are typically seen among living humans. On this basis, Krings and colleagues (1997) concluded that Neandertals and modern humans were separate species who last shared a common ancestor sometime between 550,000 and 690,000 years ago.

Critics of these results were quick to point out that the mtDNA used in this study was extracted from only one individual and that the degree of difference between the Neandertal mtDNA and that of modern humans is less than what is seen between humans and our closest living relatives, the chimpanzees. Since then, however, mtDNA has been extracted from more than a dozen additional Neandertal skeletons (Green et al. 2008; Ovchinnikov et al. 2000; Krings et al. 2000; Schmitz et al. 2002; Serre et al. 2004; Caramelli et al. 2006). All sequences have been found to fall outside the range of variation seen in modern humans, suggesting that Neandertals contributed few if any of their genes to the modern European gene pool. The sequencing of nuclear DNA from a 38,000-year-old Neandertal fossil recovered from the Vindija Cave in Croatia has also demonstrated its distinctiveness from that of modern humans (Noonan et al. 2006).

Compared to mtDNA, very little was known of Neandertal genomic DNA. We noted the *FOXP2* gene above, and Lalueza-Fox and colleagues (2007) identified a variant of the *MC1R* gene associated with pigmentation in a 43,000-year-old specimen from Spain, suggesting the possibility of fair skin and red hair. All of this changed dramatically, however, with the recent publication of a draft sequence numbering 4 billion nucleotides of the Neandertal genome (Green et al. 2010). These researchers recovered genomic DNA from four sites spanning the geographic range of Neandertals in Europe (most of the sequence was prepared from three individuals sampled from Vindija Cave, Croatia). This sequence was then compared to "libraries" of the modern human and chimpanzee genomes, as well as to data from five selected human individuals from Europe, West and Southern Africa, China, and Oceania. These comparisons point to a number of significant outcomes. While the Neandertal and modern human genomes diverged ca. 825,000 years ago, we currently share between 1% and

---

6. People with mutations of this gene have impaired speech.

4% of our genome with Neandertals! In other words, gene flow did occur between Neandertals and early modern humans in Europe (but not Africa). Their study also points to positive selection for genes in the modern human genome relating specifically to cognitive abilities and cranial morphology. It might seem perplexing that the genomic DNA picture of hybridization differs from the mtDNA results discussed above. Remember, however, that mtDNA is involved in many important attributes (including life span and brain physiology) and will itself be a target of positive selection. In other words, modern human mtDNA is derived! The Green study seems to finally settle one question regarding Neandertals—as per the Biological Species Concept, they were *Homo sapiens*!

A remarkable new discovery was announced in March 2010 in the form of a mitochondrial DNA sequence obtained from a small finger bone excavated in 2008 from Denisova Cave in the Altai Mountains of southern Siberia. Much to the surprise of the researchers conducting this study, the bone, dating to 48,000 to 30,000 years ago, yielded a mtDNA sequence that was distinctly different from that of both Neandertals and early modern humans who lived in the area, suggesting that a third hominin lineage may have been present in this region at the same time (Krause et al. 2010). While it remains to be seen whether this specimen represents a new species, it certainly adds another layer of complexity to our understanding of human evolutionary history in Late Pleistocene Eurasia.

## The Fate of Neandertals

Radiometric dating indicates that Neandertals disappeared from western Asia around 45,000 years ago and from most of Europe by 30,000 years ago, though a recently dated Neandertal site in Gibraltar suggests that Neandertals may have survived in this area until at least 28,000 years ago (Finlayson et al. 2006). Until recently, the popular explanation for their demise was that they were supplanted by modern humans who possessed a more effective technological and cultural repertoire. In other words, they were out-competed. This argument was based largely on evidence indicating substantial behavioural differences between Neandertals and modern humans. In recent years, however, it has become increasingly apparent that the technology, subsistence strategies, and symbolic behaviour of Neandertals was not markedly different from that of early anatomically modern humans (D'Errico 2003) and that the transition from the Middle to Upper Palaeolithic, discussed in more detail in the next chapter, was one of mosaic evolution rather than cultural revolution (McBrearty and Brooks 2000).

There is growing consensus that no single factor can account for the disappearance of Neandertals and that a variety of factors—including deteriorating climatic conditions and diminishing food resources—may have contributed to their decline. Paleoclimatic records reveal unstable conditions between 40,000 and 25,000 years ago, with the most severe and prolonged period of climatic stress occurring around 30,000 years ago. These unstable conditions may have precipitated the extinction of the large herd animals on which the Neandertals depended for food (Stringer 2008; Stringer et al. 2004). Archaeologist Eugène Morin of Trent University recently analyzed the faunal remains from Saint-Césaire and found that as the temperature declined, the proportion of reindeer in the Neandertal diet increased while the proportion of horses, bison, and red deer decreased. Heavier reliance on reindeer—a species whose populations are known to fluctuate widely—would have placed Neandertals at increased risk of famine and led to decreased population densities, ultimately contributing to their demise (Morin 2008).

# SUMMARY

There is increasing recognition that more than one species of hominin existed during the Middle Pleistocene and that distinct lineages evolved during this period. The relationships among them, and their connections to modern populations, however, remain uncertain. *Homo antecessor*, if we accept this taxon, likely arose from *Homo ergaster* in Africa and may have been the last common ancestor of Neandertals and modern humans. Many of the archaic fossils from Europe, Africa, and Asia have now been classified by some paleoanthropologists as *Homo heidelbergensis*, a species that may have given rise to Neandertals in Europe and the earliest *Homo sapiens* in Africa (Rightmire 2007). Long-standing debates concerning the taxonomic status of Neandertals and their morphological and genetic distinctiveness do not appear to be close to resolution. While it is now widely recognized that Neandertals were a distinct evolutionary branch that shared a common ancestor with modern humans, questions remain regarding the nature of their interactions, including the degree to which they interbred. There is also growing recognition that the cognitive abilities of Neandertals were not significantly different from those of anatomically modern humans and that aspects of behavioural modernity (see Chapter 12) were present in Neandertals (D'Errico 2003).

# CORE REVIEW

### In what ways did archaic hominins differ from Homo erectus?

Archaic hominins possessed a combination of features seen in earlier *Homo erectus* fossils, as well as those of anatomically modern humans. They had a significantly larger cranial capacity than *Homo erectus,* averaging about 1200 cc, a more rounded skull, and smaller teeth. Some archaic hominins, however, retained a large supraorbital torus and a receding forehead.

### What are the morphological characteristics of Neandertals? In what ways did they differ from modern humans?

Neandertals possessed a large skull with a low vault and low sloping forehead, a cranial capacity that in some cases exceeded that of modern humans, an occipital bun, small mastoid processes, midfacial prognathism, a large nasal cavity, large, rounded orbits, and prominent arched browridges; also, they lacked a distinct chin. Their bodies were short and stocky, with robust, heavily muscled, and slightly curved long bones and a large, barrel-shaped chest. In contrast, anatomically modern humans had a higher, more rounded skull, no occipital bun, a vertically oriented forehead, relatively small browridges, a smaller and narrower face tucked under the brain case, a well-developed chin, small teeth and jaws, and a more gracile infracranial skeleton with straighter, less robust limb bones.

### What is the adaptive significance of Neandertal cranial and infracranial morphology?

The unique cranial and infracranial morphology of classic Neandertals—most notably their large prognathic face, large nasal cavities, heavily worn incisors, and short, stocky body build—is likely the result of a combination of factors, including adaptation to cold temperatures, heavy chewing stresses resulting from the use of their teeth as tools, and a physically strenuous lifestyle.

### What do we know from the archaeological and fossil record about Neandertal lifestyles and behaviours?

Neandertals used Mousterian tools, which they manufactured using several methods, including a prepared core technique known as Levallois. Chemical analyses of their bones, and faunal remains found in association with Neandertal fossils, indicate that they relied heavily on the meat of medium to large mammals that they hunted. Neandertals may also have practised cannibalism, as indicated by cut marks on some of their bones. They adapted to the glacial climate of Europe by occupying caves and rock shelters, using fire, and wearing clothing made from animal hides. They likely lived in small groups and ranged over distances of 20 kilometres or more during their lifetime. They were the first hominins to practise intentional burial and may have produced some form of art. Their fossil remains indicate that they suffered from a variety of ailments, including traumatic injuries sustained as a result of accidents and interpersonal violence, nutritional deficiencies, and joint disease.

**What does the genetic evidence tell us about the position of Neandertals in our evolutionary history?**

The extraction and analysis of mitochondrial DNA from more than a dozen Neandertal skeletons has revealed sequences that closely resemble one another but fall outside the range of variation seen in modern humans. Those sequences are also different from the ones derived from early modern *Homo sapiens* fossils, suggesting that Neandertals contributed few if any of their genes to the modern European gene pool. However, recent genomic DNA data suggest a different story, indicating that Neandertals did contribute to the modern human gene pool (In Europe and Asia, but not Africa), and thus should be considered *Homo sapiens*.

# CRITICAL THINKING QUESTIONS

1. Much of our knowledge of Neandertals comes from studies of Neandertal fossils found in western Europe (i.e., the "classic" Neandertals). How might the anatomy and behaviour of Neandertals living in southern Europe or the Near East have differed from their western European counterparts? What factors might account for this variation?
2. Why do you think there has been such a heated debate regarding whether Neandertals interbred with modern humans?

# GROUP DISCUSSION QUESTIONS

1. Studies of Neandertal burials have led some researchers to conclude that Neandertals believed in an afterlife. What archaeological evidence would be needed to support this conclusion?
2. Neandertals have featured prominently in popular culture, appearing in books, television advertisements, and films. How does their portrayal in the media differ from what we know about them based on the archaeological and fossil evidence?

# RESOURCES AND READINGS

- C. Finlayson, *Neandertals and Modern Humans: An Ecological and Evolutionary Perspective* (Cambridge: Cambridge University Press, 2004).
- K. Harvati and T. Harrison, eds., *Neanderthals Revisited: New Approaches and Perspectives* (Netherlands: Springer, 2008).
- P. Mellars, *The Neanderthal Legacy: An Archaeological Perspective from Western Europe* (Princeton: Princeton University Press, 1996).
- I. Tattersall, *The Last Neanderthal: The Rise, Success, and Mysterious Extinction of our Closest Human Relatives* (Boulder: Westview, 1999).
- J.L. Thompson, G.E. Krovitz, and A.J. Nelson, eds., *Patterns of Growth and Development in the Genus Homo* (Cambridge: Cambridge University Press, 2003).

# 12 The Emergence of Anatomically Modern Humans

## OVERVIEW

This chapter examines the emergence and spread of anatomically modern *Homo sapiens* and their morphological and behavioural characteristics. Most paleoanthropologists now agree that fully modern humans first evolved in Africa from archaic hominins but continue to disagree on how, exactly, they came to occupy other regions of the Old World and what their relationship was to earlier hominins in these regions. We introduce you to several models for explaining the origins of modern humans, and examine each model with respect to the fossil and genetic evidence. We review the cultural and behavioural adaptations of *Homo sapiens* and assess the ongoing debate concerning the emergence of modern human behaviour. Finally, we examine the evidence for the initial human colonization of Australia and the Americas.

## CORE CONCEPTS

■ out of Africa, multiregional evolution, transitional fossils, replacement, hybridization, assimilation, last common ancestor, behavioural modernity

## CORE QUESTIONS

■ In what ways did the earliest modern humans differ anatomically from archaic hominins?

■ What models have been proposed to explain the origins of anatomically modern humans?

■ What does the fossil and genetic evidence tell us about modern human origins?

■ When did behavioural modernity emerge, and what characterized this transition?

■ When did the earliest occupants of Australia and the Americas arrive, where did they come from, and how did they get there?

*Alone among all creatures, the species that styles itself wise,*
*Homo sapiens, has an abiding interest in its distant origins,*
*knows that its allotted time is short, worries about the future*
*and wonders about the past.*

John Noble Wilford, Journalist

# PROLOGUE: DANCING WITH NEANDERTALS?

It is possible that one of the questions that prompted you to take this course is a simple one: Where did I come from? Or something similar—perhaps, "Am I *really* related to chimpanzees?" By now we hope you realize that, while the question is simple, the answer is frightfully complicated. This is true even though we have not only *more* evidence than ever before, but more *lines* of evidence, including several varieties of molecular data. Given that modern *Homo sapiens* has been around for less than 5% of our 6.5-million-year evolutionary story as hominins, one would think that having such a wealth of information relating to recent events would settle the matter! Far from the truth, as this chapter will attest.

There are, in fact, a number of interrelated questions when it comes to the appearance of those hominins collectively referred to as "anatomically modern *Homo sapiens*" (intentionally to distinguish them from something less anatomically modern, e.g., archaic forms such as Neandertals). Succinctly put, the issues are these: Where did we come from, where did we go, and what did we do when we got there? Or more bluntly: origin—migration—behaviour. Our interests here are several. We are, after all, talking about *us*—our most immediate ancestors, who by and large (and for want of a shower or a shave) could be sitting next to you as you read this. We are also talking about our ancestors who colonized the most remote parts of the planet—namely, Australia and the Americas, North and South from Nunavut to Patagonia. And—not least especially—we are talking about the advent of so much of ourselves that we presently take for granted: art, symbolism, and **signification**. Hence the complications!

As you will see in this chapter, it comes down to "sharing and caring." How much of the genome, morphology, and behaviour of our anatomically modern relatives will we find among the archaic hominins (e.g., Neandertals)? Was contact sociable or violent? Did we mingle or did we murder?

**signification**

a sign (a character, a word, an image) that identifies an entity or assigns meaning to a situation; for example, a red light at an intersection or a dollar sign

## MODERN HUMANS TAKE THE STAGE

Sometime between 150,000 and 200,000 years ago, archaic hominins began evolving into anatomically modern *Homo sapiens*. Compared to their predecessors, the latter possessed a higher, more rounded cranium, an average cranial capacity of about 1500 cc, a more vertically oriented forehead with relatively small browridges, a smaller and flatter face, smaller teeth, and a well-developed chin (Figure 12.1). The first anatomically modern humans also possessed a more lightly built infracranial skeleton with straighter, less robust limb bones than earlier hominins.

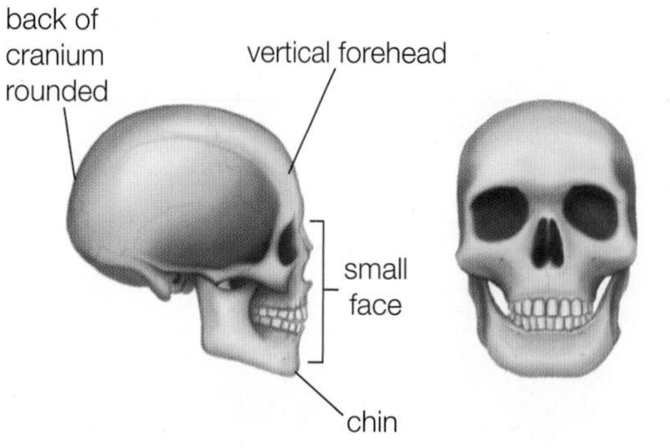

**Figure 12.1** Compared to archaic hominins, anatomically modern humans had a higher and more rounded skull, a vertical forehead, smaller browridges, a smaller, flatter face, smaller teeth, and a projecting chin.

## THE ORIGINS OF ANATOMICALLY MODERN HUMANS

Considerable debate surrounds the origins of anatomically modern humans. While we know that archaic hominins evolved into modern *Homo sapiens*, we are less certain about where and when this occurred. A number of hypotheses have been proposed to explain the emergence of our most recent ancestors, and three models have dominated the literature: (1) recent out-of-Africa, (2) assimilation, and (3) multiregional evolution. We will review these models and consider the fossil and genetic evidence for each.

## Recent Out-of-Africa Model

The recent out-of-Africa model (Figure 12.2a) proposes that modern humans first evolved in Africa between 150,000 and 200,000 years ago, then spread to Europe and Asia, replacing pre-existing archaic populations in these regions with little or no interbreeding (Stringer and Andrews 1988). It holds that Neandertals and other archaic populations were separate species that were either wiped out or driven to extinction by modern humans. This model makes several predictions: (1) that the earliest anatomically modern human fossils are found in Africa and that modern humans found in Europe and Asia are more recent; (2) that archaic and anatomically modern humans overlapped more or less briefly in areas of the Old World into which the latter moved; (3) that the archaeological record shows a sudden change in technology and behaviour during the replacement event; and (4) that genetic evidence reveals distinct differences between archaic and modern humans—that is, the genes of all modern humans in Eurasia are derived only from populations that lived in Africa 150,000 to 200,000 years ago.

## Assimilation Model

The assimilation model (Figure 12.2b), which is often grouped with the recent out-of-Africa model, proposes that modern humans first evolved in Africa and spread from there to other regions of the Old World, where they interbred with small archaic populations, genetically swamping them (Trinkaus 2005, 2007; Smith, Jankovic, and Karavanic 2005). It predicts that (1) the earliest anatomically modern human fossils are found in Africa; (2) the fossil evidence points to interbreeding between archaic and modern humans; (3) the archaeological record shows a diffusion of technological and stylistic traits between archaic and modern populations; and (4) the genetic evidence shows little or no evidence of Neandertal and other archaic genes in modern populations due to assimilation by a larger, more genetically diverse population.

## The Multiregional Evolution Model

The multiregional evolution model (Figure 12.2c) proposes that archaic humans evolved into modern *Homo sapiens* in several regions of the Old World and that extensive gene flow between regions maintained these populations as a single species (Wolpoff, Zhi, and Thorne 1984;

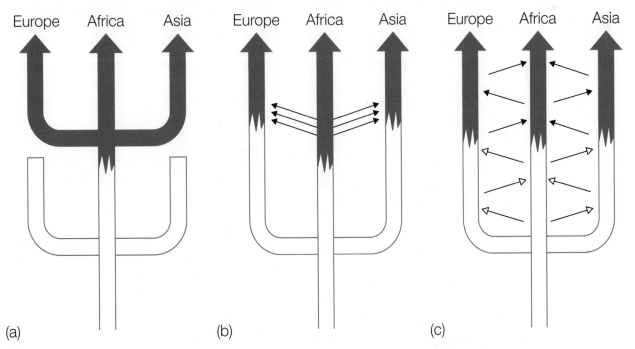

**Figure 12.2** Three models of modern human origins: (a) recent out-of-Africa; (b) assimilation; (c) multiregional evolution.

Thorne and Wolpoff 1992). At the same time, regional differences emerged because of different local selective pressures. It predicts that (1) the fossil record from Africa, Europe, and Asia shows continuity in the form of transitional fossils possessing morphological characteristics of both archaic and modern humans; (2) the archaeological record shows continuity in technology and behaviour; and (3) the genetic data show lineages emerging from several different regions of the Old World, as well as evidence of gene flow between these regions.

## What Do the Fossils Tell Us?

Fossil evidence for early modern humans has been uncovered in Africa, Europe, and Asia (Figure 12.3). There is considerable uncertainty with respect to the dating of some of these specimens, especially those from East Asia, and disagreements have surrounded the interpretation of this evidence. As you will see, some of the same fossils have been used to support more than one model of modern human origins.

With respect to the recent out-of-Africa model, the fossil evidence meets the first prediction—namely, that the earliest evidence for anatomically modern humans comes from Africa. The oldest fossils, recovered from the site of Omo Kibish and initially dated to 130,000 years ago (Butzer et al. 1969), have more recently been assigned an age of approximately 195,000 years based on argon-argon dating of the deposits in which they were found (McDougall, Brown, and Fleagle 2005). The partial remains of three individuals, including a cranium dating to 160,000 years ago, have been recovered from the site of Herto in Ethiopia. Modern features of this cranium include a high, rounded vault, a vertical forehead, and a small face (White et al. 2003). Other well-known sites that have yielded the remains of fully modern humans are Klasies River Mouth, a cave site on the coast of South Africa from which fragmentary remains dating to more than 100,000 years ago (Feathers 2002) have been recovered, and Border Cave, from which a partial cranium dating to 90,000 years ago has been found (Grün and Beaumont 2001).

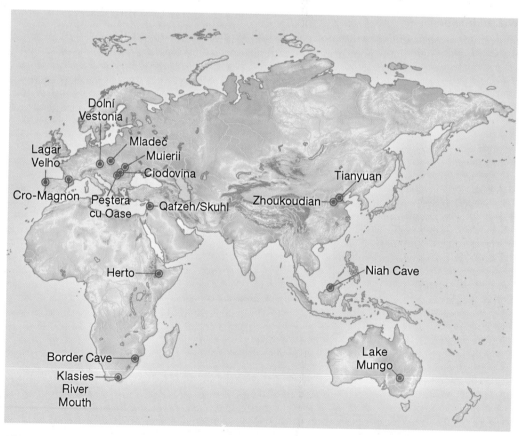

**Figure 12.3**   Sites of early anatomically modern humans.

The earliest anatomically modern humans in the Near East are currently represented by several well-known specimens. These include crania from the cave sites of Qafzeh and Skhul (Figure 12.4) in Israel, dating to between 90,000 and 110,000 years ago. In contrast, modern humans do not appear in the fossil record in Europe until after 35,000 years ago. Among the earliest sites are Peştera cu Oase (35,000 ya), Muierii Cave (30,000 ya), and Cioclovina Cave (29,000 ya) in Romania, Mladeč (31,000 ya) and Dolní Vestonice (26,000 ya) in the Czech Republic, and Cro-Magnon (28,000 ya) in southwestern France. The expansion of modern humans across Europe appears to have occurred rapidly, and the overlap between modern humans and Neandertals may have been as short as 1,000 to 2,000 years in some places (Mellars 2006).

The fossilized remains of anatomically modern humans do not appear in China until about 40,000 years ago (Shang et al. 2007). These are represented by a mandible and partial skeleton recovered from the cave site of Tianyuan and by several more recent crania (24,000 to 29,000 ya) recovered from the famous cave site of Zhoukoudian (Suzuki and Hanihara 1982). A date of 45,000 to 39,000 years ago has been assigned to modern human fossils from Niah Cave in Indonesia (Barker et al. 2007).

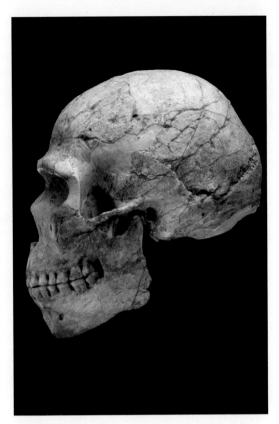

**Figure 12.4** Recovered from the site of Skhul in Israel, this 100,000-year-old cranium exhibits many modern features.

Fossil credit: Peabody Museum, Harvard University. Copyright protection notice: © 1985 David L. Brill/Brill Atlanta

Similarly, securely dated fossils from Australia indicate the presence of anatomically modern *Homo sapiens* by 40,000 years ago (see below).

The fossil evidence appears to meet the second prediction of the recent out-of-Africa model as well—namely, that archaic and anatomically modern humans overlapped briefly in areas of the Old World into which the latter moved. More specifically, a number of sites in the Near East have yielded Neandertal remains that are contemporaneous with or postdate those of modern humans, suggesting that they competed with each other for extensive periods of time.

What about the assimilation model? Several sites in Europe have yielded early modern human remains displaying a mosaic of modern features and Neandertal traits such as an occipital bun. These include specimens from Peştera cu Oase (Trinkaus et al. 2003; Rougier et al. 2007) and the Muierii and Cioclovina Caves (Soficaru, Doboş, and Trinkhaus 2006; Trinkaus 2007). One European fossil in particular, the skeleton of a four-year-old child, has gained considerable attention for its 'hybrid' status. Excavated from the site of Lagar Velho in Portugal and dating to 24,500 years ago, this skeleton exhibits the lower-limb robusticity and length typical of Neandertals, while at the same time possessing a distinct chin, dental proportions, and pubic ramus length characteristic of early modern humans (Duarte et al. 1999). The fact that this individual is a juvenile, however, makes it difficult to draw conclusions about its adult morphology, especially given that very little is known about the range of morphological variation in children during this time period. As Tattersall and Schwartz (1999, 7119) remark: "The probability must thus remain that this is simply a chunky Gravettian child."[1]

---

1. "Gravettian" refers to a phase of the Upper Paleolithic in Europe dating to 28,000 to 22,000 years ago.

What about the multiregional evolution model? The fossil record provides some support for its first prediction—namely, that continuity is evident in Africa, Europe, and Asia in the form of transitional fossils possessing morphological characteristics of both archaic and modern humans. For example, moderately heavy browridges and facial prognathism seen in the *Homo erectus* cranium from Sangiran are also found in some of the early modern human specimens recovered from Australia (Wolpoff et al. 1984; Thorne and Wolpoff 1992). Continuity is also evident in the fossil record from China, suggesting a gradual transition from *Homo erectus* to modern *Homo sapiens* (Wu 2004).

## What Does the Genetic Evidence Tell Us?

The first genetic studies to investigate modern human origins involved the use of mitochondrial DNA (mtDNA) derived from living populations. As you will recall from Chapter 3, mtDNA is inherited only from females, while nDNA comes from both mother and father. In 1987 a group of researchers from Berkeley attracted international attention when they published genetic data supporting an exclusively African origin for modern *Homo sapiens*. The team, led by Rebecca Cann (Cann, Stoneking, and Wilson 1987), took mtDNA samples from 147 modern women representing five different ethnic groups from Africa, Asia, Europe, Australia, and New Guinea. Comparisons of these samples revealed little genetic variation, indicating that these women shared a common ancestor relatively recently. Their analysis also revealed that the mtDNA of the African women exhibited the greatest amount of variation (Figure 12.5), as would be expected if they had more time to diverge or accumulate genetic differences; thus, they represented the oldest population of anatomically modern humans. The researchers concluded from these findings that the last common ancestor of all modern humans, dubbed "mitochondrial Eve," originated in Africa sometime between 90,000 and 180,000 years ago.[2]

Underlying the use of mtDNA from living humans to calculate the date at which anatomically modern humans emerged are these four assumptions: (1) the genetic variation measured in modern samples represents the total amount of variation derived from the common ancestor; (2) the rate of mutation has

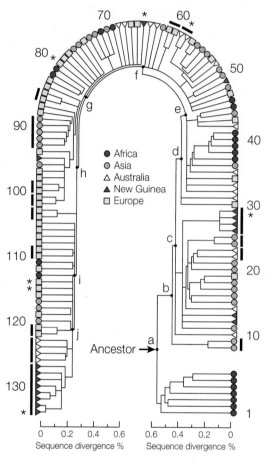

**Figure 12.5** Mitochondrial DNA data collected from 147 women were used to generate this tree. African women showed the greatest genetic diversity, suggesting that Africa was the birthplace of modern humans.

2. This is a widely used but misleading term. It does not mean that she was the mother of all who came after her, but simply the last common ancestor whose mitochondrial DNA is present in all living humans. Thus, while she tells us something about our common mitochondrial ancestor, she tells us nothing about the rest of our genome.

been constant; (3) random mating has occurred; and (4) the particular mitochondrial DNA sequence used in the analysis is selectively neutral. Critics of the Berkeley study were quick to point out flaws in the evidence presented by Cann and her colleagues, including errors in the way in which they analyzed their data and their assumption that the rate of mutation of mtDNA was constant. Their detractors claimed that additional analyses of the same data could result in many different genetic trees, not all of which point to an African origin for modern humans. The low genetic variability exhibited by the mtDNA could, they argued, be equally consistent with a much older origin for modern humans if, in fact, there was sufficient movement of people and therefore genes between populations to maintain low genetic diversity (recall from Chapter 4 that gene flow between two populations reduces the amount of variability between those populations, thereby making them more similar to each other). As well, Africans may possess the greatest amount of genetic diversity simply by virtue of having been the largest population for most of human prehistory and therefore having experienced less genetic drift (Relethford and Jorde 1999). Thus the data is compatible with both the recent out-of-Africa and multiregional evolution models.

More recent studies of Y chromosome DNA have provided additional support for an African origin for modern humans. As noted in Chapter 3, this chromosome does not undergo recombination with the X chromosome except at its tip, and its DNA therefore passes from father to son largely unchanged. Research by geneticist Michael Hammer and colleagues on a small section of DNA on the Y chromosome called Yap (for "Y Alu insertional polymorphism") revealed the presence of five Yap haplotypes, or clusters of genes, in 60 populations worldwide, with African populations showing greater haplotype diversity compared to those from other regions (Hammer et al. 1997). Further research revealed an African root for the Y-DNA tree (Hammer et al. 1998).

Analyses of other regions of our genome have provided further confirmation of a modern human lineage arising in Africa. At the same time, however, they have revealed lineages emerging in Asia as well, suggesting admixture between archaic and modern populations. Harris and Hey's (1999) study of genes found on the X chromosome, for instance, yielded evidence of two separate founding populations emerging some 200,000 years ago, one African and the other non-African. Similarly, an analysis of the beta-globin gene, one of the hemoglobin genes, has revealed evidence for an Asian lineage dating back more than 200,000 years (Harding et al. 1997). Subsequent studies of X-linked and autosomal DNA regions have provided additional support for admixture between anatomically modern humans and archaic populations of Eurasia (Garrigan et al. 2005; Plagnol and Wall 2006), thus refuting the recent out-of-Africa model.

As geneticist Alan Templeton (2005) points out, the use of only one genetic marker tells us only about the last common ancestor for that particular marker. In order to obtain a more complete picture of our evolutionary history, we therefore need to examine multiple loci. This is exemplified in Templeton's study of 25 DNA regions: mtDNA, Y chromosome DNA, 11 X-linked markers, and 12 autosomal markers. This analysis has revealed evidence for several major migrations out of Africa, the most recent of them around 100,000 years ago.

Geneticists have also examined DNA sequences in fossil *Homo sapiens*. mtDNA has been extracted from the remains of seven late Upper Paleolithic *Homo sapiens* fossils: two from southern Italy (Caramelli et al. 2003), two from the Czech Republic, and three from France (Serre et al. 2004). All exhibited sequences that are distinct from those derived from Neandertal samples, suggesting that Neandertals contributed few if any of their genes to the modern European gene pool. As Relethford (2001a) points out, however, the absence of Neandertal mtDNA in modern Europeans does not necessarily mean complete replacement without interbreeding (Relethford 2001a), as predicted by the recent out-of-Africa model. Furthermore, if there was considerable gene flow between geographic regions over time, as predicted by the multiregional evolution model, we may not *expect* to find evidence of regional affinities in mtDNA (Relethford 2001b). As you learned in Chapter 11, the Neandertal genome data (Green et al. 2010) have revealed the presence of Neandertal genes in modern humans, pointing to local (regional) contributions to later human evolution outside of Africa. Thus the genetic evidence for modern human origins is not inconsistent with the multiregional evolution or assimilation models.

The low level of genetic diversity in modern humans has long been interpreted as resulting from a **population bottleneck**. Various hypotheses have been proposed to explain the occurrence of this bottleneck. Stanley Ambrose, for instance, has posited that massive environmental change following the cataclysmic eruption of the Toba volcano on the island of Sumatra approximately 70,000 years ago reduced the world's population to about 10,000 individuals. A subsequent decline in global temperatures then forced survivors of this disaster to seek refuge in tropical areas of Africa, where they rapidly differentiated into the diverse populations that we see today (Ambrose 1998).

Premo and Hublin (2009) have challenged the view that low genetic diversity in modern humans resulted from a recent bottleneck. Citing genetic evidence indicating that the **effective population size** of the human lineage has been low for more than 500,000 years, they hypothesize that a primitive form of what they term "culturally mediated migration" may have acted to maintain low genetic diversity in modern humans, Neandertals, and our last common ancestor. More specifically, gene flow between different groups of individuals may have been constrained by cultural barriers to migration thereby mimicking the effect—at the genetic level—of a population bottleneck.

# THE EMERGENCE OF MODERN HUMAN BEHAVIOUR

The transition from the Middle to the Upper Paleolithic in Europe around 40,000 to 35,000 years ago is commonly portrayed as characterized by significant cultural and behavioural innovations in the form of more sophisticated tool technologies, changes in subsistence practices, and greater expressions of symbolic and ritual behaviour. These innovations have been interpreted by some (e.g., Klein 1995, 2000) as representing a "cultural revolution." The notion of a sudden emergence of modern human behaviour associated with the appearance of anatomically modern humans has been challenged, however, and it is becoming increasingly apparent that **behavioural modernity** emerged in Africa and Eurasia long before modern humans first appeared in Europe (McBrearty and Brooks 2000). As you learned in the previous chapter, aspects of behavioural modernity such as intentional burial and artistic expression were evident among Neandertals as well.

## Technology and Subsistence

Lithic assemblages recovered from **Middle Stone Age** sites in Africa and the Near East indicate that the earliest anatomically modern humans continued to make tools using the Levallois technique. At the same time, they began to make and use more sophisticated implements in the form of **blade tools** made by striking multiple blades from a single prepared core using a hard or soft hammer. These blades were then fashioned into a variety of different tools (Figure 12.6), including points hafted onto wooden shafts to form **composite tools**. Considerable regional variation is also evident in these assemblages.

Early modern humans—and, as we noted in the previous chapter, late Neandertals as well—also made tools from materials other than stone, including needles of bone and antler, presumably for sewing clothes from hides, and bone points and harpoons, such as those recovered from the Middle Stone Age site of Blombos Cave in South Africa, dating to 80,000 years ago (Henshilwood et al. 2001) and the site of Katanda in the Republic of Congo, also dating

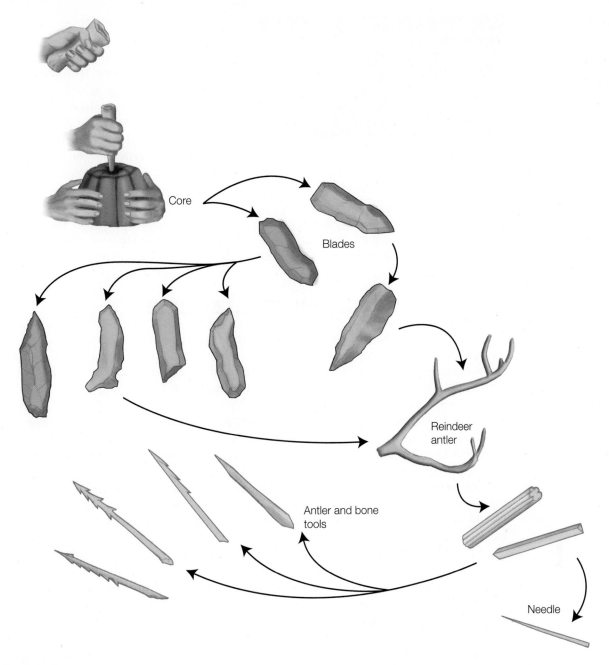

**Figure 12.6** Blades were fashioned into a variety of stone tools, some of which were used to make tools from other materials.

Peter Bull Art Studio. From *The Human Past: World Prehistory & the Development of Human Societies*, ed. Chris Scarre, Thames & Hudson, London and New York, 2005. Reprinted by permission.

to 80,000 years ago (Feathers and Migliorini 2001). Early *Homo sapiens* also made elaborate items of personal adornment, including jewellery manufactured from exotic materials that would have originated hundreds or thousands of kilometres away, pointing to long-distance exchange networks. Blombos Cave, for example, has yielded a remarkable collection of pierced shells (Henshilwood et al. 2004). Other forms of creative expression uncovered at Middle Stone Age sites include pieces of incised ochre from 70,000-year-old deposits at Blombos Cave (Figure 12.7) (Henshilwood et al. 2002) and 82,000-year-old shell beads covered in red ochre from the site of Grotte des Pigeons in Morocco (Bouzouggar et al. 2007).

**Figure 12.7**   The meaning of the incisions on this piece of ochre from Blombos Cave is unknown, but it may represent a primitive calendar.

Courtesy of the Blombos Cave Project.

Archaeological evidence recovered from Middle Stone Age sites in South Africa points to a broad subsistence base that included terrestrial herbivores such as antelope and zebras as well as, at some coastal sites, marine resources such as shellfish and tortoises. At Klasies River Mouth, for instance, modern humans appear to have relied heavily on the eland antelope, but they also consumed other food resources such as fish and shellfish. Fish remains have also been recovered from Katanda (Yellen et al. 1995) and Blombos Cave. In addition, the presence of grindstones at some Middle Stone Age sites suggests the processing of plant foods (McBrearty and Brooks 2000).

## LATER STONE AGE/UPPER PALEOLITHIC

**Later Stone Age**

the period of time spanning 40,000 to 10,000 years ago in Africa

**microliths**

small stone tools made from blades or parts of blades

**burin**

a type of stone tool used to shape bone, wood, antler, and ivory into other tools

The transition from the Middle to the **Later Stone Age** in Africa around 40,000 years ago was associated with the appearance of a greater number and variety of blade tools, including **microliths** and **burins**, and more sophisticated flaking techniques. The production and use of tools made from materials other than stone also increased.

In Europe, the Upper Paleolithic is typically divided into four main cultural periods associated with anatomically modern humans: (1) Aurignacian, (2) Gravettian, (3) Solutrean, and (4) Magdalenian. The Aurignacian (40,000 to 28,000 ya) is characterized by a variety of blade, bone, and antler tools as well as figurines. The Gravettian (28,000 to 22,000 ya) is marked by more elaborate blade technology and the production of figurines and cave paintings (see below). Tool manufacturing techniques reached a pinnacle in the Solutrean period (22,000 to 18,000 ya), best known for its exquisite leaf-shaped Solutrean blades (Figure 12.8). Finally, the Magdalenian period (18,000 to 10,000 ya) was dominated by elaborately worked tools of bone, antler, and ivory.

As noted earlier, evidence for the use of marine resources has been uncovered at a number of Middle Stone Age coastal sites. Greater reliance on marine foods is evident in the Later Stone Age, and middle to late Upper Paleolithic populations in Europe also relied on a broad spectrum of resources, which included fish and waterfowl, as indicated by faunal evidence and stable isotope analysis (Richards et al. 2001, 2005). These populations also utilized a variety of strategies to obtain their food. Finely made harpoons were used to catch fish, and large game animals were driven into bogs or over cliffs where they could be easily dispatched. Successful procurement of these animals was facilitated by specialized hunting equipment such as **atlatls**. These implements extended the arm of the thrower, making it possible to throw spears faster and farther.

**atlatl**

a device fashioned from bone, antler or wood which increases the mechanical advantage of the arm, allowing a hunter to propel a spear for much greater distances with great accuracy

Archaeological evidence for symbolic and ritual behaviour in the Later Stone Age and later Upper Paleolithic is much more plentiful than in earlier times. Among the many cultural achievements during this period was cave painting. Cave art sites have been found in Europe, Africa, and Australia, and among the most famous of these are Lascaux and Chauvet in France and Altamira in Spain. Dating to more than 30,000 years ago, the cave site of Chauvet contains more than 300 paintings, many of them depicting large game animals. So spectacular are some of these sites that increasing numbers of tourists have necessitated the construction of "replica" caves in order to preserve the original paintings from the damaging effects of humidity from human breath. Natural pigments such as red ochre and manganese were used to create the paintings, and experiments have demonstrated that some of these pigments may have been spit, blown, or stencilled onto the wall by the

**Figure 12.8** Exquisitely made Solutrean points such as these reproductions were sometimes hafted onto shafts.

Courtesy of Lithic Casting Lab

artists rather than painted on with a brush (Lorblanchet 1991). The fact that many of these paintings are located at great heights or in deep recesses of caves, necessitating the use of torches and some form of ladder to create them, suggests that they were meant to be seen by only a small number of people.

Anthropologists have long pondered the significance of cave art. Some have suggested that the paintings had magical significance and were created to protect hunters, ensure a successful hunt, or increase the fertility of large game animals and thereby ensure a plentiful supply of food. These suggestions are based on depictions in many of the paintings of wounded, trapped, pregnant, or mating animals. Others have suggested that they symbolize male and female forces in nature. Researchers have also speculated that some of the symbols in these paintings may represent **entoptic** images associated with altered states of consciousness such as trances (Lewis-Williams and Dowson 1988).

http://www.culture.gouv.fr/culture/arcnat/chauvet/en

**Figure 12.9** Venus figurines, such as the famous Venus of Willendorf, varied regionally and likely carried a variety of meanings.

© Ali Meyer/Corbis

**entoptic**
images that arise from within the eye during altered states of consciousness

BOX 12.1    **FOCUS ON... Figuratively Speaking**

In 1990 a remarkable discovery came to light when a local artist stumbled upon five ivory figurines on display in a Montreal antique store. Suspecting that they might be of scientific interest, he bought the set and took them to McGill University for evaluation. There they were examined by archaeologist Michael Bisson, who declared them to be authentic Upper Paleolithic figurines (Bisson and Bolduc 1994). This assessment was confirmed by New York University anthropologist Randall White, a leading expert in Paleolithic art, who determined that the figurines had come from the Grimaldi caves in Italy. Further investigation revealed that they had been excavated in the 1880s by amateur archaeologist and antiquities dealer Louis Jullien, who immigrated to Canada between 1895 and 1900, bringing the valuable artifacts with him. Here the story takes an interesting twist, as reports surfaced that a total of eight figurines, including the five that ended up in the antique store, had been excavated by Jullien, who not only kept them a secret for years, but was also vague about their precise provenience. In the years that followed, the significance of his treasures was overshadowed by claims that the specimens were forgeries, and he spent the remainder of his life working in Montreal as a chemist. After his death in 1928, the figurines were inherited by family members and were ultimately sold to the antique store owner. All seven were later transferred to the Musée des Antiquités Nationales in France, where they remain today.

Since the discovery of the first Upper Paleolithic figurine in the 1860s at the site of Laugerie-Basse in the Dordogne region of France, approximately 200 have been found to date, most of them in Central Europe and Russia from archaeological sites dating between 11,000 and 35,000 years ago. Made of stone, bone, ivory, or clay, and in some cases bearing the marks of the stone tools used to produce them, they range in size from about 5 to 25 cm and exhibit considerable stylistic variation, some of them unadorned and others displaying engravings that appear to represent clothing or jewellery. A large number of them are female; others lack anatomical detail. Attention has focused largely on the female representations with exaggerated sexual characteristics. Commonly referred to as Venus figurines, their significance has been debated for decades, with interpretations ranging from fertility figures to self-portraits to symbols of female power and status to Upper Paleolithic pornography (Rice 1981; McDermott 1996). In all likelihood, however, these specimens had multiple functions. Though questions remain regarding who made these figurines and why, one thing is for certain: they will continue to fascinate researchers well into the future.

Later Upper Palaeolithic people were also famous for their figurines made in various shapes and sizes (Box 12.1). The best-known figurines depict the female body with exaggerated sexual characteristics (Figure 12.9). The long-standing assumption that they were made by men for men has been challenged (Nelson 1990).

Burials associated with later Upper Paleolithic peoples were more elaborate than those of Neandertals and early modern humans, and a diversity of burial practices with respect to the position and treatment of the body (e.g., cremation and the use of red ochre), and the inclusion of grave goods with the body, have been documented. The most remarkable example comes from the 24,000-year-old site of Sungir in Russia, where archaeologists have uncovered the remains of three skeletons, including two children, whose bodies had been placed head to head in a trench and covered with red ochre and thousands of ivory beads and other artifacts (Formicola and Buzhilova 2004).

# IN SEARCH OF NEW LANDS

## Colonization of Australia

The remarkable voyage of modern humans culminated in their occupation of Australia and the Americas. The timing of the initial occupation of Australia has been the subject of controversy, with some archaeologists arguing for a date of more than 60,000 years ago (Thorne et al. 1999), and others arguing for a more recent date of no more than about 40,000 years ago (O'Connell and Allen 1998). Much of the controversy relates to the limitations of radiocarbon dating. Recall from Chapter 7 that carbon-14 dating cannot be used reliably to date organic materials more than 40,000 to 45,000 years old. In addition, erroneous dates can be obtained if samples are contaminated with carbon from other sources. Concern has also been expressed about the relationship between artifacts found at some of these "early" sites and the deposits with which they were dated. In recent years, improved sample preparation techniques have alleviated some of the problems with sample contamination, and many of the archaeological sites initially dated decades ago have been redated using newly developed techniques such as optically stimulated luminescence (OSL), ultrafiltration AMS, and U-series dating. Together this evidence points to an initial occupation of Australia sometime between 40,000 and 45,000 years ago (O'Connell and Allen 2004), though dates derived from some sites

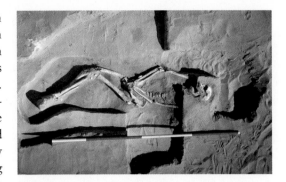

**Figure 12.10** A cremation burial and a fully articulated skeleton dubbed "Mungo Man," seen here, were excavated from the site of Lake Mungo.

Published by permission of Willandra Indigenous Elders, © J.M.Bowler.

suggest a somewhat earlier occupation (Turney et al. 2001). The oldest human remains recovered from Australia so far consist of a 40,000-year-old skeleton (Figure 12.10) and a cremation burial excavated from the site of Lake Mungo (Bowler et al. 2003). Thus modern humans appear to have reached Australia before Europe!

To appreciate the significance of these dates, it is important to recognize that Australia has been separated from southeast Asia for millions of years by a significant stretch of water. As such, colonization would have required the use of some form of watercraft and the ability to navigate (O'Connell and Allen 1998, 133, 143). This technological innovation would also have been required to colonize the Pacific Islands, which comprise Melanesia, Micronesia, and Polynesia. Most of these islands were occupied only within the last 5,000 years or so.

## Coming to America

The occupation of North and South America has also been the subject of considerable debate, much of it focusing on the date of arrival of the first migrants, and the number and location of their entry routes. In the 1920s, clues to the arrival of the first occupants of North America came in the form of a technology known as fluted projectile points[3] (Figure 12.11) found in association with the remains of extinct bison at the site of Folsom, New Mexico. Several years later, another type of fluted point was found in association with mammoth bones at a site near Clovis, New Mexico. Subsequent dating of these sites revealed that the Clovis people—**Paleo-Indians**, as we now call them—were present in North America by 12,500 years ago. In the decades that followed, however, additional archaeological sites have provided compelling evidence for an even earlier "pre-Clovis" occupation. These sites include Meadowcroft Rockshelter in Pennsylvania, which may have been occupied more than 19,000 years ago (Adovasio et al. 1998). Other possible candidates include

**Figure 12.11** Paleo-Indians used fluted projectile points to hunt large game animals.

Archaeological Research Center, South Dakota State Historical Society.

**Paleo-Indians**
the name given to the first occupants of North and South America

---

3. Archaeologists have suggested that the removal of a flake from the face of a projectile point to create a groove or 'flute' may have been done to facilitate hafting of a point onto a piece of wood.

Cactus Hill in Virginia, dated between 15,000 and 18,000 years ago (Wagner and McAvoy 2004); the Topper site in South Carolina, dated between 15,000 and 16,000 years ago (Goodyear 2005); Page-Ladson in Florida, dated to just over 14,000 BP (Dunbar and Hemmings 2004); and Paisley Caves in Oregon, which has yielded 14,000-year-old human coprolites (Gilbert et al. 2008). Possible pre-Clovis sites have also been uncovered in South America. Among the most widely accepted is Monte Verde in south-central Chile. While the dates obtained from this site point to an occupation of nearly 15,000 years ago (Dillehay 2000), its location at the southern tip of South America suggests that humans entered North America thousands of years earlier.

Where did these individuals come from, and how did they get to North and South America? Most archaeologists believe that the ancestors of the Clovis people came from Asia, and a number of early sites, including the Yana Rhinoceros Horn site, dating to 30,000 years ago (Pitulko et al. 2004), have been found in Siberia. From here these migrants crossed into North America via a land bridge that would have been exposed during the last glacial

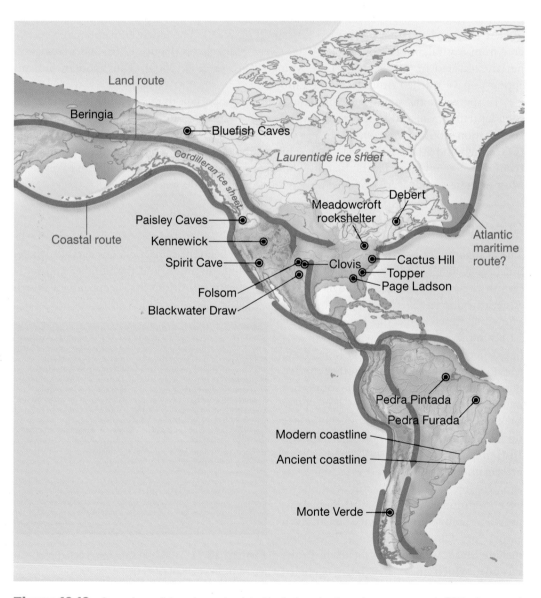

**Figure 12.12** Several possible entry routes into North America have been proposed. Of the two most frequently proposed routes, an ice-free corridor between the Cordilleran and Laurentide ice sheets, and a western coastal route, the latter is now seen as the most likely.

period, when sea levels were low.[4] Known as the Bering land bridge, or **Beringia**, it would have been a migration route not only for humans but also for herds of large game animals on which these humans depended for food. Hints of the early occupation of eastern Beringia come from the site of Swan Point in Alaska, which has yielded 14,000-year-old stone tools, and the site of Bluefish Caves in Yukon, from which tools dating to nearly 25,000 years ago have been recovered (Cinq-Mars and Morlan 1999). Once in North America, Paleo-Indians moved southward, reaching South America within a relatively short time.

Archaeologists have long believed that the earliest migrants to the Americas passed through an "ice-free corridor" between the Laurentian and Cordilleran ice sheets that covered North America during the last glacial period (Figure 12.12).[5] This belief has been challenged, however, based on environmental evidence indicating that this route would have been inaccessible between 30,000 and 11,500 years ago (Mandryk et al. 2001). An alternative route along the Pacific coast (Figure 12.12), which would have been open to humans by 15,000 years ago, is now becoming increasingly likely (Goebel, Waters, and O'Rourke 2008). Such a route implies the use of boats. Unfortunately, one of the major challenges to identifying an entry route is the fact that sites that may once have been located on Beringia or on the Pacific coast are now submerged under hundreds of metres of water.

Our knowledge of the biology of the earliest occupants of North and South America comes from only a small number of skeletons, all of them anatomically modern humans. These include the infracranial skeleton of a male found at the site of Gore Creek in Kamloops, B.C., and dating to 8250 BP (Cybulski et al. 1981), and some 8,000 to 9,000 year old teeth found at the site of Namu on the B.C. coast (Carlson and Dalla Bona 1996). The most significant find in recent years is the nearly complete skeleton of a middle-aged male discovered in 1996 on the banks of the Columbia River near the town of Kennewick in Washington. Commonly referred to as Kennewick Man (Figures 12.13 and 12.14), this

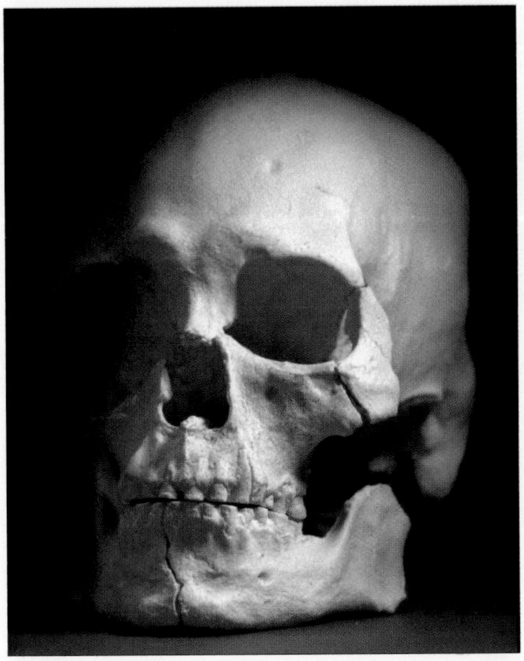

**Beringia**

a land bridge that connected Siberia and Alaska during the last glacial period

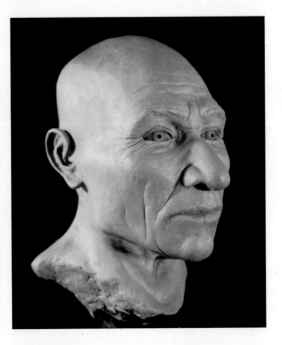

**Figure 12.13**  Kennewick Man's skull.

AP Photo/Elaine Thompson.

**Figure 12.14**  A plaster cast of Kennewick Man's skull was used to make this facial reconstruction.

Emmanuel Laurent/Eurelios/Science Photo Library

4. First Nations peoples today have their own stories about how they came to occupy North and South America.

5. This corridor, which extended from Yukon through Alberta and southern Saskatchewan, was created when the two ice sheets began to retreat after about 14,000 years ago.

9,300-year-old skeleton gained considerable attention because of its lack of resemblance to modern First Nations. In fact, initial assessments highlighted its Caucasian features (Chatters 2001), and much discussion has ensued over its relationship to modern indigenous populations. Subsequent analyses have revealed similarities between Kennewick Man and populations from southern Asia and Japan (Powell and Rose 1999), and studies of other

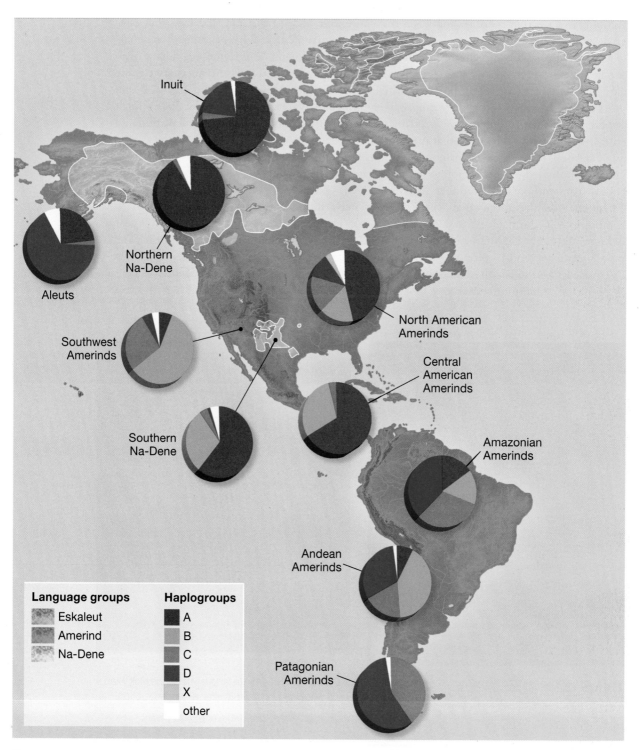

**Figure 12.15**   Map showing the distribution of Native American mtDNA haplogroups.

Theodore Schurr, (2000). Mitochondrial DNA and the peopling of the New World, *American Scientist* Vol. 88: 246. Reprinted with permission.

early modern skeletons from North America have revealed morphological features not seen in modern indigenous populations. Thus there are no grounds to reject Kennewick as being ancestral to modern First Nations.[6]

http://www.mnh.si.edu/arctic/html/kennewick_man.html

Another contentious issue concerning the occupation of the Americas is the number of migrations that occurred. In the 1980s, Greenberg and colleagues (1986) argued for three separate migrations based on linguistic, dental, and genetic evidence, the first of them giving rise to Amerindian populations, the second one to the Inuit and Aleut, and the third one to Na-Dene–speaking groups of northwestern North America and parts of the American Southwest. Recent analyses of mitochondrial DNA have revealed the presence of four main haplogroups: A, B, C, and D, into which the majority of First Nations fall (Figure 12.15; Schurr 2004).[7] These data point to an initial migration into North America between 14,000 and 20,000 years ago, thus supporting a pre-Clovis occupation. This was later followed by a dispersal of populations ancestral to modern-day Inuit, Aleuts, and Na-Dene (Schurr 2004).

# SUMMARY

Many anthropologists now agree that anatomically modern humans first evolved in Africa and dispersed from there to other regions of the Old World, ultimately reaching Australia and North and South America. Considerable disagreement remains, however, over the degree to which interbreeding occurred, if at all, between these humans and the archaic populations they came into contact with, and the various models of modern human origins continue to be modified as new data accumulate. As you have learned in this chapter, the fossil and genetic evidence can be interpreted in a number of different ways, and each has been used to support more than one model. Whatever the case, the expansion of modern humans occurred rapidly, possibly precipitated by a population expansion in Africa. Modern human behaviour appears to have emerged in Africa long before modern humans made their appearance in Europe. To date, however, the selective advantage of anatomically modern humans remains unclear.

# CORE REVIEW

**In what ways did the earliest modern humans differ anatomically from archaic hominins?**

The earliest anatomically modern humans possessed a higher, more rounded cranium, an average cranial capacity of about 1500 cc, a more vertically oriented forehead with relatively small browridges, a smaller and flatter face, a well-developed chin, and smaller teeth compared to archaic hominins. They also had a more lightly built infracranial skeleton with straighter, less robust limb bones than earlier hominins, and their body proportions most closely resembled those of modern-day populations living in Africa.

---

6. This skeleton has been the focus of a major legal battle between First Nations groups demanding repatriation under the Native American Grave Protection and Repatriation Act (NAGPRA) on the basis of affiliation, and biological anthropologists wanting to study these remains.

7. A fifth haplogroup, X, has also been identified. It is restricted almost exclusively to North America.

## What models have been proposed to explain the origins of anatomically modern humans?

The recent out-of-Africa model proposes that modern humans evolved from earlier archaic populations in Africa sometime between 150,000 and 200,000 years ago, then spread to Europe and Asia, replacing pre-existing archaic populations in these regions with little or no interbreeding. The assimilation model proposes that modern humans first evolved in Africa and spread from there to other parts of the Old World, where they interbred with local archaic populations, genetically swamping them. The multiregional evolution model proposes that archaic humans evolved into modern *Homo sapiens* in several regions of the Old World, with extensive gene flow between regions maintaining these populations as a single species.

## What does the fossil and genetic evidence tell us about modern human origins?

Most paleoanthropologists now believe that anatomically modern humans emerged in Africa and dispersed from there to other regions of the Old World. The earliest securely dated anatomically modern human fossils date to 160,000 years ago and come from Africa, pointing to this continent as the homeland of modern *Homo sapiens*. According to the fossil evidence, modern humans likely dispersed from Africa sometime after 60,000 years ago and expanded into Europe and Asia, reaching central and western Europe by 35,000 years ago, and China, southeastern Asia, and Australia by 40,000 years ago. Mitochondrial and Y chromosome DNA data indicate that modern humans evolved in Africa, and Neandertal genome data indicate the presence of Neandertal genes in modern humans, pointing to local (regional) contributions to later human evolution outside of Africa.

## When did behavioural modernity emerge and what characterized this transition?

Modern human behaviour appears to have emerged in Africa during the Middle Stone Age period, though aspects of behavioural modernity were also evident in Neandertals. The earliest anatomically modern humans made and used blades, some of which were used to make composite tools. They also made tools from bone and antler, including needles and harpoons, as well as items of art and personal adornment. They relied on a broad subsistence base that included terrestrial herbivores, marine resources, and plants. Later Stone Age and Upper Paleolithic peoples made a greater number and variety of blade tools using more sophisticated flaking techniques, as well as elaborately fashioned tools of bone, antler, and ivory. They relied on a broad spectrum of resources that included fish and waterfowl, and they utilized more complex hunting strategies and specialized hunting equipment. They also produced remarkable works of art, including cave paintings and figurines, and conducted more elaborate burials than their predecessors.

## When did the earliest occupants of Australia and the Americas arrive, where did they come from, and how did they get there?

Archaeological evidence points to an initial occupation of Australia occurring sometime between 40,000 and 45,000 years ago. Colonization of this continent would have required the use of some form of watercraft. Most archaeologists today believe that North and South America were first occupied approximately 13,000 years ago by Clovis people—whom we now refer to as Paleo-Indians—though evidence pointing to an earlier pre-Clovis occupation of at least 15,000 years ago is accumulating. The earliest occupants of the Americas were big game hunters who migrated from northeastern

**PART THREE** Ancient Currents

Siberia into North America via the Bering Land Bridge. Once in North America, they spread southward by one of two routes: through an interior ice-free corridor between the Laurentian and Cordilleran ice sheets that covered the continent during the last glacial period; and/or along the Pacific coast. By 11,000 years ago, these humans had reached the tip of South America, indicating rapid dispersal by highly mobile groups of people.

# CRITICAL THINKING QUESTIONS

1. Early modern humans spent a considerable amount of time on the move. What might have prompted them to disperse through much of the Old World, and what factors might have facilitated these migrations?
2. We often use the term "ritual" to describe human behaviours for which the significance is unclear to us. What does this term imply? Are there other terms that might be more appropriate?

# GROUP DISCUSSION QUESTIONS

1. What role did language play in modern human origins? Is the origin of modern humans associated with the emergence of complex language (i.e., was there a substantive change in language capabilities with the emergence of modern humans?), or was the capacity for complex language already present in premodern hominins?
2. How would you define modern behaviour? What cultural attributes would you include on your list? Based on the archaeological evidence from Africa and Europe, at what point do you think *Homo sapiens* reached this stage?

# RESOURCES AND READINGS

- M.H. Crawford, *The Origins of Native Americans: Evidence from Anthropological Genetics* (Cambridge: Cambridge University Press. 2001).
- D. Kaufman, *Archaeological Perspectives on the Origins of Modern Humans: A View from the Levant* (Oxford: Bergin and Garvey, 1999).
- R.G. Klein, *The Dawn of Human Culture* (New York: Wiley, 2002).
- P. Mellars, K. Boyle, O. Bar-Yosef, and C. Stringer, eds., *Rethinking the Human Revolution: New Behavioural and Biological Perspectives on the Origin and Dispersal of Modern Humans*. McDonald Institute Monographs (Cambridge: McDonald Institute for Archaeological Research, 2007).
- J.H. Relethford, *Genetics and the Search for Modern Human Origins* (New York: Wiley-Liss, 2001).
- P.R. Willoughby, *The Evolution of Modern Humans in Africa: A Comprehensive Guide* (African Archaeology Series) (Lanham: AltaMira, 2006).

# 13 Contemplating Modern Human Diversity

## OVERVIEW

One of the most divisive and harmful enterprises undertaken in the name of human biology has been the characterization and explanation of geographic variation within humankind. Beginning with the concept of race,[1] and continuing to supposedly less baggage-laden notions such as "ethnicity" or "ancestry," interpretations of phenotypic (and later genotypic) variation within and between populations have historically diminished human social and political landscapes. At the same time, scientific debates regarding human classification and its meaning have enriched our appreciation for the biocultural diversity of our species and its adaptive histories. Many fields of study in human biology have entered an era of comparative objectivity with respect to human difference; but others—including Western biomedicine—continue to struggle to integrate a nonracial/ethnic model of human population variation into their research domains.

## CORE CONCEPTS

- race, typology, cline, polytypism, polymorphism, heritability, biomedicine, intelligence, eugenics

## CORE QUESTIONS

- What role did 19th-century ideas of race play in the history of European colonial expansion?

- What is the distinction between polytypic and polymorphic variation?

- What is a cline? Why are clines useful in explaining human geographic variation?

- How has genomics modified our understanding of human population variation?

- In what way(s) is "race" problematic for biomedicine?

---

1. The term "race" in the context of human biological variation has, in the latter half of the 20th century, become extremely problematic. Here we use the term to reflect its (erroneous) historical referent as a discrete population of humans whose members share particular morphological features to the exclusion of other such populations.

# PROLOGUE: WE ARE ALL HUMAN

**adaptability**

a capacity to maintain function in response to short- or long-term ecological challenges by means of growth and development, physiology, technology, and/or behaviour

**race**

in general biology, a category often considered synonymous with "subspecies," into which individuals can be placed based on distinctive physiological, morphological, and/or ecological features; it is now generally held that the complexity of human biobehavioural variation cannot be usefully understood in terms of race

**heritability**

a measure, varying from 0 to 1, of the degree to which the phenotypic variance of a trait within a population can be attributed to the genetic variance within that population; heritability is not a measure of the degree to which a trait may be attributed to an individual's genetic make-up

In previous chapters we explored the nature and importance of "differences." We discussed, for example, how different evolutionary mechanisms produce variation within and between populations (Chapters 3 and 4) and how different behavioural, ecological, and reproductive strategies are employed by males and females within a primate species, or by one species of primate in competition with another (Chapters 5 and 6). We also looked at how paleoanthropologists identify different kinds of fossil hominins and remnants of their behaviour (Chapters 9 to 11). As we introduce this text's final section examining modern population biology, we want to emphasize one overarching reality—while modern humans are wonderfully diverse both biologically and culturally, we remain nonetheless a single species. In many ways our similarities transcend our differences, and this is certainly true of our biology, owing to the comparatively slow pace of biological evolution and our relatively recent origin as *Homo sapiens*. Thus it is a sad and unfortunate historical fact that it has been the latter—an emphasis on differences, both biological and cultural—that has defined human social relations throughout recent history.

Human variation is as fascinating as it is complex; no other organism has adapted to such a wide variety of habitats, aided by an artful melding of biology, culture, and technology. In the following chapters we explore and exemplify some of the myriad ways in which our capacity for adaptation and **adaptability** has become manifest within our species as a whole, within individual geographically circumscribed populations, and within distinct ethnic and cultural entities. As we will learn, many of these biological features set us apart and distinguish us as members of a particular instance of humankind—they are bone fide differences. But it is our ability as a species to acquire, develop, and reveal these differences while remaining at the same time alike in our fundamental biology that is something not to lose sight of—at the end of the day, it is what makes us all human. In the present chapter we delve into two central themes: (1) How do we understand past and present approaches to characterizing human diversity, in particular as they embrace or critique the concept of "**race**"? And (2), how do we interpret methods that shape our understanding of genotype, phenotype, and identity, including the especially problematic topic of the **heritability** of intelligence?

## RACE, PLACE, AND FACE

**folk taxonomy**

an informal albeit consensual classification of the world used by ordinary people in everyday life

Humans in all places and in all times classify the natural world—a process evident in all narrative traditions studied to date, written or oral. Classification is a necessary act of ordering information into groups of objects that do us good or bring us harm, of thinking about time, space, community, identity, and 'self and other'. It is a necessary part of understanding the past and predicting the future (Ghiselin and Landa 2005). Such classifications, founded on experience and tradition and used in everyday life, constitute **folk taxonomies**. Though similarities exist between folk and scientific classifications (ibid.), what sets the latter apart is the degree to which they are codified, rule-bound, hierarchically complex, and—in biology—evolutionary. Scientific classifications develop complexity as a consequence of variation in the natural world (see Chapter 4). Humans evince a high degree of biological variation (as we explore in the following chapters); how then, should we approach a biological classification of humanity?

It is next to impossible to frame a discussion of human population variation without referring to geography—a fact apparent since the first modern classification of people into discrete categories was proposed by Linnaeus (Marks 2007; see also Chapter 2). The important question is how geography arbitrates human diversity: Does biology adhere to boundaries in the same fashion as national identity? In the 18th and 19th centuries, it was logical and not at all unreasonable for European natural historians and anthropologists to divvy up humanity according to where European explorers first encountered other groups: notions of the meaning or mechanism behind population variation were still poorly developed within natural history (the forerunner of modern biological science). These early thinkers all belonged to one or another nationality defined by distinct borders: they identified with discrete spaces and lived during a time of European political expansion—a project of colonization aimed at surveying, partitioning, and exploitation. Furthermore, global travel at the time was accomplished by ship. Such long-distance travel offered at best a snapshot of apparently major differences between human populations living in far-removed places such as Africa, Asia, the East Indies, Australia, and the Americas, with relatively little appreciation for the small-scale variation occurring across intervening regions. And the differences noted were invariably those easily observed: the size and shape of bodies, the colour of skin, and features of face and hair (Figure 13.1). Differences regarding temperament, moral character, or intelligence (as depicted at the outset by Linnaeus, though disavowed by his 18th-century peers such as Blumenbach) were

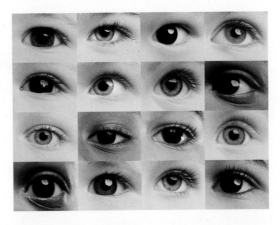

**Figure 13.1** Humans vary in many dimensions, as noted here with regard to the eye. Note differences in shape, colour, and contour.

Richard Newstead/Lifesize/Getty Images

little more than fabricated constructions—what European "geopolitics" needed other peoples to be in comparison to themselves.

Such essentialist and typological approaches to partitioning human biological diversity continued well into the 20th century (Table 13.1): humankind was decomposed into a variety of discrete races, and the transition from one to the next consisted of stepping across a geographic line rather than shifting through geographic space. Indeed, in the 1860s Alfred Russel Wallace, who had proposed along with Darwin that species evolved by means of natural selection, famously contributed to this typology by identifying Malays and Papuans as distinct races during one of his sojourns in the Malay Archipelago (Vetter 2006). The major change in the 200 years following the publication of the 10th edition of Linnaeus' *Systema Naturae* (see Chapter 2) lay not so much in whether races were real biological entities, but rather in how many distinct pieces of the human pie existed and how they should be defined. Mid-20th-century biological anthropologists such as Stanley Garn had devised a system for packaging humanity into a nested series of geographic races, local races, and microraces, characterized by ever finer degrees of presumed breeding isolation and more and more commonly held characteristics.[2]

As biological anthropologist Rachel Caspari (2003) has noted, all of these entities—from race to microrace—were viewed as closed systems with restricted gene flow, creating high degrees of similarity within geographic zones however large or small one wished to define them—for example, "micro"-geography or "local" geography. This line of reasoning falls apart because human populations are not, in fact, reproductively closed systems (see below). Nonetheless, a reasonable question to ask is whether such supposedly distinct and isolated groups could trace their beginnings to one or several points of origin. This question was especially problematic for those scholars in the 18th and 19th centuries who were trying to reconcile acceptance of the Biblical version of a single creation with the agenda of European expansion and colonization—an agenda that included the subjugation, displacement, and enslavement of indigenous peoples. Those scholars, now referred to as **monogenists**, clung to the idea that humanity was created but once and that the different races reflected various degrees of degeneration from that original form following expulsion from Eden (as per Scripture). Exposure to different climates as human populations dispersed over the landscape was argued to be the mechanism behind the formation of different varieties of people. A problem with this view, however, was time. According to Biblical accounts, the world was only 6,000 or so years old. On the other hand, a view known as **polygenesis**—most

**monogenesis**

the 18th-century view that all human populations ("races") could be traced to a single origin, specifically related to the Judeo-Christian account of human origins; the diversity of human races was ascribed to exposure to different climates following humanity's Fall from Grace as related in the Old Testament

**polygenesis**

in contrast to monogenesis, polygenesis maintains that different human races were created as separate species. Note that both monogenesis and polygenesis assign primacy to European peoples

---

2. In his 1961 text *Human Races*, Garn identified 9 geographic races corresponding to peoples inhabiting major continental landmasses (e.g., Europe) or extended island groups (e.g., Polynesia), and up to 30 local or microraces divisible within these larger zones (e.g., northwestern Europeans). The degree of "likeness" decreases as one moves from microraces to geographic races.

**Table 13.1** Human typology in the 18th and 20th centuries. The expansion in number of categories reflects increasing awareness of diversity but adherence to the concept of discreteness.

| Linnaeus, 1758 *Systema Naturae*, 10/e | Blumenbach, 1795 | Stanley Garn, 1971, *Human Races*, 3/e |
|---|---|---|
| Varieties | Varieties | Major Geographic Races |
| American | American | American |
| European | Caucasian | European, North African, and Middle Eastern |
| Asian | Mongolian | Asiatic |
|  |  | Indian |
| African | Ethiopian | African (sub-Saharan) |
|  | Malay | Melasian |
|  |  | Micronesian |
|  |  | Polynesian |
|  |  | Australian |

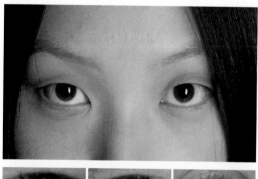
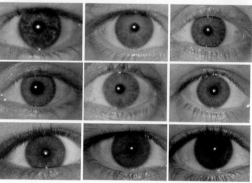

**Figure 13.2** (a) The upper and lower eyelids in some human populations, notably Central and East Asians, overlap at the medial canthus, producing an "epicanthic fold," a morphological feature distinguishing these groups from non-Asian populations. (b) European peoples are more polymorphic for iris colour than non-Europeans.

(a) © visual7/iStockphoto.com. (b) Richard A. Sturm and Tony N. Frudakis. 2004. "Eye color: Portals into pigmentation genes and ancestry," *Trends in Genetics* 20 (8). Copyright © 2004 Elsevier Ltd. All rights reserved. Photo courtesy of Richard A. Sturm.

prominent in 19th-century America and advocated by notable scientists such as Samuel George Morton and Louis Agassiz (Gould 1996)—held that races were created as *separate* biological species, a perspective that allowed polygenists to rationalize both the superiority of the European race with its dominant culture, as well as the relatively brief Old Testament history of humankind.

## If People Are Not Packages, Then Why Are Asians from Asia, Africans from Africa ...?

Whether you're shopping at Toronto's St. Lawrence Market, riding the C-Train in Calgary, attending the Solstice Festival in Yellowknife, waiting to board a flight at Vancouver's International Airport, or strolling rue Sainte-Catherine in Montréal, you will invariably see people who *look* more like one another than any of them *look* like you. We say this making no presumptions about your own ancestry because, as a student of biological anthropology, it matters not whether you're an aboriginal Canadian, a fifth-generation Québécois, or are newly arrived from Beijing, Beirut, or Botswana. The diversity around us is a fact of our multicultural, pluralistic, multiethnic society born of a long history of immigration.[3] Someone else's complexion may be differently pigmented than yours, their bodies and faces differently proportioned, their hair a different form—kinky and black rather than straight and blond. Perhaps your eyes are notable for their **epicanthic fold**, perhaps not (Figure 13.2a). The point we make is simply this: there *are* demonstrable differences, both phenotypic and genotypic, between people who can trace their ancestry to one place as opposed to another.

Such differences reflect the fact that for much of human history people have by necessity chosen mates living close by (and to this extent, Stanley Garn's reasoning holds some water). As a result, a variant for a particular trait that developed in neighbouring populations would understandably occur in much higher frequencies within those groups than in more distantly removed populations. Thus the epicanthic fold is most common among peoples from East and Central Asia, and while the frequency of ginger hair is about 4% among Europeans generally, it reaches as high as 13% in Scotland. Consequently, humans are to some degree what we call a **polytypic** species, meaning that there are broad geographic patterns (clusters) to some aspects of our biology, just as there are similar geographic patterns characterizing languages and social and cultural traditions. This reasoning also accounts for the fact that, as molecular studies indicate, the greatest amount of genetic diversity occurs *within* populations rather than between them. That is to say, at the population level, humans are also a highly **polymorphic** species. **Local breeding populations** accumulate mutations (polymorphisms) at particular genetic loci at rates that are independent of changes occurring at these same loci in other groups. As a result, different populations exhibit different degrees of phenotypic expression for a given characteristic, simply by having a greater number of alleles for that characteristic. A good example is eye colour. Europeans display a greater range of lighter iris pigmentation than is found in non-European populations (Sturm and Frukadis 2004; Figure 13.2b), a result of having more polymorphic melanin pigment coding alleles, including the genes *OCA2* on chromosome 15 and *MC1R* on chromosome 16 (the latter also contributes to the frequency of ginger hair, freckles and sensitivity to ultraviolet radiation). Population size, physical and/or cultural isolation, and history can also help modify the polymorphic structure of different populations. Recall for example the migration to New France of Louis XIV's "filles du roy" and their contribution to the higher occurrence of Leber Hereditary Optic Neuropathy among modern Québécois (see Chapter 4, p. 74).

## What About Spaces Between "Races"?

Whether we wish to consider three races, five races, or even 30 or so "microraces," the problem will always lie in the necessity of drawing lines. Two immediate difficulties arise. First, where should these lines be drawn? Second—and surely the more important question—*who gets to draw the lines?* We will address this concern later in this chapter with particular regard to the question of intelligence and aptitude. Suffice to say for now that in recent human history, "line drawing" has always been a matter of economic, political, and military clout and has invariably produced tragic consequences (see Chapters 15 and 16).

But "race" as a concept, an entity, a category, is nothing if not a boundary, and divisive by definition. From what you have already learned regarding the ways in which biological variation is produced and transmitted, does this notion make sense to you at all? You may wish to refer back to Chapters 3 and 4. Ask yourself this rather simple question: Where does one variety end and another begin? Our hope at this point is that your answer is that, for most human variation, there is neither an ending nor a beginning, but rather a matter of "more or less." More or less melanin production, more or less blood type "A," more or less sickle cell anaemia—these and other human polymorphisms are discussed in detail in

**epicanthic fold**
a fold of skin of the upper eyelid adjacent to the bridge of the nose covering the medial canthus (corner) of the eye, commonly present in peoples of Central and East Asian ancestry

**polytypism**
"many types," referring to the existence of geographic variation within species

**polymorphism**
the existence of alternative forms of a gene; e.g., eye colour in humans is a polymorphic trait

**local breeding population**
the tendency for members of a geographically dispersed species to find mates within a local region rather than from farther afield

---

3. Canadian history in this regard is not so enviable. It has been marked by several less than stellar moments, including the levying of a prohibitive and escalating "head tax" (i.e., a fee each prospective Chinese migrant had to pay) from the late 19th to the mid-20th century; the refusal in 1914 to allow more than 350 East Indian migrants, arriving aboard the Japanese freighter *Komagata Maru*, to land in Vancouver in order to thwart the so-called "brown invasion"; and in 1939, the refusal of sanctuary to German Jewish refugees aboard the *SS St. Louis*, who were forced to return to Europe prior to the outbreak of the Second World War.

BOX 13.1

## RETROSPECTION: The Cline Appears ... from Frank Livingstone (1962)

*In this paper I would like to point out that there are excellent arguments for abandoning the concept of race with reference to the living populations of Homo sapiens. Although this may seem to be a rather unorthodox position among anthropologists, a growing minority of biologists in general are advocating a similar position with regard to such diverse organisms as grackles, martens, and butterflies ... Their arguments seem equally applicable to man. It should be pointed out that this position does not imply that there is no biological variability between the populations of organisms which comprise a species, but just that this variability does not conform to the discrete packages labelled races. The position can be stated in other words as: There are no races, there are only clines.*

The aphorism with which Livingstone concludes this paragraph has achieved the status of doctrine within biological anthropology. The publication of his article in *Current Anthropology* coincided with that of Carleton S. Coon's *On the Origin of Races* (Coon 1962), a book heavily criticized for its explicitly typological approach to human population variation and its racist undertones.[4] Livingstone's article contributed to a growing movement away from "typological [toward] population thinking" in human biology—a movement led by scientists such as Ashley Montague in the 1940s and Joseph Birdsell, Sherwood Washburn, and C. Loring Brace (among others) through the 1950s and 1960s. After the Second World War ended in 1945—in particular, after a momentous

meeting at the Cold Spring Harbour Institute for Quantitative Biology in 1951 concerning the "Origin and Evolution of Man"—the idea that human populations could be catalogued into neat and tidy "discrete packages" increasingly fell out of favour within anthropology. Population genetic concepts such as selection, adaptation, genetic drift, gene flow, and founder effect have been shown to account for subtle shifts over geographic space in the frequency of phenotypic and genotypic characters—for example, skin pigmentation, blood groups, and immune system proteins, among many others. In a now classic example of research merging history and culture with biology, Livingstone himself demonstrated that the pattern of sickle cell anaemia followed a cline from high to low frequency coincident with the degree of **endemism** of Falciparum malaria and the transition to more settled, farming lifeways (Livingstone 1958; see Chapter 3). It is also important to note that the race concept, which had been used to classify *and* explain human biological variation for more than 200 years, was encountering resistance just as the Civil Rights Movement was gaining momentum in the United States. Nonetheless, its fall from favour in biological anthropology was a long and hard one (Cartmill 1998). One subfield in particular—forensic anthropology—persists in identifying race as a determinable feature in human skeletal remains (e.g., Byers 2007; see Chapter 15), and **cognate disciplines** such as medicine and psychology continue to wrestle with race as a legitimate construction of heritable human biological variation (e.g., Smedley and Smedley 2005).

Source: On the Non-Existence of Human Races. *Current Anthropology* 3: 279

**endemism**

refers to organisms which are native to a particular region, and not found elsewhere

**cognate discipline**

a field of study related to one's own by virtue of subject matter, theoretical foundations, and/or issues

**cline**

a gradient over which the frequency of expression of a character changes, observed in contiguous populations in space

http://raceandgenomics.ssrc.org

Chapter 14. The existence of gradual shifts in trait prevalence through geographic space is captured by the concept of **cline** (Box 13.1). A cline is literally a depiction of the frequency with which a character appears in one population compared to its occurrence in a neighbouring group (Figure 13.3). Unlike the concept of race, divisions marking changes in clinal frequency are transient, reflecting sources of population data (i.e., where and how observations have been taken); they are not preconceived notions of "this race lives here, and that race lives there."

The reality of clines reveals the error inherent in assuming that human populations have behaved biologically as closed systems (recall Rachel Caspari's position, noted above). Even though historically, most of our ancestors found mates close to home, people and genes did flow, through and over all divides—geographic, cultural, linguistic, and so forth—and adaptation to local circumstances followed. A fascinating example of clinal variation and adaptation is the existence of a latitudinal cline for differential susceptibility to hypertension (high blood pressure), a known leading cause of many cardiovascular diseases, including stroke and renal failure (Young et al. 2005). Young and colleagues argue that the greater likelihood of becoming hypertensive among African Americans today is in part genetic, reflecting an

4. Coon maintained that there were five distinct races of humankind, which could be identified also in the fossil record as distinct subspecies of *Homo erectus*. He further proposed that the evolution of intellect—as epitomized by civilization—did not proceed uniformly but was achieved first by "Caucasians" and last and only recently by the "Congoids" and "Capoids" of Africa (the former represented by peoples of Central Africa and the latter by those of the Southern Cape, e.g., Khoi San).

(a)

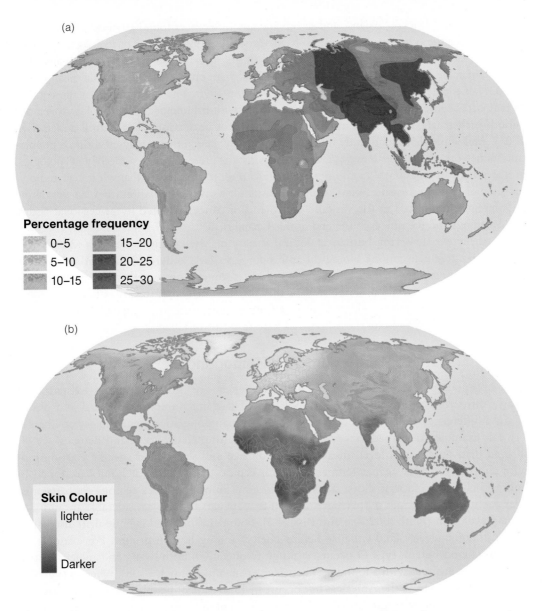

Percentage frequency

- 0–5
- 5–10
- 10–15
- 15–20
- 20–25
- 25–30

(b)

Skin Colour

lighter

Darker

**Figure 13.3** Clines are gradients of phenotypic or genotypic expression through space, as seen here for (a) blood type "B" and (b) skin pigmentation.

adaptation in our early African hominin ancestors some 150,000 years ago for water and salt **avidity**. Such an adaptation would compensate for excessive losses of these nutrients through sweating as a response to heat stress. Water loss during the heat of the day also translates into reduced blood volume, and one measure to maintain blood pressure and to ensure that organs receive sufficient blood-borne nutrition is to develop a greater ability for the heart muscle to contract and for arteries to maintain tone (known as vascular reactivity). Using data provided by the Human Genome Diversity Project, Young and colleagues showed that several genetic variants (single nucleotide polymorphisms, or SNPs) associated with high blood pressure occur with declining frequency with increasing latitude, consistent with data showing that temperate populations have reduced cardiac reactivity and a lower craving for salt.

**avidity**

having a physiological craving for a particular thing

## SIX FALLACIES CONCERNING RACE

As we suggest in Box 13.1, race has continued to appear as an organizing and explanatory factor within biological anthropology and related fields. Studies may be structured as a comparison

**CHAPTER 13** Contemplating Modern Human Diversity

among "white," "black," "Asian," and so on, and any differences found attributed to membership in one or the other specified group. Matt Cartmill's (1998) survey of its usage in articles on human variation published over three decades in the *American Journal of Physical Anthropology* saw considerable fluctuation year by year but little change on average, with equal proportions (ca. 33% of papers published) appearing in 1965 and in 1996. The suggestion that the concept of race had been progressively falling out of favour within biological anthropology over this period (Lieberman, Kirk, and Littlefield 2003) may not be warranted (Cartmill and Brown 2003). And while those who study human variation may couch their analyses within a population framework, that alone does not guarantee against the presence of an underlying typological perspective (Caspari 2003). Practitioners in the field must remain aware that while certain polymorphic or polytypic features may be characteristic for a given population, they do not define it—a premise reinforced in the various "Statements on Race" adopted by professional bodies (see Readings and Resources at the end of this Chapter).

In their text surveying human biological variation, Mielke and colleagues (2006) note the lack of agreement among biological anthropologists (and others) as to what a definition of a biological race might look like—indeed, there is some doubt whether it is even possible to contrive such a definition. They suggest that this lack of consensus arises from a number of erroneous premises as to which factors or features constitute and supposedly validate the concept of "race." We restate these premises here in terms of fallacies.

## Fallacy 1. Human Populations Are Homogenous

A homogenous population is one in which differences are minimal or non-existent, and clearly this is not so for any human population. There are numerous physical and physiological differences within and between different human populations (the subject of Chapter 14). For example, in a broad survey of published literature, Katzmarzyk and Leonard (1998) showed that, on a global level, measures of body size and shape hold specific relationships with climatic variables such as temperature. It is typical that tall, linear bodies are found in hot, arid climates and that short, stockier bodies are found in colder regions—a pattern of selection to the challenges of thermoregulation that appears to have considerable antiquity in human evolution (Ruff 2002; see also Box 11.1). Founder effect and genetic drift also act to diminish homogeneity (and enhance heterogeneity) among human groups. For example, in the ABO blood system, type O occurs at a high frequency in both living and ancient Native Americans, consistent with a founder effect (Halverson and Bolnick 2008), whereas type B is virtually nonexistent in the Americas but occurs in 15 to 25% of people living in eastern Asia (the putative region of origin for Native American peoples).

## Fallacy 2. Polygenic Traits Can Be Measured Accurately

As you learned in Chapter 3, polygenic traits are influenced by a number of genes and result in phenotypes that vary continuously rather than in the discrete, "present/absent" fashion typical of Mendelian characters. Both your height and your eye colour, for example, are influenced by several genes, though the exact number is unknown. The heritability for height is estimated to be approximately 0.80. In other words, about 80% of the variance for stature reflects underlying genetic variance in the population, with the balance of stature variance ascribed to environmental factors such as nutrition and health (see below for further discussion of heritability). Sanna and colleagues (2008) have recently identified a variant of a gene known as *HMGA2* that has an additive effect on body height of 0.44 cm on average for those with one copy of the variant, and almost a full 1.0 cm when this variant is present for both alleles. Clearly, this is a very precise and presumably accurate measure.[5] Unlike most polygenic traits,

---

5. In measurement, precision and accuracy are not the same. Precision reflects whether or not our measurements provide a consistent answer, whether they are accurate or not. Accuracy refers to the degree to which a measurement represents the true value.

a person's stature *can* be measured with a great deal of confidence. But what about other continuously varying characters, such as skin or hair colour, or polygenic systems such as the **human leukocyte antigens**, or variably expressive disease conditions such as systemic lupus erythematosus—lupus, for short? In fact, most human variation is polygenic and not at all easily quantified. Simply put, most human features that have long been at the core of human racial classifications—such as skin colour—are too complex to measure accurately, even with fairly sophisticated instrumentation.[6] Similarly, the phenotypic expression of polygenic, continuous traits invariably involves some contribution from the environment, either directly through agents such as diet or disease, or via epigenetic mechanisms during development (as discussed in Chapter 4).

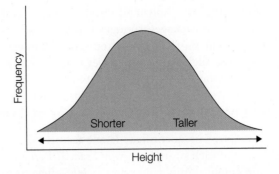

**Figure 13.4** Continuous traits do not lend themselves to nominal descriptions. A person is not *short* so much as they are *shorter than* someone who is taller, and they will be taller than someone who is even shorter.

human leukocyte antigens

HLAs are the chief component of the Major Histocompatability Complex and regulate the human immune response; six polymorphic regions on chromosome 6 alone contribute to the HLA system

## Fallacy 3. Continuously Varying Traits Can Be Marked by Discrete Boundaries

Given that measuring polygenic trait expression accurately is problematic, it is almost moot to argue that we can trace reliable geographic boundaries that would set one character state apart from another. However, the problem underlying this fallacy is as much philosophical as it is practical: a continuously varying trait has no meaningful boundaries. Even for a more or less reliably measured character such as stature, where would you draw the line between someone who is "short" and someone who is "medium-short," and so forth (Figure 13.4)? Such boundaries will always be arbitrary, and more often than not reflect some form of bias. In the case of clines, however, lines demarcating the frequency of expression for a character reflect empirical data. They are analogous to lines joining places of equal mean atmospheric temperature (isotherms) or lines of equal elevation on a map (contours)—all are transient and changeable. In the case of clines, migration and mutation alter genotypic and phenotypic frequencies, whereas global warming shifts isotherms and continental drift, erosion, and uplift modify contours. When, how, and where we take measurements are important considerations whenever we characterize continuous variation. In our example of height, it is more informative to depict the geographic distribution of population means for stature than it is to say that "Britons are taller than Basques."

## Fallacy 4. Traits Used in Racial Classification are Linked

The racial argument that people can be classified into discrete entities rests on the premise that somatic (body) features classically ascribed to a particular group always occur together as phenotypic clusters to the exclusion of members of a different group. This can easily be shown to be false, since it implies a uniform geographic distribution for each racial character—that is, clines for each so-called racial character should be concordant. But as the two clines shown in Figure 13.2 attest, individual traits develop their own patterns of variation in space as a result of their own particular histories of gene flow, drift, selection, and so on. The suggestion that human variation consists of homogenous packages of linked traits corresponding with the biological notion of "subspecies" is clearly false (Keita et al. 2004). Indeed, the action

---

6. Recent developments in 3D imaging and computation models such as the Bidirectional Reflectance Distribution Function (BDRF; Weyrich et al., 2008) appear to offer highly quantifiable resolution of variation in human skin pigmentation, though the technology is currently too cumbersome for large, population-based surveys.

of independent assortment during meiosis, as discussed in Chapter 3, prohibits traits being inherited as packages, though in some instances linkage can occur when alleles for different traits occur on the same chromosome. However, since most human variation is polygenic, involving alleles distributed over a number of different chromosomes, linkage of phenotypes is uncommon.

## Fallacy 5. A Specific Number of Traits Can Define a Race

Can "race" be quantified? Is one feature, such as ginger hair or an epicanthic fold, sufficient to assign each of us to a given "race"? Perhaps three features are necessary. If you have dark skin colour, kinky hair, and the *HbS* allele for sickle cell disease, clearly you are African. Or are you? Perhaps your parents are of Middle Eastern ancestry, or possibly even Asian, as all three of these features occur in Africa, Asia, and the Middle East, albeit with variable degrees of expression. The fact that they may collectively be more frequent in Africa does not resolve the question; you might be African or you might not.

In fact, for the same reasons as given with regard to Fallacy 4, you would be completely frustrated if you tried to enumerate a series of biological traits that could *unambiguously* assign a given individual to a specific population of origin. Even in cases of rare genetic disorders that have very high population affinity, the issue can be far from clear. Tay-Sachs disease is a case in point. Though it occurs with a very high frequency among Ashkenazi Jews (roughly 1 person in 30 carries a copy of the recessive allele), a variant of the allele can be found at similar frequencies in a few other populations, including French Canadians from the Gaspésie-Bas-St-Laurent region of Québec, and among small populations of Cajuns and Pennsylvania Dutch. In all of these instances, founder effect and culturally mediated genetic isolation are effective agents behind the high frequency of this fatal condition. Thus, while having a disease such as Tay-Sachs might focus attribution of someone to a few populations, it does not necessarily pinpoint a specific group of origin.

## Fallacy 6. Between-Group Genetic Diversity Distinguishes Geographic Races

How much genetic difference actually matters? In the case of genetically determined diseases such as Tay-Sachs, very small differences can have a huge impact on the lives of individuals, who may either express the disease or carry the allele for its expression. But does the occurrence of such a marker in a population readily distinguish it from some other population? Clearly not, as we noted above. Fallacy 6 derives from an oft-cited classic study of genetic polymorphism within and between human populations, published by Harvard geneticist Richard Lewontin (1972). Lewontin argued that upwards of 85% of the genetic diversity in *Homo sapiens* occurs among individuals within populations, leaving relatively little genetic variation capable of distinguishing one group from another.[7] Though his statistical analysis has been criticized (Edwards 2003), his fundamental conclusion has been substantiated (though the actual proportions vary slightly) by other studies examining the genetic structure of human populations. For example, Bamshad and colleagues (2004), using more powerful **multilocus** statistical methods and data for more than 400 genetic loci, showed that "pairs of individuals from different populations are often more similar than pairs from the same population" (Witherspoon et al. 2007, 351). Thus a randomly selected European will be classified as European as opposed to Asian only 62% of the time (meaning that she would be classified as Asian approximately 38% of the time). However, a number of recent studies have shown that, as the number of polymorphic loci included in the study increases, the likelihood of being able to discriminate among major geographic populations also increases (e.g., Rosenberg et al. 2005). Human variation exists as clines as we noted earlier, but also as clusters. Importantly, as Rosenberg and colleagues' study shows, the clusters themselves form

**multilocus analysis**
a method for characterizing genetic diversity at multiple sites, or loci, within the genome

---

7. In his 1972 study, Lewontin analyzed 17 polymorphic loci from populations distributed over 7 major geographical "races," including Caucasian, African, Mongoloid, South Asian Aborigines, Amerinds, Oceanians, and Australian aborigines.

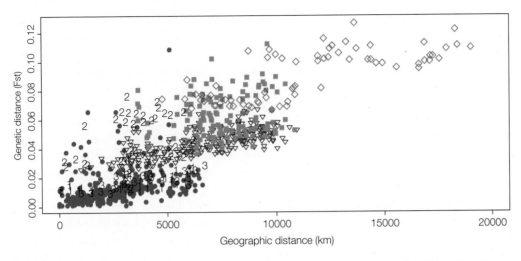

**Figure 13.5** Genetic distance increases with geographic distance, supporting the notion that an analysis based on sufficient polymorphic variation can discriminate among different clusters of human populations. However, note that the changes are linear, indicating that the clusters themselves vary in a clinal fashion through geographic space.

From N.A. Rosenberg, S. Mahajan, S. Ramachandran, et al., (2005). Clines, clusters, and the effect of study design on the inference of human population structure, *PLoS Genetics* 1:e70; Figure 6.

clines over large geographic distances (Figure 13.5). There are two profound implications to these findings. First, any classification of humankind based on only a handful of characters (genotypic or phenotypic) is meaningless, even though this has been the practice both historically and in contemporary fields such as medicine. Second, genetic analyses can provide important insight into historical patterns of human population migration and interbreeding. Thus, studies of mtDNA and Y-chromosomal variation have dramatically altered our view of major population expansions, as seen, for example, in the recent argument for a single versus multiple migration model for the peopling of the Americas from an Asian site of origin (Fagundes et al. 2008).

# DIFFERENCE ABUSED AND USED

Though modern genetic analyses lend credibility to the proposition that if enough genes are used, geographically distinct populations become identifiable, there is still no evidence that individuals from these various populations can be arranged on a scale of "better–worse," "higher–lower," or "greater–lesser." Yet the history of how the biological concept of race has been employed in the social, economic, and political arenas has emphasized just those dimensions. We close this chapter examining how "race" has been abused in Western political economic discourse, emphasizing the rise of the Eugenics Movement in North America in the early 20th century and the debate over race and intelligence (which continues to this day). We also look at how race continues to be used, ostensibly with good intentions, in Western biomedicine—though here as well it remains a thorny issue.

Web link http://www
.eugenicsarchive.org/

## "The Great Problem of Civilization..."

In January 1913, Theodore Roosevelt wrote to Charles Davenport: "The great problem of civilization is to secure a relative increase of the valuable as compared with the less valuable or noxious elements in the population." At the time, Roosevelt was a recent past president of the United States (serving from 1901–1909) and still a person of great political authority; Davenport was the leading American figure in the growing field of genetics, Director of the Cold Spring Harbor Laboratory, and founder of the Eugenics Record Office (Marks 2008). Roosevelt's admonition was written in support of Davenport's call for a state-sponsored

**eugenics**

literally "well-born," a political and philosophical policy of improving racial quality by direct intervention in the composition of society

program of **eugenics**, which he championed in his influential 1911 book *Heredity in Relation to Eugenics*. This text marked the formal marriage of the philosophical core of the Eugenics Movement (as advocated by Charles Darwin's first cousin Sir Francis Galton in the late 19th century) with the recently rediscovered principles of Mendelian genetics. The essential goal of eugenicists was to improve the racial quality of society, in the hope of removing any possible threat to the existing dominant position of Western European–derived upper classes.

The early 20th century was an era of unprecedented migration to North America. During Roosevelt's presidency almost 9 million immigrants began new lives in the United States, most arriving from eastern and southern Europe, Russia, and from the lower classes of Western Europe. Around the same time, Asian immigrants were arriving on the Pacific coast. The influx of these peoples, most of them poor, disenfranchised, uneducated, and (at least in the East) Catholic, raised alarm among the established Western European and Protestant American aristocracy. Though the numbers were smaller, a similar pattern existed in Canada, with a 20th-century record of over 400,000 migrants arriving in 1913 alone (CCR 2009). In both Canada and the United States, the initial response was to enact legislation of various kinds to restrict the numbers of new arrivals from "undesirable" countries of origin. For example, Canada's Immigration Act of 1910 allowed for prohibition against anyone "belonging to any race deemed unsuited to the climate or requirements of Canada, or of immigrants of any specified class, occupation or character." Other acts or amendments invoked "continuous journey" clauses and "head taxes" (see note 3). However, restricting immigration would not remove the threat embodied by the hundreds of thousands who had already arrived; further measures would need to be instituted.

The more sinister response of the eugenicists' program was to develop policies regulating the reproduction of those members of society deemed a threat to the status quo. Charles Davenport himself advocated that young people of the appropriate (i.e., upper) classes be persuaded "to fall in love intelligently," by which he meant to choose mates of similar class and creed (Marks 1995). But a more effective limitation was to impose programs of forced non-therapeutic sterilization targeting those deemed unfit by virtue of "**feeble-mindedness**." Though phenotypically ambiguous, feeble-mindedness was made out to be genetic in origin, supposedly following a Mendelian pattern of inheritance. Clearly, in the eugenicists' view, controlling birth was the most effective intervention to keep society from degenerating as a result of the overzealous reproductive capacity of the immigrant classes.

**feeble-mindedness**

an artificial construct which suggested that defects of personality, intellect, ethnicity, or behaviour were inborn, and thus could be selected against by policies restricting reproduction; sterilization was often the method of choice

**negative eugenics**

involved preventing successful reproduction (via conception or sterilization)

Advocates such as the notable feminist Margaret Sanger would later promote a form of "**negative eugenics**" by arguing that contraception should be made widely accessible to the lower classes.[8] Similarly in Canada, Emily Murphy—a champion in the movement to have women recognized as persons under the British North America Act—believed that a program of negative eugenics was a solution to the problem of overpopulation, especially among the lower classes. Possibly the foremost proponent of eugenics in Canada was Dr. Helen Mac-Murchy, appointed in 1915 as Ontario's "inspector of the feeble-minded." While campaigning on the one hand for a reduction in maternal and infant death rates, work for which she was recognized by being named a Commander of the British Empire, MacMurchy also argued for sterilization as a means to prevent the production of "degenerate babies." It was in Alberta and British Columbia that these measures were embraced most strongly. For example, the Alberta Sexual Sterilization Act of 1928 created a Eugenics Board that over the next 43 years approved more than 98% of cases heard. Of these individuals, almost 3,000 were subjected to forced sterilization. Most of these people were from minority groups and most were women; all had been identified as feeble-minded or otherwise deviant.

Eugenics-based sterilization programs were instituted in many countries, including social democratic states such as Sweden. Most such programs, though, fell into decline after the Second World War, when it was realized how relentlessly the Nazi regime had implemented

---

8. Sanger founded the American Birth Control League in 1921 to advocate for women's reproductive rights; the ABCL was renamed in 1942 as Planned Parenthood of America. While widely recognized as a strong feminist and activist, Sanger's eugenics philosophy, as reflected in her argument that "birth control must lead ultimately to a cleaner race" (Sanger 1922, 12) has tarnished her reputation.

BOX 13.2

# FOCUS ON... LIBERAL EUGENICS: POSSIBLE, PROBABLE, DESIRABLE?

*But with the Paradice method, there would be ninety-nine percent accuracy. Whole populations could be created that would have pre-selected characteristics. Beauty, of course; that would be in high demand. And docility: several world leaders had expressed interest in that. Paradice had already developed a UV-resistant skin, a built-in insect repellant, an unprecedented ability to digest unrefined plant material. As for immunity from microbes, what had until now been done with drugs would soon be innate.*

This passage, from Margaret Atwood's 2003 apocalyptic novel *Oryx and Crake*, captures the "con" side of the debate vis-à-vis genetic engineering applied to human reproductive choice. The idea carried within this excerpt—that we can fabricate "designer babies" at will—is but a stone's throw from early 20th-century arguments that humanity would best be served by "breeding out unsavoury kinds," identified by colour or creed—hence the mid-20th-century Nazi pogroms against, for example, Jewish and Romani peoples throughout Europe. Today the mention of "eugenics" leaves a sour taste in the mouth; the notion of "true breeding" bears a nasty history. In recent years, however, new technologies have reopened that Pandora's Box to the possibility that parents can indeed intentionally design future generations.

These methods, known by the labels "liberal eugenics" or "reprogenetics," trace their origin to the development of oral contraceptives and in vitro methods of fertilization, notably with Gregory Pincus's success in 1934 at combining rabbit egg and sperm in the inverted crystal of his watch glass and implanting the subsequent embryo into a surrogate rabbit mother (Andrews 2008).[9] Over the intervening seven decades, research has greatly extended the options available to prospective parents—including fully fertile couples—to manipulate and control their reproductive choices. As an extension of assisted reproductive technology, reprogenetics permits couples to either ensure or prevent particular genes appearing in offspring. As molecular biologist Lee Silver (2000) has noted, humans have always practised a form of reprogenetics: mating is hardly ever random in human populations, and mate choices are often made to bring phenotypic traits together (positive assortative mating) or to keep them apart (negative assortative mating). Selecting appropriate egg or sperm donors, and decisions to abort an abnormal fetus based on the results of genetic screening tests such as amniocentesis, also constitute forms of reprogenetics. But in an era of genome sequencing and germline engineering, the choices are as biologically remarkable as they are ethically complex. Genes can potentially be modified, deleted, or added in, in a nonrandom manner, to ensure a healthy, happy, long-lived, and successful baby.

But is this something we should be pursuing? Silver (1998) holds that reprogenetics simply offers one more tool for parents to provide advantages to their future offspring; there is little difference between providing good genes and providing a good environment, such as high-quality nutrition and a first-class education. On the other hand, bioethicists such as McGill University medical anthropologist Margaret Lock (2002) argue that reprogenetics, because of the high costs involved, extends much further than individual choices (of parents) and individual outcomes (of babies); indeed, it represents a new form of biocapitalism that is likely to exacerbate both social and biological/genetic inequities. In the case of germline engineering (a form of positive eugenics having the sole aim of genetically enhancing babies), Lock asks a fundamental question: Who gets to decide which genes are "good" and which are "bad"? Clearly, this is an issue with many questions; societal, political, ethical, and spiritual. The answers must come from a wider field than simply those who devise the technology.

From N.A. Rosenberg, S. Mahajan, S. Ramachandran, et al., (2005). Clines, clusters, and the effect of study design on the inference of human population structure, PLoS Genetics 1:e70; Figure 6.

American eugenic politics. In this light, it is sobering to note that legislated non-therapeutic sterilization of the "feeble-minded" continued in Alberta until 1972. Indeed, lawsuits are still before the courts in Alberta and B.C. as survivors seek redress.

## Race as Advantage

When a program of eugenics advocates sterilizing individuals on grounds of "race" or ethnicity, it is based on the belief that some peoples are innately superior to others—that is, endowed with genes that provide biological advantages. Given that geographically distant human populations have somewhat unique histories of selection and adaptation, we should not be surprised that biologically meaningful differences occur in some areas of human

---

9. Louise Joy Brown, the first human *in vitro* baby, was born July 25, 1978, in England to Lesley and John Brown, whose attempts at natural conception had proved futile owing to Lesley's blocked fallopian tubes. In 2006, Louise gave birth to her own son, conceived without the need of *in vitro* technology.

**BOX 13.3**    **FOCUS ON... RECORD-BREAKING BIOLOGY**

© Clifford White/Corbis

**Figure 13.6**  Usain Bolt's accomplishments on the track are unprecedented in the modern era.

Jamaicans reigned supreme at many track events at the Beijing 2008 Olympics, earning 11 medals, 6 of them gold. Not only did Usain Bolt (Figure 13.6) cross the finish line in record time to take the gold medal in the men's 100 and 200 metre sprints, he did so with such apparent ease that many were left wondering whether he could have run faster. This achievement prompted a flurry of newspaper articles addressing a question that has long been pondered: Why do athletes of West African heritage tend to perform better in short-distance running events? And for that matter, in professional sports leagues such as the NFL and NBA? Does the secret to this success lie in their genes or in their environment (e.g., training, coaching, history of play)? Is it nature or nurture? Recent research suggests a link between athletic performance and the *ACTN3* gene, which codes for a protein called α-actinin-3, located in muscle fibres termed "fast-twitch fibres" (Yang et al. 2003). It is these fibres that provide the explosive power exhibited by top-level sprinters by allowing for the rapid contraction of muscles. Two alleles of the gene exist in the general population, known as 577R and the less common 577X. Individuals who carry two of the latter alleles are healthy but lack the ability to produce the α-actinin-3 protein in their fast-twitch muscle fibres. In contrast, individuals who carry at least one of the 577R alleles have the ability to produce this protein. The frequency of the 577X allele has been found to be significantly lower in elite sprint athletes and significantly higher in endurance athletes such as marathon runners (MacArthur and North 2004). This observation suggests that natural selection has maintained this allele in the human population because it confers some advantage. Does this mean, however, that the key to athletic ability lies solely in the genes? The case for a so-called "speed gene" certainly sounds convincing, but as one of the scientists involved in the original study points out, when we consider the prevalence of individuals who have the R/R or R/X genotype (an estimated 5 billion people worldwide), the difference between Jamaicans and other populations is much less pronounced (MacArthur 2008). The bottom line is that athletic ability is a complex phenotype influenced by many different genetic and environmental factors. While the *ACTN3* gene does appear to play some role in athletic performance and could possibly be used to help make decisions about the type of sport at which an athlete is more likely to excel (MacArthur and North 2005), it clearly does not account for the difference in sprinting ability between Usain Bolt and other athletes. For this we have to also look at environmental factors such as the availability of funding and training facilities, and cultural attitudes toward athletic success.

endeavour—for example, in certain kinds of athleticism (see Box 13.3). But the arena in which the most effort has been exhausted arguing for the existence of inborn differences (ranking from greater to lesser) is that of "intelligence." While it is true that individuals vary with regard to different measures of aptitude—just as they do for traits such as stature, hair colour, disease risk, and so on—there is no credible evidence that populations can be hierarchically ordered along any measure of intellectual or cognitive capacity. Why, then, does the debate continue? There are at least three prominent reasons: the first relates to what intelligence *is;* the second, to the historical rootedness of racist essentialism (as we saw earlier); and the third, to the personal motives (i.e., the politics and philosophies) of a handful of individuals who assert that "average intelligence" is reflected in the classic tripartite classification of race—white, black, Asian—and that these differences are the result of natural selection and adaptation.

## Defining and Measuring Intelligence

The question "what is intelligence" has vexed scholars across disciplines. Is it "innate ability," as Galton supposed? Is it competence in "problem solving," as many educational psychologists have maintained? More than 100 years ago the English psychometrician Charles Spearman proposed a quantity known as "g" (standing for "general intelligence factor"), which could be derived from an individual's performance on specific intelligence tests[10] and from performances grouped over a larger number of cognitive tasks. The modern version of "g" is called the Full Scale Intelligence Quotient (FSIQ), a composite score of accomplishment over 11 tests of verbal and cognitive performance abilities. Measures of FSIQ have been variously shown to be positively correlated with educational outcomes, health outcomes (e.g., morbidity and mortality), occupational success, physical attributes such as body asymmetry (Prokosch, Yeo, and Miller 2005), brain volume, and cortical grey matter thickness (Narr et al. 2007). However, test outcomes have also been shown to vary across the life span and to be influenced by numerous social and economic determinants. For example, a recent study among Canadian schoolchildren aged 6 to 16 years found that "demographic" variables alone (age, sex, parental education, region of country, ethnicity) accounted for 18% of the variance in predicting (previously ascertained) FSIQ scores (Scheonberg, Lange, and Saklofske 2007). Even with a full battery of additional tests, only 70% of the variance in FSIQ could be accounted for, leaving one to wonder whether other, nonspecified social and economic factors might explain any of the remaining 30% of variance in "intelligence." Consider also that Scheonberg and colleagues' characterization of ethnicity included only white, Asian, Aboriginal and "other"—hardly a reflection of the diversity one finds in many Canadian school classrooms!

## Do Populations Differ in Intelligence?

At the root of the question of innate differences in intelligence conferring advantages to some populations over others[11] is the degree to which intelligence is inherited—that is, genetically determined. Given that defining "intelligence" is such a nebulous exercise, you might well wonder how this issue can be approached. Researchers have relied mainly on family and **monozygotic** (MZ) twin studies to investigate the genetic contribution to intelligence. Especially useful are studies of MZ twins reared together (having the same genome and similar environment) versus MZ twins raised apart (same genome, different environment). Such studies report correlation coefficients for intelligence test results ranging from 0.20 to 0.87; other degrees of biological relationship tend to report lower correlations for test results. However, as Molnar (2006) points out, it is erroneous to equate correlation with genetic causation. At issue is the concept of heritability (symbolized as $H^2$), which is often assumed—in error—to be a measure of genetic determination. For example, a heritability of 0.87 for stature (Visscher et al. 2007) does *not* mean that 87% of an individual's stature is determined by genes. Rather, in its broadest sense, this estimate of heritability means that 87% of the phenotypic variance for height *in a population* can be attributed to underlying genetic variance within that population, suggesting that 13% can be ascribed to nongenetic (environmental) variance. In fact, height is a complex polygenic trait, with genes on at least 6 chromosomes (3, 4, 8, 15, 17, and 18) having **additive effects** (Visscher et al. 2007), which explains in part why heritability for height can be so high, yet variability in trait expression so broad. Heritability is calculated as

$$H^2 = Vg/(Vg + Ve)$$

Thus, in simple terms, heritability is the proportion of genetic variance (Vg) relative to the total variance for a trait from all sources, environmental (Ve) *and* genetic.

**monozygotic**

Twins derived from a single zygote. Commonly called identical twins, they result from splitting of the fertilized egg very early in pregnancy (at the blastocyst stage), and thus possess the same genome

**additive effect**

in quantitative genetics, an additive effect refers to a genetic contribution to a trait that either increases or decreases (if the effect has a "negative value") the degree of expression

---

10. The history of intelligence testing—IQ tests—is also one fraught with controversy; see Gould (1996) for a thorough discussion.

11. Historically, this ranking has placed Caucasians on top, followed by Asians and Africans. In the late 1980s and early 1990s this was turned around in a series of controversial publications to switch the order to one of Asian–Caucasian–African. Lieberman (2001) provides an interesting political-economic analysis of this transformation.

Heritability estimates will be high for populations with high degrees of genetic variance, as well as for populations reared in environments with little environmental variance (e.g., mould in an agar medium under controlled conditions). Similarly, if Vg is low or Ve very high, heritability estimates will be low. It is also important to understand that H² is an estimate of heritability for a trait in a given population at a given time—*it is not a constant!* This is easily comprehended if we realize that environments are also not constant; thus, Ve is always changing. More to the point, as Moore (2006, 349) has stated, "the amount of variation that can be accounted for by one factor always depends on the amount of variation in the other factor." In other words, the contribution of genetic variance is not independent of the contribution of environmental variance. For this reason alone, it should be anticipated that different human populations will have different heritability estimates for all traits, including intelligence, and that such differences say nothing about the innate character of the trait in question.

## ONE INTELLIGENCE OR SEVERAL INTELLIGENCES?

A final consideration regarding intelligence is how many kinds there may be. Though psychologists measure general or full-scale intelligence, others—notably animal behaviourists and paleoanthropologists—speak of ecological intelligence, social intelligence, or technical intelligence. These "intelligences" imply specific aptitudes hypothesized to have been essential adaptations for group living and foraging, including the use of tools, in complex habitats. Remembering the location of food sources in patchy or seasonal environments, your position relative to other group members in a hierarchically ranked society, and where to build nests and how to use reeds for termite fishing, can be vital in terms of survival and reproduction, and each capacity will have significant selective pressures attached to it.

These capacities have been linked to the evolution of brain size among primates. Features such as social learning and innovation are essential components of behavioural flexibility (see Chapter 6). For example, Reader and LaLand (2002) surveyed the literature on primate behaviour, social intelligence, and brain size and found strong positive correlations with measures of behavioural flexibility and "executive" brain volume (i.e., the size of the neocortex and striatum, which are involved in processes of learning, planning, rule acquisition, and abstract thinking). Hermann and colleagues (2007) have proposed a model of **"cultural intelligence"** unique to hominins, as shown by their tests carried out with chimpanzees, orangutans, and human toddlers. They found that 2.5-year-old human children were equally adept at solving problems in the physical world, but more savvy in dealing with social problems than either of the great apes (Figure 13.7).

**cultural intelligence**

the capacity of humans to acquire early in life complex skills for negotiating social situations

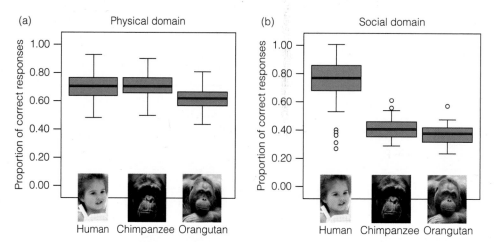

**Figure 13.7**  Human children and apes have similar capacities in dealing with the physical world, but humans have exceptional skills with respect to social situations.

From E. Herrmann, et al., (2007). Humans have evolved specialized skills of social cognition: the cultural intelligence hypothesis. *Science* 317: 1362. Reprinted with permission AAAS. Photos: Monkey Business Images/Shutterstock.com (child); Devid Camerlynck/Shutterstock.com (chimpanzee); Olga OSA/Shutterstock.com (orangutan).

The point we make here is that different cognitive capacities and abilities (skills) are necessary for survival and confer distinct but not necessarily mutually exclusive selective advantages. Some individuals may have exceptional abilities for learning, innovation, and problem solving, others for tool use, still others for spatial mapping, planning, and ecological memory. Humans in particular may have evolved special talents applied to the multifaceted world of a long-lived, socially complex, culture-bearing hominin. These variations may create differences among individuals, but not among different populations composed of such individuals.

## Race and Biomedicine

In June 2005 the U.S. Food and Drug Administration (FDA) approved a heart therapy drug known as BiDil, the first ever therapeutic measure carrying a race-specific label. The target population was African Americans. The immediate response inside and outside the medical community was by and large critical. Some suggested that it was scientifically unreasonable to render such approvals based on race rather than **pathophysiology** (Bloche 2004); others saw it as an attempt to avoid the cost of lengthy clinical trials and to "exploit race" to gain market advantage (Sankar and Kahn 2005). The response of the FDA has been to point out that their decision was founded not on the results of one clinical trial in which only black subjects were enrolled, but on three such investigations, two of which included self-identified black *and* white participants (Temple and Stockbridge 2007). In each case, BiDil was shown to have a marked benefit for health improvement and quality of life in the black cohort studied; indeed, the black-only trial was terminated early after initial results showed a 43% to 63% reduction in mortality for those participants adding BiDil to a standard therapy. Moreover, as we noted earlier in this chapter, African Americans are especially prone to hypertension and heart disease; thus, the need for such an intervention was already well established.

The controversy around BiDil ranged from biologists and medical geneticists pointing out that there is a sound evolutionary rationale for designing "race-specific" therapies, to social scientists and politicians raising spectres of racialized medicine and the entrenchment of already damaging negative stereotypes (Carlson 2005). As a case study, BiDil provides a classic example of the struggle that biomedicine has had for many years in attempting to cope with population diversity and the interplay of biology, economics, and culture (Collins 2004; Figure 13.8). Persons of African origin may well have a genetic predisposition to heart disease, but it is as important to ask what degree diet, poverty, education, access to health care, and other lifestyle factors come into play. As a further example, African-American adults and adolescents are much more likely to be diagnosed with AIDS than either white or Hispanic Americans (nine times and three times more likely, respectively); however, these disparities are founded almost exclusively in nonbiological causes (Kraut-Becher et al. 2008).

**pathophysiology**
a disturbance of normal body function as a result of disease, genetic disorder, or impaired development

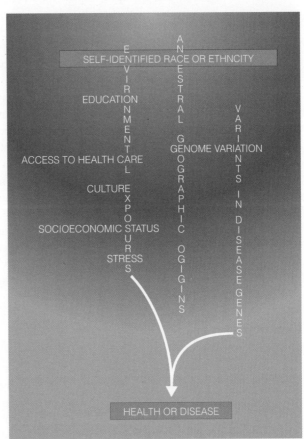

**Figure 13.8** With few exceptions, health disparities measured as disease risk involve a complex interplay of many causal factors—biologic, economic, and social-cultural.

**CHAPTER 13** Contemplating Modern Human Diversity

In modern biomedicine, the gold standard for assessing population disease risk is the randomized clinical trial, in which defined groups (populations) are evaluated for outcomes under different treatments. Subjects are randomly assigned to a treatment group receiving a new therapy under investigation or to a control group, which is administered either an experimental/proven treatment or a **placebo**. But how are such populations to be defined, and how is relative risk to be assigned? Subject groups are often identified according to known health outcomes: if there is a higher prevalence of heart disease among African Americans, it would seem reasonable to compare samples of black, white, Hispanic, and so on. Indeed, as Jackson (2008) notes, more than 113,000 scientific articles had been published and reported by the indexing service PubMed (as of March 2007) using the classic Linnaean racial classification system. But if the predisposition is genetically based, how do we control for population admixture, and what impact might *that* have on disease susceptibility? Yaeger and colleagues (2008) compared more than 100 genome markers for ancestry in 50 self-identified African Americans and 40 Nigerians and found that while the latter had about 4% European admixture, the African-American sample had 15% European ancestry—a statistically significant difference. Indeed, in the United States, the Agency for Health Care Policy and Research recommends screening *all* infants for the presence of sickle cell disease—generally considered a condition affecting primarily African Americans—since it is generally not possible to determine an infant's ancestry "by appearance, name or self-report" (Ashley-Koch et al. 2000, 844).

If the use of self-identified race or ethnicity is problematic in clinical medical research, what are the alternatives? Two possibilities have recently been suggested. First, Ng and colleagues (2008) have proposed that with increasing availability and reduced cost of obtaining full genome sequencing of patients, medicine should move away from a race-based model of pharmacological investigation and therapeutics toward one based on individual genetic variation. They argue that the design of personalized medicines would mark an endpoint to the often tragic (albeit relatively rare) adverse event, in which a prescribed drug or treatment causes harm and sometimes death instead of providing relief.

A second model, proposed by Jackson (2008) involves the use of GIS methods to create layered maps combining information collected at the local level to capture disease risk (e.g., potential for toxic exposures), social determinants of health factors (e.g., education, occupation), demography (e.g., age, sex, family size), genetic diversity measures (e.g., single nucleotide polymorphism data), cultural patterns (e.g., nutrition, behaviour), population history (e.g., immigration, admixture), and other relevant information. Collectively, these data are used to define units of analysis that Jackson refers to as geographically localized MicroEthnic Groups (MEGs).[12] While invoking several assumptions regarding population structure and history, Jackson's model of ethnogenetic layering could provide MEGs highlighting local influences on disease susceptibility and expression while avoiding the homogenizing impact of using self-identified race or ethnicity in health research.

# SUMMARY

For the better part of 300 years, humans have taken it upon themselves to classify and organize the world, including other humans. From this was born the modern concept of biological race. For disparate historical, political, and economic reasons, these early classifications of humankind were translated as fundamental divisions according to distance (geography) and worth, with Western European–derived peoples placed at the pinnacle of the hierarchy. However, arguments supporting such distinctions have been shown to be fallacious, in that phenotypic traits generally do not segregate into discrete packages. Most human variation is continuous and polygenic in any case, and geographic variation in such traits can be more

---

12. Jackson's (2008) MEGs differ from Stanley Garn's (1971) notion of microraces discussed earlier. The latter are defined as local biological populations and do not include the detailed non-biological information contained in the multiethnic group.

efficaciously depicted as clinal, with subtle changes occurring over space. Nonetheless, some scholars hold to the proposition that innate differences characterize different human populations, and some disciplines (notably biomedicine) continue to struggle with the relationship among disease susceptibility, biological ancestry, and (cultural) ethnicity.

# CORE REVIEW

### What role did 19th-century ideas of race play in the history of European colonial expansion?

In the 18th and 19th centuries, human races were not only marked in terms of visual differences (e.g., skin colour), but also ranked on a scale of high to low in terms of behaviour, attitude, and aptitude. As it was European natural history that created these classifications, it was natural to place European peoples at the pinnacle of the hierarchy, and all others as lesser forms of humankind. Such classifications were used to justify colonial expansion into Africa, the Far East, and the Americas, as well as the subjugation of the indigenous populations found therein.

### What is the distinction between polytypic and polymorphic variation?

Polytypic variants are traits that distinguish major geographic populations. They are discontinuous in nature and likely reflect recent local adaptation, founder effect, and/or low levels of gene flow between neighbouring groups. The epicanthic fold of the eye common among Asian populations is but one example. In contrast, polymorphic variation is continuously distributed over geographic space and can be readily depicted in terms of clines. Polymorphism reflects the existence of multiple alleles of a gene, the expression of which results in subtle differences among phenotypes within populations. Most human variation is polymorphic. The ABO blood type system is one example in humans.

### What is a cline? Why are clines useful in explaining human geographic variation?

Clines are maps of changes in trait expression, either genotypic or phenotypic. Such maps are based on measured frequencies within populations over geographic space. A classic example of a phenotypic cline is skin pigmentation (darker near the equator, lighter at higher latitudes). In the case of genotypes, the occurrence of the HbS allele for sickle cell disease is high in central Africa and declines in frequency elsewhere. Depicting polymorphic variation in terms of clines is useful because it is readily linked to causal factors (biological, cultural, historical). In the case of HbS, trait frequency is linked to endemism in *Falciparum* malaria, which in turn has been linked with the introduction of settled, agricultural lifeways.

### In what way(s) is "race" problematic for biomedicine?

The model that Western biomedicine has used, with some success, is to define populations of interest according to classic Linnaean racial taxonomy (e.g., Negroid, Caucasian, Asian, and—more recently—in the United States, Hispanic, and in Canada, First Nations). However, none of these "populations" constitutes a biologically distinct entity, given tens of thousands of years of migration and admixture. Especially problematic is the recent search for the genetic basis of disease risk, which is confounded by interactions with numerous nongenetic factors, including lifestyle, education, socioeconomic status, and so forth. As a result, studies that attempt to partition disease susceptibility according to "race" will find, at best, weak associations.

**How has genomics altered our understanding of human population variation?**

In the past decade, molecular genetics has vastly increased our detailed knowledge of population variation in both nuclear and mitochondrial DNA. While it was once thought that very little genetic variation could discriminate between populations, it is now clear that if enough DNA loci are studied, genetic distances do reflect geographic differences. That is, genetic polymorphism forms geographic clusters. Nonetheless, these clusters themselves also can be mapped as clines, reflecting histories of population migration and mating patterns.

# CRITICAL THINKING QUESTIONS

1. Is intelligence measurable? If so, should we measure it?
2. How do the concepts of race, ethnicity, and ancestry differ as used in fields such as anthropology, psychology, and biomedicine?

# GROUP DISCUSSION QUESTIONS

1. In conducting the 2006 census, Statistics Canada defined a visible minority as "persons, other than Aboriginal peoples, who are non-Caucasian in race or non-white in colour." (Note: Aboriginal peoples are excluded from this definition as they are enumerated in the census under an independent heading.) Should StatsCan modify this approach to appreciating Canadian diversity? If so, how should visible minorities be defined?
2. Is "race" a necessary concept?

# RESOURCES AND READINGS

• The American Association of Physical Anthropologists' "Statement on Race" is found at **http://physanth.org/association/position-statements/biological-aspects-of-race**; the American Anthropological Association's "Statement on Race" is at **http://www .aaanet.org/issues/policy-advocacy/AAA-Statement-on-Race.cfm**.

• A special issue (November 2004) of the journal *Nature Genetics* considered the issue of race and the emerging field of genomics and disease epidemiology; more recently, the May 2009 issue of *American Journal of Physical Anthropology* contained several articles on the issue of biological anthropology and race, under the heading "Race Reconciled."

# Chapter 14 Biology of Contemporary and Past Populations

## OVERVIEW

In Part III of this book we took you on a journey from our earliest ancestors to the appearance of anatomically modern humans. As you have seen, this transition was characterized by profound anatomical and behavioural changes that are evident in the fossil and archaeological record. Human populations today are a product of that evolutionary journey, and the morphological and genetic diversity we see today reflects long-term natural selection and other evolutionary mechanisms. In the first half of this chapter we explore the ways in which humans have adapted to their environments, particularly those characterized by extreme conditions. We also examine emerging and re-emerging infectious diseases, nutritional anthropology, and the human life cycle. In the second half of the chapter we examine how past populations are studied through analyses of their skeletal remains, highlighting the variety of data that such remains can provide.

## CORE CONCEPTS

■ biocultural perspective, biomedical anthropology, epidemiology, epidemiologic transition, emerging infectious diseases, human adaptability, nutritional anthropology, human life course, bioarchaeology, paleopathology, paleonutrition

## CORE QUESTIONS

■ What factors are contributing to the emergence and re-emergence of infectious diseases today?

■ In what ways can biological anthropologists contribute to the study of the human life course?

■ What are the consequences of under- and over-eating?

■ How have humans adapted physiologically to their environments?

■ What can we learn about past populations from their skeletal remains?

We do not grow absolutely, chronologically. We grow sometimes in one dimension, and not in another, unevenly. We grow partially. We are relative. We are mature in one realm, childish in another. The past, present, and future mingle and pull us backward, forward, or fix us in the present. We are made up of layers, cells, constellations.

Anaïs Nin (1903–1977)

# PROLOGUE: "THREE OF THESE THINGS BELONG TOGETHER ..."

Those of us who grew up with *Sesame Street* remember the song by that title, by Joe Raposo and Jeff Moss (written in 1970, a bit before most of you were born!), and the game in which several similar objects were shown, one of which was somehow unlike the rest. The message was about the nature and meaning of difference: How do we know when things belong together? In this chapter we explore the wonderful world of modern human variation and celebrate difference for what it means, as testimony to human adaptation throughout history, *and* as a living record of human population dynamics, including recent migration and marriage.

The dimensions along which human populations vary are as diverse as the variation itself. They range from disease experience and resistance, to patterns of growth and development, to aging, to the biology of lifestyle choices. One of the questions we have to ask when we are confronted with population variation is this: To what degree do variations reflect fundamental genetic differences acquired over many generations, as opposed to merely reflecting our ability to produce adapted phenotypes over the course of a lifetime of exposure to a particular environment? This dichotomy underlies the distinction between *adaptation* and *adaptability*, the latter referring to an intrinsic biological plasticity, or capacity to respond to specific environmental cues in an appropriate fashion. A fascinating aspect of our biology that we explore in this chapter is that different human populations have followed different routes—in some cases genetic and in others plastic—to accommodate similar environmental challenges.

One aspect of modern population biology that demands our attention is that of ethics. Whether we are studying the skeletal remains of the ancestors of contemporary First Nations peoples, or taking buccal swabs for DNA analysis from people around the world, we need to remember that what we learn has as much (or more) importance and impact for the future of those studied as it does for the future of "science." If nothing else, recognizing and respecting the truth in this should make one thing patently clear: all of us belong together.

# BIOLOGY OF CONTEMPORARY POPULATIONS

In Chapter 1 we introduced you to the biocultural approach, which recognizes that biology and culture are interrelated. Much of the research being done today by biological anthropologists is guided by this perspective (see, for example, *Medical Anthropology: A Biocultural Approach*, by Andrea Wiley and John Allen [2008]). It is also evident in the interdisciplinary nature of our field. For example, the integration of biological and medical anthropology has led to the emergence of **biomedical anthropology**. Similarly, the integration of anthropology and **epidemiology**, exemplified by the edited volume *Anthropology and Epidemiology: Interdisciplinary Approach to the Study of Health and Disease* (James, Stall, and Gifford 2002), has resulted in numerous studies of the cultural and behavioural factors underlying the spread of infectious disease. Central to this perspective has been the realization over the past several decades that a good deal of human phenotypic variation arises as a consequence of each individual's capacity to respond differentially to challenges posed by life's circumstances—a process known as adaptability. Humans are malleable in the face of varying environmental conditions (and environments are themselves diverse, ranging from the environment of the uterus to that of the International Space Station). One example of a plastic response familiar to us all is that our bodies accommodate seasonal changes in temperature and exposure to UV-B radiation. Adaptability differs from our general understanding of biological adaptation in that our responses are not (typically) passed on to future generations in a fashion akin to Lamarckian inheritance (see Chapter 2); nonetheless, as we will see in this chapter and the following ones, adaptability is essential to our capacity as a species to survive, reproduce, and expand into previously unexplored habitats.

**biomedical anthropology**

the study of health from a biocultural and epidemiological perspective

**epidemiology**

the study of the distribution and determinants of disease

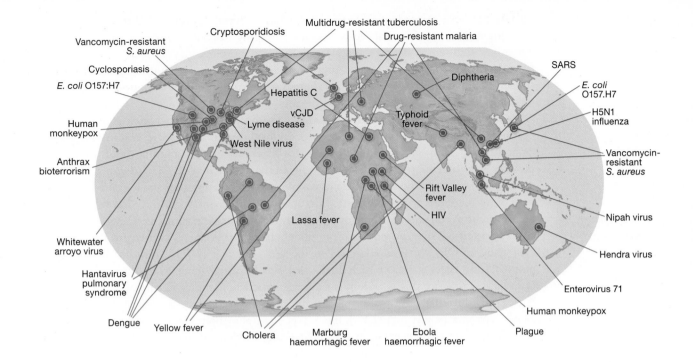

**Figure 14.1** Emerging and re-emerging infectious diseases pose a significant health threat today. While many of these diseases are appearing in North America, this may reflect greater identification and reporting on this continent than elsewhere.

F.S. Fauci, (2001). Infectious diseases: Considerations for the 21st century. *Clinical Infectious Diseases* 32: 675–685. Copyright © 2001, Infectious Diseases Society of America. Reprinted with permission of The University of Chicago Press.

# INFECTIOUS DISEASES

## Emerging and Re-emerging Infectious Diseases

You are probably all familiar with the Black Death, the outbreak of bubonic plague that struck Europe in the fourteenth century, killing an estimated one-third of the population. Over the centuries that followed, plague and other infectious diseases such as tuberculosis, smallpox, influenza, and cholera were leading causes of death, and many anthropological studies have focused on the biological and social impact of these diseases on human populations (see, e.g., Sawchuk and Burke 1998, 2003; Padiak 2008; Sattenspiel and Herring 1998).

In the early 1970s, epidemiologist Abdel R. Omran formulated what he called the **epidemiologic transition model** to explain changing patterns of health and disease over time. Integrating epidemiological and demographic data, he identified three stages: (1) the "age of pestilence and famine," characterized by high death rates from **epidemics**, famines, and war; (2) the "age of receding pandemics," marked by a decline in infectious diseases and famine resulting from improved nutrition and living conditions; and (3) the "age of degenerative and man-made diseases," characterized by an increase in chronic diseases and a reduction in infectious diseases (Omran 1971). One of the implications of Omran's model is that infectious diseases are a thing of the past. Nothing could be further from the truth, however, and today more than one-quarter of all annual deaths worldwide are estimated to be directly related to infectious diseases (Morens et al. 2004; Figure 14.1). We have thus entered what Barrett and colleagues (1998) have described as the third epidemiologic transition: the age of emerging and re-emerging infectious diseases.[1] Since 1973 alone, more than 30 new

**epidemiologic transition model**

a model developed by epidemiologist Abdel Omran to explain changing patterns of health and disease over time

**epidemic**

an outbreak of disease exceeding the normal level of occurrence

---

1. According to Barrett and colleagues (1998), the first epidemiologic transition was characterized by an increase in infectious diseases associated with the Neolithic Revolution, and the second transition was marked by a shift from infectious to chronic diseases associated with industrialization.

**pathogens**
microorganisms or other
agents that cause disease

**pathogens** have been identified, and South Asia, Central America, and tropical Africa have been highlighted as potential "hotspots" for emerging infectious diseases (Jones et al. 2008). These are defined as diseases that (1) are new to humans, (2) have been identified only recently in humans, or (3) existed previously but have reappeared after a period of decline (Lederberg et al. 1992). At the root of these diseases are human behaviours that have created ideal conditions for their outbreak and spread.

Among the most frequently identified factors underlying the emergence and re-emergence of infectious diseases are ecological changes associated with agriculture, mining, logging, and deforestation. Slash-and-burn agriculture, for example, creates standing pools of water that provide ideal breeding grounds for mosquitoes that carry malaria. The digging of irrigation ditches has facilitated the spread of schistosomiasis, and deforestation and logging have brought humans into contact with pathogenic microorganisms to which they have never been exposed before, resulting in the transmission of **zoonotic diseases** to humans. HIV, for example, is closely related to SIV, the simian immunodeficiency virus that is carried by chimpanzees as well as by an Old World monkey called the sooty mangabey. This virus is believed to have jumped from these primates to humans through hunting, butchering, and consumption of bush meat, a practice that is widespread among poorer households in parts of Central and West Africa. The hunting of primates for bush meat also appears to have caused the emergence of a new type of retrovirus, HTLV (human T-cell lymphotropic virus), among hunters in Cameroon as a result of their exposure to a related simian virus through cuts and bites on the skin (Wolfe et al. 2005).

**zoonotic diseases**
diseases that can be
transmitted from wild or
domesticated animals to
humans

Climate change and global warming have also contributed to the increased incidence of infectious diseases such as malaria, which kills 2 to 3 million people worldwide each year. As a result of rising temperatures, we are now seeing cases of malaria at higher latitudes and higher altitudes than before.[2] The mosquito that transmits dengue fever has also expanded its range as a result of global warming, from tropical regions where it is endemic to more temperate zones.

In addition to ecological disruption and climate change, economic and social disruption, poverty, sexual behaviour, and the increased movement of people (e.g., air travel, migration from rural to urban areas, flight from war) have resulted in the spread of infectious diseases. Airline travel means that pathogenic microorganisms can now be transported from one side of the globe to the other within a matter of hours. A perfect example is the 2003 outbreak of SARS (severe acute respiratory syndrome) in Toronto, which was ultimately traced to an individual who had boarded a plane in Hong Kong. Some of you may remember the fear and panic associated with that outbreak. To put this into perspective, however, keep in mind that nearly 800 individuals worldwide succumbed to SARS compared to an average of 4,000 who die of seasonal influenza *each year* in Canada alone. Travel to exotic locations also places tourists at risk of contracting diseases to which they have never been exposed. In urban areas of Indonesia, for instance, macaques trained to perform tricks for human audiences have been found to carry several retroviruses that are capable of infecting humans via scratches or bites (Schillaci et al. 2005, 2006; Engel et al. 2002). Tourist sites that are frequented by monkeys are another potential source of disease. Analyses of blood samples taken from macaques who reside in the "monkey temple" in Bali, for example, have revealed antibodies to the herpes virus, raising the possibility of its transmission to humans (Engel et al. 2002).

Large-scale food production has also come at a cost to our health. The mad cow scare in Britain in the 1990s highlighted the consequences of feeding cattle with meat from sheep that were infected with scrapie, a degenerative disease that affects sheep and goats. Consumption of meat thereby contaminated resulted in the transmission of mad cow disease (bovine spongiform encephalopathy, or BSE) to humans.[3] Closer to home, outbreaks of *E. coli* infection resulting from the ingestion of contaminated water and hamburger meat

---

2. Most cases of malaria documented in Canada each year are brought into the country from geographic areas where the disease is endemic.

3. Humans who consume BSE-infected meat develop a similar neurodegenerative disease known as new variant Creutzfeldt-Jakob disease.

have been reported in Canada and elsewhere in North America. In the town of Walkerton, Ontario, for example, contamination of the town's water supply by runoff from local farms was identified as the source of an *E. coli* outbreak in May 2000, which sickened about 2,500 individuals, killing seven.[4] The 2008 outbreak of another bacterial infection, listeriosis, was linked to contaminated meat-slicing machines at a well-known food processing plant in Ontario.[5]

Changes in the pathogenic organisms themselves are also leading to the emergence and re-emergence of infectious diseases. Like humans, disease-causing microorganisms evolve, and increased virulence can result from the exchange of genes with other organisms. Harmful strains of *Streptococcus*—once the cause of scarlet fever—have been linked to necrotizing fasciitis (flesh-eating disease) and toxic shock syndrome.[6] One of the major roadblocks to preventing and treating AIDS is that HIV constantly mutates. Similarly, the influenza virus changes its appearance from year to year, necessitating the development of a new vaccine annually to target the strains that could potentially strike. While most outbreaks of influenza are caused by Type B and Type C viruses, it is Type A that has been responsible for the flu pandemics that have occurred in human history. What makes Type A so dangerous is its ability to change dramatically by combining with a flu virus from another organism. Pigs, for instance, can become infected with both human and avian influenza A viruses, and the mixing of these two viruses within pigs can give rise to deadlier strains that can be transmitted to humans and passed from person to person. It was this mixing of flu strains that gave rise to the 1918 flu pandemic that killed 40 to 50 million people worldwide. In Canada alone, the pandemic claimed 30,000 to 50,000 lives (Herring 2000); small northern communities lacking stored food supplies and medicines were especially hard hit (Herring 1994a and b).[7] In contrast, the 2009 flu pandemic involved a new strain of H1N1 influenza that was made up of genes from human, swine, and avian flu viruses; however, it lacked the genes that made the 1918 strain so lethal.

The other major challenge facing public health officials today is the emergence of antibiotic-resistant strains of bacteria. Factors that have contributed to this trend are the overuse of antibiotics (e.g., taking them for viral infections for which they do no good), the failure by patients to take the full course of their medication, and the practice of putting antibiotics in animal feed in order to prevent infections among livestock. Tuberculosis has re-emerged as a leading killer, due in part to the rise of drug-resistant strains of the bacterium responsible for the disease, and to HIV/AIDS, with which an estimated 35 million people worldwide are now living. (Individuals with HIV are more susceptible to tuberculosis; infection with HIV can also lead to reactivation of latent tuberculosis.) Other notable examples of antibiotic-resistant bacteria include *Neisseria gonorrhoeae*, Methicillin-resistant *Staphylococcus aureus* (MRSA), and Vancomycin-resistant *Staphylococcus aureus* (VRSA).

## THE HUMAN LIFE COURSE

As we discussed in Chapter 5, in comparison to nonhuman primates, humans have slower growth, a longer period of maturation and dependency, a longer life span, and—in the case of females—a longer postmenopausal stage. As you will recall from Chapter 10, there has been much debate about the rate of growth in earlier *Homo* species such as *Homo ergaster*. Patterns of growth in modern humans have also been the focus of numerous studies (e.g., Bogin 1999; Hoppa and Fitzgerald 1999).

---

4. Millions of *E. coli* bacteria are present in our intestines and help maintain a healthy digestive system. The O157:H7 strain normally found in the intestines of cattle and other livestock, however, can cause serious illness and death in humans.

5. In this particular case, infection with *Listeria* bacteria in deli meats resulted in more than 50 cases of illness and a number of deaths.

6. Outbreaks of this syndrome in the 1980s were linked to the use of superabsorbent tampons.

7. Scientists have recently identified three genes in the 1918 flu strain that allowed the virus to invade the lungs and cause a severe form of pneumonia (Watanabe et al. 2009).

## The Early Years: Breastfeeding, Weaning, and Child Growth

**weaning**

the process by which infants gradually shift from a diet of breast milk to one consisting of other foods

Biological anthropologists have brought their unique biocultural perspective to the study of infant feeding practices in contemporary populations. Considerable variation exists in breastfeeding and **weaning** practices, with some infants being breastfed for only a short period of time, if at all, and others for several years. Factors underlying this variation include cultural beliefs about weaning, the availability of supplementary foods, a woman's reproductive status, and her role in the labour force. University of Calgary biocultural anthropologist Warren Wilson and colleagues recently examined weaning practices of the Makushi Amerindians of central Guyana in order to investigate the relationship between the length of exclusive breastfeeding and infant and child mortality (Wilson et al. 2006; see Box 16.2). This study was motivated by the controversy surrounding the World Health Organization's recommendation for exclusive breastfeeding during the first six months of life owing to the immunological benefits of breast milk. In contrast to their hypothesis that exclusive breastfeeding (EBF) for less than six months compromises the health of infants and children, Wilson and colleagues found no relationship between the length of EBF and infant and child mortality. They suggest several possible explanations for this finding, and conclude that international recommendations for exclusive breastfeeding up to six months of age must consider local cultural and environmental factors. Moffat's (2001) study of growth and **morbidity** indices in partially and exclusively breastfed infants from birth to seven months in Kathmandu, Nepal, also revealed no differences between the two groups, suggesting that a more relaxed recommendation of four to six months of EBF instead of the rigid recommendation of EBF for the first six months of life may be more bioculturally appropriate.

**morbidity**

a measure of the state of disease or disability from any cause in a population

On a broader scale, Dan Sellen's (2007) research on lactation biology and variation in breastfeeding and weaning practices also has public health implications. Humans are the only mammals to use complementary feeding, meaning that we routinely provide infants with complementary foods following a period of exclusive breastfeeding. Unfortunately, infant and child feeding practices are suboptimal in many parts of the world, resulting in high rates of illness and death. Identifying the social and cultural reasons for the failure to adopt current international recommendations for infant and child feeding is therefore crucial if we are to reduce morbidity and mortality rates in this age group.

**secular trend**

a directional change in phenotypic expression over time independent of change in the underlying genotype

Considerable research has been devoted to child growth. Taking a biocultural perspective, human biologists have examined the growth of children living in a variety of different environments and have identified multiple factors underlying variation in growth patterns. Tina Moffat's (2003) study of child growth in peri-urban Nepal, for instance, linked stunted growth—defined as low height for age—to parasitic infections associated with poor sanitation and contaminated drinking water. Closer to home, Rob Hoppa and Todd Garlie's (1998) analysis of child growth in 19th- to 20th-century Toronto revealed a **secular trend** toward increased height for age in more recent children—a trend common in industrialized countries over the past two centuries. Major contributing factors include a decline in infectious diseases and improvements in nutrition, hygiene, sanitation, and medical care.

## The Anthropology of Aging

**senescence**

the biological process by which an individual reaches an advanced age

At the other end of the human life cycle is old age. In developed countries, 20% of the population is over the age of 60, and this percentage is expected to increase to over 30% by 2030 (Kinsella and Velkoff 2001). Developing countries have increasingly aging populations, home to over half the world's senior citizens (individuals 65 years of age and older) (ibid.). The anthropological study of **senescence** has attracted considerable attention in recent years as our population becomes increasingly older (Crew 1993). Taking a biocultural approach, biological anthropologists have examined a variety of aspects of aging, including changes in life expectancy over the course of our evolutionary history, skeletal and reproductive aging, and the development of chronic diseases (Ice 2005). A variety of factors affect the rate of aging, including diet, physical activity, smoking, hormones, and genetics. Considerable individual and population variation exists, and some populations—such as the residents of the Japanese island of Okinawa—are known for being long-lived.[8] You may recall from Chapter 11 that old age for Neandertals was about 40 years! Medical advances in recent decades have allowed us to extend our life span, and people in industrialized countries are now living longer than ever. In Canada the life expectancy is currently 82.7 years for women and 78 years for men. It is considerably lower in countries where access to a healthy diet and medical care is lacking, however, and despite hopes of reaching the maximum human life span of 120 years (Ruiz-Torres and Beier 2005), few people ever come close to this age.

As we get older, our bodies begin to break down. We become shorter as our vertebral column compresses, and many of us become heavier as our metabolic rate slows down. So why do we age in the first place? Hypotheses proposed to explain aging have focused on both physiological and evolutionary mechanisms. The former include the damaging effects of mutations and **free radicals** on the somatic (i.e., body) cells, as well as wear and tear on the joints and other tissues (Ricklefs and Finch 1995). With respect to evolutionary explanations, two theories predominate: the **antagonistic pleiotropy theory** (Williams 1957) and the **disposable soma theory** (Kirkwood and Holliday 1979). In Chapter 3 we introduced you to the concept of pleiotropy, a phenomenon whereby a gene controls for more than one phenotypic trait. According to the antagonistic pleiotropy theory of aging, selection for a gene that benefits an organism early in life by enhancing fertility is harmful later on (Williams 1957). Alternatively, the disposable soma theory is based on the argument that since energy is required for both reproduction and the maintenance of the body, organisms balance these needs by directing more of their energy to reproduction and less to maintaining the body's cells (Kirkwood and Holliday 1979). The end result in both cases is aging and ultimately death.

# NUTRITIONAL ANTHROPOLOGY

## Undernutrition

If we look at *Canada's Food Guide*, a healthy diet consists of a balance of four different food groups: protein, dairy, fruits and vegetables, and grains. Yet some populations have traditionally subsisted on a diet that would not be considered "balanced" by North American standards. The Inuit are a case in point. Their traditional diet consisted primarily of protein and fat, with very little plant food and no dairy products, yet they were able to derive all of the nutrients they need from these foods. Clearly, then, what matters is not so much the types of foods you eat but what nutrients they contain.

An estimated 2 billion people worldwide suffer from nutritional deficiencies, including protein malnutrition and deficiencies of vitamins A, $B_1$, $B_3$, C, and D, as well as iron, iodine, and folic acid (see Table 14.1). Many of these deficiencies are the direct result of a lack of access to foods containing these nutrients, either because people cannot afford to buy them or because they are simply unavailable. In other cases, an overreliance on a narrow range of food items means that some populations lack key nutrients in their diet. Populations that rely heavily on cereals, for instance, are prone to protein, iron, and vitamin B deficiencies. In the past, scurvy resulting from a deficiency in vitamin C—a nutrient required for the synthesis of collagen in bones and other connective tissues—was common among sailors who spent long periods of time at sea with no fresh fruits and vegetables. Food processing also plays a role in the availability of nutrients. Some food processing methods can destroy nutrients or prevent their absorption by the intestine. The refining of rice, for instance, removes vitamin $B_1$, thereby increasing the risk of vitamin $B_1$ deficiency, or **beriberi**, among populations that rely heavily on this food item.

To prevent nutritional deficiencies from occurring, some of the foods we eat today have been fortified. For example, vitamins A and D are added to milk, vitamin C to fruit drinks, iodine to salt, iron to cereal grains, calcium to orange juice, and folic acid to flour. Scientists at the University of Toronto have recently come up with a way of fortifying salt with iron

www.statcan.gc.ca

**free radicals**
unstable molecules that react with other molecules, causing damage to the body's cells

**antagonistic pleiotropy theory**
the theory that aging is the result of a gene that benefits an organism early in life by enhancing fertility but that is detrimental later on

**disposable soma theory**
the theory that organisms balance their energy needs by directing more of their energy to reproduction and less to maintaining the body

**beriberi**
a disease caused by a deficiency of vitamin $B_1$ resulting in a number of neurological, cardiovascular, and physiological ailments

8. This particular population has been identified as having the longest life span in the world. As of 2004, approximately 1,800 individuals out of a total population of 1.35 million on Okinawa were over the age of 100 (Wiley and Allen 2009).

**Table 14.1**  Common nutritional deficiencies seen today

| Nutrient | Sources | Disease/condition | Symptoms | Individuals at Risk |
|---|---|---|---|---|
| Protein | Meat, eggs, dairy | Kwashiorkor | Swollen abdomen, loss of muscle mass, changes in skin pigmentation | Mainly young children; a high prevalence in sub-Saharan Africa |
| Vitamin A | Carrots, sweet potatoes, squash, liver | Vitamin A deficiency | Blindness, weakened immune system, impaired embryonic development, increased risk of maternal mortality | Young children; a high prevalence in Southeast Asia |
| Vitamin $B_1$ (thiamine) | Brown rice, beans, peas, | Beriberi | Fatigue, weight loss, cardiovascular, gastrointestinal, and neurological symptoms | Individuals who rely heavily on refined rice; common in parts of Asia |
| Vitamin $B_3$ (niacin) | Red meat, fish, dairy products, almonds, leafy green vegetables | Pellagra | Diarrhea, dermatitis, dementia | Individuals who rely heavily on corn and other niacin-deficient foods; common in parts of Africa and Asia |
| Vitamin D | Sunlight, egg yolks, cod liver oil | Rickets (infants and children); osteomalacia (adults) | Skeletal deformities, loss of bone mass | Infants and children, especially dark-skinned individuals living in northern climates or individuals confined to the indoors |
| Iron | Meat, fish, poultry, broccoli | Iron deficiency anemia | Fatigue, irritability, pale skin, mental impairment | Pregnant women and children |
| Iodine | Seafood, seaweed, iodized salt | Iodine deficiency | Goiter in adolescents and adults, impaired fetal development | People living in areas with iodine-poor soil and water; common in parts of Africa |
| Folic Acid | Leafy green vegetables, chickpeas, lentils, fruits | Folic acid deficiency | Birth defects; heart disease in adults | Pregnant women |

in an attempt to treat and prevent iron deficiency anemia, one of the most common health problems in the world today. When iron is combined with iodine, the reaction that occurs results in evaporation of the iodine. Thus the challenge facing this research team, led by L.L. Diosady, Professor of Food Engineering at the University of Toronto, was to add iron in such a way that the iodine would remain stable and both elements would be easily absorbed by the digestive system. After 10 years of experimenting, they developed a technique known as microencapsulation, which involves coating iodine with an agent consisting of a water-soluble starch (Diosady and Venkatesh Mannar 2000). This new double-fortified salt has already been distributed to parts of India and Africa, and further testing is currently under way.

If left untreated, nutritional deficiencies can have a profound effect on the health of an individual. Poor nutrition among females, for example, can result in low birth weight babies, which in turn can increase the risk of infant mortality. Protein-calorie malnutrition and vitamin deficiencies during childhood can impair cognitive ability and result in growth stunting, skeletal abnormalities, reduced adult stature, and reduced work capacity in adulthood. The synergistic relationship between malnutrition and infectious diseases also means that malnourished individuals are more susceptible to infectious diseases. You might be surprised to learn that nutritional deficiencies exist today not only in developing countries but also in industrialized nations. A recent study by the Canadian Paediatric Society revealed 104 confirmed cases of rickets in Canadian children between 2002 and 2004, the majority of them individuals living in the North and infants with darker skin who were breastfed without receiving supplemental vitamin D (Ward et al. 2007). Dan Sellen, Canada Research Chair in Human Ecology and Public Health Nutrition at the University of Toronto, Esteban Parra of the University of Toronto Mississauga, Tina Moffat, and Warren Wilson are currently investigating the vitamin D status among immigrants to Canada with the goal of identifying the risk factors underlying vitamin D deficiency in this community, and assessing the knowledge and adoption by new Canadians of current recommendations to supplement breastfed infants with this vitamin.

## Nutritional Excess: Overnutrition and Obesity

The past few decades have witnessed a dramatic increase in the number of people who are overweight or obese. **Anthropometric** data typically used to assess obesity and body fatness include height, weight, waist circumference, and skinfold thicknesses. The standard measure of obesity is the **body mass index** (BMI), calculated as body weight $(kg)/height(m)^2$. In Canada and elsewhere, BMI values are grouped into four categories: (1) underweight (BMI $<18.5$ kg/m$^2$); (2) normal weight (BMI ranging from 18.5 to 24.9 kg/m$^2$); (3) overweight (BMI ranging from 25 to 29.9 kg/m$^2$); and (4) obese (BMI $> 30$ kg/m$^2$). Over 300 million adults worldwide are estimated to have a BMI greater than 30, and an additional 700 million are considered to be overweight (Ulijaszek and Lofink 2006). Regions with the highest rates of obesity include the United States, much of Europe and the Middle East, parts of Latin America, South Africa, and the South Pacific. In Canada, a national survey conducted in 2004 revealed that 23.1% of adults were obese. Rates are even higher for First Nations and Inuit peoples and for long-term immigrants. Scientists studying the health effects of immigration to North America, for example, have found that new Canadians, while less likely to be overweight or obese than non-immigrants when they first arrive in the country, show higher rates of overweight and obesity after a decade or so than recently arrived immigrants, due to factors such as the transition to a less healthy diet and a decline in activity levels (Tremblay et al. 2005). This phenomenon is part of the "**healthy immigrant effect**." Other factors contributing to rising rates of obesity include the availability of ready-to-eat prepackaged foods, larger portion sizes (i.e., "supersizing"), increased snacking, aggressive marketing of cheap, high-calorie/high-fat foods, dining out, high degrees of economic inequality, and low levels of physical activity. As obesity is a major risk factor for chronic diseases such as diabetes and cardiovascular disease, reducing the incidence of this condition has become a major public health priority.

Biological anthropologists have contributed a great deal to our knowledge of the distribution and determinants of obesity, and their biocultural perspective is reflected in numerous studies of this condition (Ulijaszek and Lofink 2006). Kue Young's (1996) investigation of obesity among the Inuit of the central Arctic, for example, linked high rates of obesity to low levels of education, low socioeconomic status, and high levels of acculturation. Cultural perceptions of body image also play a role, with some cultures such as those of the South Pacific viewing a larger body size as a symbol of health, fertility, high status, and beauty.

A particularly worrying trend is the increase in the prevalence of overweight and obese children. From 1978 to 2004, the prevalence of overweight and obesity in Canadian children aged 2 to 17 jumped from 17% to 27% for boys and from 15% to 25% for girls (Shields 2006) (Figure 14.2). Given the rising rates of obesity among children, this age group has become the focus of an increasing number of studies in recent years. Richard Lazenby and colleagues, for instance, examined obesity in children from four different elementary schools in Prince George, B.C., located in neighbourhoods of differing socioeconomic status (SES) (Lazenby et al. 2007). They found a trend toward increasing rates of overweight and obesity in all four schools compared to national standards, with the trend most pronounced in the school with the lowest socioeconomic status. Similarly, Tina Moffat's and Tracey Galloway's studies of

**anthropometric**
relating to the measurement of the human body

**body mass index**
a measure of body fatness, calculated as body weight (kg)/height(m)$^2$

www.hc-sc.gc.ca

**healthy immigrant effect**
a pattern in which the initially positive health status of new immigrants declines following immigration

http://www.oecd.org

**CHAPTER 14** Biology of Contemporary and Past Populations

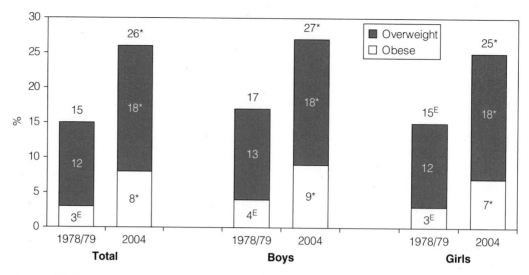

Figure 14.2  The prevalence of overweight and obesity in Canadian children aged 2 to 17 years has increased significantly from 1978/79 to 2004.

Statistics Canada, *Measured Obesity: Overweight Canadian Children and Adolescents, 2004* (Nutrition: Findings from the Canadian Community Health Survey), 82-620-M, Issue 2005001, July 6, 2006.

growth and food consumption patterns in elementary schoolchildren in Hamilton, Ontario, revealed high rates of overweight and obesity in children of lower socioeconomic status (Moffat and Galloway 2007, 2008; Moffat et al., 2005; see Box 14.1).

## BOX 14.1    PROFILE... Biocultural Research on Child Growth and Nutrition

Courtesy of Tina Moffat

Dr. Tina Moffat of McMaster University investigated the growth and nutrition of school-age children living in socio-economically contrasting neighbourhoods in the city of

Hamilton, Ontario. She used a mixed-methods approach that combined quantitative methods (anthropometric measures of height and weight, 24-hour dietary recall) with qualitative measures of the school and neighbourhood environment (observation, interview, focus groups with children) to compare the growth and nutritional outcomes of children living in diverse socioeconomic conditions. The study hypothesized that children's stature and adiposity would vary according to the socioeconomic conditions in urban North American neighbourhoods. The research compared the growth of 6- to 10-year-old children attending elementary schools in three neighbourhoods that differ in terms of socioeconomic and recent-immigrant status. Results showed that 27.4% of the total sample of children could be classified as overweight or obese. However, analysis by socioeconomic status (SES) revealed that there were approximately twice as many children in the overweight category in the two low-SES schools compared to the high SES school (Moffat et al. 2005). Further analysis by individual school indicated that children attending the school in the poorest neighbourhood had a significantly lower mean height relative to the most affluent school, despite comparable proportions of recent immigrants in each neighbourhood.

The study also examined the diet of elementary schoolchildren in socioeconomically contrasting neighbourhoods. Data were collected through 24-hour dietary recall interviews. Low intake of vegetables and fruit and milk products was found for students at all three schools, and only a small proportion drank milk during school lunch. The authors recommended that educators discourage the consumption of sugar-sweetened drinks during school lunches and promote the consumption of milk or calcium-fortified drinks (Moffat and Galloway 2008).

Dr. Tracey Galloway investigated similar growth and nutritional processes in rural Canadian communities. In her study of schoolchildren attending rural Ontario schools, she reported that 28.6% of children were overweight or obese. While obesity was as common in this population as in other North American studies, prevalence was unequally divided by gender, with 15% of boys and 7% of girls classified as obese (Galloway 2006). Dietary analysis revealed a similar pattern. There was low overall consumption of vitamins, minerals, and micronutrients, and dietary fibre, as well as high-energy intake across the sample. However, boys consumed signifi-

cantly greater energy, protein, carbohydrate, calcium, iron, and phosphorus than girls (Galloway 2007). The gendered pattern of growth and nutrition observed in this rural sample may arise from sociocultural processes such as selective child-feeding practices in favour of males and gendered body size ideals.

In combination, Moffat and Galloway's research highlights the importance of local environmental conditions in shaping children's biologies. The processes that shape children's growth patterns are often unique to the particular communities in which children reside (Moffat and Galloway 2007). Most studies of child health and nutrition tend to portray Canadian children's environments as homogenous. This practice may obscure variability that is of significant interest to researchers and health and social service providers.

Source: Written by Tina Moffat (McMaster University) and Tracey Galloway (University of Toronto). Tina Moffat is an Associate Professor in the Department of Anthropology at McMaster University. Tracey Galloway is a Post-Doctoral Fellow in the Dalla Lana School of Public Health, University of Toronto.

## What Exactly Are We Putting into Our Bodies?

How many times have you had a craving for a McDonald's Big Mac or a Tim Hortons iced cappuccino? Before you reach for that burger or drink, consider this: by eating just one of these items you run the risk of exceeding your total daily recommended intake of fat and/or calories (see Table 14.2). A quick look at the nutrition labels of many of the foods we often eat reveals that the caloric and saturated fat content of these foods is exceedingly high.[9] And beware! Foods advertised as "reduced fat" or "a source of omega-3 polyunsaturated fatty acids" are not always healthy options. So before you reach for one of these items, read the nutrition label first!

## Nutritional Adaptation

As we discussed above, many of us today have access to a seemingly limitless supply of food. Obesity was virtually nonexistent until about 10,000 years ago (Brown and Krick 2001, cited in Ulijaszek and Lofink 2006). Our earlier ancestors lived a very different existence characterized by a reliance on wild animal and plant foods. According to S. Boyd Eaton, a physician and medical anthropologist, we are genetically programmed to consume a diet very different from the one that most North Americans consume today (Eaton and Konner 1985). Significant differences between the Paleolithic and modern Western diet include a higher intake of cereals, dairy products, refined sugars, vegetable oils, saturated fat, and salt in the latter (Cordain et al. 2005). As a consequence, we are now experiencing many diet-related chronic diseases that would have been absent in the past. Among affluent nations today, these "diseases of civilization" are the leading cause of morbidity and mortality.

## Diabetes and the Thrifty Genotype

One manifestation of the disjunction between the diet to which we have genetically adapted and the diet we consume today is the rising rate of diabetes, a chronic disease characterized by high blood sugar. There are two main forms of diabetes: Type 1, also known as

9. The labelling of all prepackaged foods with their nutritional content became mandatory in Canada in 2007.

**Table 14.2** Caloric and saturated fat content of popular food items

| Food Item | # of Calories | Saturated Fat Content (g) |
|---|---|---|
| Tim Hortons triple chocolate cookie | 250 | 8 |
| Starbucks hot chocolate | 370 (grande) | 9 |
| Starbucks pumpkin spice latte | 380 (grande) | 8 |
| Starbucks eggnog latte | 470 (grande) | 13 |
| Tim Hortons breakfast sandwich with sausage | 520 | 21 |
| McDonald's Egg McMuffin with sausage | 450 | 10 |
| Wendy's chicken BLT salad | 470 | 10 |
| Orville Redenbacher's buttery popcorn | 190 (1 mini-bag) | 6 |
| Starbucks caramel frappuccino with whipped cream | 380 (grande size) | 9 |
| President's Choice Indian chicken korma | 575 | 12 |
| Mars bar | 260 | 6 |
| Baskin Robbins mint chocolate chip ice cream | 270 (one scoop) | 10 |
| President's Choice macaroni and cheese (single serving package) | 500 | 8 |
| President's Choice sirloin burgers | 340 | 12 |
| Stouffers Bistro Italiano spaghetti carbonara | 420 | 5 |
| Ben & Jerry's chocolate chip cookie dough ice cream | 270 (half cup) | 10 |
| Homestyle two-bite brownies (2) | 190 | 4 |
| Lean Cuisine meat lasagna | 310 | 4 |
| Master Choice Lifesmart Omega-3 beef burgers | 290 | 7 |

juvenile diabetes, and Type 2, also referred to as non–insulin dependent diabetes mellitus (NIDDM).[10] In individuals with Type 1 diabetes, the pancreas stops producing insulin, the hormone that allows for the absorption of glucose from the blood into the cells. This leads to blood sugar levels that are higher than normal. Type 2, in contrast, is characterized by **insulin resistance**, i.e., the failure of tissues to react to the insulin produced by the pancreas. Consequences of both types of the disease include organ damage, blindness, amputation and, if untreated, ultimately death.

Global rates of diabetes have skyrocketed in recent decades, and more than 180 million people are estimated to have either Type 1 or Type II diabetes. It is becoming more and more prevalent worldwide and is also occurring at younger ages.[11] The major contributors are obesity and decreased physical activity; other risk factors include low socioeconomic status, a high level of acculturation, high unemployment rates, and a lack of education. As with obesity, rates of diabetes are significantly higher among aboriginal populations than

**insulin resistance**
the failure of body cells to respond to insulin in order to regulate plasma glucose, resulting in elevated levels of both insulin (hyperinsulemia) and glucose (hyperglycemia)

http://www.who.int

---

10. A third form, gestational diabetes, is a temporary condition characterized by the body's inability to use insulin during pregnancy.

11. In the past, Type 2 diabetes was seen mainly in older adults but is now being diagnosed in children as young as eight (Dean et al. 1998).

non-aboriginal ones. The Pima Indians of Arizona, for example, currently have the world's highest rate of Type 2 diabetes. Rates of diabetes in Canada are also three to five times higher among First Nations populations compared to the general population.

Considerable debate has focused on the contribution of genetic versus environmental factors to the development of diabetes. The idea that diabetes has a genetic basis was first articulated by the geneticist James Neel in his classic 1962 paper "Diabetes mellitus: a 'thrifty' genotype rendered detrimental by 'progress'?" In that paper, Neel postulated that indigenous populations possessed a genotype that allowed them to store excess carbohydrates as fat in times of plenty and to draw from those stores when food was scarce. While this genotype would have been advantageous in the past, when periodic food shortages were common, in times when food was plentiful (as it is today), the genotype would promote the continuous storage of fat reserves, leading to obesity and ultimately to diabetes. Critics of this hypothesis point out that famines severe enough to cause substantial mortality are uncommon and that when they do strike, they target primarily the very young and the very old (i.e., nonreproductive members of society). Furthermore, deaths during periods of famine tend to result from disease rather than starvation, and rates of obesity do not increase between famines (Speakman 2006). Finally, these "thrifty genes" have yet to be discovered (ibid.). Higher frequencies of certain **cytokine** genotypes have been found to characterize Canadian First Nations populations compared to Caucasians, but these may be linked to selective pressures associated with parasitic and fungal infections present in the environment to which First Nations have adapted (Larcombe et al. 2005).

It is clear today that diabetes results from a complex interaction between genetic and environmental factors. Efforts to identify these factors are exemplified by a number of interdisciplinary projects in Canada and elsewhere. At the University of Toronto Mississauga, Esteban Parra is searching for genes that he believes increase the susceptibility of Mexican Americans to Type 2 diabetes. Using a technique called "admixture mapping," which involves looking at the proportions of genes derived from different populations (e.g., Native American versus European), Parra and his colleagues have estimated the proportion of Native-American admixture in a sample of individuals from Mexico City to be 65%, which suggests that Mexican Americans are at high risk for this disease (Martinez-Marignac et al. 2007).

Closer to home, a number of community-based projects have been set up to investigate the high rate of diabetes in First Nations communities in Canada. One example is the Sandy Lake Health and Diabetes Project (SLHDP), launched in 1993 in the Sioux Lookout region of northwestern Ontario. The objectives of this project are to determine the prevalence of diabetes at Sandy Lake, identify the risk factors involved, and develop a strategy to prevent the disease. Researchers from the University of Western Ontario and Mount Sinai Hospital in Toronto have already identified a genetic variant among residents of this community who have Type 2 diabetes (Hegele et al. 1999).[12] Similar community-based initiatives to prevent diabetes have been established elsewhere in Ontario as well as in other provinces.

## Lactose Intolerance

A survey of your class would probably reveal that some of you are lactose intolerant or lactase deficient, meaning that you possess a variant of the lactase gene that results in the inability of your body to produce lactase, the enzyme required to digest lactose, the sugar found in milk. As a result, when you drink a glass of milk or consume other dairy products such as ice cream, you experience gastrointestinal discomfort, diarrhoea, bloating, and gas. For most individuals, lactose intolerance develops naturally after the age of about two years, when the body begins to produce less lactase.[13] Some individuals, however, retain the

**cytokines**
proteins produced by white blood cells in response to the presence of pathogens. They interact with cells of the immune system and stimulate them to respond to the infection

---

12. This variant of the hepatic nuclear factor 1-alpha gene, known as the S319 allele, was found to be significantly more common in residents with diabetes than in those without.

13. Congenital lactose intolerance, a much rarer condition, is characterized by the inability to digest lactose at birth.

ability to digest lactose throughout life. In fact, the incidence of lactose intolerance varies greatly worldwide, from less than 5% in Swedish populations to nearly 100% in many Asian populations.

We all know the benefits of drinking milk: it helps build strong bones and teeth. Why, then, do some populations possess the ability to digest dairy products while others do not? The key lies in the cultural history of certain populations. More specifically, populations who possess this ability have a long history of cattle domestication and dairy farming. These include northern and central Europeans and African pastoralists (herders). Lactose intolerance is, in fact, the norm for most populations around the world, and this condition was present in our early ancestors, who would have had no source of milk after weaning. Under such circumstances, natural selection would have favoured an end to the production of lactase after weaning, possibly to allow the body to save energy (Weiss 2004). With the domestication of cattle some 5,000 to 10,000 years ago, however, the persistence of lactase after early childhood would have been advantageous in allowing for digestion of nutrient-rich milk. Thus natural selection would have favoured a mutation allowing for the continued production of lactase, either to allow individuals to take advantage of the nutrients in milk, or possibly to facilitate increased absorption of calcium in more northern latitudes where levels of ultraviolet radiation are lower and the production of vitamin D, required for the uptake of calcium in the body, is reduced. Being able to drink milk would also have been advantageous to those populations living in hot, arid environments where water is scarce (ibid.). The extraction of DNA from one Mesolithic and eight early Neolithic skeletons from Europe points to a recent origin for this mutation and provides support for the argument that dairy farming was the catalyst for the rapid evolution of lactose tolerance (Burger et al. 2007). Furthermore, analyses of DNA taken from modern East Africans have revealed several mutations that differ from the one found in northern Europeans, indicating that the ability to digest lactose arose independently in the two regions (Tishkoff et al. 2007).[14]

# HUMAN ADAPTABILITY

## The Adaptive Significance of Skin Colour

The largest organ in the human body is the skin. Would you believe it covers more than two square meters! The colour of your skin is directly related to the amount of melanin it produces.[15] Formed in cells called **melanocytes**, melanin production is controlled by an enzyme called **tyrosinase**. If the gene for this enzyme is defective, the end result is **albinism**, a condition in which no melanin is produced. Scientists have yet to identify the genes that underlie skin colour, though a number of candidate genes, including the *MC1R* gene (see Chapter 11), have been suggested (Norton et al. 2007).

The evolution of skin colour variation has been the focus of numerous studies, and a variety of biological, cultural, and environmental factors have been implicated. When we look at the global distribution of skin colour (Figure 14.3), we notice a close correlation between skin colour and latitude. Specifically, populations living at higher latitudes have lighter skin than those living closer to the equator.[16]

A number of hypotheses have been proposed to explain the adaptive significance of light-coloured skin. The most widely accepted hypothesis is that light skin was selected for in areas of lower ultraviolet radiation in order to allow for the adequate synthesis of vitamin D, which is crucial for bone growth and development. This explanation—commonly referred to as the vitamin D hypothesis—has gained widespread acceptance (but see Robins 2009),

**melanocytes**
cells that produce melanin

**tyrosinase**
the enzyme that controls the production of melanin

**albinism**
a condition characterized by a complete lack of melanin

---

14. This is an excellent example of convergent evolution.

15. Skin colour has traditionally been measured by reflectometry, a technique that measures the amount of light reflected off the skin. Light-coloured skin reflects more light and dark-coloured skin, less light.

16. This relationship was first described by Italian geographer Renato Basutti, who plotted the distribution on a map but extrapolated for those regions for which he had no data.

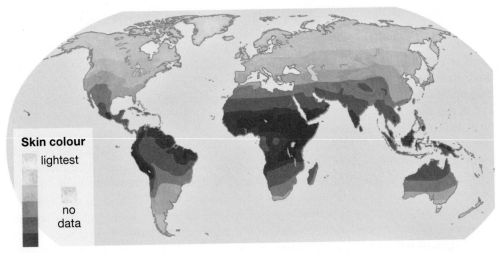

**Figure 14.3** The geographic distribution of skin colour corresponds closely with latitude. Note, however, that this pattern is stronger in the Southern Hemisphere than in the Northern Hemisphere and is more pronounced in Africa than in South America.

Jablonski, N.G. (2004). The evolution of human skin and skin colour. *Annual Review of Anthropology* 33: 585–623. Copyright © 2004. Reproduced with permission of Annual Reviews, Inc. via Copyright Clearance Center.'

and today dark-skinned populations living in northern Europe and the northeastern United States suffer from higher rates of rickets and osteomalacia than light-skinned populations living in the same areas.[17] There are, however, exceptions to the pattern of light skin in northern latitudes. The Inuit, for instance, have darker skin than we would expect, given the latitude at which they live. One explanation for this deviation from the normal pattern lies in the high vitamin D content of fish and marine mammals, foods that make up their traditional diet. As well, the Inuit are relatively recent newcomers to the Arctic, having migrated to North America only about 5,000 years ago. A recent migration also explains why populations of Bantu-speakers living in South Africa have darker skin than other populations in this region. Indeed, sub-Saharan African populations exhibit a great deal of variation in skin colour, in part reflecting their migratory history and the length of time these populations have lived in their new homeland (Relethford 2000). The same explanation holds true for indigenous populations of South America, whose lighter skin compared to populations living at similar latitudes elsewhere in the world likely reflects their more recent arrival on that continent (Jablonski and Chaplin 2000).

Hemispheric differences in skin colour are also apparent. Specifically, a greater proportion of people with dark skin are found in the Southern Hemisphere, where ultraviolet radiation is greater than in the Northern Hemisphere (Relethford 1997). Finally, sex differences in skin colour have been noted, with females generally having lighter coloured skin than males. While sexual selection has been invoked to explain this phenomenon (Darwin 1871; Frost 1994; Aoki 2002)—namely, that males prefer females with lighter skin—this observation may also reflect females' greater need for calcium—in part regulated by vitamin D—during pregnancy and lactation (Jablonski and Chaplin 2000).

What about the adaptive significance of dark skin? One of the most common explanations is that dark skin was selected for in areas of high UV radiation in order to protect the skin from cancer. One criticism of this argument is that skin cancer does not typically strike individuals until their postreproductive years and would therefore have had no effect on their reproductive fitness. Thus there would be little selective pressure for darker skin. More recently, an alternative explanation has been proposed based on the observation that exposure

---

17. Light-skinned individuals can also suffer from rickets if they spend most of their time indoors or are fully covered with clothing when they are outdoors.

**CHAPTER 14** Biology of Contemporary and Past Populations

to intense sunlight can substantially reduce folate levels in light-skinned individuals. Folate is a B vitamin that is essential for the development of the brain and spinal cord in the embryo. It is also important in spermatogenesis. In pregnant women, low levels of folate can result in neural-tube defects such as spina bifida. This is why women planning to become pregnant are advised to take folic acid supplements (folic acid is the synthetic form of folate). Because high levels of ultraviolet radiation can break down folate, dark skin was selected for, according to this argument, in order to protect the body's supply of folate and thereby increase the survival chances of a woman's offspring (Jablonski and Chaplin 2002).

What, then, was the skin colour of our earliest ancestors? According to anthropologist Nina Jablonski, early hominins probably had fair skin like chimpanzees. Moving from the forest to the savannah, however, meant greater exposure to the sun and a greater need for a more efficient cooling system. A subsequent reduction in body hair and an increase in the number of sweat glands, which were more widely distributed across the body, would have allowed early hominins to dissipate body heat.[18] Recall from Chapter 10 that *Homo ergaster* had long legs, suggesting that this hominin walked longer distances and thus would have required a more efficient cooling mechanism. At the same time, natural selection would have begun to favour darker skin in order to protect hominins from the damaging effects of high levels of ultraviolet radiation in tropical Africa. Thus, early members of the genus *Homo* would have had dark skin (ibid.). As they moved farther from the equator, however, selection for lighter coloured skin would have occurred in order to allow them to produce sufficient quantities of vitamin D.

## Living at High Altitude

Living in a high-altitude environment poses a number of challenges, including cold temperatures, low humidity, wind, and reduced food resources. The most significant challenge, however, is **hypoxia**—that is, lack of oxygen. The higher you go, the fewer the number of oxygen molecules are found per unit volume of air. At the peak of Mount Everest, for example, the lungs get only 25% of the oxygen available at sea level. The physiological responses to this condition include increased ventilation (i.e., breathing) and heart rate as the body attempts to obtain more oxygen and carry it to the tissues. Individuals born and raised at low elevation who move to high altitude later in life may experience the onset of acute mountain sickness, which is characterized by headaches, dizziness, and nausea. If you have ever travelled to a high altitude, you may have experienced some of these symptoms. Prolonged stays at high altitude can lead to pulmonary and cerebral edema—the accumulation of fluid in the lungs and brain respectively, both of which can be fatal. While native lowlanders can avoid these problems through gradual **acclimatization**,[19] a number of populations are well adapted to high-altitude environments (defined as elevations above 2500 m) and can function very well in such settings. For example, the Tibetans of the Himalayas and the Quechua and Aymara of the Andes exhibit physiological characteristics that differ from those of native lowlanders. These include greater lung volume, greater blood flow to the tissues, and a higher number of red blood cells.

Various hypotheses have been proposed to explain how these populations have adapted to their environments. The **developmental adaptation hypothesis**, put forward by human biologist Roberto Frisancho (1969, 1977), proposes that the physiological characteristics displayed by high-altitude natives are acquired during growth and development. Specifically, metabolic energy is preferentially directed toward the body's oxygen transport system at the expense of the musculoskeletal system. The end result is earlier maturation, smaller adult stature, and lower birth weight babies.

Physiological differences among high altitude populations suggest that genetic factors may also be involved and that high-altitude adaptation may be a product of natural selection. Compared to Andeans, for instance, Tibetans have higher ventilation levels, lower concentrations

**hypoxia**

lack of oxygen, as seen at high altitudes

**acclimatization**

physiological changes that occur in response to changes in the environment

**developmental adaptation hypothesis**

the hypothesis that the physiological characteristics exhibited by high-altitude populations arise during growth and development

---

18. The loss of body hair is thought to have occurred by about 1.6 mya.

19. Mountain climbers attempting to scale Mount Everest typically undertake a series of short ascents followed by descents in preparation for their final climb to the top.

of hemoglobin, lower levels of oxygen in their arterial blood, greater blood flow, and a higher density of capillaries, which are the tiny vessels that supply blood to the tissues (Beall 2007; Figure 14.4). Similarly, high-altitude Ethiopian populations seem to have adapted physiologically to their environments differently than Andeans and Tibetans (Beall et al. 2002). The search for factors underlying these differences has focused largely on genes. While a number of candidate genes have been identified, the specific genetic loci have yet to be identified.

Other factors have been implicated in the variation seen among populations living at high elevations. For instance, differences between the Andean Aymara and Quechua in the physical growth of children have been linked to differences in microclimates and consequently food availability and nutritional status of these children (de Meer et al. 1993).

## Adaptation to Temperature Extremes

Before we look at the specific ways in which humans adapt to temperature stress, it is important to understand how the body maintains its internal temperature, a process we call **thermoregulation**. Our normal body temperature is 37°C, but it can fluctuate by up to one degree depending on time of day and activity level. Greater temperatures can occur as a result of illness, unusually high activity, or exposure to extreme heat. Conversely, lower temperatures can result from exposure to extreme cold. The maintenance of a stable internal environment, or **homeostasis**, requires a balance between heat gain and heat loss. This requires a variety of physiological (i.e., involuntary) and behavioural (i.e., voluntary) mechanisms.

## Heat Stress

As you learned in Chapter 12, modern humans evolved in Africa, and our greater tolerance to heat stress than cold stress reflects, to a large extent, this evolutionary history. All human populations, regardless of where they live, have the ability to respond to heat stress both biologically and behaviourally. Those of you who have travelled to southern climates know that people living in these regions tend to dress in light clothes, live in houses that are built to absorb heat and keep it away from sleeping quarters, and schedule their activities to avoid the hottest part of the day (thus, the siesta). The dangers of overheating include muscle cramps due to salt depletion, heat exhaustion due to loss of fluids, and heat stroke, which can be life threatening. Every year many lives are lost to heat stroke during the summer months.

**thermoregulation**
the maintenance of a relatively constant body temperature

**homeostasis**
the maintenance within the body of a stable environment

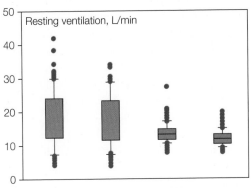
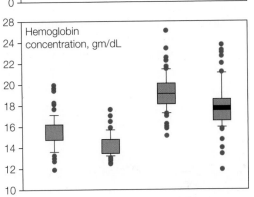
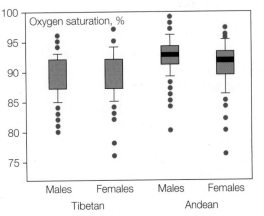

**Figure 14.4** Physiological differences are apparent among high-altitude populations. These include differences in resting ventilation, hemoglobin concentration, and oxygen saturation.

Beall, C.M., (2007). Two routes to functional adaptation: Tibetan and Andean high-altitude natives, *Proceedings of the National Academy of Sciences* 104(1): 8655–8660. Copyright 2007 National Academy of Sciences, USA. Reprinted with permission.

**CHAPTER 14** Biology of Contemporary and Past Populations

**vasodilation**

expansion of the peripheral blood vessels, resulting in increased blood flow to the skin surface

We respond biologically to heat stress in two ways: **vasodilation** and sweating. Vasodilation is characterized by the expansion of peripheral blood vessels, which allows for increased blood flow to the skin surface and, consequently, the loss of body heat. Sweating, the primary cooling mechanism, involves the sweat glands, of which we have more than a million in our bodies.[20] An increase in temperature signals the activation of these glands, and perspiration begins to form on the skin surface. The convective evaporation of this perspiration cools the body.[21]

Factors influencing responses to, and tolerance of, heat stress include sex, age, the amount of body fat, and the level of physical fitness and overall health (Hanna and Brown 1983). Women, for example, tend to sweat less than men (you have probably heard the expression "men sweat and women glow"). Also, the very young and the very old are less tolerant of heat than young and middle-aged adults because of reduced thermoregulatory capacity; individuals with greater amounts of body fat have a harder time coping with heat than those with less body fat; and fitter and healthier individuals are better able to endure heat than individuals with poor physical fitness and pre-existing health problems. Body size and shape also influence one's ability to cope with heat stress. In Chapter 11 we talked about Bergmann's and Allen's Rules with respect to Neandertals. In general, people living in warmer climates tend to have lower body mass than those living in colder climates (Bergmann's Rule), and people living in warmer climates tend to have longer appendages than those living in colder climates (Allen's Rule). It must be noted, however, that this is only a very general rule and that other factors, including diet and health, can affect body size and shape (see below).

Individuals who are fully acclimatized to hot environments respond differently to heat stress than non-acclimated individuals. For example, if you were to compare the !Kung San of the Kalahari desert with Canadians born and raised in southern Ontario, you would find that for the latter, initial exposure to heat results in high vasodilation, an increased heart rate as the body attempts to pump more blood to the skin, excessive sweating, and inefficient evaporation. With continued exposure to heat stress, however, the sweat rate decreases and evaporation of sweat becomes more efficient. Interesting variation has been observed among populations living in hot, dry regions such as desert environments and those living in hot, humid regions such as tropical rainforests. The former environments are typically characterized by high solar radiation, high daytime temperatures, cool night-time temperatures, and relatively low humidity. In contrast, the latter are characterized by less extreme temperature differences between night and day, and high humidity. Populations living in both types of environment respond to heat stress through vasodilation and sweating, but the latter is much less effective in hot, humid regions, where evaporation rates are low.

## Cold Stress

Humans are not as well adapted biologically to cold stress as they are to heat stress, so we must rely to a greater extent on cultural adaptations to cope with cold temperatures. Human populations today inhabit a variety of cold environments, some of them characterized by extremely low temperatures (e.g., the Arctic), and others by more moderate temperatures (e.g., high-altitude, subarctic, and desert environments). In addition, populations living in such environments often have to contend with other challenges, including a lack of food resources, as well as high humidity and high winds, which exacerbate the cold.

**vasoconstriction**

the narrowing of the peripheral blood vessels to reduce blood flow to the skin and thereby reduce heat loss at the skin's surface

We respond biologically to cold stress by conserving and generating body heat. The main mechanism of heat conservation is **vasoconstriction**—that is, the narrowing of the peripheral blood vessels to reduce blood flow to the skin and thereby reduce heat loss at the skin's surface.

---

20. Humans have two types of sweat glands: apocrine and eccrine. It is the latter that produce the watery secretions that help cool the body.

21. While sweating is an adaptive mechanism in allowing for heat loss, it can also be maladaptive if the water and electrolytes such as sodium and magnesium lost from the body are not replaced.

In addition, blood flow is shifted to deeper vessels in the body in order to reduce heat exchange between the core and the shell of the body. At the same time, in a process known as countercurrent blood flow, heat is exchanged between veins returning cool blood from the arms and legs, and arteries moving warm blood to the shell, thereby minimizing heat loss from the core. Heat production is facilitated by actively moving around and by involuntary shivering of the muscles, a process that increases the metabolic rate and thus releases energy in the form of heat. As in the case of heat stress, a variety of factors influence one's response to cold stress, including body size and shape, amount of body fat, age, sex, and level of physical fitness. Infants and older adults as well as individuals in poor physical health are at greater risk of cold injury. Furthermore, women are more susceptible to cold stress than men because they are less able to generate heat through shivering or exercise and they experience a faster rate of cooling in their extremities. The consumption of alcohol can also accelerate heat loss by prompting vasodilation.

Interesting physiological differences in cold response have been observed between populations living in extreme cold environments and those living in more moderate environments. For example, individuals habitually exposed to extreme cold stress (e.g., Inuit) experience not only vasoconstriction but also alternating cycles of vasodilation of the blood vessels, most notably in the hands. Known as the **Lewis hunting phenomenon**, this reaction serves to protect the fingers from frostbite that could occur from prolonged constriction of the peripheral blood vessels. This mechanism has been observed in North Atlantic fishermen who work with their bare hands in extremely cold temperatures.

**Lewis hunting phenomenon**
a physiological reaction characterized by alternating cycles of vasoconstriction and vasodilation

# INVESTIGATING THE BIOLOGY OF PAST POPULATIONS

We have spent a great deal of this chapter talking about contemporary populations. What about populations that lived hundreds or thousands of years ago? What kinds of information can we draw from the mummified or skeletonized remains of these individuals? In Chapter 1 we introduced you to the terms "skeletal biology" and "osteology," which is the study of human skeletal remains. This is an immensely popular subfield of biological anthropology, and many graduate students choose to pursue this area of research, some devoting their attention to modern human remains from legal contexts (which is the domain of forensic anthropology; see Chapter 15), and others focusing on the study of human remains from archaeological contexts, a subfield known as **bioarchaeology**.

The breadth and scope of bioarchaeology is reflected in the diversity of research topics pursued by graduate students, faculty, and other researchers. These include (1) the health and diet of past populations; (2) behaviour, lifestyle, and occupation; and (3) geographic origins and migration patterns. Since its origins in the early 20th century, this subfield has seen a dramatic shift in focus, from descriptive studies of individual specimens to studies of populations. Canadian bioarchaeologists have been involved in field projects all over the world, including Italy (Figure 14.5), Egypt, Portugal, Bulgaria (Figure 14.6), South Africa, Siberia (Figure 14.7), Antigua, Mexico, and Peru. Closer to home, samples of 19th-century human remains have also been the focus of bioarchaeological study. Among these are the remains of more than 500 individuals excavated from the St. Thomas' Anglican Church cemetery in Belleville (Saunders, Hoppa, and Southern 1993; Saunders, De Vito, and Katzenberg 1997), and the frozen and skeletonized remains of crew members of the last expedition of Sir John Franklin to the Canadian Arctic (Beattie and Geiger 2004; Keenleyside, Bertulli, and Fricke 1997).

**bioarchaeology**
the study of human remains from archaeological contexts

## Health and Disease

It is rarely possible to determine the cause of death of an individual from his or her skeleton, and acute diseases such as measles and influenza do not affect bone. Thus when we talk about skeletal lesions, we are referring to those caused by chronic conditions, and it is these lesions that can provide us with clues to the health status of past populations. Reconstructing

**Figure 14.5** Students excavating Roman period burials at the site of Vagnari (south Italy).

Courtesy of Tracy Prowse

**Figure 14.6** Excavation of a necropolis associated with the ancient Greek colony of Apollonia Pontica, on the Black Sea coast of Bulgaria, has yielded the remains of more than 1,400 individuals.

Courtesy of Anne Keenleyside.

the health of populations that lived long ago from their skeletal remains is no easy task, however. Hindering the analysis of disease in bone is the fact that some diseases affect bone in only a small percentage of cases; individuals may die before bone lesions develop; and different disease-causing microorganisms may produce similar bone lesions, making them difficult to diagnose. Incomplete and fragmentary skeletal remains also pose a challenge to reconstructing the health of past populations. For instance, evidence of disease may not be preserved, and in some cases it may even make bone more susceptible to decay. Also, small sample sizes reduce the likelihood of finding evidence of disease. The calculation of sex- and age-specific prevalence rates of disease may be hindered by the inability to accurately determine the sex and estimate the age at death of an individual from his or her skeleton,

**Figure 14.7** Anne Broadberry excavating a skeleton from the Kurma XI cemetery on Lake Baikal, Siberia.

Courtesy of Ann Broadberry.

especially if it is incomplete or poorly preserved. Another confounding factor is that skeletal samples may not represent the living population from which they are derived. Skeletal samples are, after all, samples of individuals who failed to survive. As such, they may reflect the less healthy segment of the population, and consequently they may display more lesions than the healthy group. Paradoxically, skeletons with lesions may represent the *healthier* segment of the population, whose stronger immune systems enabled them to fight off infectious agents long enough for lesions to develop on their bones (Wood et al. 1992).

Despite the limitations outlined above, a wide range of ailments suffered during life may be recorded in an individual's bones and teeth, and these indicators of stress can provide valuable information on health, diet, and nutritional status, as well as individual behavioural patterns. For example, we know from studies of skeletal remains that nutritional deficiencies were common in the past. Porous lesions on the cranial vault and on the roof of the eye socket (see Figure 1.8) have been linked to several forms of anemia, including childhood episodes of iron deficiency resulting from a low dietary intake, poor intestinal absorption, and/or excess loss of iron due to parasitic and other infections. These lesions may also result from other nutritional deficiencies such as scurvy (vitamin C deficiency) and rickets (vitamin D deficiency), as well as tumours and eye infections. Also, nutritional stress and/or infectious diseases experienced during childhood can disrupt the growth of the skeleton, leading to defects that are visible on X-rays of immature long bones.

Traumatic injuries such as fractures are often observed in archaeological samples. These injuries can provide valuable insights into the lifeways of past societies. The location and nature of fractures, for instance, can tell us something about the circumstances in which they were sustained. Unhealed fractures to the skull and facial bones are sometimes a sign of violent interactions, whereas well-healed fractures to the ribs, clavicles, long bones, and hands and feet suggest accidental injuries resulting from falls, occupation, and other mishaps. As well, the manner in which fractures have healed can provide clues to a community's knowledge of medical treatment. A fractured bone that is poorly set implies a lack of knowledge about how to properly treat a fracture, and complications resulting from a fracture can have implications in terms of an individual's ability to survive on his or her own. Severe fractures resulting in a loss of mobility, for instance, may have necessitated the care of an individual by other members of his or her group. Similarly, individuals with congenital abnormalities such as cleft palate (Figure 14.8) or clubfoot may have required assistance, though we must be cautious in drawing conclusions about the quality of life of these individuals and the manner in which they were treated (Dettwyler 1991).

A variety of infectious diseases can leave their mark on skeletal remains. Some of these diseases are nonspecific, meaning that they can be caused by a variety of different microorganisms, many of them bacteria. The lesions resulting from these infections typically take the form of a buildup of new bone on the external surface of affected elements, or lesions extending into the marrow cavity (Figure 14.9). They can occur as a result of localized infection, such as an overlying skin ulcer, or from an infection that has spread through the bloodstream from another location in the body, or from a wound. Besides nonspecific infections, there are a host of specific infectious diseases such as tuberculosis, leprosy, and venereal syphilis (Figure 14.10) that can cause alterations to the skeleton.

**Paleohistology**, the microscopic study of bones and teeth, can provide clues to the health of individuals who lived long ago. Scanning electron and light microscopy have enabled researchers to evaluate the diagnostic value of histological features (Weston 2009),

**paleohistology**
the microscopic study of ancient tissues

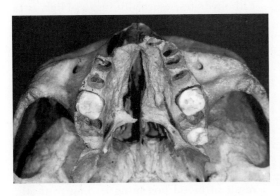

**Figure 14.8** In the past, an infant born with a cleft palate would have been unable to breastfeed and would therefore likely not have survived for very long.

Courtesy of Donald Ortner.

to diagnose osteoporosis (Agarwal and Stout 2003), syphilis (Von Hunnius et al. 2006), and sinus infections (Merrett and Pfeiffer 2000), and to identify episodes of physiological stress in teeth (Fitzgerald et al. 2006). The detection in archaeological remains of the DNA of **pathogenic** microorganisms has enabled the diagnosis of infectious diseases such as tuberculosis, leprosy, and bubonic plague. The analysis of elements such as zinc in teeth has the potential to tell us something about health and diet (Dolphin, Goodman, and Amarasiriwardena 2005; Dolphin and Goodman 2009). Finally, delayed skeletal growth, as reflected in long bones of diminished size, points to poor nutritional status and compromised health (Hoppa and Fitzgerald 1999).

## Paleonutrition

The study of ancient diets, or **paleonutrition**, is an important component of bioarchaeology, and human tissues can provide a variety of information on the foods eaten long ago.

**pathogenic**
disease causing

**paleonutrition**
the study of diet in past populations

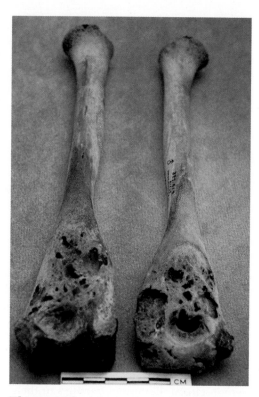

**Figure 14.9** Infection that involves the marrow cavity is referred to as osteomyelitis. It is a chronic condition that can last for months or years if untreated.

Courtesy of Anne Keenleyside.

The study of teeth, for example, can provide clues to the type and nature of foods consumed and the level of oral hygiene in past populations. Teeth can also reveal evidence of nutritional and disease stress, as well as nondietary functions (e.g., use of the teeth as tools). The level of tooth decay is an important indicator of diet, in that cavities are associated with the consumption of refined carbohydrates, especially sugars. High rates of tooth decay can lead to the loss of teeth prior to death due either to the complete destruction of the tooth or to the intentional extraction of the tooth to alleviate pain. Tooth decay, trauma, and/or heavy wear can also lead to exposure of the pulp cavity of the tooth, allowing bacteria to infiltrate the crown and root, causing inflammation and the formation of an abscess (Figure 14.11). In the days before antibiotics, abscesses could result in blood poisoning leading to death, as the bacteria spread through an affected individual's body. Nutritional stress and/ or infectious diseases can also disrupt the process of tooth enamel formation, resulting

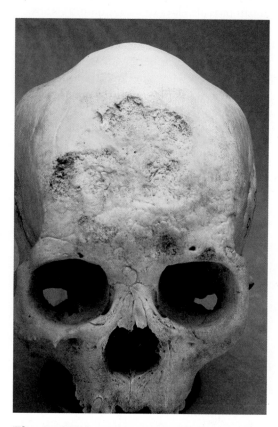

**Figure 14.10** The bacteria that cause venereal syphilis target the cranial vault, the facial region, and the anterior surfaces of the tibiae.

Courtesy of Anne Keenleyside.

in the appearance of permanent defects on the anterior surface of the teeth (see Figure 11.11). Because teeth are not physiologically altered as a normal process of aging, these defects provide a permanent record of episodes of stress in early childhood. High levels of tooth wear can result from a diet of uncooked and unrefined food items (such as coarse cereal grains), the consumption of poorly washed foods, and the consumption of foods ground with grinding stones that inadvertently introduce particles of grit into the diet.

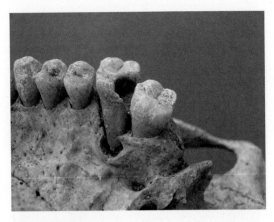

**Figure 14.11** Exposure of the pulp cavity as a result of tooth decay allows bacteria to infiltrate the cavity and root, leading to an abscess.

Courtesy of Anne Keenleyside.

The chemical analysis of bones, teeth, and other tissues can also provide valuable insight into the diet of past societies. As you learned in Chapter 10, stable carbon and nitrogen isotope analysis of collagen, the protein found in bone, yields direct evidence of the foods that were consumed. For example, it can tell us something about the types of plant foods eaten and the proportion of marine versus terrestrial foods in the diet. In southern Ontario, for instance, it has been used to detect the introduction of maize agriculture and to investigate changes in diet over time (Katzenberg et al. 1995). This technique has been applied to hair and soft tissues to investigate seasonal differences in diet (White 1993; White et al. 1999; Williams and Katzenberg 2008). It has also been a useful tool for investigating the timing and duration of breastfeeding in past populations (Dupras, Schwarcz, and Fairgrieve 2001; Prowse et al. 2008; Kwok and Keenleyside 2010; Herring, Saunders, and Katzenberg 1998; Katzenberg, Herring, and Saunders 1996; Williams, White, and Longstaffe 2005). This application is based on the fact that breastfeeding infants have $\delta^{15}N$ values that are higher than those of their mothers. Once weaning begins, however, these values begin to decline to adult levels.

**Coprolite** research, founded by the late Eric Callen, a professor of plant pathology at McGill University in Montreal (Bryant and Dean 2006), can also yield clues to ancient human diets. Studies of preserved feces can reveal evidence of **phytoliths**, which are silica particles found in plants that can be used to identify particular plant foods consumed, and pollen grains, which may tell us something about the time of year foods were eaten. Researchers have successfully extracted plant and animal DNA from coprolite samples (Poinar et al. 2001) and have even detected human myoglobin, a protein found in muscle tissue. Its presence has been interpreted as evidence of cannibalism (Marlar et al. 2000). In addition, coprolites may contain the remains of parasites that afflicted individuals during their life. Evidence of intestinal parasites has also been detected in shell midden sediments (Bathurst 2005).

**coprolite**
preserved feces

**phytoliths**
silica particles found in plants; variation in their size and shape allows scientists to identify the particular species from which they derive

## Activity Patterns

Skeletal stress indicators and the biomechanical properties of bones can provide a glimpse into the activity patterns of past populations. Osteoarthritis, or degenerative joint disease, for instance, is one of the most common conditions observed in skeletal remains, and its prevalence and distribution can tell us something about habitual activities and workloads. Nancy Lovell and her graduate students linked osteoarthritis and other markers of occupational stress in skeletons excavated from two 19th-century trading post cemeteries in Alberta to activities associated with the fur trade, including paddling, rowing, carrying, and lifting (Lai and Lovell 1992; Lovell and Dublenko 1999). Lovell (1994) also attributed vertebral arthritis in a skeletal sample from the urban Bronze Age site of Harappa in Pakistan to physical stress associated with carrying heavy loads on top of the head—a practice still seen in many parts of Africa, Asia, and Central and South America. In a more recent study, Angela Lieverse and colleagues

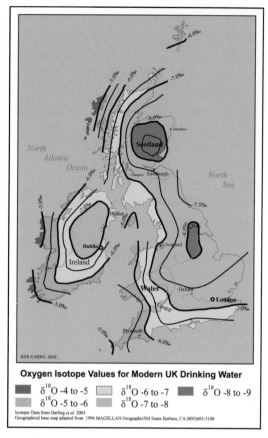

**Oxygen Isotope Values for Modern UK Drinking Water**

| | | |
|---|---|---|
| ■ $\delta^{18}O$ -4 to -5 | □ $\delta^{18}O$ -6 to -7 | ■ $\delta^{18}O$ -8 to -9 |
| ▨ $\delta^{18}O$ -5 to -6 | ▨ $\delta^{18}O$ -7 to -8 | |

Isotopic Data from Darling *et al.* 2003
Geographical base map adapted from 1996 MAGELLAN GeographixSM Santa Barbara, CA (805)685-3100

**Figure 14.12** Stable oxygen isotope analysis of bones and teeth is based on the fact that the ratio of $O^{16}$ and $O^{18}$ in local meteoric precipitation and thus in drinking water varies geographically, as seen in this map of oxygen isotope values for the United Kingdom. Thus measuring oxygen isotopic signatures in skeletal and dental tissues can provide clues to the regions where an individual was born and died.

(Lieverse et al. 2007) found the distribution of osteoarthritis to vary among foragers living in Siberia's Cis-Baikal region, pointing to changes in mobility and activity patterns over time. The geometric properties of long bones (e.g., strength, shape, asymmetry) can also shed light on the habitual behaviours of individuals who lived long ago. Stock and Pfeiffer (2001, 2004), for example, linked variability in the robusticity of long bones to the differing subsistence practices of two groups of South African foragers. Evidence of activities may also be recorded in teeth. For instance, dental modification in the form of grooves on the occlusal surfaces of teeth from Holocene period hunter-fisher-gatherers may have resulted from the processing of fibers to make implements related to fishing (Waters-Rist et al. 2010).

## Residential Histories

Stable isotope analysis of bones and teeth can be used to determine the geographic origins and movement of individuals who lived in the past. Stable oxygen isotope analysis is based on the fact that the ratio of the stable isotopes of oxygen ($O^{16}$ and $O^{18}$) in drinking water is recorded in the mineral component of an individual's bones and in their tooth enamel. Because the teeth form very early in life, they record the geographic location (i.e., source of the drinking water) of an individual during early childhood. In contrast, bones, which undergo constant remodelling throughout life, record the isotopic signature of drinking water consumed *later* in life. These signatures must be interpreted with caution, however, since they may be altered by diagenesis, or post-mortem changes, especially to bone tissue. Similar oxygen isotopic signatures in the bones and teeth of an individual thus indicate that an individual spent most of his or her life in one place. In contrast, differing values tell us that an individual was born in one place but moved to another later in life (Figure 14.12). Similarly, the ratio of the stable isotopes of strontium ($Sr^{87}$ and $Sr^{86}$), which can be detected in an individual's dental tissues, points to the geographic location in which he or she once lived—specifically, the underlying geology of the area as reflected in the food and drink that person consumed. Because diagenesis can significantly alter strontium isotopic signatures in bone, this technique can only be used on teeth. Christine White, a Canada Research Chair at the University of Western Ontario, has utilized both oxygen and strontium isotopes to investigate geographic origins and migration in Mesoamerica (White et al. 1998, 2007). Bioarchaeologists Tracy Prowse and Tosha Dupras have also used oxygen isotope analysis to identify immigrants in Roman Italy (Prowse et al. 2008) and Roman Egypt (Dupras and Schwarcz 2001) respectively. Mobility has also been inferred from stable carbon and nitrogen isotope analysis of hair samples from pre-contact burials in Peru (White et al. 2009).

# THE ETHICS OF STUDYING HUMAN REMAINS

The collection and study of human remains has encountered a long history of controversy and debate. In 1990 the U.S. Congress passed the Native American Graves Protection and Repatriation Act (NAGPRA), which laid out in detail the process by which native remains found on federally recognized tribal lands or in federally funded institutions must be handled. Specifically, the act requires federal museums and institutions to conduct an inventory of their collections of Native American skeletal remains and associated objects, and return them to culturally affiliated tribes upon request. Canada has no comparable federal legislation; the manner in which aboriginal human remains are dealt with is determined by various institutes, municipalities, provinces, and territories individually.

http://www.nps.gov/history/nagpra

http://www.civilization.ca

---

**BOX 14.2    PROFILE... The China Lake and Big Bar Burials**

Courtesy of the Canadian Museum of Civilization.

In October 2002, I approached the Canoe Creek Indian Band of British Columbia to obtain their consent to carry out mitochondrial DNA analysis on two ancient skeletons from the nearby archaeological site of China Lake. This wasn't something new to me as I had been working with Native American or First Nations bands in either the United States or Canada since 1965. In the case of Canoe Creek, I received an overwhelmingly enthusiastic response as I explained to the community at large my request and its purpose. About 50 people from Canoe Creek and three neighbouring communities came to this town meeting. I hardly expected 10, much less that many, but it quickly became obvious that there was much interest in the ancestral past and in what I might bring to bear on that knowledge through the study of human remains. Twenty

years previously, two male skeletons had been accidentally unearthed during road building. They had been radiocarbon dated to 5,000 years, they were developmentally about the same age at death, their skeletal morphology was strikingly similar and unique compared with other Plateau skeletal remains I had studied, and the bodies had been buried next to each other. Were they brothers or even twins? DNA testing might hold the answer.

After I presented my case and listened to contributions from the audience, I was treated to a tour of the Fraser Plateau, an area of British Columbia that I had not previously visited. We relocated the China Lake site thanks to the knowledge of elders and field photographs lent to me by Simon Fraser University, whose archaeologists had recovered the remains. My hosts also took me to other suspected ancient burial grounds. At nearby Big Bar Lake we identified human remains eroding from the top of a knoll within a broad area of lithic debris and pithouse depressions marking an ancient habitation site.

Over the winter, I prepared and submitted a formal request in a letter to Chief and Council. We also put our heads together to figure out what to do about the exposed human remains at Big Bar Lake. The knoll was on the path of a road leading to a provincial park and thus accessible to many tourists. The community decision was to protect those remains by removing them for reburial in a more secure context but only with rigorous scientific method and utmost respect for the deceased. An archaeological excavation and anthropological study of the remains began in 2003 as a community-based project attended by Canoe Creek band members and those from the nearby High Bar First Nation, which shared territorial jurisdiction. Comprehensive study and publication of all the remains culminated in ceremonial reburials at China Lake in 2006 and Big Bar Lake in 2008. The success of the project signified the importance of cooperation and collaboration with the descendants of those who walked this earth before us.

Source: Written by Dr. Jerome Cybulski, Curator of Physical Anthropology in the Archaeology and History Division of the Canadian Museum of Civilization.

Canadian bioarchaeologists have a history of positive collaboration with First Nations, and their calls for a cooperative and collaborative relationship with First Nations have been voiced in a series of conference papers and reports (Cybulski 1976, 2007; Cybulski, Ossenberg, and Wade 1979; Canadian Museum of Civilization 1992). A number of collaborative projects exemplify this close working relationship. These include excavations of the Greenville burial ground (Cybulski 1992) and the China Lake and Big Bar Lake burials (Cybulski et al. 2007b; Malhi et al. 2007; see Box 14.2), analyses of Cree remains from northern Manitoba (Brownlee and Syms 1999), the excavation and analysis of the Moatfield ossuary in Ontario (Williamson and Pfeiffer 2003), and Owen Beattie's investigation of Kwaday Dän Ts'inchi, an individual whose partially preserved body was found eroding from a B.C. glacier in 1999 (Beattie et al. 2000; Corr et al. 2008; Dickson et al. 2004).[22]

# SUMMARY

The biology of populations is at the very core of human variation; it is central to the notions of cline and cluster as discussed in Chapter 13. As we have seen in this chapter, population biology provides a multidimensional window through which we can measure the capacity of individuals to respond to the challenges of everyday life. This adaptive capacity may reflect many generations of selection favouring particular phenotypes, or it may call upon our inherent plasticity to provide accommodation over the life course (be it short-term and reversible or permanent, developmental change).

The avenues by which we can study human population biology are numerous. We can chart differential responses to infectious disease burden (morbidity and survivorship), or measure growth and development in terms of variation in nutritional quality and other health determinants, or differences in longevity or chronic disease experience. We can examine how people respond to very specific environmental challenges, such as cold or high altitude, cognizant that the same challenges (e.g., childbirth under hypoxic stress) may be "solved" via different pathways (genetic adaptation in the indigenous Han population in Tibet versus physiological adaptability in Andean Quechua, possibly reflecting length of residence at high elevations and/or historical population bottlenecks). It is important to note that in many cases, humans have developed highly sophisticated cultural, behavioural, and technological buffers to shield their physical selves from the full force of many environmental challenges.

Many of the questions we ask of living populations can also be asked of the dead; osteology, paleonutrition, paleopathology, and bioarchaeology can all tell us much about how people lived in the past, through markers of physical activity, trauma, disease, bone chemistry, and the use of cultural interventions. Not surprisingly, studies of past populations reflect the deep historical relationship of humankind with their biocultural and ecological environment—a relationship that continues to the present day. The life course and its numerous challenges vary with age, sex, status, and experience. Thus, for example, inadequate nutrition today impairs growth just as it did 100 or 1,000 years ago. If one thing has changed, it has been our ability to interfere with the progress of many infectious diseases, though even here, our sophisticated technology may only provide temporary solace, as diseases adapt (in a Darwinian fashion) and re-emerge with renewed virulence.

---

22. This name, given to the remains of this individual by the Champagne and Aishihik First Nations community, means "Long ago person found." Scientists have recently found 17 living relatives of Kwaday Dän Ts'inchi through DNA analysis of members of the Champagne and Aishihik communities.

# CORE REVIEW

## What factors are contributing to the emergence and re-emergence of infectious diseases today?

Factors contributing to the emergence and re-emergence of infectious diseases include ecological changes associated with agriculture, mining, logging, and deforestation; climate change and global warming; economic and social disruption; poverty; sexual behaviour; the increased movement of people; large-scale food production; and changes in pathogenic microorganisms.

## In what ways can biological anthropologists contribute to the study of the human life course?

Biological anthropologists have brought their unique biocultural perspective to the study of the human life course. Studies of infant feeding practices in contemporary populations have revealed considerable variation in these practices, and a number of factors underlying this variation have been identified, some of which have had a direct impact on implementing international guidelines for breastfeeding. A considerable body of literature has also been devoted to studies of child growth and to temporal and population variation in growth patterns. In addition, the anthropological study of aging has attracted considerable attention in recent years as our population becomes increasingly older. Biological anthropologists have examined a variety of aspects of aging, including changes in life expectancy over the course of our evolutionary history, skeletal and reproductive aging, and the development of chronic diseases.

## What are the consequences of under- and over-eating?

Reliance on a diet insufficient in quantity and quality can result in protein malnutrition and vitamin and mineral deficiencies such as iron deficiency anemia, rickets, scurvy, beriberi, and pellagra. Such deficiencies can lead to low birth weights and increased risk of infant mortality, impaired cognitive ability, growth stunting, skeletal abnormalities, reduced adult stature, reduced work capacity in adulthood, and increased susceptibility to infectious diseases. Overeating, in contrast, can lead to overweight and obesity, a major risk factor for diabetes, cardiovascular disease, and other chronic conditions.

## How have humans adapted physiologically to their environments?

Populations living in conditions of high ultraviolet radiation, low levels of oxygen, or extreme temperatures have adapted physiologically in a number of ways. Humans living closer to the equator have darker skin that protects them from the harmful effects of UV radiation; those living farther from the equator have lighter coloured skin that allows for the synthesis of adequate amounts of vitamin D at latitudes where the level of UV radiation is weaker. Populations native to high altitudes exhibit greater lung volume, greater blood flow to the tissues, and a higher number of red blood cells compared to those living at lower elevation. Finally, humans living under conditions of extreme heat respond physiologically through vasodilation and sweating, whereas those living under conditions of extreme cold respond through vasoconstriction and shivering.

**What can we learn about past populations from their skeletal remains?**

Human skeletal remains can reveal a great deal about the health, diet, and behaviour of past populations. They can tell us about the type and prevalence of certain diseases that individuals and populations suffered from, the kinds of foods they ate, their activity patterns, and the locations where they were born and died.

# CRITICAL THINKING QUESTIONS

1. Over the past number of years, there has been considerable controversy regarding the impact of "fast foods" on human health (consider Morgan Spurlock's 2004 cult documentary, *Supersize Me*). How would you justify abolishing fast food outlets in your community? Why would you argue that they are necessary?
2. Who would be more challenged in terms of day-to-day functioning—you arriving in La Paz, Bolivia, for a one-week vacation (elevation 3660 m) or a resident of La Paz taking classes at Dalhousie University in Halifax (elevation 0–145 m)?

# GROUP DISCUSSION QUESTIONS

1. In North America the excavation and analysis of First Nations skeletal remains has been surrounded by controversy. In contrast, far fewer ethical and moral objections have been raised over the excavation and study of human remains from other parts of the world. Why do you think this is?
2. Would adopting a diet like that of our Paleolithic ancestors solve many of our chronic health problems today? Why or why not?

# RESOURCES AND READINGS

- J.E. Buikstra and L. Beck, *Bioarchaeology: The Contextual Analysis of Human Remains* (Academic Press, 2006).
- D.A. Herring, and A.C. Swedlund, eds., *Human Biologists in the Archives: Demography, Health, Nutrition, and Genetics in Historical Populations* (Cambridge: Cambridge University Press, 2003).
- R.D. Hoppa and C.M. Fitzgerald, eds., *Human Growth in the Past: Studies from Bones and Teeth* (Cambridge: Cambridge University Press, 1999).
- R.D. Hoppa and J.W. Vaupel, eds., *Paleodemography: Age Distributions from Skeletal Samples* (Cambridge: Cambridge University Press, 2002).
- M.A. Katzenberg and S.R. Saunders, eds., *Biological Anthropology of the Human Skeleton*, 2nd ed. (Wiley-Liss, 2008).
- C.S. Moffat and T.L. Prowse, eds., *Human Diet and Nutrition in Biocultural Perspective*. Biosocial Society Symposium Series, edited by Catherine Panter-Brick (New York: Berghahn, 2010).

# Chapter 15

# Biological Anthropology as Applied Science

## OVERVIEW

As do all sciences, anthropology aims to reveal fundamental aspects of its subject matter—in this case, humankind. So we ask some very basic questions. Where did we come from? Why do we look the way we do? How did culture and technology develop? How have we come to dominate—and in many cases transform—the planet's varied environments and ecosystems? The answers to these questions reveal a complex history of social and ecological interactions, many of which have become strained over time. Consequently, humanity today faces a diverse array of problems, and many anthropologists are now applying this basic knowledge of who we are and what we are about toward finding solutions to these issues. This chapter explores a few of the ways in which the field of *applied anthropology* seeks to address difficulties arising from the inequities of human social, cultural, and technological relations.

## CORE CONCEPTS

■ applied anthropology, medical anthropology, evolutionary medicine, nutritional genomics, anthropometrics, ergonomics, primate conservation, forensic anthropology

## CORE QUESTIONS

■ What is medical anthropology? In what ways can it be applied?

■ What is evolutionary medicine? In what ways have anthropologists contributed to this field?

■ What is nutritional genomics, and what are some of the potential applications of this newly emerging science?

■ What is ergonomics? How has anthropometry contributed to this specialty?

■ What threats do nonhuman primates currently face? In what ways can primatology contribute to the conservation of these animals?

■ What is forensic anthropology? What contributions do forensic anthropologists make both locally and globally?

The purpose of anthropology is to make the world safe for human differences.
Ruth Benedict (1887–1948)

# PROLOGUE: REAL WORLDS, REAL PROBLEMS

In previous chapters we emphasized the ways in which anthropology generates new understandings of ourselves as a biologically and culturally diverse global species. Much of this knowledge has been gained through basic research—that is, by testing hypotheses about our place in nature, how we evolved, and why we differ from one place or time to the next. We develop or modify theories to account for these phenomena. This knowledge swirls round and round in the world of academia—it is peer reviewed and published, it is discussed and debated at conferences and in classrooms, and it justifies new grants for yet more new research. But the academic world is only a small fragment of the world at large, and over the past few decades an increasing number of anthropologists have been turning their attention away from creating more and more "new" knowledge in favour of putting that which we already possess to good use in the wider world. This is the purview of an "emerging" subfield known as **applied anthropology**.[1] The objectives of applied anthropology encompass "the integration of anthropological perspectives and methods in solving human problems throughout the world; to advocate for fair and just public policy based upon sound research; to promote public recognition of anthropology as a profession; and to support the continuing professionalization of the field" (Society for Applied Anthropology 2009). There are numerous domains within which this mission is made manifest, from health and medicine to human rights, environmental issues, and local, national, and international development policy, to name but a few.

More often than not, the problems addressed by applied anthropologists are **anthropogenic** in origin. They are the offspring of the actions and interactions of individuals and societies with one another, with the environment in which they live, and with technology. In these final two chapters, we examine a few areas in which anthropological knowledge has been, or could be, usefully brought to bear on problems both practical and distressing. In this chapter we examine five such areas: evolutionary medicine and infectious disease; nutrition and genomics; ergonomics; primate conservation; and forensic anthropology.

**applied anthropology**

a branch of anthropology that uses anthropological methods and theories to address practical issues

http://www.sfaa.net/

**anthropogenic**

literally, "of human origin," as an outcome of human actions or deliberate manufacture; e.g., urban crowding, pollution

# MEDICAL ANTHROPOLOGY

In Chapter 1 we introduced you to the field of medical anthropology, which is the study of health, illness, and healing from a cross-cultural perspective. Medical anthropologists are often employed by international organizations such as the World Health Organization, international development agencies such as CIDA (Canadian International Development Agency), public health departments, and nongovernmental organizations (NGOs) to help design and implement health policies and treatment strategies. Utilizing their expertise in ethnographic research, they may, for instance, contribute to the development of disease control campaigns by collecting data on cultural beliefs, attitudes, and behaviours of at-risk individuals, the purpose being to design treatment regimes that are culturally appropriate. University of Victoria anthropologist Eric Roth and colleagues, for example, have examined perceptions of HIV/AIDS risk in northern Kenya (Roth et al. 2006, 2009), and many other researchers have explored the relationship between sexual behaviour and HIV transmission with the goal of assessing the effectiveness of public health measures such as education programs in combating the spread of HIV.

Another good example of applied medical anthropology is the cholera control campaign that was implemented in northeastern Brazil in 1993 (Nations and Monte 1996). Attempts by public health officials to control the outbreak and spread of this disease in two urban slums were met with resistance in the form of denying the existence of the disease, downplaying its virulence, making a joke of it, and refusing treatment. Interviews conducted by anthropologists

---

1. Some authors (e.g., Rylko-Bauer, Singer, and Van Willigen 2006; Scheper-Hughes and Bourgois 2004; Weiss 2006) have noted that anthropology, be it ethnological or biological, has a long and fairly dark history as an applied science. One example is anthropology's role in constructing racial divides supporting colonial expansion, xenophobic immigration policies, and genocide (e.g., 1930s German eugenicist anthropology and the rise of National Socialism under Hitler).

revealed the true meaning behind these reactions. As they discovered, the word for cholera in Portuguese refers not only to the disease but also to rabies. Thus, for the residents of these slums, cholera was seen as a conspiracy against the poor, who in the eyes of the wealthy represented rabid dogs that had to be exterminated. An effective control campaign therefore required the elimination of harmful metaphors that stigmatize the poor (ibid.).

Another interesting example of applied medical anthropology concerns blood donation. Many people routinely donate blood to the Canadian Blood Services for use in life-saving operations. As you may know, some cultural and religious groups refuse to donate blood on the basis of certain beliefs. Objections to donating blood, may, however, pose considerable problems for people who have rare blood types or genetic blood disorders and require blood for transfusions. This situation exists in places such as France that have large immigrant populations from Africa. For one such community, originating from the Comoros Islands off the coast of Mozambique and now living in Marseille, blood is closely linked to family identity, and blood donations traditionally occur only between close relatives. As such, there is great reluctance to donate blood to nonrelated individuals, with whom sharing blood would create an "unnatural tie." To address this issue, anthropologist Dominique Grassineau and colleagues interviewed members of the Comorian community to develop a recruitment message that would address the concerns of the community (Grassineau et al. 2007). This involved identifying the barriers to blood donation, using cultural mediators to facilitate communication between the community and the blood bank and to deal with cultural misunderstandings, and recruiting political and religious leaders to spread the message.

# EVOLUTIONARY MEDICINE

In 1991, evolutionary biologists George Williams and Randolph Nesse published an influential paper titled "The Dawn of Darwinian Medicine," in which they applied Darwin's theory of evolution by natural selection to medicine (Williams and Nesse 1991). Since that time, the field of Darwinian medicine—or **evolutionary medicine**, as it is more commonly known, has become an increasingly important area of applied biological anthropology (see Trevathan 2007).[2] The premise of evolutionary medicine is that pathogens and our resistance to them have coevolved. That is, we have adapted to the challenges of disease, and disease-causing agents have in turn adapted to our responses to them.

**evolutionary (Darwinian) medicine** the application of evolutionary theory to medicine

As we noted in Chapter 4, natural selection has maintained ("balanced") certain alleles in some populations because of the advantage they provide to individuals who are heterozygous for those alleles and who are living in environments where particular diseases are endemic. Taking an evolutionary approach to the study of infectious diseases allows us to understand the ways in which populations have adapted to particular pathogens. It also enables us to determine why some strains of pathogenic microorganisms have much lower virulence than others. In recent decades, for instance, a less virulent strain of cholera known as the El Tor strain has arisen in many parts of the world. Unlike its more dangerous predecessor, this strain has the ability to infect many more people by virtue of the fact that it is not virulent enough to kill its host. The survival of infected individuals therefore ensures that the bacteria continue to be transmitted to new hosts. So in this case, low virulence is beneficial to the pathogen.

The application of evolutionary theory to infectious disease has also resulted in a shift in our way of thinking about the human body's response to pathogens (Nesse 2007). Our bodies possess a number of defence mechanisms that protect us from disease-causing microorganisms. These include physical barriers such as the skin, chemical barriers such as tears, mucous, and stomach acid, and mechanisms of expulsion such as vomiting and diarrhea that rid the body of harmful organisms that may have been ingested. While we are all familiar with some of the more unpleasant symptoms of illness, we may never have considered the possibility that they may, in fact, have some adaptive significance. Similarly, coughing allows pathogens to

---

2. While this field gained particular attention in the 1990s, anthropologists and other researchers have been doing research in this area for decades (Trevathan 2007).

be expelled. Fever also serves an adaptive function by creating an environment of elevated temperature that is inhospitable to invading bacteria or viruses, thus helping the body fight infection (Kluger 1978; Kluger et al. 1996). Even withholding iron to the point where an individual becomes anemic may deprive a pathogen of an element required for growth and development (Stuart-Macadam 1992). Thus, in a society that promotes pill popping every time we are feeling unwell, it is wise to consider the consequences of taking medication the next time you find yourself sick. It may simply prolong your illness or, worse yet, increase the likelihood of developing a secondary infection.

The concept of evolutionary medicine has also been applied to reproductive health. For example, Margie Profet (1993) has hypothesized that menstruation is an adaptive trait that evolved to protect females from pathogens carried on sperm. Because ovulation is concealed in humans (but see Chapter 6 for an alternative view on this question), sexual activity takes place throughout the year, thus potentially increasing the risk of sexually transmitted diseases. By shedding the lining of the uterus each month, females thereby rid themselves of organisms that might cause infection. Her hypothesis has been met with a great deal of criticism, however, and a number of competing hypotheses have been proposed. Some researchers have argued, for example, that menstruation may have evolved because it is more energy efficient for the body to shed the uterine lining than to permanently maintain it (Strassman 1999). Others have suggested that menstruation has no adaptive significance at all (Finn 1998). Whatever the case may be, it is interesting that women today experience far more cycles than they did in the past. Modern American women have as many as 450 monthly cycles in their lifetime compared to only 160 in women living in foraging societies, who spend more of their time pregnant or lactating (Eaton et al. 1994). In this respect, the current pattern of cycling seen in North American women can be seen as abnormal. Earlier menstruation and a greater number of menstrual cycles in modern women may, in fact, be contributing to the high rates of breast and reproductive cancers that we see today (Eaton and Eaton 1999).[3] This has important implications for the pharmaceutical industry, and efforts are currently under way to develop birth control methods that reduce the number of monthly cycles (Trevathan 2007).

Morning sickness has also been hypothesized to have evolved for a specific purpose— namely, to protect the embryo from toxins that the mother may have inadvertently ingested early in pregnancy when the developing fetus is most vulnerable to these harmful substances (Profet 1992; Flaxman and Sherman 2000). Thus medications to combat nausea may do more harm than good.[4] Similarly, an aversion to certain foods may be adaptive in preventing the mother from consuming foods that are potentially harmful to the fetus.

In recognizing the important roles that evolutionary processes play in human health, anthropologists have made valuable contributions to evolutionary medicine, and the insights that their research has provided have the potential to make a significant impact on public health (Trevathan 2007). It is important to remember, however, that natural selection "maximizes the reproductive success of genes," not health (Nesse and Williams 1998, 92). It is therefore up to us to follow a healthy lifestyle as best we can.

## NUTRITIONAL ANTHROPOLOGY

In the previous chapter we introduced you to nutritional anthropology and looked at several examples of nutritional adaptation. Recall our discussion of lactose tolerance, in which the gene coding for the enzyme (lactase) that digests lactose is maintained in high frequency in populations that have a long history of dairy farming. We also examined James Neel's thrifty genotype hypothesis with respect to Type 2 diabetes, and outlined Boyd Eaton's research on the Paleolithic diet, which highlighted the discrepancy between the diet to which

---

3. Menarche is now occurring in girls as young as nine and is linked to increased caloric intake.
4. Some of you may have heard of the drug thalidomide, used by pregnant women for morning sickness during the 1950s and 1960s. Women who took this drug gave birth to infants with severe birth defects.

we are genetically adapted and today's unhealthy diet. Research conducted by nutritional anthropologists also has an applied aspect, as illustrated in the example below.

## Nutritional Genomics

Imagine being able to design a diet to complement your genes. The newly emerging science of nutritional genomics seeks to do just that. As the study of how our genes interact with the foods we eat, **nutritional genomics** (also referred to as nutrigenomics) has the potential to enable individuals to tailor their diet to their genetic makeup in order to optimize their health and prevent or treat disease (Ordovas and Corella 2004). A well-known example of a gene–diet interaction is lactose intolerance, which we have already discussed. There are, however, a number of other monogenic diseases in which diet plays a major role in the expression and prevention of the disease.[5] These include phenylketonuria, familial hypercholesterolemia, and celiac disease. As you will recall from Chapter 3, phenylketonuria (or PKU) is an autosomal recessive disorder characterized by an inability to utilize phenylalanine due to a deficiency in the enzyme phenylalanine hydroxylase, which is necessary to break down this essential amino acid commonly found in breast milk. Without this enzyme, phenylalanine accumulates in the blood, leading to neurological problems. Fortunately, it can be prevented by avoiding foods high in phenylalanine such as meat, fish, chicken, dairy products, nuts, and beans. Familial hypercholesterolemia is a genetic disorder characterized by abnormally high levels of low-density lipoprotein in the blood (i.e., LDL, the "bad" cholesterol, which contributes to cardiovascular disease such as atherosclerosis). It has been linked to a mutation in the *LDLR* gene necessary for the production of a **receptor** that binds with low-density lipoproteins that carry cholesterol and removes them from the blood. Celiac disease is an autoimmune disorder characterized by intolerance to gluten. When affected individuals consume gluten (e.g., all wheat products), the body's immune system attacks the cells lining the small intestine, leading to gastrointestinal distress and other symptoms. A gluten-free diet eliminates these problems.

A greater challenge to researchers in nutritional genomics is identifying gene–diet interactions for polygenic diseases such as some cancers. We know that high cholesterol levels are a risk factor for heart disease, and similarly a high-fat diet has been linked to breast and colon cancer. The multifactorial nature of such diseases, however, makes it difficult to pinpoint specific gene–diet interactions. Nevertheless, some progress is being made, and a number of links between diet and chronic disease have been identified. A compound found in soy, for example, appears to be associated with a reduced risk of prostate cancer (Hamilton-Reeves et al. 2007).

A key requirement in the study of nutritional genomics is collecting accurate dietary information, and anthropologists can play an important role here. Human biologists use a variety of techniques to gather information about the types and amounts of foods eaten over a certain period of time. These include food frequency questionnaires, 24-hour dietary recalls, and food diaries. Accurate genetic data are also required in order to properly assess gene–nutrient interactions. As with any newly emerging field of study, however, nutritional genomics is experiencing growing pains. One of the major challenges it faces is demonstrating causality. While researchers may find a strong association between a disease and a particular diet or dietary component, this does not necessarily mean that eating such a diet will cause a specific disease (i.e., correlation does not equal causation!).[6] Other challenges include identifying the particular nutrients that interact with genes; determining the manner in which they interact; assessing the role of non-nutrients (i.e., chemical compounds) found in many processed food items; determining at what point in life gene–diet interactions exert

http://nutrigenomics.ucdavis.edu

**nutritional genomics**
the study of the interaction between diet and genes

**receptor**
a protein molecule to which another molecule attaches

---

5. While these diseases are described as monogenic, some of them may involve more than one gene, and the phenotype may be influenced by environmental factors.

6. A classic example used in many statistics textbooks to illustrate this concept is the correlation between violent crime and ice cream eating. Eating ice cream does not lead to violent crime! Rather, both are associated with warm weather.

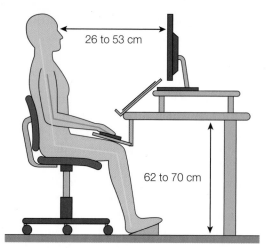

http://www.ergonomics.org

**Figure 15.1** Designing an ergonomic workspace involves considering body proportions and the range of movements of different parts of the body.

their greatest influence on health and how long individuals must be exposed to particular diets to develop conditions such as cardiovascular disease or cancer; and identifying the role of other factors (e.g., hormones) in gene–diet interactions (Ordovas and Corella 2004). Despite these difficulties, nutritional genomics promises to have a major impact on nutrition research and public health.

# ANTHROPOMETRY AND ERGONOMICS

Anthropometry is the measurement of the human body. This practice has a long and at times controversial history. First used in the 19th century to identify criminals based on their physical characteristics,[7] it was later used to distinguish between "races" and to promote eugenics policies such as the restriction of immigration based on the presumed inferiority of certain populations (Gould 1996; see Chapter 13). Today, however, anthropometric studies are conducted for very different reasons. As we noted in the previous chapter, human biologists often measure living populations to study growth and development, assess health and diet, and examine population differences in body size and proportions. From a more practical perspective, anthropometry has become an important component of ergonomics, which is the science of designing work areas and products that optimize human performance and provide the best "fit." Just as we spend one-third of our life sleeping, we spend at least one-third of our life in the workplace. The purpose of ergonomics is to ensure that our working and living environments are safe and comfortable and that they allow us to perform our daily tasks at our optimal level. Office jobs, for example, may require us to sit in front of a computer for seven or eight hours a day. It is therefore essential that we be comfortable and safe from injuries or ailments that could be debilitating (Figure 15.1). Those of you who have suffered from repetitive strain injuries like carpal tunnel syndrome or chronic neck problems from sitting in front of a computer day and night writing papers and checking e-mail or Facebook will know exactly what we mean. Outside the workplace, anthropometry is also used to design appropriately sized clothing and footwear for a number of applications, including—if not especially—the military (see Box 15.1), as well as car and airplane seats.

# PRIMATE CONSERVATION

http://www.iucnredlist.org

In Chapter 5 we noted that a number of primate species face extinction in the very near future. In fact, more than 100 of the world's nearly 300 species of primates are now endangered. Among the 25 most critically endangered, listed on the IUCN red list of threatened species, are the Western and Lowland gorillas (*Gorilla gorilla*) and the orangutans of Sumatra (*Pongo abelii*).[8] In 2000, one subspecies of red colobus monkey known as Miss Waldron's red colobus was declared extinct in the wild (Oates et al. 2000), and many more species are on the verge of disappearing forever (Wrangham 2008).

---

7. The method was developed by French criminologist Alphonse Bertillon.

8. Every year the International Union for Conservation of Nature and Natural Resources publishes a list of the 25 most endangered species.

**BOX 15.1**    **PROFILE... Applied Anthropometry in the Military**

Courtesy of Todd Garlie

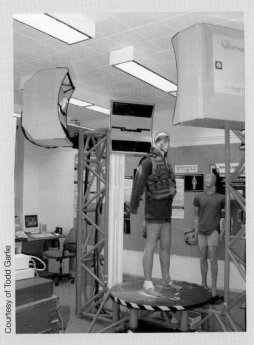

Courtesy of Todd Garlie

**Figure 15.2** 3D anthropometric laboratory with whole body laser scanner.

I obtained my Ph.D. in physical anthropology from McMaster University in Hamilton, Ontario, in 2000, investigating changes in stature and body mass of Canadian children during the last half of the 20th century. I completed a SSHRC Post-Doctoral Fellowship in 2002 at the University of Winnipeg in Manitoba, focusing on human osteology and skeletal repatriation. In 2003, I joined the Natick Soldier Research, Development and Engineering Center (NSRDEC) as a civilian biological research anthropologist with the U.S. Army. I am a member of the Ergonomics Team, a group of physical anthropologists, **human factors engineers**, and biomechanical researchers who fall under the Human Systems Integration and Sciences Division of the Warfighter Science Technology and Applied Research (WarSTAR) Directorate.

My role at NSRDEC is to conduct a combination of applied anthropological research on Warfighter body size and shape and to conduct anthropometric fit and size evaluations for the evaluation of military clothing and protective equipment. Most recently my research has focused on the estimation of percent body fat calculated from current military body fat equations employing manual body measurements and automated measures extracted from whole body 3D laser scanning technology (Figure 15.2). These results are compared to body fat estimations using dual energy X-ray absorptiometry (DEXA). One of the goals of this research is to move beyond using height, weight, and circumference measurements for estimating body fat and to evaluate individual geometry extracted from 3D

whole body scans that may provide better information on body fat estimates and distribution.

I also conduct or participate in a variety of anthropometric fit and size evaluations of Warfighter clothing and protective equipment for the Army. One of my recent projects involved leading the collection of unclothed and clothed anthropometry for a Special Forces unit to aid in the development of a side gunner's seat. Due to space restrictions, body size dimensions were critical for understanding the occupant's envelope in the design of this seat. Other ongoing projects include the evaluation of toxicological agent protective (TAP) gloves and the evaluation and development of **tariffs** for a cold-weather clothing system. In the first project, chemical personnel tasked with the destruction of chemical agents were having issues with the fit of their gloves. In order to evaluate these fit issues, a field evaluation was undertaken to obtain a series of hand measurements and fit assessments of different glove types and sizes. The goal is to try to discern issues of fit surrounding their current gloves and to provide recommendations for fixing such issues. In the other project, I have been tasked with evaluating sizing dimensions for a newly obtained cold-weather clothing system to determine whether there are any fit issues and to provide tariff estimates to the customer.

Source: Written by Todd Garlie, Biological Research Anthropologist, Ergonomics Team, Warfighter Science, Technology and Applied Research Directorate (WarSTAR), Natick Soldier Research, Development and Engineering Center (NSRDEC), US Army Research, Development and Engineering Command (RDECOM), Natick, MA

Major threats to primates include habitat destruction in the form of deforestation, logging, and forest fires, the hunting of primates for bush meat, and the trade in live animals for laboratories, zoos, and pets. The alteration of natural habitats due to global warming is also having an effect on primate populations (Dunbar 1998). To appreciate the impact of habitat destruction on primates, consider that about 90% of these animals live in tropical and subtropical forests. The destruction of tropical rainforest is occurring at an unprecedented rate. Countries with primate populations are losing an estimated 125,000 $km^2$ of forest each year (Chapman and Peres 2001). Much of the deforestation currently taking place is directly related to agriculture and resettlement. Selective logging and forest fires are also contributing to a decline in primate populations.[9] For example, in the 1980s and 1990s a series of fires in Indonesia destroyed many of the fruit trees on which orangutans depend for food, resulting in a marked decline in the orangutan population. On Madagascar, agricultural practices involving the deliberate burning of forest to create agricultural fields and grazing areas have also had devastating effects on local primate populations.

An excellent case study of the impact of habitat alteration on primates is that of Kibale National Park in Uganda. Commercial logging and the clearing of land for agriculture have led to reduced food availability and increased parasitic infections among primates (Gillespie, Chapman, and Greiner 2005). As well, studies have revealed variation in the ways in which primates have responded to selective logging within the park. Chapman and colleagues (2000) investigated the long-term effects of logging on the density of five species of primates in Kibale and found that those groups living in heavily logged areas of the park experienced more significant population declines than those living in areas that were less heavily logged. In addition, populations inhabiting less heavily logged areas recovered better from habitat destruction than those living in heavily logged ones. Based on these results, Chapman and colleagues (2000) concluded that while low-intensity logging may be compatible with primate conservation, high-intensity logging is not.

Infectious diseases originating in humans are also having a significant impact on non-human primates, especially the great apes. Genetic similarities between apes and humans mean that they are susceptible to many of the same kinds of diseases we are; indeed, many human diseases, such as HIV, originated in primates. The Ebola virus, which has killed hundreds of humans to date, has wrought havoc on gorilla and chimpanzee populations in the Congo. It is estimated that since 2002, 5,000 gorillas have been killed by the virus (Bermejo et al. 2006), and that up to one-quarter of the world's gorilla population has been killed by the disease in the past 10 years. In 2003 alone, an outbreak of Ebola in the Congo resulted in a 56% reduction in the gorilla population and an 89% reduction in the chimpanzee population (Leroy et al. 2004). Other diseases such as polio and anthrax have contributed to the decline in ape populations, and recent studies of chimpanzees in Tanzania and West Africa have revealed evidence of respiratory infections that appear to have been caused by human viruses (Kaur et al. 2008; Köndgen et al. 2008). Particularly alarming is the possibility that primatologists and ecotourists may have been the source of these viruses.

Natural disasters can also take a toll on primate populations and can have a significant impact on many aspects of primate behaviour (Figure 15.3). In Madagascar, for instance, a two-year drought (1991–92) resulted in increased mortality rates and a significant decline in the population of ring-tailed lemurs living in the Beza-Mahafaly Special Reserve (Gould, Sussman, and Sauther 1999). Similarly, Hurricane Iris, which struck Belize in October 2001, had a pronounced impact on black howler monkeys living in the Monkey River region of southern Belize. This extreme weather event resulted in a significant reduction in the howler population and the complete destruction of the forest canopy. The consequences of this included the breakdown of social groups into smaller units, an increase in the number of solitary animals, a dietary shift from frugivory to folivory, and an increase in the amount of time the monkeys spent on or near the ground (Pavelka et al. 2003; Pavelka, McGoogan, and Steffens 2007; Behie and Pavelka 2005).

---

9. Selective logging is not the same thing as deforestation—the latter involves the removal of forest to less than 10% of its original level (see Chapman and Peres 2001).

**Figure 15.3** The destruction of forest habitats by hurricanes, as seen here in Puerto Rico, can have a detrimental impact on primate populations.

Courtesy of Nicholas Brokaw

The loss of primates has a direct impact on human food availability. A number of primates act as seed dispersers, meaning that seeds from the fruits they eat are dispersed in their fecal matter as they move about. Consequently, the loss of even one species of primate can threaten the survival of plant species. On Madagascar, for example, lemurs are the primary seed dispersers and as such play a vital role in maintaining the health of its forests. Similarly, monkeys living in the Taï Forest of West Africa are key seed dispersers; their protection therefore benefits not only them but also human populations that rely on plant resources for food (Koné et al. 2008).

While the threat of extinction looms large for a number of primate species, considerable efforts are being taken to protect these animals, and primatologists are becoming increasingly involved in raising awareness of primate conservation. Through their engagement in **public anthropology**, they play a vital role in educating the public about the threats to primates and in promoting effective responses to ensure their survival. The key to designing and implementing successful conservation measures lies in identifying the factors that influence primate density in undisturbed environments and understanding how primate populations respond to, and recover from, habitat disturbance. Studies have shown, for instance, that environmental modification does not necessarily affect all primate species living in that environment in the same way. A decline in one species, for example, may result in an increase in another species. Similarly, species vary in the ways in which they respond to the fragmentation of forest, with some species remaining within isolated fragments and others moving between them (Chapman and Peres 2001). Understanding how primates respond is therefore important for the development of appropriate conservation policies. The protection of food resources on which they rely is also vital. Thus an awareness of primate diets and nutritional requirements is crucial for the construction of sound conservation plans.

Over the past few decades, a number of conservation initiatives have been launched. In 1977, the Jane Goodall Institute for Wildlife Research, Education, and Conservation was founded with the goal of increasing primate habitat conservation, expanding primate research programs, increasing awareness of primates and their relationship with their environment, and ensuring their well-being. Similarly, the Orangutan Foundation International was cofounded in 1986 with Simon Fraser University primatologist Biruté Galdikas to promote orangutan research and conservation. Other successful conservation measures include the construction of bridges across logging roads to assist the movement, interaction, and mating of nonhuman primates threatened by dwindling habitats. Besides this, national parks have been established, and the development of ecotourism—which promotes primates as tourist attractions—is providing funding needed for their protection. The implementation of CITES (Convention on International Trade in Endangered Species of Wild Flora and Fauna) has led to a decline in the live capture of and trade in primates. Ultimately, however, training local people in conservation and providing them with economic incentives to protect primates and their habitats are key to ensuring the long-term survival of these species.

**public anthropology**
an aspect of anthropology that involves writing and speaking to public audiences about social issues and concerns

http://www.janegoodall.org

http://www.orangutan.org

# FORENSIC ANTHROPOLOGY

The arena for applied biological anthropology with the highest public profile is undoubtedly that of forensic science, as witnessed by the popularity in recent years of television programs such as *CSI* and *Bones*, and crime novels such as the Temperance Brennan series written by Dr. Kathy Reichs, a practising forensic anthropologist. Because they are deeply familiar with normal population variation in skeletal and dental tissues, forensic anthropologists are able to assist government agencies (municipal, provincial, and national police forces, as well as coroners or medical examiners) in identifying and interpreting remains of individuals that would otherwise be unidentifiable as a result of decomposition, taphonomic factors (e.g., animal scavenging), and **perimortem** and **postmortem** trauma (Dupras et al. 2006). Cremation, in which bodies are partially or completely burned,[10] is another context in which the expertise of a trained human osteologist may help identify the victim and provide evidence for criminal proceedings (Correia and Beattie 2002; Fairgrieve 2007; Figure 15.4). It is important to note that in Canada, forensic anthropology does not exist as a career per se. Instead it is practised by academically trained biological anthropologists and archaeologists as an adjunct to their normal responsibilities as teachers and researchers employed in universities, colleges, and museums. Nonetheless, most are members of professional forensic science associations, such as the Canadian Forensic Science Society or the American Academy of Forensic Sciences.

**perimortem**
occurring at or around the time of death

**postmortem**
occurring after death

## From Field to Lab

Crime scene investigators are highly trained in assessing and "processing" (i.e., locating, recording, and collecting) evidence germane to reconstructing the circumstances around a suspicious death; few, however, are familiar with human skeletal anatomy, especially in cases

**Figure 15.4** Cremations are complex scenes requiring both archaeological (for recovery) and bioanthropological (for identification) expertise. Here, one of the authors (Lazenby) examines cremains of a homicide victim prior to recovery.

Courtesy of Richard Lazenby

10. The term cremains, abbreviated from "cremated remains," is often applied to such occurrences.

where bodies are fragmented, scavenged, traumatized, or burned. Subadult or fetal remains offer their own complexities, as individual bones and teeth are much smaller in size and incompletely formed and have unfused epiphyses that may easily be lost or overlooked. Thus, the presence of a forensic anthropologist/archaeologist at the site where remains are discovered can contribute immensely to the completeness of the recovery of the skeletal remains and thus to the quality of the information that can be gleaned from them. Two excellent examples of such cooperative efforts are the investigation of the World Trade Center tragedy following the "9/11" attack (Budimlija et al. 2003) and the systematic search for remains of over 60 women who had disappeared from Vancouver's notorious Downtown Eastside between 1978 and 2001. The latter search involved the laborious excavation of almost half a million cubic metres of soil from convicted serial killer Robert Pickton's 14-acre farm in Port Coquitlam, B.C. (Figure 15.5). At any given time over the course of the two-and-a-half-year project, more than 100 anthropology and archaeology students from universities and colleges across Canada assisted police investigators in the search for the remains of these women, under the direction of University of Toronto forensic anthropologist Dr. Tracy Rogers and one of the authors of this text (RL).[11]

When remains are recovered and brought back to the lab for analysis, the tasks of the forensic anthropologist are several. First, the bones must be cleaned and catalogued. This is necessary in order to observe any details of normal or abnormal morphology, as well as to determine whether more than a single individual is represented. For example, the occurrence

**Figure 15.5** The anthropological excavation of the 14-acre Pickton crime scene was a unique event in Canadian criminal history, involving the coordinated efforts of more than 100 anthropology and archaeology students and many more police investigators.

Courtesy of S/Sgt. Wayne Clary, RCMP

11. Pickton was charged in the deaths of 26 of these women, and was convicted of second degree murder in late 2007 on the first 6 counts brought forward; he is currently serving a sentence of life in prison. As this text goes to press, appeals from both defense and crown are outstanding.

commingled

the intentional or accidental mixing of bones from multiple individuals during burial or reburial

biological profile

in forensic anthropology, the fundamental biological characteristics of a person, including age, sex, body size, and ancestry

of the same portions of two left femora (thighbones) clearly indicates the presence of at least two separate individuals. In more complex situations, mass graves (see Box 15.2) may be intentionally disturbed in the weeks or months following their initial formation in order to disguise their existence or mask the identities of the perpetrators, and the skeletons interred therein may become **commingled**, presenting the anthropologist with the difficult task of sorting out one individual from another in order to complete an analysis and eventually repatriate the remains to surviving family members (Figure 15.6).

Once the remains have been cleaned and sorted, the process of identifying the individual begins. This is a multistage endeavour, which begins with deriving the **biological profile** of the remains (including age, sex, body size, and ancestry), followed by searching for any uniquely individualizing features (such as dental or osteopathic restorations, healed fractures, or developmental anomalies; see Figure 15.7) and determining how long the person may have been deceased.[12] This latter aspect is important. For example, if it is estimated that less than five years have passed since death occurred, investigators will not search through missing persons files that are much older than that for a possible identification. Indeed, the point of this stage of the analysis is to provide investigators with bounding limits on a possible identity in order to reduce the size of the pool of missing persons.

Evaluation of the biological profile is aided by the fact that the human skeleton varies in predictable ways as an individual grows from infancy to adulthood, as well as by the presence of well-studied patterns of sexual dimorphism—particularly with regard to the cranium and pelvis (Williams and Rogers 2006; Albanese, Eklics and Tuck, 2008). In addition, a wide variety of methods have been developed to calculate a person's body size (usually stature) from various intact or even fragmented bones, owing to the fact that the size of an individual bone is proportionate

**Figure 15.6** Following a complete forensic anthropological analysis, remains of victims of genocide are repatriated to their families in Guatemala.

Courtesy of Fundación de Antropología Forense de Guatemala/Guatemalan Forensic Anthropology Foundation

12. This period is known as the "postmortem interval" or, alternatively, as "elapsed time since death."

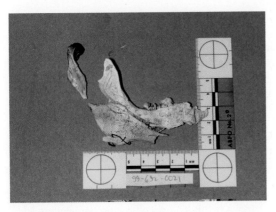

**Figure 15.7** The presence of a unique surgically implanted wire following a jaw fracture confirmed the identity of a homicide victim, even after the body had been consumed by an intentionally set fire.

Courtesy of Richard Lazenby

to that of the body overall. The most challenging component of the biological profile is that of ancestry.[13] As discussed in Chapter 13, assigning any single individual to a particular population of origin (i.e., "race") based on his or her physical features is highly problematic. At the same time, this aspect of someone's identity may be significant to a criminal investigation, as different ethnic groups (as determined, for example, by national censuses) are disproportionately represented among victims of crime. Over half the missing women from Vancouver's DTES, for example, were of aboriginal descent, though First Nations people in British Columbia comprise only 4.77% of the provincial population (Statistics Canada 2006). Ascertaining

---

**BOX 15.2    PROFILE... Anthropology, Forensic Science, and Human Rights**

Courtesy of Mark Skinner

I began doing forensic anthropology and archaeology in 1976. My predecessor at Simon Fraser University, Tom McKern, was a forensic anthropologist famous for his studies of age changes in the skeletons of young American males killed in Korea. He had already contacted the police in British Columbia offering his expertise. I stepped into his shoes along with two students, Owen Beattie and Richard Lazenby, both of whom are heavily involved today in forensic anthropology and in producing their own generations of students.

By 1978 we had been asked to apply archaeological and osteological expertise to the cremated remains of a homicide victim (a case that ultimately took 19 years to result in conviction of an American national). Even at that point we realized the significance of understanding site formation processes, taphonomic variables, and botanical and insect evidence. It was commonly stated in textbooks of the time that forensic anthropology was basically about identification and had little to

do with understanding the circumstances and timing of death. I wondered then why my tasks in Canada were so much broader than seemed to be the case in the United States.

Richard Lazenby and I decided it was time to write a field manual for death investigators with an emphasis on archaeological techniques—specifically, site formation and transformation processes as applied to crime scenes. That publication appeared in 1983. The Department of Archaeology at Simon Fraser University began to accept that our kind of applied science was scholarly activity, beneficial to the community and forensic science; consequently, it offered space and resources for such activities. This support has grown into the recently created Centre for Forensic Research at SFU, a suite of state-of-the-art dedicated forensic labs shared with Criminology and Biosciences, where we undertake casework and research on entomology, bone biochemistry, osteology, botany, and DNA. We currently handle more than one case a week, drawing on various kinds of forensic expertise for the benefit of the police and coroner's services. In addition, we are starting to solve cold cases going back as much as 40 years. Our students enjoy a remarkably rich and real exposure to almost every kind of forensic situation imaginable, ranging from floating feet to plane crashes to serial homicides.

Based on our publication Found: Human Remains, I was asked to write an article on how to apply archaeological methods to the excavation of mass graves—an emerging problem that came to the attention of the forensic community in the 1980s through the remarkable activities of Clyde Snow, who, on behalf of the American Association for the Advancement of Science, began trying to locate, excavate, and identify the "desaparicidos" of Argentina. Few had ever contemplated this kind of daunting excavation; it was hardly imaginable to me then that one would

*continued* ▶

---

13. While many forensic anthropologists are employing the term "ancestry" to connote a person's genetic heritage or population of origin, some still adhere to the more problematic, albeit historically entrenched, notion of "race" (see Byers 2007).

even be able to stand in the midst of a mass of rotting bodies, let alone do good forensic science. I wrote an article about 40 manuscript pages long titled "Planning the Archaeological Recovery of Evidence from Recent Mass Graves." It was rejected, and I was told it should be only four pages long. I could not accept that as large a topic as this could be dealt with usefully in so short a space, so I published it elsewhere. In retrospect, the article was naive but useful as, sadly, conflicts in the former Yugoslavia and elsewhere resulted in the creation of primary and secondary mass graves of an unprecedented scale and complexity.

I began to work internationally, and my youthful enthusiasm for forensics returned in full force. My first experience, back in 1997, was in Afghanistan on behalf of Physicians for Human Rights. This was my first exposure to an ongoing conflict, and I learned it was safer to be hunkered down in a 2 m² unit excavating bodies than up on top gazing about. I also learned about the naïveté of almost all concerned, including my own ignorance of explosive devices, armaments, clothing, and material culture as well as that of the UN teams of investigators, who seemed to know nothing about the potential of forensic science to figure out what had really happened as opposed to what a northern warlord said. From there I went on to Bosnia and Serbia, where I worked on and off for almost eight years. In the end, I would spend more than half my life abroad—a

sacrifice that I asked of my family and children. But with the aid of the International Commission on Missing Persons (IMCP), we tackled the largest identification problem ever faced by forensic science to that date. The ICMP applies DNA technology of its own creation to link hard-tissue DNA with that from biological relatives to derive personal identifications of great reliability. This decade-long enterprise has achieved more than 13,000 identifications of the estimated 35 to 40 thousand missing persons from the Balkans conflict. Apart from the scale of the problem, there was the unprecedented existence of secondary mass graves—the next major challenge to international forensic anthropology. These had been created by the perpetrators in a vain attempt to hide the existence of the primary graves by exhuming the bodies clandestinely and crudely burying them in remote locations in the Republika Srpska. The bodies in these graves are commingled, fragmented, and mixed up. The ICMP dealt with this situation by creating in 2005 the Lukavac Reassociation Centre, which reunites body parts scattered within and even among graves using DNA technology.

When I look back on more than 30 years of doing forensic anthropology, two feelings are paramount: each case teaches me something new, so my education has never stopped; and being able to do something for the marginalized, forgotten, or violated members of our society is deeply satisfying.

Source: Written by Mark Skinner, Department of Archaeology, Simon Fraser University

ancestry from skeletal remains, therefore, is often a necessary step toward reaching a conclusion as to identity. Using logic similar to analyzing clines for biological traits such as skin pigmentation or the HbS allele, forensic anthropologists diagnose ancestry based on features present in the skeleton that occur at higher frequencies among some populations than others. An attribute of the upper central incisors known as "incisor shovelling" (Figure 15.8) is more prevalent among peoples of Asian ancestry than, for example, among European-derived peoples; similarly, "nasal guttering" (Figure 15.9) is more common among individuals of African origin (Byers 2007). While these are reasonable determinations from a forensic science perspective and conform to prevailing views of ethnic diversity as reported in broad surveys such as censuses, such characterizations remain problematical from the perspective of a biocultural anthropology that has

moved away from the notion that humankind can be partitioned into a handful of types or categories. Furthermore, in North America perhaps more than elsewhere, three centuries of colonization, immigration, and subsequent intermarriage have blurred many cultural and biological distinctions. What traits might we expect to find in the skeleton of someone whose mother was a third-generation Métis and whose father recently arrived from Ghana?

The assessment and interpretation of perimortem and postmortem traumatic events that impart traces on bone is another significant piece of what the modern forensic anthropologist is asked to do. While it remains the purview of the coroner or

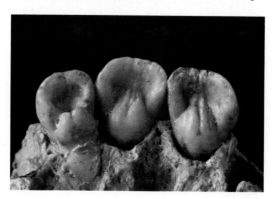

**Figure 15.8** Forensic anthropologists rely on traits that occur at higher frequencies in some populations versus others. Shovel-shaped upper incisors as seen here suggest affinity with Asian populations.

Ira Block/National Geographic Stock

medical examiner to formally determine the manner and cause of death,[14] these conclusions are often supported by evidence present in the physical (i.e., skeletal) remains. Perimortem trauma is, as the name suggests, most closely tied to actions around the time of death. In a criminal proceeding, evidence of penetrating wounds, fractures from blunt force impacts, or **tool marks** may support or refute other lines of evidence (such as witness statements) and help the "**trier of fact**" reach an informed conclusion as to guilt or innocence. After death, and prior to discovery, bones may also be modified by various elements in the environment—animal scavenging, water, sun, and wind can all change the appearance of bones and teeth, though these are in the main easily distinguished from trauma occurring at the time of death (Figure 15.10; Byers 2007).

## A New Forensic Anthropology?

As we noted in Chapter 1, almost 60 years ago, Sherwood Washburn (1951) proclaimed the arrival of a "new" physical anthropology, one that embraced the concepts of adaptation and evolutionary biology. Recently, Dennis Dirkmaat and colleagues from the Department of Applied Forensic Sciences at Mercyhurst College (2008) have borrowed a page from Washburn's thesis, announcing that a "new forensic anthropology" has materialized from a series of significant developments over the past 20 years. These advances have transformed the role of the forensic anthropologist from a bone specialist who does little more than identify bones and provide a biological profile, to one of forensic archaeologist, taphonomist, osteologist, trauma analyst, and "expert witness." They ask: "Does conventional physical anthropology training fully qualify an individual—if you can stomach the smell—as a forensic practitioner, or has forensic anthropology acquired a level of specialization and sophistication requiring special training?" (ibid., 34). A positive answer to the second of these questions would suggest, as these authors argue, that in requiring its own basic research and professional development, forensic anthropology has shifted from an applied branch of biological anthropology to a fully fledged scientific discipline in its own right.

While Dirkmaat and colleagues (2008) discuss six major developments underlying this "paradigm shift" (see Chapter 2 for a discussion of this concept), two have been particularly transformative. First, there is

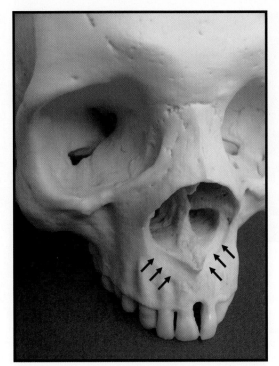

**Figure 15.9** Nasal guttering, seen here, is another feature suggestive of ancestry; in this case, African.

Courtesy of Anne Keenleyside

**tool marks**

with regard to the skeleton, these are marks left on the surface of bone that may be linked through a process of replication in the lab to a suspect instrument, e.g., knife, axe, saw

**trier of fact**

in law, the person or persons who decide which facts are to be accepted as evidence; in a jury trial, the trier of fact is the jury; in a "bench trial" in which no jury is present, the trier of fact is the judge

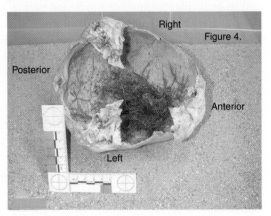

**Figure 15.10** Animal scavenging leaves distinctive gnaw marks on bone. In this case, the entire lower and facial portions of a skull have been destroyed by animals in their quest for nutrition (i.e., the brain).

Courtesy of Richard Lazenby

---

14. Manner of death refers to the circumstance in which death occurred, such as accident, homicide, or suicide, whereas cause of death refers to the specific agent responsible, e.g., gunshot, fall, or asphyxiation.

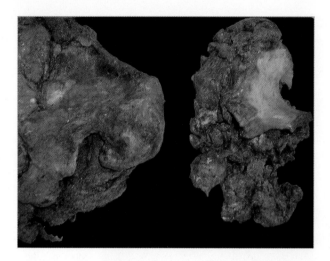

**Figure 15.11** As we learned from the World Trade Center experience, DNA may not always provide conclusive results as to identification. In the left image, two portions of right pelvis thought to belong to one individual were later shown to contain the DNA of two people; one profile from bone and the other from soft tissue.

(A) Z. Budimlijo, et al. (2003). World Trade Center Human Identification Project: Experiences with individual body identification cases. *Croatian Medical Journal* 44: 259–263. Reprinted by permission of The Croatian Medical Journal. Image courtesy of Zoran Budimlijo. (B) Helene Seligman/AFP/Getty Images

**evidentiary**

anything that constitutes evidence or that has the quality of evidence, as a substantiation of fact, related to a court proceeding

**amplifying**

a step in DNA analysis in which small quantities of DNA collected by investigators are multiplied to provide sufficient material for the subsequent steps of identifying the nucleotide sequence and comparing it with known sequences stored in databases or obtained from putative relatives

**exemplar**

a sample of DNA obtained from a known individual to be used in comparison with an unknown sample for purposes of matching and identification

the revolutionizing role of DNA as an investigative and **evidentiary** tool; second, there is the establishment within Canadian and American courts of standards determining the admissibility of expert testimony. Our DNA, mitochondrial or nuclear, is without question the most uniquely identifying feature of our biology, and by virtue of reproduction our particular version of it can be linked to those with whom we are most closely related: parents and siblings. Since the mid-1980s, techniques for collecting, **amplifying**, sequencing, and comparing DNA profiles have progressed to the point where the probability of a correct match between an unknown sample and an **exemplar** approaches 100%, and multiple comparisons can be made simultaneously. From the standpoint of identification of unknown remains, be they single and intact individuals or multiple, fragmented, and commingled, DNA analysis is orders of magnitude more efficient than the traditional biological profile described previously, though it is entirely dependent on being able to connect the unknown individual with a sample of known missing persons. While the Pickton investigation referred to earlier employed large numbers of anthropologists and archaeologists, their primary function was to locate skeletal remains—all of the personal identifications were achieved via DNA analysis, and the role of the forensic anthropologists at trial was relatively minor. This of course was made possible by the fact that there was a fairly small pool of missing individuals believed to have been associated with the Pickton site, which meant that the necessary exemplar DNA was readily obtained from relatives.

Does this mean that the traditional role of the anthropologist in identifying found remains through the analysis of "dry bones" will be usurped by test tubes and gene sequencers in sterile laboratories? Certainly not in the near future; DNA analysis is still relatively costly, and forensic labs are overwhelmed with work. Furthermore, in the case of fragmented and commingled remains involving multiple individuals (mass disasters and mass graves come to mind), the anthropologist remains an essential element in sorting and reconstructing bodies. The WTC (World Trade Center) disaster is a case in point (Figure 15.11). Budimlija and colleagues (2003), for example, note an instance in which DNA recovered from muscle mass from two isolated human fragments was matched to one individual; however, the bony portions to which the muscle was attached were duplicates from the right pelvis. When DNA was extracted from the bone fragments, two different

**348**     **PART FOUR** Modern Currents          NEL

profiles emerged, the original one found in the earlier soft tissue analysis and a new one from the bone analysis. The investigators concluded that the force of the event was so intense that soft tissue from one person had actually become fused to the skeletal remains of someone else! Perhaps somewhat disturbingly, in a recent paper, Frumkin et al. (2009) have shown that it is possible to create fake DNA that can be made to match anyone's profile. Current techniques used by police forces worldwide do not have the ability to distinguish real from fake DNA, though in the same paper, these authors demonstrate a new assay method that is able to tell one from the other based on the degree of **DNA methylation**.

Not all of the work performed by a forensic anthropologist is necessarily related to criminal cases. Skeletal remains believed to be human may prove to be nonhuman in origin, or if human may sometimes derive from unmarked archaeological gravesites. Others may be recent but represent remains of individuals who died as a result of misfortune rather than foul play. While coroners and medical examiners have an interest in resolving these occurrences, the legal community (police and Crown persecutors) generally does not. On occasion, however, the forensic anthropologist works closely with these authorities to assist in solving deaths resulting from homicide. In such cases, they may be required to appear in court as an "expert witness"[15] and to assist the trier of fact in understanding complex evidence requiring particular kinds of knowledge not commonly held by the public.

Since the 1990s, two cases, one in the United States and the other in Canada, have redefined the relationship between the expert's opinion and the courts. Known as the *Daubert* (US) and *Mohan* (Canada) rulings, they specifically require that all experts (not just forensic anthropologists) ground their expertise in methods that are "testable, replicable, reliable, and scientifically valid" (Dirkmaat et al. 2008, 35). These rulings have had a profound impact on forensic anthropology; in particular, they have resulted in a serious undertaking on the part of the forensic anthropological community to show that its methods are, in fact, as scientifically robust as practitioners assert them to be (Steadman, Adams, and Konigsberg 2006). Thus, for example, we see studies published in peer-reviewed journals testing existing methods or developing new methods such that experts can be more precise in their explanations as to how certain conclusions were reached. University of Toronto forensic anthropologist Tracy Rogers and her students have recently been "proofing" methods based on cranial morphology with the express purpose of identifying which particular features are best able to distinguish male from female (e.g., Williams and Rogers 2006; see also Albanese, Eklics and Tuck 2008) and to establish positive identification based on cranial suture patterns (Rogers and Allard 2004). It is precisely this kind of research activity which suggests to Dirkmaat and colleagues (2008) that forensic anthropology, in developing its own literature and basic science, has shifted from an applied branch of biological anthropology to become its own bone fide discipline.

**DNA methylation**

a chemical modification of DNA that adds methyl group compounds to certain base pairs (adenine and cytosine) during cell division and differentiation and which may be inherited

# SUMMARY

In recent decades, anthropologists have come to appreciate that the discipline's "knowledge of discovery," derived from formulating and testing hypotheses regarding fundamental aspects of human biological, cultural, and technological evolution, can have a significant beneficial impact on real-world problems. Anthropological knowledge not only transforms our understanding of who we are, but also provides a foundation for *changing* the way we are. Understanding how we 'came to be different in spite of being the same' allows us to amend, correct, and rectify inequities in relationships we share with one another, with our environment, and with our technology. Does an applied anthropology have all the answers to all of our problems? Certainly not. But it can provide some solutions directly (as in the case of forensic anthropology and ergonomics), and it can suggest avenues toward others (as with medical anthropology and emerging fields such as nutritional genomics). In the next and final chapter, we pursue these themes further, asking one frank question: What is the future of humankind?

---

15. The status of expert is determined by the court through a process of *qualification*, based on credentials (academic training, experience, professional status) possessed by the witness.

# CORE REVIEW

**What is medical anthropology? In what ways can it be applied?**

Medical anthropology is the study of health, illness, and healing from a cross-cultural perspective. Applied medical anthropology involves collecting ethnographic data on cultural beliefs, attitudes, and behaviours in order to design and implement health policies and treatment strategies that are culturally appropriate.

**What is evolutionary medicine? In what ways have anthropologists contributed to this field?**

Evolutionary (or Darwinian) medicine is an interdisciplinary field that involves applying the principles of evolutionary theory to medicine. Key areas of research in this field are nutrition, disease epidemiology, and reproductive health. Anthropologists have made valuable contributions to all three areas through their studies of the health impact of changing diets, chronic and infectious diseases, and population variation in reproductive patterns and outcomes.

**What is nutritional genomics, and what are some of the potential applications of this newly emerging science?**

Nutritional genomics is a newly emerging science that examines the interaction between our genes and the foods we eat. Its potential lies in enabling individuals to tailor their diet to their genetic makeup in order to optimize their health and prevent or treat disease. Well-known examples of gene–diet interactions include lactose intolerance, phenylketonuria, familial hypercholesterolemia, and celiac disease.

**What is ergonomics? How has anthropometry contributed to this specialty?**

Ergonomics is the science of designing work areas and products that optimize human performance and ensure that our working and living environments are safe and comfortable. Anthropometry, the measurement of the human body, provides the data used to design optimal workspaces, clothing and footwear, and car and airplane seats.

**What threats do nonhuman primates currently face? In what ways can primatology contribute to the conservation of these animals?**

Major threats to nonhuman primates today include habitat destruction in the form of deforestation, logging, and forest fires, the hunting of primates for bush meat, the trade in live animals for laboratories, zoos, and pets, infectious diseases transmitted from humans, and the alteration of natural habitats due to global warming. Primatologists play a key role in helping ensure the survival of these animals by studying the factors that influence primate density in undisturbed environments, as well as the ways in which species respond to and recover from habitat disturbance.

**What is forensic anthropology? What contributions do forensic anthropologists make both locally and globally?**

Forensic anthropologists apply methods of skeletal analysis to identify unknown human remains within a medico-legal framework. Locally, forensic anthropologists assist government agencies in the recovery and interpretation of human skeletal remains to ascertain who the individual was in life and the circumstances of death (e.g., misfortune, criminal act). Besides biological markers (age, sex, etc.), they provide details about traumatic and taphonomic modifications of bone and teeth, as well as elapsed time since death. Many forensic anthropologists travel the world, analyzing and interpreting human remains found in mass graves as a consequence of noncombat deaths, extrajudicial killings, and genocide.

# CRITICAL THINKING QUESTIONS

1. If "race" is not a valid biological category, as discussed in Chapter 13, on what grounds can forensic anthropologists argue that race/ancestry can be identified in human skeletal remains?
2. What impact might nutritional genomics have on the food industry and the development and consumption of genetically modified foods?

# GROUP DISCUSSION QUESTIONS

1. The great apes and other nonhuman primates are currently facing a number of threats, including loss of habitat due to logging and agriculture, hunting resulting from the demand for bush meat, and infectious diseases transmitted from humans. One possible source of these diseases is ecotourists. Given this observation, do you think the ecotourism industry should continue to be promoted? What are the advantages and disadvantages of ecotourism for humans and nonhuman primates? Does the threat to nonhuman primates outweigh the benefits to human populations that live in developing countries? What measures could be taken to help protect primates against disease?
2. Despite its history of abuse, vis-à-vis racial categorization, anthropometry has contributed greatly to the field of ergonomics. Having said that, are there any ways in which data derived from anthropometry could potentially be misused today?
3. Our perceptions of biological processes such as menstruation and morning sickness have implications in terms of medical intervention. To what extent should we be manipulating such processes?

# RESOURCES AND READINGS

- R. Brigelius-Flohé and H.-G. Joost, eds., *Nutritional Genomics: Impact on Health and Disease* (New York: Wiley-VCH, 2006).
- S.N. Byers, *Introduction to Forensic Anthropology,* 3rd ed. (New York: Allyn and Bacon, 2007).
- G. Cowlishaw and R.I.M. Dunbar, *Primate Conservation Biology* (Chicago: University of Chicago Press, 2000).
- A. Fuentes and L.D. Wolfe, eds., *Primates Face to Face: The Conservation Implications of Human-Nonhuman Primate Interconnection* (Cambridge: Cambridge University Press, 2005).
- J. Kaput and R.L. Rodriguez, eds., *Nutritional Genomics: Discovering the Path to Personalized Nutrition* (New York: Wiley-Interscience, 2006).
- S. Pheasant and C.M. Haslegrave, *Bodyspace: Anthropometry, Ergonomics and the Design of Work,* 3rd ed. (Boca Raton: CRC, 2005).
- W.R. Trevathan, E.O. Smith, and J.J. McKenna, *Evolutionary Medicine and Health: New Perspectives* (Oxford: Oxford University Press, 2007).

Chapter

# 16 Human Legacies, Human Prospects

## OVERVIEW

*A Human Voyage*, as a text, comes to an end with this chapter—but not with respect to your own lives. That voyage will go on, and will take each of you to distant corners of the world. For some that may mean a few hundred kilometres, for others many thousands. Regardless, you will be touched by events and actions far removed from your personal (or virtual) space. You will be challenged by diverse inequities—social, economic, historical, and structural—and we hope that what you have learned here will be a kind benefit to you along the way. Some of these challenges are explored in this chapter. Your generation will be required to address major issues over the next few decades: a burgeoning population rapidly depleting nonrenewable resources, consumption-driven environmental degradation, and the growing divide between rich and poor households in your own neighbourhood and nation, and between rich and poor nations within the global community. But the history of human biocultural evolution has always been one of surmounting challenges, and that will also continue.

## CORE CONCEPTS

- population growth, demography, Malthusian dilemma, population momentum, political economy, poverty, genetic load, positive selection

## CORE QUESTIONS

- How would measures of fertility distinguish between expanding and contracting populations?
- What is the relationship between population growth, fertility, and economic development?
- What is political economy, and why is it significant for the field of biological anthropology?
- Why is childhood growth and development a useful proxy for population well-being and adaptation?
- Are humans still evolving? How do we know?

*As human beings, we are endowed with
freedom of choice, and we cannot shuffle off our
responsibility upon the shoulders of God or nature.
We must shoulder it ourselves. It is our responsibility.*

Arnold J. Toynbee (1889–1975)

# PROLOGUE: PAST, PRESENT, FUTURE

Turn back to the first page of this text and you will see that we introduced the opening chapter of *A Human Voyage* with a quotation from the British historian Arnold Toynbee, as we do in this closing chapter. Toynbee suggested that the current state of humankind ("civilization") was not something that could—by any measure—be viewed as an endpoint or a destination. We hope that, having completed your reading of this book, you will agree with us (and with Toynbee) that there is no harbour waiting for humankind. As we have illustrated in the intervening chapters, *Homo sapiens* in the 21st century is simply at one particular moment on a long, historically contingent, and fascinating journey. Our understanding of that enterprise is much clearer today than it was when Charles Darwin correctly pointed toward Africa as the birthplace of our species in *The Descent of Man* (1871).

Today technological innovation occurs at a jarring, mind-numbing pace, perhaps most especially in the realm of information technologies. They shape our world physically, biologically, politically, and economically in innumerable ways (Figure 16.1). They blur cultural boundaries, and it is far from clear whether humankind is improved or burdened (or both!) by these developments. Thus, we should appreciate that our understanding of humanity in 2170 will be … well, will be what? A reasonable question to ask is just that: What will that understanding of ourselves look like at the bicentenary of *The Descent of Man*? What kind of world will that knowledge be situated within? Will people still be interested in who we are as a species, where we came from, where we are going? Will your grandchildren be attending a college or a university and reading a text such as this? Will texts or books of any sort still exist?

We have seen that as a species, humans share very close affinities—genetic, physiological, and functional—with many other organisms. Some of these, chimpanzees for example, are very closely related to us—so near in fact that some scholars have argued for their inclusion in the genus *Homo* (or humans within the genus *Pan*). Other animals, such as rodents and honeybees, are more distantly related. But in all cases the biological relationships are significant,

**Figure 16.1** Modern technology now has a global reach. It is no longer a question of adopting technology, but of finding ways to cope with its imposition in all aspects of our lives.

Joseph Van Os/Getty Images

demonstrable, and persistent. We are both mouse and chimpanzee (and mice are both chimp and human and so on).

This brings us to Toynbee's second quote. There are two ideas central to it, and to this closing chapter: human choice, and human responsibility. You might think these to be strange concepts for a text, and a course, in biological anthropology. But in fact they extend from the point just made in the previous paragraph: while there is something certainly special about humans as a species, we are simply that—one species among so many more, and all of them our relatives. Let us ask what makes us special. As Toynbee would have it, it is the power of our choice, and the breadth of our responsibility which follows from that power. As biological anthropologists, we (and you) are more aware than many others of the ways in which humans are integral to, and yet have become disenfranchised from, the biological world that nurtured us for so many millennia. Who better, then, to speak with some authority on matters of choice and responsibility? In this chapter we focus on a several pressing engagements awaiting human action: population growth, the biologies of inequity, and the future of human evolution. There are so many more—too many more—from which we could have chosen. There is a common thread to our selection, however, and it is the same thread that has brought us from Toynbee first to Toynbee last: generation and variation.

# POPULATION GROWTH

In the September 2008 issue of *National Geographic* magazine, journalist Charles Mann (2008) noted that a mere 11% of the world's land surface is devoted to growing food for over 6 billion people, and only 3% of that land can be characterized as being inherently fertile soil (the balance requiring technological interventions, such as irrigation and chemical fertilization). Moreover, in the most comprehensive study to date on the state of the world's marine fishery, Worm and colleagues (2006) note that without immediate remediation, global food fish stocks will be depleted beyond recovery by 2048 (Figure 16.2). At the same time as land and ocean productivity is dwindling, the creation of waste increases annually, including a new form of toxic waste unique to the end of the 20th century—namely, e-waste (Wong et al. 2007; Figure 16.3).[1] In Canada, per capita nonhazardous solid waste production increased 10% between 1998 and 2000 to almost 750 kilograms per person, in spite of intensified programs for reuse and recycling (Environment Canada 2003; Figure 16.4). The common threads to all of these realities are the twinned economic forces of production and consumption, both of which can be tied to one overwhelming demographic factor: population growth. However, as we explore below, the challenge is not limited to the total number of individuals on the planet; it also encompasses the inequitable distribution of people with respect to necessary resources, including space, wealth, and security. Such inequities have significant ramifications for human biology, impacting growth and development, health, fertility, and mortality.

## Measuring Population Growth

**Demographers** speak of population growth as either negative (more deaths than births) or positive (more births than deaths), though these are crude measures; more precise estimates would also consider changes due to immigration or emigration. Population growth also varies over time with changing patterns of fertility and mortality, resulting in a phenomenon known as the **demographic transition**. Such changes might come about through advancements in technology reducing the risk of dying at a given age, through improvements in nutrition, hygiene, and health care extending life spans, or through shifts in cultural attitudes

**demography**

the study of population dynamics, including measures such as fertility, mortality, migration, survivorship, and life expectancy

**demographic transition**

the change in a population's age and sex structure with changing birth and death rates. Declines in mortality are typically followed by declines in fertility, shifting a population from an expansion phase to one of stability or contraction

---

1. E-waste refers to the disposal of obsolete electronic equipment of all varieties, including computer cathode-tube televisions and computer monitors, printers, CPUs, keyboards, and so forth. These components contain a toxic mix of heavy metals, PCBs, furans, and dioxins known to be harmful to human health. Recycling of reusable components has become a major industry for developing nations with lax environmental and worker safety standards.

**CHAPTER 16** Human Legacies, Human Prospects

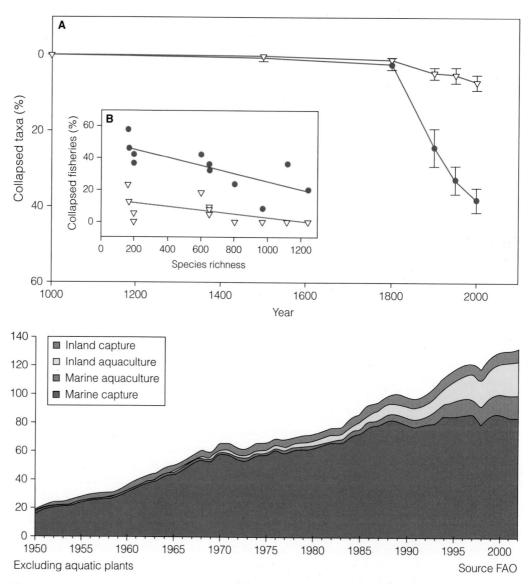

**Figure 16.2** The number of fish taxa that have collapsed (closed circles) or become extinct (open triangles) has increased dramatically over the past 200 years (a) as the total capture has increased in the marine fishery over 400% in the last 50 years alone (b).

Food and Agriculture Organization of the United Nations, (2005). Review of the state of world marine fishery resources, FAO Technical Paper 457, Figure A1.1; http://www.fao.org/docrep/009/y5852e/y5852e00.htm. Reprinted by permission. From B. Worm, et al., (2006). Impacts of biodiversity loss on ocean ecosystem services, *Science* 314: 787–790. Reprinted with permission from AAAS

**replacement rate fertility**

the rate of fertility required to replace a parental generation and to account for differences in local mortality rates

with respect to birth control, abortion, or family size thereby reducing fertility.[2] A measure of the pace at which a population is expanding or shrinking is **replacement rate fertility**. On a global scale, this measure is approximately 2.33—one child each to account for the parents and one-third of a child to make up for variations in sex ratio at birth[3] and early adult mortality. However, there is considerable variation by country in fertility rates (Table 16.1).

2. Many other factors influence the demographic structure of a population, including political or civil strife, famine, itinerant labour migration, and disease outbreaks that preferentially affect certain age/sex groups. Lifestyle choices such as smoking, alcohol consumption, and lack of exercise, long known to reduce longevity, have also been correlated with reduced reproductive output (Homan, Davies, and Norman 2007).

3. Sex ratio is calculated as the number of males to females at given periods over the life cycle (e.g., conception, birth, at puberty, and postreproductive). In humans, the birth sex ratio (also known as the secondary sex ratio) is approximately 105 males per 100 females, though this can be affected by cultural practices such as selective abortion and infanticide. For most countries, the postreproductive sex ratio favours females due to differences in longevity.

For example, in 2008 Canada had an annual population growth rate of 0.8% and a **total fertility rate** (TFR) of 1.6, while Liberia's growth rate was 3.7% with a TFR of 5.9. The fact that Canada's 2008 TFR was below replacement level indicates that future growth in the Canadian population will need to rely heavily on immigration.

There is also considerable variation within national boundaries. For example, traditional Anabaptist religious sects such as Hutterites, Mennonites, and Amish are well known for having TFRs of 10.0 or higher (Hurd 2006)—a rate supported by high levels of both economic and **social capital** within these populations. There is some indication of recent declines in fertility among these groups; TFR for Canadian Hutterite colonies in Alberta dropped from 9.99 in the 1950s to 8.80 by the mid-1980s (Nonoka, Miura, and Peter 1994), primarily through a decline in the number of children borne by women over age 35.

The other side of the population growth coin is mortality, and as we saw with birth rates, there is considerable variation among nations with respect to death rates (Figure 16.5). Here again, the causes of death are diverse and are not equitably distributed between or within national boundaries. To illustrate, consider that the infant mortality rate (per 1,000 live births) in 2003 for Canada overall was 5.3 while in Nunavut it was 19.8; and that youth suicide among Inuit in 2008 was 11 times the national average. Such disparities in rate and manner of death point to profound inequities in access to health care, in cultural dissonance, and to myriad other cultural and socioeconomic factors.

## Future Tense?

As this sentence was being written (9:41 p.m., January 13, 2009), the world's population was 6,723,223,846. In 1950 this figure was approximately 2.5 billion. It is estimated that 10 millennia ago, as settled life and agriculture were getting under way, world population was about 1 million (Michael 1993). In other words, between ca. 8000 BCE and 1950, global population increased on average by about 700,000 people per year, but in the past six decades by almost 73 million per year. Clearly, the change in the rate of growth has not been this abrupt; nonetheless, it has been dramatic over the past 200 years (Figure 16.6). Two questions are raised: How did this happen? And what are the implications going forward in the 21st century?

It is far easier to answer the first of these queries. Aside from opening the door to the nuclear age and the Cold War, the end of the Second World War led into two decadesh of economic prosperity in the developed world; to important advances in

**Figure 16.3** The disposal or recycling of non-biodegradable electronic components is a new phenomenon associated with the "information age." Many of these components contain toxic waste harmful to human health.

© Greenpeace/Natalie Behring-Chisholm

**total fertility rate**
the average number of children born per woman if all women in the country concerned lived to the end of their childbearing years and bore children according to the age-specific pattern for the region or group

**social capital**
the resources available to a person or group deriving from their connection to social networks

http://www.census.gov/ipc/www/idb/summaries.html

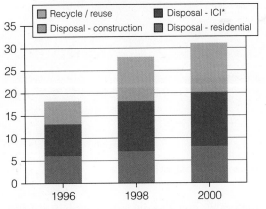

**Total non-hazardous solid waste disposal and recycling/reuse (million tonnes)**

Legend:
- Recycle / reuse
- Disposal - construction
- Disposal - ICI*
- Disposal - residential

(years shown: 1996, 1998, 2000)

**Figure 16.4** Humans create immense amounts of solid waste. In some parts of the world, such as Manila, municipal waste has become a commodity exploited by hundreds of families. In Canada, waste production continues to increase in spite of programs to reuse or recycle.

From Total non-hazardous solid waste disposal and recycling/reuse (million tonnes), *Canada's National Environmental Indicators Series, 2003*, http://www.ec.gc.ca/soer-ree/English/Indicator_series/new_issues.cfm?issue_is=13&tech_id=53#bio_pic. © Her Majesty The Queen in Right of Canada, Environment Canada, 2010. Reproduced with the permission of the Minister of Public Works and Government Services Canada

**Table 16.1** Total fertility rate (TFR) and infant mortality (IM, deaths per 1,000 live births) for selected countries, ranked in order as per TFR. The correlation of the ranks for these two measures in this table is 0.898; that is, countries with high TFR also have high IM, though some exceptions do occur (e.g., Israel).

| Country | TFR | Rank | IM | Rank |
|---|---|---|---|---|
| Mali | 7.34 | 1 | 103.83 | 8 |
| Afghanistan | 6.58 | 5 | 154.67 | 3 |
| Liberia | 5.87 | 13 | 143.89 | 4 |
| Ethiopia | 4.99 | 30 | 82.64 | 20 |
| Haiti | 4.79 | 36 | 62.33 | 37 |
| Iraq | 3.97 | 50 | 45.43 | 58 |
| Papua New Guinea | 3.71 | 55 | 46.67 | 56 |
| Guatemala | 3.59 | 58 | 28.79 | 79 |
| Bangladesh | 3.08 | 70 | 57.45 | 43 |
| Israel | 2.77 | 86 | 4.28 | 206 |
| India | 2.76 | 87 | 32.31 | 73 |
| Venezuela | 2.52 | 101 | 22.02 | 101 |
| Mexico | 2.37 | 111 | 19.01 | 113 |
| United States | 2.1 | 125 | 6.3 | 181 |
| France | 1.98 | 134 | 3.36 | 216 |
| Chile | 1.95 | 137 | 7.9 | 163 |
| Ireland | 1.85 | 150 | 5.14 | 189 |
| Sweden | 1.67 | 171 | 2.75 | 221 |
| United Kingdom | 1.66 | 172 | 4.93 | 193 |
| Canada | 1.57 | 182 | 5.08 | 190 |
| Russia | 1.4 | 194 | 10.81 | 151 |
| Japan | 1.22 | 215 | 2.80 | 220 |
| Hong Kong | 1 | 220 | 2.93 | 219 |

Source: CIA World Fact Book, 2008

medical knowledge, including antibiotic drugs; and to significant developments in agricultural science—the "Green Revolution"—which resulted in unprecedented levels of production of staple crops as new, higher yielding varieties of rice, wheat, and maize were developed (Conway and Toenniessen 1999).[4] The demographic impacts were several, including the Baby Boom in Europe, North America, Australia, and parts of Asia, the provision of sufficient calories in developing states to sustain high levels of population growth, and a reduction in levels of mortality worldwide through the application and distribution of health care advances (principally through agencies of the United Nations). Consequently, more babies were born (typically to younger women), and fewer people died in any given year. In Canada, the Baby

4. As a result of current population pressures in developing states, biological and social scientists alike are calling for greater efforts in producing a second Green Revolution, via biotechnology, to provide crops that will provide even greater yields, besides being resistant to drought, pests, and pesticides (Wollenweber, Porter, and Lübberstedt 2005).

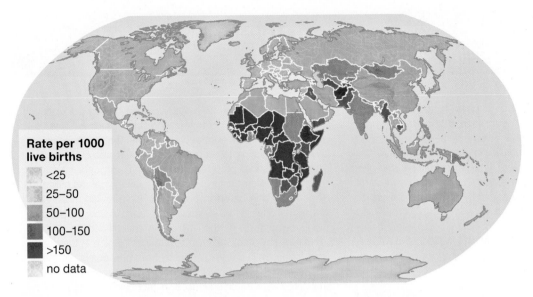

**Figure 16.5** Infant mortality rate varies globally, mainly due to intrinsic factors regarding nutrition, maternal health care, and endemic disease risk.

From World Health Organization (WHO), (2005). http://www.who.int/healthinfo/statistitcs/01.whostat2005map_under5 mortaliity.jpg. Reprinted by permission of WHO

Boom resulted in an additional 1.5 million births between 1940 and 1965 (among whom are included the authors of this text!).

## A Neo-Malthusian Dilemma?

The implications of the recent historic trend in population growth as we enter the second decade of the 21st century are profound. Though the annual rate of population increase is slowing down on a global scale (it is almost half today what it was in the early 1960s: around 1.2% versus 2.2%), the decline is not even across the board and remains beyond replacement levels in regions of the world that can least support rapidly growing populations. The ominous consequences of unsustainable growth were first pointed out more than 200 years ago by Thomas Robert Malthus (1766–1834), an English political economist whose now famous 1798 essay on population not only established the foundations of modern demography but also influenced a number of his peers and intellectual successors (see Box 16.1). Since the 1960s, social demographers (most famously the Stanford entomologist Paul Erhlich; see Ehrlich and Ehrlich 1990) have revived Malthusian prognostications for significant declines in human well-being as a result of overpopulation (Williams 2008).

While Ehrlich's dire warnings of impending demographic calamity, famine, and population decline have not been received without criticism (Lomborg 2001),

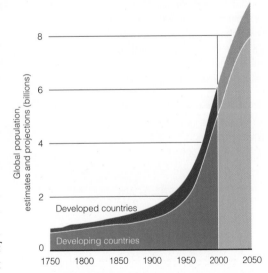

**Figure 16.6** Global population growth rate has increased dramatically since the end of the Second World War. The vast majority of this increase occurs in developing countries.

UNEP/GRID-Arendal, Trends in population, developed and developing countries, 1750–2050 (estimates and projections). Cartographer: Hugo Ahlenius, Nordpil. UNEP/GRID-Arendal Maps and Graphics Library, http://maps.grida.no/go/graphic/trends-in-population-developed-and-developing-countries-1750-2050-estimates-and-projections (accessed 7 November 2009)

BOX 16.1

# RETROSPECTION: Thomas Robert Malthus (1798) *An Essay on the Principle of Population*

*The power of population is so superior to the power of the earth to produce subsistence for man, that premature death must in some shape or other visit the human race. The vices of mankind are active and able ministers of depopulation. They are the precursors in the great army of destruction, and often finish the dreadful work themselves. But should they fail in this war of extermination, sickly seasons, epidemics, pestilence, and plague advance in terrific array, and sweep off their thousands and tens of thousands. Should success be still incomplete, gigantic inevitable famine stalks in the rear, and with one mighty blow, levels the population with the food of the world.*

T.R. Malthus's small *Essay*, originally published anonymously and reprinted through six editions, owes as much to his training as a mathematician and political economist as it does to his philosophical conversations with his father and his vocation as curate of Okewood Chapel in Surrey, England, whose parishioners were illiterate and extremely poor (Avery 2005). Combining his lived and learned experience, Malthus reasoned that all animal populations, including human, were capable of multiplying exponentially. For us, this means doubling every 25 years, quadrupling every 50, and so on; left unchecked, in theory an initial population of 100 sexually mature persons would become 1,600 after four generations! Clearly, positive checks on population growth must exist that increase mortality, as Malthus dramatically evokes in the above passage. In later editions (in response to critics), he included several "negative" checks on population growth aimed at controlling fertility. These included birth control, late marriage, and "Moral Restraint" outside of marriage.

Malthus's influence extended into numerous spheres, from politics, to theology, sociology, natural history, and beyond. National censuses were established in the United Kingdom in 1801, and birth control programs were created in the latter part of the century based on Malthusian ideas. Charles Darwin and Alfred Russel Wallace drew heavily on

Malthus's analysis of the limits by which human populations might be "improved" in formulating their principle of natural selection. Malthus's central premise was that the capacity of human population to reproduce, as noted above, exceeded that of agricultural production to sustain it. His ideas have also been incorporated into 20th-century ecological modelling of the relationship between population increase and **carrying capacity** (Figure 16.7): growth rate should slow as population size approaches the limit of the environment to support it. Failure to do so results in "overshoot," which in turn leads to a reduction in carrying capacity from previous levels. While the degree to which carrying capacity is suppressed may be mitigated by further advances in technology (e.g., genetically engineered high-yield crops that are both drought and pest resistant), an emerging consensus suggests that such innovations will have less and less impact in the future as the natural fertility of soils and available arable land is depleted (Ramankutty, Foley, and Olejniczak 2008). Both outcomes were predicted by Malthus two centuries ago.

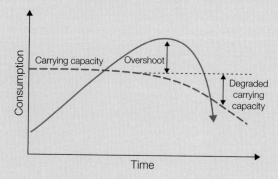

**Figure 16.7** Populations are able to grow in size to an upper limit determined by local ecological factors; typically, this limit is set by the least available essential resource.

**carrying capacity**

the population size of a given organism that a habitat could comfortably sustain given available resources, noted by the symbol K; K fluctuates with variation in resources, and for human populations these include not only space, food, and water but also variables such as sanitation, health care, and social capital

there is cause to reconsider the implications of global human expansion and local inequities in population growth. In this regard, in a series of articles published in the *American Journal of Physical Anthropology*, J. Kenneth Smail (2002, 2003a, b) argued that the world does not have the resources to support its current population, let alone one numbering over 9 billion, as projected for 2050.[5] It is worth examining Smail's argument for a number of reasons. First, global population has increased by over 500 million people since his 2002 publication. Second, Smail concludes that significant remedial action must be enacted urgently in order to ameliorate an impending and chaotic reduction in world population over the next 150 years. Finally, Smail specifically exhorts biological anthropologists to become active voices

5. Current projections, Malthus notwithstanding, are that the human population will stabilize around this figure by midcentury.

in developing recommendations germane to such action—we are, after all, consummate describers and explainers of the history of human reproduction!

Smail (2002) outlines his position as a series of 10 "inescapable realties" (see Table 16.2), five of which are demographic and five economic/ecological. The essential message is not difficult to comprehend: the bulk of future population growth will occur disproportionately in sub-Saharan Africa, India, and Asia, all centres of massive **population momentum**, while the largest per capita consumption of goods, services, and nonrenewable resources (e.g., oil, minerals, arable land, and potable water) will continue to occur in developed countries (Europe, North America, Japan, and Australia, with China rapidly joining their ranks with alarming environmental impact). Indeed, at 7.5 hectares, Canada's per capita **ecological footprint** is the third largest in the world (Mackenzie, Messinger, and Smith 2008), exceeded only by the United States and the United Arab Emirates, and tied with Finland.[6] This is not an enviable position!

While on the surface this analysis smacks of pessimism, the question needs to be asked: Can the world afford for Smail (and others in the neo-Malthusian camp) to be wrong? Even if only half-right, it buys little more than a modest reprieve from impending population collapse—perhaps a century or so. Smail argues that what is needed now is a multilateral program of guided social engineering. At first glimpse, guided social engineering looks like a euphemism for a new eugenics initiative. However, Smail's (2003b) intention is for all nations to bring a coordinated effort toward achieving a global subreplacement fertility rate of around 1.5 to 1.8, starting immediately and lasting until at least the 22nd century. Unlike eugenics

**http://www.growinggap.ca**

**population momentum**
the reproductive potential of those yet to reproduce; typically measured as the proportion of a population under 18 years of age. Expanding populations with broad-based demographic pyramids have considerable population momentum

**ecological footprint**
a measure of the ecological impact of human behaviour and activity, measured in the amount of land and seascape required to produce resources consumed and to absorb waste produced

**Table 16.2**  Ten inescapable realities regarding human population growth.

| | |
|---|---|
| 1. | In spite of geopolitical events causing major reductions in human population (world wars, disease pandemics), global population increased fourfold during the 20th century; 15% in the final decade alone. |
| 2. | Population momentum is such that it would take two to three generations of **zero population growth** implemented immediately and globally just to stabilize numbers. |
| 3. | Growth is not just fertility, but also declining mortality; life expectancy will increase in future years, especially in developing states. |
| 4. | There are no historical precedents to guide us; population growth is analogous to a malignant cancer capable of permanently destabilizing planetary ecology. |
| 5. | The time frame for remedial action lies within the life span of those already born. |
| 6. | Long-term sustainable carrying capacity is finite (consider space and potable water); technological "fixes" are incremental, not revolutionary. |
| 7. | We have likely exceeded the planet's optimal carrying capacity (vis-à-vis long-term adaptive balance with ecosystem, resources, and one another). |
| 8. | Only around 20% of the current population has an adequate standard of living; almost 5 billion live in conditions of mild deprivation to severe deficiency. |
| 9. | By the year 2100 the ecological footprint of humanity on planetary ecosystems, already demonstrably unsustainable, is expected to quadruple. This estimate takes into account future improvements in energy conservation and resource-use efficiencies through technological advancements. |
| 10. | Remedial action to reduce population size must also account for unknowns, requiring a redundancy in planning that, at a minimum, accommodates biodiversity and wilderness conservation, and the possibility of loss of ecosystem resilience. |

**zero population growth**
arises when the balance of birth and death, and the sum of net migration (immigration and emigration), is zero; ZPG denotes a stationary population that neither increases nor declines

Source: Smail 2002

6. As you might expect, our use of resources—comprised of food, housing, mobility, goods, and services—is not equitably distributed among Canadian households. The wealthiest 10% of Canadians have an ecological footprint 66% larger than the national average.

policies implemented in the 20th century that encouraged reproduction in some sectors of society and that discouraged (or eliminated) it in other select groups (see Chapter 13), guided social engineering with respect to fertility in Smail's sense targets all of humanity, across class, ethnicity, religion, and nationality. And here lies the role for sciences such as biological anthropology, which articulates both the biological and the cultural diversity of humankind, and which can undertake the kind of research necessary to support and develop such measures and policies. Such advocacy is explored further in the following section.

## BIOLOGIES OF EXCESS AND NEGLECT

In 1998, biological anthropologists Alan Goodman and Thomas Leatherman published an edited volume of essays titled *Building a New Biocultural Synthesis: Political-Economic Perspectives on Human Biology.*[7] The intent of the book was to illustrate "how sociocultural and political-economic processes affect human biologies, and then how compromised biologies further threaten the social fabric" (Goodman and Leatherman 1998, 5). In *A Human Voyage* we have explicitly noted that biology cannot be comprehended without regard to culture; for example, farming in Africa predisposes people to increased incidence of malaria by providing breeding grounds for mosquitoes, and chewing coca leaves facilitates work at high altitude in South American Quechua Indians, increasing stamina and heart rate (see Box 16.2). However, Goodman and Leatherman ask a more compelling question: How does human biology respond when challenged by a transformed and transformative global network of intertwined relations of power, influence, and wealth? Economic structures such as the World Bank and the International Monetary Fund, multinational corporations such as Coca-Cola and China Minmetals, commodity cartels such as OPEC, and trade agreements such as the North American Free Trade Act (NAFTA), are not benign with respect to the lives of people, who have no option but to live and work in the communities and countries exposed to their influence. Modernizing forces of economic development, with international movement of labour, raw material, and capital, impact not only developing states but developed ones as well. The rapid growth of the *maquiladoras* in Mexico, coincident with manufacturing job losses (especially) in the United States, have taken advantage of a considerably cheaper workforce, and has been linked to NAFTA's implementation in 1994. Job loss equates with loss of income, inevitably leading to lower standards of living, poorer nutrition, and compromised health.

Internal state politics and policies aimed at attracting foreign investment and capital can lead to the displacement of entire civilian populations (Figure 16.9) and increased disparity among classes. For example, Leatherman and Goodman (2005) have recently reviewed the impact of ecotourism and **archaeotourism** in Central America—specifically, Mexico's Yucatan Peninsula and its indigenous Mayan population. They note, for example, that Cancun—today one of the most popular destinations for tourists, with a human population of about 500,000 and a hotel room "population" of over 25,000 (Figure 16.10)—was only 35 years ago a small fishing village with a population of 426. Such rapid development affects many aspects of life: indigenous people shift from subsistence to wage labour as waiters, groundskeepers, and chambermaids; cultural artifacts and foodways are commoditized, becoming souvenirs and "ethnic cuisine"; rural populations are depleted as people move to these new centres seeking opportunity; and water and nutritional quality decline as these resources are sequestered for resort guests. Leatherman and Goodman (2005) describe the situation in the Mexican Yucatan as **"coca-colonialism,"** referring specifically to the transformative power of **"empty-calorie"** foods. The undernourishment resulting in low **height-for-age** and **weight-for-height** characteristic of predevelopment populations has been replaced by chronic obesity among adults; for example, they found that among the Mayan people of the Yucatan, 40% of men and 64% of women were obese by North American clinical standards. This is not to say that such economic development is negative in all respects, and many Maya have an improved quality of life. But it has not been universal, and especially lacking is the ability of indigenous peoples to have a voice in the

### archaeotourism

a form of tourism in which the attraction consists of archaeological sites, typically megalithic, locations (cities, pyramids, and the like)

### coca-colonialism

refers to the ability of multinational companies to usurp local traditions and lifeways, effectively replacing local customs with "Western" surrogates

### empty-calorie

in nutritional science, empty-calorie foods offer no nutrition other than energy (calories); the vast majority of "junk foods" fall into this category

### height-for-age

a measure of achieved growth in height, standardized for age. A person suffering significant growth deficits for their age compared to normal standards is considered stunted

### weight-for-height

a measure of body mass standardized for a given height; high weight-for-height values indicate overweight/ obesity

---

7. The essays were mostly derived from a conference sponsored by the Wenner-Gren Foundation, held in Mexico in 1992.

direction of future development. As Leatherman and Goodman remark (2005, 844), local Maya "are primarily seen as sources of cheap labor and ethnic backdrop at tourist sites."

The point we make here is that a "new" biocultural synthesis views the "cultural" component in its broadest sense, as influenced by global and invariably inequitable forces of change and transformation, with concomitant impact on the biologies of those less able to insulate themselves from their impact. In the following sections we illustrate this with particular regard to the biology of children.

## Children and Canaries

In the 19th and early 20th centuries, it was common practice for English and American coal miners to take caged canaries into the mines to act as sentinels, warning the miners of the presence of noxious gases such as methane or carbon monoxide (Figure 16.11). Being more

Courtesy of Warren Wilson

Dr. Warren Wilson is an Associate Professor in the Department of Archaeology at the University of Calgary, where he specializes in the relationships among human health, diet, and culture. His research interests have taken him from the rainforests of Guyana to the immigrant and refugee communities of Canada.

For the past decade the Makushi Amerindians of Guyana's rainforests and savannas have undergone a rapid cultural transformation, largely the result of a new national park established in 1996 in the traditional Makushi homelands (Figure 16.8). I started working with the Makushi in 2000 to assess the impact of this park on their children's health. To that end we collected data for weight, height, and percent body fat, measures of dietary intake, and interview data. To assess the impact of chronic under-nutrition or infectious disease among the Makushi, the anthropometric data were compared to international growth standards for healthy children created by the World Health Organization (WHO). In 2000–2001 we found that overall, the girls were doing better than the boys. Compared to the girls, the boys were significantly more likely to be quite short for their age. How might we then explain the variation in growth between boys and girls?

Part of the answer may come from work by William Greulich, who was working in Guam just after the Second World War and noticed the same phenomenon—females fared better during the privations of war than did males. Greulich hypothesized that females are physiologically more resistant to environmental insults such as chronic malnutrition. But why would this be the case? In 1973, William Stini proposed that in order for a sexually reproducing species to survive, females must produce offspring. The condition of pregnancy and lactation is extremely demanding physiologically, so Stini concluded that females should be more resistant to deprivation in order to meet the challenges of reproduction. This idea seemed to go a long way toward explaining the pattern we observed among Makushi boys and girls. Makushi boys and girls grow up in a difficult environment where there is often not enough to eat and infectious disease is prevalent.

Recall, however, that as human population biologists we are encouraged to consider both biology *and* cultural variables. I was reminded of this by my collaborator on this project, Janette Bulkan, a cultural anthropologist who has worked for years among the Makushi. Janette suggested that we may be missing another explanation. In Makushi households

*continued* ▶

daughters are favoured over sons. One reason for this is that traditional marriage practices dictate that a new husband will move into the house with his wife and her parents. For one year he is on a type of probation and must contribute to the economic well-being of his parents-in-laws' household. If he passes this probationary period, he is accepted into the household and is allowed to remain as the husband. Hence, daughters are valued as they attract this source of labour and economic support. Another reason is that the bulk of the food consumed by the Makushi comes from a root crop known as manioc, the cultivation and laborious processing of which is

the responsibility of females. Since many Makushi households remain subsistence based, healthy, robust girls would retain their high status. The presence of this bias toward females led us to ask whether parents were allocating more resources to daughters than to sons. Our dietary intake data revealed that, indeed, females had a superior diet relative to males—significantly so in the 13 to 19 year old age group. Our research among the Makushi provides a classic example of what human biologists have come to appreciate worldwide—the most rewarding interpretations result from applying a biocultural perspective to the study of human variation.

Courtesy of Warren Wilson

**Figure 16.8**  A Makushi family.

sensitive to such environmental hazards, the birds would succumb before the miners suffered adverse effects, thereby allowing the latter to escape to the surface. In modern population biology, children are de facto canaries (Pelto 2008). There are good reasons for asserting this metaphor: infants and children have less robust **adaptive immune systems** and are continually enmeshed in the shifting sands of growth and development. From conception through adolescence, there is a huge demand for resources—physical, nutritional, and psychosocial—which must be satisfied so that the child can meet standards of normal growth (Moffat and Galloway 2007). The major constraint on providing for child growth is poverty, which, as we saw with demographic measures such as fertility, is not equitably distributed around the

**Figure 16.9** International interests often usurp local rights, displacing landowners and fomenting dissent. Here, Mayan people of the community of Comitancillo, San Marcos, Guatemala, were protesting in May 2008 against the Canadian mining company Goldcorp and its Guatemalan subsidiary Montana Exploradora.

Courtesy of Catherine Nolin Geography Program, University of Northern British Columbia

globe. For example, 63.2% of Bolivia's population were living below that country's poverty line in 1997, while in Estonia, the comparable value was 8.9% (World Bank Development Indicators 2005). In Canada, the estimate of persons living at low income for 2006 for the country as a whole was 11.8% according to the Market Basket Measure,[8] though this varied considerably province by province.

The impact of inequality in household wealth is well established, with **food insecurity** and undernutrition as significant corollaries. Hong, Banta, and Betancourt (2006), for example, found that children living in the poorest 20% of Bangladeshi households were more than twice as likely to suffer growth stunting as those from the top 20%, after adjusting for numerous social and economic determinants (the World Bank estimates that 51% of *all* Bangladeshis live below the national poverty line). The UN Food and Agriculture Organization (FAO 2008) estimates that around 2 billion

**Figure 16.10** Only a generation has passed since Cancun has been converted from a small fishing village into world tourist destination, transforming local lives, culture, and biologies.

Mike Liu/Shutterstock.com

8. The Market Basket Measure (MBM) was developed by Human Resources Development Canada to track changes in low-income distribution across the country. The MBM is based on affordability of a standardized set of goods and services, including housing, transportation, food, and clothing. It is not intended as a measure of poverty per se.

**adaptive immune system**

a component of the immune response that targets specific pathogens and that requires prior exposure to establish an "immunological memory"; a short-term adaptive immune response is transferred to the newborn across the placenta and via breast milk, though it is less effective in resisting infection than that which an individual develops through its own exposure to invading organisms

**food insecurity**

the real or anticipated lack of safe, nutritious foods that would normally be available at all times and in socially acceptable ways

**Figure 16.11** Sensitive species act as early warning systems to adverse environments. In human populations the same function is served by children, whose growth and development can be impaired by lack of adequate resources (such as food and clean water) or exposure to disease.

© Trinity Mirror/Mirrorpix/Alamy

people lack food security at least part of the time owing to poverty-related issues; 15% of people worldwide are undernourished.

Recently, researchers from the Université de Montréal (Ehounoux et al. 2009) studying families enrolled in the Québec Longitudinal Study of Child Development found that four-year-old children living in households that had experienced two episodes of being unable to purchase basic needs were significantly growth delayed. In an earlier study, these same researchers found negative impacts on other health indicators, such as frequency of asthma attacks or "perceived poor health" as rated by the mother (Séguin et al. 2005). On the other side of the coin is the apparent paradox of childhood obesity: a recent study of elementary schoolchildren found that a higher proportion of children in poorer households were overweight or obese (Lazenby et al., 2007; see Chapter 14). This paradox is resolved when we recognize that the issue remains one of food insecurity: lower income households tend to purchase less expensive, calorically dense but nutritionally deficient foods. Impairments other than physical growth have also been documented, in both developed and developing nations, particularly with regard to cognition and behavioural outcomes (Morris 2008). Significantly, those aspects of neurological development most impacted by material deprivation appear to be areas associated with language and memory (Farah et al. 2006), predisposing children to learning impairment and mental health disorders. Larson (2007) observes that as many as 100,000 children in Canada are born into poverty each year, with a higher likelihood of being preterm, low birth weight babies suffering delayed cognitive development, which ultimately contributes to poor educational outcomes. While such effects manifest themselves in infancy and childhood, they are also recognized as major contributors to negative health experience in older adults. Low birth weight, for example, is a significant risk factor for coronary heart disease, hypertension, and Type II diabetes in middle-aged and older adults through a mechanism known as fetal programming (Kuzawa 2005).

What do such studies tell us, and why should a field such as biological anthropology be interested? Clearly, it is important to understand that living in a First World country such as Canada, with a stable government, a complex and well-funded medical system, a "social safety net," and a high per capita GDP, guarantees neither good quality of life nor physical and psychological well-being. The WHO (1946) defined health as "a state of complete physical, mental and social well-being and not merely the absence of disease or infirmity." Many people you know—indeed, perhaps some of your classmates or even yourself—may not satisfy this definition. And it does not take a rocket scientist (as the saying goes) to appreciate that most people living in politically tenuous, economically disadvantaged, and geographically marginal countries of the world fall far short. One need only consider the rate of desertification in Africa, a continent already ravaged by political strife and a massive burden of disease. Over 30% of nondesert land in continental Africa is vulnerable to being transformed into a desert landscape through increased aridification; 8% of this area—some 1 million km²—is considered at very high risk for becoming unsustainable for agricultural use, directly impacting more than 200 million people who already live "on the edge" (Reich et al. 2001). Here we would remind you of Goodman and Leatherman's (1998) call for an integration of political-economic variables into the analysis of human biology. As biological anthropologists, we are fundamentally interested in human variation and variability in time and space and in the genetic, epigenetic, and environmental mechanisms responsible (see Chapter 4). Through the latter half of the 20th century, and going forward into the 21st century, it has become increasingly evident that the epigenetic and environmental components of human variation are being shaped by forces far beyond the economic and ecological boundaries of households and local communities, and by events and decisions taken by governments, multinational corporations, international finance, and sectarian ideologies. Such inputs are not new to human history, but they have never before attained such a far-reaching and sinister authority to undermine the ability of individuals to provide for and control their basic well-being. Such variation, its sources and its impact on current and future generations, is inherently the subject matter of our discipline. And this of course generates the following question: What lies in wait for the evolutionary future of humankind?

# THE END OF HUMAN EVOLUTION?

Having taught university-level courses in biological anthropology for a combined total of more than 35 years, we can say that there is one question that is invariably asked by at least one student in each of our classes: Are humans still evolving? That is a reasonable question, but one that needs to be qualified: because evolution is not predictive, we cannot say what changes may occur over the next few generations. But we can look back retrospectively, and speak of recent developments. By all accounts, humans seem to be the pinnacle of evolutionary progress, the dominant species on the planet, conquerors of the highest mountains and the deepest ocean trenches, interstellar explorers mapping the origin of the universe, having played golf on the moon. We are so surrounded, embedded, and insulated from nature by our culture and our technology, how could something as base as natural selection possibly fabricate significant advances over what has previously been wrought? To some degree, we feel we should leave you to ponder this question beyond the confines of this course and this text, as it implores you to always ask: Are humans so perfect? But we feel obligated to remind you that "perfection" will always be a moving target—evolution will always be playing catch-up.[9] There is always room for 'improvement' and humans are as eligible as nematodes in that regard!

## Blondes Had More Fun?

In the fall of 2002, a number of news agencies, including Canadian Press and the BBC, reported that scientists in Germany were predicting that natural blondes would become "extinct" at some point in the next 200 years, owing to the fact that men found women with dyed blonde hair more attractive. The story turned out to be a prank, but as journalist Michael Balter (2005) noted, the fact that the story garnered so much attention reveals the public's fascination with the possibility of ongoing human evolution. In Darwinian terms, this hoax would have us believe that mate choice is entirely based on hair colour and that chemically enhanced blondes are more fit than natural blondes, whom they out-perform in the competition for males.[10] It is equally difficult to imagine non-Darwinian mechanisms such as genetic drift randomly eliminating blondes. A number of biologically valid questions could be posed with respect to such phenomena, however, including these: How are technological advances impeding the action of natural selection in human populations? What are the biological ramifications of technologically mediated reduction in selection pressure? What evidence is there for ongoing or recent Darwinian evolution within *Homo sapiens*?

---

9. This reality is captured by evolutionary biologist Leigh Van Valen's (1973) invocation of the Red Queen Hypothesis for evolutionary change, named after Lewis Carroll's character in *Through the Looking Glass*, who exclaimed: "It takes all the running you can do, to keep in the same place." Metaphorically, evolution is always "one step behind" the selective challenges imposed by a changing habitat.

10. The absurdity of the hoax should have been apparent to anyone remotely familiar with evolutionary theory, given that dyed blonde hair could not be passed on to future generations unless one ascribed to Lamarckian notions of the inheritance of acquired characters! In fact, this hoax has been resurrected many times, most recently in 2006. In response, the American satirist Stephen Colbert (*The Colbert Report*, March 6, 2006) promoted a eugenics program of selective breeding to "save blondes"!

## Technology, Genetic Load, and Adaptation

As noted above, technology surrounds us, particularly those of us living in developed postindustrial states with well-funded public and private research sectors (but see Figure 16.1). The intervention of technology into human biology is perhaps most apparent in terms of biomedicine. Thousands of people with congenital or acquired disabilities, both mild and severe, are now able to lead reasonably (if not completely) normal productive *and* reproductive lives.

From an evolutionary perspective, however, the issue is how technology interferes with the role of selection in eliminating less fit phenotypes. For example, individuals with reduced visual acuity resulting from conditions such as congenital strabismus (Figure 16.12), with its attendant loss of binocular vision and depth perception, would likely have had reduced Darwinian fitness in hunting-gathering societies (or for that matter, in automotive societies!). The several common forms of this polygenic trait, with a heritability of 73% to 82% based on monozygotic twin studies, are more prevalent in European-derived populations than in African or Asian groups (around 5% vs. < 1%, retrospectively; see Engle 2007). However, early detection and the use of corrective lenses (or in some cases surgery) lessen any negative consequences of strabismus. In a similar fashion, the adoption of softer diets and the use of technology to preprocess foods (cooking, cutlery) has removed any selective disadvantages associated with reduced mandible and maxillary size, dental crowding, or malocclusion (Varrela 2006). The result of these kinds of nonbiological interventions is that those genetic variants responsible for previously less fit phenotypes are not removed through the normal course of selection, which increases the **genetic load** borne by the population as a result of a higher proportion of deleterious alleles carried by individuals.

## Evidence for Recent Human Evolution

An alternative approach to showing how technology alleviates selective disadvantage and increases genetic load is to consider the impact of selection when such interventions are absent. This of course is how we understand the operation of Darwinian evolution—adaptation via natural selection. There are effectively two approaches by which we can identify recent evolutionary change. The first is by generating hypotheses linking a specific phenotype to a putative selective agent that itself can be historically dated. The relationship of the sickle cell phenotype with malaria and the latter's association with settled agriculture (as recounted in Chapter 14) is the paradigmatic example. But others have become known in recent years with the advent of genomic mapping as an investigative tool. For example, Perry and colleagues (2007) tested the hypothesis that populations living in regions of high starch consumption would benefit from higher levels of salivary amylase, the enzyme that breaks down complex starches. Starches form a significant portion of the diet in agricultural societies. They found that high starch-consuming populations had significantly greater **copy number variation** for the gene *AMY1*, which codes for salivary amylase, compared to those whose diets contained little in the way of starches. Genomic analysis shows that this

**genetic load**

formally, the average deviation of an individual from the best possible phenotype determined by the relative proportion of deleterious alleles he or she carries; because genetic load varies from 0 (maximum fitness) to 1.0 (minimum fitness), it can also be taken as a measure of the probability that an individual will die before reproducing

**copy number variation**

inter-individual variations in the number of copies of a gene present in the genome; classic Mendelian genetics suggests that we should possess two copies for each gene, one inherited from each parent. Recent studies suggest, however, that individuals can have more than two copies, through processes such as duplication and recombination

Esotropia

Exotropia

Hypertropia

Hypertropia

**Figure 16.12** Strabismus involves a misalignment of the eyes due a failure of the extraocular muscles to coordinate the gaze, resulting in loss of depth perception.

adaptation can be located historically within the past 10,000 years, and becomes a marker for recent human evolution. Perry and colleagues suggest that selection has favoured greater levels of salivary amylase[11] to protect against the possibility of "fitness-reducing intestinal disease," which is more prevalent among agriculturalists. Additionally, amylase breaks down starches in the oral cavity, enhancing energy absorption during bouts of diarrheal disease (a condition also more prevalent in settled societies). This is important because diarrheal diseases lead to rapid loss of hydration and important macro- and micronutrients, including calories.

Recently, population geneticists at the University of Chicago and their colleagues have argued that humans have undergone recent positive selection for two genes associated with brain size, one called *microcephalin* (Evans et al. 2005), and the other by the more cumbersome name *abnormal spindle-like microcephaly-associated protein* (*ASPM*) (Mekel-Bobrov et al. 2005). Mutations in these genes have been linked to primary microcephaly (Figure 16.13), a condition of significantly reduced brain size (ca. 400 cm$^3$ versus a normal range of 1200 to 1600 cm$^3$) but otherwise normal neuroarchitecture. A human variant of *microcephalin* is estimated to have appeared around 37,000 years ago and *ASPM* only 5,800 years ago. In a sample of 1,184 individuals from diverse ancestral backgrounds, they found that one version of the *microcephalin* gene occurred at significantly higher levels for human populations outside of sub-Saharan Africa (allele frequency around 80%), supporting the hypothesis that it arose after the divergence of anatomically modern humans. Moreover, the young date estimated for the appearance of this variant of *microcephalin* in humans (37,000 years) is associated with the appearance of anatomically modern *Homo sapiens* in Europe,[12] as well as the development and elaboration of symbolic traditions (e.g., art). The even younger *ASPM* gene variant is also argued to be due to strong positive selection for its role in regulating neural stem cell proliferation (Mekel-Bobrov et al. 2005). Again, in a survey of subjects representing diverse ancestries, they found one variant, haplotype 63, to occur at particularly high values among Europeans and people of Middle Eastern extraction (allele frequency around 40%), and at very low levels among other human populations. The very young age estimated for *ASPM* and its geographic distribution suggests it may be associated with major cultural developments in the circum-Mediterranean region over the past 5,000 to 10,000 years—notably domestication, development of writing, and the rise of cities. However, it must be remembered that the historical associations attached to the appearance of these variants of *microcephalin* and *ASPM* are merely correlative, and not necessarily causal.

The suggestion that selection has acted on genes regulating brain size in recent human history that correlate with specific transformative events in human behaviour leads one to wonder whether these genes are in any way associated with cognition (i.e., intelligence). Timpson and colleagues (2007) explored this question in a sample of 9,000 children, correlating the occurrence of the *microcephalin* and *ASPM* variants with a range of phenotypic measures, including anthropometry, physiology, and cognitive functioning (including general IQ, working memory, and verbal and motor skills). No significant associations were found, suggesting that some other selective advantage must have accrued to those individuals having the variants for these two genes. Timpson and colleagues (2007) note that

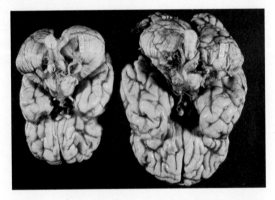

**Figure 16.13** Mutation in the *ASPM* or *microcephalin* genes leads to primary microcephaly, as seen in this image of a microcephalic 13-year-old female (left) versus a normal 11-year-old (right).

Martin M. Rotker/Photo Researchers, Inc.

---

11. The alternative hypothesis would be to propose selection for lower levels of amylase in non–starch-eating populations; this is seen as less likely, since high levels of amylase pose no selective disadvantage.

12. Some authors (e.g., Evans et al. 2006) have suggested that the *microcephalin* gene was contributed by Neandertals into the modern human genome. However, the recently published draft sequence for Neandertals (Green et al. 2010) did not identify the haplogroup for this gene.

both of these genetic variants occur in adult and fetal tissues and that both have functional roles beyond contributing to neurological development; thus, positive selection may have acted on those extraneural effects, possibly related to immune function or spermatogenesis. Interestingly, in a separate study, the University of Chicago team also found no association of the *ASPM* and *microcephalin* genotypes with standardized measures of general intelligence (Mekel-Bobrov et al., 2007).

The story of *ASPM* and *microcephalin* does not end here. Ali and Meier (2008), for example, have recently shown positive selection of *ASPM* and cerebral cortex size across nine primate lineages, but not with whole-brain size. Université Laval anthropologist Peter Frost (2008) has hypothesized that the 5,800-year-old *ASPM* variant may have been associated with the advent of alphabetical writing, and that individuals with such latent ability would occupy highly valued roles in society as scribes and secretaries. He also argues that the earlier studies discounting cognitive associations with *ASPM* (see above) may not have been sufficiently robust (adequate in scope or duration) to capture the high-level cognitive functioning underlying early alphabetical writing, which lacked punctuation and necessitated real-time recording of oral commentary—both features placing high demands on short-term memory and motor skills.

It is also informative to consider that not all genetic variants for which positive selection can be demonstrated may have been selected for by agents with which they are currently associated. For example, in the 1990s it was discovered that a mutation in the gene producing a protein known as chemokine C-C motif receptor 5 (CCR5) conferred resistance to HIV in individuals who had two copies of the mutation. This mutation, termed CCR5Δ32, is found in high frequency in peoples of European descent. However, in spite of the obviously high selective advantage conferred by CCR5Δ32 in this scenario, exposure to HIV played no role in the origin of this allele. We can say this because HIV has a relatively short epidemiological history[13] and the origin of CCR5Δ32 has been estimated at around 700 years ago based on molecular genetic studies. Selective forces such as the bubonic plague or smallpox have been proposed, as both were major diseases in the 13th and 14th centuries in Europe, but these hypotheses have not been confirmed by laboratory studies (Mecsas et al. 2005).

So we return to the question posed earlier—are we at the end of human evolution? The evidence for recent positive selection at a number of loci across the human genome associated with features such as skin pigmentation, immune response, and metabolic diseases (Barreiro et al. 2008), as well as the examples discussed above, would suggest not. But the answer may be much simpler than the one obtained through genomic analyses. As University of Calgary primatologist Mary Pavelka succinctly remarked (quoted in Balter 2005, 234): "The question, 'Are humans still evolving?' should be rephrased as 'Do all people have the same number of children?' The answer is that we do not make equal contributions to the next generation, and thus we are still evolving."

# SUMMARY

This chapter has considered where humanity is at present, and what the future might portend. Clearly, there are significant challenges ahead, fundamentally about coping with the product of our own successes as well as our excesses. It could plausibly be argued that the concept of sustainable development is an oxymoron: the weight of human numbers and the weight of human inequity will challenge every facet of our ingenuity, every gram of our compassion. There may be some solace in remembering that it was free will which brought humanity to this juncture, and we have the capacity to exercise that will in the future. The central message of this chapter is that we are now, as we have always been, part of our environment and subject as much to its generosity as to its meanness. In the 21st century, we have the capacity as never before to shape natural selection, by our political decisions, our economic choices, and our ecological attitudes. We leave you with this message: How we shape selection will ultimately determine our evolutionary future.

---

13. HIV is derived from simian immunodeficiency virus (SIV) via cross-species transfer from nonhuman primates, which still act as a reservoir for several ancestral strains of HIV (Van Heuverswyn and Peeters 2007).

# CORE REVIEW

**How would measures of fertility distinguish between expanding and contracting populations?**

Expanding populations typify early stages of the demographic transition, often seen in preindustrial/developing countries, in which fertility is high and the "base" of the demographic pyramid is relatively broad; the pyramid will have a triangular shape if mortality is also high. Conversely, in stable, developed societies in which measures of fertility control have been enacted, TFR may be below replacement level and the base of the pyramid is small (constricted) relative to the age grades above, giving the appearance of a vase shape.

**What is the relationship between population growth, fertility, and economic development?**

Though a global total fertility rate (TFR) can be calculated, it obscures the fact that there are great regional disparities in fertility. Typically, developing countries are poorer than developed industrial and postindustrial states. Measures such as gross domestic product, reflecting the wealth of a nation, tend to be inversely related to fertility: low GDP equals high TFR. The reasons for this pattern are diverse, but generally signal greater economic, educational, and lifestyle opportunities available to women in developed states, as well as reduced need for human capital (labour) and greater reproductive choices (later marriage, contraception, abortion). In short, women put more effort into production than reproduction.

**What is political economy and why is it significant for the field of biological anthropology?**

Within anthropology, political economy refers to the nexus of national and international political and economic forces that shape and regulate development, trade, and the movement of resources, goods, and capital. Its significance to biological anthropology lies in the ways in which political economy influences the distribution of wealth and access to essential resources needed to ensure health and the attainment of normal physical as well as neurocognitive growth and development. Inequities arising from political economic forces underlie poverty at all levels, from the local to the global.

**Why is childhood growth and development a useful proxy for population well-being and adaptation?**

From the moment of conception, there is a significant demand from the growing fetus, infant, and child for nutritional and psychosocial resources; at the same time, they are highly sensitive to pathogen exposure due to unsanitary conditions, poor water, and so on. Compromised child growth and ill health (physical and/or mental) are thus useful measures of the adaptive state of the population as a whole in meeting its basic needs.

**Are humans still evolving? How do we know?**

The simple answer is "yes." We can anticipate that this is so because reproduction is not equitably distributed—some of us will contribute more to succeeding generations than others, and that in itself will affect gene frequencies (microevolution). However, we can also demonstrate the occurrence of evolution through genomic analysis, relating particular distributions of genetic variation to specific historical events, such as the adoption of agriculture or major outbreaks of disease. The important point to understand is that evolution does not end simply because environments shift from natural to technological; only the character of selection changes.

# CRITICAL THINKING QUESTIONS

1. How would you account for the fact that total fertility rate and infant mortality are highly correlated (Table 16.1)?
2. To what degree should biological anthropologists advocate for social and/or political economic change? What particular issues in Canada might qualify for such an agenda?

# GROUP DISCUSSION QUESTIONS

1. As a result of technology, many people who in earlier centuries would have died in childhood are today able to survive to reach reproductive maturity and contribute to succeeding generations. Discuss the pros and cons of these technological (and cultural) achievements.
2. What are the merits of Smail's notion of "guided social engineering"? What obstacles can you imagine would stand in the way of developing such a global program?

# RESOURCES AND READINGS

- Current data on global trends in fertility can be found at **http://www.indexmundi .com/map/?v=31&l=en** and the *CIA World Factbook,* **https://www.cia.gov/ library/publications/the-world-factbook**.
- The World Health Organization site contains diverse information and links on global health disparities; see **http://www.who.int/en**.

# Bibliography

Abbate, E, Albianelli, A, Azzaroli, A, et al. 1998. A one-million-year-old *Homo* cranium from the Danakil (Afar) Depression of Eritrea. *Nature* 393: 458–460.

Abzhanov, A, Protas, M, Grant, BR, et al. 2004. *Bmp4* and morphological variation of beaks in Darwin's finches. *Science* 305: 1462–1465.

Adovasio, JM, Pedler, DR, Donahue, J, et al. 1998. Two decades of debate on Meadowcroft Rockshelter. *North American Archaeologist* 19: 317–341.

Agarwal, SC, and Stout, SD. 2003. *Bone Loss and Osteoporosis: An Anthropological Perspective*. Berlin: Springer.

Aiello, LC, and Wells, JCK. 2002. Energetics and the evolution of the genus *Homo*. *Annual Review of Anthropology* 31: 323–338.

Aiello, L, and Wheeler, P. 1995. The expensive tissue hypothesis: the brain and digestive system in human and primate evolution. *Current Anthropology* 36: 199–221.

Albanese, J, Eklics, G, and Tuck, A. 2008. A metric method for sex determination using the proximal femur and fragmentary hipbone. *Journal of Forensic Sciences* 53: 1283–1288.

Alemseged, Z, Spoor, F, Kimbel, WH, et al. 2006. A juvenile early hominin skeleton from Dikka, Ethiopia. *Nature* 443: 296–301.

Alexeev, VP. 1986. *The Origin of the Human Race*. Moscow: Progress.

Ali, F, and Meier, R. 2008. Positive selection in ASPM is correlated with cerebral cortex evolution across primates but not with whole-brain size. *Molecular Biology and Evolution* 25: 2247–2250.

Amaral, LA. 2008. Mechanical analysis of infant carrying in hominoids. *Naturwissenschaften* 95: 281–292.

Ambrose, L. 2003. Three acoustic forms of Allen's galagos (Primates; Galagonidae) in the Central African region. *Primates* 44: 25–39.

Ambrose, SH. 1998. Late Pleistocene human population bottlenecks, volcanic winter, and differentiation of modern humans. *Journal of Human Evolution* 34(6): 623–651.

Anderson, DP, Nordheim, EV, and Boesch, C. 2006. Environmental factors influencing the seasonality of estrus in chimpanzees. *Primates* 47: 43–50.

Andrews, L. 2008. Book review: Reprogenetics: Law, Policy and Ethical Issues. *New England Journal of Medicine* 358: 204–205.

Andrews, P. 2007. The biogeography of hominid evolution. *Journal of Biogeography* 34: 381–382.

Antón, SC. 2003. A natural history of *Homo erectus*. *Yearbook of Physical Anthropology* 46: 126–170.

Antón, SC, Leonard, WR, and Robertson, ML. 2002. An eco-morphological model of the initial hominid dispersal from Africa. *Journal of Human Evolution* 43: 773–785.

Antón, SC, Spoor, F, Fellmann, C, and Swisher CC III. 2007. Defining *Homo erectus*: size considered. In W Henke and I Tattersall, eds., *Handbook of Paleoanthropology*. Berlin: Springer. 1655–1693.

Anway, MD, Cupp, AS, Uzumcu, M, et al. 2005. Epigenetic transgenerational actions of endocrine disruptors and male fertility. *Science* 308: 1466–1469.

Aoki, K. 2002. Sexual selection as a cause of human skin colour variation: Darwin's hypothesis revisited. *Annals of Human Biology* 29: 589–608.

Arensberg, B, Schepartz, LA, Tillier, AM, et al. 1990. A reappraisal of the anatomical basis for speech in Middle Paleolithic hominids. *American Journal of Physical Anthropology* 83: 137–146.

Argue, D, Donlon, D, Groves, C, et al. 2006. *Homo floresiensis*: Microcephalic, pygmoid, *Australopithecus*, or *Homo*? *Journal of Human Evolution* 51: 360–374.

Arking, DE, Krebsova, A, Macek, M Sr, et al. 2002. Association of human aging with a functional variant of klotho. *Proceedings of the National Academy of Sciences* 99: 856–861.

Asfaw, B, Gilbert, WH, Beyene, Y, et al. 2002. Remains of *Homo erectus* from Bouri, Middle Awash, Ethiopia. *Nature* 416: 317–320.

Asfaw, B, White, T, Lovejoy, O, et al. 1999. *Australopithecus garhi*: a new species of early hominid from Ethiopia. *Science* 284: 629–635.

Ashley-Koch, A, Yang, Q, and Olney, RS. 2000. Sickle hemoglobin (HbS) allele and sickle cell disease: a HuGE review. *American Journal of Epidemiology* 151: 839–845.

Avery, J 2005. Malthus' Essay on the Principle of Population. http://www.learndev.org/dl/MalthusEssay-Avery.pdf, accessed January 17, 2009.

Bajpai, S, Kay, RF, Williams, BA, et al. 2008. The oldest Asian record of *Anthropoidea*. *Proceedings of the National Academy of Sciences* 105(32): 11093–11098.

Baker, M. 1996. Fur rubbing: use of medicinal plants by capuchin monkeys (*Cebus capucinus*). *American Journal of Primatology* 38: 263–270.

Balter, M. 2005. Are humans still evolving? *Science* 309: 234–237.

Bamshad, M, Wooding, S, Salisbury, BA, et al. 2004. Deconstructing the relationship between genetics and race. *Nature Reviews Genetics* 8: 598–609.

Barker, DJ. 1998. In utero programming of chronic disease. *Clinical Science* 95: 115–128.

Barker, G, Barton, H, Bird, M, et al., 2007. The 'human revolution' in lowland tropical Southeast Asia: the antiquity and behaviour of anatomically modern humans at Niah Cave (Sarawak, Borneo). *Journal of Human Evolution* 52: 243–261.

Barnett, RJ. 1986. Taosim and biological science. *Zygon Journal of Religion and Science* 21: 297–317.

Barr, J. 1984–85. Why the world was created in 4004 BC: Archbishop Ussher and biblical chronology. *Bulletin of the John Rylands University Library of Manchester* 67: 575–608.

Barreiro, LB, Guillaume, L, Quach, H, et al. 2008. Natural selection has driven population differentiation in modern humans. *Nature Genetics* 40: 340–345.

Barrett, J, Abbott, DH, and George, LM. 1993. Sensory cues and the suppression of reproduction in subordinate female marmoset monkeys, *Callithrix jacchus*. *Journal of Reproductive Fertility* 971: 301–310.

Barrett, R, Kuzawa, CW, McDade, T, and Armelagos, GJ. 1998. Emerging and re-emerging infectious diseases: the third epidemiologic transition. *Annual Review of Anthropology* 27: 247–271.

Bartel, DP. 2004. MicroRNAs: genomics, biogenesis, mechanism, and function. *Cell* 116: 281–297.

Baruch, S, Kaufman, DJ, and Hudson, K. 2008. Genetic testing of embryos: practices and perspectives of US IVF Clinics. *Fertility and Sterility* 89: 1053–1058.

Bastiaens, M, ter Huurne, J, Gruis, N, et al. 2001. The melanocortin-1-receptor gene is the major freckle gene. *Human Molecular Genetics* 10: 1701–1708.

Bathurst, RR 2005. Archaeological evidence of intestinal parasites from coastal shell middens. *Journal of Archaeological Science* 321: 115–123.

Beall, CM. 2006. Andean, Tibetan, and Ethiopian patterns of adaptation to high-altitude hypoxia. *Integrative and Comparative Biology* 46:18–24.

Beall, CM. 2007. Two routes to functional adaptation: Tibetan and Andean high-altitude natives. *Proceedings of the National Academy of Sciences* 1041: 8655–8660.

Beall, CM, Decker, MJ, Brittenham, GM, et al. 2002. An Ethiopian pattern of human adaptation to high-altitude hypoxia. *Proceedings of the National Academy of Sciences* 99(26): 17215–17218.

Beard, KC. 2004. *The Hunt for the Dawn Monkey: Unearthing the Origins of Monkeys, Apes, and Humans.* Berkeley: University of California Press.

Beard, KC, Qi, T, Dawson, MR, et al. 1994. A diverse new primate fauna from middle Eocene fissure-fillings in southeastern China. *Nature* 368: 604–609.

Beard, KC, Tong, Y, Dawson, MR, et al. 1996. Earliest complete dentition of an anthropoid primate from the late Middle Eocene of Shanxi Province, China. *Science* 272: 82–85.

Beattie, O, Apland, B, Blake, EW, et al. 2000. The Kwäday Dän Ts'ínchi discovery from a glacier in British Columbia. *Canadian Journal of Archaeology* 24: 129–147.

Beattie, O, and Geiger, J. 2004. *Frozen in Time.* Vancouver: Douglas and McIntyre.

Becquet, C, Patterson, N, Stone, AC, et al. 2007. Genetic structure of chimpanzee populations. *Public Library of Science. Genetics* 3: e66.

Begun, DR. 1992. Miocene fossil hominids and the chimp–human clade. *Science* 257: 1929–1933.

Begun, DR. 2002. European Hominoids. In Hartwig, W, ed., *The Primate Fossil Record.* Cambridge: Cambridge University Press. 339–368.

Begun, DR. 2003. Planet of the apes. *Scientific American* 2892: 74–83.

Begun, DR. 2004a. The three "Cs" of behavioral reconstruction in fossil primates. *Journal of Human Evolution* 46: 497–505.

Begun, DR. 2004b. The earliest hominins—is less more? *Science* 303: 1478–1480.

Begun, DR. 2004c. Knuckle-walking and the origin of human bipedalism. In Meldrum, DJ, and Hilton, CE, eds., *From Biped to Strider: The Emergence of Modern Human Walking, Running, and Resource Transport.* New York: Kluwer Academic. 9–34.

Begun, DR. 2005. *Sivapithecus* is east and *Dryopithecus* is west, and never the twain shall meet. *Anthropological Science* 113: 53–64.

Begun, DR. 2007a. Fossil record of Miocene hominoids. In Henke, W, and Tattersall, I, eds., *Handbook of Palaeoanthropology.* Berlin: Springer. 921–977.

Begun, DR. 2007b. How to identify (as opposed to define) a homoplasy: examples from fossil and living great apes. *Journal of Human Evolution* 52: 559–572.

Begun, DR, Richmond, BG, and Strait, DS. 2007. Comment on "Origin of human bipedalism as an adaptation for locomotion on flexible branches." *Science* 318: 1066d–1067d.

Behe, M. 1996. *Darwin's Black Box.* New York: Free Press.

Behie, AM, and Pavelka, MSM. 2005. The short-term effects of a hurricane on the diet and activity of black howlers (Alouatta pigra) in Monkey River, Belize. *Folia Primatologica* 761: 1–9.

Bellomo, RV. 1994. Methods of determining early hominid behavioral activities associated with the controlled use of fire at FxJj 20 Main, Koobi Fora, Kenya. *Journal of Human Evolution* 27: 173–195.

Benefit, BR. 1999. *Victoriapithecus*: the key to Old World monkey and catarrhine origins. *Evolutionary Anthropology* 7: 155–174.

Berge, C, Penin, X, and Pellé, É. 2006. New interpretation of Laetoli footprints using an experimental approach and Procrustes analysis: preliminary results. *Comptes Rendus Palevolution* 5: 561–569.

Berger, TD, and Trinkaus, E. 1995. Patterns of trauma among the Neandertals. *Journal of Archaeological Science* 22: 841–852.

Bermejo, M, Rodríguez-Teijeiro, JD, Illera, G, et al. 2006. Ebola outbreak killed 5000 gorillas. *Science* 314: 1564.

Bermúdez de Castro, JM, Arsuaga, JL, Carbonell, E, et al. 1997. A hominid from the Lower Pleistocene of Atapuerca, Spain: possible ancestor to Neandertals and modern humans. *Science* 276: 1392–1395.

Bermúdez de Castro, JM, Martinón-Torres, M, Carbonell, E, et al. 2004. The Atapuerca sites and their contribution to the knowledge of human evolution in Europe. *Evolutionary Anthropology* 131: 25–41.

Bhopal, R. 2007. The beautiful skull and Blumenbach's errors. *British Medical Journal* 335: 1308–1309.

Binford, LR, and Binford, SR. 1966. A preliminary analysis of functional variability in the Mousterian of Levallois facies. *American Anthropologist* 682: 238–295.

Birdsell, JB. 1993. *Microevolutionary Patterns in Aboriginal Australia.* New York: Oxford University Press.

Bisson, MS, and Bolduc, P. 1994. Previously undescribed figurines from the Grimaldi caves. *Current Anthropology* 35(4): 458–468.

Black, D. 1931a. Evidences of the use of fire by *Sinanthropus. Bulletin of the Geological Society of China* 11: 107.

Black, D 1931b. On an adolescent skull of Sinanthropus pekinensis in comparison with an adult skull of the same species and with other hominid skulls, recent and fossil. *Palaeontologica Sinica Series D* 7: 1–114.

Bloch, JI, and Silcox, MT. 2006. Cranial anatomy of the Paleocene plesiadapiform *Carpolestes simpsoni* (Mammalia, Primates) using ultra high-resolution X-ray computed tomography, and the relationships of plesiadapiforms to Euprimates. *Journal of Human Evolution* 50(1): 1–35.

Bloch, JI, Silcox, MT, Boyer, DM, et al. 2007. New Paleocene skeletons and the relationship of plesiadapiforms to crown-clade primates. *Proceedings of the National Academy of Sciences* 104(4): 1159–1164.

Bloche, MG. 2004. Race-based therapeutics. *New England Journal of Medicine* 351: 2035–2037.

Boback, SM, Cox, CL, Ott , BD, et al. 2007. Cooking and grinding reduces the cost of meat digestion. *Comparative Biochemistry and Physiology, Part A* 148: 651–656.

Bobe, R, and Behrensmeyer, A. 2004. The expansion of grassland ecosystems in Africa in relation to mammalian evolution and the origin of the genus *Homo*. *Palaeogeography, Palaeoclimatology, Palaeoecology* 207: 399–420.

Bocherens, H, Billiou, D, Mariotti, A, et al. 1999. Palaeoenvironmental and palaeodietary implications of isotopic biogeochemistry of last interglacial Neanderthal and mammal bones in Scladina Cave (Belgium). *Journal of Archaeological Science* 26: 599–607.

Bocherens, H, Drucker, DG, Billiou, D, et al. 2005. Isotopic evidence for diet and subsistence pattern of the Saint-Césaire I Neanderthal: review and use of a multi-source mixing model. *Journal of Human Evolution* 49: 71–87.

Bocklandt, S, Horvath, S, Vilain, E, et al. 2006. Extreme skewing of X chromosome inactivation in mothers of homosexual men. *Human Genetics* 118: 691–694.

Bodnar, AG, Ouellette, M, Frolkis, M, et al. 1998. Extension of life-span by introduction of telomerase into normal human cells. *Science* 279: 349–352.

Boë, L-J, Heim, J-L, Honda, K, et al. 2002. The potential Neandertal vowel space was as large as that of modern humans. *Journal of Phonetics* 30: 465–484.

Boëda, E, Geneste, JM, Griggo, C, et al. 1999. A Levallois point embedded in the vertebra of a wild ass (*Equus africanus*): hafting, projectiles and Mousterian hunting weapons. *Antiquity* 73280: 394–402.

Bordes, F. 1961. Mousterian cultures in France: artifacts from recent excavation dispel some popular misconceptions about Neanderthal man. *Science* 134(3482): 803–810.

Borries, C, Launhardt, K, Epplen, C, et al. 1999. DNA analyses support the hypothesis that infanticide is adaptive in langur monkeys. *Proceedings of the Royal Society of London B* 266: 901–904.

Boswell, R. 2006 (April 6). "Intelligent design" debate evolves into funding fracas. *CanWest News Service*.

Bouzouggar, A, Barton, N, Vanhaeren, M, et. al. 2007. 82,000-year-old shell beads from North Africa and implications for the origins of modern human behavior. *Proceedings of the National Academy of Sciences* 10424: 9964–9969.

Bowler, JM, Johnston, H, Olley, JM, et al. 2003. New ages for human occupation and climatic change at Lake Mungo, Australia. *Nature* 421: 837–840.

Boyd, B. 2006. Getting it all wrong: bioculture critiques cultural critique *American Scholar* 75: 18–30.

Boyd, WC. 1950. Taste reactions to antithyroid substances. *Science* 112: 153.

Brace, CL. 1964. The fate of the "classic" Neanderthals: a consideration of hominid catastrophism. *Current Anthropology* 51: 3–43.

Brain, CK. 1993. *Swartkrans: A Cave's Chronicle of Early Man.* Pretoria: Transvaal Museum.

Breuer, T, Ndoundou-Hockemba, M, and Fishlock, V. 2005. First observation of tool use in wild gorillas. *Public Library of Science Biology* 311: e380.

Bromage, TG, McMahon, JM, Thackeray, JF, et al. 2008. Craniofacial architectural constraints and their importance for reconstructing the early *Homo* skull KNM-ER 1470. *Journal of Clinical Pediatric Dentistry* 33(1): 43–54.

Brown, P, Sutikna, T, Morwood, MJ, et al. 2004. A small-bodied hominin from the Late Pleistocene of Flores, Indonesia. *Nature* 431: 1055–1061.

Browne, J. 2001. Darwin in caricature: a study in the popularisation and dissemination of evolution. *Proceedings of the American Philosophical Society* 145: 496–509.

Browner, WS, Kahn, AJ, Ziv, E, et al. 2004. The genetics of human longevity. *American Journal of Medicine* 117: 851–860.

Brownlee, K, and Syms, L. 1999. *Kayasochi Kikawenow—Our Mother from Long Ago. An Early Cree Woman and Her Personal Belongings from Nagami Bay, Southern Indian Lake.* Winnipeg: University of Manitoba Press.

Brunet, M, Guy, F, Pilbeam, D, et al. 2002a. A new hominid from the Upper Miocene of Chad, Central Africa. *Nature* 418: 145–151.

Brunet, M, Guy, F, Pilbeam D, et al. 2002b. Reply to Wolpoff et al. '*Sahelanthropus* or *Sahelpithecus*?' *Nature* 419: 582.

Brunet, M, Guy, F, Pilbeam D, et al. 2005. New material of the earliest hominid from the Upper Miocene of Chad. *Nature* 434: 752–755.

Bryant, VM, and Dean, GW. 2006. Archaeological coprolite science: the legacy of Eric O. Callen (1912–1970). *Palaeogeography, Palaeoclimatology, Palaeoecology* 237: 51–66.

Bshary, R, and Noë, R. 1997. Red colobus and Diana monkeys provide mutual protection against predators. *Animal Behaviour* 54: 1461–1474.

Budimlija, Z, Prinz, M, Zelson-Mundorff, A, et al. 2003. World Trade Center Human Identification Project: experiences with individual body identification cases. *Croatian Medical Journal* 44: 259–263.

Burger, J, Kirchner, M, Bramanti, B, et al. 2007. Absence of the lactase-persistence-associated allele in early Neolithic Europeans. *Proceedings of the National Academy of Sciences* 104: 3736–3741.

Burkhardt, F, ed. 1996. *Charles Darwin's Letters: A Selection.* Cambridge: Cambridge University Press.

Burton, FD, Bolton, K, and Campbell, V. 1999. Soil-eating behaviour of the hybrid macaque of Kowloon. *Natural History Society of Nepal Bulletin* 9(1–4): 14–20.

Butzer, KW, Brown, FH, and Thurber, DL. 1969. Horizontal sediments of the lower Omo Valley: the Kibish Formation. *Quaternaria* 11: 15–29.

Byers, SN. 2007. *Introduction to Forensic Anthropology,* 3rd ed. Boston: Allyn and Bacon.

Cachel, S. 2006. *Primate and Human Evolution.* Cambridge: Cambridge University Press.

Caillaud, D, Levréro, F, Cristescu, R, et al. 2006. Gorilla susceptibility to Ebola virus: the cost of sociality. *Current Biology* 1613: R489–R491.

Cameron, D, Patnaik, R, and Sahni, A. 2004. The phylogenetic significance of the Middle Pleistocene Narmada hominin cranium from Central India. *International Journal of Osteoarchaeology* 14: 419–447.

Canadian Museum of Civilization. 1992. *Turning the Page: Forging New Partnerships between Museums and First Peoples.* A Task Force Report jointly sponsored by the Assembly of First Nations and the Canadian Museums Association. Ottawa.

Cane, M, and Molnar, P. 2001. Closing of the Indonesian seaway as a precursor to east African aridification around 3–4 million years ago. *Nature* 411: 157–163.

Cann, RL, Stoneking, M, and Wilson, AC. 1987. Mitochondrial DNA and human evolution. *Nature* 325: 31–36.

Cannon, DS, Baker, TB, Piper, ME, et al. 2005. Associations between phenylthiocarbamide gene polymorphisms and cigarette smoking. *Nicotine and Tobacco Research* 7: 853–858.

Caramelli, D, Lalueza-Fox, C, Condemi, S, et al. 2006. A highly divergent mtDNA sequence in a Neandertal individual from Italy. *Current Biology* 1616: R630-R632.

Caramelli, D, Lalueza-Fox, C, Vernesi, C, et al. 2003. Evidence for a genetic discontinuity between Neandertals and 24,000-year-old anatomically modern Europeans. *Proceedings of the National Academy of Sciences* 100: 6593–6597.

Carbonell, E, Bermúdez de Castro, JM, Parés, JM, et al. 2008. The first hominin of Europe. *Nature* 452: 465–470.

Carlson, RJ. 2005 (October 11). The case of BiDil: a policy commentary on race and genetics. *Health Affairs.*

Carlson, RL, and Dalla Bona, L, eds. 1996. *Early Human Occupation in British Columbia.* Vancouver: UBC Press.

Carrai, V, Borgognini-Tarli, SM, Huffman, MA, et al. 2003. Increase in tannin consumption by sifaka (*Propithecus verreauxi verreauxi*) females during the birth season: a case for self-medication in prosimians? *Primates* 441: 61–66.

Cartmill, M. 1972. Arboreal adaptations and the origin of the order Primates. In Tuttle, RH, ed., *The Functional and Evolutionary Biology of Primates.* Chicago: Aldine-Atherton. 97–122.

Cartmill, M. 1992. New views on primate origins. *Evolutionary Anthropology* 1: 105–111.

Cartmill, M. 1994 (April 1). Reinventing anthropology: American Association of Physical Anthropologists annual luncheon address. *Yearbook of Physical Anthropology* 37: 1–9.

Cartmill, M. 1998. The status of the race concept in physical anthropology. *American Anthropologist* 100: 651–660.

Cartmill, M, and Brown, K. 2003. Surveying the race concept: a reply to Lieberman, Kirk, and Littlefield. *American Anthropologist* 105: 114–115.

Caspari, R. 2003. From types to populations: a century of race, physical anthropology, and the American Anthropological Association. *American Anthropologist* 105: 65–76.

Cassell, J. 2002. Perturbing the system: "Hard Science," "Soft Science," and Social Science, the anxiety and madness of method. *Human Organization* 61: 177–185.

Cavalli-Sforza, LL. 1997. Genes, peoples, and languages. *Proceedings of the National Academy of Sciences* 94: 7710–7724.

Cawthon, R, Smith, K, O'Brien, E, et al. 2003. Association between telomere length in blood and mortality in people aged 60 years or older. *The Lancet* 361: 393–395.

CCR. 2009. Canadian Council for Refugees. http://www.ccrweb.ca/history.html. Accessed January 4, 2009.

Chan, AW, Dominko, T, Luetjens, CM, et al. 2000. Clonal propagation of primate offspring by embryo splitting. *Science* 287: 317–319.

Changizi, MA, Zhang, Q, and Shimojo, S. 2006. Bare skin, blood, and the evolution of primate colour vision. *Biology Letters* 22: 217–221.

Chapais, B. 1995. Alliances as a means of competition in primates: evolutionary, developmental, and cognitive aspects. *Yearbook of Physical Anthropology* 38: 115–136.

Chapman, CA, Balcomb, SR, Gillespie, TR, et al. 2000. Long-term effects of logging on African primate communities: a 28-year comparison from Kibale National Park, Uganda. *Conservation Biology* 141: 207–217.

Chapman, CA, and Pavelka, MSM. 2005. Group size in folivorous primates: ecological constraints and the possible influence of social factors. *Primates* 46: 1–9.

Chapman, CA, and Peres, CA. 2001. Primate conservation in the new millennium: the role of scientists. *Evolutionary Anthropology* 10: 16–33.

Charles-Dominique, P, and Martin, RD. 1970. Evolution of lorises and lemurs. *Nature* 227: 257–260.

Chase, PG. 1986. The Hunters of Combe Grenal. Approaches to Middle Paleolithic subsistence in Europe. B.A.R. International Series #286, Oxford.

Chase, PG, and Nowell, A. 1998. Taphonomy of a suggested Middle Paleolithic bone flute from Slovenia. *Current Anthropology* 39: 549–553.

Chatters, JC. 2001. *Ancient Encounters: Kennewick Man and the First Americans.* New York: Simon and Schuster.

Chevalier-Skolnikoff, S. 1990. Tool use by wild cebus monkeys at Santa Rosa National Park, Costa Rica. *Primates* 31: 375–383.

Chimpanzee Sequencing and Analysis Consortium. 2005. Initial sequence of the chimpanzee genome and comparison with the human genome. *Nature* 437: 69–87.

Churchill, S. 2008. Bioenergetic perspectives on Neanderthal thermoregulatory and activity budgets. In K Harvati and T Harrison, eds., *Neanderthals Revisited: New Approaches and Perspectives.* Netherlands: Springer. 113–133.

Cinq-Mars, J, and Morland, RE. 1999. Bluefish Caves and Old Crow Basin: a new rapport. In R Bonnichsen and KL Turnmire, eds., *Ice Age Peoples of North America: Environments, Origins, and Adaptations of the First Americans.* Corvallis: Oregon State University Press. 200–212.

Ciochon, RL, Olsen, J, and James, J. 1990. *Other Origins: The Search for the Giant Ape in Human Prehistory.* New York: Bantam.

Clark, AG, Glanowski, S, Nielson, R, et al. 2003. Inferring non-neutral evolution from human–chimp–mouse orthologous gene trios. *Science* 302: 1960–1963.

Clarke, RJ. 1998. First ever discovery of a well-preserved skull and associated skeleton of *Australopithecus*. *South African Journal of Science* 94: 460–4.

Cobb, SN. 2008. The facial skeleton of the chimpanzee–human last common ancestor. *Journal of Anatomy* 212: 469–485.

Collins, FS. 2004. What we do and don't know about "race," "ethnicity," genetics, and health at the dawn of the genome era. *Nature Genetics Supplement* 36: S13–S15.

Collins, FS, Morgan, M, and Patrinos, A. 2003. The Human Genome Project: lessons from large-scale biology. *Science* 300: 286–290.

Colquhoun, I. 2006. Predation and cathemerality: comparing the impact of predators on the activity patterns of lemurids and ceboids. *Folia Primatologica* 77: 143–165.

Comuzzie, AG, and Allison, DB. 1998. The search for human obesity genes. *Science* 280: 1374–1377.

Comuzzie, AG, Cole, SA, Martin, L, et al. 2003. The baboon as a nonhuman primate model for the study of the genetics of obesity. *Obesity Research* 11: 75–80.

Conroy, GC. 1987. Problems of body-weight estimation in fossil primates. *International Journal of Primatology* 82: 115–137.

Conroy, GC. 1990. *Primate Evolution.* New York: Norton.

Conroy, GC. 2005. *Reconstructing Human Origins,* 2nd ed. New York: Norton.

Conroy, GC, Pickford, M, Senut, B, et al. 1992. *Otavipithecus namibiensis,* first Miocene hominoid from southern Africa. *Nature* 356: 144–148.

Conservation International. 1999. Biodiversity Hotspots.

Conway, G, and Toenniessen, G. 1999. Feeding the world in the twenty-first century. *Nature* 402: C55–C58.

Coon, CS. 1962. *The Origins of Races.* New York: Knopf

Cooper, A, and Poinar, HN. 2000. Ancient DNA: do it right or not at all. *Science* 289: 1139.

Cordain, L, Eaton, SB, Sebastian, A, et al. 2005. Origins and evolution of the Western diet: health implications for the 21st century. *American Journal of Clinical Nutrition* 81: 341–354.

Cormack, J. 2000. The scientific influence that Dr. Davidson Black (Bu Dasheng) had on Chinese prehistory. In Conference Proceedings: International Symposium on Paleoanthropology. *Acta Anthropologica Sinica Supplement* 19: 292–298.

Cormack, J. 2003. Davidson Black and his role in Chinese palaeoanthropology. In C Shen and SG Keates, eds., *Current Research in Chinese Pleistocene Archaeology,* B.A.R. International Series #1179, Oxford. 9–19.

Corr, LT, Richards, MP, Jim, S, et al. 2008. Probing dietary change of the Kwäday Dän Ts'ìnchì individual, an ancient glacier body from British Columbia: I—Complementary use of marine lipid biomarker and carbon isotope signatures as novel indicators of a marine diet. *Journal of Archaeological Science* 35: 2102–2110.

Corsi, P. 2005. Before Darwin: transformist concepts in European natural history. *Journal of the History of Biology* 38: 67–83.

Crews, DE. 1993. Biological anthropology and human aging: some current directions in aging research. *Annual Review of Anthropology* 22: 395–423.

Crews, DE. 2004. *Human Senescence: Evolutionary and Biocultural Perspectives.* Cambridge: Cambridge University Press.

Crews, DE, and Garruto, RM, eds. 1994. *Biological Anthropology and Aging: Perspectives on Human Variation over the Life Span.* Oxford: Oxford University Press.

Crompton, R, Vereecke, E, and Thorpe, S. 2008. Locomotion and posture from the common hominoid ancestor to fully modern humans, with special reference to the last common panin/hominin ancestor. *Journal of Anatomy* 212: 501–543.

Cross, A, Collard, M, and Nelson, A. 2008. Body segment differences in surface area, skin temperatures, and 3D displacement and the estimation of heat balance during locomotion in hominins. *Public Library of Science ONE* 3: e2464.

Crubézy, E, and Trinkaus, E. 1992. Shanidar 1: A case of hyperostotic disease (DISH) in the Middle Paleolithic. *American Journal of Physical Anthropology* 89: 411–420.

Cybulski, JS. 1976. Scientific aspects of archaeology in Canada: a physical anthropologist's view. In AG McKay, ed., *Symposium on New Perspectives in Canadian Archaeology,* October 22–23, 1976, Theatre Auditorium, Royal Ontario Museum, Toronto. Ottawa: Royal Society of Canada. 177–184.

Cybulski, JS. 1992. A Greenville burial ground: human remains and mortuary elements in British Columbia coast prehistory. Archaeological Survey of Canada, Mercury Series #146. Hull: Canadian Museum of Civilization.

Cybulski, JS. 2007. Bioarchaeology, ethics, cooperation, collaboration. Paper presented at the 35th Annual Meeting of the Canadian Association for Physical Anthropology, Banff, Alberta, November 15–17.

Cybulski, JS, Howes, DE, Haggarty, JC, et al. 1981. An early human skeleton from south-central British Columbia: dating and bio-archaeological inference. *Canadian Journal of Archaeology* 5: 49.

Cybulski, JS, McMillan, AD, Malhi, RS, et al. 2007. The Big Bar Lake burial: middle period human remains from the Canadian plateau. *Canadian Journal of Archaeology* 31: 55–79.

Cybulski, JS, Ossenberg, NS, and Wade, WD. 1979. Committee report: statement of the excavation, treatment, analysis, and disposition of human skeletal remains from archaeological sites in Canada. *Canadian Review of Physical Anthropology* 1: 32–36.

Dagosto, M, Gebo, DL, Beard, KC, et al. 1996. New primate postcranial remains from the middle Eocene Shanghuang fissures, southeastern China. *American Journal of Physical Anthropology* 22 (Suppl.): 92–93.

Dagosto, M, and Terranova, CJ. 1991. Estimating the body size of Eocene primates: a comparison of results from dental and postcranial variables. *International Journal of Primatology* 13: 307–344.

Darling, WC, Bath, AH, and Talbot, JC. 2003. The O and H stable isotopic composition of fresh waters in the British Isles: 2, surface waters and groundwaters. *Hydrology and Earth System Sciences* 7: 183–195.

Darwin, C. 1871. *The Descent of Man and Selection in Relation to Sex.* London: John Murray.

Dausmann, KH, Glos, J, Ganzhorn, JU, et al. 2005. Hibernation in the tropics: lessons from a primate. *Journal of Comparative Physiology B: Biochemical, Systemic, and Environmental Physiology* 175: 147–155.

De A Moura, AC, and Lee, PC. 2004. Capuchin stone tool use in Caatinga dry forest. *Science* 306: 1909.

Dean, C, Leakey, MG, Reid, D, et al. 2001. Growth processes in teeth distinguish modern humans from *Homo erectus* and earlier hominins. *Nature* 416: 628–631.

Dean, HJ, Young, TK, Flett, B, et al. 1998. Screening for type-2 diabetes in aboriginal children in northern Canada. *Lancet* 352: 523–4.

De Boo, HA, and Harding, J. 2006. The developmental origins of adult disease (Barker) hypothesis. *Australian and New Zealand Journal of Obstetrics and Gynaecology* 46: 4–14.

de Lumley, H. 1969. Une cabane acheuléenne dans la Grotte du Lazaret. *Mémoires de la Société Préhistorique Française,* Volume 7.

Defleur, A, White, T, Valensi, P, et al. 1999. Neanderthal cannibalism at Moula-Guercy, Ardéche, France. *Science* 286: 128–131.

DeGusta, D, Gilbert, WH, and Turner, SP. 1999. Hypoglossal canal size and hominid speech. *Proceedings of the National Academy of Sciences* 96: 1800–1804.

De Meer, K, Bergman, R, Kusner, JS, et al. 1993. Differences in physical growth of Aymara and Quechua children living at high altitude in Peru. *American Journal of Physical Anthropology* 90(1): 59–76.

D'Errico, F. 2003. The invisible frontier: a multiple species model for the origin of behavioural modernity. *Evolutionary Anthropology* 12: 188–202.

Dettwyler, KA. 1991. Can paleopathology provide evidence for "compassion"? *American Journal of Physical Anthropology* 84: 375–384.

de Waal, F. 1990. *Peacemaking among The Primates.* Cambridge, MA: Harvard University Press.

de Waal, F. 1982. *Chimpanzee Politics: Power and Sex Among Apes.* New York: Harper and Row.

Dickson, JH, Richards, MP, Hebda, RJ, et al. 2004. Kwäday Dän Ts'inchi, the first ancient body of a man from a North American glacier: reconstructing his last days by intestinal and biomolecular analyses. *The Holocene* 14: 481–486.

Di Fiore, A. 2003. Molecular genetic approaches to the study of primate behaviour, social organization, and reproduction. *Yearbook of Physical Anthropology* 46: 62–99.

Dillehay, TD. 2000. *The Settlement of the Americas: A New Prehistory.* New York: Basic.

Diosady, LL, and Mannar, MGV. 2000. Double fortification of salt with iron and iodine. In RM Geertman, ed., *8th World Salt Symposium.* Amsterdam: Elsevier. 971–976.

Dirkmaat, DC, Cabo, LL, Ousley, SD, et al. 2008. New perspectives in forensic anthropology. *Yearbook of Physical Anthropology* 51: 33–52.

Dolphin, AE, Goodman, AH, and Amarasiriwardena, DD. 2005. Variation in elemental intensities among teeth and between pre- and postnatal regions of enamel. *American Journal of Physical Anthropology* 128: 878–888.

Dominy, NJ. 2004. Fruits, fingers, and fermentation: the sensory cues available to foraging primates. *Integrative and Comparative Biology* 44: 295–303.

Dominy, NJ, and Lucas, PW. 2001. Ecological importance of trichromatic vision to primates. *Nature* 410: 363–366.

Donoghue, HD, Marcsik, A, Matheson, C, et al. 2005. Co-infection of Mycobacterium tuberculosis and Mycobacterium leprae in human archaeological samples: a possible explanation for the historical decline of leprosy. *Proceedings of the Royal Society of London B* 272: 389–394.

Doran, GH, Dickel, DN Jr, Ballinger, WE Jr, et al. 1986. Anatomical, cellular, and molecular analysis of 8000-yr-old human brain tissue from the Windover archaeological site. *Nature* 323: 803–806.

Drew, AP. 1997. Genes and human behavior: the emerging paradigm. *Zygon* 32: 41–50.

Duarte, C, Mauricio, J, Pettitt, PB, et al. 1999. The early Upper Paleolithic human skeleton from the Abrigo do Lagar Velho (Portugal) and modern human emergence in Iberia. *Proceedings of the National Academy of Sciences* 9613: 7604–7609.

Dudar, JC, Waye, JS, and Saunders, SR. 2003. Determination of a kinship system using ancient DNA, mortuary practice, and historic records in an upper Canadian pioneer cemetery. *International Journal of Osteoarchaeology* 13: 232–246.

Dunbar, JS, and Hemmings, CA. 2004. Florida Paleoindian points and knives. In BT Lepper and R Bonnichsen, eds., *New Perspectives on the First Americans.* College Station: Texas A&M University Press. 65–72.

Dunbar, RIM. 1998. Impact of global warming on the distribution and survival of the gelada baboon: a modelling approach. *Global Change Biology* 4: 293–304.

Dupras, T, Schultz, JJ, Wheeler, SA, et al. 2006. *Forensic Recovery of Human Remains: Archaeological Approaches.* Boca Raton: CRC.

Dupras, T, Schwarcz, HP, and Fairgrieve, SI. 2001. Infant feeding and weaning practices in Roman Egypt. *American Journal of Physical Anthropology* 115: 204–212.

Dupras, T, and Tocheri, M. 2007. Reconstructing infant weaning histories at Roman period Kellis, Egypt, using stable isotope analysis of dentition. *American Journal of Physical Anthropology* 134: 63–74.

Eaton, SB, and Eaton, SB. III 1999. Breast cancer in evolutionary context. In W Trevathan, EO Smith, and JJ McKenna, eds., *Evolutionary Medicine.* New York: Oxford University Press. 429–442.

Eaton, SB, and Konner, M. 1985. Paleolithic nutrition: a consideration of its nature and current implications. *New England Journal of Medicine* 312: 283–289.

Eaton, SB, Pike, M, Short, R, et al. 1994. Women's reproductive cancers in evolutionary context. *Quarterly Review of Biology* 69: 353–367.

Edwards, AWF. 2003. Lewontin's fallacy. *BioEssays* 25: 798–801.

Ehounoux, NZ, Zunzunegui, M-V, Séguin, L, et al. 2009. Duration of lack of money for basic needs and growth delay in the Quebec Longitudinal Study of Child Development birth cohort. *Journal of Epidemiology and Community Health* 63: 45–49.

Ehrlich, P, and Erhlich, A. 1990. *The Population Explosion.* New York: Simon and Schuster.

Eldridge, N. 1989. *Macroevolutionary Dynamics.* New York: McGraw-Hill.

Eldridge, N, and Gould, S. 1972. Punctuated equilibrium: an alternative to phyletic gradualism. In TMJ Schopf, ed., *Models in Paleobiology.* San Francisco: Freeman, Cooper. 82–115.

Elton, S. 2008. The environmental context of human evolutionary history in Eurasia and Africa. *Journal of Anatomy* 212: 377–393.

Enard, W, Przeworski, M, Fisher, SE, et al. 2002. Molecular evolution of *FOXP2*, a gene involved in speech and language. *Nature* 418: 869–872.

Engel, GA, Jones-Engel, L, Schillaci, MA, et al. 2002. Human exposure to herpesvirus B-seropositive macaques, Bali, Indonesia. *Emerging Infectious Diseases* 8. http://www.cdc.gov/ncidod/EID/vol8no8/01–0467.htm.

Engle, EC. 2007. Genetic basis of congenital strabismus. *Archives of Ophthalmology* 125: 189–195.

Enoch, MA, Harris, CR, and Goldman, D. 2001. Does a reduced sensitivity to bitter taste increase the risk of becoming nicotine addicted? *Addictive Behaviour* 26: 399–404.

Environment Canada. 2003. Canada's National Environmental Indicator Series. http://www.ec.gc.ca/soer-ree. Accessed January 11, 2009.

Eriksson, J, Hohmann, G, Boesch, C, et al. 2004. Rivers influence the population genetic structure of bonobos (*Pan paniscus*). *Molecular Ecology* 13: 3425–3435.

Evans, PD, Gilbert, SL, Mekel-Bobrov, N, et al. 2005. *Microcephalin*, a gene regulating brain size, continues to evolve adaptively in humans. *Science* 309: 1717–1720.

Evans, PD, Mekel-Bobrov, N, Vallender, EJ, et al. 2006. Evidence that the adaptive allele of the brain size gene *microcephalin* introgressed into *Homo sapiens* from an archaic *Homo* lineage. *Proceedings of the National Academy of Sciences* 103: 18178–18183.

Faccia, KJ, and Williams, RC. 2007. Schmorl's Nodes: clinical significance and implications for the bioarchaeological record. *International Journal of Osteoarchaeology* 18: 28–44.

Faerman, M, Bar-Gal, GK, Filon, D, et al. 1998. Determining the sex of infanticide victims from the Late Roman era through ancient DNA analysis. *Journal of Archaeological Science* 25: 861–865.

Fagundes, NJR, Kanitz, R, Eckert, R, et al. 2008. Mitochondrial population genomics supports a single pre-Clovis origin with a coastal route for the peopling of the Americas. *American Journal of Human Genetics* 82: 583–592.

Fairgrieve, S. 2007. *Forensic Cremations—Recovery and Analysis.* Boca Raton: CRC.

Falk, D, Hildebolt, C, Smith, K, et al. 2005. The Brain of LB1, *Homo floresiensis. Science* 308: 242–245.

FAO. 2008. http://www.fao.org/docrep/011/i0291e/i0291e00.htm. Accessed January 22, 2009.

Farah, MJ, Sherab, DM, Savagea, JH, et al., 2006. Childhood poverty: specific associations with neurocognitive development. *Brain Research* 1110: 166–174.

Feathers, JK. 2002. Luminescence dating in less than ideal conditions: case studies from Klasies River main site and Duinefontein, South Africa. *Journal of Archaeological Science* 292: 177–194.

Feathers, JK, and Migliorini, E. 2001. Luminescence dating at Katanda—a reassessment. *Quaternary Science Reviews* 20: 961–966.

Fedigan, LM, Carnegie, SD, and Jack, KM. 2008. Predictors of reproductive success in female white-faced capuchins (*Cebus capucinus*). *American Journal of Physical Anthropology* 137: 82–90.

Fedigan, LM, and Pavelka, MSM. 2001. Is there adaptive value to reproductive termination in Japanese macaques? A test of maternal investment hypotheses. *International Journal of Primatology* 22(2): 109–125.

Fernández-Jalvo, Y, Díez, JC, Cáceres, I, et al. 1999. Human cannibalism in the Early Pleistocene of Europe (Gran Dolina, Sierra de Atapuerca, Burgos, Spain). *Journal of Human Evolution* 37: 591–622.

Fiedel, SJ. 2000. The peopling of the New World: present evidence, new theories, and future directions. *Journal of Archaeological Research* 81: 39–103.

Finlay, BL, and Darlington, RB. 1995. Linked regularities in the development and evolution of mammalian brains. *Science* 268: 1578–1584.

Finlayson, C, Pacheco, FG, Rodríguez-Videl, J, et al. 2006. Late survival of Neanderthals at the southernmost extreme of Europe. *Nature* 443: 850–853.

Finn, CA. 1998. Menstruation: a nonadaptive consequence of uterine evolution. *Quarterly Review of Biology* 732: 163–173.

Firestone, RB, West, A, Kennett, JP, et al. 2007. Evidence for an extraterrestrial impact 12,900 years ago that contributed to the megafaunal extinctions and the Younger Dryas cooling. *Proceedings of the National Academy of Sciences* 104: 10616–10621.

Fisher, RA, Ford, EB, and Huxley, J. 1939. Taste-testing the anthropoid apes. *Nature* 144: 750.

Fisher, RA. 1936. Has Mendel's work been rediscovered? *Annals of Science* 1: 115–137.

Fitzgerald, C, Saunders, S, Bondioli, L, et al. 2006. Health of infants in an Imperial Roman skeletal sample: perspective from dental microstructure. *American Journal of Physical Anthropology* 1302: 179–189.

Fizet, M, Mariotti, A, Bocherens, H, et al. 1995. Effect of diet, physiology, and climate on carbon and nitrogen isotopes of collagen in a late Pleistocene anthropic paleoecosystem (France, Charente, Marillac). *Journal of Archaeological Science* 22: 67–79.

Flaxman, SM, and Sherman, PW. 2000. Morning sickness: a mechanism for protecting mother and embryo. *Quarterly Review of Biology* 75: 113–148.

Fleagle, JG. 1985. New primate fossils from Colhuehuapian deposits at Gaiman and Sacanana, Chubut Province, Argentina. *Armeghinians* 21: 266–274.

Fleagle, JG. 1999. *Primate Adaptation and Evolution,* 2nd ed. London: Academic Press.

Fleagle, JG. 2000. The century of the past: one hundred years in the study of primate evolution. *Evolutionary Anthropology* 92: 87–100.

Fleagle, JG, Kay, RF, and Anthony, MRL. 1997. Fossil New World monkeys. In RF Kay, RH Madden, RL Cifelli, et al., eds., *Vertebrate Paleontology in the Neotropics: The Miocene fauna of La Venta, Colombia.* Washington: Smithsonian Institution Press. 473–495.

Formicola, V, and Buzhilova, AP. 2004. Double child burial from Sunghir, Russia: pathology and inferences for Upper Paleolithic funerary practices. *American Journal of Physical Anthropology* 124: 189–198.

Fossey, D. 1983. *Gorillas in the Mist*. Boston: Houghton Mifflin.

Fox, AL. 1932. The relationship between chemical constitution and taste. *Proceedings of the National Academy of Sciences* 18: 115–120.

Frayling, TM, Timpson, NJ, Weedon, MN, et al. 2007. A common variant in the FTO gene is associated with body mass index and predisposes to childhood and adult obesity. *Science* 316: 889–894.

Frisancho, AR. 1969. Human growth and pulmonary function of a high altitude Peruvian Quechua population. *Human Biology* 91: 365–379.

Frisancho, AR 1977. Developmental adaptation to high altitude hypoxia. *International Journal of Biometeorology* 212: 135–146.

Frost, P. 1994. Geographic distribution of human skin colour: a selective compromise between natural selection and sexual selection? *Human Evolution* 92: 141–153.

Frost, P. 2008. The spread of alphabetical writing may have favored the latest variant of the ASPM gene. *Medical Hypotheses* 70: 17–20.

Frumkin, D, Wassertrom, A, Davidson, A, et al. 2009. Authentification of forensic DNA samples. *Forensic Science International: Genetics*. 4(2): 95–103.

Gabunia, L, and Vekua, A. 1995. A Plio-Pleistocene hominid from Dmanisi, East Georgia, Caucasus. *Nature* 373: 509–512.

Gabunia, L, Vekua, A, Lordkipanidze, D, et al. 2000. Earliest Pleistocene hominid cranial remains from Dmanisi, Republic of Georgia: taxonomy, geological setting, and age. *Science* 288: 1019–1025.

Gagneux, P, Wills, C, Gerloff, U, et al. 1999. Mitochondrial sequences show diverse evolutionary histories of African hominoids. *Proceedings of the National Academy of Sciences* 96: 5077–5082.

Galdikas, B. 1982. Orangutan tool-use at Tan Jung Reserve, Central Indonesian Borneo (Kalimantan Tengah). *Journal of Human Evolution* 11: 19–33.

Galdikas, BMF. 1995. *Reflections of Eden: My Years with the Orangutans of Borneo*. Boston: Little, Brown.

Galdikas, B, and Wood, JW. 1990. Birth spacing patterns in humans and apes. *American Journal of Physical Anthropology* 83: 185–191.

Galloway, T. 2006. Obesity rates among rural Ontario schoolchildren. *Canadian Journal of Public Health* 97: 353–356.

Galloway, T. 2007. Gender differences in growth and nutrition in a sample of rural Canadian schoolchildren. *American Journal of Human Biology* 19: 774–788.

Gangstad, SW, Thornhill, R, and Garver, CE. 2002. Changes in women's sexual interests and their partners' mate retention tactics across the menstrual cycle: evidence for shifting conflicts of interest. *Proceedings of the Royal Society of London, Series B* 269: 975–982.

Garber, PA, Estrada, A, Bicca-Marques, JC, et al., eds. 2008. *South American Primates: Comparative Perspectives in the Study of Behavior, Ecology, and Conservation*. New York: Springer.

Gardner, JP, Li, S, Srinivasan, SR, et al. 2005. Rise in insulin resistance is associated with escalated telomere attrition. *Circulation* 111: 2171–2177.

Gargett, RH. 1989. Grave shortcomings: the evidence for Neandertal burial. *Current Anthropology* 302: 157–190.

Gargett, RH 1999. Middle Paleolithic burial is not a dead issue: the view from Qafzeh, Saint-Césaire, Kebara, Amud, and Dederiyeh. *Journal of Human Evolution* 371: 27–90.

Garn, SM. 1971. *Human Races*, 3rd ed. Springfield: Charles C. Thomas.

Garrigan, D, Mobasher, Z, Severson, T, et al. 2005. Evidence for archaic Asian ancestry on the human X chromosome. *Molecular Biology and Evolution* 22: 189–192.

Gebo, DL, MacLatchy, L, Kityo, R, et al. 1997. A hominoid genus from the early Miocene of Uganda. *Science* 276: 401–404.

Ghiselin, M, and Landa, S. 2005. The economics and bioeconomics of folk and scientific classification. *Journal of Bioeconomics* 7: 221–238.

Gibbons, A. 2007. Swapping guts for brains. *Science* 316: 1560.

Gibbs, RA, Rogers, J, Katze, MG, et al. 2007. Evolutionary and biomedical insights from the rhesus macaque genome. *Science* 316: 222–234.

Gibbs, WW, 2003. The unseen genome: gems among the junk. *Scientific American* 289: 46–53.

Gilardi, KV, Shideler, SE, Valverde, CR, et al. 1997. Characterization of the onset of menopause in the rhesus macaque. *Biology of Reproduction* 57: 335–340.

Gilbert, MTP, Jenkins, DL, Götherstrom, A, et al. 2008. DNA from pre-Clovis human coprolites in Oregon, North America. *Science* 320: 786–789.

Gillespie, TR, Chapman, CA, and Greiner, EC. 2005. Effects of logging on gastrointestinal parasite infections and infection risk in African primates. *Journal of Applied Ecology* 42: 699–707.

Gingerich, P. 1975. Dentition of *Adapis parisiensis* and the evolution of lemuriform primates. In I Tattersall and R Sussman, eds., *Lemur Biology*. New York: Plenum. 65–80.

Glander, KE. 1994. *Eating on the Wild Side*. Tucson: University of Arizona Press.

Goebel, T, Waters, MR, and O'Rourke, DH. 2008. The Late Pleistocene dispersal of modern humans in the Americas. *Science* 319: 1497–1502.

Gonzalez-Suarez, E, Samper, E, Flores, JM, et al. 2000. Telomerase-deficient mice with short telomeres are resistant to skin tumorigenesis. *Nature Genetics* 26: 114–117.

Goodall, J. 1986. *The Chimpanzees of Gombe: Patterns of Behavior*. Cambridge, MA: Belknap.

Goodall J, Bandora A, Bergman E, et al. 1979. Intercommunity interactions in the chimpanzee population of the Gombe National Park. In DA Hamburg and ER McCown, eds., *The Great Apes*. Menlo Park: Benjamin/Cummings. 13–53.

Goodman, M. 1999. The genomic record of humankind's evolutionary roots. *American Journal of Human Genetics* 64: 31–39.

Goodman, AH, and Leatherman, TL. 1998. Traversing the chasm between biology and culture: an introduction. In *Building a New Biocultural Synthesis. Political-Economic Perspectives on Human Biology*, AH Goodman and TL Leatherman (Ed.), University of Michigan Press, Ann Arbor, pp. 3–41.

Goodyear, AC. 2005. Evidence of pre-Clovis sites in the eastern United States. In R Bonnichsen, B Lepper, D Standford, et al., eds., *Paleoamerican Origins: Beyond Clovis*. College Station: Texas A&M University Press. 103–112.

Gould, L, Sussman, RW, and Sauther, ML. 1999. Natural disasters and primate populations: the effects of a two-year drought on a naturally occurring population of ring-tailed lemurs (*Lemur catta*) in southwestern Madagascar. *International Journal of Primatology* 20: 69–84.

Gould, L, Sussman, RW, and Sauther, ML. 2003. Demographic and life-history patterns in a population of ring-tailed lemurs (Lemur catta) at Beza Mahafaly Reserve, Madagascar: a 15-year perspective. *American Journal of Physical Anthropology* 120: 182–194.

Gould, S. 1996. *The Mismeasure of Man*, 2nd ed. New York: WW Norton.

Gould, S, and Lewontin, R. 1979. The spandrels of San Marco and the Panglossian paradigm. *Proceedings of the Royal Society of London Series B* 205: 581–598.

Gowlett, JJ, Harris, JWK, Walton, D, et al. 1981. Early archaeological sites, hominid remains, and traces of fire from Chesowanja, Kenya. *Nature* 294: 125–129.

Grammer, K, Fink, B, and Neave, N. 2005. Human pheromones and sexual attraction. *European Journal of Obstetrics and Gynecology and Reproductive Biology* 118: 135–142.

Grassineau, D, Papa, K, Ducourneau, A, et al. 2007. Improving minority blood donation: anthropologic approach in a migrant community. *Transfusion* 47: 402–409.

Gravlee, CC, Russell, BH, and Leonard, WR. 2003. Boas's "Changes in Bodily Form": the immigrant study, cranial plasticity, and Boas's physical anthropology. *American Anthropologist* 105: 326–332.

Green, RE, Malaspinas, A-S, Krause, J, et al. 2008. A complete Neandertal mitochondrial genome sequence determined by high-throughput sequencing. *Cell* 134: 416–426.

Green, RE, Krause, J, Briggs, AW, et al. 2010. A draft sequence of the Neandertal genome. *Science* 328: 710–722.

Greenberg, J, Turner, C, and Zegura, S. 1986. The settlement of the Americas: a comparison of the linguistic, dental, and genetic evidence. *Current Anthropology* 27: 477–497.

Greenfield, LO. 1992. Origin of the human canine: a new solution to an old enigma. *Yearbook of Physical Anthropology* 35: 153–185.

Gregory, TR. 2004. Macroevolution, hierarchy theory, and the C-value enigma. *Paleobiology* 30: 179–202.

Groombridge, B, and Jenkins, MD, eds. 1994. *Biodiversity Data Sourcebook*. Compiled by the World Conservation Monitoring Centre. Cambridge: World Conservation Press.

Groves, CP. 1989. *A Theory of Human and Primate Evolution*. New York: Oxford University Press.

Groves, CP. 2007. Species concepts and speciation: facts and fantasies. In W Henke and I Tattersall, eds., *Handbook of Paleoanthropology*. Berlin: Springer. 1861–1879.

Groves, CP, and Mazek, V. 1975. An approach to the taxonomy of the Hominidae: gracile Villafranchian hominids of Africa. *Casopis pro Mineralogii A Geologii* 20: 225–247.

Grün, R, and Beaumont, PB. 2001. Border Cave revisited: a revised ESR chronology. *Journal of Human Evolution* 40: 467–482.

Grün, R, Huang, PH, Huang WP, et al. 1998. ESR and U-series analyses of teeth from the palaeoanthropological site of Hexian, Anhui province, China. *Journal of Human Evolution* 34:555–564.

Guatelli-Steinberg, D. 2009. Recent studies of dental development in Neandertals: implications for Neandertal life histories. *Evolutionary Anthropology* 18: 9–20.

Guatelli-Steinberg, D, Larsen, CS, and Hutchinson, DL. 2004. Prevalence and the duration of linear enamel hypoplasia: a comparative study of Neandertals and Inuit foragers. *Journal of Human Evolution* 47: 65–84.

Guatelli-Steinberg, D, Reid, DJ, Bishop, TA, et al. 2005. Anterior tooth growth periods in Neandertals were comparable to those of modern humans. *Proceedings of the National Academy of Sciences* 102: 14197–14202.

Guy, F, Mackaye, H-T, Likius, A, et al. 2008. Sympyseal shape variation in extant and fossil hominoids, and the symphyses of *Australopithecus bahrelghazali*. *Journal of Human Evolution* 55: 37–47.

Haeusler, M, and McHenry, HM. 2007. Evolutionary reversals of limb proportions in early hominids? Evidence from KNM-ER 3735 (*Homo habilis*). *Journal of Human Evolution* 53: 383–405.

Hager, LG. 1997. Sex and gender in paleoanthropology. In L Hager, ed., *Women in Human Evolution*. London: Routledge. 1–28.

Haile-Selassie, Y. 2001. Late Miocene hominids from the Middle Awash, Ethiopia. *Nature* 412: 178–181.

Haile-Selassie, Y, Saylor, BZ, Deino, A, et al. 2010. New hominid fossils from Waranso-Mille (Central Afar, Ethiopia) and taxonomy of early Australopithecus. *American Journal of Physical Anthropology* 141: 406-417.

Haile-Selassie, Y, Suwa, G, and White, TD. 2004. Late Miocene teeth from Middle Awash, Ethiopia, and early hominid dental evolution. *Science* 303: 1503–1505.

Haleem, AA. 1995. (translation) Al-Jahiz, *Chance or Creation? God's Design in the Universe*. Attributed to al-Jahiz, AD 776–869. Reading: Garnet.

Hall, BK. 2001. Evo-devo or devo-evo—does it matter? *Evolution and Development* 2: 177–178.

Hall, BK, ed. 2007. *Fins and Limbs: Evolution, Development, and Transformation*. Chicago: University of Chicago Press.

Hallgrímsson, B, Lieberman, DE, Liu, W, et al. 2007. Epigenetic interactions and the structure of phenotypic variation in the cranium. *Evolution and Development* 9: 76–91.

Hallgrímsson, B, Willmore, K, and Hall, BK. 2002. Canalization, developmental stability, and morphological integration in primate limbs. *Yearbook of Physical Anthropology* 45: 131–158.

Halverson, MS, and Bolnick, DA. 2008. An ancient DNA test of a founder effect in Native American ABO blood group frequencies. *American Journal of Physical Anthropology* 137: 342–347.

Hamer, DH, Hu, S, Magnuson, VL, et al. 1993. A linkage between DNA markers on the X chromosome and male sexual orientation. *Science* 261: 321–327.

Hamilton-Reeves, JM, Rebello, SA, Thomas, W, et al. 2007. Isoflavone-rich soy protein isolate suppresses androgen receptor expression without altering estrogen receptor-ß expression or serum hormonal profiles in men at high risk of prostate cancer. *Journal of Nutrition* 137: 1769–1775.

Hammer, MF, Karafet, T, Rasanayagam, A, et al. 1998. Out of Africa and back again: nested cladistic analysis of human Y chromosome variation. *Molecular Biology and Evolution* 15: 427–441.

Hammer, MF, Spurdle, AB, Karafet, T, et al. 1997. The geographic distribution of human Y chromosome variation. *Genetics* 145: 787–805.

Hanna, JM, and Brown, DE. 1983. Human heat tolerance: An anthropological perspective. *Annual Review of Anthropology* 12: 259–284.

Harcourt-Smith, WEH. 2007. The origins of bipedal locomotion. In W Henke and I Tattersall, eds., *Handbook of Paleoanthropology*. Berlin: Springer. 1483–1518.

Harding, RM, Fullerton, SM, Griffiths, RC, et al. 1997. Archaic African and Asian lineages in the genetic ancestry of modern humans. *American Journal of Human Genetics* 60: 772–789.

Harris, E, and Hey, J. 1999. X chromosome evidence for ancient human histories. *Proceedings of the National Academy of Sciences* 96: 3320–3324.

Harrison, T. 1989. New postcranial remains of *Victoriapithecus* from the middle Miocene of Kenya. *Journal of Human Evolution* 18: 3–54.

Hartl, DL, and Fairbanks, DJ. 2007. Mud sticks: on the alleged falsification of Mendel's data. *Genetics* 175: 975–979.

Hegele, RA, Cao, H, Harris, SB, et al. 1999. The hepatic nuclear factor-1 G319S variant is associated with early-onset Type 2 diabetes in Canadian Oji-Cree. *Journal of Clinical Endocrinology and Metabolism* 84: 1077–1082.

Heilbron, JL. 2003. *The Oxford Companion to the History of Modern Science*. Oxford: Oxford University Press.

Hemmer, H. 2007. Estimation of basic life history data of fossil hominoids. In W Henke and I Tattersall, eds., *Handbook of Paleoanthropology*. Berlin: Springer. 587–619.

Henke, W, and Tattersall, I. eds. 2007. *Handbook of Paleoanthropology*. Berlin: Springer.

Henshilwood, C, d'Errico, F, Marean, CW, et al. 2001. An early bone tool industry from the Middle Stone Age at Blombos Cave, South Africa: implications for the origins of modern human behaviour, symbolism, and language. *Journal of Human Evolution* 41: 631–678.

Henshilwood, C, d'Errico, F, Vanhaeren, M, et al. 2004. Middle Stone Age shell beads from South Africa. *Science* 304(5669): 404.

Henshilwood, CS, d'Errico, F, Yates, R, et al. 2002. Emergence of modern human behavior: Middle Stone Age engravings from South Africa. *Science* 295: 1278–1280.

Hernandez-Aguilar, RA, Moore, J, and Pickering, TR. 2007. Savanna chimpanzees use tools to harvest the underground storage organs of plants. *Proceedings of the National Academy of Sciences* 104: 19210–19213.

Herring, DA. 1994a. "There were young people and old people and babies dying every week": The 1918–1919 influenza pandemic at Norway House. *Ethnohistory* 41: 73–105.

Herring, DA. 1994b. The 1918 influenza epidemic in the central Canadian subarctic. In A Herring and L Chan, eds., *Strength in Diversity: A Reader in Physical Anthropology*. Toronto: Canadian Scholars' Press. 365–384.

Herring, DA. 2000. Mundane diseases can kill: the 1918 influenza pandemic in Canada. *Journal of the Ontario Occupational Health Nurses Association* 19: 6–11.

Herring, DA, and Sattenspiel, L. 2007. Social contexts, syndemics, and infectious disease in northern aboriginal populations. *American Journal of Human Biology* 19: 190–202.

Herring, DA, Saunders, SR, and Katzenberg, MA. 1998. Investigating the weaning process in past populations. *American Journal of Physical Anthropology* 105: 425–439.

Herrmann, E, Call, J, Hernàndez-Lloreda, MV, et al. 2007. Humans have evolved specialized skills of social cognition: the cultural intelligence hypothesis. *Science* 317: 1360–1366.

Hey, J. 2001. The mind of the species problem. *Trends in Ecology and Evolution* 16: 1326–1329.

Hey, J. 2009. The divergence of chimpanzee species and subspecies as revealed in multi-population isolation-with-migration analyses. *Molecular Biology and Evolution*, doi:10.1093/molbev/msp298.

Hill, A, Ward, S, Deino, A, et al. 1992. Earliest *Homo. Nature* 355: 719–722.

Hobolth, A, Christensen, OF, Mailund, T, et al. 2007. Genomic relationships and speciation times of human, chimpanzee, and gorilla inferred from a coalescent hidden Markov model. *Public Library of Science Genetics* 3: e7.

Hoffstetter, R. 1974. Phylogeny and geographical deployment of the primates. *Journal of Human Evolution* 3: 327–350.

Hoffstetter, R. 1980. Origin and deployment of New World monkeys emphasizing the southern continent's route. In R Ciochon and AB Chiarelli, eds., *Evolutionary Biology of the New World Monkeys and Continental Drift*. New York: Plenum. 103–122.

Hohmann, G, and Fruth, B. 2003. Culture in bonobos? Between-species and within-species variation in behaviour. *Current Anthropology* 44: 563–571.

Hohmann, G, and Fruth, B. 2003. Intra- and inter-sexual aggression by bonobos in the context of mating. *Behaviour* 140: 1389–1413.

Holloway, RL, Broadfield, DC, and Yuan, MS. 2003. Morphology and histology of chimpanzee primary visual striate cortex indicate that brain reorganization predated brain expansion in early hominid evolution. *Anatomical Record* 273A: 594–602.

Holloway, RL, Clarke, RJ, and Tobias, PV. 2004. Posterior lunate sulcus in *Australopithecus africanus:* was Dart right? *Comptes Rendus Paleoevolution* 3: 287–293.

Holmes, R. 2006. *The Hottentot Venus*. London: Bloomsbury.

Homan, GF, Davies, M, and Norman, R. 2007. The impact of lifestyle factors on reproductive performance in the general population and those undergoing infertility treatment: a review. *Human Reproduction Update* 13: 209–223.

Hong, R, Banta, JE, and Betancourt, JA. 2006. Relationship between household wealth inequality and chronic childhood under-nutrition in Bangladesh. *International Journal for Equity in Health* 5: 15.

Hooper, J. 2003. *Of Moths and Men: The Untold Story of Science and the Peppered Moth*. New York: Norton.

Hoppa, RD, and Garlie, TN. 1998. Secular changes in the growth of Toronto children during the last century. *Annals of Human Biology* 25: 553–561.

Houle, A. 1999. The origin of platyrrhines: an evaluation of the Antarctic scenario and the floating island model. *American Journal of Physical Anthropology* 109: 541–559.

Hrdy, SB. 1977. *The Langurs of Abu: Female and Male Strategies of Reproduction*. Cambridge, MA: Harvard University Press.

Hrdy, SB, Janson, C, and Van Schaik, C. 1995. Infanticide: let's not throw the baby out with the bath water. *Evolutionary Anthropology* 3: 151–154.

Hrdy, SB, and Whitten, PL. 1987. Patterning of sexual activity. In BB Smuts, DL Cheney, RM Seyfarth, et al., eds., *Primate Societies*. Chicago: University of Chicago Press. 370–384.

Hu, S, Pattatucci, AML, Patterson, C, et al. 1995. Linkage between sexual orientation and chromosome Xq28 in males but not in females. *Nature Genetics* 11: 248–256.

Huang, W, Ciochon, R, Yumin, G, et al. 1995. Early *Homo* and associated artifacts from Asia. *Nature* 378: 275–278.

Huber, SK, and Podos, J. 2006. Beak morphology and song features covary in a population of Darwin's finches (*Geospiza fortis*). *Biological Journal of the Linnean Society* 88: 489–498.

Huffman, MA. 1997. Current evidence for self-medication in primates: a multidisciplinary perspective. *Yearbook of Physical Anthropology* 40: 171–200.

Huffman, MA, Gotoh, S, Turner, LA, et al. 1997. Seasonal trends in intestinal nematode infection and medicinal plant use among chimpanzees in the Mahale Mountains, Tanzania. *Primates* 382: 111–125.

Hull, D. 2005. Deconstructing Darwin: evolutionary theory in context. *Journal of the History of Biology* 38: 137–152.

Hunt, KD. 1994. The evolution of human bipedality: ecology and functional morphology. *Journal of Human Evolution* 26: 183–202.

Hunt, KD. 2003. The single species hypothesis: truly dead and pushing up bushes, or still twitching and ripe for resuscitation? *Human Biology* 75: 485–502.

Hurd, JP. 2006. The shape of high fertility in a traditional Mennonite population. *Annals of Human Biology* 33: 557–569.

Huxley, TH. 1863. *Man's Place in Nature*. London: Williams and Norgate.

Ice, GH. 2005. Biological anthropology and aging. *Journal of Cross-Cultural Gerontology* 20: 87–90.

IHGSC. International Human Genome Sequencing Consortium. 2001. Initial sequencing and analysis of the human genome. *Nature* 409: 860–921.

IHGSC. International Human Genome Sequencing Consortium. 2004. Finishing the euchromatic sequence of the human genome. *Nature* 431: 931–45.

Isaac, GL. 1978. The food-sharing behaviour of proto-human hominids. *Scientific American* 238: 90–108.

Isbell, LA. 2006. Snakes as agents of evolutionary change in primate brains. *Journal of Human Evolution* 51: 1–35.

Isler, K, and van Schaik, C. 2006. Costs of encephalization: the energy trade-off hypothesis tested on birds. *Journal of Human Evolution* 51: 228–243.

Jablonka, E, and Lamb, M. 2005. *Evolution in Four Dimensions—Genetic, Epigenetic, Behavioral, and Symbolic Variation in the History of Life*. Cambridge, MA: MIT.

Jablonka, E, and Lamb, M. 2007. The expanded evolutionary synthesis—a response to Godfrey-Smith, Haig, and West-Eberhard. *Biology and Philosophy* 22: 453–472.

Jablonski, NG. 2004. The evolution of human skin and skin color. *Annual Review of Anthropology* 33: 585–623.

Jablonski, NG, and Chaplin, G. 2000. The evolution of skin coloration. *Journal of Human Evolution* 391: 57–106.

Jablonski, NG, and Chaplin, G. 2002. Skin deep. *Scientific American* 287: 74–82.

Jackson, FLC. 2008. Ancestral links of Chesapeake Bay region African Americans to specific Bight of Bonny (West Africa) microethnic groups and increased frequency of aggressive breast cancer in both regions. *American Journal of Human Biology* 20: 165–173.

Jacob, T. 2001. Biological aspects of *Homo erectus* through the time-space continuum. In T Simanjuntak, B Prasetyo, R Handini, et al., eds., *Sangiran: Man, Culture and Environment in Pleistocene Times*. Jakarta. 19–23.

Jacobs, B. 2004. Paleobotanical studies from tropical Africa: relevance to the evolution of forest, woodland, and savannah biomes. *Philosophical Transactions of the Royal Society London B* 359: 1573–1583.

James, CR, Stall, R, and Gifford, SM. 2002. *Anthropology and Epidemiology: Interdisciplinary Approach to the Study of Health and Disease*. New York: Springer.

Jantz, RL, and Spencer, F. 1997. Boas, Franz (1858–1942). In F Spencer, ed., *A History of Physical Anthropology*, Vol. I, *A-L*. New York: Garland. 186–190.

Jeffery, B, Abonyi, S, Labonte, R, et al. 2006. Engaging numbers: developing health indicators that matter for First Nations and Inuit people. *Journal of Aboriginal Health* (September): 44–52.

Jerkic, S. 2001. The influence of James E Anderson on Canadian physical anthropology. In L Sawchuk and S Pfeiffer, eds., *Out of the Past: The History of Human Osteology at the University of Toronto*. Toronto: CITD. http://citdpress.utsc.utoronto.ca/osteology/pfeiffer.html.

Jones, KE, Patel, NG, Levy, MA, et al. 2008. Global trends in emerging infectious diseases. *Nature* 451: 990–993.

Jones, PR. 1980. Experimental butchery with modern stone tools and its relevance for Palaeolithic archaeology. *World Archaeology* 12(2): 153–165.

Kaiser, J. 2003. Sipping from a poisoned chalice. *Science* 302: 376–379.

Kaplan, H. 1996. A theory of fertility and parental investment in traditional and modern human societies. *Yearbook of Physical Anthropology* 39: 91–135.

Katzenberg, MA, Schwarcz, HP, Knyf, M, et al. 1995. Stable isotope evidence for maize horticulture and paleodiet in southern Ontario, Canada. *American Antiquity* 602: 335–350.

Katzenberg, MA, and Saunders, S, eds. 2008. *Biological Anthropology of the Human Skeleton*, 2nd ed. New York: Wiley.

Katzenberg, MA, Herring, DA, and Saunders, SR. 1996. Weaning and infant mortality: evaluating the skeletal evidence. *Yearbook of Physical Anthropology* 39: 177–200.

Katzmarzyk, PT. 2008. Obesity and physical activity among aboriginal Canadians. *Obesity* 16: 184–190.

Katzmarzyk, PT, and Leonard, WR. 1998. Climatic influences on human body size and proportions: ecological adaptations and secular trends. *American Journal of Physical Anthropology* 106: 483–503.

Kaur, T, Singh, J, Tong, S, et al. 2008. Descriptive epidemiology of fatal respiratory outbreaks and detection of a human-related metapneumovirus in wild chimpanzees (*Pan troglodytes*) at Mahale Mountains National Park, Western Tanzania. *American Journal of Primatology* 70: 755–765.

Kaurah, P, MacMillan, A, Boyd, N, et al. 2007. Founder and recurrent *CDH1* mutations in families with hereditary diffuse gastric cancer. *JAMA* 297: 2360–2372.

Kay, R 1984. On the use of anatomical features to infer foraging behavior in extinct primates. In J Cant and P Rodman, eds., *Adaptations for Foraging in Nonhuman Primates*. New York: Columbia University Press. 21–53.

Kay, RF, Cartmill, M, and Balow, M. 1998. The hypoglossal canal and the origin of human vocal behaviour. *Proceedings of the National Academy of Sciences* 95: 5417–5419.

Keenleyside, A, Bertulli, M, and Fricke, HC. 1997. The final days of the Franklin expedition: new skeletal evidence. *Arctic* 50(1): 36–46.

Keenleyside, A, and Panayotova, K. 2006. Cribra orbitalia and porotic hyperostosis in a Greek colonial population (5th to 3rd centuries BC) from the Black Sea. *International Journal of Osteoarchaeology* 16: 373–384.

Keita, S, Kittles, R, Royal, C, et al. 2004. Conceptualizing human variation. *Nature Genetics* 36: S17–S20.

Kelly, R. 2001. Tripedal knuckle-walking: a proposal for the evolution of human locomotion and handedness. *Journal of Theoretical Biology* 213: 333–358.

Kemppainen, J, Aalto, S, Fujimoto, T, et al. 2005. High intensity exercise decreases global brain glucose uptake in humans. *Journal of Physiology* 568(1): 323–332.

Kimbel, WH, Lockwood, CA, Ward, CV, et al. 2006. Was *Australopithecus anamensis* ancestral to *A. afarensis*? A case of anagenesis in the hominin fossil record. *Journal of Human Evolution* 51: 134–152.

Kimbel, WH, Walter, RC, Johanson, DC, et al. 1996. Late Pliocene *Homo* and Oldowan tools from the Hadar formation (Kada Hadar Member), Ethiopia. *Journal of Human Evolution* 31(6): 549–561.

Kimura, M. 1983. *The Neutral Theory of Molecular Evolution*. Cambridge: Cambridge University Press.

Kinsella, K, and Velkoff, VA. 2001. *An Aging World: 2001*. US Census Bureau, Series P95/01–1. Washington: US GPO.

Kirk, EC, and Simons, EL. 2001. Diets of fossil primates from the Fayum Depression of Egypt: a quantitative analysis of molar shearing. *Journal of Human Evolution* 40: 203–229.

Kirkwood, TBL, and Holliday, R. 1979. The evolution of ageing and longevity. *Proceedings of the Royal Society of London Series B, Biological Sciences* 2051161: 531–546.

Kivell T, and Schmitt, D. 2009. Independent evolution of knuckle-walking in African apes shows that humans did not evolve from a knuckle-walking ancestor. *Proceedings of the National Academy of Sciences* 106(34): 14241–14246.

Klein, N, Fröhlich, F, and Krief, S. 2008. Geophagy: soil consumption enhances the bioactivities of plants eaten by chimpanzees. *Naturwissenschaften* 95: 325–331.

Klein, RG. 1995. Anatomy, behavior, and modern human origins. *Journal of World Prehistory* 92: 167–198.

Klein, RG. 2000. Archaeology and the evolution of human behavior. *Evolutionary Anthropology* 91: 17–36.

Kluger, MJ. 1978. The evolution and adaptive value of fever. *American Scientist* 661: 38–43.

Kluger, MJ, Kozak, W, Conn, C, et al. 1996. The adaptive value of fever. *Infectious Disease Clinics of North America* 101: 1–20.

Kociba, RJ, Keyes, DG, Beyer, JE, et al. 1978. Results of a two-year chronic toxicity and oncogenicity study of 2, 3, 7, 8-tetrachlorodibenzo-p-dioxin in rats. *Toxicology and Applied Pharmacology* 46: 279–303.

Kohn, D, Murrell, G, Parker, J, et al. 2005. What Henslow taught Darwin. *Nature* 436: 643–645.

Köndgen, S, Köhl, H, N'Goran, PK, et al. 2008. Pandemic human viruses cause decline of endangered great apes. *Current Biology* 18: 260–264.

Koné, I, Lambert, JE, Refisch, J, et al. 2008. Primate seed dispersal and its potential role in maintaining useful tree species in the Taï region, Côte-d'Ivoire: implications for the conservation of forest fragments. *Tropical Conservation Science* 1: 293–306.

Kordos, L, and Begun, DR. 2001. A new cranium of *Dryopithecus* from Rudabánya, Hungary. *Journal of Human Evolution* 41: 689–700.

Kordos, L, and Begun, DR. 2002. Rudabánya: a late Miocene subtropical swamp deposit with evidence of the origin of the African apes and humans. *Evolutionary Anthropology* 112: 45–57.

Krause, J, Lalueza-Fox, D, Orlando, L, et al. 2007. The derived *FOXP2* variant of modern humans was shared with Neandertals. *Current Biology* 17: 1908–1912.

Krause, J, Orlando, L, Serre, D, et al. 2007. Neanderthals in central Asia and Siberia. *Nature* 449: 902–904.

Kraut-Becher, J, Eisenberg, M, Voytek, C, et al. 2008. Examining racial disparities in HIV Lessons from sexually transmitted investigations research. *Journal of Acquired Immune Deficiency Syndromes* 47 (Suppl 1): S20–S27.

Krings, M, Capelli, C, Tschentscher, F, et al. 2000. A view of Neandertal genetic diversity. *Nature Genetics* 26: 144–146.

Krings, M, Stone, A, Schmitz, RW, et al. 1997. Neandertal DNA sequences and the origin of modern humans. *Cell* 901: 19–30.

Krishnamani, R, and Mahaney, WC. 2000. Geophagy among primates: adaptive significance and ecological consequences. *Animal Behaviour* 59: 899–915.

Kuhn, T. 1962. *The Structure of Scientific Revolutions*. Chicago: University of Chicago Press.

Kurki, HH, Ginter, JK, Stock, JT, et al. 2008. Adult proportionality in small-bodied foragers: a test of ecogeographic expectations. *American Journal of Physical Anthropology* 136: 28–38.

Kurosu, H, Yamamoto, M, Clark, JD, et al. 2005. Suppression of aging in mice by the hormone Klotho. *Science* 309: 1829–1833.

Kuzawa, C. 2005. Fetal origins of developmental plasticity: are fetal cues reliable predictors of future nutritional environments? *American Journal of Human Biology* 17: 5–21.

Kwok, C, and Keenleyside, A. 2010. Baby bones, food, and health: Isotopic evidence for infant feeding practices in the Greek colony of Apollonia Pontica (5th–2nd centuries B.C.). In M Richards and A Papathanasiou, eds., *Stable Isotope Dietary Studies of Prehistoric and Historic Greek Populations*. Occasional Weiner Laboratory Series from Hesperia.

Laberge, A-M, Jomphe, M, Houde, L, et al. 2005a. A "fille du Roy" introduced the T14484C Leber Hereditary Optic Neuropathy mutation in French Canadians. *American Journal of Human Genetics* 77: 313–317.

Laberge, A-M, Michaud, J, Richter, A, et al. 2005b. Population history and its impact on medical genetics in Quebec. *Clinical Genetics* 68: 287–301.

Lahn, BT, and Page, DC. 1999. Four evolutionary strata on the human X chromosome. *Science* 286: 964–967.

Lai, P, and Lovell, NC. 1992. Skeletal markers of occupational stress in the fur trade: a case study from a Hudson's Bay Company fur trade post. *International Journal of Osteoarchaeology* 2: 221–234.

Lalueza-Fox, C, Römpler, H, Caramelli, D, et al. 2007. A melanocortin 1 receptor allele suggests varying pigmentation among Neanderthals. *Science* 318: 1453–55.

Larcombe, L, Rempel, JD, Dembinski, I, et al. 2005. Differential cytokine genotype frequencies among Canadian Aboriginal and Caucasian populations. *Genes and Immunity* 6: 140–144.

Larson, CP. 2007. Poverty during pregnancy: its effects on child health outcomes. *Paediatrics and Child Health* 12: 673–677.

Lazenby, R, Angus, S, Galloway T, et al. 2007. Social determinants of childhood overweight and obesity in elementary school children. 35th Annual Meeting of the Canadian Association for Physical Anthropology, Banff, Alberta.

Lazenby, R, Cooper, DML, Angus, S, et al. 2008a. Articular constraint, handedness, and directional asymmetry in the human second metacarpal. *Journal of Human Evolution* 54: 875–885.

Lazenby, R, Tilgner, R, Hublin, J-J, et al. 2008b. 3D trabecular microarchitecture in SKX 5020, a first metacarpal attributed to *Paranthropus robustus*, compared with *Pan* and *Homo*. Paleoanthropology Society Meetings, Vancouver, Canada.

Leakey, LSB, Tobias, PV, and Napier, JR. 1964. A new species of genus *Homo* from Olduvai Gorge. *Nature* 202: 7–9.

Leakey, M, Feibel, C, McDougall, I, et al. 1995. New four-million-year-old hominid species from Kanapoi and Allia Bay, Kenya. *Nature* 376: 565–571.

Leakey, MD, and Hay, RL. 1979. Pliocene footprints in the Laetoli beds at Laetoli, northern Tanzania. *Nature* 278: 317–323.

Leakey, M, Spoor, F, Brown, FH, et al. 2001. New hominin genus from eastern Africa shows diverse middle Pliocene lineages. *Nature* 410: 433–440.

Leatherman, TL, and Goodman, AH. 2005. Coca-colonization of diets in the Yucatan. *Social Science and Medicine* 61: 843–866.

Lebatard, A-E, Bourle, D, Duringer, P, et al. 2008. Cosmogenic nuclide dating of *Sahelanthropus tchadensis* and *Australopithecus bahrelghazali*: Mio-Pliocene hominids from Chad. *Proceedings of the National Academy of Sciences* 105: 3226–3231.

Lederberg, J, Shope, RE, and Oaks, SC Jr., eds. 1992. *Emerging Infections: Microbial Threats to Health in the United States*. Washington: Institute of Medicine, National Academy Press.

Leduc,, C, Coonish, J, Haddad, JP, et al. 2006. Plants used by the Cree Nation of Eeyou Istchee (Quebec, Canada) for the treatment of diabetes: a novel approach in quantitative ethnobotany. *Journal of Ethnopharmacology* 105: 55–63.

Lee, AC, Kamalam, A, Adams, SM, et al. 2004. Molecular evidence for absence of Y-linkage of the hairy ears trait. *European Journal of Human Genetics* 12: 1077–1079.

Lee-Thorp, J, Thackeray, JF, and van der Merwe, N. 2000. The hunters and the hunted revisited. *Journal of Human Evolution* 39: 565–576.

Lehmann, J, Korstjens, AH, and Dunbar, RIM. 2007. Fission–fusion social systems as a strategy for coping with ecological constraints: a primate case. *Evolutionary Ecology* 21:613–634.

Lehmann, J, Korstjens, AH, and Dunbar, RIM. 2007. Group size, grooming, and social cohesion in primates. *Animal Behaviour* 74: 1617–1629.

Leonard, WR, and Crawford, M. 2003. *Human Biology of Pastoral Populations*. Cambridge: Cambridge University Press.

Leonard, WR, Snodgrass, J-J, and Robertson, M. 2007. Effects of brain evolution on human nutrition and metabolism. *Annual Review of Nutrition* 27: 311–327.

Leroy, EM, et al. 2004. Multiple Ebola virus transmission events and rapid decline of central African wildlife. *Science* 303: 387–390.

Lewis, RJ, and Kappeler, PM. 2005. Seasonality, body condition, and timing of reproduction in *Propithecus verreauxi verreauxi* in the Kirindy Forest. *American Journal of Primatology* 67: 347–364.

Lewis-Williams, JD. 2001. The enigma of Palaeolithic cave art. BM Fagan, ed., *The Seventy Great Mysteries of the Ancient World: Unlocking the Secrets of Past Civilisations*. London: Thames and Hudson. 96–100.

Lewis-Williams, JD, and Dowson, TA. 1988. The signs of all times: entoptic phenomena in Upper Palaeolithic art. *Current Anthropology* 29(2): 201–245.

Lewontin, RC. 1972. The apportionment of human diversity. In T Dobzhansky et al., eds., *Evolutionary Biology* 6. New York: Appleton-Century-Crofts. 381–398.

Lieberman, DE, McBratney, M, and Krovitz, G. 2002. The evolution and development of cranial form in *Homo sapiens*. *Proceedings of the National Academy of Sciences* 93: 1134–1139.

Lieberman, L. 2001. How "Caucasoids" got such big crania, and why they shrank. From Morton to Rushton. *Current Anthropology* 42: 69–95.

Lieberman, L, Kirk, RC, and Littlefield, A. 2003. Perishing paradigm—race 1931–1999. *American Anthropologist* 105: 110–113.

Lieberman, P, and Crelin, ES. 1971. On the speech of Neanderthal man. *Linguistic Inquiry* 2: 203–222.

Lieverse, AR, Weber, AW, Bazaliiskiy, VI, et al. 2007. Osteoarthritis in Siberia's Cis-Baikal: skeletal indicators of hunter-gatherer adaptation and cultural change. *American Journal of Physical Anthropology* 132(1): 1–16.

Liman, ER, and Innan, H. 2003. Relaxed selective pressure on an essential component of pheromone transduction in primate evolution. *Proceedings of the National Academy of Sciences* 100: 3328–3332.

Lindefors, P, Nunn, CL, and Barton, RA. 2007. Primate brain architecture and selection in relation to sex. *BMC Biology* 5: 20.

Livingstone, F. 1958. Anthropological implications of sickle cell gene distribution in West Africa. *American Anthropologist* 60: 533–562.

Livingstone, F. 1962. On the non-existence of human races. *Current Anthropology* 3: 279.

Lock, M. 2002. Utopias of health, eugenics, and germline engineering. In M Nichter and M Lock, eds., *New Horizons in Medical Anthropology: Essays in Honour of Charles Leslie*. London: Routledge. 239–266.

Lockwood, CA, Kimbel, WH, and Lynch, JM. 2004. Morphometrics and hominoid phylogeny: support for a chimpanzee-human clade and differentiation among great ape species. *Proceedings of the National Academy of Sciences* 101: 4356–4360.

Lomborg, B. 2001. *The Skeptical Environmentalist: Measuring the Real State of the World*. Cambridge: Cambridge University Press.

Lorblanchet, M. 1991. Spitting images: replicating the spotted horses. *Archaeology* 44: 26–31.

Lovejoy, CO. 1981. The orgin of man. *Science* 211: 341–350.

Lovejoy, CO. 2005. The natural history of human gait and posture. Part 1. Spine and pelvis. *Gait and Posture* 21: 95–112.

Lovejoy, CO. 2009. Re-examining human origins in light of *Ardipithecus ramidus*. *Science* 326: 74e1–74e8.

Lovejoy, CO, Suwa, G, Simpson, SW, et al. 2009. The great divides: *Ardipithecus ramidus* reveals the postcrania of our last common ancestors with African apes. *Science* 326: 73.

Lovell, NC. 1994. Spinal arthritis and physical stress at Bronze Age Harappa. *American Journal of Physical Anthropology* 932: 149–164.

Lovell, NC, and Dublenko, AA. 1999. Further aspects of fur trade life depicted in the skeleton. *International Journal of Osteoarchaeology* 9: 248–256.

Lucas, PW, Constantino, PJ, and Wood, BA. 2008. Inferences regarding the diet of extinct hominins: structural and functional trends in dental and mandibular morphology within the hominin clade. *Journal of Anatomy* 212: 486–500.

Lycett, SJ, Collard, M, and McGrew, WC. 2007. Phylogenetic analyses of behavior support existence of culture among wild chimpanzees. *Proceedings of the National Academy of Sciences* 104: 17588–17592.

Lyn, H, Franks, B, and Savage-Rumbaugh, ES. 2008. Precursors of morality in the use of the symbols "good" and "bad" in two bonobos (*Pan paniscus*) and a chimpanzee (*Pan troglodytes*). *Language and Communication* 28: 213–224.

MacArthur, D. 2008. The gene for Jamaican sprinting success? No, not really. *Genetic Future* www.genetic-future.com. Accessed August 21, 2008.

MacArthur, D, and North, K. 2004. A gene for speed? The evolution and function of alpha-actinin-3. *Bioessays* 26: 786–95.

MacArthur, D, and North, K. 2005. Genes and human elite athletic performance. *Human Genetics* 116: 331–339.

Mackenzie, H, Messinger, H, and Smith, R. 2008. *Size Matters: Canada's Ecological Footprint, by Income*. Toronto: Centre for Policy Alternatives, Toronto.

MacLeod, CE, Zilles, K, Schleicher, A, et al. 2003. Expansion of the neocerebellum in Hominoidea. *Journal of Human Evolution* 44: 401–429.

Maggioncalda, AN, Czekala, NM, and Sapolsky, RM. 2002. Male orangutan subadulthood: A new twist on the relationship between chronic stress and developmental arrest. *American Journal of Physical Anthropology* 118: 25–32.

Malhi, RS, BM Kemp, J Eshleman, et al. 2007. Mitochondrial haplogroup M discovered in prehistoric North Americans. *Journal of Archaeological Science* 34: 642–648.

Malthus, TR. 1798. *An Essay on the Principle of Population*. Reprint. New York: Norton.

Mandryk, CAS, Josenhans, H, Fedje, DW, et al. 2001. Late Quaternary paleoenvironments of Northwestern North America: implications for inland versus coastal migration routes. *Quaternary Science Reviews* 20(1-3): 301–314.

Mann, C. 2008. Our Good Earth. *National Geographic* 214: 88–106.

Marean, CW. 1998. A critique of the evidence for scavenging by Neandertals and early modern humans: new data from Kobeh Cave (Zagros Mountains, Iran) and Die Kelders Cave 1 Layer 10 (South Africa). *Journal of Human Evolution* 35: 111–136.

Marean, CW, and Kim, SY. 1998. Mousterian large-mammal remains from Kobeh Cave: behavioral implications for Neanderthals and early modern humans. *Current Anthropology* 39(S1): S79–S113.

Margulis, SW, Atsalis, S, Bellem, A, et al.. 2007. Assessment of reproductive behaviour and hormonal cycles in geriatric western lowland gorillas. *Zoo Biology* 262: 117–139.

Marks, J. 1995. *Human Biodiversity: Genes, Races, and History*. New York: Aldine.

Marks, J. 1997. Buffon's Natural History. In F Spencer, ed., *A History of Physical Anthropology*, Vol I, *A-L*. New York: Garland. 231–234.

Marks, J. 2007. Long shadow of Linnaeus's human taxonomy. *Nature* 447: 28.

Marks, J. 2008. Race across the physical-cultural divide in American anthropology. In H Kuklick, ed., A *New History of Anthropology*. New York: Blackwell. 242–258.

Marlar, RA, Leonard, BL, Billman, BR, et al. 2000. Biochemical evidence of cannibalism at a prehistoric Puebloan site in southwestern Colorado. *Nature* 407: 74–78.

Marmor, M, Sheppard, HW, Donnell, D, et al. 2001. Homozygous and heterozygous CCR5-Δ32 genotypes are associated with resistance to HIV infection. *Journal of Acquired Immune Deficiency Syndromes* 27: 472–481.

Marques-Bonet, T, Ryder, OA, and Eichler, EE. 2009. Sequencing primate genomes: what have we learned? *Annual Review of Genomics and Human Genetics* 10: 355–386.

Martin, RD. 1980. Adaptation and body size in primates. *Zeitschrift für Morphologie und Anthropologie* 71: 115–124.

Martinez-Marignac, VL, Valladares, A, Cameron, E, et al. 2007. Admixture in Mexico City: implications for admixture mapping of Type 2 diabetes genetic risk factors. *Human Genetics* 120: 807–819.

Marvan, R, Stevens, JMG, Roeder, AS, et al. 2006. Male dominance rank, mating, and reproductive success in captive Bonobos (*Pan paniscus*). *Folia Primatologica* 77: 364–376.

Mayne Correia, P, and Beattie, O. 2002. A critical look at methods for recovering, evaluating, and interpreting cremated human remains. In WD Haglund and MH Sorg, eds., *Advances in Forensic Taphonomy: Method, Theory, and Archaeological Perspectives*. Boca Raton: CRC. 435–450.

Mayr, E. 1942. *Systematics and the Origin of Species*. New York: Columbia University Press.

Mayr, E. 1950. Taxonomic categories in fossil hominids. *Cold Spring Harbor Symposium in Quantitative Biology* 15: 109–118.

Mayr, E. 1982. *The Growth of Biological Thought: Diversity, Evolution, and Inheritance*. Cambridge, MA: Belknap.

McBrearty, S, and Brooks, AS. 2000. The revolution that wasn't: a new interpretation of the origin of modern human behaviour. *Journal of Human Evolution* 39: 453–563.

McBrearty, S, and Jablonski, NG. 2005. First fossil chimpanzee. *Nature* 437: 105–108.

McConkey, EH, and Varki, A. 2000. A primate genome project deserves high priority. Letters. *Science* 289: 1295–1296.

McDermott, L, 1996. Self-representation in Upper Paleolithic female figurines. *Current Anthropology* 372: 227–275.

McDougall, I, Brown, FH, and Fleagle, JG. 2005. Stratigraphic placement and age of modern humans from Kibish, Ethiopia. *Nature* 433: 733–736.

McHenry, H, and Coffing, K. 2000. *Australopithecus* to *Homo*: transformations in body and mind. *Annual Reviews in Anthropology* 29: 125–146.

Meagher, S, Penn, DJ, and Potts, WK. 2000. Male–male competition magnifies inbreeding depression in wild house mice. *Proceedings of the National Academy of Sciences* 97: 3324–3329.

Mecsas, J, Franklin, G, Kuziel, W, et al. 2005. CCR5 mutation and plague protection. *Nature* 427: 606.

Medin, DL, and Atran, S. 2004. The native mind: biological categorization and reasoning in development across cultures. *Psychological Review* 111: 960–983.

Mekel-Bobrov, N, Gilbert, SL, Evans, PD, et al. 2005. Ongoing adaptive evolution of *ASPM*, a brain size determinant for *Homo sapiens*. *Science* 309: 1720–1722.

Mekel-Bobrov, N, Posthuma, D, Gilbert, SL, et al. 2007. The ongoing adaptive evolution of *ASPM* and *Microcephalin* is not explained by increased intelligence. *Human Molecular Genetics* 16: 600–608.

Mellars, P 1996. *The Neanderthal Legacy: An Archaeological Perspective from Western Europe*. Princeton: Princeton University Press.

Mellars, P. 2006. A new radiocarbon revolution and the dispersal of modern humans in Eurasia. *Nature* 439: 931–935.

Mendel, G. 1866. Versuche über pflanzen-hybriden. Verhandlungen des naturforschenden vereines. *Abh. Brünn* 4: 3–47. (Reprinted in 1951 in the *Journal of Heredity*, Volume 42).

Mercader, J, Barton, H, Gillespie, J, et al. 2007. 4,300-year-old chimpanzee sites and the origins of percussive stone technology. *Proceedings of the National Academy of Sciences* 104: 3043–3048.

Mercader, J, Panger, M, and Boesch, C. 2002. Excavation of a chimpanzee stone tool site in the African rainforest. *Science* 296: 1452–1455.

Merrett, DC, and Pfeiffer, S. 2000. Maxillary sinusitis as an indicator of respiratory health in past populations. *American Journal of Physical Anthropology* 111: 301–318.

Michael, M. 1993. Population growth and technological change: one million BC to 1990. *Quarterly Journal of Economics* 108: 681–716.

Mielke, JH, Konigsberg, LW, and Relethford, JH. 2006. *Human Biological Variation*. New York: Oxford University Press.

Miller, G, Tybur, JM, and Jordan, BD. 2007. Ovulatory cycle effects on tip earnings by lap dancers: economic evidence for human estrus? *Evolution and Human Behavior* 28: 375–381.

Milton, K. 1981. Food choice and digestive strategies of two sympatric primate species. *American Naturalist* 117: 496–505.

Mitani, JC, Hasegawa, T, Gros-Louis, J, et al. 1992. Dialects in wild chimpanzees? *American Journal of Primatology* 27: 233–243.

Mitani, JC, Merriwether, DA, and Zhang, C. 2000. Male affiliation, cooperation, and kinship in wild chimpanzees. *Animal Behaviour* 59: 885–893.

Mitchel, REJ, Jackson JS, Morrison DP, et al. 2003. Low doses of radiation increase the latency of spontaneous lymphomas and spinal osteosarcomas in cancer-prone, radiation-sensitive Trp53 heterozygous mice. *Radiation Research* 159: 320–327.

Mithen, S, and Reed, M. 2002. Stepping out: a computer simulation of hominid dispersal from Africa. *Journal of Human Evolution* 43: 433–462.

Mitteroecker, P, and Bookstein, F. 2008. The evolutionary role of modularity and integration in the hominoid cranium. *Evolution* 62: 943–958.

Moffat, T. 2001. A biocultural investigation of the weanling's dilemma in Kathmandu, Nepal: do universal recommendations for weaning practices make sense? *Journal of Biosocial Science* 33: 321–338.

Moffat, T. 2002. Breastfeeding, wage labor, and insufficient milk in peri-urban Kathmandu, Nepal. *Medical Anthropology* 21: 207–230.

Moffat, T. 2003. Diarrhea, respiratory infections, protozoan gastrointestinal parasites, and child growth in Kathmandu, Nepal. *American Journal of Physical Anthropology* 1221: 85–97.

Moffat, T, Galloway, T, and Latham, J. 2005. Stature and adiposity among children in contrasting neighborhoods in the city of Hamilton, Ontario, Canada. *American Journal of Human Biology* 17: 355–367.

Moffat, T, and Galloway, T. 2007. Adverse environments: investigating local variation in child growth. *American Journal of Human Biology* 19: 676–683.

Moffat, T, and Galloway, T. 2008. Food consumption patterns: in elementary school children. *Canadian Journal of Dietetic Practice and Research* 69: 152–154.

Moffat, T, and Herring, DA. 1999. The historical roots of high rates of infant death in Aboriginal communities in Canada in the early twentieth century: the case of Fisher River, Manitoba. *Social Science and Medicine* 48: 1821–1832.

Molnar, S. 2006. *Human Variation: Races, Types, and Ethnic Groups*, 6th ed. Upper Saddle River: Prentice-Hall.

Moore, DS. 2006. A very little bit of knowledge: re-evaluating the meaning of the heritability of IQ. *Human Development* 49: 347–353.

Morens, DM, Folkers, GK, and Fauci, AS. 2004. The challenge of emerging and re-emerging infectious diseases. *Nature* 430: 242–249.

Morin, E. 2008. Evidence for declines in human population densities during the early Upper Paleolithic in western Europe. *Proceedings of the National Academy of Sciences* 1051: 48–53.

Morris, K. 2008. Shedding light on the role of poverty in brain development. *The Lancet Neurology* 7: 676–677.

Morwood, MJ, O'Sullivan, PB, Aziz, F, et al. 1998. Fission-track ages of stone tools and fossils on the east Indonesian island of Flores. *Nature* 392: 173–176.

Morwood, MJ, Soejono, RP, Roberts, RG, et al. 2004. Archaeology and age of a new hominin from Flores in eastern Indonesia. *Nature* 431: 1087–1091.

Morwood, MJ, Sutikna, T, Saptomo, EW, et al. 2009. Preface: research at Liang Bua, Flores, Indonesia. *Journal of Human Evolution* 57: 437–449.

Moya-Sola, S, Alba, D, Almecija, S, et al. 2009. A unique Middle Miocene European hominoid and the origins of the great ape and human clade. *Proceedings of the National Academy of Sciences* 106(24): 9601–9606.

Moya-Sola, S, Kohler, M, Alba, DM, et al. 2004. *Pierolapithecus catalaunicus*, a new Middle Miocene great ape from Spain. *Science* 306(5700): 1339–1344.

Müller, AE, and Soligo, C. 2005. Primate sociality in evolutionary context. *American Journal of Physical Anthropology* 128: 399–414.

Mulligan, CJ. 2006. Anthropological applications of ancient DNA: problems and prospects. *American Antiquity* 71: 365–380.

Mustanski, BS, DuPree, MG, Nievergelt, CM, et al. 2005. A genomewide scan of male sexual orientation. *Human Genetics* 116: 272–278.

Myers Thompson, JA. 2003. A model of the biogeographical journey from Proto-*Pan* to *Pan paniscus*. *Primates* 44: 191–197.

Nakatsukasa, M, Pickford, M, Egi, N, et al. 2007. Femur length, body mass, and stature estimates of *Orrorin tugenensis*, a 6 Ma hominid from Kenya. *Primates* 48: 171–178.

Narr, KL, Woods, RP, Thompson, PM, et al. 2007. Relationships between IQ and regional cortical gray matter thickness in healthy adults. *Cerebral Cortex* 17: 2163–2171.

Nations, MK, and Monte, CG. 1996. "I'm not dog, no!": cries of resistance against cholera control campaigns. In PJ Brown, ed., *The Anthropology of Infectious Disease: International Health Perspectives.* London: Routledge. 439–481.

Neel, JV. 1962. Diabetes mellitus: a "thrifty" genotype rendered detrimental by "progress"? *American Journal of Human Genetics* 14: 353–362.

Nelson, SM. 1990. Diversity of the Upper Paleolithic "Venus" figurines and archeological mythology. In SM Nelson and AB Kehoe, eds., *Powers of Observation, Alternative Views in Archaeology.* Archeological Papers of the American Anthropological Association. 11–22.

Nelson, RJ, and Chiavegatto, S. 2001. Molecular basis of aggression. *Trends in Neurosciences* 24: 713–719.

Nesse, R.M. 2007. The importance of evolution for medicine. In WR Trevathan, JJ McKenna, and EO Smith, eds., *Evolutionary Medicine,* 2nd ed. New York: Oxford University Press. 416–432.

Nesse, RM, and Williams, GC. 1998. Evolution and the origins of disease. *Scientific American* 279: 86–93.

Ng, PC, Zhao, Q, Levy, S, et al. 2008. Individual genomes instead of race for personalized medicine. *Clinical Pharmacology and Therapeutics* 84: 306–309.

Ni, X, Wang, Y, Hu, Y, et al. 2004. A euprimate skull from the early Eocene of China. *Nature* 427: 65–68.

Niewoehner, WA. 2008. Neanderthal hands in their proper perspective. In K Harvati and T Harrison, eds., *Neanderthals Revisited: New Approaches and Perspectives.* Netherlands: Springer. 157–190.

Nonoka, K, Miura, T, and Peter, K. 1994. Recent fertility decline in Dariusleut Hutterites: An extension of Eaton and Mayer's Hutterite fertility study. *Human Biology* 66: 411–421.

Noonan, JP, Coop, G, Kudaravalli, S, et al. 2006. Sequencing and analysis of Neanderthal genomic DNA. *Science* 314: 1113–1118.

Norton, HL, Kittles, RA, Parra, E, et al. 2007. Genetic evidence for the convergent evolution of light skin in Europeans and East Asians. *Molecular Biology and Evolution* 24: 710–722.

Nunn, CL, Gittleman JL, and Antonovics, J. 2000. Promiscuity and the primate immune system. *Science* 290(5494): 1168–1170.

O'Connell, JF, and Allen, J. 1998. When did humans first arrive in Greater Australia and why is it important to know? *Evolutionary Anthropology* 6: 132–146.

O'Connell, JF, and Allen, J. 2004. Dating the colonization of Sahul (Pleistocene Australia–New Guinea): a review of recent research. *Journal of Archaeological Science* 31: 835–853.

O'Connell, JF, Hawkes, K, and Blurton Jones, NG. 1999. Grandmothering and the evolution of *Homo erectus. Journal of Human Evolution* 36: 461–485.

O'Connor, CF, Franciscus, RG, and Holton, NE. 2005. Bite force production capability and efficiency in Neandertals and modern humans. *American Journal of Physical Anthropology* 127: 129–151.

Oates, JF, Abedi-Lartey, M, McGraw, WS, et al. 2000. Extinction of a West African Red Colobus Monkey. *Conservation Biology* 14: 1526–1532.

Ogilvie, MD, Curran, BK, and Trinkaus, E. 1989. Incidence and patterning of dental enamel hypoplasia among the Neandertals. *American Journal of Physical Anthropology* 791: 25–41.

Ohigashi, H, Huffman MA, Izutsu D, et al. 1994. Toward the chemical ecology of medicinal plant use in chimpanzees: the case of *Vernonia amygdalina,* a plant used by wild chimpanzees possibly for parasite-related diseases. *Journal of Chemical Ecology* 20: 541–553.

Ohl, M. 2007. Principles of taxonomy and classification: current procedures for naming and classifying organisms. In W Henke and I Tattersall, eds., *Handbook of Paleoanthropology.* Berlin: Springer. 141–166.

Ohman, JC, Wood, C, Wood, B, et al. 2002. Stature-at-death of KNM-WT 15000. *Human Evolution* 17: 129–141.

Omran, AR. 1971. The epidemiologic transition: a theory of the epidemiology of population change. *Milbank Memorial Fund Quarterly* 49(1): 509–538.

Ordovas, JM, and Corella, D. 2004. Nutritional genomics. *Annual Review of Genomics and Human Genetics* 5: 71–118.

Ossenberg, NS. 2001. Lawrence Oschinsky: the contribution to Canadian osteology of a classical anthropologist. In L Sawchuk and S Pfeiffer, eds., *Out of the Past: The History of Human Osteology at the University of Toronto,* Toronto: CITD. http://citd-press.utsc.utoronto.ca/osteology/pfeiffer.html.

Ostner, J, Nunn, CL, and Schülke, O. 2008. Female reproductive synchrony predicts skewed paternity across primates. *Behavioral Ecology* 19: 1150–1158.

Ovchinnikov, IV, Götherström, A, Romanova, GP, et al. 2000. Molecular analysis of Neanderthal DNA from the northern Caucasus. *Nature* 404: 490–493.

Pääbo, S. 1985. Preservation of DNA in ancient Egyptian mummies. *Journal of Archaeological Science* 12: 411–417.

Padiak, J. 2008. The contribution of tuberculosis to the mortality of British soldiers 1830–1913. In *Multiplying and Dividing: Tuberculosis in Canada and Aotearoa New Zealand.* J Littleton, J Park, A Herring, et al., *Research in Anthropology and Linguistics*-e Number 3, 103–112.

Parker, M, and Harper, I. 2006. The anthropology of public health. *Journal of Biosocial Science* 38: 1–5.

Partridge, TC, Granger, DE, Caffee, MW, et al. 2003. Lower Pliocene hominid remains from Sterkfontein. *Science* 300: 607–12.

Paterson, HEH. 1985. The recognition concept of species. In E Vrba, ed., *Species and Speciation.* Transvaal Museum Monographs No. 4, Pretoria, pp. 21–29.

Patterson, N, Richter, DJ, Gnerre, S, et al. 2006. Genetic evidence for complex speciation of humans and chimpanzees. *Nature* 441: 1103–1108.

Pavelka, MSM. 1999. Primate gerontology. In P Dolhinow and A Fuentes, eds., *The Nonhuman Primates.* Mountain View: Mayfield. 220–224.

Pavelka, MSM, Brusselers, OT, Nowak, D, et al. 2003. Population reduction and social organization in *Alouatta pigra* following a hurricane. *International Journal of Primatology* 24: 1037–1055.

Pavelka, MSM, and Fedigan, LM. 1991. Menopause: A comparative life history perspective. *Yearbook of Physical Anthropology* 34: 13–38.

Pavelka, MSM, and Fedigan, LM. 1999. Reproductive termination in female Japanese monkeys: a comparative life history perspective. *American Journal of Physical Anthropology* 109: 455–464.

Pavelka, MSM, Fedigan, LM, and Zohar, S. 2002. Availability and adaptive value of reproductive and postreproductive Japanese macaque mothers and grandmothers. *Animal Behaviour* 64(3): 407–414.

Pavelka, MSM, McGoogan, KC, and Steffens, TS. 2007. Population size and characteristics of *Alouatta pigra* before and after a major hurricane. *International Journal of Primatology* 28: 919–929.

Pawlowski, B. 2007. Origins of homininae and putative selection pressures acting on the earliest hominins. In W Henke and I Tattersall, eds., *Handbook of Paleoanthropology*. Berlin: Springer. 1409–1440.

Pearson, OM, Cordero RM, and Busby, AM. 2008. How different were Neanderthals' habitual activities? A comparative analysis with diverse groups of recent humans. In K Harvati and T Harrison, eds., *Neanderthals Revisited: New Approaches and Perspectives*. Netherlands: Springer. 135–156.

Peccei, JS 2001. Menopause: adaptation or epiphenomenon? *Evolutionary Anthropology* 10: 43–57.

Pellan, MJ, and Matzke, NJ. 2006. From *The Origin of Species* to the origin of bacterial flagella. *Nature Reviews Microbiology* 4: 784–790.

Pelto, GH. 2008. Taking care of children: applying anthropology in maternal and child nutrition and health. *Human Organization* 67: 237–243.

Perry, GH, Dominy, NJ, Claw, KG, et al. 2007. Diet and the evolution of human amylase gene copy number variation. *Nature Genetics* 39: 1256–1260.

Perry, MJ. 2008. Effects of environmental and occupational pesticide exposure on human sperm: a systematic review. *Human Reproduction Update* 14: 233–242.

Pilbeam, D, and Young, N. 2004. Hominoid evolution: synthesizing disparate data. *Comptes Rendus Paleoevolution* 3: 305–321.

Pilcher, H. 2005. Apeing our language. *News@Nature.com* doi:10.1038/050829–8.

Pitulko, VV, Nikolsky, PA, Girya, EY, et al. 2004. The Yana RHS site: humans in the Arctic before the last glacial maximum. *Science* 303: 52–56.

Plagnol, V, and Wall, JD. 2006. Possible ancestral structure in human populations. *Public Library of Science Genetics* 2: 972–979.

Plavcan, JM. 2000. Inferring social behavior from sexual dimorphism in the fossil record. *Journal of Human Evolution* 39: 327–344.

Plavcan, JM. 2003. Scaling relationships between craniofacial sexual dimorphism and body mass dimorphism in primates: implications for the fossil record. *American Journal of Physical Anthropology* 120: 38–60.

Plavcan, JM, and Kelley, J. 1996. Evaluating the "dual selection" hypothesis of canine reduction. *American Journal of Physical Anthropology* 99: 379–387.

Poinar, H, Kuch, M, Sobolik, K, et al. 2001. A molecular analysis of dietary diversity for three archaic Native Americans. *Proceedings of the National Academy of Sciences* 98: 4317–4322.

Poolman, EM, and Galvani, AP. 2007. Evaluating candidate agents of selective pressure for cystic fibrosis. *Journal of the Royal Society Interface* 4: 91–98.

Ponce de León, MS, Golovanova, L, Doronichev, V, et al. 2008. Neanderthal brain size at birth provides insights into the evolution of human life history. *Proceedings of the National Academy of Sciences* 105: 13764–13768.

Pontzer, H, and Wrangham, R. 2006. Ontogeny of ranging in wild chimpanzees. *International Journal of Primatology* 27: 295–309.

Pope, GG. 1989. Bamboo and human evolution. *Natural History* 10: 49–56.

Potts, R. 1999. Variability selection in hominid evolution. *Evolutionary Anthropology* 7: 81–96.

Powell, JF, and Rose, JC. 1999. Report on the Osteological Assessment of the "Kennewick Man" Skeleton (CENWW.97. Kennewick). www.cr.nps.gov/aad/kennewick/powell_rose.htm (accessed May 9, 2010).

Prat, S, Brugal, J-P, Tiercelin, J-J, et al. 2005. First occurrence of early *Homo* in the Nachukui Formation (West Turkana, Kenya) at 2.3–2.4 myr. *Journal of Human Evolution* 49: 230–240.

Premo, LS, and Hublin, J-J. 2009. Culture, population structure, and low genetic diversity in Pleistocene hominins. *Proceedings of the National Academy of Sciences* 106(1): 33–37.

Profet, M. 1992. Pregnancy sickness as adaptation: A deterrent to maternal ingestion of teratogens. In JH Barkow, L Cosmides, and J Tooby, eds., *The Adapted Mind: Evolutionary Psychology and the Generation of Culture*. New York: Oxford University Press. 327–366.

Profet, M. 1993. Menstruation as a defense against pathogens transported by sperm. *Quarterly Review of Biology* 68: 335–386.

Prokosch, MD, Yeo, RA, and Miller, GF. 2005. Intelligence tests with higher g-loadings show higher correlations with body symmetry: evidence for a general fitness factor mediated by developmental stability. *Intelligence* 33: 203–213.

Prowse, TL, Saunders, SR, Schwarcz, HP, et al. 2008. Isotopic and dental evidence for infant and young child feeding practices in an Imperial Roman skeletal sample. *American Journal of Physical Anthropology* 137: 294–308.

Prowse, TL, Schwarcz, HP, Garnsey, P, et al. 2007. Isotopic evidence for age-related immigration to Imperial Rome. *American Journal of Physical Anthropology* 132: 510–519.

Prowse, TL, Schwarcz, HP, Saunders, SR, et al. 2004. Isotopic paleodiet studies of skeletons from the Imperial Roman-age cemetery of Isola Sacra, Rome, Italy. *Journal of Archaeological Science* 31: 259–272.

Pruetz, JD, and Bertolani, P. 2007. Savanna chimpanzees, *Pan troglodytes verus*, hunt with tools. *Current Biology* 17: 412–417.

Pusey, AE, Williams, J, and Goodall, J. 1997. The influence of dominance rank on the reproductive success of female chimpanzees. *Science* 277: 828–831.

Raff, RA. 2007. Book review: intelligent design judged and found wanting. *Evolution and Development* 9: 402–404.

Raichlen, D, Pontzer, H, and Sockol, M. 2008. The Laetoli footprints and early hominin locomotor kinematics. *Journal of Human Evolution* 54: 112–117.

Rak, Y. 1986. The Neanderthal: a new look at an old face. *Journal of Human Evolution* 15: 151–164.

Rak, Y, and Arensburg, B. 1987. Kebara 2 Neanderthal pelvis: first look at a complete inlet. *American Journal of Physical Anthropology* 73(2): 227–231.

Ramankutty, N, Foley, JA, and Olejniczak, NJ. 2008. Land-use change and global food production. In AK Braimoh and PLG Vlek, eds., *Land Use and Soil Resources*. Netherlands: Springer. 23–40.

Ramirez Rozzi, FV, and Bermúdez de Castro, JM. 2004. Surprisingly rapid growth in Neanderthals. *Nature* 428: 936–939.

Rankinen, T, Zuberi A, Chagnon YC, et al. 2006. The human obesity gene map: the 2005 update. *Obesity* 14: 529–644.

Rasmussen, DT. 2007. Fossil record of the primates from the Paleocene to the Oligocene. In W Henke and I Tattersall, eds., *Handbook of Palaeoanthropogy*, Berlin: Springer. 889–920.

Reader, SM, and LeLand, K. 2002. Social intelligence, innovation, and enhanced brain size in primates. *Proceedings of the National Academy of Sciences* 99: 4436–4441.

Reed, KE. 2008. Paleoecological patterns at the Hadar hominin site, Afar Regional State, Ethiopia. *Journal of Human Evolution* 54: 743–76.

Reich, PF, Numbem, ST, Almaraz, RA, et al. 2001. Land resource stresses and desertification in Africa. *Agro-Science* 2: 1–10.

Relethford, JH. 1997. Hemispheric difference in human skin colour. *American Journal of Physical Anthropology* 104: 449–457.

Relethford, JH. 2000. Human skin color diversity is highest in sub-Saharan African populations. *Human Biology* 72: 773–780.

Relethford, JH. 2001a. Ancient DNA and the origin of modern humans. *Proceedings of the National Academy of Sciences* 982: 390–391.

Relethford, JH. 2001b. Absence of regional affinities of Neandertal DNA with living humans does not reject multiregional evolution. *American Journal of Physical Anthropology* 115: 95–98.

Renner, R. 2003. Nietzsche's toxicology. *Scientific American* 289: 28–30.

Research Project Steering Committee. 2006. Northern Saskatchewan HIV/AIDS and HEPATITIS C Awareness Initiative: Research Project. SPHERU, University of Saskatchewan, Saskatoon. Available online at http://www.spheru.ca/www/html/Reports/Reports_aboriginal.htm.

Rice, G, Anderson, C, Risch, N, and Ebers, G. 1999. Male homosexuality: absence of linkage to microsatellite markers at Xq28. *Science* 284: 665–667.

Rice, PC. 1981. Prehistoric venuses: symbols of motherhood or womanhood? *Journal of Anthropological Research* 37: 402–404.

Richards, MP, Harvati, K, Grimes, V, et al. 2008. Strontium isotope evidence of Neanderthal mobility at the site of Lakonis, Greece, using laser-ablation PIMMS. *Journal of Archaeological Science* 35: 1251–1256.

Richards, MP, Jacobi, R, Cook, J, et al. 2005. Isotope evidence for the intensive use of marine foods by Late Upper Palaeolithic humans. *Journal of Human Evolution* 49: 390–394.

Richards MP, Pettitt, PB, Stiner, MC, et al. 2001. Stable isotope evidence for increasing dietary breadth in the European mid-Upper Paleolithic. *Proceedings of the National Academy of Sciences* 9811: 6528–6532.

Richards, MP, Pettitt, PB, Trinkaus, E, et al. 2000. Neanderthal diet at Vindija and Neanderthal predation: the evidence from stable isotopes. *Proceedings of the National Academy of Sciences* 9713: 7663–7666.

Richards, MP, and Schmitz, RW. 2008. Isotope evidence for the diet of the Neanderthal type specimen. *Antiquity* 82: 553–559.

Richmond, B, Begun, D, and Strait, DS. 2001. Origin of human bipedalism: the knuckle-walking hypothesis revisited. *Yearbook of Physical Anthropology* 44: 70–105.

Richmond, B, and Jungers, W. 2008. *Orrorin tugenensis* femoral morphology and the evolution of hominin bipedalism. *Science* 319: 1662–1665.

Ricklefs, RE, and Finch, CE. 1995. *Aging: A Natural History.* New York: Scientific American Library.

Rightmire, GP. 1998. Human evolution in the Middle Pleistocene: The role of *Homo heidelbergensis*. *Evolutionary Anthropology* 6: 218–227.

Rightmire, GP. 1998. Evidence from facial morphology for similarity of Asian and African representatives of *Homo erectus*. *American Journal of Physical Anthropology* 106: 61–85.

Rightmire, GP. 2007. Later Middle Pleistocene *Homo*. In W Henke and I Tattersall, eds., *Handbook of Paleoanthropology*, Berlin: Springer. 1695–1715.

Rightmire, GP, Lordkipanidze, D, and Vekua, A. 2006. Anatomical descriptions, comparative studies, and evolutionary significance of the hominin skulls from Dmanisi, Republic of Georgia. *Journal of Human Evolution* 502: 115–141.

Rilling, JK, and Seligman, RA. 2002. A quantitative morphometric comparative analysis of the primate temporal lobe. *Journal of Human Evolution* 42: 505–533.

Roberts, MB, and Parfitt, SA. 1999. A Middle Pleistocene hominid site at Eartham Quarry, Boxgrove, West Sussex. English Heritage Archaeological Report No. 17. London: English Heritage.

Roberts, RG, Westaway, KE, Zhao, J, et al. 2009. Geochronology of cave deposits at Liang Bua and of adjacent river terraces in the Wae Racang valley, western Flores, Indonesia: a synthesis of age estimates for the type locality of *Homo floresiensis*. *Journal of Human Evolution* 57(5): 484–502.

Robins, AH. 2009. The evolution of light skin color: role of vitamin D disputed. *American Journal of Physical Anthropology* 139(4): 447–450.

Robinson, JT. 1972. *Early Hominid Posture and Locomotion.* Chicago: University of Chicago Press.

Rodman, PS, and McHenry, H. 1980. Bioenergetics and the origin of hominid bipedalism. *American Journal of Physical Anthropology* 52: 103–106.

Rogers, TL, and Allard, T. 2004. Expert testimony and positive identification of human remains through cranial suture patterns. *Journal of Forensic Sciences* 49: 203–207.

Rosenberg, K, and Trevathan, W. 2003. The evolution of human birth. *Scientific American Special Edition* 13: 80–85.

Rosenberg, NA, Mahajan, S, Ramachandran, S, et al. 2005. Clines, clusters, and the effect of study design on the inference of human population structure. *Public Library of Science Genetics* 1: e70.

Ross, CF. 2000. Into the light: the origin of *Anthropoidea*. *Annual Review of Anthropology* 29: 147–194.

Roth, E, Ngugi, E, and Fujita, M. 2006. Self-deception does not explain high risk sexual behaviour in the face of HIV/AIDS: a test from northern Kenya. *Evolution and Human Behavior* 27: 53–62.

Roth, EA, Ngugi, E, and Fujita, M. 2009. HIV/AIDS risk and worry in Northern Kenya. *Health, Risk and Society* 11(3): 231–239.

Rougier, H, Milota, S, Rodrigo, R, et al. 2007. Peştera cu Oase 2 and the cranial morphology of early modern Europeans. *Proceedings of the National Academy of Sciences* 104: 1165–1170.

Rozen, S, Skaletsky, H, Marszalek, JD, et al. 2003. Abundant gene conversion between arms of palindromes in human and ape Y chromosomes. *Nature* 423: 873–876.

Rudolph, KL, Millard, M, Bosenberg, MW, et al. 2001. Telomere dysfunction and evolution of intestinal carcinoma in mice and humans. *Nature Genetics* 28:155–159.

Ruff, CB. 2002. Variation in human body size and shape. *Annual Reviews of Anthropology* 31: 211–232.

Ruff, CB. 2008. Relative limb strength and locomotion in *Homo habilis*. *American Journal of Physical Anthropology* 1381: 90–100.

Ruff, CB, and Walker, A. 1993. Body size and body shape. In A Walker and R Leakey, eds., *The Nariokotome Homo erectus Skeleton*. Cambridge, MA: Harvard University Press. 234–263.

Ruiz-Torres, A, and Beier, W. 2005. On maximum human lifespan: interdisciplinary approach about its limits. *Advances in Gerontology* 16: 14–20.

Ruse, M. 1992. Darwinism. In EF Keller and EF Lloyd, eds., *Keywords in Evolutionary Biology*. Cambridge, MA: Harvard University Press.

Russell, MD. 1987. Mortuary practices at the Krapina Neandertal site. *American Journal of Physical Anthropology* 72: 381–397.

Rylko-Bauer, B, Singer, M, and Van Willigen, J. 2006. Reclaiming applied anthropology: its past, present, and future. *American Anthropologist* 108: 178–190.

Sanger, M. 1922. *Woman, Morality, and Birth Control*. New York: New York Publishing.

Sankar, P, and Kahn, JD. 2005 (October 11). BiDil: race medicine or race marketing? *Health Affairs*.

Sanna, S, Jackson, AU, Nagaraja, R, et al. 2008. Common variants in the GDF5-UQCC region are associated with variation in human height. *Nature Genetics* 40: 198–203.

Sanz, C, Morgan D, and Gulick S. 2004. New insights into chimpanzees, tools, and termites from the Congo Basin. *American Naturalist* 164: 567–581.

Sapolsky, RM. 2005. The influence of social hierarchy on primate health. *Science* 308: 648–652.

Sarich, VM, and Wilson, AC. 1967. Immunological time scale for hominoid evolution. *Science* 158: 1200–1203.

Sato, A, Tichy, H, O'hUigin, C, et al. 2001. On the origin of Darwin's finches. *Molecular Biology and Evolution* 18: 299–311.

Sattenspiel, L, and Herring, DA .1998. Structured epidemic models and the spread of influenza in the central Canadian subarctic. *Human Biology* 701: 91–115.

Saunders, SR, DeVito, C, and Katzenberg, MA. 1997. Dental caries in nineteenth century Upper Canada. *American Journal of Physical Anthropology* 1041: 71–87.

Saunders, SR, Hoppa, R, and Southern, R. 1993. Diaphyseal growth in a nineteenth century skeletal sample of subadults from St Thomas' church, Belleville, Ontario. *International Journal of Osteoarchaeology* 3: 265–281.

Savage, TS. 1847. Notice of the external characters and habits of *Troglodytes gorilla*, a new species of orang from the Gaboon River. With J. Wyman. *Boston Journal of Natural History* 5: 417–443.

Sawchuk, LA, and Burke, SDA. 1998. Gibraltar's 1804 yellow fever scourge: the search for scapegoats. *Journal of the History of Medicine and Allied Sciences* 53: 3–42.

Sawchuk, LA, and Burke, SDA. 2003. The ecology of a health crisis: Gibraltar and the 1865 cholera epidemic. *Cambridge Studies in Biological and Evolutionary Anthropology* 34: 178–215.

Sayers, K, and Lovejoy, CO. 2008. The chimpanzee has no clothes. *Current Anthropology* 49: 87–114.

Schell, L, Ravenscroft, J, Gallo, M, et al. 2007. Advancing biocultural models by working with communities: a partnership approach. *American Journal of Human Biology* 19: 511–524.

Scheonberg, MR, Lange, RT, and Saklofske, DH. 2007. A proposed method to estimate premorbid full scale intelligence quotient (FSIQ) for the Canadian Wechsler Intelligence Scale for Children–Fourth Edition (WISC-IV) using demographic and combined estimation procedures. *Journal of Clinical and Experimental Neuropsychology* 29: 867–878.

Scheper-Hughes, N, and Bourgois, P. 2004. Introduction: Making sense of violence. In N Scheper-Hughes and P Bourgois, eds., *Violence in War and Peace: An Anthology*. Malden: Blackwell. 2–31.

Schick, KD, Toth, N, Garufi, G, et al. 1999. Continuing investigations into the stone tool-making and tool-using capabilities of a bonobo (*Pan paniscus*). *Journal of Archaeological Science* 26: 821–832.

Schillaci, MA, Jones-Engel, L, Engel, GA, et al. 2005. Prevalence of enzootic simian viruses among urban performance monkeys in Indonesia. *Tropical Medicine and International Health* 10: 1305–1314.

Schillaci, MA, Jones-Engel, L, Engel, GA, et al. 2006. Exposure to human respiratory viruses among urban performing monkeys in Indonesia. *American Journal of Tropical Medicine and Hygiene* 75: 716–719.

Schino, G. 2001. Grooming, competition, and social rank among female primates: a meta-analysis. *Animal Behaviour* 62: 265–271.

Schmitt, D, Churchill, SE, and Hylander, WL. 2003. Experimental evidence concerning spear use in Neandertals and early modern humans. *Journal of Archaeological Science* 301: 103–114.

Schmitz, RW, Serre, D, Bonani, G, et al. 2002. The Neandertal type site revisited: interdisciplinary investigations of skeletal remains from the Neander Valley, Germany. *Proceedings of the National Academy of Sciences* 99(20): 13342–13347.

Schoetensack, O. 1908. Der Unterkiefer des *Homo Heidelbergensis* aus den Sanden von Mauer bei Heidelberg. Ein Beitrag zur Paläontologie des Menschen. *Molecular and General Genetics* 11: 408–410.

Schrago, CG, and Russo, CAM. 2003. Timing the origin of New World monkeys. *Molecular Biology and Evolution* 2010: 1620–1625.

Schrenk, F, Bromage, T, Beltzer, CG, et al. 1993. Oldest *Homo* and Pliocene biogeography of the Malawi Rift. *Nature* 365: 833–836.

Schrenk, F, Kullmer, O, and Bromage, T. 2007. The earliest putative *Homo* fossils. In W Henke and I Tattersall, eds., *Handbook of Paleoanthropology*. Berlin: Springer. 1611–1631.

Schurr, TG. 2004. The peopling of the New World. *Annual Review of Anthropology* 33: 551–583.

Schwartz, JH, and Tattersall, I. 1996. Whose teeth? *Nature* 381: 201–202.

Sclater, A. 2006. The extent of Darwin's knowledge of Mendel. *Journal of Biosciences* 31: 191–193.

Searle, JB. 1998. Speciation, chromosomes, and genomes. *Genome Research* 8: 1–3.

Séguin, L, Nikiéma, B, Gauvin, L, et al. 2007. Duration of poverty and child Health in the Quebec Longitudinal Study of Child Development: Longitudinal analysis of a birth cohort. *Pediatrics* 119: e1063–e1070.

Sellen, DW. 2007. Evolution of infant and young child feeding: implications for contemporary public health. *Annual Review of Nutrition* 27: 123–148.

Sellers, WI, Dennis, LA, and Crompton, RH. 2003. Predicting the metabolic energy costs of bipedalism using evolutionary robotics. *Journal of Experimental Biology* 206: 1127–1136.

Semaw, A, Simpson, S, Quade, J, et al. 2005. Early Pliocene hominids from Gona, Ethiopia. *Nature* 433: 301–305.

Semaw, S, Rogers, MJ, Quade, J, et al. 2003. 2.6-million-year-old stone tools and associated bones from OGS-6 and OGS-7, Gona, Afar, Ethiopia. *Journal of Human Evolution* 452: 169–177.

Semendeferi K, and Damasio H. 2000. The brain and its main anatomical subdivisions in living hominoids using magnetic resonance imaging. *Journal of Human Evolution* 38(2): 317–332.

Semendeferi, K, Lu, A, Schenker, A, et al. 2002. Humans and great apes share a large frontal cortex. *Nature Neuroscience* 5: 272–276.

Senut B, Pickford, M, Gommery, D, et al. 2001. First hominid from the Miocene (Lukeino Formation, Kenya). *Comptes Rendus de l'Académie des Sciences—Series IIA—Earth and Planetary Science* 332: 137–144.

Sepulchre, P, Ramstei, G, Fluteau, F, et al. 2006. Tectonic uplift and eastern African aridification. *Science* 313: 1419–1423.

Serre, D, Langaney, A, Chech, M, et al. 2004. No evidence of Neandertal mtDNA contribution to early modern humans. *Public Library of Science Biology* 2: 313–317.

Shang, H, Tong, H, Zhang, S, et al. 2007. An early modern human from Tianyuan Cave, Zhoukoudian, China. *Proceedings of the National Academy of Sciences* 10416: 6573–6578.

Shephard, R, and Rode, A. 1996. *The Health Consequences of 'Modernization': Evidence from the Circumpolar North*. New York: Oxford University Press.

Shipman, P. 1986. Scavenging or hunting in early hominids. *American Anthropologist* 88: 27–43.

Shipman, P, and Rose, J. 1983. Evidence of butchery and hominid activities at Torralba and Ambrona: an evaluation using microscopic techniques. *Journal of Archaeological Science* 10(5): 465–74.

Sibley, C, and Ahlquist, JE. 1984. The phylogeny of the hominoid primates as indicated by DNA-DNA hybridization. *Journal of Molecular Evolution* 20: 2–15.

Sibley, CG, and Ahlquist, JE. 1987. DNA hybridization evidence of hominoid phylogeny: results from an expanded data set. *Journal of Molecular Evolution* 26: 99–121.

Sibley, CG, Comstock, JA, and Ahlquist, JE. 1990. DNA hybridization evidence of hominoid phylogeny: a reanalysis of the data. *Journal of Molecular Evolution* 30: 202–236.

Silk, JB. 2002. The form and function of reconciliation in primates. *Annual Review of Anthropology* 31: 21–44.

Silver, LM. 1998. *Remaking Eden: How Genetic Engineering and Cloning Will Transform the American Family*. New York: Avon.

Silver, LM. 2000. Reprogenetics: third millennium speculation. *EMBO Reports* 1: 375–378.

Simons, EL. 1995. Egyptian Oligocene primates: a review. *Yearbook of Physical Anthropology* 38: 199–238.

Simons, EL. 2008. Eocene and Oligocene Mammals of the Fayum, Egypt. In JC Fleagle and CC Gilbert, eds., *Elwyn Simons: A Search for Origins*. New York: Springer. 87–105.

Simons, EL, and Bown, TM. 1985. *Afrotarsius chatrathi*, first tarsiiform primate (? Tarsiidae) from Africa. *Nature* 313: 475–477.

Skaletsky, H, Kuroda-Kawaguchi, T, Minx, PJ, et al. 2003. The male-specific region of the human Y chromosome is a mosaic of discrete sequence classes. *Nature* 423: 825–837.

Skinner, MF, and Sterenberg, J. 2005. Turf wars: authority and responsibility for the investigation of mass graves. *Forensic Science International* 151: 221–232.

Skinner, MM, and Wood, BA. 2006. The evolution of modern human life history. In K Hawkes and RR Paine, eds., *The Evolution of Human Life History*. Albuquerque: School of American Research Press. 331–400.

Skinner, MM, Wood, BA, Boesch, C, et al. 2008. Dental trait expression at the enamel-dentine junction of lower molars in extant and fossil hominoids. *Journal of Human Evolution* 54: 173–186.

Slocombe, KE, and Zuberbühler, K. 2006. Food-associated calls in chimpanzees: responses to food types or food preferences? *Animal Behaviour* 72: 989–999.

Smail, JK. 2002. Remembering Malthus—a preliminary argument for a significant reduction in global human numbers. *American Journal of Physical Anthropology* 118: 292–297.

Smail, JK. 2003a. Remembering Malthus II—establishing sustainable population optimums. *American Journal of Physical Anthropology* 122: 287–294.

Smail, JK 2003b. Remembering Malthus III—implementing a global population reduction. *American Journal of Physical Anthropology* 122: 295–300.

Small, M. 1989. Female choice in nonhuman primates. *Yearbook of Physical Anthropology* 32: 103–127.

Small, M. 1995. *What's Love Got to Do with It?* New York: Doubleday.

Smedley, A, and Smedley, BD. 2005. Race as biology is fiction, racism as a social problem is real: anthropological and historical perspectives on the social construction of race. *American Psychologist* 60: 16–26.

Smith, AC, et al. 2003. The effect of colour vision status on the detection and selection of fruits by tamarins (Saguinus spp.). *Journal of Experimental Biology* 206: 3159–3165.

Smith, BH. 1993. The physiological age of KNM-WT 15000. In A Walker and R Leakey, eds., *The Nariokotome Homo erectus Skeleton*. Cambridge, MA: Harvard University Press. 195–220.

Smith, FH, Jankovi´c, I, and Karavani´c, I. 2005. The assimilation model, modern human origins in Europe, and the extinction of Neandertals. *Quaternary International* 137: 7–19.

Smith, SL. 2004. Skeletal age, dental age, and the maturation of KNM-WT 15000. *American Journal of Physical Anthropology* 125: 105–120.

Smith, T, Olejniczak, A, Reh, S, et al. 2008. Brief communication: enamel thickness trends in the dental arcade of humans and chimpanzees. *American Journal of Physical Anthropology* 136: 237–241.

Smith, T, Rose, KD, and Gingerich, P. 2006. Rapid Asia–Europe–North America geographic dispersal of earliest Eocene primate *Teilhardina* during the Paleocene–Eocene thermal maximum. *Proceedings of the National Academy of Sciences* 103: 11223–11227.

Society for Applied Anthropology. 2009. Mission Statement. http://www.sfaa.net/sfaagoal.html (accessed 2008–12–21).

Sockol, MD, Raichlen, DA, and Pontzer, H. 2007. Chimpanzee locomotor energetics and the origin of human bipedalism. *Proceedings of the National Academy of Sciences* 104: 12265–12269.

Soficaru, A, Doboș, A, and Trinkaus, E. 2006. Early modern humans from the Peștera Muierii, Baia de Fier, Romania. *Proceedings of the National Academy of Sciences* 103(46): 17196–17201.

Solecki, R. 1971. *Shanidar: The First Flower People.* New York: Knopf.

Sommer, JD. 1999. The Shanidar IV 'flower burial': a re-evaluation of Neanderthal burial ritual. *Cambridge Archaeological Journal* 9: 127–129.

Sparks, CS, and Jantz, RL. 2003. Changing times, changing faces: Franz Boas's immigrant study in modern perspective. *American Anthropologist* 105: 333–337.

Speakman, JR. 2006. Thrifty genes for obesity and the metabolic syndrome—time to call off the search? *Diabetes and Vascular Disease Research* 31: 7–11.

Spencer, F. 1990. *Piltdown: A Scientific Forgery.* Oxford: Oxford University Press.

Spigelman, M, Matheson C, Lev G, et al. 2002. Confirmation of the presence of *Mycobacterium tuberculosis* complex-specific DNA in three archaeological specimens. *International Journal of Osteoarchaeology* 12: 393–401.

Spoor, F, Leakey, MG, Gathogo, PN, et al. 2007. Implications of new early *Homo* fossils from Ileret, east of Lake Turkana, Kenya. *Nature* 448: 688–691.

Stanford, C, Allen, JS, Anton, SC, and Lovell, NC. 2000. *Biological Anthropology.* Canadian Edition. Toronto: Pearson Prentice Hall.

Statistics Canada, 2006. Census. www.statcan.gc.ca.

Steadman, DW, Adams, BJ, and Konigsberg, LW. 2006. Statistical basis for positive identification in forensic anthropology. *American Journal of Physical Anthropology* 131: 27–32.

Stephens, D, and Dudley, R. 2004. The drunken monkey hypothesis: the study of fruit-eating animals could lead to an evolutionary understanding of human alcohol abuse. *Natural History* 113: 40–44.

Stern JT, Jr. 1975. Before bipedality. *Yearbook of Physical Anthropology* 19: 59–68.

Steudel-Numbers, K, and Tilkins, MJ. 2004. The effect of lower limb length on the energetic cost of locomotion: implications for fossil hominins. *Journal of Human Evolution* 47: 95–109.

Steudel-Numbers, K, Weaver, TD, and Wall-Scheffler, CM. 2007. The evolution of human running: Effects of changes in lower-limb length on locomotor economy. *Journal of Human Evolution* 53: 191–196.

Stock, JT, and Pfeiffer, SK. 2001. Linking structural variability in long bone diaphyses to habitual behaviors: foragers from the southern African Later Stone Age and the Andaman Islands. *American Journal of Physical Anthropology* 115: 337–348.

Stock, JT, and Pfeiffer, SK. 2004. Long bone robusticity and subsistence behaviour among Later Stone Age foragers of the forest and fynbos biomes of South Africa. *Journal of Archaeological Science* 31: 999–1013.

Stone, AC, Milner GR, Pääbo S, et al. 1996. Sex determination of ancient human skeletons using DNA. *American Journal of Physical Anthropology* 99: 231–238.

Strassmann, BI. 1999. Menstrual cycling and breast cancer: an evolutionary perspective. *Journal of Women's Health* 82: 193–202.

Strier, KB 2003. *Primate Behavioral Ecology,* 2nd ed. Toronto: Allyn and Bacon.

Stringer, CB. 2001. Modern human origins—distinguishing the models. *African Archaeological Review* 182: 67–75.

Stringer, CB. 2008. The Neanderthal–*H. sapiens* interface in Eurasia. In K Harvati and T Harrison, eds., *Neanderthals Revisited: New Approaches and Perspectives.* New York: Springer. 315–324.

Stringer, CB, and Andrews, P. 1988. Genetic and fossil evidence for the origin of modern humans. *Science* 239 (4845): 1263–1268.

Stringer, CB, Palike H, van Andel TH, et al. 2004. Climatic stress and the extinction of the Neanderthals. In TH van Andel and W Davies, eds., *Neanderthal and Modern Humans in the European Landscape of the Last Glaciation,* Mcdonald Institute Monographs. Toronto: Brown Book Company. 233–240.

Struhsaker, TT, Cooney, DO, and Siex, KS. 1997. Charcoal consumption by Zanzibar red colobus monkeys: its function and its ecological and demographic consequences. *International Journal of Primatology* 181: 61–72.

Strum, S, and Fedigan, LM, eds. 2000. *Primate Encounters.* Chicago: University of Chicago Press.

Stuart-MacAdam, P. 1992. Porotic hyperostosis: A new perspective. *American Journal of Physical Anthropology* 87: 39–47.

Stumpf, RM, Thompson, ME, and Nott, CD. 2008. A comparison of female mating strategies in *Pan troglodytes* and *Pongo* spp. *International Journal of Primatology* 29: 865–884.

Sturm, RA, and Frudakis, TN. 2004. Eye colour: portals into pigmentation genes and ancestry. *Trends in Genetics* 20: 327–332.

Susman, RL. 2008. Brief communication: evidence bearing on the status of *Homo habilis* at Olduvai Gorge. *American Journal of Physical Anthropology* 137: 356–361.

Sussman, RW, Cheverud, JM, and Bartlett, TQ. 1995. Infant killing as an evolutionary strategy. *Evolutionary Anthropology* 3: 149–151.

Sussman, RW. 1991. Primate origins and the evolution of angiosperms. *American Journal of Primatology* 23: 209–223.

Suwa, G, and Kono, R. 2005. A micro-CT based study of linear enamel thickness in the mesial cusp section of human molars: re-evaluation of methodology and assessment of within-tooth, serial, and individual variation. *Anthropological Science* 113: 273–289.

Suwa, G, Kono, RT, Katoh, S, et al. 2007. A new species of great ape from the late Miocene epoch in Ethiopia. *Nature* 448, 921–924.

Suzuki, H, and Hanihara, K. 1982. *The Minatogawa Man: The Upper Pleistocene Man from the Island of Okinawa.* Tokyo: University of Tokyo Press.

Swedell, L. 2006. *Strategies of Sex and Survival in Hamadryas Baboons: Through a Female Lens.* Upper Saddle River: Pearson.

Swindler, DR. 1998. *Introduction to the Primates.* Seattle: University of Washington Press.

Swisher, CC III, Curtis, GH, Jacob, T, et al. 1994. Age of the earliest known hominids in Java, Indonesia. *Science* 263: 1118–1121.

Swisher, CC, III, Rink, WJ, Antón, SC, et al. 1996. Latest *Homo erectus* of Java: potential contemporaneity with *Homo sapiens* in Southeast Asia. *Science* 274: 1870–1874.

Szalay, FS, and Costello, RK. 1991. Evolution of permanent estrus displays in hominids. *Journal of Human Evolution* 20: 439–464.

Szathmary, EJE. 1994. Non-insulin dependent diabetes mellitus among aboriginal North Americans. *Annual Review of Anthropology* 23: 457–480.

Tattersall, I. 1982. *The Primates of Madagascar.* New York: Columbia University Press.

Tattersall, I. 2007. *Homo ergaster* and its contemporaries. In W Henke and I Tattersall, eds., *Handbook of Paleoanthropology.* Berlin: Springer. 1633–1653.

Tattersall, I, and Schwartz, JH. 1999. Hominids and hybrids: the place of Neanderthals in human evolution. *Proceedings of the National Academy of Sciences* 96: 7117–7119.

Teaford, MF. 1988. Scanning electron microscope diagnosis of wear patterns versus artifacts on fossil teeth. *Scanning Microscopy* 2: 1167–1175.

Teaford, MF, and Walker, A. 1984. Quantitative differences in dental microwear between primate species with different diets and a comment on the presumed diet of *Sivapithecus. American Journal of Physical Anthropology* 64: 191–200.

Teichroeb, JA, and Sicotte, P. 2008. Infanticide in ursine colobus monkeys (*Colobus vellerosus*) in Ghana: new cases and a test of the existing hypothesis. *Behaviour* 145: 727–755.

Temple, R, and Stockbridge, NL. 2007. BiDil for heart failure in black patients: the U.S. Food and Drug Administration perspective. *Annals of Internal Medicine* 146: 57–62.

Templeton, AR. 2005. Haplotype trees and modern human origins. *Yearbook of Physical Anthropology* 48: 33–59.

Thieme, H. 1997. Lower Palaeolithic hunting spears from Germany. *Nature* 385: 807–810.

Thompson, JL, and Nelson, AJ. 2000. The place of Neandertals in the evolution of hominid patterns of growth and development. *Journal of Human Evolution* 38: 475–495.

Thorne, AG, and Wolpoff, MH. 1992. The multiregional evolution of humans. *Scientific American* 266: 76–83.

Thorne, AG, Grün, R, Mortimer, G, et al. 1999. Australia's oldest human remains: age of the Lake Mungo 3 skeleton. *Journal of Human Evolution* 36: 591–612.

Thorpe, S, Holder, R, and Crompton, R. 2007. Origin of human bipedalism as an adaptation for locomotion on flexible branches. *Science* 316: 1328–1331.

Tiemei, C, Quan, Y, and En, W. 1994. Antiquity of *Homo sapiens* in China. *Nature* 368: 55–56.

Timpson, N, Heron, J, Smith, GD, et al. 2007. Comment on papers by Evans et al. and Mekel-Bobrov et al. on evidence for positive selection of *MCPH1* and *ASPM. Science* 317: 1036a.

Tishkoff, SA, Reed, FA, Ranciaro, A, et al. 2007. Convergent adaptation of human lactase persistence in Africa and Europe. *Nature Genetics* 39: 31–40.

Tobias, PV. 1991. *Olduvai Gorge,* Vol. 4. *The Skulls, Endocasts, and Teeth of Homo habilis.* Cambridge: Cambridge University Press.

Tobias, PV, Wang, Q, and Cormack, J. 2000. Davidson Black and Raymond A. Dart: Asian-African parallels in palaeoanthropology. *Acta Anthropologica Sinica Supplement* 19: 299–306.

Tobias, PV, Wang, Q, and Cormack, J. 2001. The establishment of palaeoanthropology in South Africa and China: with especial reference to the remarkably similar roles of Raymond A. Dart and Davidson Black. *Transactions of the Royal Society of South Africa* 561: 1–9.

Tocheri, MW, Marzke, MW, Liu, D, et al. 2003. Functional capabilities of modern and fossil hominid hands: three-dimensional analysis of trapezia. *American Journal of Physical Anthropology* 122: 101–112.

Tocheri, MW, Orr, CM, Jacofsky, et al. 2008. The evolutionary history of the hominin hand since the last common ancestor of *Pan* and *Homo. Journal of Anatomy* 212: 544–562.

Tocheri, MW, Orr, CM, Lasen, SJ, et al. 2007. The primitive wrist of *Homo floresiensis* and its implications for hominin evolution. *Science* 317: 1743–5.

Toro, R, and Burnod, Y. 2005. A morphogenetic model for the development of cortical convolutions. *Cerebral Cortex* 15: 1900–1913.

Tosi, AJ, Morales, JC, and Melnick, DJ. 2000. Comparison of Y chromosome and mtDNA phylogenies leads to unique inferences of macaque evolutionary history. *Molecular Phylogenetics and Evolution* 17: 133–144.

Toth, N, Schick, KD, Savage-Rumbaugh, ES, et al. 1993. Pan the tool-maker: investigations into the stone tool-making and tool-using capabilities of a bonobo (*Pan paniscus*). *Journal of Archaeological Science* 20: 81–91.

Townsend, SW, Slocombe, KE, Thompson, ME, et al. 2007. Female-led infanticide in wild chimpanzees. *Current Biology* 1710: R355–R356.

Tremblay, MS, Perez, CE, Ardern, CI, et al. 2005. Obesity, overweight, and ethnicity. *Health Reports* 16(4): 23–32.

Tremblay, MS, and Willms, JD. 2000. Secular trends in the body mass index of Canadian children. *Canadian Medical Association Journal* 16311: 1429–1433.

Trevathan, W. 2007. Evolutionary medicine. *Annual Review of Anthropology* 36: 139–154.

Trinkaus, E. 1983. *The Shanidar Neanderthals.* New York: Academic Press.

Trinkaus, E. 1984. Neandertal pubic morphology and gestation length. *Current Anthropology* 25: 500–514.

Trinkaus, E. 1985. Cannibalism and burial at Krapina. *Journal of Human Evolution* 14: 203–216.

Trinkaus, E. 1995. Neanderthal mortality patterns. *Journal of Archaeological Science* 221: 121–142.

Trinkaus, E. 2005. Early modern humans. *Annual Review of Anthropology* 34: 207–230.

Trinkaus, E. 2007. European early modern humans and the fate of Neandertals. *Proceedings of the National Academy of Sciences* 104: 7367–7372.

Trinkaus, E, Moldovan, O, Milota, S, et al. 2003. An early modern human from the Peştera cu Oase, Romania. *Proceedings of the National Academy of Sciences* 100: 11231–11236.

Trinkaus, E, and Zimmerman, MR. 1982. Trauma among the Shanidar Neandertals. *American Journal of Physical Anthropology* 571: 61–76.

Trivers, RL. 1972. Parental investment and sexual selection. In B Campbell, ed., *Sexual Selection and the Descent of Man, 1871–1971.* Chicago: Aldine. 136–179.

Turk, Ivan, ed. 1997. *Mousterian Bone Flute.* Znanstvenoraziskovalni Center Sazu, Ljubljana, Slovenia.

Turney, CSM, Bird, MI, Fifield, LK, et al. 2001. Early human occupation at Devil's Lair, Southwestern Australia, 50,000 years ago. *Quaternary Research* 55: 3–13.

Twitchett, RJ. 2006. The palaeoclimatology, palaeoecology, and palaeoenvironmental analysis of mass extinction events. *Palaeogeography, Palaeoclimatology, Palaeoecology* 232: 190–213.

Ulijaszek, SJ, and Lofink, H. 2006. Obesity in biocultural perspective. *Annual Review of Anthropology* 35: 337–360.

Ungar, P. 2004. Dental topography and diets of *Australopithecus afarensis* and early *Homo*. *Journal of Human Evolution* 46: 605–622.

Ungar, PS 1996. Dental microwear of European Miocene catarrhines: evidence for diets and tooth use. *Journal of Human Evolution* 31: 335–366.

Ungar, PS, Grine, FE, and Teaford, MF. 2006. Diet in early *Homo*: a review of the evidence and a new model of adaptive versatility. *Annual Review of Anthropology* 35: 209–228.

Ungar, PS, Grine, FE, and Teaford, MF. 2008. Dental microwear and diet of the Plio-Pleistocene hominin *Paranthropus boisei*. *Public Library of Science ONE* 3: e2044.

Ungar, PS, Grine, FE, Teaford, MF, et al. 2006. Dental microwear and diets of African early *Homo*. *Journal of Human Evolution* 50: 78–95.

Valderrama, X, Robinson, JG, Attygalle, AB, et al. 2000. Seasonal anointment with millipedes in a wild primate: a chemical defense against insects? *Journal of Chemical Ecology* 2612: 2781–2790.

VandeBerg, JL, Williams-Blangero, S, Dyke, B, et al. 2000. Examining priorities for a primate genome project. Letters. *Science* 290(5496): 1504–1505.

van Heuverswyn, F, and Peeters, M. 2007. The origins of HIV and implications for the global epidemic. *Current Infectious Disease Reports* 9: 338–346.

van Oostdam, J, Donaldson, SG, Feeley, M, et al. 2005. Human health implications of environmental contaminants in Arctic Canada: a review. *Science of the Total Environment* 351–352: 165–246.

van Schaik, CP, Ancrenaz, M, Borgen, G, et al. 2003. Orangutan cultures and the evolution of material culture. *Science* 299(5603): 102–105.

van Schaik, CP, and Janson, CH. 2000. *Infanticide by Males and Its Implications*. Cambridge: Cambridge University Press.

van Valen, L. 1973. A new evolutionary law. *Evolutionary Theory* 1: 1–30.

Varki, A. 2000. A chimpanzee genome project is a biomedical imperative. *Genome Research* 10: 1065–1070.

Varki, A, and Nelson, DL. 2007. Genomic comparisons of humans and chimpanzees. *Annual Review of Anthropology* 36: 191–209.

Varrela, J. 2006. Masticatory function and malocclusion: a clinical perspective. *Seminars in Orthodontics* 12: 102–109.

Vasey, PL. 1995. Homosexual behavior in primates: a review of the evidence and theory. *International Journal of Primatology* 16(3): 173–204.

Vekua, A, Lordkipanidze, D, Rightmire, GP, et al. 2002. A new skull of early *Homo* from Dmanisi, Georgia. *Science* 297(5578): 85–89.

Venter, JC, Adams, MD, Myers, EW, et al. 2001. The sequence of the human genome. *Science* 291: 1304–1351.

Veraska, A, Del Campo, M, and McGinnis, W. 2000. Developmental patterning genes and their conserved functions: from model organisms to humans. *Molecular Genetics and Metabolism* 68: 85–100.

Vetter, J. 2006. Wallace's *other* line: human biogeography and field practice in the Eastern colonial tropics. *Journal of the History of Biology* 39: 89–123.

Videan, EN, and McGrew, WC. 2001. Are bonobos (*Pan paniscus*) really more bipedal than chimpanzees (*Pan troglodytes*)? *American Journal of Primatology* 54: 233–239.

Visscher, PM, Macgregor, S, Benyamin, B, et al. 2007. Genome partitioning of genetic variation for height from 11,214 sibling pairs. *American Journal of Human Genetics* 81: 1104–1110.

von Hunnius, TE, Roberts, CA, Boylston, A, et al. 2006. Histological identification of syphilis in pre-Columbian England. *American Journal of Physical Anthropology* 129: 559–566.

Wagner, DP, and McAvoy, JM. 2004. Pedoarchaeology of Cactus Hill, a sandy Paleoindian site in southeastern Virginia, USA. *Geoarchaeology* 19: 297–322.

Waldram, J, Herring, A, and Kue Young, T. 2006. *Aboriginal Health in Canada: Historical, Cultural, and Epidemiological Perspectives*, 2nd ed. Toronto: University of Toronto Press.

Walker, AC, and Leakey, REF, eds. 1993. *The Nariokotome Homo erectus Skeleton*. Cambridge, MA: Harvard University Press.

Walker, J, Cliff, R, and Latham, A.2006. U-Pb isotopic age of the StW 573 hominid from Sterkfontein, South Africa. *Science* 314: 1592–1594.

Wall-Scheffler, CM, Geiger, K, and Steudel-Numbers, K. 2007. Infant carrying: the role of increased locomotory costs in early tool development. *American Journal of Physical Anthropology* 133: 841–846.

Ward, LM, Gaboury, I, Ladhani, M, et al. 2007. Vitamin D-deficiency rickets among children in Canada. *Canadian Medical Association Journal* 1772: 161–166.

Washburn, SL. 1951. The new physical anthropology. *Transactions of the New York Academy of Science* 13 (2d ser.): 298–304.

Washburn, SL. 1960. Tools and evolution. *Scientific American* 203: 63–75.

Watanabe, T, Watanabe, S, Shinya, K, et al. 2009. Viral RNA polymerase complex promotes optimal growth of 1918 virus in the lower respiratory tract of ferrets. *Proceedings of the National Academy of Sciences* 106: 587–591.

Waters-Rist, A, Bazaliiskii, VI, Weber, A, et al. 2010. Activity-induced dental modification in Holocene Siberian hunter-fisher-gatherers. *American Journal of Physical Anthropology* (published online May 3, 2010).

Watson, J, Payne, R, Chamberlain, A, et al. 2009. The kinematics of load carrying in humans and great apes: implications for the evolution of human bipedalism. *International Journal of Primatology* 80: 309ff.

Weaver, TD, Roseman, CC, and Stringer, CB. 2007. Were Neandertal and modern human cranial differences produced by natural selection or genetic drift? *Journal of Human Evolution* 53: 135–145.

Weiner, JS. 1979. Beyond physical anthropology. *RAIN* 32: 3–7.

Weiner, S, Xu, Q, Goldberg, P, et al. 1998. Evidence for the use of fire at Zhoukoudian, China. *Science* 281: 251–253.

Weiss, K. 2004. The unkindest cup. *The Lancet* 363: 1489–1490.

Weiss, SF. 2006. Human genetics and politics as mutually beneficial resources: the case of the Kaiser Wilhelm Institute for Anthropology, human heredity, and eugenics during the Third Reich. *Journal of the History of Biology* 39: 41–88.

Weyrich, T, Matusik, W, Pfister, H, et al. 2008. Analysis of human faces using a measurement-based skin reflectance model. Accessed online at http://people.csail.mit.edu/addy/research/weyrich06-skin.pdf October 25, 2008.

Wheeler, PE. 1994. The foraging times of bipedal and quadrupedal hominids in open equatorial environments (a reply to Chaplin, Jablonski, and Cable, 1994). *Journal of Human Evolution* 27: 511–517.

Whitcome, KK, Shapiro, LJ, and Lieberman, DE. 2007. Fetal load and the evolution of lumbar lordosis in bipedal hominins. *Nature* 450: 1075–1078.

White, CD, Spence, M, and Stuart-Williams, H. 1998. Oxygen isotopes and the identification of geographical origin: the Valley of Oaxaca vs. the Valley of Mexico. *Journal of Archaeological Science* 25: 643–657.

White, CD. 1993. Isotopic determination of seasonality of diet and death in ancient Nubian hair. *Journal of Archaeological Science* 20: 657–666.

White, CD, ed. 1999. *Reconstructing Ancient Maya Diet*. Salt Lake City: University of Utah Press.

White, CD, Longstaffe, FJ, and Law, KR. 1999. Seasonal stability and variation in diet as reflected in human mummy tissues from the Kharga Oasis and the Nile Valley. *Paleogeography, Paleoclimatology, Palaeoecology* 147: 209–222.

White, CD, Nelson, AJ, Longstaffe, FJ, et al. 2009. Landscape bioarchaeology at Pacatnamu, Peru: inferring mobility from $\delta13C$ and $\delta15N$ values of hair. *Journal of Archaeological Science* 36(7): 1527–1537.

White, TD. 1986. Cut marks on the Bodo cranium: a case of prehistoric defleshing. *American Journal of Physical Anthropology* 69: 503–509.

White, TD. 2006. Early hominid femora—the inside story. *Comptes Rendus Palevolution* 5: 99–108.

White, TD, Asfaw, B, Beyene, Y, et al. 2009. *Ardipithecus ramidus* and the paleobiology of early hominids. *Science* 326: 75–86.

White, TD, Asfaw, B, DeGusta, D, et al. 2003. Pleistocene *Homo sapiens* from Middle Awash, Ethiopia. *Nature* 423: 742–747.

White, TD, Suwa, G, and Asfaw, B. 1994. *Australopithecus ramidis*, a new species of early hominid from Aramis, Ethiopia. *Nature* 371: 306–312.

White, TD, Suwa, G, and Asfaw, B. 1995. *Australopithecus ramidis*, a new species of early hominid from Aramis, Ethiopia—a corrigendum. *Nature* 372: 88.

White, TD, and Toth, N. 1991. The question of ritual cannibalism at Grotta Guattari. *Current Anthropology* 32(2): 118–138.

White, TD, WoldeGabriel, G, Asfaw, B, et al. 2006. Asa Issie, Aramis, and the origin of *Australopithecus*. *Nature* 440: 883–889.

Whitelaw, E. 2006. Sins of the fathers, and their fathers. *European Journal of Human Genetics* 14: 131–132.

Whiten, A. 2007. *Pan* African culture: Memes and genes in wild chimpanzees. *Proceedings of the National Academy of Sciences* 104: 17559–17560.

Whiten A, Goodall, J, McGrew, WC, et al. 1999. Cultures in chimpanzees. *Nature* 399: 682–685.

WHO. 1946. Preamble to the Constitution of the World Health Organization as adopted by the International Health Conference, New York, June19–July 22, 1946.

WHO. 1996. *Fighting Disease, Fostering Development*. Geneva.

Wildman, DE, Uddin, M, Liu, G, et al. 2003. Implications of natural selection in shaping 99.4% nonsynonymous DNA identity between humans and chimpanzees: Enlarging genus Homo. *Proceedings of the National Academy of Sciences* 10012: 7181–7188.

Wiley, A, and Allen, JS. 2008. *Medical Anthropology: A Biocultural Approach*. Oxford: Oxford University Press.

Williams, B, and Rogers, T. 2006. Evaluating the accuracy and precision of cranial morphological traits for sex determination. *Journal of Forensic Sciences* 51: 729–735.

Williams, GC. 1957. Pleiotropy, natural selection, and the evolution of senescence. *Evolution* 11: 398–411.

Williams, GC, and Nesse, RM. 1991. The dawn of Darwinian medicine. *Quarterly Review of Biology* 661: 1–22.

Williams, JS, and Katzenberg, MA. 2008. Investigating season of death using carbon isotope data from the hair of 500 year old Peruvian mummies. Proceedings of the VI Mummy Congress (February 2007), Teguise, Lazarote: University of Las Palmas de Gran Canaria.

Williams, J, White, C, and Longstaffe, F. 2005. Trophic level and macronutrient shift effects associated with the weaning process in the Maya Postclassic. *American Journal of Physical Anthropology* 128: 781–790.

Williams, N. 2008. The population bomb. *Current Biology* 18: R535–R536.

Williamson, RF, and Pfeiffer, S (ed). 2003. *Bones of the Ancestors: the Archaeology and Osteobiography of the Moatfield Ossuary*. Mercury Series Archaeology Paper No. 163. Hull: Canadian Museum of Civilization.

Wilmé, L, Goodman, SM, and Ganzhorn, JU. 2006. Biogeographic evolution of Madagascar's microendemic biota. *Science* 312: 1063–1065.

Wilson, AC, and Sarich, VM. 1969. A molecular time scale for human evolution. *Proceedings of the National Academy of Sciences* 63: 1088–1093.

Wilson, W, Milner, J, Bulkan, J, et al. 2006. Weaning practices of the Makushi of Guyana and their relationship to infant and child mortality: a preliminary assessment of international recommendations. *American Journal of Human Biology* 18: 312–324.

Winkler, LA. 2005. Morphology and relationships of the orangutan fatty cheek pads. *American Journal of Primatology* 17: 305–319.

Witherspoon, DJ, Wooding, S, Rogers, AR, et al. 2007. Genetic similarities within and between human populations. *Genetics* 176: 351–359.

Wolfe, LD. 1991. Human evolution and the sexual behavior of female primates. In JD Loy and CB Peters, eds., *Understanding Behavior: What Primate Studies Tell Us About Human Behavior*. New York: Oxford University Press. 121–151.

Wolfe, ND, Heneine, W, Carr, JK, et al. 2005. Emergence of unique primate T–lymphotropic viruses among central African bushmeat hunters. *Proceedings of the National Academy of Sciences* 102(22): 7994–7999.

Wollenweber, B, Porter, JR, and Lübberstedt, T. 2005. Need for multidisciplinary research towards a second green revolution. *Current Opinion in Plant Biology* 8: 337–341.

Wolpoff, MH, Hawks, J, Senut, B, et al. 2006. Is the Toumaï cranium TM 266 a hominid? *PaleoAnthropology* 2006: 36–50.

Wolpoff, MH, Senut, B, Pickford, M, et al. 2002. *Sahelanthropus or Sahelpithecus? Nature* 419: 581–582.

Wolpoff, MH, Zhi, WX, and Thorne, AG. 1984. Modern *Homo sapiens* origins: a general theory of hominid evolution involving the fossil evidence from east Asia. In FH Smith and F Spencer, eds., *The Origins of Modern Humans.* New York: Alan R. Liss. 411–484.

Wong, MH, Wu, SC, Deng, WJ, et al. 2007. Export of toxic chemicals—a review of the case of uncontrolled electronic-waste recycling. *Environmental Pollution* 149: 131–140.

Wood, BA. 1991. *Koobi Fora Research Project,* Vol. 4. Oxford: Clarendon. 230–254.

Wood, BA. 1993. Early *Homo*: how many species? In WH Kimbel and LB Martin, eds., *Species, Species Concepts, and Primate Evolution.* New York: Plenum. 485–522.

Wood, BA, and Chamberlain, AT. 1987. The nature and affinities of the "robust" australopithecines: a review. *Journal of Human Evolution* 16: 625–641.

Wood, BA, and Collard, M. 1999. The human genus. *Science* 284: 65–71.

Wood, BA, and Lonergan, N. 2008. The hominin fossil record: taxa, grades, and clades. *Journal of Anatomy* 212: 354–376.

Wood BA, Wood CW, and Konigsberg, LW. 1994. *Paranthropus boisei*: an example of evolutionary stasis? *American Journal of Physical Anthropology* 95: 117–136.

Wood, JW, Milner, GR, Harpending, HC, et al. 1992. The osteological paradox: problems of inferring prehistoric health from skeletal samples. *Current Anthropology* 33: 343–370.

Wooding, S. 2004. Natural selection: sign, sign, everywhere a sign. *Current Biology* 14: R700–R701.

Wooding S, Bufe, B, Grassi, C, et al. 2006. Independent evolution of bitter-taste sensitivity in humans and chimpanzees. *Nature* 440: 930–4.

Wooding, S, and Jorde, LB. 2006. Duplication and divergence in humans and chimpanzees. *BioEssays* 28: 35–338.

World Bank Development Indicators 2005. http://devdata.worldbank.org/wdi2005/Table2_5.htm. Accessed January 20, 2009.

Worm, B, Barbier, EB, Beaumont, N, et al. 2006. Impacts of biodiversity loss on ocean ecosystem services. *Science* 314: 787–790.

Wrangham, R, and Peterson, D. 1996. *Demonic Males: Apes and the Origins of Human Violence.* Boston: Mariner.

Wrangham, RW. 2008. The International Primatological Society as a coalition: primatologists and the future of primates. *International Journal of Primatology* 29: 3–11.

Wrangham, RW, Jones, JH, Laden, G, et al. 1999. The raw and the stolen: cooking and the ecology of human origins. *Current Anthropology* 40: 567–594.

Wu, X. 2004. On the origin of modern humans in China. *Quaternary International* 117: 131–140.

Yaeger, R, Avila-Bront, A, Abdul, K, et al. 2008. Comparing genetic ancestry and self-described race in African Americans born in the United States and in Africa. *Cancer Epidemiology Biomarkers and Prevention* 17: 1329–1338.

Yamei, H, Potts, R, Baoyin, Y, et al. 2000. Mid Pleistocene Acheulean-like stone technology of the Bose Basin, South China. *Science* 287: 1622–26.

Yang, DY. 1997. *DNA Diagnosis of Thalassemia from Ancient Italian Skeletons.* Ph.D. diss., Department of Anthropology, McMaster University, Hamilton, Ontario.

Yang, DY, and Watt, K. 2005. Contamination controls when preparing archaeological remains for ancient DNA analysis. *Journal of Archaeological Science* 32: 331–336.

Yang, N, MacArthur, D, Gulbin, J, et al. 2003. *ACTN3* genotype is associated with human elite athletic performance. *American Journal of Human Genetics* 73: 627–631.

Yellen, JE, Brooks, AS, Cornelissen, E, et al. 1995. A Middle Stone Age worked bone industry from Katanda, Upper Semliki Valley, Zaire. *Science* 268: 553–556.

Yoder, AD, Cartmill, M, Ruvolo, M, et al. 1996. Ancient single origin for Malagasy primates. *Proceedings of the National Academy of Sciences* 93: 5122–5126.

Young, JH, Chang, YP-C, Kim, JD-O, et al. 2005. Differential susceptibility to hypertension is due to selection during the out-of-Africa expansion. *Public Library of Science Genetics* 1: e82.

Young, R. 2003. Evolution of the human hand: the role of throwing and clubbing. *Journal of Anatomy* 202: 165–174.

Young, TK. 1996. Sociocultural and behavioural determinants of obesity among Inuit in the central Canadian Arctic. *Social Science and Medicine* 43: 1665–1671.

Young, TK, Reading, J, Elias, B, et al. 2000. Type 2 diabetes mellitus in Canada's First Nations: status of an epidemic in progress. *Canadian Medical Association Journal* 163: 561–566.

Yuan, Q, Joiner, WJ, and Sehgal, A. 2006. A sleep-promoting role for the *Drosophila* serotonin receptor 1A. *Current Biology* 16: 1051–1062.

Zeller, A. 2007. What's in a picture? A comparison of drawings by apes and children. *Semiotica* 166: 181–214.

Zhu, RX, Potts, R, Xie, F, et al. 2004. New evidence on the earliest human presence at high northern latitudes in northeast Asia. *Nature* 431: 559–562.

Zilles, K, Armstrong, E, Schleicher, A, et al. 1988. The human pattern of gyrification in the cerebral cortex. *Anatomy and Embryology* 179: 173–179.

Zollikofer, CPE, Ponce de León, MS, Lieberman, DE, et al. 2005. Virtual cranial reconstruction of *Sahelanthropus tchadensis. Nature* 434: 755–759.

Zollikofer, CPE, Ponce de León, MS, Vandermeersch, B, et al. 2002. Evidence for interpersonal violence in the St. Césaire Neanderthal. *Proceedings of the National Academy of Sciences* 99: 6444–6448.

# Index

Note: Figures and tables are denoted by *f* or *t* following the page number. Footnotes are denoted by *n* following the page number.

Nutritional deficiencies, 309–311, 323
Nutritional genomics, 337–338
Nutritional value, 313, 314t

## O

Obesity. *See* Overweight and obese
    (OW-OB)
Obesity gene map, 65
Obligate, 110
Obligate bipeds, 161
Occipital bun, 247
Occipital torus, 224
Occlusal, 144
Occlusal plane, 174
O'Connell, J.F., 222
O'Connor, C.F., 247
Oldowan tool industry, 221
Oldowan-type tools, 218, 221f, 229
Olduvai Gorge, 218
Old World monkeys, 107, 148
Olfactory, 97
Oligocene, 146–148
Omnivorous, 99
Omomyids, 145, 146f
Omran, Abdel R., 305
Oogonia, 58
Opposable thumbs, 97, 97f
Orangutan Foundation International, 341
Orangutans
    aggression, 123
    birth spacing, 124
    characteristics, 109
    divergence time, 153
    face, 152f
    language and communication, 131
    locomotion, 168–170
    social living, 103, 119
    tool use, 120–121, 121f
*Oreopithecus*, 151
*Orrorin*, 186, 194, 199, 212
*Orrorin tugenensis*, 193, 196–197, 197f
Orthognathic, 205
Orthograde, 162
Orthograde clamber, 168
Oschinsky, Larry, 19–20
Ossuary, 20
Osteoarthritis, 250, 325–326
Osteology, 10–11
Osteomyelitis, 324f
*Otavipithecus namibiensis*, 150
*Ouranopithecus*, 151
*Ouranopithecus macedoniensis*, 151
Overnutrition, 311–312
Overweight and obese (OW-OB), 7, 65,
    311–312
Ovulation, concealed, 126, 171

Owen, Robert, 42
Oxygen isotope analysis, 141, 326f

## P

Paleoanthropology, 11–12, 161, 190t
Paleobiology, 143
Paleobotany, 141
Paleocene, 144–145
Paleo-DNA Laboratory, Lakehead
    University, 68
Paleoecology, 141
Paleoenvironments, 190–193
Paleohistology, 323f
Paleo-Indians, 273
Paleomagnetism, 137
Paleoneurology, 177
Paleontology, 31, 141
Paleonutrition, 324–325
Paleopathology, 11
Paley, William, 31, 37
Palynology, 141
Panayotova, K., 11
Pandemic, 7, 8
Pangaea, 139, 139f
Pangenesis, 39
Panins, hominins in relation to, 160, 162,
    167–168, 171, 174–177, 179–181,
    192, 194. *See also* Chimpanzees
Paradigm, 30
*Paranthropus*, 186, 205, 209n, 211
*Paranthropus aethiopithecus*, 209–210
*Paranthropus boisei*, 199, 209–211, 210f, 218
*Paranthropus robustus*, 187, 209, 211
Parapatric, 79
Parapatry, 80
Parapithecids, 146
Parental investment, 126
Parra, Esteban, 311, 315
Partridge, T.C., 207
Paterson, H.E.H., 80
Paterson, James, 20
Pathogenic, 324
Pathogens, 306
Pathophysiology, 297
Patterson, N., 79, 193–194
Pavelka, Mary, 116, 125, 370
Pedal phalange, 199
Pedigree, 63
Peking Man, 227–228, 228
Pelvis, 167, 168f
Pendants, 253f
Pentadactyly, 97
Percussive stone tools, 199, 206, 218, 221
Perimortem, 341
Perry, G.H., 368
Pfeiffer, S.K., 326

Phalanx, 196
Pharynx, 254
Phenotype, 61
Phenotypic plasticity, 77
Phenylketonuria (PKU), 65, 337
Phenylthiocarbamide (PTC), 61–62
Pheromone, 26
Philopatric, 103
Phyletic evolution, 82
Phyletic sequence, 201
Phylogenetic, 27
Physical anthropology, 17n7
Physicians for Human Rights, 346
Phytoliths, 325
Pickford, Martin, 196
*Pierolapithecus catalaunicus*, 150
Piltdown Man, 18, 201, 228
Pincus, Gregory, 293
*Pithecanthropus erectus*, 227
Placebo, 298
Planned Parenthood of America, 292n
Plato, 32–33
Platyrrhini, 106–107
Pleiotropy, 65, 309
Pleisomorphic, 91
Plesiadapiforms, 144–145
*Plesiadapis*, 145
Pliocene, 191
Plio-Pleistocene hominins, 234
Pluripotent, 52
Point mutation, 53
Polar bodies, 58
Polyandry, 102
Polydactyly, 87
Polygenesis, 283–284, 288–289
Polygenic traits, 65
Polygynous, 102
Polymerase chain reaction (PCR), 68
Polymorphism, 87, 285
Polypeptide, 57
Polytypism, 87, 285
Ponce de Léon, M.S., 249
*Pongo*, 151
Population bottleneck, 268
Population genetics, 75
Population growth, 355–362
    implications, 359–362
    limits, 360f
    measuring, 355–357
    rate of, 359f
    realities concerning, 361t
    trends, 357–359
Population momentum, 361
Populations, homogeneity of
    human, 288
Populations, local breeding, 285
Population size, effective, 268